THE
WINE
BUYER'S
GUIDE

THE
WINE
BUYER'S
GUIDE

ROBERT
PARKER

DORLING KINDERSLEY · LONDON

A Jill Norman Book

First published in Great Britain in 1987
by Dorling, Kindersley Limited.
9 Henrietta Street, London WC2E 8PS

Drawings by Christopher Wormell
Maps by Jeanyee Wong

British Library Cataloguing in Publication Data

Parker, Robert
    The wine buyers guide, 1987–88.
    1. Wine——Catalogs
    I. Title
    641.2'2'0294 TP548

    ISBN 0-86318-234-8

Data Capture by Stenton Associates
Computerset in 10/11pt Linotron 202 Perpetua
by MFK Typesetting Ltd, Hitchin, Herts

Printed and Bound in Great Britain
by R. J. Acford Ltd, Chichester, Sussex

ACKNOWLEDGMENTS

It is the world's finest winemakers who merit a hefty endorsement and acknowledgment. Always risking foul weather, the uncertainty of supply and demand, the headaches of fluctuating international currency rates, as well as merciless and relentless wine critics, they take all the risks and work extraordinarily hard to produce the magical beverage that gives so many people so much pleasure.

I would like to thank the following people for their support and encouragement: Victor Morgenroth, Bob Cline, Paul Evans, Joel Fleishman, Steve Gilbertson, Thomas Hoving, Alan Krasner, Jay Miller, Annette Piatek, Frank Prial, Jancis Robinson, Bob Schindler, Ila Stanger, Elliott Staren, Ed Sands and Dan Green, whose idea this was.

To Eve Metz and Frank Metz at Simon & Schuster, my appreciation for the book's design, which make it at once elegant and easy to use. And special thanks to Jeanyee Wong for her beautiful maps.

Finally, special recognition is due to my magnificent seven "sitters" who are always there to offer counsel and provide reassurance when needed. I owe a great deal of thanks to my wonderfully capable team at Simon & Schuster, Carole Lalli and Nancy Kalish, their British counterpart, Jill Norman of Dorling Kindersley, my formidable yet always compassionate literary representative, Bob Lescher, my ever smiling, meticulous secretary, Joan Passman, and lastly, the two women in my life that I love so dearly, my dear and adored mother and the woman who started my obsession with wine, my wife.

This book is dedicated to my beloved wife, Patricia, my mother and father, and to Jean Claude Vrinat, a man who embodies all the finest qualities of the true oenophile—unselfishness, enthusiasm, knowledge, and remarkable passion for the subject.

CONTENTS

HOW TO USE THIS BOOK

This book is both a wine educational and buying manual; it is not an encyclopaedic listing of wine producers and growers. It is intended to make you a more formidable, more confident wine buyer by providing you with sufficient insider's information to permit the most intelligent choices possible when buying wine. The finest producers and growers of the world's greatest viticultural regions are evaluated, as well as many of the current releases available in the marketplace. If you cannot find a specific vintage of a highly regarded wine, you still have at your fingertips a wealth of information and evaluations concerning the best producers for each viticultural area. You should be confident in knowing that you will rarely make a mistake (unless, of course, the vintage is absolutely dreadful) with a producer rated 'outstanding' or 'excellent' in this buying manual. These producers are the finest and most consistent in the world.

However, to make the most of this guide, you must know how to use it.

ORGANIZATION

The general organization of each specific viticultural region is arranged as follows:
1 The name of the viticultural region
2 A short introduction to the area
3 A summary of the quality of recent vintages for the area
4 A quick reference chart of that area's best producers/growers
5 A buying strategy to follow for the next two years for the wines of that area
6 And, where deemed relevant, tasting commentaries, a specific numerical rating for the wine, and the approximate retail price for a bottle (750 ml) of that grower/producer's wine.

VITICULTURAL AREAS COVERED

This guide covers the world's major viticultural regions. In Western Europe, France receives the most detailed coverage, followed by Italy, Spain, Portugal and Germany. In North America, California receives much more significant coverage than other viticultural areas, with the exception of America's new emerging wine star, Oregon. The wine regions of the world that dominate the marketplace are given priority and more detailed coverage than minor areas whose wines are rarely seen. Consequently, the sections dealing with Bordeaux, Burgundy, Champagne, Alsace, the Rhône in France, Piedmont and Tuscany in Italy, Rioja, Penedès, and the Duero in Spain, the northern viticultural area of California, and the Mosel in Germany receive an inordinate amount of coverage herein simply because those regions produce the world's greatest wines.

RATING THE PRODUCERS/GROWERS

Who's who in the world of wine becomes readily apparent after years of tasting and visiting the vineyards and wine cellars of the world's producers and growers. Great producers are, unfortunately, still quite rare, but certainly more growers and producers today are making better wine, with better technology and more knowledge than ever before. The charts that follow rate the producers on a five-star system, awarding five stars and an 'outstanding' rating to those producers deemed to be the very best, four stars to those who are 'excellent', three stars to 'good' producers, and two stars or one star to 'average' and 'below average' producers. Since the aim of this book is to provide you with the names of the very best producers, the content is dominated by the top producers rather than the less successful ones. Those few growers/producers who have received five-star ratings are indeed those who make the world's finest wines. They have been selected for this rating because of two reasons: they make the greatest wine of their particular viticultural region, and they are remarkably consistent and reliable even in mediocre and poor vintages. Ratings, whether they be specific numerical ratings of individual wines or classifications of growers, are always likely to create controversy not only among the growers but among wine tasters too. But, if done impartially, with a global viewpoint and with first hand 'sur place' knowledge of the wines, the producers, and the type and quality of the winemaking, such ratings can be reliable and powerfully informative. The important thing for readers to remember is that those growers/producers who receive either a four-star or five-star rating are producers to search out; I suspect few consumers will ever be disappointed with one of their wines. The three-star-rated growers/producers are less consistent, but can be expected to make fine wines in the very good to excellent vintages. Their weaknesses come either from the fact that their vineyards are not so strategically placed, or because for financial or other reasons they are unable to make the rigorous selections necessary to make only the finest-quality wine.

The importance of rating the growers/producers of the world's major viticultural regions is perhaps the single salient point to this book. Years of wine tasting have taught me many things, but the more one tastes and assimilates the knowledge of the world's regions, the more one begins to isolate the handful of truly world-class growers and producers who seem to rise above the crowd in great as well as mediocre vintages. I always admonish consumers against blind faith in one grower or producer, or one specific vintage, but the producers and growers rated 'outstanding' and 'excellent' are as close to a guarantee of high quality as you are likely to find.

VINTAGE SUMMARIES

Everyone is exposed to wine advertisements proclaiming 'a great vintage', but I have never known more than several viticultural areas of the world to have a great vintage in the same year. The chances of a uniformly great vintage are extremely remote simply because of significantly different micro-climates, soils and so on, in every wine-producing region. It is easy to fall into the trap of thinking that because Bordeaux had a great vintage in 1982 everywhere else in France did too. Nothing, of course, could be further from the truth. Nevertheless, a Bordeaux vintage's reputation unfortunately seems to dictate what the world thinks about many other wine-producing areas. This obviously creates many problems, since in poor Bordeaux vintages the Rhône or Alsace or Champagne could have excellent vintages, and in great Bordeaux vintages those same areas could have bad years because of poor climate conditions. For California, many casual observers seem to think *every* year is a top year and this image is, of course, promoted by that state's publicity-conscious Wine Institute. It may be true that California rarely has a disastrous vintage, but tasting certainly proves that 1981, 1982, and 1983 are far more irregular in quality than either 1984 or 1985. In this guide, there are vintage summaries for each viticultural area because the vintages are so very different in both quantity and quality. Never make the mistake of assuming that one particular year is great everywhere or poor everywhere. I know of no year when that has happened.

TASTING NOTES AND RATINGS

For many of the major viticultural areas, the growers/producers are listed alphabetically and their current wines are reviewed, scored, and commented upon. In this instance, great attention has been given to trying to provide an overview of the style and quality level of the producer/grower. Such factors as whether the producer is steadily improving the wine's quality, resting on its allegedly superior reputation, or slipping in quality because of mismanagement, replanting, or simple negligence are issues that I deem extremely important for consumers to be aware of. Virtually all of my tastings are done in peer group, single, blind conditions – meaning that the same type of wines are tasted against each other one at a time and the producers' names are not known. The ratings reflect an independent, critical look at the wines. Neither price nor the reputation of the producer/grower affect the rating in any way. I spend three months of every year tasting in vineyards, and the other nine months of the year are devoted solely to tasting and writing. I do not participate in wine judgings or trade tastings for many reasons, the principal of which are the following: **1** I prefer to taste from an entire bottle of wine, **2** I find it essential to have properly sized and cleaned professional tasting glasses, **3** the temperatures of the wine must be correct, and **4** I alone will determine the time allocated to the number of wines to be assessed. The numerical rating given is a guide to what I think of the wine *vis-à-vis* its peer group. Certainly, wines rated above 85 are very good to excellent, and any wine rated 90 or above will be outstanding for its particular type. While some have suggested that scoring wines is unfair when they have been so romantically extolled for centuries, the fact of the matter is that wine is no different from any product being sold to a consumer – there are specific standards of quality that full-time wine professionals recognize, and there are benchmark wines against which all others can be judged. I know of no one with three or four different glasses of wine in front of him, regardless of how good or bad the wines might be, who cannot say 'I prefer this one to that one'. Scoring wines is simply taking a professional's opinion and applying some sort of numerical system to it on a consistent basis. Scoring permits rapid communication of information to expert and novice alike.

The rating system I employ in my wine journal, *The Wine Advocate*, is the one I have utilized in this buying manual. It is a 100-point scale, the most repugnant of all wines meriting 50, and the most glorious, perfect gustatory experience commanding 100. I prefer my system to the more widely quoted 20-point scale called the Davis Scale, of the University of California at Davis, because it permits much more flexibility in scoring. It is also easier to understand because it corresponds to the grading system most of us have experienced in school, and it avoids the compression of scores from which the Davis Scale suffers. It is not without its own problems, though, because readers will often wonder what the difference is between an 86 and an 87, both very good wines. The only answer I can give is a simple one, that when tasted side by side, I thought the 87-point wine slightly better than the 86-point wine.

The score given for a specific wine reflects the quality of the wine at its best. Wines from obviously badly corked or defective bottles are re-tried, since a wine from a single bad bottle does not indicate an entirely spoiled batch. Many of the wines reviewed here have been tasted several times, and the score represents a sort of cumulative average of the wine's performance in tastings to date. However, the written commentary that accompanies the ratings is often a better source of information regarding the wine's style and personality, its relative quality level *vis-à-vis* its peers, and its relative value and ageing potential than any score could ever possibly indicate. Here, then, is a general guide to interpreting the numerical ratings:

90–100 is equivalent to an A and is given for an outstanding or excellent special effort. Wines in this category are the very best produced for their type and, like a three-star Michelin restaurant, worth a special effort to find and try. There is a big difference between a 90 and a 99, but both are top marks. As you will note throughout the text, there are very few wines that actually make it into this top category simply because there just are not so many truly great wines.

80–89 is equivalent to a B and such a wine, particularly in the 85–89 range, is very, very good. Many of the wines that fall into this range are often great value as well; I would not hesitate to have any of these wines in my own personal collection.

70–79 represents a C, or average mark, but obviously 79 is a much more desirable score than 70. Wines that receive scores between 75 and 79 are generally pleasant, straightforward wines that simply lack complexity, character, and depth.

Below 70 is a D; for wine it is a sign of an imbalanced, flawed, terribly dull or diluted wine that will be of little interest to the smart wine consumer.

In terms of awarding points, my scoring system gives a wine 50 points to start with. The wine's general colour and appearance merit up to 5 points. Since most wines today have been well made due to modern technology and the increased use of professional oenologists, they tend to receive at least 4, often 5 points. The aroma and bouquet merit up to 15 points. Obviously, the intensity of the aroma and bouquet are important, and equally so is the wine's cleanliness. The flavour and finish merit up to 20 points, and again, intensity of flavour, balance, cleanliness, and depth and length on the palate are all important considerations when giving out points. Finally, the overall quality level or potential for further evolution and improvement – ageing merits up to 10 points.

Scores are important for the reader to gauge a professional critic's overall qualitative placement of a wine in relation to its peers. However, don't ignore the accompanying description of the wine's style, personality, and potential, which is just as important. No scoring system is perfect, but a system that provides for flexibility in scores, if applied without prejudice and fairly, can quantify different levels of wine quality. If implemented properly, then this guide will lead you to the finest wines as well as the very finest wine values. But no scoring system could ever convey the hedonistic experience of wine that might arise from the ambience, gorgeous setting, excellent food, and fine company that may accompany it.

QUOTED PRICES

The most important thing for a wine consumer to realize when shopping for wine is that there is no one definitive price for a bottle of wine. Wine prices fluctuate widely due to an enormous number of factors. The percentage of mark-up over cost taken by the importer and/or merchant may vary significantly because of the type of wine, the demand for it, and the type of shop and degree of service provided by it. Merchants who provide personal attention, hire informed wine consultants, and publish comprehensive and educational wine catalogues, have more overhead costs and no doubt have a much higher mark-up on their wines than a no-frills discount outlet, whose staff is there simply to sell and not to give advice and counsel as well. Consequently, prices for the same wines may vary by at least 20%–30% from merchant to merchant.

The great disparity in wine pricing is particularly acute in the case of the wines of Bordeaux. A merchant who has taken an aggressive position with respect to a top vintage of claret very early on, when the wines first came on the market (usually in the spring following the vintage), can often offer Bordeaux wine as a future or 'en primeur' at prices 50% or even 100%–200% below what the wine may ultimately sell for when it is bottled and released by the respective châteaux two and a half years after the vintage. Recent history proves convincingly that those merchants who offered the great 1982 Clarets in spring 1983 to their customers saved their clients considerable amounts of money as international demand for these wines sent prices soaring 100%–200% above their opening base price. A merchant who did not move quickly to purchase wines from this vintage had to pay a much higher price for the 1982 Bordeaux and, obviously, that price was passed on to the client. One should remember, though, that buying Bordeaux futures from a good year in the spring following the vintage does not automatically guarantee that one is going to get Claret at the bottom price. Take for example the 1985 Clarets, an excellent vintage, which came on the market in spring 1986 at what were very high prices. The French franc had strengthened against the pound sterling over the previous year, reducing the latter's purchasing power considerably. In addition, the Bordelais had in many instances taken hefty price hikes on their wines to take into account their own inflationary pressure. Given the record-breaking size of the crop, the surplus of fine Bordeaux already in the distribution pipeline throughout the world, and the high quality and enormous quantity of the new 1986 crop waiting in the wings, it seems quite illogical to assume that 1985

Claret prices will appreciate, as did the 1982s, and cost the consumer significantly more when they are bottled and released on the market in spring 1988. Consequently, except for a handful of the superstars of this vintage, buying futures in 1985 will probably not save many consumers a great deal of money, although no one will be disappointed in the quality of the wine they receive.

It is not only with Bordeaux wines that the vagaries of the international currency market have a great impact. Certainly, one only has to look at how the value of the pound sterling has fared in relation to the main European currencies to see a vivid display of why wines can differ in price by 40%–50%, simply depending on when the importer and/or merchant purchased the wine. The wide swings in currency values is a pattern that has emerged in the eighties that is unlikely to disappear.

For this *Buyer's Guide*, each wine has been placed in one of five different price categories. That placement should be regarded as a general indication of the price of the wine. Some wines will no doubt sometimes be sold at a lower or higher price than their category. It is simply impossible to precisely gauge the specific price of a wine given the number of factors that influence wine prices. The categories used in the *Buyer's Guide* are:

① Inexpensive = wines priced under £5
② Reasonable = wines priced between £5 and £8
③ Moderate = wines priced between £9 and £12
④ Expensive = wines priced between £13 and £20
⑤ Luxury = wines priced over £20

LOOKING AT TODAY'S MARKETPLACE

Before I predict what will happen over the next several years in the wine world, I want first to go back a dozen years to 1975 and look at the situation in the wine market then, simply because to know the past will help to understand the events that will fashion and shape the future.

First, there was a tremendous glut from European wine-producing countries being dumped on the market. Wine investors (you hear that same term applied today) had determined that wine was a great investment. These investors, largely corporations heavily involved in the spirits and beer business, relied significantly on worldwide interest in the 1970 Bordeaux vintage and purchased large portions of that and subsequent vintages such as 1972, 1973, and 1974. While 1970 was a wonderful vintage, 1972, 1973, and 1974 were poor years. Then when the international oil crisis arrived in 1974, the wine market collapsed. The international oil crisis had an unsettling effect on major wine-buying markets, particularly their economies; investors from countries holding large wine inventories, principally England and America, became nervous and began to unload their wine stocks at English auction houses. This was led by the bureaucratic beer and spirits corporations, which, not knowing a whole lot about wine, decided to dump huge stocks of mediocre to poor Bordeaux on a market unwilling and financially unable to accept it. The result was a massive crash and subsequent reorganization of the entire wine trade, particularly that of Bordeaux, where many large companies were either crippled or put out of business.

It is hard to believe, but in America in 1975 California's wine star had barely begun to ascend. Although California had just finished two consecutive top-notch vintages, 1973 and 1974, these wines had not yet been released for sale. 1975 was a whole year before Steven Spurrier's now famous tasting in Paris, when French Bordeaux were tasted against California's best Cabernets, and white Burgundy against California's best Chardonnays. As everyone who follows wine news knows, the California wines scored unanimous and consistent triumphs over their more highly esteemed French counterparts. A year later, after the results of this historic tasting had been ballyhooed over and over by the international wine press, the California wine industry was on an upward surge in fame, prosperity, optimism, and vineyard expansion and development. California wines, largely ignored in Britain in 1975, are now represented and sold by many merchants. Because of the shipping costs and the ever tumultuous currency market, prices for California wines are high and availability unpredictable, but most of the best known wineries are represented to some extent in Britain.

In short, in 1975, European wine prices were depressed and there was a glut of mediocre, even poor wine on the market from a succession of poor European harvests in 1972, 1973, and 1974. California wines were beginning to make serious noises in America and have an effect on that marketplace, but were virtually unknown in the United Kingdom.

What is the state of wine today? First, while there is a glut of wine in the marketplace, and also a strong possibility of a downward shift in wine prices, there is no likelihood that a wine crash is imminent. Like the early seventies, there has been tremendous buying and investment in top-quality wines, but it has been done worldwide by consumers rather than by corporations and financial entities which can then control large chunks of the wine market. Furthermore, the high quality of Europe's vintages in the eighties has been unprecedented and the situation is not at all like that in 1975 since the glut of wine that exists today is at least a glut of very good-quality wine.

What has happened to California's stardom? There is no question that the remarkable period of growth and enthusiasm for

California wines in America that started in 1976 and declined in 1981 was due to a number of factors:

1 There were wide swings in styles of wine. In the seventies, California winemakers went for full extract, high-intensity, very tannic, big, rich wines. Some of these wines met with criticism because they did not go well with food and, in turn, there was a lemming-like rush in the other direction by winemakers in the late seventies and early eighties to fashion wines that were often referred to as 'food' or 'sculptured' wines. In fact, most of these wines were just expensive wines which were innocuous, bland, and very simple.

2 The proliferation of wineries and the multitude of offerings available to the wine consumer. For example, when a major winery such as Château St.-Jean produces as many as six different Chardonnays in a given vintage, most consumers find it overwhelmingly confusing.

3 The game of musical chairs played by so many of California winemakers has added to the chaotic situation. One has only to look at some of the best and most talented winemakers in that state, Chuck Ortman, Rick Forman, Jerry Luper, and Bill Bonetti, to see that they were switching wineries every several years. They took their style of winemaking with them, and just when the consumer had settled in to thinking that he or she liked a particular winery's wine, the winemaker would abruptly leave and a totally different style of wine would emerge from that winery.

4 Perhaps the biggest reason California's image suffered was a result of the very strong American dollar between 1981 and 1985 which made imported wines remarkably inexpensive. It's ironic but true that this surge in strength coincided with a remarkable succession of top-quality, big-quantity vintages from Europe, and there was an inundation of lower-priced but very high-quality imported wines in the American marketplace. This did significant damage to the California wine trade.

What should wine consumers be buying today? There is no question that the wine merchant as well as the wine consumer today is better educated than ever before. It is increasingly difficult for the wine trade to unload poor wine or poor vintages. Intelligent merchants and consumers will go anywhere that excellence in wine is offered. One sees shrewd wine buyers at both the trade and consumer level selecting wines from the Rhône Valley, from Alsace, from New Zealand and Australia, from numerous viticultural regions in Italy, as well as from Spain and Portugal. The wine merchants and consumers of 1987 are not loyal to or captives of any one wine region; it is a global market, and they have taken full advantage of that.

Perhaps the most important development in 1987 is the emergence of viticultural regions that to all intents and purposes were ignored a mere twelve years ago. There has been tremendous development and interest in the underrated, glorious wines of the Rhône Valley, and in Alsace and Loire Valley wines. Many of the less glamorous yet impeccably run Cru Bourgeois estates of Bordeaux are finally getting more and more attention. The remarkable progress French vintners have made in Provence, the Languedoc, and Roussillon has not been lost on merchants and consumers. In Italy, the wines of the north in the Piedmont area have at long last been given their due as world-class, outstanding, complex wines. The new breed of light, white, crisp, and fresh wines of Friuli and the Alto Adige regions of Italy, which offer great value and quality, are also being recognized for their satisfying personalities. In Tuscany, the innovative blends of the Sangiovese and Cabernet Sauvignon grapes have impressed both consumers and professionals. The best wines from Australia and New Zealand have become much more widely available in Britain than they were twelve years ago, as are the better wines from Chile and Argentina. Lastly, there has been a recognition of the remarkable quality of red wine from Spain's emerging viticultural regions, particularly Penedès and Ribero del Duero. Portugal, Spain's neighbour, may have even greater potential for producing outstanding dry, red table wine as modern technology is just beginning to get a foothold in this country.

What do I think will be happening over the next several years?

Prediction 1. The glamorous French wines, meaning those from the top two dozen Bordeaux châteaux as well as the best Grands Crus and Premiers Crus from Burgundy, will become increasingly more expensive and, unfortunately, affordable only by the super-rich. The simple reason for this is that the quantities are finite. The great vineyards cannot be expanded, and they are already at their maximum level of production. Given the continuing worldwide demand for these wines from an increasingly aware wine-drinking public, demand will continue to outstrip supply and push prices for these wines into a very expensive élitist arena.

Prediction 2. Other French wine prices, as well as wine prices from countries such as Italy, Spain, Germany, and Portugal, will remain largely stable, perhaps even soften, simply because these areas are producing quantities of wine at a rate that far outstrips current demand. In addition to the huge, sound crop of 1985 there is now another bumper crop in 1986 and this has resulted in an ocean of fine imported wine in the pipeline.

Prediction 3. The greatest values in imported wines in 1987 will come from Australia, Chile, Spain, and New Zealand.

Prediction 4. California will continue its strong rebound in the American marketplace which started in 1986, largely because of the two outstanding vintages of 1984 and 1985 which have generated considerable excitement over the wines from that area. This will have a significant effect on the sales of expensive Bordeaux and Burgundy in the American market, which is currently saturated with unsold quantities of 1981 and 1983 Bordeaux, as well as 1982 and 1983 Burgundy. The increased interest in America's own wines in that marketplace will squeeze out the more expensive wines from France, and the Bordelais in particular will have to take much of their business elsewhere. But, I do not see any other country capable of absorbing such large quantities of wine. This will put tremendous downward pressure on Bordeaux prices worldwide, with the exception of the top two dozen châteaux.

Prediction 5. Italy, always known for its production of fine red wine, will become wider known as a major supplier of excellent-quality white wine at very reasonable prices.

Prediction 6. The glut of wine will continue to grow at a staggering rate. There is entirely too much fine wine in the marketplace. Where will the slack be taken up as more vineyards are being planted than ever before, and modern technology allows wineries to make much better wine in mediocre vintages and produce much more wine in great vintages? Who is going to drink all this wine? The two leading wine-drinking countries in the world, France and Italy, have seen their consumption of wine per person drop by almost 25% between 1975 and today. Certainly, it will not be America, simply because that country is not and is unlikely ever to be a wine-drinking country. In 1987 America ranked thirtieth in the world in wine consumption per person. Although there is a healthy 30% growth rate, even if Americans increased their consumption by 50% by the year 1995, America will only move up to twenty-fifth place (based on today's figures), behind such wine-thirsty countries as Rumania, Bulgaria, Czechoslovakia, and, yes, the vodka kingdom, Russia. There is the possibility that Japan, which has doubled its consumption in the last ten years from 0.5 litres per person to 1 litre per person, may be developing a keen interest in wine. In fact, many Japanese are visiting the vineyards of France and at least one of their major companies, Suntory, has purchased a major château in Bordeaux. There may also be help from Britain, which has quadrupled its wine consumption from 2.7 litres per person in 1975 to more than 10 litres per person in 1987. However, it is impossible to anticipate that the international wine glut will evaporate significantly because of the increased wine consumption of relatively small countries like Britain and Japan. This means that there will be tremendous competition and stability in prices except for the top wines from France and a few other rare wines of limited production.

Prediction 7. Technology, so useful and necessary for providing the world with higher-quality wines, will go too far. Although it allows winemakers to produce better wine, the continuing and growing obsession with technically perfect wines is unfortunately stripping wines of their identifiable and distinctive character. Whether it is excessive filtration, excessive emulation of winemaking styles, or a lemming-like rush by winemakers to produce only wine from the two super grapes, Cabernet Sauvignon and Chardonnay, it seems to be the tragedy of modern winemaking that it is now increasingly difficult to tell the difference between an Italian Chardonnay and one made in France, California or Australia. When the corporate winemakers of the world begin to make wines all in the same manner and designed to offend the least number of people, wine will no doubt lose its fascinating appeal and individualism, and become no better than a popular brand of whisky, gin, or vodka. One must not forget that the great appeal of wine is that it is a unique, distinctive, fascinating product and different every time one drinks it. Winemakers and owners of wineries have become hypnotized by such wonderful technological devices as centrifuges and micropore filter machines in the pursuit of technically perfect, clean wines. Unfortunately, this pursuit has led many to eviscerate their wines of both character and charm. It is these winemakers and owners who must learn to take more risks, and at all costs preserve the individual character of their wines. It is the distinctive regional differences in the quality and taste of wines that will ensure their future.

Prediction 8. Is it possible that the perception of wine as an élitist drink for snobs will change over the next several years? It is this ridiculous notion, which is fostered unfortunately not only by restaurant wine pricing but also by absurd, élitist advertizing from the wine industry, that discourages many people from ever enjoying the benefits of a good bottle of wine. Certainly, things are better today than they were twelve years ago as there are more and more progressive, forward-thinking restaurants that have eliminated mark-ups of 200%–400% over their cost and are offering a greater array of wines at more reasonable 50%–100% mark-ups. However, the great majority of restaurant wine prices, as well as advertising from the wine industry, continues to reinforce an image of wine that is neither correct nor true.

GENERAL BUYING GUIDELINES FOR 1988

Knowledge of the international financial climate, as well as the top vintages that are in demand, can always put you ahead of the pack in developing an intelligent buying strategy for wine. The pound has slipped over the last several years against the French franc, German mark, and Italian lira, and its decline has had a negative impact on prices for imported wines compounded by the fact that producers have also raised their prices because of inflationary pressures. In short, the international wine market in 1987 is in a state of rapid change. However, on the positive side, there are bumper crops in the pipelines and aside from the most expensive, luxury-priced wines, prices should at least remain stable and may drop over the next eighteen months.

With respect to French wine prices that have reached dangerously high levels, my advice with regard to red and white Burgundies is to avoid them altogether. I see no reason whatsoever to buy white Burgundies such as Meursault and Puligny-Montrachet that are selling for £20–£40 a bottle when better Chardonnays from New Zealand and Australia, not to mention Italy, are available at a quarter of the price. The situation for red Burgundies is the same. You have to have the income of a movie star or superstar athlete to afford them. The area in France that still merits considerable consumer interest is Bordeaux. It remains the leader in the world for producing large quantities of superb wines. The 1986 vintage, a gigantic and certainly very good crop, followed the 1985 vintage, which also set records in terms of quantity and was another excellent vintage in terms of quality. The prices asked for these wines, which will not be released until spring 1988 for the 1985s and spring 1989 for the 1986s, are approximately double and sometimes triple the prices asked for the 1981s, a vintage of comparable quality.

Furthermore, the fact that there is so much unsold Bordeaux means that prices could conceivably soften for the less glamorous châteaux of this region. However, do not forget for one second that there are many delicious, charming wines from other vintages that are still available at remarkably modest prices, and that today's best Bordeaux bargains are not the very good 1985s or the monumentally great 1982s, but the 1979s and 1981s, two vintages that produced very good, stylish, elegant wines that have been ignored since all the media and consumer attention was directed towards the 1982 and subsequently the 1983 vintage. Prices for the 1979s and 1981s, wines which by and large can be drunk now and over the next decade, are approximately half those asked for the 1985 futures and a third of the asking price for the few 1982s that remain in stock. Be sure to consult the reviews herein, but the following châteaux merit a serious look by interested consumers for these two vintages: Gruaud-Larose, Talbot, Ducru-Beaucaillou, Léoville-Las Cases, Branaire-Ducru, Giscours, Chasse-Spleen, and Cos D'Estournel. These châteaux are all making some of Bordeaux's finest wines.

Elsewhere in France, Champagne prices, like those of Bordeaux, have increased significantly, but there are still bargains to be had. Non-vintage Champagne prices have remained more stable than those of vintage and luxury cuvées. Be sure to try some of the higher-rated producers of non-vintage Champagne and after deciding on the style you prefer, stock up. Other bargains are also available from France. The 1985 wines of Beaujolais were as good as these wines can be, and prices remain reasonable, particularly those from the best producer of that region, Georges Duboeuf. The 1986s are not as flashy and exuberantly fruity as the 1985s, but still are well made and again reasonably priced. In addition, look for the 1985s from the Loire, where many producers consider it the best vintage in over 20 years. Many Loire wines, particularly those from Muscadet, are still quite reasonable, selling for £3–£6 a bottle. Even such highly regarded wines as those of Sancerre and Pouilly Fumé, while more expensive, are still attractively priced and are superb in 1985. Still one of the great values in French wines are the distinctive wines produced in scenic Alsace on the German border. By and large, they represent the greatest white wine values in all of Europe. From the spicy Gewürztraminers and smoky Tokays to the steely Rieslings and straightforward Pinot Blancs, there are plenty of top-notch wines at excellent prices. 1983 is an outstanding vintage for Alsace, but 1985 is almost as good and the marketplace is now swamped with wines from both these vintages. If you like opulence over elegance, then 1983 would be your choice. If it is the reverse, 1985 offers a bit more finesse, but not as much exotic fruit.

Italy produces and consumes more wine than any other country in the world; however, last year's international furore over the criminal adulteration of cheap wine with lethal chemical additives had far-reaching effects on Italian wine sales in 1986. Of course, this is now history, but a cloud still seems to hang over the Italian wine producers. This is unfortunate, for the top producers in Italy make majestic wine and for years have tried to improve the image of Italy as a producer of great, not cheap, wine. My buying strategy with respect to the white wines of Italy would be to concentrate on two areas that offer spectacular values. The vibrant, zesty, light, refreshing, white wines of Fruili-Venezia Giulia at around £5 a bottle have no peers in the world for freshness and lightness. These wines, made from such grapes as Riesling, Ribolla, Chardonnay, Pinot Grigio, and Müller-Thurgau, never see an oak barrel and are bottled and sold just months after the wines are made to retain their vivacity and freshness. The 1985s and 1986s are excellent and these are the wines I would look for. There is no need to look for older vintages since these wines are meant to be drunk young, not cellared. The other white wines of Italy that offer great value are from the scenic countryside of Tuscany. Vernaccia di San Gimignano is a dry, medium-bodied wine that is refreshingly crisp and flavourful, and an ideal complement to fish and poultry. Again the 1985s and 1986s are the stars and excellent across the board; they can be bought for about £4 a bottle.

Italy has made tremendous progress with its white wines, but the real glories of this country continue to be its majestic, long-lived reds. Italy's finest red wines come from Piedmont and the best of them are the massive, very tannic, rather tough, stern Barolos and the more elegant, yet no less complex Barbarescos. Both are made from the Nebbiolo grape and are not inexpensive. Expect to pay anywhere from £10 and up for the greatest wines from the greatest producers, but remember, these are world-class wines that in a great vintage such as 1982 or 1985 require a full decade of cellaring to reach their summit of maturity. A less expensive and less time-consuming way to introduce yourself to the glories of the red wines of Piedmont is to try a wine called Nebbiolo D'Alba, often called the poor man's Barolo or Barbaresco, or Piedmont's answer to a French Beaujolais, the soft, fruity but rich and velvety Dolcettos. Both of these wines have broad, popular appeal in Italy but have yet to be discovered by wine enthusiasts in this country. Consequently, the prices are often less than £5 a bottle.

With respect to other imports, Australia merits more and more attention from quality-conscious, serious wine consumers. Traditionally, the big, high-alcohol reds have been the stars here. However, with modern winemaking technology, the quality of this country's white wines has increased dramatically. Australia is now turning out beautifully made Chardonnays for around £6 a bottle. Most of them compete with the best Chardonnays of California and with the highest-quality French white Burgundies at a fraction of the price. Distribution has improved significantly in the last several years and it is not difficult to find Chardonnays from any of the top producers.

South American wines are normally relegated to the back shelf by wine merchants, but I have only praise for the wines from Chile's best winery, Cousino Macul, which merit plenty of attention from consumers looking for value rather than prestige.

With respect to Spain, prices, like those for wines from the other less glamorous wine-producing countries, should remain completely stable and offer the best rapport in quality and price. In Spain, the three areas that often have great wine buys are the Rioja, Penedès, and the Ribera del Duero. Just remember that the Spanish style of wine is usually more noticeably oaky in taste than others; this has considerable appeal to an increasing number of wine enthusiasts, but it is different if you have not been exposed to it.

German wines: wine consumers seem to find it difficult to take these wines seriously, but they should be looked at, particularly the Kabinetts and Spätleses from the 1983 vintage and the 1985 vintage. Prices have generally remained stable, despite the increasing strength of the German mark.

With respect to California wines, it would appear that this

beautiful state in America has had in 1984 and 1985 its best two vintages since the legendary 1974. However, in Britain prices are generally quite high when compared with European wines. Should you want to splurge on some California wines, I suggest you look for any of the top producers of Chardonnay from both 1984 and 1985. Unless I knew the wine well, I would ignore any Chardonnay older than 1983. While California's best Cabernets are again on the verge of challenging the French for supremacy in the American market, they are not priced competitively enough to offer any challenge to the best values from Bordeaux in the British market. The 1982 vintage in California turned out fruity, immensely drinkable wines, although irregularity tends to plague many wineries in this vintage. However, the excellent and opulent 1984s which are just now coming on the market, and the classic 1985s which will be available in the next year, are two vintages that should bring California plenty of attention. Of the 1984s, those that look potentially outstanding (and quite expensive) are the three different Cabernets of Diamond Creek, Ridge's Monte Bello, Ravenswood's Merlot, Santa Cruz's Mountain Vineyards, Dunn, William Hill, Caymus, Joseph Phelps, Monticello, Buehler, Carmenet, Dominus, Forman, Girard, Groth, Laurel Glen, Lyeth, Château Montelena, Rubicon, the three separate Cabernets from Silver Oak Vineyards, and the Matanzas Creek Merlot. Certainly, 1984 will be the best vintage for California Cabernet and Merlot since 1974.

TEN PROPOSITIONS TO CONSIDER FOR 1988

Despite all the insider's information you have at your disposal, I hope that every reader will seriously consider and accept the following propositions for satisfying both the palate and purse.

1 For dry white wines under £5, try some of the best 1983 and 1985 Pinot Blancs from Alsace. In a quality sense, they are worth at least twice the price.

2 For serious white wines, there are numerous alternatives to overpriced white Burgundy. Try a 1983 or 1985 Pinot Gris (also called Tokay) from Alsace, or the 1984 and 1985 Chardonnays from Australia and New Zealand.

3 Until prices come down, avoid red Burgundy; there are far better wines made at significantly lower prices in the Rhône Valley as well as elsewhere in the world. Unfortunately, if you have a thirst for Pinot Noir the only Pinot Noir you will find that is comparable to a great red Burgundy will be from Oregon, and as yet few of the wines from these tiny wineries are available in England.

4 As for great, rich, complex, red wines, make a special effort to try a Côte Rôtie, Hermitage, Crozes Hermitage, Cornas, St.-Joseph,

Gigondas, or Châteauneuf-du-Pape from one of the excellent or outstanding growers listed in this Guide. The vintages to look for are 1982, 1983, and 1985.

5   For a wonderfully fresh, crisp, delicious apéritif wine, look no further than a 1983 or 1985 German Kabinett or Spätlese, or 1985 Italian white wine from Friuli-Venezia Giulia, or from the vineyards surrounding Tuscany's medieval town of San Gimignano.

6   Buy, taste, and recognize that Spanish red wines offer the greatest quality/price rapport in the world. Try a bottle each of the 1981 or 1982 Torres Gran Coronas, the 1978 Torres Black Label Gran Coronas, the 1982 or 1983 Cabernet Sauvignon-based wine from Remelluri, or the 1982 or 1983 Pesquera Tinto from Ribera del Duero. These are among the world's greatest wines, regardless of their modest prices.

7   Try one of the three wines made by the excellent Chilean winery of Cousino Macul. The 1985 Chardonnay for about £4, the 1982 Cabernet Sauvignon priced the same, or the 1980 Cabernet Sauvignon Antiguas Reserva for under £6 will quite convincingly prove that quality-wise these wines are worth twice the price, and if they had a Bordeaux label on them, they would sell for that.

8   Until Bordeaux prices moderate, search out the following twelve properties in Bordeaux which are very conspicuous overachievers—châteaux that make great wine at modest prices— Potensac (Médoc), Haut Marbuzet (St.-Estèphe), Les Ormes de Pez (St.-Estèphe), Meyney (St.-Estèphe), Bon Pasteur (Pomerol), L'Enclos (Pomerol), La Dominique (St.-Emilion), L'Arrosée (St.-Emilion), La Louvière (Graves), Sociando Mallet (Médoc), Chasse-Spleen (Moulis), Belles Graves (Lalande de Pomerol), and Balestard-La Tonnelle (St.-Emilion). There are a number of vintages to look for, the 1981s, the extraordinary 1982s, the excellent 1983s, and the 1985s, which will be released late in 1987 and in early 1988.

9   If you want to try a California wine, stick to the 1984 and 1985 vintages, and approach any white wine made earlier with a great deal of caution. As far as California red wines go, be extremely selective from the two erratic years of 1982 and 1983, and concentrate on the excellent 1984s now coming on the market.

10   Lastly, seek out some of the red wines now being made in Provence to discover what remarkable progress is being made in that region. From the Coteaux Aix-en-Provence make an effort to find the monumental and exquisite red wines from the Domaine Trevallon and the very good wines from Château Vignelaure. From the scenic seaside resort of Bandol, the red wines from Domaine Tempier will provide an exhilarating tasting experience, as will the red wine from the Côte de Provence estate called the Domaine Richeaume, which produces excellent wines with enchanting scents and flavours.

CHAPTER ONE

FRANCE

ALSACE

France's Least-Known Great White Wines

For years I thought that my unabashed fondness for the distinctive, spicy, unique wines of Alsace was because my first exposure to wine and France was in this highly picturesque region as a visiting student in 1967. As I have learned more about the great wines of France as well as the world, I have come to realize that these wines are among the greatest white wines of France. Furthermore, they are curiously and terribly undervalued, and, to a large part, misunderstood by the wine-drinking public.

Alsace, in the northeastern section of France, sits strategically between the Vosges Mountains and the Rhine. Although it remains fervently French in its free spirit, Alsace looks as if it belongs in Bavaria. The plethora of cute little villages overflowing with quaint, timbered houses with windows bursting with boxes of vividly coloured flowers makes Alsace France's loveliest wine region. The 70-mile stretch of Alsace's 'Route du Vin' goes through one fairy-tale village after another. The most picturesque towns, Riquewihr, Ribeauvillé, Colmar, Kaysersberg, Eguisheim, and of course, the major city of the area, Strasbourg, with its magnificent rose-coloured cathedral that still dominates the skyline, are alone reason enough to devote significant attention to this largely undiscovered area of France.

At first glance, Alsace should be the easiest region for a wine consumer to understand. All the wines are named after the grape variety they are made from. Consequently, the major wines of Alsace, the Riesling, Gewürztraminer, Muscat, Pinot Gris (also called Tokay), Pinot Blanc, and Sylvaner, are labelled as such. So why is there confusion? I suspect that many wine consumers think the wines of Alsace are similar to the German wines made further north up the Rhine. True, the grape varieties are the same. However, nothing could be further from the truth. The German wines balance crisp, tart acidity, low alcohol, and a captivating sweetness to produce light, elegant, refreshing, clean wine. In Alsace, the great majority of the wines are totally dry, much fuller-bodied than their German counterparts and a good 2-4 degrees higher in alcohol. In fullness, richness and size, the wines of Alsace come much closer to white Burgundies than to German Rieslings.

Second, Alsace has not had a 'Grand Cru' system of evaluating its top vineyard sites, as do Burgundy and Bordeaux. This changed in 1983, when Alsace developed a 'Grand Cru System' that was effectively put into action with what is coincidentally the greatest vintage for Alsace since 1971. The system recognizes 25 hillside vineyards as 'Grands Crus', chosen for their proven ability to produce outstanding and distinctive wines. The 'Grand Cru' vineyard notation will appear on the label of an Alsace wine when 100% of the grapes used for the wine have come from one of these specific vineyards. However, do not think for a moment that only the wines so designated are the best. Many of this area's top firms will continue to blend their best lots of wine under their own designations of quality such as 'Réserve' or 'Réserve Personnelle' rather than by vineyard designation. Many high-quality firms such as Hugel, Trimbach, Beyer, Domaine Weinbach, Kuentz-Bas, and Dopff produce specific lots or Cuvées that are as fine as any single-vineyard Alsace wine that you are likely to find.

In addition, the new system gives legal authority to the two types of late-harvest wines currently produced in Alsace. The 'Vendange Tardive' wines and 'Sélection de Grains Nobles' are now wines which meet specific requirements. Contrary to what most consumers believe, the Vendange Tardive wines are totally dry but harvested much later than the normal wines, for extra ripeness and richness. For example, the minimum alcohol for a Vendange Tardive Gewürztraminer or Pinot Gris is 14.3%; for Riesling 12.9%. These are rich, dry, full-bodied wines, not sweet as many consumers assume. Should you want a sweet dessert wine from Alsace, search out the wines with the designation 'Sélection de Grains Nobles'. It is these wines, representing less than 1% of the total production of Alsace, that are unctuous dessert wines and though they have the sweetness of German Beerenauslese, they are considerably higher in alcohol. Legally, the minimum requirements for these wines are 16.4 degrees potential alcohol for Gewürztraminer and Pinot Gris, and 15.1 degrees potential alcohol for Riesling and Muscat. They are indeed powerful wines.

These changes in the wine laws of Alsace could not have come at a better time as the 1983 vintage was a monumental year. The wines are opulently fruity, powerful, rich, and deep. Furthermore, they are still available in abundant quantities at the retail level. Looking ahead, 1985 is another excellent vintage, so there is a plentiful supply of fine Alsace. You will be in for some unbelievable gustatory experiences with these wonderful 1983s and 1985s from Alsace.

What does one eat with a wine from Alsace? The most spicy and distinctive of the Alsatian wines are the fragrant, rich Gewürztraminers. These full-flavoured and full-bodied wines require full-flavoured foods. Perfect matches include oriental or Indian cuisine, rich pâtés, and duck or quail. The Riesling of Alsace is a drier, fuller-bodied wine than its German counterpart; it is less aromatic, spicy, and unique than Gewürztraminer and much more flexible when paired with food. All fish and chicken dishes are

ALSACE AOC AREAS
ROUTE DE VIN
VINEYARD AREAS

MILES

KILOMETERS

Northern Alsace

Southern Alsace

ALSACE AOC AREAS
ROUTE DE VIN
VINEYARD AREAS

HAUT RHIN

Orschwiller
St-Hippolyte
Rodern
Rorschwihr
Bergheim
Ribeauvillé
Hunawihr
Zellenberg
Riquewihr
Beblenheim
Kientzheim
Mittelwihr
Kaysersberg
Bennwihr
Sigolsheim
Ammerschwihr
Katzenthal
Ingersheim
Turckheim
Wintzenheim
Colmar
Zimmerbach
Wettolsheim
Eguisheim
Husseren-le-ch.
Herrlinsheim
Voegtlinshoffen
Hattstatt
Gueberschwihr
Pfaffenheim
Rouffach
Soultzmatt
Westhalten
Orschwihr
Bergholtz
Guebwiller
Thann
Cernay
Mulhouse

Strasbourg
Paris
Alsace

0   5 MILES
0 5 10 KILOMETERS

excellent. The Pinot Gris or Tokay d'Alsace can be Alsace's biggest, richest, fullest wine. I have often mistaken a top-notch Pinot Gris for a great white Burgundy. Yes, I did say that. Pinot Gris is smoky, buttery, nutty, and very flavourful. It goes marvellously well with richly sauced fish and fowl dishes, and is superb with fresh foie gras. Lastly, but for different reasons, Pinot Blanc and Muscat are perfect apéritif wines. Pinot Blanc is light, fresh, medium-bodied, and fruity. The Muscat is softer, more perfumed, often rounder and slightly sweeter.

Most of the rich, dry, intense, full-bodied Vendange Tardive (or late-harvest) wines and the sweet dessert Sélection de Grains Nobles wines are very rare and much more expensive. Keep in mind that the top Gewürztraminers will evolve and improve in the bottle for five to ten years and the top Rieslings for five to fifteen years in vintages such as 1983 and 1985. The Vendange Tardive and Sélection de Grains Nobles wines will last twenty or more years.

ALSACE · QUICK VINTAGE GUIDE

1986 Because of significant rainfall as well as rot, it is expected that Alsace's 1986 crop will range in quality from average to above average. The size of the crop is much smaller than in 1985 or in 1983 because of the rot and hailstorms that plagued this area. Most growers hope that the wines will turn out as good as the light yet charming 1979s.

1985 An excellent vintage, the 1985 Alsace appears to be a match for the exceptional 1983s. There was less intense, full-bodied Vendange Tardive wine made and the wines are less opulent, rich, and alcoholic than the 1983s, but otherwise this is a lovely vintage of top wines that should drink well for five to seven years, if not longer. Cask samples of 1985s from Domaine Weinbach, Hugel, Zind-Humbrecht, Sparr, and Gustave Lorentz look like more elegant, finesse-styled competitors to their great 1983s. Interestingly, the Rieslings of 1985 look overall to be the strongest group, although the other varietals are certainly very good.

1984 As in all of France, a difficult year, but not disastrous as press reports indicated. Most wines are quite light, a trifle too acidic, and less intensely fruity than their 1983 and 1985 counterparts. If priced reasonably, the best of these wines offer decent drinking for the next few years.

1983 A great vintage, the best since 1976 and 1971, the 1983s from scenic Alsace have everything – intense, pungent, aromatic bouquets, long, rich, ripe flavours, plenty of body, and great balance and length. At the top levels, the wine will last until the mid- to late nineties. It was also a splendid year for the Titans of Alsace, the rich, alcoholic, but generally dry Vendange Tardive wines.

1982 A huge crop of rather sound, commercial wines that are soft, fruity, and pleasant. They are ageing fast and should, by and large, be drunk up before the end of this decade.

1981 Forgotten in all the justifiable hype surrounding 1983 and 1985, this is a good, sometimes very good, vintage of medium-bodied, fruity, well-defined wines. They have good acidity and structure, and though now at their peak, can be drunk with a good deal of pleasure over the next four to five years.

1980 A mediocre to below-average-quality vintage. Interestingly, the wines, which were tart and green when first released in 1982/1983, have mellowed substantially with ageing. Nothing exciting to be found here, but, as elsewhere in France, the wines are better than their initial reputation.

1979 A huge crop of sound, fruity, medium-bodied wines was produced in 1979. The wines have aged nicely, surprising most observers who felt they would not last. All of the wines should be drunk up over the next four to five years. This vintage can render a number of surprises, particularly in Gewürztraminer, Tokay, and Riesling.

Older Vintages

The 1976s are luscious – intense, full-blown, rather powerful wines of great dimension. The sweet, nectar-like Sélection de Grains Nobles wines are just now coming of age. Two other great vintages for Alsace were 1971 and 1967. Except for the well-cellared examples of Gewürztraminer, Tokay, and Riesling, particularly the richer, fuller-bodied Vendange Tardive wines, the glory days of these wines have passed.

A GUIDE TO ALSACE'S BEST PRODUCERS

★ ★ ★ ★ ★ Outstanding Producers

Dopff 'Au Moulin' (Riquewihr)
Hugel (Riquewihr)
Josmeyer (Wintzenheim)
Kuentz-Bas
  (Husseren-les-Châteaux)

Weinbach (Kientzheim)
Zind-Humbrecht
  (Wintzenheim)

★ ★ ★ ★ Excellent Producers

Léon Beyer (Eguisheim)
Gustave Lorentz (Bergheim)
Jerome Lorentz (Bergheim)
René Schaefle (Rouffach)

Charles Schleret (Turckheim)
Schlumberger (Guebwiller)
Pierre Sparr (Sigolsheim)
Trimbach (Ribeauvillé)

Willm (Barr)   A. Zimmerman (Orschwiller)

★ ★ ★ Good Producers

Bennwihr Cooperative
E. Boekel (Mittelbergheim)
Joseph Cattin (Voegtlinshoffen)
Bott Frères (Ribeauvillé)
Caves Vinicole d'Eguisheim
Dopff & Irion (Riquewihr)
W. Gisselbrecht
    (Dambach-La-Ville)

Klipfel (Barr)
Muré (Rouffach)
Ostertag (Epsig)
Preiss Henny (Mittelwihr)
Martin Schaetzel
    (Ammerschwihr)
René Schmidt (Riquewihr)
Louis Sipp (Ribeauvillé)

★ ★ Average Producers

Baumann (Mittelwihr)
Gaschy (Wettolsheim)

Klack (Riquewihr)
H. Krick (Wintzenheim)

IN SEARCH OF THE BEST WINES OF ALSACE

Some of the Very Best Producers and Their Best Wines

Gewürztraminer

Léon Beyer: Comtes
    D'Eguisheim
Dopff & Irion: Les Sorcières
Dopff 'Au Moulin' Eichberg
Hugel Réserve Personnelle
Josmeyer Hengst Vyd.
Kuentz-Bas Réserve
    Personnelle
Gustave Lorentz
    Altenberg Vyd.
Muré: Clos St.-Landelin
Ostertag: Moenchberg Vyd.
Schleret Cuvée Speciale

Schlumberger Christine
    Schlumberger
Schlumberger Kessler Vyd.
Pierre Sparr Mambourg Vyd.
Trimbach Ribeaupierre
Weinbach Cuvée Théo
Weinbach Réserve Personnelle
Willm Clos Gaensbroennel
Zind-Humbrecht Hengst
    Wintzenheim Vyd.
Zind-Humbrecht
    Gueberschwihr Vyd.

Riesling

Léon Beyer Ecaillers
Dopff 'Au Moulin'
    Schoenenberg
Hugel Réserve
    Personnelle
Josmeyer Hengst
Kuentz-Bas Réserve
    Personnelle
Gustave Lorentz
    Altenberg Vyd.
Ostertag Moenchberg Vyd.
Schaetzel Kaefferkopf

Schlumberg Saering Vyd.
Schmidt Schoenenberg
L. Sipp Kirchberg
Pierre Sparr Altenbourg
Trimbach Frédérick Emile
Trimbach Clos St.-Hune
Weinbach Schlossberg
Weinbach Sainte Catherine
Willm Kirchberg
Zind-Humbrecht Brand
Zind-Humbrecht Clos
    Hauserer

Zind-Humbrecht	Zind-Humbrecht Rangen
Herrenweg Turkheim	

Tokay D'Alsace (Pinot Gris)

L. Beyer Réserve	Schaetzel
Hugel Réserve Personnelle	Weinbach
Kuentz-Bas Réserve	Zind-Humbrecht Rangen
Personnelle	Zind-Humbrecht
Gustave Lorentz Altenberg	St.-Urbain Rangen

ALSACE'S VERY BEST WINE VALUES · PINOT BLANC AND CRÉMANT

Virtually all of Alsace's white wines offer good values in the world-wide wine market, but two stand out as particularly fine values: Pinot Blanc and the sparkling wine of Alsace called Crémant d'Alsace. Pinot Blanc is the poor man's Chardonnay; fresh, lively, crisp, and pleasantly fruity. It is not a wine to buy in lean, tart vintages such as 1980 and 1984 because it is then too acidic. However, it flourishes in vintages such as 1983 and 1985, rivalling in quality Chardonnays that sell for two or three times the price. Pinot Blanc, a dry, spicy wine, but not one to age well, is best drunk up within three to four years of the vintage. Alsace's other bargain, Crémant d'Alsace, is hardly known outside of the area where it is produced. This inexpensive, sparkling alternative to Champagne can be a delicious, fairly priced, dry wine.

Alsace's best Pinot Blancs

Josmeyer Hengst	
Josmeyer Les Lutins	Schlumberger Princess Abbes
Hugel Cuvée les Amours	Weinbach Réserve
M. Schaetzel	Willm Cordon d'Alsace

Alsace's best Crémants

Caves Vinicole d'Eguisheim	Muré
Dopff	Willm
Laugel	

TWO ALSACE WINES THAT RARELY MERIT ATTENTION

Not everything in Alsace is a great bargain. One of Alsace's biggest selling wines is Sylvaner. It can be good – Domaine Weinbach's is in fact always pleasant – but, in general, it is a rather dull, flat wine with little charm. It is best avoided. Alsace also makes red wines from the Pinot Noir grape. They are fashionable and rather expensive, and the local cognoscenti have a great deal of pride in the wine. However, it usually looks like a blush or rosé wine in colour and often tastes insipid and diluted, although the 1983 Muré could have been confused for a minor red Burgundy. One can find an exception or two, but Pinot Noirs from Alsace are by and large mediocre.

ALSACE · TODAY'S BUYING STRATEGY

The primary thrust in buying Alsace wines should be to search out the better 1983s that are still around on the shelves. Most of these wines will offer splendid drinking for the rest of this decade, with the Vendange Tardive wines lasting well into the next decade. The 1984s are light and somewhat acidic. They are not bad wines, but the 1983s are generally outstanding, and the newly released 1985s excellent. Buy 1983s and 1985s – you are not likely to be disappointed.

BAUMANN *MITTELWIHR* ★★
1983 Riesling Schoenenbourg .... ② **86**
Quite an excellent Riesling, this rather large-framed, big, rich wine is quite full-bodied, with an exotic, smoky, spicy bouquet, long, deep flavours, and at least three to five years of evolution ahead of it.

BENNWIHR COOPERATIVE ★★★
These wines represent very good value and on occasion can be excellent (for example, the 1983 Gewürztraminer is amazing for the price).

1983 Gewürztraminer .... ② **86**
A great value in Gewürztraminer, this rich, spicy, surprisingly intense wine has excellent depth and richness, full body, some round, ripe sweetness in the long finish, and a powerful, heady bouquet. Quite impressive.

1983 Riesling .... ① **75**
Rather tart and lean, with some herbal overtones, this dry, austere Riesling may develop more flesh and character with several more months of bottle age.

LÉON BEYER *EGUISHEIM* ★★★★
1978 Gewürztraminer Cuvée des Comtes Eguisheim .... ② **87**
The 1978 is still quite youthful but showing excellent ripeness, full body, and the rich, exotic bouquet that typifies Gewürztraminer. Quite a successful wine for the 1978 vintage in Alsace, this wine will last for at least another decade.

1981 Gewürztraminer Cuvée des Comtes Eguisheim .... ② **85**
No doubt 1981 for Alsace has been forgotten with all the justified hoopla over 1983. However, 1981 was a good vintage. This wine is still quite young and unevolved, but has oodles of the rich, exotic Gewürztraminer fruit, a powerful,

heady punch to it, and long finish. Its bouquet has yet to open and develop, but that will come.

1983 Gewürztraminer Cuvée des Comtes Eguisheim .... ② 88

A powerful, authoritative, spicy, exotic Gewürztraminer for sure, but at present this wine, despite considerable promise, is quite closed. The bouquet hints at rich, ripe fruit but remains tight and generally restrained. On the palate, the wine is full-bodied, very concentrated, but like a spring flower in bud, it has yet to blossom. Quite dry, quite concentrated, and impeccably vinified, this wine will merit a higher score in two to three years when it is showing all its considerable charm.

1983 Riesling .... ① 80
1983 Riesling Cuvée des Écaillers .... ② 82

Here is a case where the regular Riesling is almost as good as the special Cuvée and is considerably less expensive. Both wines are medium-bodied with light-intensity, floral, spicy bouquets, dry, nicely textured flavours and good crisp finishes. Both should last for four to six years.

1983 Tokay (Pinot Gris) Réserve .... ② 86
1983 Tokay (Pinot Gris) Sélection de Grains Nobles .... ⑤ 92

The Réserve is another very fine Pinot Gris in what looks to be an outstanding vintage for this grape variety. In Alsace, the Pinot Gris in this great vintage has a buttery, creamy richness that is not unlike a fine Chardonnay. This example from Beyer is a big wine like most 1983 Alsatian Pinot Gris wines, yet more restrained and elegant than others. A flowery yet buttery, creamy bouquet is just beginning to emerge. On the palate, the wine is full-bodied, relatively rich, quite long, and should improve for three to five years. As for the nectar-like 1983 Tokay Sélection de Grains Nobles, it is like tasting a blend of a great Montrachet and Yquem. Powerful, unctuous, rich, dense, and incredibly long on the palate, this wine will age for fifteen or more years.

E. BOEKEL *MITTELBERGHEIM* ★ ★ ★

Boekel is a good, even very good, producer that offers solid, well-flavoured wines at very reasonable prices.

1983 Gewürztraminer Réserve .... ② 86

This is not an overly aggressive, intense Gewürztraminer, but it is well balanced and spicy, with rich fruit and a fine, dry finish.

1983 Pinot Blanc .... ① 84

Boekel's Pinot Blanc is one of the vintage's best. It is rather fresh, ripe, rich, and full-bodied, and all in all quite impressive.

1983 Riesling... ① **84**
The 1983 Riesling from Boekel is a good, solid Riesling with flowery, spicy flavours and excellent balance.

1983 Riesling Zotzenberg.. ② **86**
An excellent Riesling with a fragrant, intense bouquet; it is very long on the palate, and has a fine balance. An impressive wine.

BOTT FRÈRES *RIBEAUVILLÉ* ★ ★ ★

This tiny firm in the lovely town of Ribeauvillé produces a small amount of wine from its own vineyards. The only wines I have experienced are the 1983s, which are excellent and very reasonably priced.

1983 Gewürztraminer Cuvée Exceptionnelle.......... ② **86**
1983 Gewürztraminer Réserve Personnelle............. ② **87**
Both of these wines are textbook Gewürztraminers at prices that are simply superb. The only difference between them I could perceive was that the Réserve Personnelle had a slightly more exaggerated bouquet and perhaps a little more depth. They are both rather big, intense wines with excellent concentration, but also possess a measure of elegance and avoid the heaviness that can sometimes be found in Gewürztraminer. Both wines will drink well for three to five years.

1983 Riesling Réserve Personnelle............................ ② **86**
An excellent Riesling, rather full yet wonderfully balanced with dry, rich, spicy, medium-bodied flavours, plenty of concentration, and a long finish. A textbook example of a dry, rather full-flavoured Alsace Riesling from an outstanding vintage. Drink over the next four to five years.

1983 Tokay d'Alsace Cuvée Exceptionelle.............. ② **80**
Light golden with a rich, smoky, spicy, almost buttery and bacon-scented bouquet, this nicely proportioned wine is not as rich and opulent on the palate as some Alsatian Tokays, but has good flavour authority, balancing acidity, and a good finish.

CAVES VINICOLE D'EGUISHEIM ★ ★ ★

This cooperative has one of the best reputations in France and now also makes the wines of the famous firm of Willm. The Aussay wines showed especially well in comparative blind tastings and, as the prices indicate, they offer excellent value. The style of the wines emphasizes crisp, dry fruitiness and medium body. They are not opulent wines, but all are faithful to their grape varieties.

1983 Crémant d'Alsace .... ② **83**
This sparkling wine from Alsace no doubt has a proportion of Pinot Gris in its composition, as the buttery, spicy bouquet suggests. The bubbles are persistent and a little large, but this sparkling wine is quite dry and has surprising flavour and character.

1983 Gewürztraminer .... ① **84**
With a flowery, almond-scented, fruity bouquet, this wine is less spicy than normal for Gewürztraminer, but this medium-bodied, stylish wine has good concentration and very fine length; it is dry, crisp and well made.

1983 Pinot Blanc d'Alsace .... ① **81**
Light- to medium-bodied, fresh, fruity, dry yet very refreshing and quite cleanly made, this is a charming wine for drinking now.

1983 Pinot Gris d'Alsace .... ① **85**
A lovely wine, as are so many 1983s from Alsace, this wine has a subtle, smoky, buttery, creamy bouquet that is reminiscent of a good white Burgundy. Medium to full body with very good length, adequate acidity, and good dryness make this wine excellent value.

1983 Riesling .... ① **84**
Quite an attractive Riesling, this medium-bodied wine is aromatic, spicy, and fresh, with solid fruit flavours.

DOPFF & IRION *RIQUEWIHR* ★★★
One of the most important firms of Alsace, Dopff & Irion produce significant quantities of wines that are usually good but rarely spectacular. The firm has excellent vineyards, but the wines have been criticized for having a commercial dullness rather than any individualistic or unique style. I would tend to agree with such observations for the 1983s from Dopff & Irion, with the exception of the firm's sensational top-of-the-line Gewürztraminer, Les Sorcières. Certainly the prices for Dopff & Irion wines remain quite reasonable.

1982 Gewürztraminer .... ① **70**
1983 Gewürztraminer .... ② **83**
The 1983 Gewürztraminer shows good ripeness, a typically big, rich, smoky, lychee-scented aroma, a touch of coarseness in the finish, and medium body. The 1982 is quite light, rather

soft and flabby, and should be drunk soon. The 1983 will keep well for the balance of this decade.

1981 Gewürztraminer Les Sorcières............................ ③ **83**
1982 Gewürztraminer Les Sorcières............................ ③ **70**
1983 Gewürztraminer Les Sorcières............................ ③ **89**

These three wines illustrate the greatness of the 1983 vintage. The 1981 is good, delicate, spicy, rather restrained for a Gewürztraminer, but stylish and well made. The 1982 is a trifle diffuse and borders on being watery and bland. However, the 1983 is the finest wine made by Dopff & Irion in at least a decade. An intense, powerful bouquet of ripe, spicy fruit is followed by a wine that has layers of flavour, full body, an intense, lingering finish and great balance. The 1983 is quite a big wine that begs for a rich pâté, or a duck or quail dish. It should improve for at least four to five more years and last well until the nineties before fading.

1982 Riesling... ① **72**
1983 Riesling... ② **82**

The 1983 regular Riesling shows good, crisp acidity, medium body and an attractive perfume of spicy, floral fruit. It is stylish and well made rather than dramatic and concentrated. The 1982 is quite light, lacks flavour authority, and finishes short and pale.

1983 Sylvaner.. ① **72**

I have never been a great admirer of Sylvaner, a wine I find acidic, with little charm and often some bitterness. I suspect these wines have turned out better than usual in 1983 because of the exceptional ripeness attained in this vintage, but I have yet to find many 1983 Sylvaners that I can enthusiastically recommend. This is a clean yet rather thin, bland wine that is neutral and, one might say, honest, but even at its low price is no bargain.

DOPFF 'AU MOULIN' *RIQUEWIHR* ★ ★ ★ ★ ★

A top house of Alsace, Dopff 'Au Moulin' has an impressive list of vineyards and also produces the best sparkling wine of Alsace. The wines drink young but age well. They are definitely wines to seek out.

N.V. Crémant d'Alsace .... ② **84**

A fresh, lively wine with good concentration of fruit and medium body. Very stylish.

1983 Gewürztraminer Eichberg................................. ③ **90**

The 1983 Gewürztraminer Eichberg is simply extraordinary.

A spectacular bouquet of lychees and exotic fruit, great concentration and length, plus super balance all combine to make this an outstanding wine.

1983 Gewürztraminer Réserve..................................... ③ **87**
The 1983 Réserve has an exceptional nose – ripe, spicy, deep, long, massive fruit on the palate – and it is very rich and deep.

1983 Riesling Réserve.. ② **86**
A fragrant, rich, flowery, spicy nose, and deep, long, rich flavours combine to produce a very well-made wine.

1983 Riesling Schoenenberg Vendange Tardive..... ③ **90**
This wine is a superb Riesling. It has a long, rich, fabulous bouquet, long finish, and is quite dry on the palate. Should last ten years.

GASCHY *WETTOLSHEIM* ★★
These wines are quite inexpensive and offer sound, rather one-dimensional, simple drinking at very fair prices. On occasion, this winery can turn out something special, as it did in 1983 with its Vendange Tardive Riesling and Gewürztraminer.

1983 Gewürztraminer Cuvée Tradition.................... ① **75**
1983 Gewürztraminer Pfersigberg Vendange Tardive... ② **85**
1983 Gewürztraminer Réserve Personnelle............. ① **75**
The star here is the dry, rich, full-bodied Pfersigberg, which has an exotic, smoky, spicy bouquet, and soft, round, clean flavours. It is quite spicy and should be served with pâté or game. The Réserve Personnelle is clean, pleasant, but of standard quality, and the Cuvée Tradition is quite palatable, but very simple and short in the finish.

1983 Pinot Gris Réserve Personnelle......................... ① **70**
Faint, spicy, creamy aromas suggest a rather watery Pinot Gris. On the palate, the wine is light, but clean and fresh.

1983 Riesling Cuvée Tradition..................................... ① **72**
1983 Riesling Réserve Personnelle............................. ① **75**
1983 Riesling Steingrubler Vendange Tardive........ ② **84**
The Riesling Steingrubler is a finely made wine, rather concentrated, full and spicy, with good acidity and length. It should age well for one to three years. The Réserve Personnelle is lean and tart, the Cuvée Tradition even more so.

WILLY GISSELBRECHT *DAMBACH-LA-VILLE* ★★★
A reliable rather than exciting producer of wine; Gisselbrecht's wines often represent very good value.

1983 Gewürztraminer Cuvée Réserve .... ② **84**
The Cuvée Réserve has rather deep colour, is ripe and round, juicy and concentrated. It tends to be one-dimensional, but is still quite satisfying.

1983 Pinot Blanc .... ① **83**
A ripe, flavourful, rather plump and succulent wine.

1983 Riesling .... ① **83**
Gisselbrecht's 1983 Riesling has a rather ripe peach-like nose with a good, supple palate.

HEYDT – see TRIMBACH

HUGEL *RIQUEWIHR* ★ ★ ★ ★ ★

Alsace's most famous wine firm, this family-run operation began in the lovely town of Riquewihr in 1637 and is now run by the ebullient Jean (or 'Johnnie') Hugel. For many Alsace enthusiasts, the name Hugel is synonymous with these special and distinctive wines. The quality here is very high and, fortunately, the wines are easy to find. The style of the wine is quite rich, concentrated, opulent, and full-bodied. The Gewürztraminers and late-harvest Sélection de Grains Nobles wines, whether they be Gewürztraminer, Riesling, Muscat, or Tokay, are truly brilliant. In addition, Hugel wines keep exceptionally well, though one suspects that most of them are drunk when they are still in a pre-pubescent state for the simple reason that they show so well. The 1983s of Hugel are truly superb, easily the equals of the great wines this firm produced in 1976 and 1971.

1976 Gewürztraminer Grains Nobles .... ⑤ **95**
1976 Gewürztraminer Grains Nobles .... ⑤ **95**
1976 Gewürztraminer Réserve Personnelle .... ⑤ **88**
1976 Gewürztraminer Vendange Tardive .... ⑤ **87**
All four of these excellent wines can still be found. Consumers are unaware that these wines, particularly the two nectar-like Sélections de Grains Nobles, are as spectacular in their own distinctive style as a great vintage of Yquem, and therefore have let them sit. The 1976 Beerenauslese-styled Gewürztraminers are still adolescents in terms of their evolution, but are truly stunning wines. Claimed by the Hugel firm as the greatest Sélection de Grains Nobles wine they have ever produced, these wines have layers of exotic tropical fruit, finishes that last a full 60 seconds (which is extremely long), intense, magnificently aromatic bouquets, and unbelievable balance. It is worth latching onto a bottle to celebrate the year 2000. The Vendange Tardive is very, very good, but lacks the depth, dimension, and balance of the Sélection de Grains

Nobles wines. As for the totally dry, intense 1976 Réserve Personnelle, it smells of ripe pineapples, almonds, candied lychees, has a powerful, heady punch to its full-bodied, rich texture, and is ready to drink now.

1979 Gewürztraminer Réserve Personnelle............ ③ **85**
Hugel produced an excellent Gewürztraminer in 1979. It may not rival the 1983 or 1976 Réserve Personnelle, but it is still quite full-bodied, rather powerful, nicely balanced, and dry with ample length and acidity. Drink over the next two to three years.

1981 Gewürztraminer Réserve Personnelle............ ③ **86**
1981 Gewürztraminer Vendange Tardive................ ④ **85**
These two 1981 Gewürztraminers are very fine, but when compared to the great efforts of Hugel in 1983 and 1976, lack the breadth and depth of the wines of the two latter vintages. Both are typically 'Hugelian', concentrated, ripe, plump, deep, but not yet complex. The Vendange Tardive is a trifle soft and leans towards being flabby. However, it and the Réserve Personnelle are authoritative examples of Gewürztraminer from one of France's great wine families.

1983 Gewürztraminer.. ② **86**
1983 Gewürztraminer Réserve Personnelle............ ③ **88**
1983 Gewürztraminer Vendange Tardive................ ④ **92**
Three outstanding examples of the Hugel style of Gewürztraminer, these wines all share this firm's rich, powerful, deep, full-bodied style. The late-harvest Vendange Tardive is not sweet, but rather incredibly ripe and rich, powerfully built, with a full-blown bouquet of almonds and flowers. It is quite long and sensationally concentrated. It should drink well for ten to twenty years. Slightly less exuberant, but still an authoritatively rich, dense, full-bodied wine, the Hugel Réserve Personnelle is probably the finest in a long line of superb Gewürztraminers since Hugel's great 1971. Even the regular Gewürztraminer shows surprising richness and strength, with a big, rich, spicy bouquet, lush, full-bodied flavours, and good balance.

1983 Pinot Blanc Cuvée les Amours.......................... ① **84**
1985 Pinot Blanc Cuvée les Amours.......................... ① **84**
Hugel's Pinot Blanc has rarely been one of the firm's better wines, but in the 1983 they are justifiably proud of the quality. This dry wine is spicy, quite fruity, round and generous, with good, crisp balance and acidity. The 1985 is slightly less opulent and lush, but stylish, quite well made, and ready to drink.

1983 Riesling.. ② *84*
1983 Riesling Réserve Personelle .... ② *85*
Hugel's regular Riesling has a wonderfully fresh, perfumed
character, medium to full body, is quite dry, but round, fruity
and surprisingly long. The Réserve Personnelle is riper, longer
on the finish, slightly deeper and fuller, with oodles of ripe
Riesling fruit. These are rather big wines with alcohol contents of 12.5%, an interesting contrast to their German
counterparts with 8% alcohol.

1983 Tokay Réserve Personnelle................................. ③ *86*
The poor man's Meursault? Many of the 1983 Tokays from
Alsace are so buttery, smoky, full-bodied, and rich that one
could easily assume one was drinking a great Meursault. Full-
bodied and rather powerful, this strongly scented, big, rich
wine will age well for four to seven years.

JOSMEYER *WINTZENHEIM* ★ ★ ★ ★ ★
One of the least known of the great wine firms of Alsace, the family-
run winery of Joseph Meyer, which appears on the label as Josmeyer,
produces outstanding wines, particularly Gewürztraminer, Pinot
Blanc, and Riesling. His Pinot Blanc is unquestionably the best in
Alsace, and is remarkably cheap. Josmeyer's wines are very rich and
concentrated, yet slow to mature, and older examples such as the
1966 Riesling and 1964 Gewürztraminer Vendange Tardive can be
incredible wines and are among the least-known great dry white
wines of the world.

1983 Gewürztraminer Cuvée des Centenaire-
Hengst.. ③ *91*
1983 Gewürztraminer Les Archenets .... ② *87*
Josmeyer's successes extend throughout his line of wines, but
certainly his 1983 Gewürztraminers are quite special. His
blended Gewürztraminer from different vineyard sites, the
Les Archenets, is splendid enough, rich, powerful, deep, quite
dry, rather alcoholic, but exotically fruity and big. However,
the special Gewürztraminer Cuvée des Centenaire, from the
chalky soil of the Hengst vineyard, is magical in 1983. It is one
of the greatest dry Gewürztraminers I have ever tasted.
Decadently rich and opulent, this full-bodied, intensely perfumed wine has stupendous length and layers of ripe, rich
fruit. It is drinking well now and will last for well over a
decade.

1983 Pinot d'Alsace Les Lutins.................................... ① *82*
1983 Pinot Auxerrois Hengst-Vieilles Vignes .... ① *85*

1983 Pinot Blanc Réserve Fourways............................ ① *84*
The 1983 Vieilles Vignes from the chalky soil of the Hengst vineyard, made from a Pinot clone called Pinot Auxerrois, is a remarkably stylish, spicy, clean, medium-bodied, dry, flavourful wine with real elegance and breeding. It is ideal for drinking over the next three to four years. The 1983 Pinot Blanc Fourways has ripe flavours and surprising richness and length. The Les Lutins is Josmeyer's blend of Pinot Blanc grapes. It is quite good and certainly one of the best Pinot Blancs from the 1983 vintage, but it gets upstaged by the firm's other two wines.

1983 Riesling Les Pierrets .... ② *84*
1983 Riesling Vendange Tardive Hengst .... ③ *87*
The Les Pierrets, the firm's blend of Riesling from different sites, is opulent, lovely, spicy, very flowery, quite dry, with well-defined flavours, good depth, and a solid finish. It should be drunk soon. The Hengst Vendange Tardive is as expected, quite rich, medium- to full-bodied, spicy, ripe, and concentrated, with a long, round, luscious finish. It is very impressive and will last more than a decade.

1983 Sylvaner d'Alsace .... ① *77*
Not a bad Sylvaner, this effort from Josmeyer shows good ripeness, a touch of acidity in the finish, but is generally pleasing, albeit simple.

KLACK *RIQUEWIHR* ★★
Apparently, Klack is a very small producer or secondary label, and the only wines I have seen from this firm are the 1983s, which are quite good.

1983 Gewürztraminer... ② *84*
Rather soft, ripe, and lush, this aromatic wine has the Gewürztraminer spicy character, medium to full body, and good length. Drink over the next one to two years.

1983 Riesling.. ② *85*
A distinctive Riesling, smoky, quite spicy, with rather dramatic, intense flavours, this is an impressive Riesling for drinking over the next three to four years.

KLIPFEL *BARR* ★★★
I know little about this estate except that it is in the very northern section of Alsace's viticultural region. With little tasting experience of the wines, it is hard to say anything about the house style. The 1983s were good rather than spectacular.

1983 Gewürztraminer Clos Zisser............................ ② **85**
A rich, authoritative, spicy, intense wine.

1983 Pinot Gris Freiberg... ① **80**
A satisfactory rather than excellent Pinot Gris, this offering from Klipfel is round, slightly sweet, quite spicy and fruity, but it lacks acidity and finishes a little short.

1983 Riesling.. ① **84**
1983 Riesling Kirchberg... ① **86**
The standard Cuvée of Riesling is quite good, fresh, aromatic, dry, with a bouquet suggestive of walnuts and flowers; it is a nicely textured wine, but the Kirchberg has a big, complex, fragrant bouquet, spicy, fresh, rather concentrated flavours, and an impressive finish. The Kirchberg should drink well for four to five years.

KUENTZ-BAS *HUSSEREN-LES-CHÂTEAUX* ★ ★ ★ ★
This tiny firm has an excellent reputation in Alsace, and the quality of its wines and in particular the 1983s should do much to establish this tiny, family firm's place among the most successful of Alsace's producers. My favourite wines of Kuentz-Bas have been the splendidly rich Gewürztraminers and Tokays. The Pinot Blancs and Rieslings do not seem to be of the same calibre. The firm believes its Muscat is the best. The style of wines produced by Kuentz-Bas is neither the most full-bodied and opulent à la Weinbach, Schlumberger, or Hugel, nor the most restrained and elegant à la Trimbach or Beyer. It lies somewhere between these two general approaches to making Alsace wines.

1983 Gewürztraminer Cuvée Tradition.................... ① **88**
1983 Gewürztraminer Réserve Personnelle............. ② **89**
1983 Gewürztraminer Vendange Tardive Cuvée
Caroline.. ③ **91**
Here are three very fine Gewürztraminers, two of which are sold very inexpensively. The regular or standard Cuvée, called Cuvée Tradition, is a powerful wine with a huge, smoky bacon fat and exotic fruit bouquet, rich, concentrated flavours, a good measure of alcohol, and long finish. It should be drunk over the next three to four years. One of my favourites here is the Réserve Personnelle (which is also a great buy), because it is a powerful, authoritative, deeply concentrated Gewürztraminer with a big aromatic, smoky, almond-like bouquet, long, gorgeously fruity flavours, a full body, and I would guess at least 13.5% alcohol. The Vendange Tardive is immense in stature, and a remarkably alcoholic and powerful wine that has more in common with a great Montrachet than a typical Alsace wine.

1983 Muscat Réserve Personnelle .... ② **82**
Very aromatic, as one would expect, this is one of the Kuentz-Bas wines that is certainly good, but a trifle heavy and lacking in acidity. Drink over the next year. Curiously, Kuentz-Bas regards Muscat as one of the firm's specialities.

1983 Pinot Blanc Cuvée Tradition .... ① **78**
For the price, this wine may merit a look, but it is not one of the top Pinot Blancs of the vintage. It has a good, clean, spicy, fruity nose, but has a touch of harshness in the finish.

1983 Riesling Réserve Personnelle .... ① **84**
1983 Riesling Sélection de Grains Nobles .... ⑤ **90**
The Réserve Personnelle is a good, clean, stylish, dry medium-bodied Riesling with a concentration of fruit and good acidity. The Sélection de Grains Nobles has 15.2% alcohol, a gorgeous, perfumed, fragrant bouquet, intense and powerful flavours, and an amazing finish. It should age for twenty to twenty-five years.

**1983 Tokay d'Alsace Pinot Gris Réserve
Personnelle** .... ② **87**
**1983 Tokay d'Alsace Pinot Gris Vendange
Tardive** .... ③ **85**
The 1983 Tokay Réserve Personnelle is splendidly concentrated, rich, buttery, smoky, and better than 85% of the white Burgundies on the market. It is a dry, full-bodied, very rich wine with stunning length. The Vendange Tardive would have scored higher, but some slight sulphur in the nose kept the score low.

GUSTAVE and JEROME LORENTZ *BERGHEIM* ★ ★ ★ ★

Two separate firms, Gustave Lorentz and Jerome Lorentz are managed by the same staff, and although the wines come from different vineyards, both the winemaking philosophy and care of the wines are under the control of Charles Lorentz, Jr. The Gustave Lorentz operation is twice the size of Jerome's, but both are rather moderate in size – a production of 160,000 cases for Gustave and 80,000 for Jerome. Both firms are highly respected for their Gewürztraminers, which usually come from the two Grand Cru vineyards of Altenberg and Kanzlerberg. I would enthusiastically agree with such observations, since these wines are clearly both firms' best. However, I would not disregard the Riesling of Jerome Lorentz from the Altenberg vineyard or the Muscat and Tokay (from Altenberg) from Gustave Lorentz. The basic Cuvées, or regular bottlings, from both Jerome and Gustave Lorentz are generally sound, but usually not on the same level of quality as the regular

Cuvées of Hugel, Trimbach or Zind-Humbrecht. The style of wine produced at Lorentz is one that emphasizes ripeness, power, and opulent flavours. The specific vineyard wines are the wines to search out from these two firms.

GUSTAVE LORENTZ

1983 Gewürztraminer	①	78
1983 Gewürztraminer Altenberg	③	90
1983 Gewürztraminer Réserve	①	84
1983 Gewürztraminer Sélection de Grains Nobles	⑤	98
1983 Gewürztraminer Vendange Tardive	④	88

The standard Cuvée of Gewürztraminer I found to be a little lacking in character and a disappointment. The Réserve is a big step up in quality as it is a rather fat, ripe, full-bodied, well-made wine. The other three wines are all huge, ripe, intense, monumental Gewürztraminers. The Altenberg has an immense structure, a chewy texture, great ripeness and length, and staggering concentration. It will drink well and improve for over a decade. The Vendange Tardive is similarly styled, even more powerful, with a head-spinning alcohol content of 14.5-15%, a dry finish, and enough body and flesh to make one think it is an old-style Chalone Chardonnay. Finally, the Sélection de Grains Nobles, which is 90% from the Grand Cru vineyard Altenberg, is a legendary wine, virtually perfect, with an incredible perfume, richness and concentration, a simply outlandish length (over 90 seconds), and fifteen to thirty years of evolution. It held up without oxidation for eight days in an open bottle. An astonishing wine!

1983 Muscat	②	85

One of the best Alsatian Muscats I have tasted, this full-bodied wine has plenty of fruit, a long, lingering finish and adequate acidity.

1983 Riesling Altenberg	③	88
1983 Riesling Réserve	①	83

The Riesling Altenberg ranks as one of the outstanding Rieslings from this great vintage. A lovely bouquet of spices and ripe pineapple gives way to a complex, rich, dry, medium- to full-bodied Riesling with excellent presence in the mouth. It should improve for six to eight years. The Réserve Riesling is more austere, with a steely, mineral-scented bouquet and tight, austere flavours.

1983 Sylvaner Réserve	①	74

Not very interesting, but clean, spicy, with a rather herbal, weedy character and some acidity in the finish, this wine is rather typical of the common Sylvaner grape.

1983 Tokay d'Alsace Altenberg...................................... ③ **87**

This wine is a dead ringer for a fat, buttery, smoky Meursault. The intense bouquet is followed by a wine that is spicy, unctuous, rich, and full-bodied, with a super finish. Quite powerful, creamy, and rich, one should think of this wine as one would a great white Burgundy – serve it with fowl or fish.

JEROME LORENTZ

1983 Gewürztraminer... ② **85**
1983 Gewürztraminer Vendange Tardive................. ④ **87**

The regular Gewürztraminer is quite fat and forward, with the superb ripeness and richness of this special vintage very capably displayed. It is intensely spicy, light golden in colour, lush, ripe, and very opulent. Because of its forward character, I would opt for drinking this wine over the next several years. As for the Vendange Tardive, it is very long and rich on the palate, with considerable alcohol, a deep, full-bodied, concentrated texture, and intensely aromatic bouquet. It should be drunk over the next four to six years.

1983 Pinot Blanc.. ① **82**

Another lovely Pinot Blanc, the 1983 has a light golden colour, medium body, and a crisp finish. It is spicy, very attractive, and fruity. Drink now.

1983 Riesling.. ① **78**

Very crisp, a little lean and ungenerous for an Alsace Riesling, this is an acceptable but undramatic wine. Drink over the next three to four years.

1983 Sylvaner... ③ **76**

Pleasant, simple, light, cleanly made and medium-bodied, this Sylvaner is free of the annoying acidity and blandness that this grape variety usually possesses.

MURÉ-CLOS SAINT-LANDELIN *ROUFFACH* ★★★

The firm of Muré, which owns 44 acres of the excellent vineyard Clos St.-Landelin, produces full-flavoured, rather strongly scented wines that usually have been put through a malolactic fermentation for additional complexity and lower acidity. I have generally found the wines of Muré good, but I am less enthusiastic about them than other well-regarded growers in Alsace. Not infrequently, the wines seem to have a rather flabby character and a slightly bizarre bouquet. The Gewürztraminers tend to be the best wines.

1983 Gewürztraminer Clos St.-Landelin .... ② **85**

1983 Gewürztraminer Clos St.-Landelin Sélection de Grains Nobles ...... ③ 90

The regular Gewürztraminer has a relatively deep colour, a typical ripe, exotic bouquet, and soft, fat flavours that taste a little low in acidity but do have plenty of length and concentration. It should be drunk over the next two to three years. The Sélection de Grains Nobles has a full-blown bouquet of ripe peaches and apricots, very concentrated, sweet, fruity flavours, full body, a huge finish, and at least 8 years of evolution.

1983 Muscat Clos St.-Landelin ...... ① 85

One of the best 1983 Muscats I tasted from Alsace, this dry, very aromatic, spicy, fruity wine has delicious flavours, medium body, and a crisp, clean, long finish. Drink it as a distinctive apéritif.

1983 Pinot Blanc Clos. St.-Landelin ...... ① 76

Quite different from the other Alsatian Pinot Blancs, the Muré has a fennel-dominated bouquet, is rather austere and tart, with some harshness in the finish.

1983 Pinot Noir ...... ② 80

This wine has surprisingly good colour, but resembles a good Beaujolais rather than a Pinot Noir.

1983 Riesling Clos St.-Landelin ...... ② 83

For a 1983 Riesling, this offering is lean, with an earthy yet pleasant bouquet, good, solid, varietal, Riesling flavours, and a moderate finish.

1983 Sylvaner Clos St.-Landelin ...... ① 72

Not much of interest can be found in this Sylvaner, which is straightforward and has a touch of acidity.

1983 Tokay Clos St.-Landelin ...... ② 80

Somewhat unusual in that this wine has a slight rosé blush to it, Muré Tokay is very ripe, a trifle too soft and flabby, but full-bodied and unctuous. Drink over the next several years because of its low acidity.

OSTERTAG EPSIG ★ ★ ★
1983 Gewürztraminer Moenchberg ...... ③ 87

This is a firmly structured, young, potentially outstanding Gewürztraminer. The bouquet is just beginning to open and emerge. The flavours show wonderful richness, ripeness and concentration. Quite deep and full-bodied, this wine should continue to develop for three to six years.

1983 Pinot Gris (Tokay)... ① 84
A plump, substantial wine with plenty of round, creamy, buttery Tokay fruit, a heady alcoholic punch, and rather long finish. Not so complex as many of the Tokays, but still a big, hefty, husky wine.

1983 Riesling.. ① 68
1983 Riesling Moenchberg............................... ③ 85
The regular Riesling is so tart and green that it is hard to believe it could have come from the 1983 vintage. This is certainly not the case with the Moenchberg, which has very good ripeness, deep, medium- to full-bodied flavours, a mineral-scented bouquet, and good acidity.

PREISS HENNY *MITTELWIHR* ★ ★ ★
A little-known but generally well-regarded producer. The several 1983s I tasted of this firm were well-made, attractive wines, with the Gewürztraminer particularly good.

1983 Gewürztraminer Château de Mittelwihr........ ② 87
Close to being a superb Gewürztraminer, this is a very powerful, rich, deep, spicy, almond-scented wine with excellent palate presence, full body, a strong, alcoholic punch to it, and very firm length. It is an extrovert, big, luscious, dry Gewürztraminer for drinking over the next two to three years.

1983 Riesling Château de Mittelwihr....................... ② 83
Rather reserved and restrained as to smell, this youthful Riesling is lean and tight, but shows good fruit, medium body, and a crisp, fruity finish. Drink over the next two to three years.

MARTIN SCHAETZEL *AMMERSCHWIHR* ★ ★ ★
Schaetzel has very high-quality wines that retail at excellent prices. His 1983s are rich, rather full-bodied, with oodles of ripe fruit present. They may well be the sleepers of the 1983 vintage in Alsace.

1982 Gewürztraminer Réserve.................................. ① 78
1983 Gewürztraminer.. ① 86
The 1982 is rather thin and high in acidity, whereas the 1983 is rich, full-bodied, deeply fruity, long on the palate and so, so lush. It should be drunk over the next one to two years.

1983 Pinot Blanc... ① 84
One of the finest Pinot Blancs on the market, the 1983 Schaetzel is quite concentrated and rather full for a Pinot Blanc, with plenty of spice and length. Drink now.

1983 Riesling Kaefferkopf Cuvée Réserve .... ① 85

Quite a complex wine, the Riesling has a bouquet suggestive of flowers, mint, and pineapple. Quite youthful on the palate, with good acidity and a long finish, this wine will improve for four years or more.

1983 Sylvaner .... ① 77

Certainly a good Sylvaner, but typically herbaceous, spicy, dry, and aromatic, this light- to medium-bodied wine should be drunk over the next year.

1983 Tokay d'Alsace .... ① 87

A Meursault look-alike, this dry, big, full-bodied wine is quite rich and powerful, with a smoky, butterscotch aroma, long, deep flavours, and good balancing acidity. Drink over the next two to three years.

CHARLES SCHLERET *TURCKHEIM* ★ ★ ★ ★

Schleret's wines are quite popular among connoisseurs. My only exposure with Schleret's wines are the 1983s, which are all quite good and among the finest regular Cuvée wines I have tasted from any grower in Alsace. The prices are quite modest given the quality.

1983 Gewürztraminer Cuvée Speciale .... ② 87

One of the most smoky, exotically rich bouquets I have ever encountered was from this gorgeously perfumed, complex wine. Medium- to full-bodied, with excellent concentration and balance, this spicy, totally dry Gewürztraminer is a delight to drink now.

1983 Riesling .... ① 84

This is not a flamboyant Riesling, but rather a well-knit, clean, fresh, dry, fruity, medium-bodied wine that has impressive structure. Drink over the next four to five years.

SCHLUMBERGER *GUEBWILLER* ★ ★ ★ ★

In the drab town of Guebwiller, one of the few in Alsace that has little tourist value, the Schlumberger firm produces a bevy of good Alsatian wines that are well coloured, fat, ripe, sometimes heavy and too alcoholic, but always interesting. This firm's best wines are its intense, rich, almost unctuous Gewürztraminers, which run the gamut from dry regular Cuvées like the Fleur de Guebwiller and Kessler to the late-harvest Vendange Tardive wines called Cuvée Christine Schlumberger and Cuvée Anne Schlumberger. As for the other wines, I have often been left unexcited and have even found a few rather tiresome to drink. The Riesling Kitterlé has the best reputation, though it rarely inspired me. This is a firm where lovers of the lusty, rich Gewürztraminers will find a great deal of pleasure, but the other wines can be flabby and heavy.

1983 Gewürztraminer Cuvée Christine Schlumberger .... ④ 90
The Cuvée Christine Schlumberger is a dessert wine with a nectar-like, honeyed sweetness, and sensational length and concentration. It will improve for ten or more years.

1983 Gewürztraminer Kessler .... ② 88
I was struck by the sheer power, richness, and balance of this huge, rather massive Gewürztraminer. Power and ripeness are the two principal assets of this wine.

1983 Gewürztraminer Kitterlé .... ② 88
The Kitterlé is ripe and exotic, with plump, luscious, big flavours. A very big, assertive wine.

1983 Pinot Blanc Cuvée Princess Abbes .... ① 85
This dry Cuvée is one of the market's great values in white wine. It is full-bodied, ripe, spicy, long, and deep on the palate.

1983 Riesling Saering .... ② 86
A classic, deeply flavourful, well-textured, fruity Riesling with class and complexity.

RENÉ SCHMIDT *RIQUEWIHR* ★★★
This small firm, in the quaint, touristy town of Riquewihr, produces sound, good-quality wines that I have always found to be a little high in acidity and austere in personality. The 1983s, no doubt because of the superb vintage, taste considerably rounder and richer, with a creamier texture than I normally associate with this grower. Schmidt's wines tend to be quite fairly priced.

1983 Gewürztraminer Cuvée Particulière .... ① 85
Surprisingly round, fruity and ripe, with a floral, peach-like bouquet, this lush Gewürztraminer has good spice and length, medium to full body, and a soft finish. It should be drunk over the next one to two years.

1983 Muscat Schoenenberg Cuvée Particulière ..... ① 75
One rarely sees Muscat from the Schoenenberg vineyard, and I could hardly get excited about this one, which is rather lean, bland, and characterless.

1983 Riesling Réserve .... ① 83
1983 Riesling Schoenenberg .... ② 86
The Réserve Riesling is quite attractive, nicely concentrated, dry, a little tart, medium-bodied, and crisp. The Schoenen-

berg has a complex bouquet of ripe fruit and cinnamon, is rather rich and deeply concentrated with a ripe, long finish. It is an excellent, medium-bodied Riesling.

1983 Tokay d'Alsace Cuvée Particulière.................. ① *82*
A rather light Tokay for Alsace in 1983, but nevertheless charming and ready for drinking now, this medium-bodied, pleasant wine has round, creamy flavours.

LOUIS SIPP *RIBEAUVILLÉ* ★ ★ ★
This firm in Ribeauvillé specializes in Riesling and Gewürztraminer. The firm's reputation is for good rather than spectacular wines. The 1983s look quite good.

1983 Gewürztraminer Medaille d'Or........................ ② *88*
1983 Gewürztraminer Sigille Qualité....................... ② *83*
Both of these wines are quite powerful Gewürztraminers. However, the Medaille d'Or has the ultimate class and distinction because it has the balance to go along with its huge power, ripeness and length. It should be drunk young, preferably over the next three to four years. The Sigille Qualité has the same power and richness, but an otherwise much higher score is brought down by some coarseness and bitterness in the finish.

1983 Riesling Kirchberg de Ribeauvillé .... ② *85*
1983 Riesling Sigille Qualité... ② *78*
The Sigille Qualité Riesling is pleasant, a little tart and green, but varietal and correct. The Grand Cru Kirchberg is very flavourful, with quite well-defined, long, rich flavours and a medium-bodied texture and finish. It needs one to two years to exhibit all its charm.

PIERRE SPARR *SIGOLSHEIM* ★ ★ ★ ★
I was unable to track down many wines from Sparr, a producer with a good reputation and some good vineyards, particularly Brand in Turckheim.

1981 Gewürztraminer Réserve..................................... ② *86*
1983 Gewürztraminer Cuvée Particulière............... ② *83*
**1983 Gewürztraminer Mambourg Cuvée
Centenaire**.. ③ *90*
These are all robust, rather rich, spicy Gewürztraminers that offer power rather than finesse. The 1981 Réserve is showing very well, with excellent ripeness, length, and full body. The 1983 Cuvée Particulière is a less rich and less weighty Gewürztraminer, but it finishes well. However, the 1983 Mambourg is a real head-turner. A very powerful, opulent,

full-bodied, dry, rich wine with a perfumed, exotic aroma of lychees and tropical fruits. This wine has sensational ripeness, excellent structure, and a finish that lasts over 40 seconds.

1983 Riesling Altenbourg Centenaire .... ③ *84*
1983 Riesling Carte d'Or .... ① *75*
The Carte d'Or is a nice yet simple Riesling with some tartness and austere qualities, but lacking a bit in the middle as well as the finish. However, the Altenbourg, although quite light in colour, exhibits very good ripeness, medium to full body, a spicy, perfumed bouquet, and good finish.

TRIMBACH *RIBEAUVILLÉ* ★ ★ ★ ★

Along with the firm of Hugel, Trimbach is one of the very best-known as well as largest Alsace firms that is capable of producing high-quality wines. The style of wine aimed at here is for wines less powerful and opulently fruity, but more delicate, crisp, refined, and austere. As with many producers, their 1983s are particularly successful. This is a firm that can often be a bit spotty in perform-ance, particularly in years where the crop is enormous and the wines a little light. It seems that in such years the Trimbach wines lack concentration and stuffing. However, in the superb vintages for Alsace, 1971, 1976, 1983 and 1985 this firm produces very refined, beautiful wines. The top wines are always the special bottlings of Riesling called Frédéric Emile and Clos Saint-Hune (the latter an uncompromisingly brilliant wine), and the special Gewürztraminer called Cuvée des Seigneurs de Ribeaupierre.The firm also produces Vendange Tardive wines with these Cuvée designations. Trimbach's wines have the virtue of being widely available, and the 1983s, particularly the regular Cuvées, are very fairly priced. Trimbach wines are also marketed under the Heydt label.

1983 Gewürztraminer .... ② *83*
1983 Gewürztraminer Ribeaupierre .... ③ *92*
**1983 Gewürztraminer Ribeaupierre Vendange
Tardive** .... ⑤ *96*
Trimbach's 1983s, like so many growers in Alsace in this marvellous vintage, are very, very successful. The standard Cuvée of Gewürztraminer is less flamboyant and extroverted than many of the vintage, but exhibits lovely balance, a seductive, spicy fruitiness, medium body, and surprising elegance. It will drink well for one to two years. The Cuvée Ribeaupierre is simply sensational. Extraordinarily deep, rich, and full-bodied, yet impeccably balanced and elegant, it is a winemaking *tour de force*. Even better is the Ribeaupierre Vendange Tardive. This is a 'must have' wine for connoisseurs, for it is as rich, opulent, and complex as the greatest Yquem or

German Eiswein. Words hardly do it justice – just let me say that it is pure nectar; honeyed, and so, so powerful and rich, but brilliantly balanced by crisp acidity.

1983 Pinot Blanc... ① **83**
Quite a good wine as well as value, this lovely Pinot Blanc offers uncomplicated charm and fruity flavours in a dry, medium-bodied format.

1982 Pinot Gris Réserve.. ① **82**
1983 Pinot Gris Réserve.. ① **84**
These are two very stylish Pinot Gris wines. The 1983 has more concentration and character, a buttery, almost toasty character, excellent, round, ripe fruit flavours, and a crisp finish. The 1982 is softer, more diffuse, but still very enjoyable and quite a bargain.

1983 Riesling... ① **82**
1983 Riesling Frédéric Emile.. ③ **88**
1983 Riesling Frédéric Emile Vendange Tardive.... ⑤ **93**
Again, one sees the progression in quality in Trimbach's wines since the special Cuvées are notably superior to the standard Cuvées. The standard Riesling is rather light for a 1983, but fragrant, crisp, clean and lively and very much in the Trimbach style of lighter, leaner wines. The Cuvée Frédéric Emile is a textbook Riesling: spicy, clean, crisp, rich in flavour, medium-bodied, concentrated, but so well-knit that it will not be until 1992–1995 that it is fully mature. The Vendange Tardive Frédéric Emile is an almost perfect wine. With layers and layers of Riesling fruit, impeccable balance, great length and richness, this powerful wine is worth knowing about now because of its greatness.

1983 Sylvaner... ① **79**
Given my hostility to Sylvaners, I was surprised by the fact that Trimbach's Sylvaner has good fruit, some character, and a touch of finesse. Drink it now for its freshness.

DOMAINE WEINBACH (THÉO FALLER) *KIENTZHEIM*
NEAR KAYSERSBERG ★ ★ ★ ★ ★

It would be unfair to state that the Domaine Weinbach is producing Alsace's greatest wines; however, there is no question that some of the finest, most concentrated, powerful, and opulent wines from this beautiful region are being made at this estate. Madame Faller runs this property with a fanatical dedication to quality. The entire line of wines is excellent, but the Rieslings made here are definitely the best in Alsace and the specific vineyard wines from the Clos des Capucins vineyard are nothing short of spectacular. The top wines are designated by the words 'Cuvée Théo' across the top of the label, a tribute to the founder of the estate, Théo Faller, who died in 1979. To reiterate, the Domaine Weinbach provides intense, very rich, strikingly powerful wines. The 1983s of this small firm are particularly outstanding; however, should you run across any of the 1981s of Weinbach, they too were quite good. They are expensive, but the high quality justifies the price.

1983 Gewürztraminer..	②	**84**
1983 Gewürztraminer Cuvée Théo	③	**92**
1985 Gewürztraminer Cuvée Théo	④	**87**
1983 Gewürztraminer Réserve Personnelle.............	②	**91**
1985 Gewürztraminer Réserve Personnelle.............	④	**88**

Weinbach consistently produces superb Gewürztraminer, but it is hard to top the splendidly concentrated, exotically perfumed 1983 Cuvée Théo and 1983 Réserve Personnelle. The bouquets explode with aromas of rosebuds, lychees, and grapefruit. They are both very rich and full-bodied, and to my palate there is little difference between them. They both should provide sensational drinking over the next four to five years. The regular Gewürztraminer is just a down-sized version of the other two wines. It is quite full-bodied, spicy, slightly sweet, and deep. The 1985s are significantly more expensive, less intense than the 1983s, but both wines are admirably concentrated, rich, and excellent examples of their types. The Réserve seems to have slightly more elegance.

1983 Pinot Réserve..	①	**85**

What makes 1983 such a special vintage for Alsace is that the rank-and-file wines, notably Pinot Blanc, are so good and inexpensive. This is a full-throttle Pinot Blanc, rich, spicy, full-bodied, dry and just oozing with fruit. Drink over the next year.

1983 Riesling Cuvée de la Sainte-Catherine............	③	**91**
1985 Riesling Cuvée de la Sainte-Catherine............	④	**90**
1983 Riesling Schlossberg	③	**88**
1985 Riesling Schlossberg	④	**88**

I can't recall ever tasting a dry, young Riesling from Alsace with as much promise and potential as these wines. The Sainte-Catherines in both vintages in particular are breathtakingly beautiful wines that are oh, so fragrant, so pure and concentrated, so well balanced, and so long and deep that they are a true gustatory *tour de force*. Both overwhelm the lovingly proportioned but less expensive Schlossbergs, two wines which would be considered classic Rieslings from Alsace. Both are dry wines and will improve for three to five years.

1983 Sylvaner... ① **83**
I do not like Sylvaner, but this is the best of this normally dull,
bland variety that I have found. It is surprisingly good and
interesting, spicy, fruity, dry, and flavourful. Drink over the
next year for its freshness.

1983 Tokay d'Alsace Vendange .... ③ **91**
A luxuriously rich, velvety wine with adequate acidity, full
body, stupendous length and concentration. This young,
potentially great wine will drink well (and continue to
develop) for at least a decade.

A. WILLM *BARR* ★ ★ ★ ★

The firm of Alsace Willm is generally well known, but the production of 42,000 cases per year is not very large. The firm specializes in
Gewürztraminer and Riesling, although there is an entire range of
wines, including a sparkling Crémant d'Alsace. The pride of the firm
is the intense, rich Gewürztraminer from the seventeen-acre Clos
Gaensbroennel. It starts off life slowly but ages magnificently. The
Cuvée Emile Willm in both Riesling and Gewürztraminer is quite
good, as is the bottom-of-the-line Cordon d'Alsace, made from
Pinot Blanc.

1983 Gewürztraminer.................................... ① **85**
1983 Gewürztraminer Cuvée Emile Willm.............. ② **87**
1983 Gewürztraminer Cuvée Emile Willm
Vendange Tardive.................................... ③ **89**
1983 Gewürztraminer Clos Gaensbroennel .... ② **89**
1983 Gewürztraminer Clos Gaensbroennel
Vendange Tardive.................................... ③ **90**
Given the prices for these wines, the Willm line-up of
Gewürztraminers offers a Bacchanalian paradise. The regular
Gewürztraminer is richly varietal, with lovely aromas of
almonds, roses, and grapefruit. Rich and full-bodied, with
surprising power and length, it is a wine that Gewürztraminer
fanatics should buy by the carload. The Cuvée Emile Willm is
even richer, fuller-bodied and dry and rich, with the Emile
Willm Vendange Tardive exceptionally powerful (14.6%
alcohol) and heady. At the pinnacle, however, are the two
Gewürztraminers from the famous Clos Gaensbroennel. The
regular Clos Gaensbroennel is still almost totally unevolved,
but behind the bouquet of spice and flowers is an enormously
rich, well-structured, powerful, full-bodied wine. The Clos
Gaensbroennel Vendange Tardive is slightly richer and fuller,
if you can believe that. It is almost too overpowering and rich,
but remember, it is dry and capable of a decade of
improvement.

1983 Pinot Blanc Cordon d'Alsace............................. ① **83**
Another surprisingly good Pinot Blanc from Alsace, this crisp, fresh, vibrantly fruity, medium-bodied wine has solid fruit and a crisp finish.

1983 Riesling... ① **76**
1983 Riesling Cuvée Emile Willm............................. ① **78**
1983 Riesling Cuvée Emile Willm Vendange Tardive.. ② **86**
1983 Riesling Réserve Kirchberg............................. ② **83**
Willm's Rieslings are no match for the firm's Gewürztraminers in 1983. They are sound, cleanly made, but generally uninteresting wines, except for the Emile Willm Vendange Tardive, which is quite good, round, dry, medium- to full-bodied, long, intense, and very flavourful.

ZIND-HUMBRECHT *WINTZENHEIM* ★ ★ ★ ★ ★

Léonard Humbrecht of the Domaine Humbrecht produces wines from some of Alsace's best vineyards – Herrenweg, Hengst, Brand, Clos Hauserer and Rangen – three of which are Grand Cru under the new law. The wines of Zind-Humbrecht, many of which are vineyard-designated, are among the most palatable, intellectually satisfying and distinctive wines of Alsace. The wines, particularly the top-of-the-line specific vineyard wines, can be absolutely brilliant as well as rare and quite expensive. Léonard Humbrecht is a fanatical perfectionist and his wines reflect the great care he obviously gives them.

1983 Gewürztraminer..................................... ① **85**
1983 Gewürztraminer Hengst Wintzenheim.......... ③ **90**
1983 Gewürztraminer Gueberschwihr Vendange Tardive.. ⑤ **92**
1983 Gewürztraminer Rangen Vendange Tardive . ⑤ **90**
Four excellent Gewürztraminers, of which three are close to being called monumental. That is quite an achievement. The 1983 regular is a great buy and has an exotic, spicy, full-bodied character. However, it cannot compare to the other three Gewürztraminers, which are truly sublime. The Hengst Wintzenheim is a marvellous wine with a big, rich, spicy bouquet of honey and almonds, full body, long, classic flavours, and a superb finish. Between the two *très cher* Vendange Tardive Gewürztraminers, there is hardly any difference. I rank the Gueberschwihr the finer, a truly great wine of sensational intensity and power, dry to taste, yet with a framework akin to the greatest white Burgundies. It will age for fifteen to twenty years. The Rangen is less open but equally spectacular in its perfect balance of power, opulence, finesse, and richness.

1983 Muscat d'Alsace... ② **75**

Pleasant, slightly aromatic, clean, and fresh, this is a decent wine, but given all the outstanding wines and values from Alsace in 1983, this wine hardly merits much attention.

1983 Riesling.. ① **84**
1983 Riesling Brand Vendange Tardive.................... ⑤ **86**
1983 Riesling Clos Hauserer... ④ **82**
1983 Riesling Clos Saint-Urbain Rangen.................. ③ **85**
1983 Riesling Herrenweg Turckheim........................ ③ **87**

Zind-Humbrecht's Rieslings are made in a rather high-acid, lean style; however, each has a very distinctive personality that justifies his vineyard-designating these wines. For high quality, the Herrenweg, with its highly aromatic bouquet, and the Rangen are very good, albeit expensive, examples of top-notch Rieslings. The Brand Vendange Tardive is dry, rather long, but has nowhere near the same richness that Zind-Humbrecht's Tokays and Gewürztraminers do. The Clos Hauserer has a great reputation, but I find it lean, rather tart, with a bouquet of stones and herbs, and needing a decade to develop.

1983 Tokay d'Alsace Rangen Vendange Tardive.... ⑤ **91**
1982 Tokay d'Alsace Saint-Urbain Rangen............. ③ **82**
1983 Tokay d'Alsace Saint-Urbain Rangen............. ③ **92**
1982 Tokay d'Alsace Vieilles Vignes.......................... ③ **84**

Here are four Tokays, two from the outstanding 1983 vintage and two from the rather average 1982 vintage. The two 1983 Tokays are as good a dry Tokay or Pinot Gris as one is likely to find anywhere. The straight Rangen is intense and concentrated, with an incredible bouquet of smoky bacon, butter, and rich ripe fruit. The palate impression is similar to that of a great white Burgundy: creamy, powerful, very concentrated, and long. The Rangen Vendange Tardive is less evolved, but very rich, dry, full-bodied and powerful, and very much like the normal Rangen, only less evolved. The 1982 Rangen is good, but lacks the overall dimension and complexity of the 1983. The Vieilles Vignes is also good, but finishes a little hot and seems short in acidity.

BORDEAUX
The World's Largest Supplier of High-Quality Wine

Bordeaux's 'Golden Age' continues unabated. The succession of good to extraordinary vintages that began in 1975 has, except for 1977, continued uninterrupted. Never in the history of this great wine region has so much fine wine been produced in so many back-to-back vintages. Of course, the consumer has been the beneficiary of Bordeaux's good fortune, with an array of high-quality wine available in all price ranges. On the negative side, insatiable world-wide demand for Bordeaux's best wines and best vintages has caused prices to rocket. However, one remarkable thing about Bordeaux is that the quality level of wine is very high, even at the lower price levels, and that is where bargains continue to exist. With two high-quality, enormous crops of wine in 1985 and 1986 now ageing in the cellars, Bordeaux wine prices may begin to moderate and even decline as production begins to outdistance demand.

BORDEAUX · QUICK VINTAGE GUIDE

Bordeaux provides the greatest rewards of cellaring and the least risk because, when mature, a well-stored bottle of Bordeaux from a very good vintage can stay at its peak of maturity longer than any red wine in the world (except for vintage port). Even in poor and mediocre vintages, Bordeaux lives for longer than anyone gives it credit.

1986 Bordeaux has a problem. In 1986 there was a record crop in terms of abundance, a staggering 14.7% larger than 1985, which itself produced more wine than any recent vintage. The trade, saturated with wine to sell from past vintages such as 1983, 1984, and 1985, will find it hard to accept that in the Médoc a number of properties produced exceptionally classic, very long-lived, powerful wines likely to age well for up to three decades. In St.-Julien and Pauillac, 1986 is the finest vintage since 1982 – yes, even superior to 1985 and 1983. The wines are very tannic as the level of tannins in many cases is the highest ever measured. However, in the top wines the great fruit and ripeness behind the tannins is obvious.

In St. Estèphe and Margaux, most growers seem to like their 1986s slightly better than their 1985s, but the quality is less consistent, and picking a favourite seems to go strictly on the lines of personal taste. However, there is no doubt that Château Margaux, given the great number of successes it has had in the late seventies and eighties, has produced a wine this

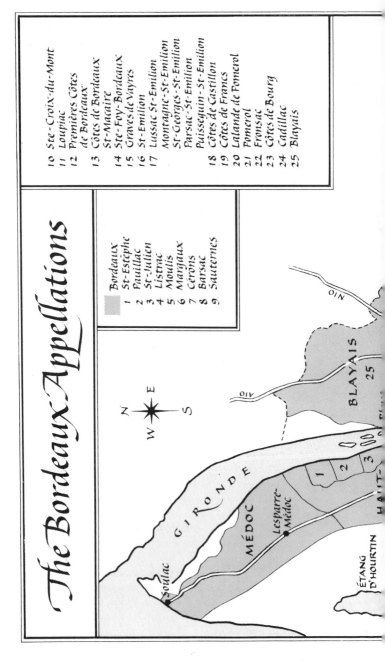

The Bordeaux Appellations

Bordeaux
1 St-Estèphe
2 Pauillac
3 St-Julien
4 Listrac
5 Moulis
6 Margaux
7 Cérons
8 Barsac
9 Sauternes

10 Ste-Croix-du-Mont
11 Loupiac
12 Premières Côtes de Bordeaux
13 Côtes de Bordeaux
14 Ste-Foy-Bordeaux
15 Graves de Vayres
16 St-Emilion
17 Lussac St-Emilion
    Montagne-St-Emilion
    St-Georges-St-Emilion
    Parsac-St-Emilion
    Puisseguin-St-Emilion
18 Côtes de Castillon
19 Côtes de Francs
20 Lalande de Pomerol
21 Pomerol
22 Fronsac
23 Côtes de Bourg
24 Cadillac
25 Blayais

vintage of aweseome, monumental proportions. In Graves, St.-Emilion, Pomerol, Fronsac, and Canon-Fronsac, the heavy rains of September 23rd caused a dilution in quality in the Merlot grapes, and for growers in these areas, while several notable exceptions exist, 1985 is far and away a superior vintage. Prices are being forced down for the 1986s simply because production of high-quality Bordeaux wine has outstripped demand. Consequently, the 1986s may well represent decent bargains if prices drop by at least 20% as is being predicted. Unlike 1983 and 1985, this is a vintage in the Médoc to lay down at least a decade or more before consuming. The dry white wines are not nearly as successful as the 1985s, but the Sauternes promise to be better than the 1985s. For a look at how the top growers fared, see the chart on pages 141–2.

1985 An excellent vintage, not up to 1982, but right on its heels. The strength of the vintage was the Merlot grape so Pomerol and St. Emilion have done exceptionally well. In the Médoc and Graves, the huge yield of juice makes selection especially critical as some wines lack both depth and body. The wines should be at their best between 1990–2005. In terms of quantity, it was the largest crop ever harvested. For an analysis of the best wines of the vintage and those wines that may merit purchasing as futures, see pages 140–1 which contains a chart of the best wines of 1985 based on cask evaluations done in March 1986 and October 1986.

1984 The wine press wrote it off before the harvest, but the quality of the Médoc and Graves wines is at least good, in many cases very good.

Due to a bad crop of Merlot grapes, St. Emilion and Pomerol produced mediocre wines at best, with some of the top châteaux declassifying their entire crop. This will be a vintage to consume within its first ten years of life.

1983 A difficult year because of rot in the vineyards. The wines, initially believed to be harder, tougher, more typical or classical wines than the more massive, intense 1982s, have turned out soft, very fruity, delicious, but destined in most cases to mature well before the fuller-bodied, richer 1982s. The sweet wines are outstanding in 1983, as are the red wines from the Margaux appellation.

1982 The greatest vintage since 1981, the 1982s have begun to close up and their considerable tannin content is now becoming very apparent. The masses of fruit are still present, but as the wines have recovered from their voyage, the huge structure and potential for extended longevity are obvious. The petits châteaux are marvellous in this vintage and can be drunk now or aged for five to seven years. As for the big shots of this vintage, 1995–2010 would be the likely period for these wines to enter their plateau of maturity.

1981 Almost all of the 1981s are developing quickly. Most will be ready to drink by 1990, but not Pétrus, Margaux, or Lafite-Rothschild.

1980 The top wines from this vintage are delicious now and quite appealing (e.g. Pichon Lalande, Domaine de Chevalier, Gruaud-Larose). Except for Margaux, these are wines to drink over the next two to three years. The sweet wines of Sauternes and Barsac are especially good in 1980 and represent very good value.

1979 A vintage that continues to show more and more class every time I go back to it. The petits châteaux are quite mixed, but the classified growths are developing a harmonious charm, show a lovely fruitiness, and may, in the best cases, turn out like the terribly underrated 1962s. For the top wines, 1987 to 1997 looks to be the decade of enjoyment for the 1979s.

1978 This is a wonderful vintage for the classified growths of the Médoc and Graves. The wines are just beginning to open up and develop. The petits châteaux are surprisingly not up to the quality one might expect and must be picked carefully. The Pomerols are generally ready to drink, the St. Emilions need another one to two years, and the Médocs and Graves need five years. Peak drinkability for the Médocs and Graves should be 1990–2000.

1977 All the 1977s require drinking now.

1976 A very irregular vintage that could have been great had the harvest rains not bloated the grapes. The best 1976s are almost always from the Médoc. They offer deliciously supple, charming drinking now. In restaurants, this is the Bordeaux vintage I look for. Drink over the next two to four years, except for Ausone and the great Lafite-Rothschild, both of which need until 1992 to be fully ready. The sweet wines of Barsac and Sauternes are remarkably rich and unctuous and will continue to drink well for one or two more decades.

1975 More irregular in quality than initially believed, 1975 still produced a bevy of very great, rich, big, tannic wines that will turn out to be some of the longest-lived Bordeaux of the last several decades. For the top wines, their bouquets are just now emerging from behind a wall of tannin. Peak drinkability for the best wines will be 1990–2010. The petits châteaux can be excellent and are now ready to drink.

1974 The sleepers of this vintage are the Graves, which turned out quite well. However, these are wines to drink over the next three to four years, save for La Mission-Haut-Brion, which will last for ten more years.

1973 Unless you have Pétrus cellared, run, don't walk, to your cellar, because these wines have been fully mature for the last seven to eight years and are now almost comatose. Beware!

1972 Drink now if ever.

1971 Virtually every 1971 is fully mature and is not likely to get better. One must pick carefully in this vintage, but the rewards are there. The Pomerols and Graves are particularly seductive at present.

1970 A great vintage that several writers naïvely criticized when released. They were said to be the product of Bordeaux's new vinification. The critics thought that because the wines had so much supple fruit, they would not last until 1980. It's 1987, and the top wines are still not ready – this vintage is unquestionably the most totally satisfying vintage after 1961 and before 1982. The petits châteaux are fully mature. The Graves, St.-Emilions, and Pomerols have reached their plateau of maturity, but will hold for at least another decade. The Médocs need two to five more years, but are drinking well now. This is a marvellous vintage at all levels.

1969 I have never tasted a 1969 claret that I did not dislike. Avoid.

1968 Avoid.

1967 All of the wines have been mature for a decade. However, the top wines are still holding together and can be revelations to drink, provided they have been well stored.

1966 Initially this was believed to be a classic, a potentially excellent vintage. After nineteen years, the wines have developed so slowly, and in some cases even lost fruit, that the opinion of this vintage has been revised downward. There are some very fine wines, but they are generally somewhat lean and austere. Most 1966s should be drunk over the next ten years.

1965 Avoid.

1964 For Graves, St.-Emilion, and Pomerol, a beautiful vintage of wines that are in full bloom. For the Médoc, caution is the watchword since persistent harvest rains plagued growers in this area. Drink over the next five to eight years.

1963 Avoid.

1962 Apparently this vintage never went through an awkward stage of development. Delicious young, delicious old, well-stored bottles of 1962 claret are beautifully harmonious wines that have been mature for a decade but have been able to stay at their plateau of maturity without fading. However, all of the 1962s require consumption now. If you are buying them, they must be from good, cool cellars or you may end up with expensive vinegar.

1961 This is, of course, a great vintage, not as consistently great as 1982, but the top 1961s have incredible concentration and richness that is unmatched in any Bordeaux vintage this century. Most can be drunk now, but the top wines will go on improving for decades.

Older Vintages
The 1959s are powerful and where well stored, excellent. The 1955s are more spotty than initially predicted, but overall very good. The 1953s are beginning to tire, but well-cellared examples of this vintage can be incredibly satisfying, rich, luxurious wines with great intensity of flavour and finesse. The 1952s are hard, the 1950s underrated, and the trio of vintages in the forties, 1945, 1947, 1949, can be pure perfection if well-cellared, good examples can be found, particularly the 1949s.

A GUIDE TO BORDEAUX'S BEST PRODUCERS – DRY RED WINES AND SAUTERNES/BARSAC

★ ★ ★ ★ ★ Outstanding Producers

L'Arrosée (St.-Emilion)
Ausone (St.-Emilion)
Canon (St.-Emilion)
Certan de May (Pomerol)
Cheval Blanc (St.-Emilion)
Domaine de Chevalier (Graves)
Cos d'Estournel (St.-Estèphe)
Ducru-Beaucaillou (St.-Julien)
L'Evangile (Pomerol)
De Fargues (Sauternes)
Giscours (Margaux)
Gruaud-Larose (St.-Julien)
Haut-Brion (Graves)
Lafite-Rothschild (Pauillac)
Lafleur (Pomerol)
La Lagune (Ludon)
Latour (Pauillac)
Latour à Pomerol (Pomerol)
Léoville-Barton (St.-Julien)
Léoville-Las Cases (St.-Julien)
Lynch-Bages (Pauillac)
Château Margaux (Margaux)
La Mission-Haut-Brion (Graves)
Mouton-Rothschild (Pauillac)
Palmer (Margaux)
Pétrus (Pomerol)
Pichon-Longueville, Comtesse
 de Lalande (Pauillac)

Raymond-Lafon (Sauternes)
Rieussec (Sauternes)
Trotanoy (Pomerol)
Yquem (Sauternes)

★ ★ ★ ★ Excellent Producers

Beychevelle (St.-Julien)
Bon Pasteur (Pomerol)
Boyd-Cantenac (Margaux)
Branaire-Ducru (St.-Julien)
Cadet-Piola (St.-Emilion)
Calon-Ségur (St.-Estèphe)
Cantemerle (Macau)
Chasse-Spleen (Moulis)
Climens (Barsac)
La Conseillante (Pomerol)
Coutet (Barsac)
La Dominique (St.-Emilion)
L'Eglise Clinet (Pomerol)
La Fleur Pétrus (Pomerol)
Forts de Latour (Pauillac)
Le Gay (Pomerol)
Gilette (Sauternes)
Gloria (St.-Julien)
Grand Puy Lacoste (Pauillac)
La Grave Figeac (St.-Emilion)
Haut-Bailly (Graves)
Haut-Marbuzet (St.-Estèphe)
Issan (Margaux)
Lafaurie-Peyraguey (Sauternes)
Langoa-Barton (St.-Julien)
Larmande (St.-Emilion)
Lascombes (Margaux)
Léoville-Poyferre (St.-Julien)
Magdelaine (St.-Emilion)
Montrose (St.-Estèphe)
Pavillon Rouge de Margaux
  (Margaux)
Pez (St.-Estèphe)
Le Pin (Pomerol)
Prieuré-Lichine (Margaux)
St.-Pierre-Sevaistre (St.-Julien)
Sociando-Mallet (Haut-Médoc)
Suduiraut (Sauternes)
Talbot (St.-Julien)
La Tour-Haut-Brion (Graves)
Vieux-Château-Certan
  (Pomerol)

★ ★ ★ Good Producers

L'Angélus (St.-Emilion)
Angludet (Margaux)
Balestard-La-Tonnelle
  (St.-Emilion)
Bastor-Lamontagne (Sauternes)
Batailley (Pauillac)
Beauséjour (Duffau-Lagarrosse)
  (St.-Emilion)
Bel Air (Lalande-de-Pomerol)
Belair (St.-Emilion)
Belles Graves (Lalande-de-
  Pomerol)
Le Boscq (Médoc)
Brane-Cantenac (Margaux)
Brillette (Moulis)
Camensac (Haut-Médoc)
Canon (Canon-Fronsac)
Canon de Brem (Canon-
  Fronsac)
Cantenac-Brown (Margaux)
Cap de Merle (Lussac-
  St.-Emilion)
Cap de Mourlin (St.-Emilion)
Les Carmes Haut-Brion (Graves)
Certan-Giraud (Pomerol)
Cissac (Haut-Médoc)
Clarke (Listrac)
Clerc-Milon (Pauillac)
Clos du Clocher (Pomerol)
Clos des Jacobins (St.-Emilion)
Clos René (Pomerol)
Corbin (St.-Emilion)
Corbin-Michotte (St.-Emilion)
Coufran (Haut-Médoc)
Couvent des Jacobins
  (St.-Emilion)
La Croix (Pomerol)
La Croix de Gay (Pomerol)
Croque-Michotte (St.-Emilion)
La Dauphine (Fronsac)

Destieux (St.-Emilion)
Doisy-Daëne (Barsac)
Doisy-Védrines (Barsac)
Duhart-Milon-Rothschild
    (Pauillac)
Durand-Laplagne (Puisseguin-
    St.-Emilion)
Durfort-Vivens (Margaux)
L'Enclos (Pomerol)
Faurie-de-Souchard (St.-
    Emilion)
Ferrand (St.-Emilion)
Fieuzal (Graves)
Fonbadet (Pauillac)
Fonplégade (St.-Emilion)
Fonroque (St.-Emilion)
Fourcas-Hosten (Listrac)
La Gaffelière (St.-Emilion)
Gazin (Pomerol)
Grand-Ormeau (Lalande-
    de-Pomerol)
Grand-Puy-Ducasse (Pauillac)
La Grave Trigant de Boisset
    (Pomerol)
Greysac (Médoc)
Guiraud (Sauternes)
La Gurgue (Margaux)
Haut-Bages-Libéral (Pauillac)
Haut-Batailley (Pauillac)
Haut-Brisson (St.-Emilion)
Haut-Sarpe (St.-Emilion)
Hortevie (St.-Julien)
Kirwan (Margaux)
Labégorce-Zédé (Margaux)
Lafon-Rochet (St.-Estèphe)
Lagrange (St.-Julien)
Lalande Borie (St.-Julien)
Lanessan (Haut-Médoc)
Larose Trintaudon (Haut-Médoc)
Liversan (Médoc)
La Louvière (Graves)
Maison Blanche (Montagne-
    St.-Emilion)
Malescot St.-Exupéry (Margaux)
Marquis-de-Terme (Margaux)
Maucaillou (Moulis)

Mazeris (Canon-Fronsac)
Meyney (St.-Estèphe)
Mouton-Baronne-Philippe
    (Pauillac)
Nairac (Barsac)
Les-Ormes-de-Pez (St.-Estèphe)
Pape-Clément (Graves)
Patache d'Aux (Médoc)
Pavie (St.-Emilion)
Pavie-Decesse (St.-Emilion)
Petit-Village (Pomerol)
Phélan Ségur (St.-Estèphe)
Pichon (Haut-Médoc)
Pichon Longueville, Baron de
    Pichon Longueville (Pauillac)
Pitray (Côtes de Castillon)
Plagmac (Médoc)
Pontet-Canet (Pauillac)
Pontensac (Médoc)
Pougeaux (Moulis)
Pouget (Margaux)
Rahoul (Graves)
Rausan-Ségla (Margaux)
Rauzan-Gassies (Margaux)
Roudier (Montagne-St.-Emilion)
Rouet (Canon-Fronsac)
Rouget (Pomerol)
Sales (Pomerol)
Sigalas Rabaud (Sauternes)
Siran (Margaux)
Soudars (Haut-Médoc)
Soutard (St.-Emilion)
Tayac Prestige (Côtes de Bourg)
Terrey-Gros-Cailloux (St.-
    Julien)
Tertre (Margaux)
Tertre-Daugay (St.-Emilion)
La Tonnelle (Côtes de Blaye)
La Tour Figeac (St.-Emilion)
La Tour-de-Mons (Margaux)
La Tour-du-Pin-Figeac
    (St.-Emilion)
La Tour St.-Bonnet (Médoc)
Tronquoy-Lalande (St.-Estèphe)
Troplong-Mondot
    (St.-Emilion)

Vieux-Château Guibeau
  (Puisseguin-St.-Emilion)
Villars (Fronsac)

Villermaurine (St.-Emilion)
La Violette (Pomerol)

★★ Average Producers

Agassac (Haut-Médoc)
Arche (Sauternes)
L'Arrivet-Haut-Brion (Graves)
Beau Séjour-Bécot (St.-Emilion)
Beaumont (Haut-Médoc)
Bel-Orme-Tronquoy-de-
  Lalande (Haut-Médoc)
Belcier (Côtes de Castillon)
Belgrave (Haut-Médoc)
Bonalgue (Pomerol)
Bouscaut (Graves)
Broustet (Barsac)
Caillou (Barsac)
Canon-La-Gaffelière
  (St.-Emilion)
Carbonnieux (Graves)
La Cardonne (Médoc)
Caronne-Ste.-Gemme
  (Haut-Médoc)
Clinet (Pomerol)
Clos L'Eglise (Pomerol)
Clos Fourtet (St.-Emilion)
Clos des Templiers
  (Lalande-de-Pomerol)
La Clotte (St.-Emilion)
La Commanderie (St.-Emilion)
Cos Labory (St.-Estèphe)
Croizet-Bages (Pauillac)
Curé-Bon-La-Madeleine
  (St.-Emilion)
Dauzac (Margaux)
Desmirail (Margaux)
Domaine de L'Eglise (Pomerol)
Ferrière (Margaux)
Filhot (Sauternes)
La Fleur Gazin (Pomerol)
Fombrauge (St.-Emilion)
Fourcas-Dupré (Listrac)
Garraud (Lalande-de-Pomerol)
Glana (St.-Julien)
Gombaude-Guillot (Pomerol)

Grand-Corbin-Despagne
  (St.-Emilion)
Gressier Grand-Poujeaux
  (Moulis)
Hanteillan (Médoc)
Haut Chatain (Lalande-de-
  Pomerol)
Haut Plantey (St.-Emilion)
Haut Sociando (Côtes de Blaye)
Labégorce (Margaux)
Lagrange (Pomerol)
Lamarque (Haut-Médoc)
Larcis-Ducasse (St.-Emilion)
Lestage (Listrac)
Loudenne (Médoc)
Malartic-Lagravière (Graves)
Marquis d'Alesme-Becker
  (Margaux)
Monbousquet (St.-Emilion)
Moulin des Carruades (Pauillac)
Nenin (Pomerol)
Les Ormes-Sorbet (Médoc)
Peyrabon (Haut-Médoc)
Plince (Pomerol)
La Pointe (Pomerol)
Rabaud-Promis (Sauternes)
Ramage La Batisse
  (Haut-Médoc)
Rayne-Vigneau (Sauternes)
Ripeau (St.-Emilion)
La Rivière (Fronsac)
Romer du Hayot (Sauternes)
St.-Bonnet (Médoc)
Smith-Haut-Lafitte (Graves)
Tailhas (Pomerol)
Taillefer (Pomerol)
La Terrasse (Côtes de Castillon)
La Tour Blanche (Sauternes)
La Tour de By (Médoc)
La Tour-Carnet (Haut-Médoc)
Trottevieille (St.-Emilion)

Verdignan (Médoc)	Vraye-Croix-de-Gay (Pomerol)

★ Other Producers

Beauregard (Pomerol)	La Garde (Graves)
Bel-Air-Marquis d'Aligre (Pomerol)	Moulinet (Pomerol)
	Olivier (Graves)
Bourgneuf-Vayron (Pomerol)	Tayac (Margaux)
La Bridane (St.-Julien)	La Tour-Martillac (Graves)
Citran (Haut-Médoc)	Villegeorge (Haut-Médoc)
Ferrande (Graves)	

A GUIDE TO BORDEAUX'S BEST PRODUCERS — DRY WHITE WINES

★ ★ ★ ★ ★ Outstanding Producers

Domaine de Chevalier (Graves)	Haut-Brion Blanc (Graves)
Fieuzal (Graves) (starting in 1985)	Laville-Haut-Brion (Graves)

★ ★ ★ ★ Excellent Producers

La Louvière (Graves)	Pavillon Blanc de Château
Malartic-Lagravière (Graves)	Margaux (Margaux)
	La Tour-Martillac (Graves)

★ ★ ★ Good Producers

L'Arrivet-Haut-Brion (Graves)	Olivier (Graves)
Bouscaut (Graves)	Pirou (Graves)
Caillou Blanc de Talbot (Bordeaux)	Pontac-Monplaisir (Graves)
	Rahoul (Graves)
Carbonnieux (Graves)	Respide (Graves)
Loudenne (Bordeaux)	Smith-Haut-Lafitte (Graves)

THE BEST WINE VALUES IN BORDEAUX

St.-Estèphe

Haut-Marbuzet	Les-Ormes-de-Pez
Marbuzet	Pez
Meyney	

Pauillac

Fonbadet	Haut-Bages-Libéral
Haut-Bages-Averous	Haut-Batailley

St.-Julien

Branaire-Ducru	Léoville-Barton
Clos du Marquis	St.-Pierre
Gruaud-Larose	Talbot
Hortevie	

Margaux

Angludet	La Gurgue
Issan	Tertre

Médoc & Haut-Médoc

Chasse-Spleen	Greysac

Lanessan	Larose-Trintaudon
Plagnac	Sociando-Mallet
Potensac	La Tour St.-Bonnet

Sauternes/Barsac
Bastor-Lamontagne	Doisy-Daëne

Pomerol
Clos René	Rouget
L'Enclos	Sales

St.-Emilion
L'Arrosée	Clos des Jacobins
Balestard-La-Tonnelle	Destieux
Cadet-Piola	La Dominique
Cap de Mourlin	La Grave-Figeac

Côtes de Bourg
La Grolet	Tayac

Côtes de Blaye
Haut-Sociando	La Tonnelle

Fronsac & Canon-Fronsac
Canon	Haut-Laroque
Canon de Brem	Mazeris
Dalem	Rouet
La Dauphine	Villars
La Grave	

Lalande-de-Pomerol
Belle Graves	Clos des Templiers
Bertineau St.-Vincent	Grand-Ormeau

Graves
Cheret-Pitres	Picque-Caillou
Haut-Bailly	Rahoul
La Louvière	

Montagne St.-Emilion
Roudier	Tour Musset

Côtes de Castillon
Pitray	

Lussac St.-Emilion
Bel Air	Tour de Grenat
Cap de Merle	Villadière
Carteyron	

BORDEAUX · TODAY'S BUYING STRATEGY

Because of the recent succession of high-quality Bordeaux crops and also because Bordeaux has traditionally been offered for sale on a pre-arrival 'futures' basis, the Bordeaux wine market has been quite active each year. Buying Bordeaux futures makes a lot of sense if you are sure you are buying top wines from a top vintage that are likely to be in great demand and cost considerably more when they arrive on the market. However, due to worldwide supply and demand, and the wide fluctuations in currency values, buying futures only makes sense with specific wines in specific vintages. Regardless of all the wine trade hype insisting that you buy Bordeaux futures, there are only three reasons to invest your money in unbottled Bordeaux wines two years prior to taking delivery. They are:

1 To buy great wine from an excellent or great vintage.

2 To save money based on the assumption that the wines will be at least 25-50% more expensive when they arrive on the market.

3 To guarantee getting wines of high quality from estates that have small productions, for example, Pomerols and St.-Emilions.

If any of these three criteria can be satisfied, then buying futures may make sense. If none of these conditions exist, then save your money until the wines arrive on the market. The 1982 was the best recent case demonstrating the wisdom of buying as much as one could afford at the earliest possible time. Since the futures were offered, the prices doubled and tripled as the demand for the 1982s was unparalleled. The 1978, 1979, and 1981 vintages, and to a lesser extent 1985, are the best recent examples for not buying futures since the wines came on the market at the same price (or lower in some cases) than the price consumers had paid for them as futures two years in advance of their arrival.

Today, the best values in Bordeaux vintages are the 1979s, which are drinking deliciously, the 1981s, similarly styled to the 1979s, and the 1983s, a rather overlooked, very good vintage that just got lost in the huge shadow cast by the great 1982s. As for the 1982s, they are great, but the famous as well as glamorous wines are very rare and very expensive. However, the top 1982 Crus Bourgeois still represent great value given their splendid quality in this vintage. The highly regarded 1985s also appear rather costly.

All things considered, there is a tremendous glut of high-quality Bordeaux in the marketplace. Those top two dozen or so estates that represent the summit of quality, have become extremely expensive in the last several years but there are hundreds of lesser-known châteaux, the Crus Bourgeois, and top wines from less renowned but up-and-coming regions such as Lalande de Pomerol, Fronsac, and Canon Fronsac, that represent remarkable rapports of quality and price.

When buying Bordeaux, remember one cardinal fact – in the last five years, the quality difference between the top Crus Bourgeois and petits châteaux and the grand classified growths has got narrower and narrower. Yet the difference in price has only widened between these two groups of Bordeaux wines. The message to the shrewd, value conscious consumer is obvious – search out the top Crus Bourgeois. Wouldn't you rather have four or five cases of the luscious Lalande-de-Pomerol Grand-Ormeau than one case of La Conseillante?

AGASSAC *HAUT-MÉDOC* ★★

1982	②	*82*
1983	②	*80*

This property has been off form for some time, but the first several vintages of the 1980s have offered encouraging new evidence that the wine is improving in quality. The 1983 is spicy, rather tannic and backward, and the 1982 more richly supple and fruity.

L'ANGELUS *ST.-EMILION* ★★★

1981	③	*84*
1982	③	*85*
1983	③	*87*

L'Angelus, like many wines, has recently made a strong effort to improve its quality. The wine still tastes better out of barrel than out of bottle, but the last couple of vintages have looked promising. The 1983 is an exuberantly fruity, ripe, lush wine; the 1982, no ugly duckling, is precocious, simple and sumptuous. The 1981 is light but herbaceous and ready to drink.

ANGLUDET *MARGAUX* ★★★

1981	③	*83*
1982	③	*84*
1983	③	*88*
1984	②	*80*

The highly respected Bordeaux winebroker Peter A. Sichel lives at Angludet and has taken this modest property from obscurity to international prominence. It tends to be a spicy, elegant, supple wine with a decade of ageing potential in the top vintages. The best recent vintage is the superb 1983, a rich, intense, remarkable wine that will make people take more notice of Angludet. The 1984 is light and ready to drink, the 1982 supple and easy to understand.

ARCHE *SAUTERNES* ★★

1981		
1982	③	80
1983	③	86

A property in Sauternes that can make solid, reliable wines that represent good value. The 1983 is their best wine in several decades.

L'ARRIVET-HAUT-BRION *GRAVES* ★★

1982	③	83

L'Arrivet-Haut-Brion produces a rather fruity, soft, but interesting red wine of which 1982 is a good example.

L'ARROSÉE *ST.-EMILION* ★★★★★

1981	③	86
1982	④	90
1983	③	90
1984	③	86

L'Arrosée is one of the least known great wines of Bordeaux and is to be sought out for its expansive, broad flavours of burgundian-like richness. The 1984 may be St.-Emilion's best wine in a very difficult vintage, fragrant, rich, and showing surprising ripeness. The 1983 has a big bouquet of black cherries, and is wonderfully spicy and lush. The 1982 is equally deep but perhaps more tannic, a lovely, wonderful wine, and the 1981 is elegant, lighter, but still very attractive.

AUSONE *ST.-EMILION* ★★★★★

1981	⑤	80
1982	⑤	90
1983	⑤	89

One of the most impressive châteaux and remarkable locations of all the châteaux in Bordeaux, Ausone has emerged from a period of long mediocrity and since 1976 has made classic, long-lived wines that should last well given their firm tannic structures. There is no 1984 as it was declassified. The 1983 is rich and jammy, with very soft flavours but a good deal of power. The 1982 was extraordinary, virtually perfect from cask, but has closed up and seems rather unyielding and backward despite an impressive colour and enormous richness and power. The 1981 is rather light and a little lean and angular, the least attractive of the vintages in the 1980s.

BALESTARD-LA-TONNELLE *ST.-EMILION* ★★★

1981	②	84
1982	②	85
1983	②	85

Balestard is an immensely enjoyable wine. The style of wine produced here is dense, big, deep, and rich with a chewy texture. Both the 1983 and 1982 are beefy, full-tilt St.-Emilions with little finesse but plenty of power and hedonistic flavours. The 1981 is lighter but also fruity and uncomplicated.

BASTOR-LAMONTAGNE *SAUTERNES* ★★★
1982 .... ② **85**
1983 .... ② **87**
This is a wonderful property making very fine Sauternes at a very good price. The 1983 is voluptuous and luscious. The 1982 is a distinct success for the vintage.

BATAILLEY *PAUILLAC* ★★★
1982 .... ④ **87**
1983 .... ③ **83**
Batailley produces wines that are never in the top class of Pauillac but are solid, well coloured, and somewhat one-dimensional in quality. The 1983 is straightforward, chunky, pleasant, but not complex. The 1982 is similarly styled only more concentrated and longer on the palate.

BEAUMONT *HAUT-MÉDOC* ★★
1982 .... ② **83**
1983 .... ② *81*
Beaumont can make very good wine at very reasonable prices. The 1983 is slightly herbaceous, but the 1982 shows more depth of fruit and character. Both are made in a very quick-maturing, soft, commercial style.

BEAUREGARD *POMEROL* ★
1982 .... ④ *81*
1983 .... ④ **80**
Beauregard generally makes light-style Pomerols that lack a little in body and richness, with sometimes pronounced her-baceous bouquets. Both the 1982 and 1983 are ready-to-drink, fruity, soft, easy wines.

BEAUSÉJOUR (DUFFAU-LAGARROSSE) *ST.-EMILION* ★★★
1981 .... ③ **82**
1982 .... ④ **87**
1983 .... ④ **88**
One of the two Beauséjours in St.-Emilion, this estate pro-duced numerous mediocre wines in the 1960s and 1970s, but

has come on strongly in the 1980s. The 1983 is a wonderfully rich, complex wine with a bouquet of roasted fruit and subtle herbs. The 1982 is also intense, expansive, rich and quite delicious now. The 1981 is much lighter than the latter two wines and a little more angular and harsh on the palate. A property to watch.

BEAU-SÉJOUR BÉCOT *ST.-EMILION* ★★

1981	③	**70**
1982	③	**78**
1983	③	**86**

A property involved in a boiling controversy since it was demoted in the new St.-Emilion classification, after which the owner appealed to the French government and lost his case. The demotion was probably justified, based on the vintages in the 1960s and 1970s, but Bécot is now making much better wines, as its 1983 and unclassified 1985 dramatically attest. The 1983 is the best recent effort with a ripe, raspberry, oaky bouquet and lush flavours.

BEL-AIR *LALANDE-DE-POMEROL* ★★★

1982	②	**83**
1983	②	**82**

Bel-Air produces ripe, fruity wines that are among the best in Lalande-de-Pomerol.

BEL-AIR-MARQUIS D'ALIGRE *HAUT-MÉDOC* ★

1983	③	**78**

This wine can be well coloured but generally lacks harmony and finesse.

BEL-ORME-TRONQUOY-DE-LALANDE *HAUT-MÉDOC* ★★

1981	②	**75**
1982	②	**83**

This property can make outstanding wine, but recent vintages have not looked as strong as one might have hoped, compared with older vintages that sometimes appear to have been made in a higher-quality, longer-lasting style. The 1982 is supple, chunky, but uncomplex. The 1981 is an austere, mean, tannic wine.

BELAIR *ST.-EMILION* ★★★

1981	③	**74**
1982	③	**85**
1983	③	**90**

The sister château of Ausone, Belair shares the winemaking and recent efforts have shown remarkable improvements in quality, particularly since 1976. There was no 1984 from Belair, but the 1983 is the best in over twenty years, a rich, surprisingly powerful, deep wine that is better than the more famous 1982. The 1981 is light, fruity, soft, and lacking concentration.

BELCIER *CÔTES DE CASTILLON* ★★
1982	①	82
1983	①	78

De Belcier is a largely unknown yet fine Côtes de Castillon representing excellent value for the money. The 1982 is the best recent vintage.

BELGRAVE *HAUT-MÉDOC* ★★
1982	③	84
1983	②	65

Although a classified growth, Belgrave has fallen into great disrepair and only considerable amounts of money invested by its owners have brought it up in quality. The 1982 is a fruity, supple, early-maturing wine. The 1983 is disappointingly thin and light.

BELLES-GRAVES *LALANDE-DE-POMEROL* ★★★
1982	②	86
1983	②	84

One of the leading estates in Lalande-de-Pomerol, Belles Graves produces very rich, blackberry scented wines with considerable character. The 1983 is delicious; the 1982 is rich, plummy, and has five to six more years of ageing potential.

BEYCHEVELLE *ST.-JULIEN* ★★★★
1981	④	84
1982	⑤	92
1983	④	85
1984	③	80

Beychevelle is one of the most scenic châteaux of Bordeaux's Route du Vin. The wines tend to be smooth, supple, and very fruity, forcing them to be drunk at a very young age. Recent vintages have shown a bit more backbone and tannin than the quick-maturing wine that was made here in most vintages of the 1960s and 1970s. The 1984 is a good, straightforward wine that should be drunk over the next three to four years. The 1983 is more aggressive, with more tannin in the finish and a good concentration of fruit. The 1982 has a wonderful, sweet, ripe nose and deep, rich, long flavours. It is very impressive. The 1981 is light and ready to drink now.

BON PASTEUR *POMEROL* ★ ★ ★ ★

1982	⑤ **90**
1983	④ **86**
1984	③ **80**

Bon Pasteur is owned and managed by one of the gifted oenologists of Bordeaux, Michel Roland. His commitment to quality is no better evidenced than in his own property, which makes wonderfully fruity, rich wines that can age for up to ten years. The 1984 is a modest success given the difficulties of the vintage; the 1983 ripe, rich, quite supple and destined for early maturity; the 1982 an atypically powerful wine with a wonderful aroma and flavours of ripe black cherries and toffee.

BONALGUE *POMEROL* ★ ★

1981	③ **83**
1982	③ **85**
1983	④ **82**

The wines of Bonalgue exhibit surprising strength and rich-ness. While not complex, they are well made with deep, black cherry fruitiness and medium to full body. The 1982 is the best of the vintages in the 1980s so far.

LE BOSCQ *MÉDOC* ★ ★ ★

1982	② **84**
1983	① **83**

Le Boscq has rewarded me on more than one occasion with its rather impressive richness and straightforward, robust, fleshy character. It is always quite reasonably priced.

BOURGNEUF-VAYRON *POMEROL* ★

1981	④ **75**
1982	③ **78**

Bourgneuf is a relatively unknown wine, well situated, and generally makes satisfying wines with richness, power, and ageing potential of five to eight years.

BOUSCAUT *(RED) GRAVES* ★ ★

1982	④ **85**
1983	③ **84**

This property has potential but has yet to live up to it. The wine is always a little lean and lacking in character, although the 1982 and 1983 are two of the best wines in the last fifteen to twenty years.

BOUSCAUT *(WHITE) GRAVES* ★★★

1983 .... ③ *84*
1984 .... ③ *82*
1985 .... ③ *85*

I have always enjoyed the white wine of Bouscaut more than the red. It is usually a lean, rather austere wine that is best drunk within five to eight years of the vintage. The 1985 is the best of the recent vintage.

BOYD-CANTENAC *MARGAUX* ★★★★

1981 .... ③ *70*
1982 .... ④ *86*
1983 .... ③ *88*
1984 .... ② *80*

Boyd-Cantenac, for whatever reason, remains largely unknown, yet offers a full-bodied, rich, plump, quite long-lived style of Margaux that remains somewhat undervalued given its quality. The 1984 is one dimensional but cleanly made and ready to drink. The 1983 is one of this property's top wines, very dark in colour, full-blown, spicy with a ripe plummy aroma, and plenty of tannin for longevity. The 1982 is not unlike the 1983, only softer with unctuous, fat, fleshy flavours. The 1981 has proved to be soft and diluted with a distinct vegetal character.

BRANAIRE-DUCRU *ST.-JULIEN* ★★★★

1981 .... ③ *86*
1982 .... ④ *93*
1983 .... ③ *85*
1984 .... ② *83*

Branaire-Ducru is one of those curiously underrated, under-valued properties that somehow gets forgotten when wine enthusiasts discuss their favourite wines. Nevertheless, it can make splendid wines, as it has in 1975, 1976, and 1982, which rivalled the best Bordeaux could produce. The 1984 is supple, richly fruity with a cedary, berry-scented bouquet. The 1983 is rather soft and lacking concentration for Branaire, but nevertheless charming. The 1982 is a superlative wine and one of the great successes for this château. Its smoky, opulent, and exotic qualities give it tremendous appeal. The 1981 is more understated in personality, but very supple, fruity, and drinking very well now.

BRANE-CANTENAC *MARGAUX* ★★★

1981 .... ④ *83*
1982 .... ④ *87*

1983 .... ④ **88**
1984 .... ③ **73**
Brane-Cantenac produces a tremendous amount of wine and although it has enjoyed a large measure of commercial success throughout the world because of its official classification as a second-growth, the wine in the period between 1967 and 1977 was quite mediocre, if not poor. However, the vintages in the 1980s have gone from one strength to another. The 1981 is a charming, fruity wine that is ready to drink. The 1982 is a rich, deep, fat, and intensely perfumed wine with lovely fruity flavours. The 1983 is the best wine this property has made since 1961. The 1984 is straightforward and rather thick.

LA BRIDANE *ST.-JULIEN* ★
1982 .... ② **82**
La Bridane produces solid, reliable, unexciting wines. The 1982 is its most recent good vintage and it is ready to drink. It is fruity, quite ripe, and soft.

BRILLETTE *MOULIS* ★★★
1981 .... ② **84**
1982 .... ③ **86**
1983 .... ③ **82**
The wines of Brillette are not yet well known, but the quality of winemaking here is very high. The wine produced is in the spicy, oaky, richly fruity style that appeals to many tasters. The 1983 is not up to the quality of either the 1981 or 1982, but is still an attractive, soft, plummy wine dominated by the smell of new oak. The 1982 is a rich, concentrated, rather exotic wine with plenty of character. The 1981 is a more elegant and lighter version of the 1982.

BROUSTET *BARSAC* ★★
1978 .... ③ **80**
1980 .... ③ **82**
This is a property to watch since great improvements are being made to the vineyard and *chai* and improved quality is expected.

CADET-PIOLA *ST.-EMILION* ★★★★
1982 .... ④ **87**
1983 .... ④ **86**
The Jabiol family, who make this wine, are conservative winemakers and the wine produced has a wonderful black ruby colour and, usually, an intense, full-bodied, rich fruitiness. It is generally good value. The 1983 is good; the 1982

rich, full-bodied, and quite concentrated, and the unreleased 1985 quite impressive. A very underrated estate worth more attention.

CAILLOU *BARSAC* ★★

1982	②	**78**
1983	②	**80**

Caillou produces straightforward, fruity, easy-going wine that can age well and should generally be drunk young. The 1983 vintage, an outstanding one for Sauternes and Barsac, produced a very rich wine.

CALON-SÉGUR *ST.-ESTÈPHE* ★★★★

1981	③	**83**
1982	⑤	**95**
1983	④	**82**
1984	③	**75**

The white château of Calon-Ségur has a magical name to it, but the wines continue to be very spotty in their performance record. The 1981, 1983, and 1984 are not notable successes, though decent wines in their respective vintages. However, Calon-Ségur did everything right in 1982 and this is probably the best vintage for this property since 1947. It is a voluptuous, tannic, and very backward wine with great potential.

CAMENSAC *HAUT-MÉDOC* ★★★

1981	③	**81**
1982	③	**85**
1983	③	**84**

Camensac is one of the least known of the 1855 classified growths. The wine is made in a very supple, soft style that is meant to be drunk young, although it is capable of ageing in top vintages like 1982 and 1985 for at least ten years. The 1981 is elegant and spicy with a taste of blackcurrants. The 1982 is quite richly concentrated, with plenty of fruit and obvious vanillin character. The 1983 is almost as good as the 1982.

CANON *CANON-FRONSAC* ★★★

1982	②	**84**
1983	②	**84**

Canon makes a more supple style of wine than many Canon-Fronsacs and both the 1982 and 1983 are superlative, richly fruity, interesting, elegant wines.

CANON *ST.-EMILION* ★★★★★

1981	④	**75**

1982 .... ⑤ **93**
1983 .... ⑤ **90**

The wines of Canon have increased in quality greatly, and although this has always been one of St.-Emilion's best wines, it is also, curiously, one of its best-kept secrets. The wines are splendidly rich, deep, and concentrated, and this can be seen in both the excellent tobacco-scented, rich, classic 1983 and sublime, extraordinarily rich 1982. The 1981 comes up short when compared to these two vintages as it lacks the fruit to handle the tannin and leanness.

CANON DE BREM *CANON-FRONSAC* ★★★
1982 .... ② **86**
1983 .... ② **86**

The top estate of Canon-Fronsac, this property makes very forceful, aggressive, rich, big, robust, intense wines that can last for ten to fifteen years. Both the 1982 and 1983 are quite good.

CANON-LA-GAFFELIÈRE *ST.-EMILION* ★★
1981 .... ② **70**
1982 .... ③ **83**
1983 .... ③ **82**

Rather light, bland, mediocre wines are produced by this property; both the 1982 and 1983 showed adequate, supple, fruit and a fresh berry character.

CANTEMERLE *MACAU* ★★★★
1981 .... ③ **85**
1982 .... ④ **85**
1983 .... ④ **92**
1984 .... ④ **86**

Cantemerle, a 'Sleeping Beauty' château in a park just north of Bordeaux, is in full form in the 1980s after a period of mediocrity and inconsistency in the 1970s. The 1984 has wonderful intensity and richness for a wine of this vintage, and the 1983 is one of the very top wines of the vintage with a remarkable bouquet of ripe plums, flowers, and oak. The 1982 is elegant, soft, and loaded with berry fruit, and the 1981 a lighter version of the 1982.

CANTENAC-BROWN *MARGAUX* ★★★
1981 .... ③ **85**
1982 .... ④ **85**
1983 .... ④ **84**
1984 .... ④ **82**

Cantenac-Brown, after a long period of mediocrity and a history of producing rather charmless, coarse, hard wines, has made a number of changes in its winemaking with a new team of people and the results have been increasingly impressive in the 1980s. The 1984 is supple and easy to drink, with an attractive bouquet. The 1983 is a full-bodied wine that needs five full years of cellaring. The 1982 is quite rich, with long, ripe flavours and excellent concentration, and the 1981, a big, tannic, chocolaty, rich wine, will age for a long time.

CAP DE MERLE *LUSSAC-ST.-EMILION* ★★★
1982 .... ① **84**
1983 .... ① **84**
The leading estate of Lussac-St.-Emilion, Cap de Merle's 1982 and 1983 are both deliciously fruity, spicy, ripe wines with plenty of character.

CAP DE MOURLIN *ST.-EMILION* ★★★
1982 .... ③ **85**
1983 .... ③ **85**
There were always two Cap de Mourlin estates, but since 1983 there is only one, under the name Jacques Capdemourlin. The wine here is powerful, dense, rather huge, and massive, with little complexity but tremendous richness and power. Both the 1982 and 1983 are of this style.

CARBONNIEUX *(RED) GRAVES* ★★
1982 .... ④ **82**
1983 .... ③ **80**
Another property better known for its white wine than red, Carbonnieux tends to make very fruity, easy-to-like, easy-to-drink, soft red wine. Both 1982 and 1983 are typical of its style.

CARBONNIEUX *(WHITE) GRAVES* ★★★
1983 .... ④ **85**
1984 .... ④ **80**
1985 .... ④ **85**
Carbonnieux produces a large quantity of very reliable, crisp, fruity, elegant white Graves. The 1983 is a textbook white Graves that should keep for five to ten years. The 1985 is slightly fruitier and less ageworthy, but very attractive.

LA CARDONNE *MÉDOC* ★★
1982 .... ② **80**
This is an interesting Cru Bourgeois owned by the Rothschild

family (of Lafite Rothschild). There has been a tremendous amount of money invested, but to date the wines have been rather light and lacking in character.

LES CARMES HAUT-BRION *GRAVES* ★★★

1982 .... ③ *82*

Rarely seen, Les Carmes Haut-Brion's vineyard is well placed and in 1982 made a rich, lush, easy-to-drink wine that will mature quickly.

CARONNE-STE.-GEMME *HAUT MÉDOC* ★★

1982 .... ③ *84*

This is a big, powerful, richly fruity, tannic wine that needs another three to five years of cellaring to reach its peak.

CERTAN-GIRAUD *POMEROL* ★★★

1982 .... ⑤ *89*
1983 .... ⑤ *88*
1984 .... ⑤ *81*

Certan-Giraud is a Pomerol on the move upward in quality. The 1984, given the difficulties of the vintage, is a success. The 1983 is filled with the scent of garden herbs and ripe fruit, and is an unctuous, rich wine for dinking in the near future. The 1982 is a big, dense, full-bodied Pomerol loaded with flavour.

CERTAN DE MAY *POMEROL* ★★★★★

1981 .... ⑤ *90*
1982 .... ⑤ *97*
1983 .... ⑤ *87*

The tiny property of Certan de May has in the last ten years emerged from a period of mediocrity into the top echelon of Pomerols. It is a connoisseur's wine, slow to evolve, but powerful, rich, and multidimensional in personality. The 1983, which will need long cellaring, is perhaps too tannic and oaky for its own good, the 1982 a fantastic wine with unbelievable concentration and one of the truly colossal efforts from this vintage. The 1981, broodingly dark and backward, is a powerful, rich, fruity wine.

CHASSE-SPLEEN *MOULIS* ★★★★

1981 .... ③ *84*
1982 .... ③ *87*
1983 .... ③ *87*

Chasse Spleen is an outstanding property that produces one of Bordeaux's best wines as well as best wine values. The wine is always characterized by a very pronounced deep ruby colour, a bouquet of plummy ripeness, and rich, round substantial flavours. The 1983 and 1982 are two very fine vintages for Chasse-Spleen, producing big, full-flavoured, rich, large-scaled wines with enormous potential. The 1981 is ready to drink and is a bit lighter and more precocious in style.

CHEVAL BLANC *ST.-EMILION* ★ ★ ★ ★ ★

1981	⑤	90
1982	⑤	98
1983	⑤	93
1984	⑤	75

Cheval Blanc, certainly one of Bordeaux's greatest wines, is also unique, being made from more than two-thirds Cabernet Franc, the only major wine in Bordeaux to have that distinction. The wine is exotic, rich, very easy to drink young but cunningly made to last. The 1984, from a disastrous vintage for St.-Emilion, is light, herbaceous, and should be drunk soon. The 1983 is a rich, exotic, full-bodied, lush wine with a sweet, long finish. The 1982 is Cheval Blanc's greatest wine since some of its legendary vintages in the late 1940s. It is voluptuous and extremely intense, with a cascade of exotic, rich aromas. There is plenty of tannin, but the immense concentration of fruit will cause many to drink the wine before it is fully mature. The 1981 is a lighter wine, but very elegant, spicy, plummy, with soft, silky, lovely flavours.

DOMAINE DE CHEVALIER *(RED) GRAVES* ★ ★ ★ ★ ★

1981	④	85
1982	⑤	90
1983	④	87
1984	④	85

For sheer elegance and consistency the tiny Domaine de Chevalier has always been a connoisseur's favourite. Recent vintages have all been very successful and this is also a property to look for in off vintages such as 1980 and 1984. The 1984 is, in fact, a top success of the vintage, the 1983 rather hard, tough, and tannic, and just needing seven to eight years of patience. The 1982 is rich, long, fat, and quite concentrated, and the 1981 elegant, with a pronounced vanillin oakiness.

DOMAINE DE CHEVALIER *(WHITE) GRAVES* ★ ★ ★ ★ ★

1982	⑤	88
1983	⑤	93
1984	⑤	88

On average, only 500-600 cases of this exceptional white wine are produced each year. It is remarkably long-lived and though usually overpoweringly oaky when young, becomes increasingly more complex with age. The 1983 is a monumental effort; both the 1982 and 1984 are very fine.

CISSAC HAUT-MÉDOC ★★★

1981	② 78
1982	② 84
1983	② 80

Cissac is one of the best of the Cru Bourgeois properties in the Médoc. The wine is generally made in a very long-lived, tannic style. The 1982 shows more supple richness and is quite full-bodied and powerful. The 1981 is rather austere and a little too lean, and the 1982 plump and showing an uncomplicated fruitiness and character.

CITRAN HAUT-MÉDOC ★

1981	① 65
1982	② 73
1983	① 70

This winery produces a significant amount of wine that is often highly promoted. However, it is also often quite diluted and emaciated in taste and texture. The latter comment would characterize the 1981, 1982, and 1983.

CLARKE LISTRAC ★★★

1982	③ 81
1983	③ 80

The Baron Edmond de Rothschild has totally restored and rejuvenated this property and when the 1985 is released people will see how far in quality it has come. Both the 1982 and 1983 reflect the youth of the vineyard and while they are adequate wines, they lack the richness and depth we will see in the upcoming 1985.

CLERC-MILON PAUILLAC ★★★

1982	④ 84
1983	④ 83
1984	④ 85

A great effort has been made by the Baron Philippe du Rothschild to improve the quality of Clerc-Milon in the 1980s. Ironically, the 1984 (the vintage of the least pedigree) is the best vintage of Clerc-Milon, even better than the 1983 and 1982. The 1984 is richer, with a lush, fruity quality and should be drunk in the near future. The 1983 seems rather lightweight for the vintage. The 1982 is again charming and very forward, an open-knit wine with a very pleasing bouquet.

CLIMENS BARSAC ★★★★

1980	⑤	90
1982	⑤	80
1983	⑤	90

Climens is the best sweet wine for sheer racy and stylish elegance. It is never overpowering, but oh so delicious and crisp, with great balance. The 1983 is superb, the 1982 a disappointment, and the 1980 a fabulous vintage for this château, with an exotic bouquet of tropical fruit, pineapples, and melons.

CLINET POMEROL ★★

1982	③	75
1983	③	80

I have usually found the wines of Clinet to be rather light and lacking the exuberant, fleshy, rich fruit for which Pomerols are so renowned. The 1982 and 1983 are typical.

CLOS DU CLOCHER POMEROL ★★★

1982	④	85
1983	③	83

This is a terribly under-publicized property that generally makes very good wine. The 1982 is surprisingly dense, concentrated, and deeply fruity, and the 1983 elegant, spicy, well coloured, and ready to drink.

CLOS L'EGLISE POMEROL ★★

1982	③	82
1983	③	80

Clos L'Eglise produces one of the more Médoc-like, and austere wines of Pomerol, with a heavy reliance on the Cabernet Franc and Cabernet Sauvignon grapes. The 1983 is slightly herbaceous and a little shallow. The 1982 is rather light for the vintage but attractive in a simple, fruity way.

CLOS FOURTET ST.-EMILION ★★

1981	③	80
1982	④	86
1983	③	78

Clos Fourtet's main claim to fame is its remarkable wine cellars, but the wine has been off form for some time, though recent vintages look more promising. The 1983 is soft, fruity, and rather commercial. The 1982 is the best recent vintage, with a full-blown bouquet of toasty oak and berry fruit, and the 1981 pleasant but rather one-dimensional.

CLOS DES JACOBINS *ST.-EMILION* ★★★

1981	④	86
1982	④	89
1983	④	87
1984	③	80

The well-known *négociant*, Cordier, owns this little château and produces deeply coloured, rich, creamy, plummy wines that have a cedary fragrance when mature. Recent vintages have all been successful, including the 1984, which is ready to drink. The 1983 is lush, ripe, fat, and alcoholic, the 1982 sweet with layers of voluptuous fruit, and the 1981 herbaceous but intensely fruity and elegant.

CLOS RENÉ *POMEROL* ★★★

1982	④	87
1983	④	86

After a period of rather uninspired activity, Clos René has come on strongly in the 1980s with a succession of good vintages. Both the 1983 and 1982 are ready to drink; they are rich, lush, fat wines with considerable flavour and power, but lacking a little in finesse.

CLOS DES TEMPLIERS *LALANDE-DE-POMEROL* ★★

1982	①	83
1983	①	80

A very good, reliable estate in Lalande-de-Pomerol making supple, silky wines for drinking within the first five to six years.

LA CLOTTE *ST.-EMILION* ★★

1982	③	84
1983	②	75

The owners of the lovely little bistro in St.-Emilion, Logis de la Cadène, also own this vineyard. The wine, made to be drunk young, is supple, fat, fruity, as well as delicious, as in 1982.

LA COMMANDERIE *ST.-EMILION* ★★

1982	③	81
1983	②	84

A tiny property next to Cheval Blanc that in 1983 made a delicious, densely coloured, chunky wine.

LA CONSEILLANTE *POMEROL* ★★★★

1981	⑤	90

1982 .... ⑤ **90**
1983 .... ⑤ **87**
La Conseillante makes one of Pomerol's most elegant and Burgundian wines. It always seems to have a smell of toasty oak and raspberry fruit not unlike a fine Chambolle Musigny. The 1983 is creamy, velvety with lovely fruit, the 1982 voluptuous, decadently ripe, a rather big wine from La Conseillante, but with a smell of raspberry fruit. The 1981, lighter than both the 1982 and 1983, is a remarkably elegant, balanced wine with layers of gorgeous plummy, sweet fruit.

CORBIN *ST.-EMILION* ★ ★ ★
1982 .... ④ **87**
1983 .... ④ **86**
Corbin, which borders Pomerol, tends to make wine in a very lush, fruity style. It seems to excel in the hot, sunny years. Both the 1983 and 1982 are supple, fat, jammy, ripe wines that offer wonderful drinking for the next five to six years.

CORBIN-MICHOTTE *ST.-EMILION* ★ ★ ★
1982 .... ③ **85**
1983 .... ③ **84**
A sound, reliable, fat, plummy, deeply coloured, Graves-like St.-Emilion that is excellent in both 1982 and 1983.

COS D'ESTOURNEL *ST.-ESTÈPHE* ★ ★ ★ ★ ★
1981 .... ⑤ **86**
1982 .... ⑤ **97**
1983 .... ⑤ **87**
1984 .... ⑤ **87**
Cos d'Estournel has risen not only to the top of its class in St.-Estèphe, but is now among the great wines in all of Bordeaux. Since 1976 the wines have improved, going from strength to strength. The 1984 is one of the top successes of the vintage; the 1983 is certainly the best St.-Estèphe, though not a great wine. The 1982 is a monumental wine of explosive richness and length on the palate, and the 1981 is elegant, a much lighter-weight wine than the 1982 or 1983. The unreleased 1985 from the cask looked to have enough potential to be the wine of the vintage – no small accomplishment.

COS LABORY *ST.-ESTÈPHE* ★ ★
1982 .... ③ **78**
1983 .... ③ **73**
1984 .... ③ **78**
Cos Labory, although a classified growth, is one of the most

disappointing. Improvements continue to be made, but the wine is generally fruity, bland, and light, often feebly coloured as well. The 1984 is light and pleasant, the 1983 again very light, and the 1982 a decent wine, but in the context of the vintage, a disappointment.

COUFRAN *HAUT-MÉDOC* ★ ★ ★

1982	③	86
1983	③	84

Coufran is one of the most unusual wines in the Médoc since it is made of a very high percentage of Merlot (85%). Consequently, the wine tends to be richly fruity and very precocious in style. The 1983 is a succulent, juicy, grapy wine, ready to drink, and the 1982 a more serious effort with greater richness and length.

COUTET *BARSAC* ★ ★ ★ ★

1981	③	78
1983	④	87

A lighter-styled wine from Barsac, Coutet makes very fresh, easy-to-drink wines with a lemony, melon fruitiness. The 1983 is their best of the most recent vintages.

COUVENT-DES-JACOBINS *ST.-EMILION* ★ ★ ★

1981	③	78
1982	③	85
1983	③	85

The gorgeous Château Couvent-des-Jacobins is one of the most interesting in all of Bordeaux, and its underground cellars are among the most impressive. The wine is increasingly well-made by the owners, the Joinaud-Borde family. The 1983 is a soft, supple, fruity, deliciously styled, elegant wine. The 1982 has an impressive colour and a complex bouquet of cedar and rich, fruity scents. The 1981 is a bit herbaceous and lacking the concentration of the latter two vintages. The 1984 was declassified totally by this meticulously run property.

LA CROIX *POMEROL* ★ ★ ★

1981	③	84
1982	③	86
1983	③	86

La Croix produces a very plump, fat, deliciously fruity, uncomplex style of Pomerol that has wide appeal. The 1982 and 1983 are both big wines with a lot of alcohol and flavour, but not much finesse. The 1981 is lighter in style.

LA CROIX DE GAY *POMEROL* ★ ★ ★

1982 .... ④ **75**
1983 .... ④ *84*

La Croix de Gay had a great reputation in the forties and fifties, but by the seventies the wine became rather light in style. Now in the eighties, the 1982 was somewhat of a disappointment given the vintage, but the 1983 shows effusively fruity, round, supple texture and good fruit, and the unreleased 1985 is perhaps the best la Croix de Gay in more than two decades. A property to watch as greater efforts are being made to upgrade the quality.

CROIZET-BAGES *PAUILLAC* ★ ★

1982 .... ③ **75**
1983 .... ② **68**
1984 .... ② **70**

Croizet-Bages is among the lightest and quickest maturing of all the Pauillacs. The wine is often lacking in class as well as concentration. The 1984 is surprisingly fruitier and more interesting than the disappointing 1983. The 1982 has simple cherry flavours and a rather flabby structure.

CROQUE-MICHOTTE *ST.-EMILION* ★ ★ ★

1982 .... ③ **86**
1983 .... ② **80**

This is a rather uncomplicated style of wine, fruity, fleshy and alcoholic in style. The 1983 is a bit too alcoholic and lacking acidity; the 1982 ripe, savoury, very flavourful, and quite full-bodied.

CURÉ-BON-LA-MADELEINE *ST.-EMILION* ★ ★

1982 .... ④ **87**
1983 .... ④ **84**

Despite a remarkable reputation, this wine is rarely seen due to the tiny production of 1,500 cases. The 1983 is herbaceous but soft and very fruity, the 1982 is richer, denser, riper, and ready to drink.

LA DAUPHINE *FRONSAC* ★ ★ ★

1982 .... ② **85**
1983 .... ② **85**

The star of Fronsac, La Dauphine, produces fragrant, rich, medium- to full-bodied wines that can age up to ten years. Both the 1982 and 1983 are very successful here.

DAUZAC *MARGAUX* ★★

1981	②	**80**
1982	③	**82**
1983	②	**80**

Despite a new ownership in 1978 that has invested considerable sums of money, Dauzac remains one of the least impressive wines in Margaux. The wine is rather simple, with decent cherryish flavours and medium body. The best recent vintage is the 1982, which is plump, fruity, with good colour and an attractive ripeness on the palate.

DESMIRAIL *MARGAUX* ★★

1981	②	**75**
1982	②	**82**
1983	②	**80**

This property has been resurrected by the owner of the famous Brane-Cantenac, Lucien Lurton. The wine to date has been uncomplicated, fruity, with attractive suppleness and richness, but is meant to be drunk young.

DESTIEUX *ST. EMILION* ★★★

1982	②	**84**
1983	②	**85**

Destieux makes an attractive, plummy, fleshy, open-knit wine with plenty of alcohol. The 1983 is the best of the recent vintages because it has a bit more concentration and flesh to it. These wines are to be drunk young.

DOISY-DAËNE *BARSAC* ★★★

1982	③	**82**
1983	③	**90**

One of the most ambitiously and innovatively run estates in Bordeaux, Doisy-Daëne is capable of making very fine sweet wines fom the Barsac region. The 1983 is one of their best vintages in recent history, with a big, ripe bouquet of pineapples, peaches, and spring flowers, and a very concentrated, full-bodied, unctuous feel on the palate.

DOISY-VÉDRINES *BARSAC* ★★★

1982	③	**84**
1983	③	**87**

This well-placed estate in Barsac can make very good wines that tend to be fatter, richer, more intense than many of the Barsacs. The 1983 is excellent and the 1982 is a success for the vintage; both are viscous, ripe, coconut-scented wines with sweet, rich flavours.

LA DOMINIQUE *ST.-EMILION* ★★★★

1981	③	**84**
1982	⑤	**92**
1983	④	**87**

A remarkably underrated wine from St.-Emilion, La Dominique is making wines on a level with any St.-Emilion save for Cheval Blanc. The property has produced a number of great wines in recent vintages, including an incredibly opulent, rich, sublime 1982, a well-structured, flavourful, full-bodied 1983, and a lighter, but complex, fully mature 1981. No 1984 was made.

DUCRU-BEAUCAILLOU *ST.-JULIEN* ★★★★★

1981	⑤	**90**
1982	⑤	**96**
1983	⑤	**88**
1984	⑤	**83**

Ducru-Beaucaillou is one of Bordeaux's most famous properties and has been elevated to greatness by its modest owner, Jean Eugène Borie. The top vintages for Ducru-Beaucaillou in recent decades have all been excellent. This wine seems to combine the cedary, majestic richness of a Pauillac with the ripe, intense fruitiness of a classic St.-Julien. The 1984 is one of the more tannic wines of the vintage and needs several more years to fully develop. The 1983 is a very good rather than great vintage for Ducru. It is tannic and needs a good decade of ageing. The 1982, along with the 1953 and 1961, is one of the three greatest Ducrus I have ever tasted. It is closed at present, but with another ten years of ageing should reveal its voluptuous, extremely concentrated, stunning density of extract and power. The 1981 is a more elegant, lighter version of the intense 1982. It is a beautifully crafted wine made to last and last.

DUHART-MILON-ROTHSCHILD *PAUILLAC* ★★★

1981	④	**84**
1982	④	**88**
1983	④	**86**
1984	④	**80**

Duhart-Milon is one of the Pauillac châteaux owned by the Rothschilds. The vineyard is still quite young and while there were many disappointing wines produced in the 1970s, the 1980s have shown greater consistency and quality. The 1984 is light but pleasant; the 1983 has good colour, a firm structure, and some pleasant cassis flavours. The 1982 is the best Duhart-Milon I have tasted in the last several decades, rich, full-bodied, with loads of tannin and fruit. The 1981 is light, but extremely elegant, with a cedary, rich bouquet.

DURAND LAPLAGNE *PUISSEGUIN-ST.-EMILION* ★ ★ ★

1982 .... ② **82**
1983 .... ② **84**

This is the top estate of Puisseguin-St.-Emilion; both 1982 and 1983 produced surprisingly rich and fruity wines with generous textures.

DURFORT-VIVENS *MARGAUX* ★ ★ ★

1981 .... ③ **74**
1982 .... ④ **85**
1983 .... ④ **86**
1984 .... ③ **73**

Durfort-Vivens, one of the principal properties of the Lurton family, has a record of twenty years of mediocrity. However, vintages since 1978 have shown improvement, particularly in 1982 and 1983, both years having produced rather rich, ripe, lovely wines with good concentration and ageing ability. The 1981 is angular and weedy and 1984 rather light and thin.

L'EGLISE-CLINET *POMEROL* ★ ★ ★ ★

1982 .... ④ **86**
1983 .... ④ **86**
1984 .... ④ **84**

L'Eglise-Clinet is one of the properties to watch in Pomerol since it is making great strides in quality. The 1984 is one of Pomerol's top wines in what was a disappointing vintage. The 1983 and 1982 are fat, powerful, with rich black cherry bouquets and chewy, dense textures. The unreleased 1985 (which rivals Pétrus) will make L'Eglise-Clinet justifiably famous.

DOMAINE DE L'EGLISE *POMEROL* ★ ★

1982 .... ③ **80**
1983 .... ③ **82**

Domaine de L'Eglise has not distinguished itself in recent vintages and remains a dull, chunky Pomerol with little character. However, the unreleased 1985 may prove to be a move towards making a better-quality wine than formerly.

L'ENCLOS *POMEROL* ★ ★ ★

1982 .... ③ **87**
1983 .... ③ **86**

L'Enclos is always a supple, fruity wine with an opulent,

blackberry fruitiness. Both the 1982 and 1983 are very smooth and velvety, and delicious for drinking over the next five to six years. As Pomerols go, this wine represents good value.

L'EVANGILE *POMEROL* ★ ★ ★ ★ ★
1981	⑤	**73**
1982	⑤	**96**
1983	⑤	**91**
1984	⑤	**78**

L'Evangile is one of the most complex and interesting Pomerols, and in the last few vintages has been a worthy rival to the great Pétrus itself. The 1984 is light, flavourful, but rather simple. The 1983 is the top wine of Pomerol, dark, with a full-blown, blackberry bouquet and plenty of tannin. The 1982 is extraordinary, with explosive, jammy, blackcurrant fruit and a full-bodied, unctuous texture. The 1981 is diffuse and a disappointment for this property. Lastly, keep an eye out for the great 1985, which is likely to turn out to be among the top four or five wines of the vintage.

FARGUES *SAUTERNES* ★ ★ ★ ★ ★
1980	⑤	**91**
1981	⑤	**90**

The ancestral home of the Lur Saluces family (who own Yquem), Château de Fargues is under the Yquem management and given exactly the same winemaking and cellar treatment. In fact, it resembles Yquem much more closely in character, style, and texture than the Lur Saluces family would like to admit. The 1981 may even be better than Yquem, a rich, sweet, exotic, concentrated wine; the 1980 is a great vintage, with an opulence and power that is exceptional for a wine. In short, the Yquem junior of Sauternes wines.

FAURIE-DE-SOUCHARD *ST.-EMILION* ★ ★ ★
1982	③	**85**
1983	③	**85**

This little-known but excellent property makes rather firm, rich, muscular wines that can take up to ten years of ageing.

FERRAND *ST.-EMILION* ★ ★ ★
1982	③	**86**
1983	③	**84**

The famous ballpoint pen king, Baron Bich, owns this up-and-coming property and is sparing no expense to produce one of St.- Emilion's top wines. The unreleased 1985 is superb, but the 1982 is a good introduction to the rich, full-bodied, yet balanced style of this wine. The 1983 is a little lean and hard. Prices can only go up once the quality of this wine is no longer a secret.

FERRANDE *GRAVES* ★

1981 .... ② *82*
1982 .... ② *82*

Ferrande produces supple, round, warm, soft red wines for drinking within the first five to six years of their lives.

FERRIÈRE *MARGAUX* ★★

1981 .... ③ *79*
1982 .... ④ *84*
1983 .... ④ *82*

The obscure and tiny property of Ferrière produces wine that is largely sold in France. The wine is made at Lascombes and shows a similarity in style. The 1983 is supple and earthy, with a nice plummy fruitiness. The 1982 shows more depth than the 1983 and better colour than the 1981, with a very forward elegance that makes it drinkable over the next couple of years.

FIEUZAL *(RED) GRAVES* ★★★

1982 .... ④ *84*
1983 .... ④ *83*

Fieuzal is a relatively unknown property in the southern Graves area making both red and white wine. The soon-to-be-released 1985 shows the great potential of this well-placed property, but though the 1982 and 1983 are good, they are nothing exciting given their vintages. However, this is a property on the move upward.

FIEUZAL *(WHITE) GRAVES* ★★★★★

1983 .... ④ *86*
1984 .... ④ *86*
1985 .... ⑤ *92*

Starting in 1985, due to a huge effort on the part of the owners to put Fieuzal in the top class of white Graves wines, Fieuzal can now challenge Laville-Haut-Brion, Haut-Brion Blanc, and Domaine de Chevalier. The 1985 is fabulous; both the 1984 and 1983 quite good. Prices, unfortunately, are rocketing.

FIGEAC *ST.-EMILION* ★★★★

1981 .... ④ *82*
1982 .... ⑤ *92*
1983 .... ④ *87*
1984 .... ④ *70*

Figeac makes the wine that is most commonly compared to Cheval Blanc. It seems to be less consistent than Cheval Blanc in recent vintages and in some years has a distinctive, if not annoying, vegetal, overtly herbaceous character to it. The 1984 is disappointing; the 1983 soft, rich, fruity, and a lovely wine for drinking over the next decade; the 1982 a sensational Figeac and the best since the property's outstanding 1964. The 1981 is dull, herbaceous, but soft and fruity.

FILHOT *SAUTERNES* ★★
1982 .... ③ *78*
1983 .... ③ *85*

This property makes fruity, aromatic, delicate wines that lack a little in power and richness but are attractively elegant. The 1983 is the best in recent vintages.

LA FLEUR GAZIN *POMEROL* ★★
1982 .... ④ *83*

The tiny vineyard of La Fleur Gazin produces a rather supple, fruity, uncomplicated style of wine that should be drunk before its sixth or seventh birthday.

LA FLEUR PÉTRUS *POMEROL* ★★★★
1981 .... ⑤ *84*
1982 .... ⑤ *90*
1983 .... ⑤ *86*

Although this property has a famous name, it is a much lighter wine than Pétrus, but often shows very elegant, forward flavours and can be drunk quite young. Whether it has the requisite power to last with the great Pomerols is questionable. The 1983 is fruity, very charming, plummy, and ready. The 1982 is a bigger, denser wine with a good future ahead of it, and the 1981 soft, a trifle jammy, but very supple and charming.

FOMBRAUGE *ST.-EMILION* ★★
1982 .... ② *82*
1983 .... ② *82*

A very commercial wine that is made to be drunk within its first four to five years. It is sold at reasonable prices and has appeal for its forward and fruity flavours.

FONBADET *PAUILLAC* ★★★
1982 .... ④ *87*
1983 .... ③ *86*
1984 .... ③ *72*

This rather unknown property in Pauillac makes very intense, chewy, rich wines that have very good style and character. The 1984 is somewhat of a disappointment for Fonbadet – light, rather diluted, and vegetal. The 1983 is quite concentrated, rich, full-bodied, with moderate tannins. The 1982 is a gorgeous wine, with intense blackberry aromas and viscous, rich flavours.

FONPLÉGADE ST.-EMILION ★★★

1981	②	82
1982	③	84

Fonplégade makes uncomplicated, fruity, soft wines that drink well for the first five to eight years of life. The 1982 is soft and fruity, the 1981 plummy, slightly lighter, but enjoyable.

FONROQUE ST.-EMILION ★★★

1981	③	84
1982	③	84
1983	③	87

Fonroque has a splendid location in St.-Emilion and is a property to watch carefully as huge efforts have been made to upgrade its quality. The 1983 may be the best Fonroque in over two decades – ripe, rich, full-bodied, lush with plenty of toasty, new oak aromas. The 1982 does not have the same concentration, nor does the more open knit, lighter 1981. This is a property on the move up.

LES FORTS DE LATOUR PAUILLAC ★★★★

1975	⑤	84
1976	⑤	82
1978	⑤	90

The second wine of Latour is often as good as some classified growths of Bordeaux. The 1978 is the best Forts de Latour I have ever tasted – rich, complex, with great bouquet and long, rich flavours. The 1976 is beginning to dry out. The 1975 is hard, unyielding, but still showing promise if it ever softens.

FOURCAS-DUPRÉ LISTRAC ★★

1982	②	84
1983	②	80

Fourcas-Dupré is usually an unexciting but generally reliable and consistent wine although certain vintages, the 1982 and 1978, have been excellent. The 1982 shows a great deal of richness and a plump, fat texture. The 1983 is a rather light, short, uninteresting wine.

FOURCAS-HOSTEN *LISTRAC* ★ ★ ★

1981	②	**84**
1982	②	**84**
1983	②	**85**

Fourcas-Hosten is perhaps the leading vineyard of Listrac. The wine is made in a very intelligent style that combines supple richness and adequate tannin for longevity of eight to ten years. The best recent vintage, the 1983, is a classic, elegantly styled wine with a complex, spicy, richly fruity bouquet and good length. The 1982 is soft and drinkable already, as is the 1981.

LA GAFFELIÈRE *ST.-EMILION* ★ ★ ★

1981	④	**78**
1982	④	**87**
1983	④	**86**

No one doubts the fabulous location of La Gaffelière, but its track record until 1982 had been one of mediocrity. Since 1982, La Gaffelière seems to be getting serious about turning out high-quality wines. The 1983 and 1982 are a big step in the right direction, fruity, ripe, elegant, not deep or powerful, but well-balanced, graceful wines for drinking at a young age.

LA GARDE *GRAVES* ★

1982	②	**75**

A soft, fruity, medium-bodied, rather one-dimensional wine that should be drunk young.

GARRAUD *LALANDE-DE-POMEROL* ★ ★

1982	①	**82**
1983	①	**75**

This can be a well made, chunky, robust, often tannic Lalande de Pomerol that takes some time to age.

LE GAY *POMEROL* ★ ★ ★ ★

1981	④	**72**
1982	⑤	**89**
1983	⑤	**85**

Le Gay is a tiny property that makes deep-coloured, robust, tannic, backward wines that need cellaring. The 1983 is alcoholic, tannic but a powerful and ripe wine. It seems a good bet for cellaring. The 1982 is even more powerful, very rich, with a blackberry, earthy, peppery bouquet. The 1981 is disappointing and flawed because of dirty barrels.

GAZIN *POMEROL* ★ ★ ★

1981	④	*81*
1982	④	*84*
1983	④	*83*

There is no question that the vineyard of Gazin has one of the better locations in Pomerol, but the wine produced has been rather light and uninspiring given what should be expected. Both the 1982 and 1983 are light, supple, and fruity, but not up to the quality one expects given the location of this vineyard and the price charged for the wine.

GILETTE *SAUTERNES* ★ ★ ★ ★

1953	⑤	*86*
1955	⑤	*88*
1959	⑤	*94*

Gilette's proprietor does not release his wines until they have had 20–25 years of ageing; consequently the vintages that are now available are all from the 1950s. The 1955 is deep golden with a honey bouquet, the 1953 less rich and fat, with a bouquet suggesting melted caramel. The 1959 is extraordinary, a hedonistic symphony of earthly and heavenly delights. These are wines that are unique and remarkably well made.

GISCOURS *MARGAUX* ★ ★ ★ ★ ★

1981	④	*87*
1982	④	*87*
1983	④	*88*
1984	④	*85*

The vast estate of Giscours is impeccably managed by the Tari family and the wines are consistently rich and supple, with robust body and fleshiness. They can be especially good in off vintages such as 1984 and 1980. The 1984 is very perfumed, very supple, a notable success. The 1983 is delicious to drink now, will evolve quickly, but offers a silky texture and oodles of fruit. The 1982 is similarly styled but slightly fatter, perhaps not so well balanced overall. The 1981 is a totally charming wine with a supple, graceful fruitiness, and rich, spicy, berry fruit bouquet.

GLANA *ST.-JULIEN* ★ ★

1982	①	*83*
1983	①	*82*
1984	①	*75*

Glana is a sizeable vineyard that had a very spotty record of achievement until 1978. Since then reliable wines have been made. The 1982 is fat, concentrated, full-bodied and supple.

The 1983 has been irregular in tasting, but is fruity, soft and ready to drink.

GLORIA ST.-JULIEN ★ ★ ★ ★
1981 .... ③ 80
1982 .... ③ 85
1983 .... ② 82
1984 .... ② 82

Gloria has lightened its style of winemaking, but the wine still remains a very stylish, delicious, richly fragrant and fruity wine meant to be drunk young, and capable of ageing for up to a decade. The 1984 is simple and fruity; the 1983 very spicy and somewhat herbaceous. The 1982 is gloriously fruity, grapy, velvety, and ready to drink. The 1981 is light, supple, and a tifle disappointing for this property.

GOMBAUDE-GUILLOT POMEROL ★ ★
1982 .... ⑤ 82

This is a middle-of-the-road Pomerol that is generally sold to private customers in France. The wine can be good but is rarely exciting.

GRAND-CORBIN-DESPAGNE ST.-EMILION ★ ★
1982 .... ② 82
1983 .... ② 83

A well-situated property that makes a great deal of wine that tends to be rather stern, darkly coloured, chunky and robust in flavour. The 1983 looks quite good.

GRAND-ORMEAU LALANDE-DE-POMEROL ★ ★ ★
1982 .... ② 86
1983 .... ② 78

Another of the up-and-coming stars of Lalande-de-Pomerol, this estate made an excellent 1982 which was rich, fruity, and loaded with extract. The unreleased 1985 also looks to be a knockout.

GRAND-PUY-DUCASSE PAUILLAC ★ ★ ★
1981 .... ② 82
1982 .... ③ 86
1983 .... ② 84

Grand-Puy-Ducasse is one of the most ignored wines in Pauillac, which is rather unfortunate. The wine is made in a style that is supple and easy to drink young. Yet the wines have a way of holding their own for eight to ten years. The 1983 is herbaceous, cedary, silky, and attractively fruity and ready.

The 1982 is richer, fuller-bodied, but also ripe, round, and will drink well for five to ten more years. The 1981 is quite light and ready to drink now. For a classified-growth Pauillac, these wines are always fairly priced.

GRAND-PUY-LACOSTE *PAUILLAC* ★ ★ ★ ★

1981	....	③	**78**
1982	....	⑤	**91**
1983	....	④	**85**
1984	....	③	**75**

Grand-Puy-Lacoste is still not as well known as its quality merits. It has always been a somewhat inconsistent property, but under the current ownership, which has run the property since 1978, the wine has been a textbook Pauillac. The 1984 is good but rather simple. The 1983, a tannic, somewhat angular wine, has yet to show its full pleasures. The 1982 is a stupendous vintage for Grand-Puy-Lacoste, with a great intensity of fruit, very dark colour, and a huge aroma, even though it will not be ready to drink for ten years. The 1981 is very light, rather elegant, but soft and ready to drink.

LA GRAVE FIGEAC *ST.-EMILION* ★ ★ ★ ★

1982	....	③	**87**
1983	....	③	**89**

This is a tiny gem of a property located right next to Cheval Blanc that produces only 1,500 cases per year. The wines are rich, fragrant, and very, very concentrated. The 1983 is absolutely sensational, with lots of ripe blackberry fruit, and the 1982 is equally good but with a lusher, more opulent texture.

LA GRAVE TRIGANT DE BOISSET *POMEROL* ★ ★ ★

1981	....	④	**83**
1982	....	⑤	**88**
1983	....	⑤	**86**

The personal property of Christian Moueix, the brilliant winemaker of Pétrus and other major Pomerols, La Grave Trigant sits on lighter soil and produces a very fruity, more elegant wine than some of the larger-scaled Pomerols from better-situated vineyards. It has been a wine that has got better and better as the vineyard has got older. The 1983 is a big, richly fruity wine, the 1982 is gorgeously ripe, richly scented with significant power for La Grave Trigant. The 1981 is elegant and a wine more of finesse than power. This is certainly a Pomerol to drink young, before its tenth birthday, but also one to watch as the vineyard gets older.

GRESSIER GRAND-POUJEAUX *MOULIS* ★★

1981 .... ③ *81*
1982 .... ③ *83*

This tiny estate in Moulis makes good but not exciting wines. The 1982 shows good body and depth and potential for improvement of four to five years.

GREYSAC *MÉDOC* ★★★

1981 .... ① *80*
1982 .... ① *82*
1983 .... ① *83*

A popular Cru Bourgeois wine, Greysac combines suppleness and elegant complexity and consistency even in weaker vintages. The 1983 needs a few years to soften, the 1982 is plump, quite soft and ripe, and the 1981 a little light for Greysac. This wine is capable of ageing in good vintages for five to eight years.

GRUAUD-LAROSE *ST. JULIEN* ★★★★★

1981 .... ④ *88*
1982 .... ⑤ *96*
1983 .... ⑤ *90*
1984 .... ④ *84*

Gruaud-Larose produces a tremendous amount of wine and is probably St.-Julien's most popular wine. Its style is big, richly fruity, and full-bodied. The 1984 is a chunky wine with very good flavour, not much complexity, but satisfying palate impressions. The 1983, one of the top wines of the vintage, is a deep, plummy wine with an excellent extract of fruit, and very dark colour for the vintage. The 1982 is a massive, incredibly rich and concentrated wine that is extremely tannic and should live for 30 or more years. It's one of the greatest wines Gruaud-Larose has ever made. The 1981, another top success for the vintage, is dark in colour, with a full-intensity bouquet of ripe blackcurrants, spicy oak, plums, and tarry scents.

GUIRAUD *SAUTERNES* ★★★

1981 .... ④ *85*
1982 .... ④ *78*
1983 .... ④ *88*

One of the larger estates of Sauternes, now run by an ambitious Canadian, the wines of Guiraud bear watching as the quality seems to get better with each vintage. The best current release is the marvellous 1983, which has excellent balance and a full-bodied, lush, rich fruitiness.

LA GURGUE *MARGAUX* ★★★

1982 .... ② 85
1983 .... ② 87

This superb little property in the village of Margaux is making itself noticed because of its rich, ripe, intense style of wine. The 1982 is very, very good, but the 1983 is a superior wine with an intense, blackcurrant fruitiness and plenty of quality and tannin. This is an up-and-coming star.

HANTEILLAN *MÉDOC* ★★

1982 .... ② 75
1983 .... ② 77

A great deal of effort is being made at Hanteillan, but to date the wines have continued to be rather lean and cleanly made, lacking intensity and charm. However, I am convinced this is a property to keep an eye out for.

HAUT-BAGES-LIBÉRAL *PAUILLAC* ★★★

1982 .... ③ 87
1983 .... ③ 87
1984 .... ③ 80

Haut-Bages-Libéral is one of Pauillac's best-kept secrets and great values. The wine is easy to understand and is fat, rich, and, since the mid-seventies, increasingly well made. The 1984 is above average in quality and ready to drink, the 1983 is a big, brash, aggressive wine with intense colour and excellent ripeness. The 1982 is very similarly styled, a voluptuous, silky wine that will drink well for the next five to six years.

HAUT-BAILLY *GRAVES* ★★★★

1981 .... ③ 84
1982 .... ④ 87
1983 .... ③ 85
1984 .... ③ 78

Haut-Bailly produces one of the lightest Graves wines, which at first may seem to lack power and richness but has an uncommon elegance and finesse. Many of the vintages in the 1970s turned out very poorly due to the declining health of the former owner. Since 1979 the property has been in full form, making wines that are voluptuous, ripe, and easy to drink young. The 1982, 1983, and 1985 are the best recent vintages.

HAUT-BATAILLEY *PAUILLAC* ★★★

1981 .... ④ 83
1982 .... ④ 86

1983 .... ③ *84*
1984 .... ③ *77*

This Pauillac sits on the border of St.-Julien and perhaps because of this is a lighter, more elegant, yet very frangrant, silky style of wine. The 1984 is light and not very substantial, but clean and pleasant if drunk young. The 1983 is good, rather soft, with decent concentration. The 1982 started life promisingly but is now in a rather awkward, closed stage and one will have to wait another four to five years to see its real potential. The 1981 is quite silky, velvety, and ready to drink.

HAUT-BRION *(RED) GRAVES* ★★★★★
1981 .... ⑤ *84*
1982 .... ⑤ *96*
1983 .... ⑤ *88*
1984 .... ⑤ *87*

The only official first-growth of Graves, American-owned Haut-Brion makes magnificently elegant, early-to-mature wines that have a way of lasting in the bottle longer than most people think. They develop very characteristic tobacco smells with age. The 1984 is one of the top successes of this vintage, with an open knit fruitiness and lush flavours. The 1983 is rather light and elegant but very forward and should be fully mature in three to four years. The 1982 is Haut-Brion's best since the great 1959; densely coloured with a gorgeous bouquet and long, lush, intense flavours. The 1981 is a bit light, angular, and lean for a first-growth.

HAUT-BRION *(WHITE) GRAVES* ★★★★★
1983 .... ⑤ *84*
1984 .... ⑤ *87*
1985 .... ⑤ *90*

The tiny production of Haut-Brion's white wine (around 1,500 cases in a good vintage) guarantees a high price for the wine. In vintages such as 1985 it is well worth it, rich, distinctive and capable of fifteen to twenty years longevity. In other years, 1983 for example, it is not worth its high price.

HAUT-BRISSON *ST.-EMILION* ★★★
1982 .... ② *84*
1983 .... ② *84*

This vineyard, planted on very gravelly soil and using a high percentage of Merlot, produces ripe, stylish, fruity, moderately concentrated, cleanly made wines. Both the 1982 and 1983 will provide delicious drinking over the next four to five years.

HAUT-CHATAIN *LALANDE-DE-POMEROL* ★★
1982 .... ② *84*
1983 .... ② *65*

Haut-Chatain made a wonderful, fruity, delicious, complex 1982 but a disappointing 1983. The as yet unreleased 1985 is also poor.

HAUT-MARBUZET *ST.-ESTÈPHE* ★★★★
1981 .... ③ *85*
1982 .... ④ *92*
1983 .... ④ *88*
1984 .... ③ *78*

Haut-Marbuzet is an immensely popular wine because it is a unique tasting experience. Aged in 100% new oak barrels, it has an opulent, almost overwhelming intensity that appeals to those who love powerful, rich, extroverted wines. The 1984 is a somewhat disappointing wine for Haut-Marbuzet; however, the 1983 is ripe, plummy, fat – simply a hedonistic drinking experience. The 1982 is a ravishing, decadently rich wine with extraordinary concentration and the potential to live for another seven to eight years. The 1981 is another intriguing Haut-Marbuzet, deeply coloured, ripe, spicy, very oaky, but loaded with fruit.

HAUT-PLANTEY *ST.-EMILION* ★★
1982 .... ② *84*
1983 .... ② *84*

A typical, uncomplicated style of St.-Emilion, with fat, plummy, chewy texture, and good concentration in the top vintages.

HAUT-SARPE *ST.-EMILION* ★★★
1981 .... ③ *83*
1982 .... ③ *85*

This is another rustic, rather generously flavoured, firm St.-Emilion that needs three to four years to show its best. The 1982 has aromas and flavours of ripe blackberry fruit with good tannin, while the 1981 is rather lean and medium-bodied.

HAUT-SOCIANDO *CÔTES DE BLAYE* ★★
1982 .... ① *82*
1983 .... ① *78*

A very good Côtes de Blaye property that can excel in the really good vintages such as 1982 and 1985.

HORTEVIE *ST.-JULIEN* ★★★

1982 .... ③ **86**
1983 .... ② **85**

Hortevie is a selection of the oldest part of the vineyard of Terrey-Gros-Cailloux and shares with it much the same character – a silky, lush, rich, jammy quality, although Hortevie, since it is made from older vines, has more depth and richness.

ISSAN *MARGUAX* ★★★★

1981 .... ③ **86**
1982 .... ③ **86**
1983 .... ④ **88**
1984 .... ③ **78**

Issan, one of the prettier châteaux in Bordeaux, produces a very elegant, plummy, supple wine that has plenty of appeal and, of all wines, tends to remind me of Palmer. The 1984 is light but clean, and destined to be drunk very young. The 1983 is one of Issan's most impressive recent efforts, with rich, cherry, fruity flavours and a lush texture. The 1982 is spicy and earthy, and displays good black cherry fruit. The 1981 is ready to drink with an oaky, plummy bouquet, and soft, light tannins in the finish.

KIRWAN *MARGAUX* ★★★

1981 .... ③ **78**
1982 .... ④ **84**
1983 .... ③ **85**
1984 .... ③ **84**

An underachiever in Margaux for most of the sixties and seventies, Kirwan's wines of the eighties have taken on a higher quality as a result of an extensive rehabilitation programme begun in the early 1970s. The 1984 is a success, with supple, spicy fruit. The 1983 is one of the best Kirwans ever produced, rich, tannic with very good length. The 1982 is charming, with a very precocious personality, and the 1981 sound but uninspiring.

LABÉGORCE *MARGAUX* ★★

1982 .... ③ **82**
1983 .... ② **75**

Labégorce produces rather light but fragrant, typical Margaux wines that offer good value. The 1982 is particularly supple, fruity, and distinctive. The 1983 is rather unexciting for a Margaux.

LABÉGORCE-ZÉDÉ *MARGAUX* ★ ★ ★
1981 .... ② *82*
1982 .... ② *86*
1983 .... ③ *87*
Labégorce-Zédé produces solid, plump, chunky, flavourful wines. The 1983 is excellent, rich, full-bodied, and long on the palate. The 1982 is very similarly styled. The 1981 is a little light, but elegant.

LAFAURIE-PEYRAGUEY *SAUTERNES* ★ ★ ★ ★
1981 .... ④ *89*
1982 .... ④ *87*
1983 .... ④ *92*
Owned by the Cordier family, this is the least-known of the great wines of Sauternes, but due to a concentrated effort to improve the quality, the vintages of the 1980s have been nothing short of spectacular, topped by the fabulous apricot-flavoured, unctuous 1983, a delicious, fresh, lively, stunningly balanced 1982, and an exceptionally rich, intense 1981.

LAFITE-ROTHSCHILD *PAUILLAC* ★ ★ ★ ★ ★
1981 .... ⑤ *92*
1982 .... ⑤ *96*
1983 .... ⑤ *88*
1984 .... ⑤ *84*
Bordeaux's most famous wine, Lafite-Rothschild is among the most elegant and lightest of all of the famous wines of Bordeaux. Its reputation rests on its fabulous bouquet, rather than on the power and intensity of its flavours. For that reason, it can often be disappointing and too light in poor years. The 1984, though good, is hardly worth the price. The 1983 is still a very tannic, closed wine, but has not aged as well as I would like. The 1982, along with the 1975, is the best Lafite since 1959, a powerful, rich, fabulous wine with a great bouquet and decades of evolved evolution ahead of it. The 1981 is another classic Lafite with a fabulous bouquet and rich, complex, elegant flavours.

LAFLEUR *POMEROL* ★ ★ ★ ★ ★
1981 .... ⑤ *78*
1982 .... ⑤ *95*
1983 .... ⑤ *90*
Lafleur is the only wine in Pomerol capable of matching the power and majesty of Pétrus in certain vintages. The 1983 is even more powerful and richer wine than Pétrus. The 1982 is

an enormous wine with great potential and depth, and the 1981 a somewhat flawed, very inconsistent wine that has turned out disappointingly.

LAFON-ROCHET *ST.-ESTÈPHE* ★ ★ ★

1982	③	85
1983	③	86
1984	②	82

Lafon-Rochet gets little publicity these days, but the wine can be very good and often a good value. The 1984 is attractively fruity and well coloured for the vintage. The 1983 is quite backward, very tannic, and in need of long-term cellaring. The 1982 is not as impressive as it should be given the vintage, but has plenty of ripe, lush, fat flavours, and a good measure of tannin.

LAGRANGE *POMEROL* ★ ★

1982	④	84
1983	④	78

Lagrange is a rarely seen Pomerol that produces rather hard, burly wines with plenty of body and tannin but little charm. Both the 1982 and 1983 are typical wines.

LAGRANGE *ST.-JULIEN* ★ ★ ★

1981	③	78
1982	③	84
1983	③	86
1984	③	85

Lagrange has suffered numerous blows to its reputation because of its poor track record in the 1960s and 1970s. However, the property looks to have a brilliant future since it is now owned by a Japanese firm that has pumped tremendous amounts of money and expertise into the property. The 1984 is a good wine for the vintage, chunky, tannic, and well coloured. The 1983 is surprisingly rich and long, and is certainly one of the top values of that vintage. The 1982, less successful than 1983 at Lagrange, is a big wine but a little awkward.

LA LAGUNE *MARGAUX* ★ ★ ★ ★

1981	④	83
1982	⑤	92
1983	④	87
1984	③	87

La Lagune is one of Bordeaux's shining success stories. From virtual obscurity in the late 1950s and early 1960s, La Lagune has become in 25 years one of the most conscientiously run properties, making top-quality wine consistently in all vintages. The style of wine is rich and fleshy with a sometimes overpowering bouquet of oak and plummy fruit. The 1984 is an outstanding success in this vintage, with ripe, rich, plummy fruit. The 1983 suffers only in comparison with the incredible 1982, which the château believes is the greatest wine it has ever made. The 1981 is a plummy, cherryish-flavoured wine that is medium-bodied and ready to be drunk now.

LALANDE BORIE ST.-JULIEN ★ ★ ★

1982	③	85
1983	③	84

The highly respected Jean-Eugène Borie produces this wine from a young vineyard planted in 1971–1972. The 1982 is dense and gorgeously coloured with deep flavours. The 1983 is tannic and more angular.

LAMARQUE HAUT-MÉDOC ★ ★

1982	②	82
1983	②	78

Lamarque is one of the prettier and more interesting châteaux in the Médoc. The wines are made in an elegant, light style, meant to be drunk within the first six to seven years. The 1983 is light, somewhat herbaceous, and the 1982 is supple, fruity, and ready to drink.

LANESSAN HAUT MÉDOC ★ ★ ★

1981	②	78
1982	③	86
1983	③	83

Lanessan produces wine of a big, rich, gutsy style that often lacks finesse but more than compensates for that deficiency with plenty of power and flavour authority. The 1982 is the best recent vintage, a powerful, unique wine of great colour and depth on the palate. The 1983 is a little disjointed and needs several years of ageing. The 1981 is light for a Lanessan and fully mature.

LANGOA-BARTON ST.-JULIEN ★ ★ ★ ★

1981	④	84
1982	④	88
1983	④	85
1984	③	78

Langoa-Barton is an impressive château sitting directly on the heavily travelled Route du Vin in the Médoc. It shares its cellar with Léoville Barton, which has no château or wine-making facilities. The wine is very traditionally made, easily taking years to show its true character. The 1984 is an uninspiring wine but flavourful and drinkable over the next few years. The 1983 is tannic and rather angular; good, but not special. The 1982 looks to be one of the best in the last several decades, with its rich, intense bouquet and big, tough, full-bodied framework. The 1981 is spicy and ready to drink but will not be long lived.

LARCIS-DUCASSE *ST.-EMILION* ★★
1981	③	**75**
1982	③	**80**
1983	③	**72**

A well-respected property, well situated on the Côtes of St.-Emilion. The wines have yet to make an impression, though a 1945 drunk several years ago was remarkable. The wines are light and simple.

LARMANDE *ST.-EMILION* ★★★★
1981	②	**83**
1982	③	**86**
1983	③	**87**

This is a relatively unknown yet up-and-coming estate in St.-Emilion that should be sought out for its high quality wines. The 1983 is rich, full bodied, deep and lush, the 1982 is very, very similar in style, and the 1981 is the lightest and most elegant of these three vintages, with a slightly more herbaceous bouquet. Also keep an eye out for the 1985, which showed enormous potential from the cask.

LAROSE-TRINTAUDON *HAUT-MÉDOC* ★★★
1982	②	**84**
1983	②	**84**

This huge vineyard in the Médoc produces over 65,000 cases of wine in a very silky, supple, intelligent style that shows well young but can also age for five to eight years. The wine is always clean and fruity with a certain spiciness to it. Both the 1982 and 1983 are very good values and attractive wines for drinking over the next four to five years.

LASCOMBES *MARGAUX* ★★★★
1981	③	**74**
1982	④	**87**
1983	④	**87**
1984	③	**83**

One of the largest estates in the Médoc, Lascombes has produced many great vintages in the 1950s and 1960s, but then in the 1970s fell from grace with a succession of mediocre wines. However, since 1982 the property has been back on track. The 1984 is a lovely, plummy, spicy, supple wine for drinking soon. The 1983 is quite an impressive wine, with deep intensity of flavours and a rich, spicy, berry-like aroma. The 1982 is similarly styled, perhaps slightly deeper and fatter on the palate. The 1981 is the last of a poor line of Lascombes wines that began with the 1976.

LATOUR *PAUILLAC* ★ ★ ★ ★ ★

1981	⑤	90
1982	⑤	98
1983	⑤	90
1984	⑤	88

Latour is one of France's and the world's greatest wines, known for its remarkable longevity and majestic richness. The 1984 is a successful wine that will develop fast. The 1983 is much more evolved and ready to drink than one usually expects of a Latour, but it is excellent. The 1982, the best Latour since the 1961, is incredibly deep and rich, and is very, very tannic. The 1981, an elegant, complex, silky Latour, will also mature quite quickly.

LATOUR À POMEROL *POMEROL* ★ ★ ★ ★ ★

1981	⑤	87
1982	⑤	93
1983	⑤	90

Another of the outstanding Pomerols that is hard to find and expensive as well. The 1983 is a muscular, brawny, big, ripe wine with plenty of tannin to carry it into the next century. The 1982 is even more powerful, decadently rich and multidimensional with explosive fruit, and the 1981 is supple, rich, elegant, and drinking beautifully now.

LAVILLE-HAUT-BRION *(WHITE) GRAVES* ★ ★ ★ ★ ★

1983	⑤	92
1984	⑤	86
1985	⑤	90

Arguably the greatest dry white wine produced in Bordeaux, Laville-Haut-Brion can easily age and improve for fifteen to twenty years in the bottle. The last three vintages have been superb; a great, rich, deep 1985, a fragrant, early-to-mature 1984, and a splendidly rich, long, honeyed, dense 1983.

LÉOVILLE-BARTON *ST.-JULIEN* ★ ★ ★ ★ ★

1981	....	④ **78**
1982	....	④ **93**
1983	....	④ **86**
1984	....	③ **84**

The late Ronald Barton was one of Bordeaux's great personalities and since he passed away the winemaking and management of the very traditionally made Léoville-Barton is run by his nephew, Anthony Barton. This is a wine that has as much of the character of a Pauillac as it does a St.-Julien. The 1984 is good, with a cedary, spicy, blackcurrant bouquet. The 1983 seems hard and in need of at least five to six years of cellaring to develop. The 1982 is a great wine and one of the best that Léoville Barton has made in the last three decades. It is a big wine and will take ten years to develop further. The 1981 is good, but not special in this vintage. The unreleased 1985 should propel this estate into the same league as such stars of St.-Julien as Ducru-Beaucaillou, Léoville-Las Cases, and Gruaud-Larose.

LÉOVILLE-LAS CASES *ST.-JULIEN* ★ ★ ★ ★ ★

1981	....	④ **88**
1982	....	⑤ **99**
1983	....	⑤ **90**
1984	....	④ **86**

One of the great wines of Bordeaux, the wines of Léoville-Las Cases are in demand the world over. They are very slow to develop and in the great vintages behave like the best first-growths – possessing majestic depth of flavour and remarkable tannins for longevity. The 1984 is quite a successful wine for the vintage and can be drunk over the next five to six years for its round fruitiness. The 1983 is also a top success in an irregular vintage. It is quite tannic and backward, shows a very classic cedary bouquet and has very ripe flavours. In 1982 this property made a monumental wine that its owner, Michel Delon, feels is the greatest wine he could ever possibly make. It is extraordinary in its flavours and richness, but will not be ready to drink before the turn of the century. The 1981 is a very elegant rendition of Las Cases. It has a spicy, oaky, berryish bouquet and long, ripe flavours.

LÉOVILLE-POYFERRÉ *ST.-JULIEN* ★ ★ ★ ★

1981	....	④ **81**
1982	....	⑤ **92**
1983	....	④ **87**
1984	....	④ **75**

Léoville-Poyferré has long been considered to have one of the greatest vineyards in all of the Médoc. The problem has been one of unrealized potential. However, things in the 1980s have improved considerably, with the 1982 being a really great wine and the best that this property has made in over three decades. The 1983, which was so promising from the cask, seems extremely hard and tannic and needs at least seven to ten years to prove its quality. The 1984 has turned out to be rather shallow, but adequate. The 1981 is soft, jammy, and lacking in complexity.

LESTAGE *LISTRAC* ★ ★
1982 .... ① *82*
1983 .... ① *80*
Both vintages produced very fruity, supple, straightforward wines that are meant to be drunk within their first four to five years of life.

LIVERSAN *MÉDOC* ★ ★ ★
1982 .... ② *84*
1983 .... ② *82*
Liversan is one of the up-and-coming Crus Bourgeois of the Médoc and its owners are giving it a great deal of attention, both financially and personally. The 1983 is rather soft, yet elegant, fruity, and easy to drink. The 1982 is a bit richer and more multidimensional.

LOUDENNE *(RED) MÉDOC* ★ ★
1982 .... ② *83*
1983 .... ② *80*
The showpiece château of the northern Médoc produces very light, picnic-style claret for drinking young. The 1982 is the best of recent vintages since it shows a bit more richness and flesh than one normally finds in this wine.

LA LOUVIÈRE *(RED) GRAVES* ★ ★ ★
1982 .... ③ *86*
1983 .... ② *87*
1984 .... ② *79*
La Louvière is making great progress in the southern part of the Graves area, producing very supple, rather rich, gloriously fruity and fleshy wines of considerable character. The 1984 is satisfactory; however, the 1983 and 1982 are both rich with wonderful ripeness, balance, concentration and ageing potential of five to ten years.

LA LOUVIÈRE *(WHITE) GRAVES* ★★★★

1983 .... ③ **87**
1984 .... ③ **84**
1985 .... ③ **86**

La Louvière shows equal ability to its red with its fleshy, ripe, fruity white wines that are made in a style perfect for drinking young. The 1985 and 1983 are both top successes.

LYNCH-BAGES *PAUILLAC* ★★★★★

1981 .... ④ **85**
1982 .... ⑤ **93**
1983 .... ⑤ **90**
1984 .... ④ **87**

Lynch-Bages is one of the Médoc's most popular wines. Impressively coloured, substantial, full-bodied, and savoury, it is always a satisfying wine. The last several vintages have been extremely strong for Lynch-Bages, including a very fragrant, supple, rich 1984, a ripe, big, full-blown, substantial 1983, a super-concentrated, extroverted, intense 1982, and a great (not yet released) 1985. The 1981 is the lightest of this quartet of wines, but is rich in blackcurrant fruit and ready to drink.

MAGDELAINE *ST.-EMILION* ★★★★

1981 .... ④ **80**
1982 .... ⑤ **90**
1983 .... ④ **85**

Although Magdelaine does not produce a lot of wine, there is a great deal of demand for it among knowledgeable connoisseurs. It tends to be a very-slow-to-evolve wine despite the fact that it is made from over 80% Merlot. It is also rather expensive. The 1983 has been an incredibly inconsistent though certainly very good wine. It is quite tannic and closed. The 1982 is powerful, rich, deep, and opulent and the 1981 lean, overly oaky, and lacking in fruit.

MAISON BLANCHE *MONTAGNE-ST.-EMILION* ★★★

1981 .... ② **82**
1982 .... ② **85**

A top estate in Montagne-St.-Emilion, this property made a delicious 1982 with excellent power and ripeness.

MALARTIC-LAGRAVIÈRE *(RED) GRAVES* ★★

1982 .... ③ **84**
1983 .... ③ **80**

This property tends to make better white wine than red, but the red has a likeable ripe cherry fruitiness, moderately intense flavours, and rather light to medium body. The 1982 is the best recent vintage.

MALARTIC-LAGRAVIÈRE *(WHITE) GRAVES* ★★★★

1983	....	④ **85**
1984	....	④ *84*
1985	....	④ *84*

This property produces very fresh, lively, crisp, rather lighter-styled white wines with a distinctively pungent, herbaceous bouquet. The 1983 looks to be the best in the last three vintages.

MALESCOT ST.-EXUPÉRY *MARGAUX* ★★★

1981	....	③ **78**
1982	....	④ **85**
1983	....	④ **83**
1984	....	③ **80**

Malescot St.-Exupéry has always had an excellent reputation for making very long-lived, traditional, firm, hard wines. However, they have never fared particularly well in my tastings. The 1984 and 1981 are rather light and lack charm and flesh. The 1983, though good, is not one of the leaders in a vintage that was extremely successful in the Margaux region. The 1982 is round, lusciously fruity, but not as deep as other top wines from this vintage.

MARGAUX *MARGAUX* ★★★★★

1981	....	⑤ **92**
1982	....	⑤ **98**
1983	....	⑤ **98**
1984	....	⑤ **90**

After a period of mediocrity in the sixties and seventies, the wines of Château Margaux, since 1978, have been as grand as any in Bordeaux. One wonders how such greatness at this high level can continue to be maintained. The 1984 is one of the top two wines of the vintage, rich, intense, and surprisingly dark-coloured given the year. The 1983 is the wine of the vintage, with a remarkable aroma of violets and ripe cassis fruit and vanillin oakiness; it will develop for at least another fifteen to twenty years. The 1982, another celestial wine, is creamier and fuller-bodied than normal for Margaux, and extremely rich and intense. The 1981 is lighter, but only in comparison to recent vintages from Margaux. It is a fabulous wine with an exceptional bouquet and great class and finesse.

MARQUIS D'ALESME-BECKER *MARGAUX* ★★
1982 .... ③ *84*
1983 .... ② *85*
     This wine is not well known and although it is well coloured it often tastes rather simple and one-dimensional. The 1983 is the most recent top success, with a rich and solid texture and very good length. The 1982 is solid and reliable, but not complex.

MARQUIS-DE-TERME *MARGAUX* ★★★
1982 .... ③ *83*
1983 .... ② *80*
     This is another wine that is little known in England but is widely available in the Benelux countries. The 1983 is chunky and fruity, but lacks finesse. The 1982 shows a bit more depth and a fragrant, precocious, soft texture.

MAUCAILLOU *MOULIS* ★★★
1981 .... ② *83*
1982 .... ② *86*
1983 .... ② *83*
     Maucaillou in Moulis is a wine made in an early-maturing style, but it offers a savoury, supple character and relatively complex, fragrant bouquet. The 1981 and 1983 are good wines, but the 1982 is very rich, quite deeply flavoured, and undoubtedly a great buy in a vintage that has become very expensive because of worldwide demand.

MAZERIS *CANON-FRONSAC* ★★★
1982 .... ① *83*
1983 .... ① *80*
     This is a forceful, aggressive, dense, chunky, tannic wine that can excel. The unreleased 1985 is excellent.

MEYNEY *ST.-ESTÈPHE* ★★★
1981 .... ③ *85*
1982 .... ③ *87*
1983 .... ② *85*
1984 .... ② *82*
     Meyney is an extremely large property and one of the most reliable wines in Bordeaux. Shrewd consumers have been beating a path to Meyney for years, knowing of the fine value of the wines and their potential for fifteen to twenty years of longevity. The 1984 is a surprisingly elegant, deeply coloured wine for the vintage. The 1983 is extremely successful, with rich, ripe, deep flavours. The 1982 is jammy, very intense,

very full-bodied, and will take at least ten years to mature. The 1981 is delicate, elegant, and attractive for early drinking.

LA MISSION-HAUT-BRION *GRAVES* ★ ★ ★ ★ ★

1981	⑤	**90**
1982	⑤	**96**
1983	⑤	**89**
1984	⑤	**86**

One of the greatest wines of Bordeaux, La Mission-Haut-Brion is first-growth in quality, if not in name. It is always a rather big, rich, powerful wine that has had remarkable consistency in even the worst Bordeaux vintages over the last four decades. The 1984 is quite attractive and rich, with a big, tobacco-scented bouquet. The 1983 is full-bodied, rather tannic, and more austere than usual, the 1982 a monumental bottle of rich, intense, fruity flavours, and with a very long evolution ahead of it. The 1981 is rather elegant, but quite well balanced, fairly rich and powerful for a 1981, and impressively long on the palate.

MONBOUSQUET *ST.-EMILION* ★ ★

1982	②	**78**
1983	②	**80**

This is a rather large estate owned by the amiable Querre family that makes very commercial, yet fruity, supple, delicious wines. Both the 1982 and 1983 were rather mediocre and not up to some of the previous vintages.

MONTROSE *ST.-ESTÈPHE* ★ ★ ★ ★

1981	③	**84**
1982	④	**87**
1983	④	**83**
1984	③	**83**

Montrose is one of the best-kept and best-situated vineyards in all of the Médoc. However, the style since 1978 has changed from a huge, massive, tannic wine to a rather elegant, lighter style that is still quite attractive but a disappointment to the old Montrose fans. The 1984 is again a success for the vintage and is ready to drink. The 1983 is rather medium-bodied and light for Montrose, but attractive and elegant. The 1982, probably the best Montrose since 1970, is a rich, full-bodied wine with an unctuous texture. The 1981 is ready to drink, light, fruity, and very pleasant.

MOULIN DES CARRUADES *PAUILLAC* ★ ★

1981	④	**82**

1982 .... ④ **83**

The second wine of Lafite-Rothschild is not nearly so attractive as its name might suggest. The wine tends to be rather light and not so impressive as the second wines of some other notable first-growths, Latour's Fort de Latour or Château Margaux's Pavillon Rouge de Margaux, to name two.

MOULINET *POMEROL* ★

1982 .... ③ **75**
1983 .... ③ **72**

Moulinet produces a very light, rather unsubstantial Pomerol that is faintly perfumed and very commercial in style. At its best it is round, fruity, and elegant, but it is generally rather bland.

MOUTON-BARONNE-PHILIPPE *PAUILLAC* ★★★

1982 .... ③ **86**
1983 .... ③ **85**
1984 .... ③ **75**

Mouton-Baronne-Philippe's 1984 is rather light and lacking in concentration. The 1983 is more amply proportioned and noticeably richer and fruitier on the palate. The 1982 is the best effort recently with a rich, cedary, blackcurrant bouquet, and long, rich, full-bodied flavours.

MOUTON-ROTHSCHILD *PAUILLAC* ★★★★★

1981 .... ⑤ **88**
1982 .... ⑤ *100*
1983 .... ⑤ **90**
1984 .... ⑤ **89**

Mouton-Rothschild is the brilliant wine that has been produced for over six decades by the Baron Philippe de Rothschild. Like its owner, it is a flamboyant, extroverted wine that, in great vintages, has no equal. The 1984 is an outstanding success for the vintage. Ripe, exotic, and rich, it is delicious already. The 1983 is also an exotic wine that should mature rather rapidly and is very fine. The 1982 is perhaps the single greatest young wine this writer has ever tasted, and certainly a wine of legendary proportions. Don't touch it until 1995 or later. The 1981 is rather light for Mouton, but elegant, stylish, and ready to drink now.

NAIRAC *BARSAC* ★★★

1981 .... ③ **83**
1982 .... ③ **84**
1983 .... ④ **87**

This is a meticulously and passionately operated Barsac estate making better and better wines as time goes on. The 1983 is powerful and rich, the 1982 has a spicy, pineapple and vanillin bouquet and flavours, and the 1981 is plump, fat but perhaps a little dull.

NENIN *POMEROL* ★★

1982	④	**70**
1983	④	**72**
1984	④	**75**

Nenin has always produced a rustic-style Pomerol, but the early vintages of the 1980s have looked increasingly poor, except for the unreleased 1985, which exhibits the kind of richness and style one expects from this property.

OLIVIER *(RED) GRAVES* ★

1982	③	**78**
1983	②	**72**

The wines here are no better than a shipper's blend – light, innocuous, and lacking richness and character.

LES-ORMES-DE-PEZ *ST.-ESTÈPHE* ★★★

1981	②	**82**
1982	③	**87**
1983	②	**84**
1984	②	**84**

Le-Ormes-de-Pez is one of Bordeaux's most popular wines because it is made by the owner of Lynch-Bages. It is a supple, very fruity, fragrant, delicious wine to drink young, yet it has the uncanny ability to age well. The 1984 is a top success in this vintage. The 1983 is fat, ripe, round, and very fruity; the 1982 is deep, seductive, very soft in the finish, but will last well; the 1981 is the least successful of the last four vintages. Always good value.

LES ORMES-SORBET *(MÉDOC)* ★★

1982	②	**82**

This is always a rather one-dimensional but solid, well-coloured wine lacking finesse but possessing good richness and a chunky, satisfying feel on the palate.

PALMER *MARGAUX* ★★★★★

1981	⑤	**82**
1982	⑤	**86**
1983	⑤	**94**
1984	⑤	**82**

Until the resurgence of Château Margaux, Palmer was usually the finest wine made in the Margaux appellation. Although it now takes a back seat to the greatness of Margaux, Palmer can be an exceptional wine. The vintages in the 1980s have not been among the great Palmer successes except for the fabulous 1983. The 1984 is light, straightforward, supple, and fruity. The 1983 is a powerful, deep, concentrated, chewy wine with a fabulous bouquet. The 1982, from a legendary vintage, is not as good as it should be, but it does offer precocious, fat, oaky flavours and early maturity. The 1981 is also good, but given Palmer's level of quality, somewhat of a disappointment.

PAPE-CLÉMENT *GRAVES* ★★★

1981	③	68
1982	④	68
1983	④	75
1984	④	80

One of the best-placed vineyards in all of Graves, Pape-Clément made fabulous wines in the 1950s and 1960s and then fell on hard times due to neglect in the 1970s, particularly after the 1975 vintage. The above vintages are all rather poor and not representative of what this property can produce. Look for the unreleased yet excellent 1985, which will resurrect the reputation of Pape-Clément and begin to put this property back in the forefront of the Graves properties.

PATACHE D'AUX *MÉDOC* ★★★

1981	②	73
1982	②	84
1983	②	84

Patache d'Aux makes a solid, firm wine which in 1982 and 1983 resembles a California Cabernet with its olive-scented, rich, blackcurrant bouquet. The 1981 is rather meagrely endowed, but both the 1982 and 1983 are rich, medium-to-full-bodied wines with lots of character.

PAVIE *ST.-EMILION* ★★★

1981	④	83
1982	⑤	89
1983	④	86
1984	④	80

Pavie produces elegant, fruity, attractive wines with a great deal of style. While the 1984 is ready to drink and rather light, 1983 is backward and tannic, and the 1982 uncommonly rich and full for Pavie. The most recent typical vintage for Pavie may be the 1981, which is classy and complex, and has a bouquet of ripe cherries.

PAVIE-DECESSE *ST.-EMILION* ★ ★ ★

1982	③	86
1983	②	86
1984	②	77

This tiny vineyard behind and further up the hill from Pavie is making better and better wines with each vintage. The 1984, from a terrible vintage, is light and slightly herbaceous. The 1983 is tannic, rich, tough, and brawny, the 1982 lush and full-bodied, with an excellent extract of fruit.

PAVILLON ROUGE DE MARGAUX *MARGAUX* ★ ★ ★ ★

1978	④	85
1979	④	86
1981	④	87
1982	④	87

The second wine of Margaux, Pavillon Rouge is a supple, fragrant, ripe, very seductive wine that is released only by the château when they deem it ready to drink. The first three vintages released have all shown well, with much of the character of the Gran Vin. Expect these wines to drink well for five to six years.

PETIT-VILLAGE *POMEROL* ★ ★ ★

1981	③	84
1982	④	89
1983	③	85

The highly respected Bruno Prats owns this château and has improved the quality dramatically in the 1980s. The 1981 is fully mature, elegant, and very supple and fruity. The 1982 has an explosive bouquet of blackberry fruit and spicy oak. It should be fully mature by 1989–1990. The 1983 is chunky, not complex, but very satisfying, round, and ready to drink.

PÉTRUS *POMEROL* ★ ★ ★ ★ ★

1981	⑤	95
1982	⑤	*100*
1983	⑤	89
1984	⑤	84

Pétrus, in the short 35 years since it was first introduced to the United States, has become the most expensive and sought after red wine, not only in France but in the world. Its character is one of great, concentrated intensity of flavour that comes from being made primarily from Merlot. It ages incredibly well despite its accessibility as a young wine. The 1984, a disastrous vintage for Pomerol, is good, though rather light, and does show some of the Pétrus character. The 1983 is a bit clumsy, but a big, full-bodied, chewy, powerful wine that has yet to show much finesse. The 1982 is considered by the owners to be the greatest Pétrus ever made, a powerful, rich, yet so perfectly balanced wine it should last for 30–40 years.The 1981 is not far behind and is incredibly rich, full-bodied, and still quite backward.

PEYRABON *HAUT-MÉDOC* ★★
1982 .... ② 78
This is a one-dimensional, soft, supple, fruity wine with little character.

PEZ *ST.-ESTÈPHE* ★★★★
1981 .... ② 81
1982 .... ③ 86
1983 .... ③ 85
1984 .... ② 82
Pez is one of the most carefully and well-run Cru Bourgeois properties and always represents one of the better wines and better wine values for long-term cellaring. The 1984 is ready to drink, clean, and fruity. The 1983 is ripe, has a good amount of tannin, and needs plenty of cellaring. The 1982 is rounder and richer than the 1983 and will be drinkable at an earlier age. The 1981 is not a great success for Pez, but is a pleasant, elegant, somewhat austere wine.

PHÉLAN-SÉGUR *ST.-ESTÈPHE* ★★★
1981 .... ② 74
1982 .... ③ 84
1983 .... ② 82
1984 .... ② 75
Phélan-Ségur is one of the lesser-known wines of St.- Estèphe, but it can be very good, although its problem has been its inconsistency. The 1984 is rather light, but pleasant; the 1983, which tasted poorly from cask samples, has turned out to be a pleasant, fruity, elegant wine with decent body. The 1982, which showed poorly early on, has turned out to be a very fruity, very soft, grapy, but quite enjoyable wine for drinking over the next few years. The 1981 is herbaceous and beginning to brown in colour, which is a bad sign.

PICHON *HAUT-MÉDOC* ★★★
1982 .... ② 85
1983 .... ② 85

Pichon is an up-and-coming star from the southernmost portion of the Médoc. The vineyard is still extremely young, but the first several vintages of the 1980s have been surprisingly good. Each vintage is stronger as the vines get older. Both the 1982 and 1983 are deeply coloured, rich in fruit, very supple, and delicious to drink now and over the next several years.

PICHON LONGUEVILLE BARON DE PICHON LONGUEVILLE *PAUILLAC* ★★★

1981	④	**83**
1982	④	**86**
1983	④	**84**

Pichon Baron is the noble-looking château sitting across from the more famous Pichon Lalande. It can make great wines, as it did in the forties, fifties, and early sixties, but it has been casually run since and many of the wines have turned out to be extremely disappointing. The three vintages in the 1980s are all successes, but one wishes, and one suspects, that they could have been a lot better. The 1983 Pichon Baron looked to be one of the best Pichon Barons since 1961, but as it has turned out, the wine lacks a little bit of richness on the palate and should have been more concentrated than it is. Nevertheless, it is a good wine. The 1982 is fat, very low in acidity, and should be drunk over the next four to five years. The 1981 is rather oaky, fairly light for a Pauillac in that vintage, and is fully mature now.

PICHON LONGUEVILLE, COMTESSE DE LALANDE *PAUILLAC* ★★★★★

1981	⑤	**91**
1982	⑤	**96**
1983	⑤	**95**
1984	⑤	**90**

At present, Pichon Lalande is unquestionably the most popular and consistently successful wine in the Médoc. The vintages since the late 1970s have been brilliant expressions of winemaking at its best. The 1984 is a revelation given the mediocre vintage overall. Rich, intense, exotic, and so, so delicious, it is a candidate for the wine of the vintage. The 1983 is also one of the greatest wines of the vintage, even better than the first growths that year. The 1982 is superb, creamy, intense, with layers of ripe, rich, cedary fruit. The 1981 is a more elegant example and slightly lighter, but again, a lovely, medium- to full-bodied wine that is drinking beautifully now.

LE PIN *POMEROL* ★★★★

1982 .... ⑤ **91**
1983 .... ⑤ **87**
1984 .... ⑤ **81**

This is a brand new vineyard owned by the famous Thienpont family of Pomerol, and the wine is given the attention of a spoiled child, à la Pétrus. It is a rich, unctuous wine dominated by Merlot. The 1984 is supple and ready to drink, the 1983 rich, oaky, lush, and fruity, and the 1982 extraordinarily voluptuous, filled with the smell of ripe blackcurrants and spicy oak. The unreleased 1985 is sensational.

PITRAY *CÔTES DE CASTILLON* ★★★

1982 .... ① **84**
1983 .... ① **82**

Pitray is the classic Côtes de Castillon wine, very supple, fruity, and early maturing. The unreleased 1985 and the 1982 can rival some classified growths.

PLAGNAC *MÉDOC* ★★★

1982 .... ① **84**
1983 .... ① **83**

This Cru Bourgeois of the large broker Cordier seems to get little attention, but like all the Cordier wines is quite well made and very reasonably priced. The 1983 is supple, quite fruity, elegant, and ready to drink. The 1982 is similarly styled, with a touch more richness.

PLINCE *POMEROL* ★★

1982 .... ③ **84**
1983 .... ③ **82**

Plince produces a rather peppery, chunky, fruity wine with good body but not much complexity. The 1983 is good but a trifle dull and the 1982 rather rich and unctuous.

LA POINTE *POMEROL* ★★

1982 .... ③ **75**
1983 .... ③ **80**

La Pointe tends to make mediocre Pomerols, but this may be changing because the gifted oenologist Michel Roland has been making the wines since 1983; the unreleased 1985 is the best La Pointe I have seen in some time.

PONTET-CANET *PAUILLAC* ★★★

1982 .... ④ **85**
1983 .... ③ **86**
1984 .... ③ **82**

Pontet-Canet has one of the largest productions of any Médoc classified growth. The property is quite capable of making top-quality wine, but in the period between 1961 and 1981 slipped considerably. Recently there has been much improvement. The 1984 is undoubtedly a success and should be drunk over the next three to four years for its medium-bodied, savoury fruitiness. The 1983 is quite tannic and needs four to five years to soften. The 1982 is the deepest in colour and is a big, corpulent wine that is just a little over weight.

POTENSAC *MÉDOC* ★★★

1981	②	82
1982	②	87
1983	②	84

Potensac is one of the very finest wines produced in the Médoc. Recent vintages, particularly the 1982 and 1983, have been excellent. The property is managed by Michel Delon, who has remarkable winemaking talents; the wine made here is dark in colour, rich, medium- to full-bodied, and capable of ageing for up to ten years. It remains stunning value. The 1982 is superb, 1981 elegant and ready to drink, the 1983 also very good, deep, and capable of living ten years in the bottle.

POUGET *MARGAUX* ★★★

1982	④	83
1983	③	82

Pouget's wines tend to be sturdy and robust, rather well coloured, but lacking in charm or finesse. Both the 1983 and 1982 are compact, sturdy wines that have decent colour but taste severe and hard; it is quite difficult to know what direction they will take.

POUJEAUX *MOULIS* ★★★

1981	②	82
1982	②	87
1983	②	86

Poujeaux, another excellent wine value from Bordeaux, is known for producing full-bodied, deeply coloured wine that lasts and lasts. Both the 1983 and 1982 are quite excellent, with the 1983 more austere and the 1982 very rich and full-bodied. The 1981 is the most elegant and lightest of this trio, and can be drunk now.

PRIEURÉ-LICHINE *MARGAUX* ★★★★

1981	③	78
1982	④	87

1983 .... ④ **87**
1984 .... ③ **75**

The home of one of the world's most famous wine writers, Alexis Lichine, Prieuré makes light but complex, elegant wines which are supple and fast maturing but have enough tannin to last eight to twelve years. The 1984 and 1981 are perhaps too light for further ageing, but the 1983 is a top success that should age well for at least ten to twelve years. The 1982 should do the same with its rich, blackcurrant aroma and sumptuous, fragrant bouquet and long flavours.

RABAUD-PROMIS *SAUTERNES* ★★
1981 .... ③ **80**
1983 .... ③ **85**

This estate, which has been run down for years, is beginning to experience a renaissance in quality and recent vintages have shown quite decently, particularly the 1983 which is light, rich, and has a good deal of flavour and intensity.

RAHOUL *GRAVES* ★★★
1981 .... ③ **81**
1982 .... ③ **84**
1983 .... ③ **80**

Rahoul is an up-and-coming property in the Graves area making rather oaky red wines with character. The 1982 is the best recent vintage.

RAMAGE LA BATISSE *HAUT-MÉDOC* ★★
1982 .... ③ **75**
1983 .... ③ **74**

After producing a bevy of good wines during the period of 1978-1980, this property has fallen on hard times. Recent vintages have lacked charm and fruit, and have tasted severe and tannic. Both the 1982 and 1983 are disappointments given the vintages.

RAUSAN-SÉGLA *MARGAUX* ★★★
1981 .... ③ **74**
1982 .... ④ **87**
1983 .... ④ **87**
1984 .... ③ **75**

Rausan-Ségla has always been considered to have one of Bordeaux's great vineyards, but over the recent decades the wine has rarely lived up to its outstanding reputation. However, while the 1984 is a bit vegetal, soft, and undistinguished, the 1983 is rich, spicy, intense, and very long on the palate.

The 1982 is similarly styled, perhaps slightly softer, but rich and very fragrant and showing a great deal of complexity. The 1981 is light, one-dimensional though interesting.

RAUZAN-GASSIES *MARGAUX* ★★★

1981	③	74
1982	④	85
1983	④	84

Rauzan-Gassies tends to produce rather hard wines that lack a great deal of the famous Margaux fragrance and finesse. The 1983 is tannic and chunky, and lacks charm. The 1982 is fat, plummy, and very precocious, with quite low acidity. The 1981 lacks depth and richness, and is rather disappointing.

RAYMOND-LAFON *SAUTERNES* ★★★★★

1980	④	90
1982	⑤	86
1983	⑤	93

The up-and-coming superstar of the Sauternes region, this wine is made by the winemaker at Yquem; it is a decadently rich, full-bodied wine with layers of viscous, sweet fruit. The 1983 is astonishing, the 1982 a total success from a difficult vintage, and the 1980 a truly great wine that is just now coming into its plateau of maturity.

RAYNE-VIGNEAU *SAUTERNES* ★★

1982	③	75
1983	③	82

These are straightforward, fruity, wines that lack much character.

RIEUSSEC *SAUTERNES* ★★★★★

1981	④	86
1982	④	82
1983	④	94

Rieussec produces powerful wines with the smell of crème brulée and deep, rich flavours that are neither heavy nor cloying. The 1983 is an extraordinary vintage for Rieussec. The 1982 is a good wine in a difficult vintage and 1981 one of the best wines of a so-so vintage for the region.

RIPEAU *ST.-EMILION* ★★

1982	③	82
1983	③	78

This property has always had good potential, but has been an inconsistent performer. The 1983 is a little light and herbaceous, the 1982 medium-weight but richer and of more interest.

LA RIVIÈRE *FRONSAC* ★★
1982 .... ② **84**
1983 .... ② **80**
La Rivière is one of the most splendid châteaux, with some of the most remarkable underground cellars in all of Bordeaux. The wines tend to be a bit inconsistent, but at their best, as in 1982, rich, fruity, soft, and delicious to drink within the first seven to eight years of life.

ROMER DU HAYOT *SAUTERNES* ★★
1982 .... ② **80**
1983 .... ② **84**
Romer du Hayot makes fruity, fresh, medium-bodied wines of no great character but with a satisfying flavour.

ROUDIER *MONTAGNE-ST.-EMILION* ★★★
1982 .... ② **85**
1983 .... ② **84**
The top estate in Montagne-St.-Emilion, Roudier makes very fleshy, rich, ripe wines with a lot of character and intensity. The 1982 is drinking deliciously now and the 1983 is also very good.

ROUET *CANON-FRONSAC* ★★★
1982 .... ① **82**
1983 .... ① **83**
Rouet makes very fragrant, supple, fruity wines in Canon-Fronsac that represent very good values.

ROUGET *POMEROL* ★★★
1982 .... ④ **88**
1983 .... ④ **83**
Rouget is potentially one of the best wines of Pomerol but it is made in a very traditional manner, is often very tannic when released, and so needs a minimum of eight to ten years, which is relatively typical in order for a Pomerol to show its best. The 1983 is a rather big, full-bodied, moderately tannic wine, and the 1982 quite concentrated, very tannic, with layers of fleshy fruit, but very backward.

ST.-BONNET *MÉDOC* ★★
1982 .... ① **84**
1983 .... ① **78**

This can be an excellent, very modestly priced wine to look for in the very good Bordeaux vintages. The 1982 is an example of a full-flavoured, very well made, rich Cru Bourgeois that should last at least seven to eight years.

ST.-PIERRE-SEVAISTRE *ST.-JULIEN* ★★★★

1981	....	④	**89**
1982	....	④	**87**
1983	....	④	**88**
1984	....	③	**84**

A terribly underrated property in St.-Julien, St.-Pierre tends to produce a big, hefty, beefy style of wine with great colour and wonderful richness, if somewhat lacking in finesse and charm. The 1984 is quite a success for the vintage, as is the 1983, which is very seductive in its lushness and full-bodied appeal. The 1982 is similarly styled, even softer. The 1981, one of the true great successes of the vintage, is impressively coloured, with a great depth of fruit and richness that is rather surprising for a 1981.

SALES *POMEROL* ★★★

1982	....	③	**87**
1983	....	③	**85**
1984	....	③	**78**

Sales makes a very commercial, very easy to enjoy and easy to understand wine of suppleness and early maturity. It satisfies virtually everyone who tastes it. The 1984 is light but pleasant, the 1983 a touch overripe but soft, low in acidity, and delicious now. The 1982 is an exceptionally elegant, richly fruity, round, and generous wine. It is a good value for a Pomerol.

SIGALAS RABAUD *SAUTERNES* ★★★

1982	....	③	**75**
1983	....	④	**86**

This is a lighter-style Sauternes that must be drunk young, generally before seven to eight years of age. The 1983 is the best recent vintage, with a wonderfully fruity bouquet suggestive of pineapples.

SIRAN *MARGAUX* ★★★

1981	....	③	**84**
1982	....	④	**85**
1983	....	④	**86**

This is an up-and-coming property in Margaux that has been making consistently delicious, fragrant, and deeply coloured wines in the 1980s. The 1983 looks to be the best; it is the most powerful and densely coloured. The lush, supple 1982 makes for lovely drinking now, and the stylish, lighter 1981 is quite pleasant. A property to watch.

SMITH-HAUT-LAFITTE *(RED) GRAVES* ★★

1982	③	*82*
1983	③	*82*

Another property in Graves better known for its white wines than its reds, Smith-Haut-Lafitte tends to produce very light, very easy to drink, pleasant wines of no particular character. Both the 1982 and 1983 represent this style.

SMITH-HAUT-LAFITTE *(WHITE) GRAVES* ★★★

1983	③	*85*
1985	③	*85*

A better producer of white wine than red, both the 1985 and 1983 are crisp, lively, fresh, medium-bodied wines of character.

SOCIANDO-MALLET *HAUT MÉDOC* ★★★★

1981	②	*81*
1982	③	*90*
1983	③	*87*
1984	③	*82*

Sociando-Mallet has in the last four or five years become one of the most sought after wines of France's wine connoisseurs. Its reputation for excellence and longevity has surged to the forefront because of the fanatical and meticulous winemaking style of its owner, Jean Gautreau. This is an inky black/ruby wine with great concentration and plenty of tannin. The 1981 can be approached now but ideally needs several more years. The 1982 is a fabulous wine that won't be ready to drink until the early 1990s. The 1983 is almost as good as the 1982, and the 1984 is light but well made and will be drinkable relatively soon.

SOUDARS *HAUT-MÉDOC* ★★★

1982	②	*82*
1983	②	*84*

This relatively new estate is making very good wine from a high percentage of Merlot. The 1983 is fat, ripe, round, and very playful. The 1982 is also lovely to drink in a supple, smooth, velvety style. This is a wine to search out because, as the vineyard gets older, one suspects the wine will get even better.

SOUTARD *ST.-EMILION* ★ ★ ★

1981	④	**84**
1982	④	**88**
1983	④	**86**

Soutard is another one of St.-Emilion's best-kept secrets. However, the wine is made in such a backward, rich, tannic style that one must usually wait eight to ten years for its tannic ferocity to subside. The 1983 is very dark, full-bodied, quite rich; the 1982 opulent and huge, but also tannic and broodingly backward. The 1981 is not as impressive, but has plenty of ripe, spicy, plummy fruit.

SUDUIRAUT *SAUTERNES* ★ ★ ★ ★

1981	④	**84**
1982	④	**90**
1983	④	**87**

An outstanding yet often inconsistent property that can make great wines in certain vintages. Curiously, the 1982 Suduiraut is the sweet wine of the vintage, fabulously honeyed, luscious, deep, with great concentration in a difficult vintage. The 1983 is very, very good, rather elegant, and the 1981 attractive, rich, with less power than normal but drinking well now.

TAILHAS *POMEROL* ★ ★

1981	③	**72**
1982	③	**84**
1983	③	**82**

Tailhas is a fairly well-respected vineyard that makes a full-bodied, robustly styled Pomerol with good richness and weight. The 1983 is loaded with good berry fruit, has medium body, and is very soft. The 1982 is a deeper and richer wine, the 1981 disappointingly thin and dirty to smell.

TAILLEFER *POMEROL* ★ ★

1982	②	**77**
1983	②	**75**

Taillefer produces one of Pomerol's lightest-styled wines. It never has a great deal of depth, but is soundly made, round, fruity, and capable of evolving for five to seven years before losing its fruit. The 1982 is the best of the recent vintages, but is hardly an inspiring wine.

TALBOT *ST.-JULIEN* ★ ★ ★ ★

1981	③	**85**
1982	④	**89**
1983	④	**89**

1984 .... ③ **84**

Talbot is owned by the famous Bordeaux family, Cordier, and tends to produce a rather robust yet fruity, full-bodied wine that offers excellent value. Recent vintages since 1978 have been particularly successful. The 1984 is ripe, medium-bodied, and quite fruity. The 1983 is a big, full-bodied, tannic, rich wine that will last a long time. The 1982 is massive, dense, earthy, with a very powerful, round, ripe, rich taste and long finish. The 1981 is more elegant and ready to drink.

TAYAC *MARGAUX* ★
1981 .... ② **75**
1982 .... ② **78**

Tayac produces easy-to-drink, decent wines that lack complexity, but are generally soundly made.

TAYAC PRESTIGE *CÔTES DE BOURGE* ★★★
1982 .... ② **87**
1983 .... ② **84**

The leading property of the Côtes de Bourg, Tayac produces a number of different wines, but their top label is their special cuvée called Prestige. The 1982 could be mistaken for a first-rate Pomerol, a rich, intense, very full-bodied wine with excellent character.

LA TERRASSE *CÔTES DE CASTILLON* ★★
1982 .... ① **82**
1983 .... ① **80**

A deliciously fruity, fragrant, easy-to-drink wine that should be drunk before its fifth birthday. Both the 1982 and 1983 are quite delicious now.

TERREY-GROS-CAILLOUX *ST.-JULIEN* ★★★
1982 .... ② **84**
1983 .... ② **83**

Both wines are jammy, meaty, fleshy mouthfuls of wine without a great deal of finesse, but they show good concentration and potential for evolution of five to seven years.

TERTRE *MARGAUX* ★★★
1982 .... ③ **87**
1983 .... ③ **87**
1984 .... ② **75**

Tertre has yet to become well-known, but great efforts are being made to elevate the quality of wine produced here. The vintages since 1978 have been quite successful. The 1984 is light, but cleanly made and ready to drink. The 1983 is a full-bodied, rather tannic, tough wine that needs time to round out. The 1982 promised well when young, but has now closed up and needs at least another five years of ageing. The 1981 is light and rather lean.

TERTRE-DAUGAY *ST.-EMILION* ★★★

| 1982 | ③ | *82* |
| 1983 | ③ | *84* |

One of St.-Emilion's oldest estates, this property completely lost credibility for its poor wines in older vintages, but the new owners are making a strong effort to bring it back to form. The 1982 and 1983 are both more impressive efforts.

LA TONNELLE *CÔTES DE BLAYE* ★★★

| 1982 | ① | *84* |
| 1983 | ① | *84* |

La Tonnelle is one of the leading estates of the Côtes de Blaye, making very delicious wine for drinking upon release. Both the 1982 and 1983 represent excellent bargains for drinking over the next three to four years.

LA TOUR BLANCHE *SAUTERNES* ★★

| 1982 | ② | *79* |
| 1983 | ② | *84* |

La Tour Blanche, run by the French Ministry of Agriculture, tends to make a very light, fruity wine that lacks character. The 1983 seems to be a step in the right direction, but this probably has more to do with the vintage, which was superb in this area.

LA TOUR DE BY *MÉDOC* ★★

| 1982 | ① | *84* |
| 1983 | ② | *81* |

La Tour de By is another of the very reliable, well-made, good values from the upper Médoc. The wine can last very well and both the 1983 and the 1982 (which is richer and fleshier than the 1983) are good candidates for lasting five to seven years.

LA TOUR CARNET *HAUT-MÉDOC* ★★

| 1982 | ③ | *80* |
| 1983 | ③ | *83* |

La Tour Carnet has been extensively replanted and the disappointing wines from the 1970s seem to be giving way in the 1980s to wines with a bit more character and richness. The

1983 wines are riper and richer than those of any recent vintage. The 1982 is also good. A property to watch.

LA TOUR-FIGEAC ST.-EMILION ★★★
1982 .... ② **85**
1983 .... ② *84*

La Tour-Figeac consistently produces fat, supple and fruity wines rarely worth keeping beyond five to six years, but they offer delicious fruit and an uncomplicated style. The 1982 is the best recent vintage; the 1983 also has plenty of appeal.

LA TOUR-HAUT-BRION GRAVES ★★★★
1981 .... ⑤ **85**
1982 .... ⑤ **95**
1983 .... ④ **85**
1984 .... ④ **82**

A separate vineyard in principle, La Tour-Haut-Brion has traditionally been the second wine of La Mission-Haut-Brion, with a bit more tannic press wine added in to give it its character; in some vintages, it has been identical, but for that addition. The 1984 is very soft, fruity, and straightforward; the 1983 good, but a lot more supple than past vintages. The 1982 is a blockbuster – rich, massive, very tannic, and every bit as good as La Mission-Haut-Brion, at half the price. The 1981 lacks some finesse and is rather robust and aggressive.

LA TOUR-MARTILLAC GRAVES ★
1982 .... ③ **83**
1983 .... ③ **82**

La Tour-Martillac makes relatively light, sometimes hard, tannic wines that consistently taste mediocre. The quality of the 1982 and 1983 is more encouraging than other efforts have been.

LA TOUR-DE-MONS MARGAUX ★★★
1981 .... ② **72**
1982 .... ② **82**

This property made wonderful wines in the sixties and seventies but has been inconsistent since the late 1970s. The 1981 is light, herbaceous, and rather high in acidity, and the 1982 supple, fruity, but not terribly complicated.

LA TOUR-DU-PIN-FIGEAC ST.-EMILION ★★★
1982 .... ③ **85**
1983 .... ② *81*

One of the many châteaux in St.-Emilion with the name

Figeac, this moderately sized vineyard produces rather straightforward, fleshy, fruity wines with good body. The 1982 is the best recent effort, with an attractive ripe berryish, spicy bouquet and silky, rather lengthy flavours.

LA TOUR ST.-BONNET *MÉDOC* ★★★

1982	②	85
1983	②	84

La Tour St.-Bonnet makes a rather full-bodied, fleshy, deeply coloured wine that is supple enough to drink young, but can keep six to eight years. Both the 1982 and 1983 are rather serious wines with a lot of character and intensity.

TRONQUOY-LALANDE *ST.-ESTÈPHE* ★★★

1981	②	81
1982	②	83
1983	②	80

Tronquoy-Lalande is one of the more attractive châteaux in St.-Estèphe. The wine is a rather clumsy one, very earthy, very rich in colour, often lacking finesse but compensating for that with plenty of power. The 1983 is extremely tannic and perhaps too austere and hard for its own good. The 1982 is corpulent, very high in concentration as well as tannin, and very exaggerated in style. The 1981 is immense as well, but very tough and hard.

TROPLONG-MONDOT *ST.-EMILION* ★★★

1982	③	84
1983	③	84

The wines of Troplong-Mondot have generally been very light in style, but the last few vintages have shown a bit more concentration and stuffing. The 1983 is elegant, fruity, and medium-bodied, the 1982 soft, supple, with a lovely berry fruitiness.

TROTANOY *POMEROL* ★★★★★

1981	⑤	87
1982	⑤	96
1983	⑤	86
1984	⑤	83

If there is one wine that often resembles Pétrus in tastings, it is Trotanoy. The 1984 is light, but charming and tasty; the 1983 a little disappointing for Trotanoy, but a very good wine. The 1982 is a powerful, exotic, chocolaty, rich, massive wine, and the 1981 elegant, yet authoritatively flavoured with good concentration.

TROTTEVIEILLE *ST.-EMILION* ★★

1981 .... ④ **70**
1982 .... ④ **85**
1983 .... ④ **72**

One of the more celebrated Premiers Grands Crus of St.-Emilion, this property has produced an embarrassing array of wines that have lacked concentration and character, and were often disturbingly light and dull. However, the vintages of the 1980s have shown improvement, with the unreleased 1985 perhaps the best yet. The vintages of the 1980s are light but fruity and soft, with 1982 being your best bet.

VIEUX CHÂTEAU CERTAN *POMEROL* ★★★★

1982 .... ⑤ **88**
1983 .... ④ **87**
1984 .... ④ **82**

Vieux Château Certan for decades was considered the second best wine of Pomerol. It has lost some of its appeal as other Pomerols have surpassed it. However, for elegance and a more Médoc style of wine, it is hard to beat. The 1984 is spicy, cedary, and light; the 1983 slightly minty, with attractive berry flavours and good body; the 1982, a rich, deep, perfumed wine with layers of lush fruit, can be drunk now.

VIEUX CHÂTEAU GUIBEAU
PUISSEGUIN-ST.-EMILION ★★★

1982 .... ① **82**
1983 .... ① **82**

Another leading estate in Puisseguin-St.-Emilion, both the 1983 and 1982 are soft, fruity, and quite delicious.

VILLARS *FRONSAC* ★★★

1982 .... ① **84**
1983 .... ① **82**

Villars tends to produce supple, fruity wines of good concentration. Recent vintages have been quite successful and the unreleased 1985 may be the best yet.

VILLEGEORGE *HAUT-MÉDOC* ★

1981 .... ② **72**
1982 .... ② **80**
1983 .... ② **83**

This property has a good reputation in Europe and the best recent vintage has been 1983 – the wine is generously fruity, supple, spicy, with good concentration and smooth texture.

VILLEMAURINE *ST.-EMILION* ★ ★ ★

1982 .... ③ *84*
1983 .... ③ *82*

Named after an ancient Moorish encampment, the enormous underground cellars here have considerable tourist interest. The wine, after a period of mediocrity, is better made in the 1980s than in previous decades. Both the 1982 and 1983 are fruity, supple, and soft.

LA VIOLETTE *POMEROL* ★ ★ ★

1981 .... ④ *78*
1982 .... ④ *87*
1983 .... ④ *83*

This rather obscure Pomerol produces only 1,800 cases, but the wine is made primarily from the Merlot grape and can be stunningly rich, as in 1982. The 1983 has a ripe berry fruit bouquet and flavours and soft tannins, but is a rather simple wine. The 1981 is rather light and watery.

VRAYE-CROIX-DE-GAY *POMEROL* ★ ★

1982 .... ③ *84*
1983 .... ③ *80*

One sees very little of this tiny property in Pomerol, which usually makes darkly coloured, dense, powerful, very flavourful and tannic wine. It suffers from inconsistency, though both the 1982 and 1983 are smoky, exotic, chocolatey flavoured wines.

YQUEM *SAUTERNES* ★ ★ ★ ★ ★

1979 .... ⑤ *88*
1980 .... ⑤ *93*
1981 .... ⑤ *90*
1982 .... ⑤ *93*

The world's most expensive wine to produce, Yquem is unique, costs a fortune, but the owners have never made a profit trying to produce it. Its nectar-like richness and legendary ageing potential are indeed all for real. The 1981 is an outstanding rather than great Yquem; both the 1980 and 1982 are perfect examples of fabulous Yquems from two vintages that were not considered textbook years for the Sauternes region. The 1979 is very, very good, but lacks the honeyed richness and incredible power and intensity that this wine seems to possess in most vintages.

THE 1985 RED BORDEAUX • A PREVIEW GUIDE

Exceptional Potential (94-96 points)

Cos d'Estournel (St.-Estèphe)   Pétrus (Pomerol)
L'Evangile (Pomerol)   Trotanoy (Pomerol)

Outstanding Potential (90-93 points)

Canon (St.-Emilion)
Cheval Blanc (St.-Emilion)
Ducru-Beaucaillou (St.-Julien)
L'Eglise-Clinet (Pomerol)
Haut-Brion (Graves)
Lafite-Rothschild (Pauillac)
Lafleur (Pomerol)
Léoville-Barton (St.-Julien)

Léoville-Las Cases (St.-Julien)
Lynch-Bages (Pauillac)
Magdelaine (St.-Emilion)
Margaux (Margaux)
La Mission-Haut-Brion (Graves)
Mouton-Rothschild (Pauillac)
Pichon Lalande (Pauillac)
Le Pin (Pomerol)

Very Good Potential (86-89 points)

L'Angélus (St.-Emilion)
L'Arrosée (St.-Emilion)
Ausone (St.-Emilion)
Beauséjour-Duffau (St.-Emilion)
Belair (St.-Emilion)
Beychevelle (St.-Julien)
Bon Pasteur (Pomerol)
Boyd-Cantenac (Margaux)
Cadet-Piola (St.-Emilion)
Clerc-Milon (Pauillac)
La Conseillante (Pomerol)
Destieux (St.-Emilion)
Ferrand (St.-Emilion)
Fieuzal (Graves)
Figeac (St.-Emilion)
Le Gay (Pomerol)
Grand-Puy-Lacoste (Pauillac)
La Grave Trigant (Pomerol)
Gruaud-Larose (St.-Julien)
Haut-Bages-Libéral (Pauillac)

Issan (Margaux)
Lafleur Pétrus (Pomerol)
Lagrange (St.-Julien)
La Lagune (Médoc)
Langoa-Barton (St.-Julien)
Larmande (St.-Emilion)
Lascombes (Margaux)
Latour à Pomerol (Pomerol)
Meyney (St.-Estèphe)
Palmer (Margaux)
Pape-Clément (Graves)
Pavie (St.-Emilion)
Pontet-Canet (Pauillac)
St.-Pierre (St.-Julien)
Sociando-Mallet (Médoc)
Soutard (St.-Emilion)
Talbot (St.-Julien)
Le Tertre-Roteboeuf
   (St.-Emilion)
Vieux Château Certan (Pomerol)

Sleepers of the Vintage (The underpublicized high-quality wines that represent great values)

L'Arrosée (St.-Emilion)
Belles-Graves
   (Lalande-de-Pomerol)
Bertineau St.-Vincent
   (Lalande-de-Pomerol)
Bon Pasteur (Pomerol)
Cadet-Piola (St.-Emilion)

Canon de Brem
   (Canon-Fronsac)
Destieux (St.-Emilion)
L'Eglise-Clinet (Pomerol)
Ferrand (St.-Emilion)
Fieuzal (Graves)
Lagrange (St.-Julien)

140

Larmande (St.-Emilion)
La Louvière (Graves)
Mazeris (Canon-Fronsac)
Le Pin (Pomerol)

Sociando-Mallet (Médoc)
Le Tertre-Roteboeuf
  (St.-Emilion)

THE 1986 RED BORDEAUX PREVIEW REPORT – A MÉDOC YEAR

Exceptional Potential (95-100 points)
Margaux (Margaux)
Mouton Rothschild (Pauillac)

Pétrus (Pomerol)
Pichon Lalande (Panillac)

Outstanding Potential (90-94 points)
L'Arrosée (St.-Emilion)*
Ausone (St.-Emilion)
Beychevelle (St.-Julien)*
Canon (St.-Emilion)
Certan de May (Pomerol)
Chambert Marbuzet
  (St.-Estèphe)
Cheval Blanc (St.-Emilion)
Cos d'Estournel (St.-Estèphe)
Ducru-Beaucaillou (St.-Julien)
L'Eglise-Clinet (Pomerol)
Figeac (St.-Emilion)

Gruaud-Larose (St.-Julien)*
Haut-Brion (Graves)
Issan (Margaux)
Léoville-Barton (St.-Julien)
Léoville-Las Cases (St.-Julien)
Lynch-Bages (Pauillac)
La Mission-Haut-Brion (Graves)
Montrose (St.-Estèphe)
Poujeaux (Moulis)
Sociando-Mallet (Haut-Médoc)
Talbot (St.-Julien)
Vieux Château Certan (Pomerol)

Very Good Potential (86-89 points)
L'Angélus (St.-Emilion)*
Angludet (Margaux)
Bahans-Haut-Brion (Graves)
Balestard-La-Tonnelle
  (St.-Emilion)
Batailley (Pauillac)
Bon Pasteur (Pomerol)*
Cadet-Piola (St.-Emilion)*
Calon-Ségur (St.-Estèphe)
Chasse-Spleen (Moulis)*
Domaine de Chevalier (Graves)
Clerc-Milon (Pauillac)
Clos Fourtet (St.-Emilion)
Clos des Jacobins (St.-Emilion)
Clos du Marquis (St.-Julien)
La Conseillante (Pomerol)
Couvent-des-Jacobins
  (St.-Emilion)
Destieux (St.-Emilion)
La Dominique (St.-Emilion)
Domaine de l'Eglise (Pomerol)
L'Evangile (Pomerol)

Fonplegade (St.-Emilion)
Grand-Puy-Lacoste (Pauillac)*
Gressier Grand-Poujeaux
  (Moulis)*
Haut-Bages-Libéral (Pauillac)
Haut-Bailly (Graves)
Haut-Batailley (Pauillac)*
Haut-Corbin (St.-Emilion)
Haut-Marbuzet (St.-Estèphe)
Haut-Sarpe (St.-Emilion)
Hortevie (St.-Julien)
Le Jurat (St.-Emilion)
Lafleur (Pomerol)*
Lafleur de Gay (Pomerol)
Lafon-Rochet (St.-Estèphe)
La Lagune (Ludon)
Langoa-Barton (St.-Julien)
Larmande (St.-Emilion)
Lascombes (Margaux)
Latour (Pauillac)*
Latour à Pomerol (Pomerol)
Latour-Haut-Brion (Graves)

Liversan (Haut-Médoc)
Magdelaine (St.-Emilion)*
Marquis-de-Terme (Margaux)*
Meyney (St.-Estèphe)*
Mont-Brison (Margaux)
Moulin Rouge (Haut-Médoc)
Mouton-Baronne-Philippe
 (Pauillac)*
Les-Ormes-de-Pez
 (St.-Estèphe)
Palmer (Margaux)*
Pavie (St.-Emilion)

Pavie-Decesse (St.-Emilion)
Le Pin (Pomerol)
Potensac (Medoc)
Prieuré Lichine (Margaux)
Roudier (Montagne-St.-Emilion)
Terrey-Gros-Cailloux
 (St.-Julien)
Tertre-Daugay (St.-Emilion)
Tertre-Roteboeuf (St.-Emilion)
Troplong-Mondot (St.-Emilion)
Trotanoy (Pomerol)
Trottevieille (St.-Emilion)

Good Potential (82–85 points)

Androw Blanquet (St.-Estèphe)
Beaumont (Médoc)
Beauséjour-Bécot (St.-Emilion)
Beauséjour-Duffau (St.-Emilion)
Belair (Lussac St.-Emilion)
Belles-Graves
 (Lalande-de-Pomerol)
Bertineau-St.-Vincent
 (Lalande-de-Pomerol)
Boyd-Cantenac (Margaux)
Brillette (Moulis)
Canon de Brem
 (Canon Fronsac)
Canon-la-Gaffelière
 (St.-Emilion)
Canon-Moueix (Canon-Fronsac)
Cantemerle (Macau)
Carbonnieux (Graves)
Carles (Fronsac)
Certan-Giraud (Pomerol)*
Clinet (Pomerol)
Clos l'Eglise (Pomerol)
Clos des Templiers
 (Lalande-de-Pomerol)
Corbin (St.-Emilion)
Le Crock (St.-Estèphe)
La Croix de Gay (Pomerol)
Dassault (St.-Emilion)
Dauzac (Margaux)
Durand Laplagne
 (Puisseguin-St.-Emilion)
L'Enclos (Pomerol)

Faurie-de-Souchard
 (St.-Emilion)
Ferrand (St.-Emilion)
Fieuzal (Graves)
Fonbadet (Pauillac)
Fonroque (St.-Emilion)
Fontenil (Fronsac)
La Gaffelière (St.-Emilion)*
Le Gay (Pomerol)
Gloria (St.-Julien)
Grand-Maison (Cotes-de-Bourg)
Grand-Pontet (St.-Emilion)
Grand-Puy-Ducasse (Pauillac)
La Grave Trigant (Pomerol)
La Grolet (Cotes de Bourg)
Haut-Bailly (Graves)
La Joye (Bordeaux-Superior)
Kirwan (Margaux)
Labégorce-Zédé (Margaux)
Lafleur-Pétrus (Pomerol)
Lagrange (Pomerol)
Lalande Borie (St.-Julien)
Latour-St.-Bonnet (Médoc)
Léoville-Poyferré (St.-Julien)
Malartic-Lagravière (Graves)
Malescot-St.-Exupéry
 (Margaux)
Marbuzet (St.-Estèphe)
Mazeris (Canon Fronsac)
Moulin-Pez-Labrie
 (Canon-Fronsac)
Pape-Clément (Graves)

Patache d'Aux (Médoc)
Petit-Village (Pomerol)
Picque-Caillou (Graves)
Pitray (Côtes de Castillon)
Plagnac (Médoc)
La Pointe (Pomerol)
Prieuré Lescours (St.-Emilion)
Rauzan Gassies (Margaux)

Rocher-Bellevue-Figeac
(St.-Emilion)
Sales (Pomerol)*
La Serre (St.-Emilion)
Soudars (Médoc)
La Tonnelle (Cotes-de-Bourg)
Villars (Fronsac)
Villemaurine (St.-Emilion)

Sleepers of the Vintage (The underpublicized high quality wines that represent great value)

Angludet (Margaux)
L'Arrosée (St.-Emilion)
Bahans-Haut-Brion (Graves)
Balestard-La-Tonnelle
(St.-Emilion)
Cadet-Piola (St.-Emilion)
Chambert-Marbuzet
(St.-Estèphe)
Chasse-Spleen (Moulis)
Clos du Marquis (St.-Julien)
Destieux (St.-Emilion)
L'Eglise-Clinet (Pomerol)
Gressier Grand-Poujeaux
(Moulis)
Haut-Marbuzet (St.-Estèphe)
Haut-Sarpe (St.-Emilion)
Hortevie (St.-Julien)
Le Jurat (St.-Emilion)

Larmande (St.-Emilion)
Liversan (Haut-Médoc)
Marquis-de-Terme (Margaux)
Meyney (St.-Estèphe)
Mont-Brison (Margaux)
Mouton-Baronne-Philippe
(Pauillac)
Les-Ormes-de-Pez (St. Estèphe)
Potensac (Médoc)
Poujeaux (Moulis)
Roudier (Montagne St.-Emilion)
Sociando-Mallet (Médoc)
Terrey-Gros-Cailloux
(St.-Julien)
Le Tertre-Roteboeuf
(St.-Emilion)
Troplong-Mondot
(St.-Emilion)

*Wines marked with an asterisk have the potential to move up in rank.

BURGUNDY

The Côte de Nuit and Côte de Beaune

Burgundy is by far the most challenging wine region one could encounter. The notorious range in the quality of wine here is greater than anywhere else. The top wines are often produced in such minute quantities that the exhilaration of finding and tasting a great Burgundy is dashed when the grower tells you that only 50 cases will be sent to Britain. Combine this with the fact that truly excellent vintages here are far less frequent than elsewhere in France. Furthermore, the demand for Burgundy, whether it be poor, mediocre, or superb, is far greater than the supply, and prices are therefore excruciatingly high. Unfortunately, for far too many growers there is simply no incentive to produce smaller yields and greater quality wines. In short, small quantities, high prices, a plethora of mediocre vintages, and greedy as well as incompetent growers are an integral part of Burgundy's story – whether it be past, present, or future.

Even where high-quality wines are produced from recognized excellent vineyards and carefully vinified by good growers, there is no guarantee that what is in the barrel will make it into the bottle. The commercial madness of today's modern wine world has caused many good growers to overfilter their wines so no sediment will form in the bottle. The result of sterile filtrations through German-made micropore filters – is that most of the character, flavour intensity, and ageing potential is left behind in the filter pads.

The Pinot Noir grape produces rather fragile, very subtle wines. Overzealous filtration or flash pasteurization will literally kill off its character. Even if a wine somehow miraculously survives the trauma of filtration, many growers and *négociants* are making sure that no 'living wine' is sent abroad, since the wines are also put through a flash pasteurization prior to bottling. Even the great Burgundies that are famous for their expansive fragrance and broad, rich, velvety flavours resemble carafe wines with cooked, compact aromas and cardboard flavours after they are subjected to this abusive treatment. Yet there are advantages for those importers who insist on this treatment for their wines. They will never have to contend with stupid consumers or ignorant restaurants that send back the wine because it has some sediment in it. And of course they will save money because these wines, now castrated and sterile, are generally incapable of developing in the bottle. Consequently, they do not have to be protected and shipped in temperature-controlled containers. Unfiltered, natural wines can spoil or become unstable if exposed to extremes of heat. However, filtered and pasteurized wines are not so vulnerable; they can take all kinds of abuse, because, to all intents and purposes, they are already dead.

Why the difficulty in finding the best wines? Finding the top producers of great red Burgundy is as difficult as hunting for one of France's other remarkable sensory and culinary treasures, the truffle. It takes patience, plenty of time, plenty of money, and the realization that there are just not so many great Burgundy wine producers who are committed to making outstanding red wine. Combined with Burgundy's troublesome and unpredictable climate for Pinot Noir, which usually results in no more than three excellent vintages a decade, wine enthusiasts the world over have the right to lament the Herculean task of finding fine Burgundy. In short, Burgundy is a wine perfectly suited for masochists...you must suffer a great deal of abuse and pain to find pleasure!

However, the fact remains that both good and bad Burgundies are expensive, and that really top Burgundy wines are incredibly hard to find. Why? you might ask. Unlike Bordeaux, where on average a moderate-sized estate or vineyard may produce 15,000–20,000 cases of wine per year, a top-notch grower in Burgundy may make only 300–500 cases of wine from a specific Premier or Grand Cru vineyard. Divide that production up around the world and you can easily see how exasperating it can be to find the top Burgundies. Scarcity is only part of the problem, however. Take one of Burgundy's most famous and expensive wines, Clos de Vougeot. There are 125 acres of vineyard at Clos de Vougeot, which makes it about the size of one moderate château in Bordeaux. However, in 1985 there were more than 80 different growers who owned a part of these 125 acres, whereas in Bordeaux, the château's vineyard is under one management and ownership. Not all of these 80+ growers bottle their own wine of course, some sell to the large brokers in Burgundy. However, there are at least 30 or more different Clos de Vougeot wines on the market in any given vintage. Some are totally insipid wines made by incompetent growers who overcrop and carelessly vinify their wines, whereas a few are splendid wines, rich, majestically scented, and truly representative of what a great Burgundy should be. Yet whether that wine is poor, mediocre, or superb, there is one constant – the wine will always be expensive, and when it is from one of the top growers, very hard to find as well, because knowledgeable Burgundy connoisseurs rush to snap up the limited supplies of the real thing. In short, the problem facing top-quality Burgundy is a classic example of supply and demand. The region's top vineyards are entirely too small to produce enough wine to satisfy the world demand. Take a look at Burgundy's most famous estate, the Domaine de la Romanée-Conti (DRC). This estate is the sole owner of such fabulously expensive and famous vineyards as Romanée-Conti and La Tâche. The Romanée-Conti vineyard comprises a full 4.75 acres, whereas the La Tâche comprises 15 acres.

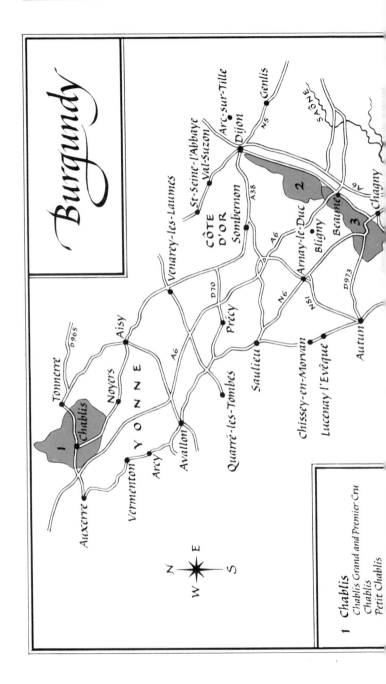

Burgundy

Genlis
Arc-sur-Tille
Dijon
St-Seine-l'Abbaye
Val-Suzon
SAÔNE
N5
A38
2
A6
Chagny
Venarey-les-Laumes
CÔTE D'OR
Sombernon
Arnay-le-Duc
Bligny
Beaune
3
D70
A6
N6
N81
D973
Tonnerre
D965
Aisy
Noyers
Y O N N E
A6
Précy
Saulieu
Autun
Chissey-en-Morvan
Lucenay l'Evêque
Chablis
1
Vermenton
Arcy
Avallon
Quarré-les-Tombes
Auxerre

N
E
W
S

1 **Chablis**
Chablis Grand and Premier-Cru
Chablis
Petit Chablis

146

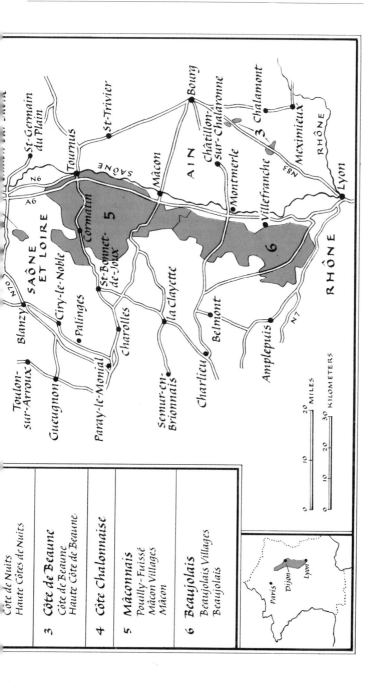

Côte de Nuits
Haute Côtes de Nuits

3 Côte de Beaune
Côte de Beaune
Haute Côte de Beaune

4 Côte Chalonnaise

5 Mâconnais
Pouilly-Fuissé
Mâcon Villages
Mâcon

6 Beaujolais
Beaujolais Villages
Beaujolais

These two wines fetch prices of £40 or more a bottle, regardless of how good the vintages are. There are simply too many people wanting to buy these wines in spite of their price or quality. However, if you are going to buy Burgundy, you must rely not just on the prestige of the vineyard, but rather on the quality and competence of the grower. In Burgundy, the French have an expression that sums it all up, 'C'est l'homme qui fait la différence' (it is the man who makes the difference). These words alone sum up the realities of buying Burgundy yesterday, today, and tomorrow. In summary, the good growers in Burgundy make much better wine in mediocre and poor years than the careless and sloppy growers make in the great years.

BURGUNDY · QUICK VINTAGE GUIDE

1986 Due to heavy rains before the harvest and rains at the end of the harvest, Burgundy will be a very difficult area to generalize about. Production was much higher than in 1985 and early reports suggest that the white wines should be very good and the red wines very irregular, with quality depending in large part on when the grower picked. The size of the crop should help stabilize prices, which at the time of writing are absurdly high.

1985 Overall, 1985 looks to be the most promising vintage since 1978. The drought during the late summer and autumn caused the grapes to ripen well. The wines are deeply coloured, very fruity and ripe, with clean, rich, very fruity aromas. They have much less tannin and more charm than the irregular, rather massive 1983s. Despite early reports that the quantity was small, the vintage has turned out a good-sized yield of wine. Most of the wines have excellent balance, and though they will be approachable in their youth, should age well for a decade. Prices are already absurdly high, so the wines will continue to be extremely expensive. The white wines, even more expensive, are fat, supple and lush, and will have to be drunk early. In style, they resemble the 1982 white Burgundies. Cask tastings showed a remarkably high level of quality wines from such red wine producers as Faiveley, Domaine de la Romanée-Conti, Bruno Clair, Dujac, Jean Gros, Hubert Lignier, Maume, Mongeard-Mugneret, Georges Mugneret, Ponsot, Pothier Rieusset, Pousse d'Or, Joseph Roty, A. Rousseau, and Mérode.

1984 All of us remember 1984. This year, like 1980, was declared by several wine writers to be a major catastrophe long before they ever tasted the wines. In 1980, the source of information was the *négociant* Louis Latour, who had all sorts of problems with the vintage, and indeed made poor wine that year. As all Burgundy lovers know, 1980 has turned out some of the most delicious and best-balanced wines of the last seven to eight years, and some of the wines from the Côte de Nuits (e.g. Domaine de la Romanée-Conti and Robert Arnoux) are superb. Well, 1984 is not likely to be as good as 1980, but many of the good growers have made wines that I predict will be better-balanced, richer wines than the 1982s. The vintage was late, and everyone had to chaptalize because the natural alcohol content was only 9%–10%. However, the resulting red wines are often quite elegant, very cleanly made, fruity, soft, and agreeable. The yields were low because of a poor flowering. There is the normal irregularity, but the wines of the Côte de Nuits are better coloured and richer than those of the Côte de Beaune. I would guess that the good 1984s will reach full maturity between 1988 and 1990. They will certainly not be long-lived, but when well chosen, will be very pleasant wines.

1983 A knowledgeable oenologist once asked me, 'Is 1983 really a great vintage or the Burgundy sham of the century?' It is hard to judge any vintage in black and white terms because of the innumerable variables that affect quality, but I have always felt that only 10% of the wines I tasted had the potential, concentration, and overall balance to be considered great. The severe hailstorms that hit the Côte de Nuits in July and the rampant rot in the vineyards from the tropical heat and rain in August and early September created significant problems. Many wine journalists, who do not look very closely at all the facts or laboriously taste across the field of play, obviously read that the hot dry weather in late September and October caused sugar readings to soar in the grapes, and that the harvest occurred under textbook conditions. So they concluded it must surely be a great vintage, and like the prophets of doom who also talk and write before tasting, the reports went out that this *was* truly a great vintage. One single thing was forgotten – it is difficult to make wine from unhealthy grapes, and in 1983 there were plenty of rot-infested and scarred grapes from both rot and hail damage.

The key to making great Burgundy in 1983 was to separate the rotten grapes from the healthy ones. This had to be done at the time of picking. It was extremely time-consuming, but absolutely essential if one was to produce a clean, well-balanced wine. There were, of course, other factors that would have a significant effect on the outcome. Because the grape skins were extremely thick and ripe, one had to be careful with the vinification so as not to extract an excess of tannin. Some growers pulled the fermenting grape juice off the skins too fast for fear of obtaining a taste of rot and getting too much tannin. Their wines tend to be lighter in colour and much more precocious in style. Other growers went for maximum extract and produced wines so tannic that 1976 Burgundies (known for their tannic ferocity) almost look supple in comparison. Other growers used too much new wood, some obviously in an attempt to hide or mask the smell of rot. Some did not use enough new wood. Some growers fined their wines excessively, hoping the egg white fining would help soften the bite from the harsh tannins. This worked in some cases, but in others both colour and flavour were also removed by the fining. And, of course, some growers have overzealously filtered and/or pasteurized their wines, destroying any taste or smell that would identify their place of origin.

For the red Burgundies of 1983, you will find many abrasive, harsh, tannic, dry wines with a 'goût de sec' and 'goût de moisi'. This is the smell and taste of rot most closely resembling damp, mouldy cardboard in aroma, and in flavour, a sharp bitter, very dry impression is created. There are also wines that have lost significant colour because of the rot. Unlike the terribly underrated 1980 Burgundy vintage in which the wines seemed to deepen in colour and flavour concentration as they aged in the cask, the 1983s have lightened considerably in colour with some taking on orange, brownish edges, a particularly dangerous sign. If you do not like the 1976 red Burgundies because of their hard tannins and firmness, don't imagine for a moment that the 1983s will be more pleasant.

As for the white Burgundies, they are simply the most enormous white wines from Burgundy I have ever tasted. Ranging to 14%–16% in alcohol, they are extremely alcoholic, heavy, clumsy wines that will leave your head spinning. Some can be magnificent if the balancing acidity is present (e.g. Leflaive, Sauzet, Coche Dury, Jadot, Jobard), but many are rather oafish wines that will please when young but fall apart within three to four years as the fruit fades and the ugly level of alcohol becomes dominant.

Does all of this sound very pessimistic? You bet it does, but there are small quantities of very good to superb wines that were produced in 1983 that should permit connoisseurs of Burgundy to replenish their cellar stocks. Of course, it will not be cheap, as many of the very best Burgundies were made in exceptionally small quantities because the grower ruthlessly discarded any tainted grapes. For a few growers, 1983 is truly a great vintage. For the rest, the vintage is a mixed bag of high alcohol, harsh, rather imbalanced wines that taste a little bizarre. For those lucky enough to get a hold of any of the greatest wines, they will undoubtedly be real treasures. However, everyone should remember that these wines are quite tannic and most of them will not be ready to drink before 1993–1995. If you don't want to wait that long – and that is minimum – then take a look at the dozen or so top 1982s, which by and large are delicious now. But whatever you decide to do, remember that 1983 is an extremely irregular and overrated vintage. Only the very best wines are worth the high price.

1982 A huge crop of grapes was harvested in 1982. Had it not been for the extremely wet month of August, this year could have been quite special. However, the enormous yield produced very fragile wines, somewhat watery, but generally charming, soft, and fruity. Where the conscientious growers were able to pick before the harvest rains and control the vinification temperature, some good, round, adequately concentrated wines have been produced. As for the white wines, they have turned out to be extremely successful – fat, lush, ripe wines for drinking over the next two to three years while waiting for the 1981s to open. Most top growers compare their white Burgundies with the 1973 vintage.

In general, the wines of the Côte de Beaune are more consistent than those of the Côte de Nuits. However, the Domaine de la Romanée-Conti and Georges Mugneret, both in Vosne-Romanée, the Armand Rousseau, Maume, Philippe and René Leclerc, all in Gevrey-Chambertin, the Domaine Dujac and Pierre Amiot in Morey St.-Denis, as well as the *négociant* Faiveley, did quite well in the Côte de Nuits.

1981 A difficult vintage for certain, the great majority of 1981 red Burgundies lack flesh and charm, and are too hard, shallow, and austere. Several optimistic reports have indicated they will turn out like the 1972s, but the 1972s had significantly more concentration. For white Burgundies it is a very good year, but for reds one must pick very carefully. Notable successes among the small growers include the wines of Philippe Leclerc in Gevrey-Chambertin, Pierre Amiot and Domaine Dujac in Morey St.-Denis, Robert Chevillon in Nuits St.-Georges, and Domaine de la Pousse d'Or and Michel Lafarge in Volnay. Among the *négociants*, the wines of Faiveley are excellent and perhaps the finest 1981s produced.

1980 A disappointing to mediocre year for the white wines, and an average year for the reds of the Côte de Beaune. As for the Côte de Nuits, a vastly underrated vintage in which there are considerable numbers of rich, medium-bodied, very elegant, cleanly made, technically sound red Burgundies that can be drunk now or cellared for another three to five years. The reds of the Côte de Nuits are probably the best bargains of Burgundy today.

1979 A good to very good year for white Burgundy. The wines are fully mature and should be consumed. For the red Burgundies, the wines are generally showing their age, are soft, rather frail and best drunk up.

1978 The most consistently pleasing and successful vintage for Burgundy over the period 1972–1984. The whites, which are just now reaching full maturity, are classic wines with power, richness, depth, and balance. The reds from the Côte de Beaune are quite good and ready to drink; from the Côte de Nuits, the red wines can be drunk, but the best of them need a few more years. Interestingly, the greatest red wines of the 1983 vintage are better than the greatest red wines of the 1978 vintage. However, in 1978 there is a general level of consistent good quality, whereas in 1983 there are numerous failures.

1977 For red Burgundies, a terrible year, and one in which even the most conscientious growers could not overcome Mother Nature's cruel blows. For the white Burgundies a surprisingly good year of wines that seemed acidic at first, but which have matured well. The 1977 white Burgundies are in beautiful condition today and are real sleepers.

1976 Along with the 1983, 1976 must surely be the most controversial Burgundy vintage of recent years. A hot drought year resulted in tiny berries with thick skins. The major difference from 1983 is that there was no hail or rot damage. The reds, very deeply coloured, very tannic and very concentrated, continue to lack charm and character, but they have all the characteristics necessary to age well. Since they have richer, more concentrated fruit than the 1983s, I suspect that all they need is more time – four to seven more years. As for the whites, they were low in acidity, powerful, rich, alcoholic wines that in size resembled the 1983s, but without the taint of rot. They should be drunk immediately since they are not likely to get any better.

1975 An undisputably terrible vintage for virtually everyone.

Several very good wines were made in Chablis, otherwise this is a vintage to avoid.

1974 When it rains, it pours, and 1974 was another very bad vintage for the growers and *négociants* of Burgundy. The palatable wines I have had have all been white Burgundies from Meursault and Chassagne-Montrachet.

1973 A very good, sometimes excellent vintage for the white wines. Like the 1982s, the white wines tasted good from the beginning, and while lacking some firmness and acidity, were full of fruit and charm. They should have been consumed by now because they no longer hold up. The reds were watery, pale, light and generally in full retreat into oblivion by 1978. They are now comatose.

1972 Like 1980, at first a maligned, poorly regarded vintage that has developed so well that lovely vinous surprises are everywhere and the vintage's reputation clearly on the rise. The reds, deeply coloured but high in acidity and dumb when first assessed in 1973–1974, have developed slowly but surely. The top wines have rich, complex bouquets, deep flavours, and a touch of firmness. A keeping vintage of wine that should be drunk over the next five to eight years. The whites were less successful, but certainly good. They are now cracking up and must be drunk.

1971 A splendid vintage of ripe, rich, voluptuous, deeply scented red and white wines. The only disappointment has been how fast these wines have matured. Virtually all the wines have been mature for several years and the tell-tale orange/amber colours have become apparent. The whites are somewhat risky unless stored in a cold cellar. The reds are just beginning to lose some fruit, but the well-preserved red Burgundies of this vintage are delectably opulent and fragrant.

1970 A good vintage of round, fruity, soft wines was produced everywhere in Burgundy. If both the whites and reds lacked greatness, there were plenty of satisfying wines produced. They matured quickly and should be drunk without delay.

1969 An excellent vintage for the red wines, a very good one for the white wines. The wines were slow to mature because they were powerful but backward and quite firm. The reds are all mature and should be drunk up. The only recent white Burgundies I have tasted from this vintage seemed to be losing their fruit and becoming oxidized. Nevertheless, this is a vintage to look for at auction.

RATING THE RED BURGUNDY GROWERS, PRODUCERS, AND NÉGOCIANTS

No one will ever have a great deal of success selecting a Burgundy without a thorough knowledge of the finest growers and *négociants*. The most meticulous producers often make better wine in mediocre vintages than many less dedicated growers and producers make in great vintages. Knowing the finest producers in Burgundy is unquestionably the most important factor in your success in finding the best wines.

The following is a guide to the best red Burgundy producers. Consistency from year to year among the producers' total range of wines was the most important consideration. One should be cognizant of the fact that many lower-rated producers may make specific wines that are qualitatively above their placement here.

A GUIDE TO RED BURGUNDY'S BEST PRODUCERS

★ ★ ★ ★ ★ Outstanding Producers

Faiveley (Nuits St.-Georges)
Henri Jayer (Vosne-Romanée)
Leroy (Meursault)

Domaine de la Romanée-Conti
  (Vosne-Romanée)

★ ★ ★ ★ Excellent Producers

Robert Arnoux
  (Vosne-Romanée)
Pierre Bourée
  (Gevrey-Chambertin)
Castagnier (Vosne-Romanée)
Cathiard Molinier
  (Vosne-Romanée)
Robert Chevillon
  (Nuits St.-Georges)
Bruno Clair (Marsannay)
Clair-Daü (Marsannay)
Courcel (Pommard)
Joseph Drouhin (Beaune)
Drouhin Larose
  (Gevrey-Chambertin)
Dujac (Morey St.-Denis)
Michel Gaunoux (Pommard)
Pierre Gelin (Fixin)
Machard de Gramont
  (Nuits St.-Georges)
Jean Grivot (Vosne-Romanée)
Jean Gros (Vosne-Romanée)
Gros Soeur et Frère
  (Vosne-Romanée)

Hospices de Beaune
Hudelot Noëllat
  (Vosne-Romanée)
Louis Jadot (Beaune)
Lucien Jayer (Vosne-Romanée)
Michel Lafarge (Volnay)
Clos des Lambrays
  (Morey St.-Denis)
Philippe Leclerc
  (Gevrey-Chambertin)
René Leclerc
  (Gevrey-Chambertin)
Hubert Lignier
  (Morey St.-Denis)
Maume (Gevrey-Chambertin)
Prince Florent de Mérode
  (Ladoix-Serrigny)
Moine Hudelot
  (Chambolle-Musigny)
Hubert de Montille
  (Volnay)
Albert Morot (Beaune)
Mongeard Mugneret
  (Vosne-Romanée)

Georges Mugneret
(Vosne-Romanée)
Mussy (Pommard)
Pernot Fourrier
(Gevrey-Chambertin)
Ponsot (Morey St.-Denis)
Pothier-Rieusset (Pommard)
Pousse d'Or (Volnay)
Joseph Roty
(Gevrey-Chambertin)

Armand Rousseau
(Gevrey-Chambertin)
Roumier (Chambolle-Musigny)
Bernard Serveau
(Morey St.-Denis)
Tollot-Beaut
(Chorey-les-Beaune)
Tollot-Voarick (Aloxe-Corton)

★ ★ ★ Good Producers

Pierre Amiot (Morey St.-Denis)
Marquis d'Angerville (Volnay)
Comte Armand (Pommard)
Barthod Noëllat
(Chambolle-Musigny)
Adrian Belland (Santenay)
Guy Berthaut (Fixin)
Berthaut (Chambolle-Musigny)
Besancenot-Mathouillet
(Beaune)
Bichot-Clos Frantin (Beaune)
Billard Gonnet (Pommard)
Simon Bize
(Savigny-les-Beaune)
Bouchard Aîné (Beaune)
Bouchard Père (Beaune)
Henri Boillot (Volnay)
Lucien Boillot
(Gevrey-Chambertin)
L. J. Bruck
(Nuits St.-Georges)
Georges Bryczek
(Morey St.-Denis)
Alain Burguet
(Gevrey-Chambertin)
Champy Père (Beaune)
Domaine Chandon de Briailles
(Savigny-les-Beaune)
Domaine de la Charrière
(Santenay)
Jean Chauvenet
(Nuits St.-Georges)
George Clerget (Vougeot)
Edmond Cornu (Ladoix)

Deroubaix-Indelli
(Clos Vougeot)
Armande Douhairet (Monthelie)
Dubreuil-Fontaine
(Pernand-Vergelesses)
Duchet (Beaune)
M. Ecard (Savigny-les-Beaune)
René Engel (Vosne-Romanée)
Robert Groffier
(Morey St.-Denis)
Jaffelin (Beaune)
Jacqueline Jayer
(Vosne-Romanée)
Domaine Jacqueson (Chagny)
Jayer Gilles
(Nuits St.-Georges)
Philippe Joliet (Fixin)
Lamy Pillot
(Chassagne-Montrachet)
Domaine Comte Lafon
(Meursault)
Henri Lamarche
(Vosne-Romanée)
Lejeune (Pommard)
Lequin-Roussot (Santenay)
Georges Lignier
(Morey St.-Denis)
Château de la Maltroye
(Chassagne-Montrachet)
Manière-Noirot
(Vosne-Romanée)
Matrot (Meursault)
Jean Meo (Vosne-Romanée)
Mestre (Santenay)

Alain Michelot
(Nuits St.-Georges)
Moillard (Nuits St.-Georges)
Charles Moncault (Beaune)
Gerard Mugneret
(Vosne-Romanée)
Charles Noëllat
(Vosne-Romanée)
André Nudant
(Nuits St.-Georges)
Jacques Parent (Pommard)
Pierre Ponnelle (Beaune)
M. Prunier (Auxey Duresses)
Rapet (Savigny-les-Beaune)
Henri Rebourseau
(Gevrey-Chambertin)
Remoissenet (Beaune)

Daniel Rion (Nuits St.-Georges)
Philippe Rossignol
(Gevrey-Chambertin)
Daniel Senard (Aloxe-Corton)
Servelle Tachot (Clos Vougeot)
Robert Siruge
(Vosne-Romanée)
Robert Suremaine (Monthelie)
Gabriel Tortochot
(Gevrey-Chambertin)
Louis Trapet
(Gevrey-Chambertin)
Vachet Rousseau
(Gevrey-Chambertin)
Domaine des Varoilles
(Gevrey-Chambertin)

★ ★ Average Producers

Arlaud (Nuits St.-Georges)
Bernard Bachelet
(Chassagne-Montrachet)
Bertagna (Vougeot)
Chanson (Beaune)
F. Chauvenet
(Nuits St.-Georges)
Chevalier (Aloxe-Corton)
Coron (Beaune)
Damoy (Gevrey-Chambertin)
Albert Derey (Marsannay)
Henri Gouges
(Nuits St.-Georges)
Jaboulet-Vercherre (Beaune)
Labouré Roi (Beaune)
Louis Latour (Beaune)
Lupé Cholet
(Nuits St.-Georges)

J. P. Magien
(Gevrey-Chambertin)
Monmessin (Macon)
Naigeon-Chauveau
(Gevrey-Chambertin)
Patriarche (Beaune)
Jacques Prieur (Meursault)
Prosper Maufoux (Santenay)
Charles Quillardet (Marsannay)
A. Rodet (Beaune)
Charles Viénot
(Nuits St.-Georges)
Henri de Villamont (Beaune)
Comte de Vogüé
(Chambolle-Musigny)

★ Other Producers

Thomas Bassot
(Gevrey-Chambertin)
Robert DuBois
(Nuits St.-Georges)

Geisweiler (Nuits St.-Georges)
Pascal (Meursault)
La Reine Pedanque (Beaune)

THE BEST WINE VALUES IN RED BURGUNDY AND COTE D'OR

The glamorous appellations of the Côte de Nuits and Côte de

Beaune offer exorbitant prices as well as irregular quality. Consequently, more and more wine-lovers are simply looking elsewhere
for Pinot Noir wines or are considering some of the less grand
appellations of Burgundy where values can still be found. The
following chart lists the best red wine appellations when quality/
price rapport is important to you. In addition, the best producers of
these appellations are noted.

Auxey-Duresses   (Côte de Beaune)
An up-and-coming appellation for both red and white Burgundy,
Auxey-Duresses does not have a charming, lyrical name, but Leroy
and Michel Prunier make very fine wine here.

Chassagne-Montrachet   (Côte de Beaune)
Internationally famous for its splendidly perfumed, rich, white
wines, Chassagne-Montrachet does not get enough respect for the
fragrant, supple, red wines made here by such top growers as
Château de la Maltroye and Lequin-Roussot.

Fixin   (Côte de Nuits)
The only reasonable value left among the extravagantly expensive
wines of the Côte de Nuits. Located next to Gevrey-Chambertin,
the wines of Fixin tend to be rustic, big, rather full red Burgundies.
The top four producers to look for are Pierre Gelin, Philippe Joliet,
Guy Bertheau, and Bruno Clair.

Monthelie   (Côte de Beaune)
The neighbour of the much sought-after, elegant, suave, lush wines
of Volnay, Monthelie is terribly overlooked for robust, quality,
fragrant Pinot Noir. Robert Suremaine and Armande Douhairet are
two growers to take note of.

Pernand-Vergelesses   (Côte de Beaune)
Perhaps the varying assessments of this appellation have kept its
wines from an expensive notoriety. They are light, fragrant, and
aromatic, and resemble good Beaunes or Aloxe-Cortons at a much
lower price. Three producers stand out here—Robert Rapet,
Dubreuil-Fontaine, and Domaine Chandon des Briailles.

Santenay   (Côte de Beaune)
Perhaps the most underrated appellation in the entire Cote d'Or,
the quality level of wine made in Santenay is particularly high. The
wines are sturdy and ageworthy, particularly for a Côte de Beaune,
with rather deep, rich, long flavours when made by the likes of
Lequin-Roussot, Adrian Bellan, Domaine de la Charrière, Domaine
de Bousse d'Or, Phillipe Mertre, and the *négociants* Joseph Drouhin
and Remoissenet. All make delicious Santenays in the good vintages.

Savigny-les-Beaune   (Côte de Beaune)
A terribly underrated appellation, the Savigny wines often have a
good ripe, rich, strawberry and cherry fruitiness. Simon Bize, Ecard,
Tollot-Beaut, Bruno Clair, and Tollot Voarick have very high
standards.

VALUES FROM BURGUNDY'S UNDERBELLY · THE CÔTE CHALONNAISE

Smart people who enjoy red Burgundy but cannot afford the luxurious prices of the famous wines have been seeking relief in the wine of the Côte Chalonnaise for decades. There is much good, not great, red Burgundy made here that normally sells for £6-£10 a bottle. The following are the wines to look for and their best producers. The 1982s and 1985s from these appellations are more consistently successful than the 1983s and 1984s.

Givry

My favourite wines of this area come from Givry. They have more richness and more colour than the other appellations. The Givry from Baron Thénard is top class, followed by those of Gardin, who owns a vineyard called Clos Saloman.

Mercurey

Mercurey, though hardly world famous, is the best known of the appellations of the Côte Chalonnaise. The best wines are made by the excellent *négociants* Faiveley, Michel Juillot, Yves de Launay and Chanzy Frères.

Montagny

Of the red wines of the Côte Chalonnaise, the wines of Montagny offer the least appeal. On the bright side, they are not expensive, but I know of no grower here making red wine as good as the aforementioned producers.

Rully

Rully is best known as the closest wine village to the drab town of Chagny, which contains one of France's greatest restaurants, the hotel/restaurant Lameloise. There are five top red wine producers making very good Rully. The best are the Domaine de la Folie and Henri Jacqueson, then Jean-François Delorme, Chanzy, and the *négociant* Faiveley.

BURGUNDY · TODAY'S BUYING STRATEGY

More than for any other French wine, buying Burgundy is fraught with the risk of paying top prices for a mediocre or poor wine – it is a classic example of buying the proverbial pig in a poke. However, you have the names of the best producers. Mediocre vintages like 1982 and 1984 are very risky, but then so is a generally accepted top vintage like 1983. Thankfully, 1985 looks much more consistent in quality, with supple, fruity wines that are easy to taste and to understand. What does one do? In lieu of avoiding the region altogether, concentrate on buying only the very finest wines from the finest growers. They will be hard to find and very expensive, but if you want to taste what some experts think is the world's greatest wines, then this is the only way, as painfully expensive as it is. Look out also for any remaining 1980s that may turn up on the shelves, and if you can afford them, have a go at the consistently good and excellent 1985s, Burgundy's most consistent vintage for red wines since 1978. Some 1983s will be fabulous, but proceed with great caution since the great majority of wines from this vintage are harsh and astringent. And remember even the great 1983s need eight to ten years of cellaring. To buy intelligently, you must learn – memorize is a better word – who the greatest producers are and then buy only their wines. They will make better wines in vintages such as 1984 and 1982 than less conscientious growers will in high-quality years such as 1985. Worldwide demand for Burgundy is simply too great for the tiny quantities of wines made; it will never be cheap, or even reasonably priced.

PIERRE AMIOT *MOREY ST.-DENIS* ★ ★ ★

In my experience, Amiot is one of Burgundy's most hospitable vignerons. More important, he is an excellent winemaker. In contrast to many of his peers who produced poor and insipid wines in 1981 and 1982, Amiot did quite well in both vintages. His 1983s are also quite good, though not spectacular. Amiot's style of Burgundy emphasizes velvety, soft, ripe, rich flavours. His wines are round and fruity with considerable charm and flavour. My instinct tells me that they are not candidates for long-term cellaring, but then how many Burgundies are? Amiot was also very successful in 1984 and his wines will be worth looking for in that terribly maligned vintage.

1983 Clos de la Roche	⑤	**85**
1983 Gevrey Chambertin Aux Combottes	⑤	**84**
1983 Morey St.-Denis Aux Charmes	⑤	**84**
1983 Morey St.-Denis Les Baudes	④	**84**
1983 Morey St.-Denis Millandes	④	**82**
1983 Morey St.-Denis Villages	④	**80**

As the scores indicate, the wines are quite consistently successful, if not at the very highest level of quality. In general, Amiot's 1983s typify the Michael Broadbent expression, 'an iron fist in a velvet glove'. They have a good measure of tannin but also more supple, lush, voluptuous fruit than one usually finds in the 1983s.

Most of Amiot's 1983s need a good five to six years of cellaring, but are clearly much more accessible, fragrant, and precocious than other 1983s. Comparing them, the Clos de la Roche has the most class, slightly more concentration and complexity, but both the Morey St.-Denis Les Baudes and Morey St.-Denis Aux Charmes are delicious, rich, and fruity wines with broad, authentic Pinot Noir flavours. The Les Baudes is slightly more tannic and darker in colour and will evolve less quickly. The Gevrey-Chambertin Aux Combottes is perhaps the biggest wine Amiot made in 1983, rather substantial and alcoholic, with ripe, earthy flavours. It clearly begs for five to six years. The Morey St.-Denis Villages has lovely, open-knit, broad, round, fruity flavours and at present is the most easily drunk wine of Amiot. In contrast, the Morey St.-Denis Millandes is Amiot's darkest coloured as well as his most backwardly tannic wine. It needs eight years of cellaring.

1982 Clos de la Roche...	⑤	**86**
1982 Gevrey-Chambertin Aux Combottes...............	④	**83**
1982 Morey St.-Denis Aux Charmes	④	**83**

There are not many 1982s, particularly from the Côte de Nuits, that are this good. Unlike the 1983s, which require some patience, these wines are best drunk over the next one to three years. Amiot's 1982s are more concentrated than many of his peers, quite perfumed, fruity, and lush with low acidity, soft tannins, and good, round yet long finishes. The Clos de la Roche is very, very good and has quite a complex bouquet of raspberries, flowers, and spicy oak. It should be drunk over the next three years. Both the Morey St.-Denis Aux Charmes and Gevrey-Chambertin Aux Combottes are lighter in weight and less rich. The Gevrey-Chambertin is also more spicy and earthy.

DOMAINE ARLAUD *NUITS ST.-GEORGES* ★★

Located on the back streets of Nuits St.-Georges, the Domaine Arlaud has twelve hectares spread throughout the Côte de Nuits. The wines produced here in 1982 and 1983 are rather fat, highly chaptalized, well-coloured wines that purists might criticize as being too sweet, but they are inexpensive and actually quite delicious to taste. Surprisingly, the 1982s had more colour and richness than the 1983s.

1983 Chambolle-Musigny	③	**85**
1983 Charmes-Chambertin..	④	**84**

These two 1983s from Arlaud have the tannic toughness of the vintage but also show the apparent house style in that they are rather fat, alcoholic, jammy, and richly fruity. There is quite a lot of Pinot Noir flavour and a pleasing lushness. No doubt both should be drunk over the next two to four years. The Chambolle-Musigny is much the better value.

1982 Clos de la Roche...	④	**86**
1982 Morey St.-Denis...	④	**85**

Two legitimate 'sleepers', these two succulent 1982s are surprisingly deep coloured, have rather sweet tastes with some powerful alcohol present, but do indeed exhibit masses of fruit, a rich, perfumed, spicy, ripe, plummy bouquet, and round, velvety finishes. They should be drunk over the next few years because of low acidity, but do offer quite a mouthful of Burgundy.

ROBERT ARNOUX *VOSNE-ROMANÉE* ★★★★

The towering, somewhat formidable-looking Robert Arnoux has received excellent reviews for his fragrant, rich, spicy, deeply flavoured Burgundies. Both his 1978s and 1980s were among the very best wines of those respective vintages. I find the style of wine of Arnoux to be somewhat like that of the famous Domaine de la Romanée-Conti, perhaps not as broad and deep, but similarly rich, expansive, pure Pinot Noir wines. The 1982s are somewhat weak by Arnoux's standards, and I doubt that his 1983s are better than either his best 1978s or 1980s. Interestingly, he bottled his 1983s very early, in late winter of 1985. Arnoux employed 30% new oak barrels for the 1983 vintage, and does not filter his wines. His 1984s looked mediocre from the cask; his 1985s are great successes.

1983 Clos Vougeot	⑤	87
1983 Nuits St.-Georges Les Corvées-Paget	⑤	79
1983 Nuits St.-Georges Les Poisets	④	82
1983 Vosne-Romanée	③	78
1983 Vosne-Romanée Les Chaumes	⑤	85
1983 Vosne-Romanée Les Suchots	⑤	86
1983 Vosne-Romanée Premier Cru	④	78

As the above scores indicate, Arnoux made good 1983s, but given a choice, I would opt for his line-up of 1980s and 1978s over these wines, if they can still be found. My main criticism of the Arnoux 1983s is that, with the possible exception of the Clos Vougeot and Vosne-Romanée Les Suchots and Les Chaumes, they are extremely tannic, perhaps to excess. From cask and from bottle, the Clos Vougeot looks to be the best. It has the deepest colour of all Arnoux's wines, with an exotic bouquet of toasty oak, licorice, and blackcurrants. Full-bodied, tannic, but balanced, it needs eight to ten years of cellaring. Next best, and usually the top wine from Arnoux, the Vosne-Romanée Les Suchots shows less complexity than the 1980 and 1978 did at a similar stage, but has a deep colour, hard tannin, plenty of power and fruit, and a dry finish. It needs seven to eight years to develop fully. Les Chaumes is also very good, but lacks dimension in flavour and depth compared to the Clos Vougeot and Les Suchots. Arnoux's two selections from Nuits St.-Georges are good, but given the reputation of Arnoux and the vintage, not terribly exciting wines. Les Poisets is deeper and more attractive, with a spicy blackcurrant fruitiness. The Les Corvées-Paget has less colour, is rather light, with an excess of tannin in the finish. Both the Vosne-Romanée and Vosne-Romanée Premier Cru share adequate colour, body, and depth, but are extremely harsh and astringent. I doubt seriously that the fruit can outlast the tannin.

1982 Bourgogne	②	**76**
1982 Clos Vougeot	⑤	**84**
1982 Nuits St.-Georges Les Corvées-Paget	④	**80**
1982 Nuits St.-Georges Les Poisets	④	**75**
1982 Romanée St.-Vivant	⑤	**84**
1982 Vosne-Romanée Les Chaumes	④	**80**
1982 Vosne-Romanée Les Suchots	④	**82**

All of these wines are sound, generally above-average examples of the 1982 vintage. Fruity, medium ruby wines with soft textures, decent concentration, the Nuits St.-Georges Les Poisets is the most tannic, angular, and charmless. The two best wines are the Clos Vougeot and Romanée St.-Vivant. The latter has broad, soft, raspberry fruit flavours with a nice touch of vanillin oakiness. It will make a fine bottle for drinking over the next one to two years, but at a very high price. The former wine, the Clos Vougeot, is elegant, rather light, medium-bodied, and soft, but effusively fruity, clean, and charming. Les Suchots is marked more by new oak, but is an agreeable, fruity wine.

BERNARD BACHELET *CHASSAGNE-MONTRACHET* ★★

This small estate in Chassagne-Montrachet makes both red and white Burgundy of good quality. Most consumers probably ignore the red wines for more prestigious appellations, but red wines from Chassagne-Montrachet indeed represent good values.

1983 Chassagne-Montrachet	③	**80**
1983 Côte de Beaune-Villages	③	**78**
1983 Santenay	③	**84**

These three wines exhibit the irregularity one finds in the 1983 vintage. The Côte de Beaune-Villages is quite alcoholic and big, with an aggressive finish. Rather awkward at the moment, it should be better in one to two years. The Chassagne-Montrachet has very fine colour, but suffers from an excessively high level of hard tannins, though the underdeveloped bouquet of leather and berry fruits hints at finer things. My favourite is the Santenay, a dark, rather tannic but full-bodied, rich, deep wine that provides the concentration of fruit to outlast the tannins. It needs four years.

BARTHOD NOËLLAT *CHAMBOLLE-MUSIGNY* ★ ★ ★

The elderly Monsieur Barthod is one of the tiny growers in Burgundy who makes good, natural, pure Pinot Noir wine that is unfiltered. He is rather aloof, perhaps even shy, but seems to warm up when sufficient interest is taken in his wines. His 1983s are full of charm and elegance, without the excess of tannin one so often finds in the wines of this vintage. He is also another viticulteur who succeeded admirably in overcoming the problems of both the 1982 and 1984 vintages and managed to make good wine. Barthod's winemaking style produces rather lightly coloured wines that are much more flavourful and rich than their colour suggests. His 1983s are likely to be drunk young because of their soft textures, although there is good tannin in the finish.

1983 Chambolle-Musigny .... ④ *84*
1983 Chambolle-Musigny Les Charmes .... ④ *86*
Both of these wines were rather light in colour, particularly for 1983s, but one whiff of the rather rich, complex, fruity, smoky, spicy bouquet leaves no doubt that some serious wine is in the glass. They are rather ripe, fat, fleshy wines with surprisingly soft tannins. The Les Charmes has more to it in both aroma and flavour. Somewhat hard to resist even at this early stage, but four to six years will reveal more pleasures.

ADRIAN BELLAND *SANTENAY* ★ ★ ★

I only wish more and more consumers wanting to enjoy reasonably priced red Burgundy would seek out the wines of Santenay. This sleepy little town is in the southern part of the Côte de Beaune and its treasures are a bevy of under-publicized wines and producers. When I visited Belland, I was struck by the quality of his wines and the reasonable prices. He makes a range of wines (even a Chambertin), but in 1983 most of his best came from the surrounding vineyards. His wines are deeply coloured, tannic, quite concentrated and full-bodied, and if they have a flaw at all, it is a lack of finesse. Nevertheless, these are Burgundies with flavour.

1983 Chambertin .... ⑤ *84*
1983 Corton Clos de la Vigne au Saint .... ④ *87*
1983 Corton Grèves .... ④ *80*
1983 Santenay .... ② *83*
1983 Santenay Les Gravières .... ③ *85*
The near-classic in this group is the lovely Corton Clos de la Vigne au Saint, which is a very rich, beautifully concentrated, full-bodied wine with an impressive, leathery, rich, plummy bouquet, and very long finish. The Santenay Les Gravières is also very good and quite a fine value given its quality. It has a big, toasty, spicy, rather full-blown bouquet, ripe, rich

flavours, deep colour, and a clean, moderately tannic finish. Neither of the aforementioned wines will be at their peaks before 1990. The Santenay is big and alcoholic, but very tannic, and though I have scored it high, I am concerned about the fruit/tannin balance. The Corton Grèves is the lightest, and while there is plenty to like – a leathery, spicy aroma, rich, alcoholic flavour – I believe there is an excess of tannin and a touch of rot in the taste that has also caused the colour to lighten. Belland makes some Chambertin, and the 1983 is quite good, smoky, rather light in colour, but rich and powerful, with plenty of alcohol. It is, however, too expensive.

DOMAINE GUY BERTHAUT *FIXIN* ★ ★ ★

Fixin is, of course, the little town that sits several kilometres north of Gevrey-Chambertin. The wines have always represented good values. Berthaut's wines are quite robustly styled, big, and rather forceful. He is quite an honest winemaker and willing to discuss problems he has had in a particular year. Interestingly, his 1983s tasted severe and dry, with traces of the ominous *'goût de sec'*. Berthaut's wines are rather modestly priced, but quite limited in availability. No filtering occurs at this estate.

1983 Fixin Les Arvelets	③	80
1983 Fixin Les Clos	③	78
1983 Fixin Les Crais	③	75
1983 Gevrey-Chambertin	④	78

All of these wines are terribly tannic in a rather severe way. Since they have not yet been bottled, additional egg white fining may help to soften the severe tastes, but with the exception of Les Arvelets, I just could not detect enough fruit to balance out the tannins. Perhaps ten years of cellaring will prove me wrong, but I think Berthaut's 1983s are real gambles.

1982 Fixin Clos d'Entre Deux Velles	③	85
1982 Fixin Les Arvelets	③	85
1982 Fixin Les Clos	②	84
1982 Fixin Les Crais	②	82
1982 Gevrey-Chambertin	③	75

Berthaut's production per acre was significantly less than most growers in 1982, and the results are wines that are deeply coloured, rich in ripe fruit, and quite well balanced. They are much better than his 1983s and are perfect examples of why vintage charts are not to be blindly relied upon. All of these wines, save for the mediocre, light, and diluted Gevrey-Chambertin, are rich, fruity, and delicious. They will all last four to six years minimum. The Les Arvelets is simply lovely, sweet, ripe, rich, and full-bodied, and will be a fine bottle of wine in four to five years. The Les Clos is nearly its equal, deeply coloured, a little bigger and more tannic, but shockingly deep for a 1982. The Clos d'Entre Deux Velles is the most precociously styled, with ripe, rich fruit, a fleshy fatness, and a lively, robust, leathery, and peppery bouquet.

DOMAINE BESANCENOT-MATHOUILLET *BEAUNE* ★★★
This small, well-run domaine right outside the walls of Beaune makes very elegant, fragrant, supple, silky, easy to enjoy wines from vineyards in the Côte de Beaune. In previous years (1979 and 1980) the wines tasted fully mature when released, but in 1983 Besancenot's wines will need four to five years to reach their peak. The two top wines tasted were very, very fine, exhibiting no signs of rot and showing excellent balance.

1983 Beaune Cent Vignes	③	**86**
1983 Beaune Clos du Roi	③	**85**

Both of these wines were quite impressive from the cask, showing rich, concentrated cherry fruit, spicy, fragrant bouquets, long, lush textures, and moderate, ripe, round tannins. They had a good measure of alcohol (13–13.5%), as do most 1983s, but were impeccably clean and well-made wines for drinking over the near future.

BICHOT-CLOS FRANTIN *BEAUNE* ★★★
This firm makes a lot of mediocre Burgundy, but at the top level its estate-bottled wines from the Domaine du Clos Frantin and Chablis from their estate called Long-Depaquit can be excellent. The 1983 reds from Clos Frantin are irregular, and will need time in the bottle to shed their tannins.

1983 Clos Vougeot	⑤	**87**
1983 Corton	④	**82**
1983 Echézeaux	④	**80**
1983 Gevrey-Chambertin	③	**75**
1983 Vosne-Romanée Malconsorts	④	**85**

The star here is the Clos Vougeot, which is ripe, rich, very tannic and well coloured. The Vosne-Romanée Malconsorts is more advanced but still in need of five to seven years of ageing. As for the other wines, the Gevrey-Chambertin is tough and severe, the Echézeaux, very tannic but light on the palate, and the Corton, very closed, dry, and rather astringent.

DOMAINE BILLARD-GONNET *POMMARD* ★★★
My experience with Billard-Gonnet's wines has been very young vintages, all of which have tasted rather tough, closed, and quite

backward. Not surprisingly, his 1983s were reserved and restrained wines obviously made for long-term cellaring. His Pommards looked to be the best, but if you are not willing to wait a minimum of ten years, then you had best seek out a more supple style of Burgundy from these pages.

1983 Beaune La Lune Montrevenots........................ ④ **72**
1983 Pommard.. ④ **80**
1983 Pommard Les Chaponnières........................... ⑤ **85**
1983 Pommard Les Rugiens .... ⑤ **86**

> The Beaune is very light in colour, has a pleasant bouquet, but tastes weak and simple on the palate. The Pommard is certainly a good run-of-the-mill wine, but lacks excitement and personality. The Pommard Les Chaponnières has considerably more personality, a dark ruby colour, a chocolate and spice box aroma, long, ripe, sufficiently deep flavours, but hard, rather dry tannins. It has the balance, but one must wait until 1995. The Pommard Les Rugiens is an even bigger, richer, more alcoholic wine, with considerable depth, flavour, and mouth-searing tannins. It may be ready by 1995.

LUCIEN BOILLOT *GEVREY-CHAMBERTIN* ★★★

There are a number of Boillots making wine in Burgundy. Lucien usually does a respectable job (his 1982s were lovely); however, the 1983s tasted were terribly tannic and astringent, and may be totally tainted by the rot and mildew that was such a problem for many winemakers in 1983. They have good colour, but are totally out of balance. The Nuits St.-Georges Les Pruliers is the best of an otherwise dreary lot of wines.

1983 Côte de Nuits-Villages .... ③ **62**
1983 Gevrey-Chambertin...................................... ④ **55**
1983 Gevrey-Chambertin Les Cherbandes .... ⑤ **75**
1983 Nuits St.-Georges Les Pruliers .... ⑤ **82**
1983 Pommard.. ④ **60**
1983 Volnay Les Angles .... ⑤ **70**

DOMAINE PIERRE BOURÉE *GEVREY-CHAMBERTIN* ★★★★

This has always been an intriguing *négociant* to follow. There is no Pierre Bourée, but instead a shy yet very professional Monsieur Vallet, who runs the operation. The wines of the Bourée firm have, justifiably so, a loyal following. Generally well coloured, chunky and slow to develop, I have always found them to be of a good level of quality, but stubbornly backward. This is a very traditionally run operation. The 1983s were bottled directly from the barrel (no assemblage to avoid barrel-to-barrel differences) and, thankfully, there was no flavour-stripping filtration. The firm is excited about the 1983s, which they claim are better than the 1978s. Quite a few wines are produced here, and while I tasted no great wines, I tasted quite a few good to very good wines.

Bourée • *Côte de Beaune*

1983 Beaune Premier Cru	③	84
1983 Bourgogne Passetout Grain	①	80
1983 Chassagne-Montrachet	③	80
1983 Corton	④	87
1983 Pernand-Vergelesses	③	80
1983 Santenay Gravières	③	87
1983 Volnay	③	79

As the above scores reflect, there is a greater range in quality in Bourée Côte de Beaune wines than those from the Côte de Nuits, where, of course, the firm is based. The two stars from the Côte de Beaune are the wonderful Santenay Gravières and the powerful Corton. The Santenay Gravières may ultimately merit a higher score. It was among the very finest Santenays I tasted and could clearly hold its own against many Grand Cru red Burgundies. Fleshy, deeply coloured with rich, ripe, concentrated fruit, it should prove to be a real eye-opener between 1995 and 2000. The Corton is equally impressive, perhaps a trifle more rustic, alcoholic, and powerful, but very, very fine, and again having enough fruit to outlast the tannins. Like the Santenay, 1990–2000 should be this wine's glory years.

Bourée • *Côte de Nuits*

1983 Bonnes Mares	⑤	86
1983 Chambertin	⑤	85
1983 Chambolle-Musigny	④	74
1983 Charmes-Chambertin	④	84
1983 Clos Vougeot	⑤	87
1983 Côte de Nuits-Villages	②	83
1983 Echézeaux	⑤	87
1983 Gevrey-Chambertin Clos de la Justice	④	88
1983 Gevrey-Chambertin Premier Cru	④	86
1983 Latricières-Chambertin	⑤	84
1983 Morey St.-Denis	④	84
1983 Nuits St.-Georges	④	78
1983 Vosne-Romanée	④	78

The Bourée firm produces an extensive range of red Burgundies from the Côte de Nuits, as the above list reflects. In 1983 the quality here was quite consistently good. The *villages* or commune wines, Morey St.-Denis, Vosne-Romanée, Nuits St.-Georges, Chambolle-Musigny, and so on, are what one expects. The Morey is much better than the others; the

Chambolle-Musigny too dry and severe and perhaps affected by the hail that hit this commune. Certainly, the Gevrey-Chambertin Clos de la Justice, always one of Bourée's best wines, is especially rich, tannic, full-bodied, and concentrated in 1983. Its smoky, plummy, earthy bouquet and big, rich flavours beg for five to seven years of cellaring. The Gevrey-Chambertin Premier Cru is almost as good, more supple, but rich, savoury, fat, and quite forward-tasting. It should be at its best in four to five years. Curiously, the Grand Cru Latricières-Chambertin is less rich than the Clos de la Justice or Premier Cru. Nevertheless, it is quite flavourful, robust and in need of three to six years of cellaring. The Clos Vougeot is excellent, with a rich bouquet of berry fruit, some toasty, vanillin oakiness, long, deep, rich flavours, immense body, and very good length. It will be excellent in 1990–1995. Both the Echézeaux and Bonnes Mares are rather atypical 1983s in that they are surprisingly light in colour, very lush and accessible, and should be ready to drink soon, say in three to four years. Both are lovely wines with the bouquet of the Echézeaux particularly fine. The Charmes-Chambertin looked and felt promising, but was quite closed, and the Chambertin was alcoholic, fat, spicy, long in the finish, but rather forward. I suspect it will be ready by 1990–1992. Lastly, don't overlook Bourée's Côte de Nuits-Villages, which in 1983 is like previous renditions of this wine, always a good value and one of the better wines of its type. It should be drunk over the next two to three years.

L. J. BRUCK *NUITS ST.-GEORGES* ★ ★ ★

A medium-sized *négociant* in Nuits St.-Georges, this firm produces wines that are generally well coloured, tannic, and firm, but perhaps a little dry and dull. The wines from vineyards in Nuits St.-Georges and Gevrey-Chambertin have been, in my opinion, the best.

1983 Chambolle-Musigny	④	68
1983 Côte de Nuits-Villages	③	80
1983 Echézeaux	⑤	84
1983 Gevrey-Chambertin	④	81
1983 Gevrey-Chambertin Lavoux St.-Jacques	⑤	85
1983 Hautes Côte de Nuits	②	78
1983 Nuits St.-Georges Corvées-Pagets	⑤	86

One sees the house style in all of these Burgundies, from the lower-priced Hautes Côte de Nuits to the Echézeaux. The wines have good colour, full body, some tough tannin, but a trace of dullness. The Nuits St.-Georges Corvées-Pagets, aged in 100% new oak barrels, is a big, forceful, rich, ripe wine with plenty of concentration, and a big, alcoholic finish. It certainly was the best of the red wines I tasted from Bruck. The Gevrey-Chambertin Lavaux St.-Jacques also stood out for having the requisite richness of fruit to balance out the hard tannins of the 1983 vintage. The expensive Echézeaux is well made, perhaps a little too alcoholic, but tasty and rather precociously styled.

ALAIN BURGUET *GEVREY-CHAMBERTIN* ★★★

This small grower only makes a Gevrey-Chambertin, but it is usually quite concentrated and powerful, and for a straight *village* appellation wine, perhaps the best one can find.

1983 Gevrey-Chambertin .... ④ **72**
1982 Gevrey-Chambertin .... ④ **83**
1981 Gevrey-Chambertin .... ④ **80**

The highly touted 1983 vintage has produced a wine that is quite darkly coloured but abrasively tannic. Ten years of cellaring is the bare minimum, but will the fruit hold? In contrast, the forward, rich, ripe, fruity 1982 has oodles of berry fruit, good spice and colour, and can be drunk over the next four years. The 1981 is tannic and has power, but lacks elegance and charm.

CHAMPY PÈRE *BEAUNE* ★★★

This is the oldest *négociant* in all of Burgundy, dating from 1720. The 1983s I tasted were not that impressive, but acceptable, save for the Clos Vougeot. They seemed to be made in a rather old, heavy style.

1983 Beaune Avaux .... ④ **83**
1983 Clos Vougeot .... ⑤ **75**
1983 Savigny Dominode... ③ **78**

Considering how very successful the wines of Clos Vougeot were in 1983, I was surprised by the lack of quality apparent in this bottle, which was good but not special. The Savigny Dominode is robust and beefy, a solid, rather heavy, rustic sort of wine which should be at its best in 1990. The Beaune Avaux was the best of these Champy wines. It had a vivid bouquet of cherry fruit and oak, a full-bodied texture, and twelve years of evolution ahead of it.

DOMAINE DE LA CHARRIÈRE *SANTENAY* ★★★

The wines from this estate are another example of why consumers should take more notice of the good values that emanate from Santenay. Monsieur Girardin makes solid wines at this estate that are chunky, robust, deeply fruity, and ageworthy.

1983 Santenay La Combe .... ③ **85**
1983 Santenay Maladière .... ③ **85**
 Both of these wines are quite robust, well coloured, fleshy, and ripe. They should age well for up to a decade. The Maladière has more interest to its aroma and flavour. It is hard to find Burgundies of this quality for this price.

1982 Santenay .... ② **78**
1982 Santenay Clos Roussot .... ③ **81**
 The *village* Santenay is round, gentle, light, and pleasant. The Clos Roussot has more flavour and character. Both should be drunk soon.

JEAN CHAUVENET *NUITS ST.-GEORGES* ★ ★ ★

This moderate-sized grower located just north of Nuits St.-Georges makes very elegant, medium-bodied wines that are well balanced and clean. Based on the vintages I have tasted in the 1980s, his wines are best drunk within the first five to six years, but the more tannic 1983s are likely to require longer. Chauvenet also made above-average quality wines in both 1984 and 1982. His best wine looks to be consistently the Les Vaucrains, the Premier Cru Nuits St.-Georges. Chauvenet does not filter his wines.

1983 Mazis-Chambertin .... ⑤ **87**
1983 Nuits St.-Georges .... ③ **83**
1983 Nuits St.-Georges La Perrière .... ④ **83**
1983 Nuits St.-Georges Les Vaucrains .... ④ **85**
1983 Vosne-Romanée .... ④ **81**
 Chauvenet's Vosne-Romanée and Nuits St.-Georges are rather understated but graceful wines, yet typical of his winemaking style. They should drink well within the first four years of life, but will not be for the long term. The Nuits St.-Georges La Perrière has more weight and richness but in effect is still on the charming lighter side for a 1983. The Mazis-Chambertin Nuits St.-Georges Les Vaucrains has the broadest and most expansive flavours, shows very good winemaking, some subtle, smoky notes, and firm tannins. Both should be at their best by 1990 and hold for five to seven years thereafter.

1982 Nuits St.-Georges .... ③ **78**
1982 Nuits St.-Georges Les Vaucrains .... ④ **85**
 Chauvenet's 1982 Les Vaucrains is every bit as good as his 1983. Softer and quite ready to drink, it is a very classy, supple wine with a smooth, broad, gentle berry fruitiness, some subtle, spicy oak, and a good finish. The Nuits St.-Georges is pleasant, cleanly made, but a little too simple and bland.

ROBERT CHEVILLON *NUITS ST.-GEORGES* ★★★★

Robert Chevillon has, since 1978, clearly established his domaine as one of the very finest in the Cote d'Or. If one were to judge the 1983 vintage by his wines, then all the hoopla and hype would be totally justified. His 1983s are marvellous and among the very finest and best-balanced wines of this overrated vintage. His 1982s are especially good for the vintage.

1983 Nuits St.-Georges	④	*81*
1983 Nuits St.-Georges La Perrière	⑤	*87*
1983 Nuits St.-Georges Les Cailles	⑤	*86*
1983 Nuits St.-Georges Les Saint Georges	⑤	*90*
1983 Nuits St.-Georges Les Vaucrains	⑤	*88*

One wishes that all producers of red Burgundy had been as successful as Chevillon in 1983. The wines from La Perrière Les Vaucrains, and Les Saint Georges are rich and intense, pure and clean, and show no evidence of rot or hail damage. The colours are dark, the bouquets explosive, and the length and balance truly superb. They are bigger and much more full-bodied than usual, with a powerful alcoholic clout. Expect these three wines to be at their best between 1992 and 2000. As the scores note, the Les Saint Georges is one of the great wines of this vintage. As for the other 1983s, Les Cailles is slightly tougher and more tannic and I have less confidence that it will hit the heights of Chevillon's other wines. The *village* wine is good, a little stern and unyielding, but well made.

1982 Nuits St.-Georges	③	*78*
1982 Nuits St.-Georges La Perrière	④	*80*
1982 Nuits St.-Georges Les Roncières	④	*81*
1982 Nuits St.-Georges Les Saint Georges	④	*83*
1982 Nuits St.-Georges Les Vaucrains	④	*88*

All of these wines are above average 1982s except for Les Vaucrains, which is very good. Les Vaucrains has an open-knit, smoky, spicy, marvellous bouquet, a ripe raspberry fruitiness, good body, and a round, gentle finish. It should be drunk over the next two to three years. Chevillon's other 1982s are lighter in weight yet generally ready for consumption, since they are only moderately concentrated and have light, soft tannins.

BRUNO CLAIR *MARSANNAY* ★★★★

I doubt that many Burgundy-lovers spend much time in Marsannay, the tiny village between Dijon and Fixin that is known for producing Burgundy's best rosé wine. This new domaine was started in 1979 by Bruno Clair after he left the famous Domaine Clair-Daü because of a family squabble. The young Bruno Clair is a very serious winemaker. His 1984s are quite good and the few 1983s he made even more noteworthy. There is also a little bit of a white Fixin made here from Pinot Blanc that is outstanding for its quality and low price. The 1985s here are marvellous.

1983 Bourgogne	③	*82*
1983 Fixin La Colle Blanche	③	*84*
1983 Morey St.-Denis	③	*81*
1983 Savigny-Les-Beaune Dominode	④	*88*

One look at the scores might cause some to think there is a typo for the Savigny 'Dominode'. But, yes, the darkly coloured wine does merit the score. It is extremely powerful, dense, rich, full-bodied wine with plenty of tannin and a great finish. Clair told me it was made from 80-year-old vines. It will need eight to ten years of cellaring. The Fixin La Colle Blanche may suffer in comparison, but it is a rich, beefy, ripe, very well-made wine that should be ready in four to five years. The Morey St.-Denis is above average, but a little tough and perhaps excessively tannic. The generic Bourgogne is one of the best of its type, fruity, fat, clean and very attractive, for drinking over the next several years.

DOMAINE CLAIR-DAÜ *MARSANNAY* ★★★★

Between 1971 and 1980 this estate produced quite mediocre wines that in no way merited the price demanded for them nor reflected the excellent reputation this very important domaine had in the sixties. Several 1970s tasted recently were extremely rich, fine wines. Well, the 1983s were among the finest red Burgundies I sampled. Rich in colour and extract, there was none of the *'goût de sec'* or *'goût de moisi'* (dryness or musty flavours) that taints many 1983 red Burgundies. The prices for the Clair-Daü 1983s seem reasonable, given the quality, and I urge readers to try these wines as examples of some of the best 1983s I saw. In 1985, the Clair-Daü firm was purchased by the large, important Beaune *négociant,* Louis Jadot.

1983 Bonnes Mares	⑤	*90*
1983 Bourgogne	①	*83*
1983 Chambertin Clos de Bèze	⑤	*89*
1983 Chambolle-Musigny Les Amoureuses	⑤	*88*
1983 Chapelle-Chambertin	⑤	*86*
1983 Clos Vougeot	⑤	*87*
1983 Gevrey-Chambertin Clos de Fonteny	④	*86*
1983 Gevrey-Chambertin Clos St.-Jacques	⑤	*85*
1983 Gevrey-Chambertin Les Cazetiers	④	*89*
1983 Vosne-Romanée Champs Perdrix	⑤	*85*

It is easy to start with superlatives concerning the 1983 Clair-Daü wines, certainly this domaine's best vintage since 1970. All of the wines have excellent colour and clean, ripe Pinot Noir aromas. They all possess various degrees of rich, fat character, good, ripe tannins, and very good to great depth. Most of the 1983 Clair-Daü wines should reach maturity between 1990 and 1995. The Bourgogne is very good value. At the top level, the Bonnes Mares was dense, ripe, rich, and close to being spectacular. It already had a hauntingly great perfume. The Chambertin Clos de Bèze and Gevrey-Chambertin Les Cazetiers are both strong, robust, alcoholic, rich wines; they have powerful bouquets, deep colours, layers of Pinot Noir fruit and a total absence of any taste or smell of rot. The Chambolle-Musigny Les Amoureuses is notable for its sheer elegance and lush seductiveness; it is named appropriately in 1983. The Clos Vougeot is a very big wine, perhaps a little rustic and overblown in size and weight, but if it reveals some finesse with bottle ageing, it could well prove to be outstanding. Of all these wines, the Chapelle-Chambertin and Clos St.-Jacques have the lightest colour and appear to be the two wines (along with the Bourgogne) that should mature fully before 1990. Both are still packed with fruit and are simply more precocious than the others. The Clair-Daü 1983s were extremely exciting wines to taste and mark a return of this domaine to being one of the leaders in Burgundy.

DOMAINE GEORGE CLERGET *VOUGEOT* ★★★

There are several Clergets in Burgundy, but to my knowledge, this is the only one from the Côte de Nuits. My only experiences with this estate's wines were the five different 1983s. The wines were rather good, with surprisingly rich, deep colours and enough fruit to stand up to the tannins.

1983 Bourgogne	③	*82*
1983 Chambolle-Musigny	④	*82*
1983 Chambolle-Musigny Les Charmes	⑤	*86*
1983 Echézeaux	⑤	*88*
1983 Vosne-Romanée La Violette	④	*84*

All of these wines have surprisingly deep colours and show none of the bitter, harsh, dry, dusty tannins that frequently show up elsewhere. The simple Bourgogne is inexpensive and offers robust, ripe, plummy fruit. It should be drunk over the next one to two years. I liked it as much as the Chambolle-Musigny, which is a solid, chunky, fruity wine but, for its appellation, lacks a little complexity. The Vosne-Romanée La Violette is a rather rich, fat, moderately tannic wine with good concentration, clean, pure Pinot Noir flavours, and five to six years of development ahead of it. The two best wines are the Chambolle-Musigny Les Charmes, which is quite concentrated, chewy and rich, with full body and a deep, dark colour, and the Echézeaux, a dark ruby-coloured wine that has rich cassis and plum-like fruit, medium to full body, and a lingering finish. It should be at its best between 1988 and 1995.

DOMAINE EDMOND CORNU *LADOIX* ★★★

The tall, lean Edmond Cornu is not yet one of Burgundy's best-known producers. I have followed his wines since 1981; they are very good quality and are reasonably priced. His wines are generally from Burgundy's least-known appellations of Chorey-Les-Beaune, Ladoix, and Savigny, but as any connoisseur knows, this is where the values are. He did not produce great 1983s—few producers did—but he did make very attractive wines.

1983 Aloxe-Corton	③	85
1983 Aloxe-Corton Les Moutottes	④	83
1983 Chorey-Les-Beaune	③	83
1983 Corton Bressandes	④	87
1983 Ladoix	④	84
1983 Savigny-Les-Beaune	③	82

The obvious star from Cornu's 1983 wines is the Corton Bressandes. It is a powerful wine, rich in colour and extract, with layers of ripe fruit, and good, firm, but not astringent tannins. However, it will need eight to ten years of cellaring. Those who cannot defer their gratification would be better advised to try the less expensive Chorey-Les-Beaune, with its bouquet of leather and cherries, medium body, and good, clean fruit, or the spicy, cherry-scented, medium-bodied Ladoix. Two tough, tannic customers are the Savigny-Les-Beaune, which may turn out to be too tannic for its own good, although it seems to have ample fruit, and the Aloxe-Corton Les Moutottes, a leathery, spicy yet hard, très dur wine, as the French say. The Aloxe-Corton is a contrast to these two wines, almost jammy with rather deep, alcoholic, rich flavours. It needs five to eight years.

ALBERT DEREY *MARSANNAY* ★★

A little-known, yet from what I have seen, competent producer of red Burgundy; this man's wines are generally quite reasonably priced.

1983 Bourgogne Coteaux de Couchey	②	83
1983 Bourgogne Les Vignes Marie	②	81
1983 Fixin	②	60

The two generic wines represent good values for Burgundy. The Les Vignes Marie is a good, medium-bodied, somewhat robust, earthy wine for drinking over the next one to two years. It has plenty of appeal. The Coteaux de Couchey is somewhat of a sleeper in this vintage of mixed results. Supple, ripe, rather broad Pinot Noir flavours show good depth, an alcoholic punch, and some complexity. It is best drunk over the next one to two years. The Fixin had an orange rim and a smell of rot. It is a real risk.

JOSEPH DROUHIN *BEAUNE* ★★★★

This popular firm in Beaune has a large international following. After slumping a bit in the early 1970s, the wines have recently been back to top form. As a general rule, I prefer the Drouhin white wines to the red, but the red wines are well made, very clean, generally elegant, medium-bodied, well-balanced, and ready to drink within five to seven years. The 1983s were given an intense filtration, no doubt because many of them are sold to American restaurants, where one is unlikely to find many who understand the virtues of sediment.

1983 Beaune Clos des Mouches	⑤	**86**
1983 Chambolle-Musigny	④	**80**
1983 Chambolle-Musigny Les Amoureuses..............	⑤	**84**
1983 Clos Vougeot	⑤	**87**
1983 Griottes-Chambertin...............................	⑤	**82**
1983 Santenay	③	**81**
1983 Vosne-Romanée Les Suchots...........................	⑤	**82**

The Santenay is a spicy, fruity, medium-weight wine that has a good finish but little excitement. It should be at its best in two to three years. The red Beaune Clos des Mouches, always one of this firm's best wines, has a moderately deep colour, a lovely ripe cherry and spicy oak bouquet, good flavour concentration, and moderate tannins. It should be at its best between 1988 and 1995. The Chambolle-Musigny has some very dusty, astringent tannins and a very dry finish. It has plenty of fruit, but I sensed a touch of rot. The Clos Vougeot, absurdly costly, was clearly the star, although not a great wine – only priced that way. It had a dark ruby colour, excellent fat, sweet fruit, full body and a rich, long finish. It should peak between 1990 and 2000. The Vosne-Romanée Les Suchots lacked balance, seemed awkward, its colour seemed light, and the tannins were very hard and severe. The Chambolle-Musigny Les Amoureuses was somewhat perplexing to evaluate. It had very good colour, ripe, rich fruitiness and good body, but once again, very astringent, almost bitter tannins. I liked it, but one will have to wait seven to eight years for it to mature. The Griottes-Chambertin seems to have a *'goût de sec'* very severe, and is very astringent in the finish without sufficient underlying fruit.

DROUHIN-LAROSE *GEVREY-CHAMBERTIN* ★★★★

This is a very wealthy estate – its cellars well hidden by large iron gates (monitored 24 hours by cameras) – in the town of Gevrey-Chambertin. Bernard Drouhin, the cocky, self-assured owner, feels no one makes better wine than he does, and for that reason prices his wines accordingly. The style of wine here is hardly classic, but one which produces rich, alcoholic, fat wines with plenty of fragrance, body, sweetness, and colour. They are hedonistic rather than classic wines. Unfortunately, Bernard Drouhin recently began to filter the wines that are sent to America because it is 'the safe thing to do'. By his own admission, the 1983 vintage is 'great because the journalists said it was'. Outspoken Drouhin prefers his 1980s and 1978s. For the record, his 1983s are quite good, with the Clos de Bèze quite outstanding.

1983 Bonnes Mares	⑤	**78**
1983 Chambertin Clos de Bèze	⑤	**89**
1983 Chapelle-Chambertin	⑤	**85**
1983 Clos Vougeot	⑤	**87**
1983 Gevrey-Chambertin	⑤	**87**

With the exception of the Clos Vougeot and Chambertin Clos de Bèze, the 1983s from Drouhin-Larose were light in colour but, surprisingly, had broad flavours. The Gevrey-Chambertin is a good, ripe, round wine that will be ready in one to two years. The Chapelle-Chambertin has plenty of clean, supple, ripe berry fruitiness, an attractive, oaky note in the bouquet, and a long, sweet finish. It should be ready in four to five years. The Clos Vougeot is much darker in colour with an intense perfume of vanillin oak and raspberries. Long, rich, deep and moderately tannic, it should be ready by 1990–1992. The Bonnes Mares had a slight taste of rot and dry bitterness in the finish. Light in colour with dusty tannins, it shows all the warning signs of having been afflicted by both rot and hail. The Chambertin Clos de Bèze ('la fleur de la cave') of Drouhin-Larose is a wonderful wine, long, ripe, succulent, rich and fruity, with excellent depth and a great finish. It should be ready by 1990–1992.

DOMAINE DUJAC *MOREY ST.-DENIS* ★★★★

This is one of my favourite estates in Burgundy. The wines are filled with ripe, rich Pinot Noir fruit and aromas but are never heavy or overly chaptalized. The colour of the Dujac wines is never very dark, even in years such as 1978, and the wines have never been filtered, so they must be shipped and stored properly because they are very much alive. It is no secret that this estate did not have the success in 1983 that one might have expected. Jacques Seysses was apprehensive about the rampant rot in the vineyards and pulled the skins off the macerating grape juice very quickly in order to avoid the taste of rot in his wines. Consequently, the wines are less coloured than other 1983s. They are, however, certainly very, very good. With respect to the 1982s, Dujac was extremely successful, and along with the Domaine de la Romanée-Conti, produced what must certainly be the best wines of the vintage.

1983 Bonnes Mares..	⑤	86
1983 Clos de la Roche....................................	⑤	86
1983 Clos St.-Denis..	⑤	85
1983 Gevrey-Chambertin Les Combottes................	⑤	85
1983 Morey St.-Denis.....................................	⑤	82

No doubt the Bonnes Mares, the best of Dujac's 1983s, will be impossible to obtain for only two barrels, or 50 cases, were produced. It is a very fragrant, richly perfumed wine with only a medium ruby colour, but with long, spicy flavours suggestive of berry fruit and cinnamon. Some firm tannins are present, so expect the Bonnes Mares to be at its peak by 1992–1995. The same can be said for the very fine Clos St.-Denis and Gevrey-Chambertin Les Combottes. The Clos St.-Denis is Dujac's darkest-coloured 1983, has a rich, ripe, deep, fruity texture, medium to full body, and a long finish. The Gevrey-Chambertin Les Combottes is extremely spicy on the nose, with big, rich, alcoholic flavours and a powerful finish. The Morey St.-Denis tasted much less complex and serious than the other wines and appears to be quite precocious, perhaps ready to drink by 1987. The Clos de la Roche is undoubtedly very good, but rather closed, quite tannic, and unyielding. It should be given at least five to seven years of cellaring. For the moment, I prefer the 1982 Clos de la Roche.

1982 Clos de la Roche.....................................	⑤	89
1982 Clos St.-Denis..	⑤	85
1982 Gevrey-Chambertin Les Combottes................	⑤	84

Jacques Seysses was one of only a handful of growers to make a rosé wine by running off some of the juice from the bloated Pinot Noir grapes. The result was that he got more concentration in his red wines, which are among the very best 1982s. The Clos de la Roche is quite excellent. Ready to drink now but capable of improving for two to five years, it is loaded with spicy, earthy, rich berry fruit, and has a succulent sweetness and long finish. The Gevrey-Chambertin Les Combottes is not so concentrated, but is very spicy, fragrant, and fruity, and should be drunk over the next one to two years. The Clos St.-Denis is richly fruity, medium-bodied, sweet, fat, and altogether charming and elegant.

DOMAINE RENÉ ENGEL *VOSNE-ROMANÉE* ★★★
This estate has been highly regarded for some time. The 1983s are good rather than exciting or great. The wines here are filtered.

1983 Clos Vougeot	④	**84**
1983 Echézeaux	⑤	**85**
1983 Grands-Echézeaux	⑤	**84**
1983 Vosne-Romanée	④	**78**
1983 Vosne-Romanée Les Brûlées	④	**75**

Given the vineyards that this domaine owns, one would have expected a greater level of quality. However, the Clos Vougeot is certainly fine with a rich, sweet texture, very good depth, a spicy, leathery, jammy bouquet, and five to eight years of ageing potential. Both the Grands-Echézeaux and Echézeaux have a lovely, rich, sweet fruitiness, medium body, and lush texture, but also a trace of hard, dry astringent tannins that are due to the rot. They have plenty of appeal and character, but they are not sure bets. The Vosne-Romanée Les Brûlées has even more noticeable rot in its flavours. As for the straight Vosne-Romanée, it is supple and fruity, with a very attractive colour. It should be drunk over the next two to three years.

FAIVELEY *NUITS ST.-GEORGES* ★★★★★
This moderate-sized firm in Nuits St.-Georges is unquestionably the most underrated producer of great red Burgundy. Most consumers probably don't realize that while Faiveley is a *négociant*, 85% of the wines they produce come from their own vineyards, which are some of the best in the Cote d'Or. The business is now run by François Faiveley, a young man in his mid-thirties who is meticulous and conservative. His father, the jovial Guy, still provides assistance. Faiveley refuses to filter his wines, refuses to shorten the long barrel-ageing period, and refuses to make a commercial Burgundy that is fully mature by age three or four, and comatose by age six. These are lusty, rich, powerful, full-bodied wines that, quite truthfully, are among the very finest made. They age magnificently. Importers who do not ship these unfiltered, natural wines in temperature-controlled containers and store them properly are doing both Faiveley and their clients a great injustice. The 1981s of this firm are excellent, by far the best wines I tasted from this vintage in Burgundy. In richness and strength, they are superior to many

producers' 1983s. They make a joke of any vintage chart. The 1982s are typically soft but generally much better than most producers'; the 1983s look to be outstanding. Burgundy-lovers, take note; Faiveley may be your best bet.

1983 Chambertin Clos de Bèze .... ⑤ **90**
1983 Clos Vougeot .... ⑤ **89**
1983 Corton Clos des Cortons .... ⑤ **87**
1983 Gevrey-Chambertin Combe aux Moines .... ⑤ **88**
1983 Gevrey-Chambertin Les Cazetiers .... ⑤ **87**
1983 Mazis-Chambertin .... ⑤ **89**
1983 Nuits St.-Georges Clos de la Maréchale .... ④ **85**

None of the Faiveley 1983s show signs of the astringent, dry tannins and mouldy flavours caused by rot. They are very powerful, rich, deep, tannic wines that ideally need eight to ten years of cellaring. The firm regards them very highly. The Gevrey-Chambertin Les Cazetiers and Combe aux Moines are very brawny, fleshy, rich and tannic, full-bodied wines and have excellent underlying sweetness and length. The colours are dark, but the Combe aux Moines is the darker. These two wines may deserve a higher score in 1995 when they reach maturity. The Nuits St.-Georges Clos de la Maréchale has plenty of rich, meaty fruitiness, a heady alcoholic content, wonderful texture, and firm tannins. One must wait until 1990–1992. The Corton was very closed on the nose, but dark in colour, with a very big framework; it will need plenty of time. The Clos Vougeot is one of the richest and biggest wines of Faiveley's 1983s. With great depth of flavour and length, it has plenty of alcohol, rich, round tannins, and an exceptional finish. It needs a decade of cellaring. The Mazis-Chambertin has a bouquet of leather and berry fruit, great density, an explosive fruitiness, and superb length. The Chambertin Clos de Bèze has even more. Huge, powerful, dense, and rich, it is truly a great red Burgundy from the 1983 vintage. These wines are among the very finest produced in 1983. Bravo!

1982 Chambertin Clos de Bèze .... ⑤ **87**
1982 Corton Clos des Corton (Tastevinage) .... ⑤ **86**
1982 Fixin (Tastevinage) .... ③ **84**
1982 Gevrey-Chambertin Combe aux Moines
(Tastevinage) .... ④ **86**
1982 Gevrey-Chambertin Les Cazetiers .... ④ **85**
1982 Mercurey .... ② **84**
1982 Nuits St.-Georges Clos de la Maréchale .... ④ **85**
1982 Nuits St.-Georges Les Saints Georges .... ④ **86**

I am not a great admirer of the 1982 vintage for red Burgundy. The wines are generally quite watery, but there are some notable exceptions. The DRC, Dujac, the Leclerc brothers, Georges Mugneret, and Faiveley have done better jobs than just about everyone else. These eight wines will please anybody. They are ready to drink, but will last for at least one to two more years. They have some real depth. The Fixin and Mercurey are very good value, the two wines from Nuits St.-Georges surprisingly big and rich. The Clos de la Maréchale has a smoky, ripe Pinot nose, and lovely, round flavours. The Les Saint Georges is dominated more by the smell of new oak barrels, has some tannin to lose, but is quite good. Both Les Cazetiers and Combe aux Moines are extraordinarily deep, with the latter wine showing a significant concentration of ripe fruit and full body. The Clos des Cortons actually needs three to four years to reveal its big fleshy character. Lastly, the firm's top wine is the Chambertin Clos de Bèze. It is a deeply scented, rich, full-bodied, particularly concentrated wine in 1982. It will drink well for at least four to five years. I am amazed by how good these 1982s are.

1981 Chambertin Clos de Bèze	⑤	90
1981 Chambolle-Musigny	④	85
1981 Charmes-Chambertin	⑤	88
1981 Clos Vougeot	⑤	87
1981 Côte de Nuits-Villages (Tastevinage)	③	84
1981 Echézeaux	⑤	85
1981 Gevrey-Chambertin	④	85
1981 Gevrey-Chambertin Les Cazetiers	④	87
1981 Latricières-Chambertin	⑤	88
1981 Morey St.-Denis	④	85

The quality Faiveley obtained in 1981 is hard to believe. Some of the wines are better than many producers' 1983s. The 1981 is not a good vintage for red Burgundy, but Faiveley made exceptional wines that, quite frankly, overwhelm anything else I have tasted from this vintage. I urge retailers and consumers to try these wines and compare them against the likes of the DRC, Leclerc, Maume, whomever you want. They have no qualitative peers in 1981. Start with the smoky, spicy Côtes de Nuits-Villages that tastes like it came from Gevrey-Chambertin. This is a rich, fruity wine that will drink well for three to four years. The Gevrey-Chambertin is similarly styled, only bigger and more concentrated. Less virile but more elegant and charming is the Chambolle-Musigny, which has broad, pure, sweet Pinot Noir flavours. It is supple and will drink well over the next three to four years. The Morey St.-Denis is softer, quite deep, rich and fruity, and a real crowd-pleaser. The surprises continue with the Gevrey-

Chambertin Les Cazetiers, which is big, rich, deep, smoky, full-bodied, and so flavourful that one would never guess it was a 1981. If I sound enthusiastic, I was stunned by the quality of Faiveley's 1981s. The Latricières-Chambertin is a powerful wine, full-bodied, spicy, rich, with extremely long, pure flavours, and a lovely balance. It will drink well for five to eight years. The story is the same for the Clos Vougeot. Not smoky or spicy like the wines from Gevrey-Chambertin, it possesses full-blown, ripe, rich, fleshy, berry fruitiness, full body, super length, and five to ten years of ageing potential. As good as the Echézeaux is, it suffered in comparison with the other Faiveley Grand Cru wines. The Charmes-Chambertin also is a full-bodied, ripe, rich, very flavourful wine with considerable character. It will be at its best between 1988–1995. Lastly, the Chambertin Clos de Bèze is a powerhouse of a wine; its aromas of fresh leather, berry fruit, and exotic spices are top-notch. Quite big, full-bodied and deep, this superb wine should be drunk between 1990 and 2000. This unbelievably fine line of 1981 red Burgundies must be tasted to be believed.

DOMAINE HENRI GOUGES *NUITS ST.-GEORGES* ★★

This famous and important estate historically produced some of the finest red Burgundies in the Côte d'Or. However, the wines of the seventies slipped considerably in quality, and in good vintages like 1971, 1976 and 1978 the wines have looked strikingly pale and tasted meagerly endowed when compared to their peers. I know Michel Gouges and his son Christian well, having visited them on three different occasions; therefore, it is all the more difficult to say that I do not believe their wines are nearly as concentrated and as rich as they should be. Nevertheless, I write for the consumer, not the wine trade, and that is my opinion. The 1983s are quite frankly very light in colour and seem also lacking in concentration except for the Les Saints Georges. The 1984s also were rather weak. Gouges does filter his wines, perhaps too aggressively. This famous old firm, whose wines of the sixties still remain superb, has sadly dropped in quality significantly since 1970.

1983 Nuits St.-Georges	③	**72**
1983 Nuits St.-Georges Les Chaignots	④	**75**
1983 Nuits St.-Georges Les Porets	④	**75**
1983 Nuits St.-Georges Les Pruliers	④	**80**
1983 Nuits St.-Georges Les Saints Georges	⑤	**86**
1983 Nuits St.-Georges Les Vaucrains	⑤	**83**

The only wines of interest here are Les Vaucrains and Les Saints Georges. The other four wines have the colour of most

1982s, and lack richness and concentration. The Les Vaucrains is quite good, has medium ruby colour, and should be at its peak by 1992. The Les Saints Georges is deep ruby in colour, has a concentrated richness to it, and is clearly the best wine Gouges made in 1983. Expect it to be fully mature by 1992.

MACHARD DE GRAMONT *NUITS ST.-GEORGES* ★ ★ ★ ★
This estate has been going through a family dispute, the vineyards being divided among family members. The 1983s are the first Machard de Gramont wines I have seen since the excellent 1978s and 1979s. These are very good, deeply coloured, richly fruity wines that are quite well made.

1983 Nuits St.-Georges Les Damodes .... ④ **85**
1983 Nuits St.-Georges Les Hauts-Pruliers .... ④ **84**
1983 Nuits St.-Georges La Perrière Noblot .... ④ **84**
1983 Pommard Clos Blanc .... ⑤ **86**

If none of these wines can be called outstanding, they can certainly be considered very good. Dark in colour with no trace of rot or hail damage, these plummy, rather chunky wines have good tannins and fleshy textures. The Pommard Clos Blanc is the richest and deepest and suggests that it needs five to six years to reach its prime. The Nuits St.-Georges Les Damodes is similarly styled, a little more lush and less tannic. Both the Nuits St.-Georges Perrière and Hauts-Pruliers have the same house style, but are slightly less elegant and complex.

DOMAINE JEAN GROS *VOSNE-ROMANÉE* ★ ★ ★ ★
Madame Gros is the mayor of Vosne-Romanée in addition to looking after this highly respected domaine. The 1983s here have very fine colour, a silky, lush richness wrapped in a velvet, but firm, glove. As the notes below indicate, two of the Gros wines are very special.

1983 Hautes Côtes de Nuits .... ② *81*
1983 Richebourg .... ⑤ **90**
1983 Vosne-Romanée .... ④ **84**
1983 Vosne-Romanée Clos des Réas .... ④ **90**

The Hautes Côtes de Nuits is a pleasant, soft, very agreeable wine with good fruit and some complexity. If it were less than £5 I would be more interested. The Vosne-Romanée has supple, sweet, plummy fruitiness, medium body, good length and five to six years of potential evolution. The Vosne-Romanée Clos des Réas is outstanding. It is dark ruby with an explosive blackberry bouquet complemented by vanillin oak and scents of licorice. Rich and full-bodied, with very fine extract, this is a wine to lay away for five to six years. It will last until 2000. It is as good as the

Richebourg, which has a remarkably complex bouquet, layers of fruit, medium to full body, and firm tannins. It needs all of six to seven years to develop.

DOMAINE GROS SOEUR ET FRÈRE
VOSNE-ROMANÉE ★ ★ ★ ★

This estate was somewhat of a discovery. Gustave Gros is the son of Madame Gros and has his own small cellar. He owns what is generally considered the better part of the Clos Vougeot vineyard, a tiny section next to Musigny. His 1983 Clos Vougeot is fabulous, one of the single greatest red Burgundies I tasted from this vintage. His other wines are inconsistent.

1983 Clos Vougeot	⑤	**92**
1983 Richebourg	⑤	**83**
1983 Vosne-Romanée	④	**83**

Inexplicably, neither the Richebourg, which was extremely tannic and dry, nor the Vosne-Romanée, which was spicy but simple, approach the Clos Vougeot made here. The 1983 Clos Vougeot has exceptional colour, a huge bouquet of intense berry fruit, coconut, ripe oranges, and spices. Enormous on the palate, with layers of ripe, very concentrated fruit, this moderately tannic wine will be a real vinous treasure for those lucky to find a bottle or two.

1982 Richebourg	⑤	**87**
1982 Vosne-Romanée	④	**84**

Two very good 1982s, both surprisingly deep in colour, have obviously been chaptalized, but offer ripe, sweet, supple fruit in a medium-bodied, high-alcohol style. The Richebourg has significantly more fragrance and greater length and class.

HOSPICES DE BEAUNE ★ ★ ★ ★

I did not taste the entire selection of Hospices wines, but did have the opportunity to sample several of the more famous names.

1983 Corton Cuvée Charlotte Dumay	⑤	**87**
1983 Corton Cuvée Docteur Peste	⑤	**85**
1983 Mazis-Chambertin Madeleine Collignon	⑤	**88**
1983 Savigny-Les-Beaune Arthur Girard	④	**87**

All of these wines are very well made. I must admit to being a little disappointed with the Cuvée Docteur Peste, perhaps because I expected much more. It is extremely tannic and severe, with good underlying sweet fruit and medium to full body. It needs a full ten to twelve years. Just as tannic, but showing considerably better, is the Cuvée Charlotte Dumay which appears to have a greater concentration of sweet Pinot fruit, full body, some strong scents of new oak barrels, and very good length. It needs ten years. Curiously, the Savigny-Les-Beaune Cuvée Arthur Girard was darker in colour and every bit as concentrated as the two Hospices de Beaune Cortons. It is a powerful, full-bodied, rich and tannic Savigny that needs seven to nine years of cellaring. It is a sleeper! Lastly, the Mazis-Chambertin Madeleine Collignon is very rich, smoky, earthy, and rather ponderous, but excellent depth of fruit and structure are present. It may well merit an outstanding score when mature in 1995–1998.

One final comment about the Hospices wines. They are extremely expensive and have been widely criticized for not always being as good as they should be. However, since 1977 a totally new team has been responsible for the management of the vineyards and the making of the wines. They are aged in 100% new oak and since 1978 have generally been models of excellence. Of course, the competence of the buyer of these wines and the manner in which they are cellared can make a difference. In my experience, the best wines from Hospices are:

Red Wines
Nicolas Rolin (Beaune-les-Avaux)
Maurice Drouhin (Beaune)
Charlotte Dumay (Corton)
Cuvée Docteur Peste (Corton)
Madeleine Collignon (Mazis-Chambertin)
Arthur Girard (Savigny)
Jehan de Massol (Volnay Santenots)

White Wines
François de Salins (Corton-Charlemagne)
Cuvée Goureau (Meursault)
Cuvée Loppin (Meursault-Charmes)
Albert Grivault (Meursault-Charmes)

DOMAINE JACQUESON *CHAGNY* ★ ★ ★
The only experience I have had with this small domaine is with the vintages 1982 and 1983. The wines offer good value, are cleanly made, with rather vivid and rich, chewy flavours. This is definitely a domaine to seek out when it comes to good values.

1983 Mercurey Les Naugues	③	82
1983 Rully Les Chaponnières	③	85
1983 Rully Les Clouds	③	85

These wines are all similar. They have deep, bright ruby colours, moderately intense bouquets of black cherries, a lovely, silky, ripe concentration of fruit, and light tannin. The Les Clouds is a very seductive, medium-weight, lush wine.

The Les Chaponnières has a very attractive Pinot fragrance, and the Mercurey Les Naugues soft, spicy, chewy flavours. Jacqueson's 1985s were even better than his 1983s, rich, supple and loaded with flavour.

LOUIS JADOT BEAUNE ★ ★ ★ ★

This excellent firm in Beaune has now been purchased by its American importer, Kobrand, Inc. I hope the quality of the wine will remain at its current level, which is very high. For white wines, Jadot's wines are as good as anybody's; both the elegant, rich 1982s and powerful 1983s belong in everyone's collection, provided you have the funds of a rock star. The red wines here don't receive the publicity of the white wines, but no wine cellar has any better management than André Gagey and his enthusiastic cellarmaster, Jacques Lardière. Gagey and Lardière succeeded in 1983, but admitted that it was a tough year and there are frequent failures elsewhere in the Côte d'Or. Their red wines are not filtered (the only other major *négociant* not to filter is Faiveley). The 1983 red wines here are of very high quality.

1983 Beaune Boucherottes	④	85
1983 Beaune Clos des Ursules	④	85
1983 Bourgogne	③	82
1983 Chambertin Clos de Bèze	⑤	88
1983 Clos Vougeot	⑤	90
1983 Corton Pougets	⑤	88
1983 Côte de Beaune-Villages	③	83
1983 Côte de Nuits-Villages	④	84
1983 Nuits St.-Georges Clos de Corvées	④	86
1983 Pernand-Vergelesses Clos de Vergelesses	④	85

There is a lot to like in these wines from Jadot. The lower-priced wines, the Bourgogne, Côte de Beaune-Villages, and Côte de Nuits-Villages, offer good value and are ready to drink, with solid Pinot Noir flavours. The Côte de Nuits-Villages is particularly fine for its class. The Pernand-Vergelesses tastes like many people's Corton, ripe, rich, rustic, big and full, and in need of seven to eight years of cellaring. Jadot's Beaune Boucherottes and Clos des Ursules already exhibit big, complex bouquets of black cherries and vanillin oak. The Boucherottes has richer and riper fruit; the Clos des Ursules has more body and is more marked by oak. Both should be *en pleine forme* in five to six years. The Nuits St.-Georges Clos des Corvées is smoky, robust, quite aromatic, full-bodied, and tannic. It needs five to seven years of cellaring. The Corton Pougets should make a delicious bottle of savoury, ripe, broadly flavoured wine. It is already extremely impressive, with excellent concentration, super ripeness, a long finish, and moderate tannins. Drink it in 1990–1995. The Clos Vougeot is outstanding. Great colour, great fragrance, great richness – this wine has the texture and intensity of a top 1982 Bordeaux. It will need eight to ten years to fully develop. Lastly, the Chambertin Clos de Bèze is surprisingly forward and accessible, with a voluptuous, seductive richness, long, deep flavours and ripe tannins. The secret to Jadot's success in 1983 was to avoid the hail and rot damage. After severe selections were made, the wines were fermented at very hot temperatures for a short period. It obviously worked.

JAFFELIN *BEAUNE* ★★★

This firm is run by Robert Drouhin, the owner of the Drouhin firm. Both firms share the same facility for bottling, but the wines are different. The Jaffelin wines are certainly above average in quality but rarely exciting.

1983 Aloxe-Corton	④	**78**
1983 Chambertin	⑤	**87**
1983 Chambolle-Musigny	④	**80**
1983 Clos Vougeot	⑤	**86**
1983 Corton	⑤	**83**
1983 Côte de Nuits-Villages	③	**75**
1983 Echézeaux	⑤	**83**
1983 Gevrey-Chambertin	④	**80**
1983 Volnay	④	**82**

There are hardly any exciting wines here, though technically the wines are pleasant, fruity, medium-bodied, with some tough tannin in the fruit. The best of the lot are the Clos Vougeot, an appellation that did extremely well in 1983, and the rich, perfumed, ripe, and sensual Chambertin. It has an extra measure of depth and length on the palate, and needs six years of cellaring.

DOMAINE HENRI JAYER *VOSNE-ROMANÉE* ★★★★★

This small domaine is consistently one of the greatest producers of red Burgundy. Everything is aged in new oak, never filtered, and Jayer is the only Burgundian I know to have a fully temperature-controlled wine cellar. He is a passionate winemaker. Several brokers in Burgundy suggested his 1983s were not as good as they should have been. Perhaps this is true, because Jayer lost a significant portion of his crop due to hail and rot. I found his 1983s to be sumptuous wines, slightly better than his unreleased, and excellent 1985s.

1983 Echézeaux	⑤	**88**
1983 Nuits St.-Georges Meurgers	⑤	**86**

1983 Richebourg	⑤	**92**
1983 Vosne-Romanée	⑤	*84*
1983 Vosne-Romanée Clos Parantoux	⑤	*89*
1983 Vosne-Romanée Les Beaumonts	⑤	*87*
1983 Vosne-Romanée Les Brûlées	⑤	*85*

There is no question that Jayer's Richebourg is his finest wine in 1983, but he only made 25 cases of it, so the chances of getting any are slim. There are 175 cases of Vosne-Romanée Clos Parantoux, which is extremely elegant with broad, deep flavours tinged with spicy oak. It has the best length of all Jayer's Vosne-Romanées and should be ready to drink by 1990. The Vosne-Romanée Les Brûlées is a more spicy, more expressive wine with harder tannins, a very good colour, full body, but less concentration. The Vosne-Romanée Les Beau-monts is a fat yet tannic wine with dark ruby colour, clean flavours of ripe, sweet Pinot Noir, and a long finish. It has more concentration than the Les Brûlées. The Nuits St.-Georges Meurgers is quite good, with fat, fleshy flavours, rather supple for a 1983, and will probably be mature by 1990. The Echézeaux is excellent, elegant, complex, highly aroma-tic, with seductive, round, rich flavours wrapped in a glove of tannin. Jayer's straight Vosne-Romanée is good.

DOMAINE JACQUELINE JAYER *VOSNE-ROMANÉE* ★★★

Another Jayer, this lady is a relative of both Henri and Lucien. Her 1983s did not show very well at all; however, the 1982s produced by this estate are very good and will make excellent drinking over the next two to three years.

1983 Echézeaux	⑤	?
1983 Nuits St.-Georges Les Lavières	⑤	?
1983 Vosne-Romanée	④	?
1983 Vosne-Romanée Les Rouges	⑤	?

These wines were so abrasively tannic and astringent, and seemed so devoid of fruit, that I must raise serious reserva-tions about their balance. I will be shocked if there is enough fruit here to outlive the excessive tannin levels.

1982 Echézeaux	⑤	**86**
1982 Nuits St.-Georges Les Lavières	④	**85**
1982 Vosne-Romanée	④	**79**

J. Jayer produced very good 1982s. They have a healthy dosage of vanillin oakiness, lovely, seductive, very lush Pinot Noir fruit, and fleshly textures. They are extremely enjoyable to drink now, but should last one to three years. The Echézeaux is a very fine 1982, with a top-rank bouquet of ripe berry fruit, spicy oak, coconuts, and plums. The Nuits St.-

Georges Les Lavières is almost as good. It has a healthy deep ruby colour, a big, plummy, oaky bouquet, and soft, lush flavours. It should be drunk over the next few years. The Vosne-Romanée is quite pleasant, but finishes short.

DOMAINE MICHEL LAFARGE *VOLNAY* ★ ★ ★ ★

This is a very serious domaine making excellent red Burgundy with richness, complexity, elegance, and power. The top wine is always the Volnay Clos des Chênes, and in both 1981 and 1983 it is excellent.

1983 Beaune Grèves	⑤	86
1983 Volnay	③	86
1983 Volnay Clos des Chênes.....................................	④	90
1983 Volnay Premier Cru	③	87

All of these wines have a rich ruby colour, deep, seductive, velvety black cherry fruitiness interlaced with smells of vanillin oakiness, and medium to full body. The tannins are obvious but not astringent or harsh. The Beaune Grèves is more open-knit and has a lighter colour and a strong alcoholic finish. It should be ready by 1990. The Volnay has very harmonious flavours, a smoky, ripe berry fruit bouquet, and long finish. The Volnay Premier Cru is slightly deeper, with layers of rich fruit and five to eight years of further evolution. The Volnay Clos des Chênes is excellent, the richest, most aromatic, deepest and most complete of all these wines. It should be at its peak by 1990–1995.

DOMAINE COMTE LAFON *MEURSAULT* ★ ★ ★

This estate has a deservedly high reputation for white Meursaults (its 1982s were fabulous, the 1983s less so), but moderate quantities of red Volnay are produced here as well that can be very, very good. The 1983s were not filtered.

1983 Volnay Champans..	④	83
1983 Volnay Santenots..	④	86

These two 1983s show no signs of rot or astringent bitterness. The Champans is a velvety yet big, fruity wine that will mature by 1990. The Santenots is bigger-framed, quite ripe, rich, fat, alcoholic, with a good, firm edge and tannins for support. It should be mature between 1990 and 1995.

1982 Volnay Champans..	④	80
1982 Volnay Santenots..	④	84

Neither of these wines has the concentration or power of the 1983s, but they offer immediate drinkability. The Champans is soft, well made, but a trifle simple and straightforward. The Santenots has more richness, a lush, supple texture, and good finish. It should be drunk over the next one to two years.

DOMAINE CLOS DES LAMBRAYS
MOREY ST.-DENIS ★★★★

This famous estate, now under the new ownership of Louis and Fabien Saier, is making numerous changes in an effort to modernize the style of wine produced at the Clos des Lambrays. The wine is now aged in one-third new oak barrels and bottled after 18–22 months. Based on the 1982, 1983, and 1984 I tasted, the wine is lighter and fruitier than the old style, which had a tendency towards heaviness and inconsistency, although some vintages—the 1945, 1947, and 1949—could be sublime. The 1983s were filtered prior to bottling.

1983 Clos des Lambrays	⑤	**84**
1983 Mercurey Les Chevelots......................................	④	**81**
1983 Morey St.-Denis..	④	**83**

The Clos des Lambrays exhibits good winemaking. It needs eight to ten years to fully develop, but shows an elegant, complex, cherry fruit, and spicy bouquet. It has good concentration, but very hard tannins in the finish. The Morey St.-Denis is a medium-weight, very stylish wine with charm and sufficient tannins to age nicely for eight to ten years. The Mercurey has a complex bouquet of ripe cherries and leather, but finishes hard and tannic. If the fruit holds, it will be better than the above score.

DOMAINE LAMY-PILLOT *CHASSAGNE-MONTRACHET* ★★★

René Lamy's 1983s did not fare well in comparative tastings. The prices are reasonable, but with the exception of the Blagny, the wines had very vegetal, rather bizarre aromas.

1983 Blagny La Pièce sous le Bois..............................	③	**80**
1983 Chassagne-Montrachet Clos Saint-Jean..........	③	**73**
1983 Saint-Aubin Les Castets	③	**72**
1983 Santenay Les Charrons	③	**65**

Unless you get excited over vegetal aromas interlaced with the scent of manure, there is nothing much to like about these wines except the Blagny, which has some tobacco, vegetal aromas but also more clean berry ripeness and richness. The Blagny should be at its best by 1988.

PHILIPPE LECLERC *GEVREY-CHAMBERTIN* ★★★★

This wild and crazy man, who seems to be the most unlikely sort to make wine, has become one of the Côte d'Or's finest growers and *vignerons*. His wines have been consistently brilliant almost regardless of the vintage. His 1980s, 1981s, 1982s and 1983s are among the very finest of those vintages. His 1984s are exceptionally good. The secret is severe pruning in the vineyard, a very slow, hot, highly extractive vinification, two and a half years in new oak barrels, and absolutely no filtration. The intensity and majesty of flavour he succeeds in obtaining make his wines worth a special search of the marketplace. Don't pass up his 1985s, which will be excellent when he releases them in 1988.

1983 Gevrey-Chambertin..	④	**84**
1983 Gevrey-Chambertin Combe aux Moines........	⑤	**89**
1983 Gevrey-Chambertin Les Cazetiers....................	⑤	**87**
1983 Gevrey-Chambertin Les Champeaux..............	⑤	**84**

Not surprisingly, all of these are powerful, deeply scented wines that show no trace of rot or bitter tannins. The Gevrey-Chambertin is alcoholic, well coloured, rich, and in need of one to three years' cellaring. The Les Champeaux is soft and surprisingly accessible, but has broad, spicy, ripe flavours. The two stars here are Les Cazetiers, a powerful, rich, substantial wine with layers of sweet Pinot Noir fruit. It is a full-bodied, big, alcoholic wine that will be close to full maturity by 1990 – 1992. The top wine is Combe aux Moines, which has an intense old-vine flavour, a rich, chewy, lush texture, moderate rather than excessive tannins, and a huge finish. It should be superb between 1990 and 1995.

1982 Gevrey-Chambertin..	③	**83**
1982 Gevrey-Chambertin Combe aux Moines........	④	**86**
1982 Gevrey-Chambertin Les Cazetiers....................	④	**85**
1982 Gevrey-Chambertin Les Champeaux..............	④	**84**

Leclerc did very well in 1982. All of these wines are ready to drink, but both the Les Cazetiers and Combe aux Moines will easily last four to five years. Soft, fat, chewy, plummy flavours complemented by vanillin oak and long, clean finishes are the rule here. If the Les Cazetiers is very good, the Combe aux Moines is slightly denser, richer, and longer on the palate.

RENÉ LECLERC *GEVREY-CHAMBERTIN* ★ ★ ★ ★

Another long-haired Leclerc, René is the brother of Philippe. Like his brother, he produces very rich, intense, broodingly dark col-oured Pinot Noir. His vinification and approach to long-term barrel ageing and his policy against filtration are exactly the same as Philippe's. However, there is one big difference. René uses no new oak barrels; his brother uses 100% new oak. Consequently, René's wines have less tannin and a richer, more accessible fruitiness. Obviously this is another small grower worth a special effort to seek out.

1983 Gevrey-Chambertin Clos Prieur	⑤	**85**
1983 Gevrey-Chambertin Combe aux Moines........	⑤	**90**

1983 Gevrey-Chambertin Lavaux St.-Jacques .... ⑤ 89

All three of these wines are rich, robust, darkly coloured, and full-bodied, with excellent extract and potential. I could have rated the Clos Prieur a little higher because it is rich, long, typically alcoholic, but also very hard. It will need ten years. The Lavaux St.-Jacques is a dense, very fat, rich, immense wine with ten to twelve years of positive evolution ahead of it. The layers of flavour are very impressive. However, the Combe aux Moines is clearly one of the great wines of this vintage. It is very concentrated, dense, and powerful, and has a huge finish. It is much better than most growers' Chambertins.

1982 Gevrey-Chambertin Combes aux Moines .... ④ 86
1982 Gevrey-Chambertin Lavaux St.-Jacques .... ④ 84

Like his brother Philippe, René also made very fine 1982s that have a surprising intensity of colour and richness, though they are ready to drink. If you have a choice to make, go for the Combe aux Moines, which resembles the Lavaux St.-Jacques but is larger in the mouth, and has more concentration and character.

DOMAINE LEQUIN-ROUSSOT *SANTENAY* ★ ★ ★

This moderate-sized estate in Santenay is extremely well run. They make excellent white wines and quite good red wines. The honesty of the two brothers is refreshing, and they, like many growers, are concerned about the ferocity of tannin in the red Burgundies of 1983. The 1983s were aged in 50% new wood. The red wines have plenty of character but are quite hard and tannic. The 1982s, both red and white, were successful here.

1983 Chassagne-Montrachet Morgeot .... ④ 78
1983 Corton .... ④ 85
1983 Pommard .... ④ 68
1983 Santenay .... ③ 83
1983 Santenay Clos de Haut Villages .... ③ 78
1983 Santenay La Combe .... ④ 85

The Pommard was so hard, tough, and tannic that I am quite concerned that it will never be balanced. Otherwise, Lequin-Roussot produced a very good, spicy, full-bodied Santenay for drinking in 1990, a very hard, tannic Chassagne-Montrachet Morgeot and Santenay Clos de Haut Villages. The Santenay La Combe exhibits much riper, plummier fruit, a big, spicy bouquet, deep colour, and long finish. Equally good is the Corton, which has a healthy, deep colour, full body, very good depth, but is also very tannic. It will need ten years of cellaring.

LEROY *MEURSAULT* ★ ★ ★ ★ ★

Mme. Lalou Bize-Leroy is certainly one of Burgundy's, if not France's, most dynamic and respected wine producers. She calls herself the 'Gardienne des Grands Millésimes', and with a stock in excess of 2.2 million bottles, no one argues. Her wines are extremely expensive, but are also consistently among the greatest made in Burgundy, and perhaps are *the* greatest. She has the habit of releasing vintages when they are just beginning to show some maturity. Leroy's Burgundies are capable of 15–30 years of life in the bottle and are natural, unfiltered wines of profound character and complexity. I cannot recommend them enthusiastically enough, but be prepared to pay a premium for such glories. The great vintages (for Leroy) are the 1964s, 1969s, and 1971s. While all of Leroy's wines are special, she seems to be at her impeccable best with respect to the wines from such appellations as Gevrey-Chambertin, Chambolle-Musigny, Nuits St.-Georges, and Pommard. Yet, as the following scores show, Leroy produces an unparalleled line of great wines, even from lesser appellations. Burgundy's single greatest producer? No doubt about it!

1955 Mazis-Chambertin	⑤	90
1961 Gevrey-Chambertin Les Cazetiers	⑤	95
1964 Chambolle-Musigny Les Amoureuses	⑤	92
1964 Chambolle-Musigny Les Charmes	⑤	88
1964 Chapelle-Chambertin	⑤	95
1964 Gevrey-Chambertin Les Combottes	⑤	92
1964 Gevrey-Chambertin Les Cazetiers	⑤	95
1964 Mazis-Chambertin	⑤	97
1964 Pommard Grand Epenots	⑤	90
1964 Pommard Rugiens	⑤	90
1966 Gevrey-Chambertin Les Cazetiers	⑤	92
1966 Musigny	⑤	87
1966 Pommard Grand Epenots	⑤	87
1969 Clos Vougeot	⑤	80
1969 Gevrey-Chambertin Lavaux St.-Jacques	⑤	89
1969 Gevrey-Chambertin Les Cazetiers	⑤	90
1969 Mazis-Chambertin	⑤	90
1972 Chambolle-Musigny	⑤	85
1976 d'Auveney Bourgogne	③	84
1976 Monthelie	③	82
1978 d'Auveney Bourgogne	③	84
1978 Auxey-Duresses	③	85
1978 Beaune	④	85
1978 Chassagne-Montrachet	④	85
1978 Côte de Beaune-Villages	④	85
1979 Gevrey-Chambertin	④	86

1979 Pommard	④	85
1979 Santenay	④	86
1979 Vosne-Romanée	④	86

DOMAINE HUBERT LIGNIER *MOREY ST.-DENIS* ★★★★

There are two separate Ligniers, Georges and Hubert, making wines in Morey St.-Denis. Both are highly respected. Hubert produces velvety, rich, and graceful wines and has been on a good streak of late, producing very fine wine in 1978, 1979, 1980, 1981, 1982, and 1983. His 1984s are good, his 1985s superb, so Lignier is clearly a grower who knows what he is doing. His wines are bottled unfiltered. He gets tremendous colour in his wines and they are magnificently scented red Burgundies.

1983 Clos de la Roche	⑤	90
1983 Morey St.-Denis	④	85

Lignier's Morey St.-Denis is quite attractive, rich, supple, yet powerful and firm. It has dark colour, a lovely bouquet, and still needs four to six years to develop fully. His Clos de la Roche is truly superb, deep, ripe, with the scent of ripe plums and violets; it is remarkably fruity and complex, but needs six to eight years to shed the moderate tannins that are present.

1982 Clos de la Roche	④	83
1982 Morey St.-Denis	④	82

Lignier made good 1982s. Both wines are much more open-knit than usual with some spicy vanillin oakiness, soft, supple, ripe fruit, good concentration, but not much tannin. They should be drunk over the next year.

LUPÉ-CHOLET *NUITS ST.-GEORGES* ★★

This firm produces rather standard-quality wine, their best being the Château Gris. The wines are commercially made and unexciting.

1983 Beaune Clos de Roi	④	78
1983 Château Gris Nuits St.-Georges	⑤	85
1983 Pommard	④	70

The Pommard is stemmy and harsh. The Beaune has a pleasant, light, strawberry fruitiness, and the Château Gris a ripe, rich, yet aggressively tannic texture. It needs eight to nine years of age, but it may not have the fruit to last that long.

CHÂTEAU DE LA MALTROYE
CHASSAGNE-MONTRACHET ★★★

One thinks of this estate usually as a very fine white wine producer. However, they also produce several red wines. The 1983s were all quite good.

1983 Chassagne-Montrachet Clos de la Maltroye.. ④ **85**
1983 Chassagne-Montrachet Clos Saint-Jean .... ④ **85**
1983 Santenay La Comme .... ④ *84*

All three wines have moderately intense bouquets of leather, spice, and ripe cherry fruit. Rather elegant for 1983s, but still rather powerful and fuller-bodied than one might normally expect, these wines need a minimum of five years to mature. The Clos Saint-Jean is slightly more forward than the others; the Clos de la Maltroye more tannic and tough; the La Comme the lightest.

DOMAINE MAUME *GEVREY-CHAMBERTIN* ★ ★ ★ ★

This traditionally run estate makes very powerful, almost inky-coloured wines. When I first visited Maume in 1981, I could not believe the colour he obtained from Pinot Noir grapes. His 1980s are impenetrably deeply coloured wines that will not be fully mature until 1990. His 1982s are among the best made in this vintage, his 1983s are extremely dense and robust with no trace of astringence or rot, and his 1985s are rich, intense, and the best I have tasted yet from this estate. Maume's wines are not filtered.

1983 Gevrey-Chambertin .... ④ **83**
1983 Gevrey-Chambertin Lavaux St.-Jacques .... ⑤ **87**
1983 Mazis-Chambertin .... ④ **89**

The *village* Gevrey-Chambertin has plenty of good, ripe fruit, but its score is kept low by some hard tannins in the finish. Both the Lavaux St.-Jacques and Mazis-Chambertin are powerfully built wines meant to mature slowly. Both should not be mature until 1993–1995. The Mazis-Chambertin has a huge aroma of violets, leather, and ripe plums. It is dense and rather huge on the palate, with full body and outstanding length. The Lavaux St.-Jacques is almost identically styled, perhaps more tannic, but equally rich and full-proportioned.

DOMAINE JEAN MÉO *VOSNE-ROMANÉE* ★ ★ ★

The Domaine Méo is one of the small but important estates in the Côte de Nuits. I tasted through the 1983s and was extremely impressed; this appears to be a domaine that succeeded admirably in this difficult vintage.

1983 Corton Clos Rognet .... ④ **87**
1983 Nuits St.-Georges Boudots .... ④ **85**
1983 Nuits St.-Georges Meugers .... ④ **68**
1983 Richebourg .... ⑤ **86**
1983 Vosne-Romanée Les Brûlées .... ④ *84*

The 1983s are not tainted by rot, although the Nuits St.-Georges Meugers was clearly bizarre and unusual when I last tasted it. The Nuits St.-Georges Boudots is quite excellent, potentially outstanding. Deep ruby in colour, with a full-intensity bouquet of spicy new oak, plums, truffles and licorice, this rich, concentrated wine will make a fine bottle in 1990–1995. The Corton Clos Rognet and Richebourg had similarly dark colours, excellent extract, clean, well-delineated Pinot Noir flavours and pure, ripe characters. The Richebourg tasted slightly less tannic. Give both wines a full five to six years of cellaring. The Vosne-Romanée Les Brûlées was in the same style, only by comparison showed less depth and fragrance.

PRINCE FLORENT DE MÉRODE *LADOIX-SERRIGNY* ★ ★ ★ ★

This well-known estate has long held a very fine reputation for graceful and elegant wines produced from vineyards at Aloxe-Corton and Pommard. The wines are made by Pierre Bitouzet, an engaging man who knows his business and is responsive to queries. The 1983s were aged in oak barrels (50% of which were new) and bottled surprisingly early. The wines here are filtered. They are surprisingly light and less powerful than most 1983s, yet totally free of any traces of rot. Mérode also made good 1984s and excellent 1985s that will mature much faster than his 1983s.

1983 Aloxe-Corton	④	*82*
1983 Corton Bressandes	⑤	*86*
1983 Corton Clos du Roi	⑤	*85*
1983 Corton Maréchaudes	④	*83*
1983 Corton Renardes	④	*84*
1983 Pommard Clos de la Platière	④	*84*

The Aloxe-Corton and Corton Maréchaudes have good fruit, light to medium ruby colours, spicy vanillin aromas intermixed with cherry fruit, and rather short finishes. They are clean, elegant, rather understated wines. The Pommard Clos de la Platière is a more serious wine with ripe, round, forward, cherry fruit, better colour, and some depth and weight. It can be drunk now or aged for four to five years. The Corton Renardes bouquet is all cherry and vanillin. On the palate, it is a medium-bodied, pleasant, elegant wine that will be ready to drink soon. The star of the Mérode 1983s is the Corton Bressandes. It is by far the richest and deepest of these wines, fragrant, loaded with ripe, cherry fruit complemented by spicy new oak. Fuller, richer, and more complex than the others, the Bressandes should be fully mature by 1990–1992. The Corton Clos du Roi is almost as good, only its toughness and dryness kept it from scoring higher. It does seem to have the concentration of fruit to outlast the tannins. It will need six to eight years.

DOMAINE MOILLARD *NUITS ST.-GEORGES* ★ ★ ★

Moillard is a large *négociant* with some very important vineyard holdings. The wines are always quite dark in colour, beefy, robust, and concentrated. In fact, they are very pleasing wines, but my experience with older vintages is that they do not develop much bouquet. Perhaps this is because the wines are pasteurized; while such a practice (also employed by the *négociant* Louis Latour) has its proponents, the result is wines that often taste very much alike and have slightly cooked bouquets and flavours. Moillard's best wines are those from the firm's own vineyard holdings. These tend to be big, rich, chocolaty wines that have little complexity, but deliver chunky, mouth-satisfying flavours. The 1983s are more alcoholic than usual but continue this style.

1983 Auxey-Duresses	②	75
1983 Beaune	③	73
1983 Beaune Grèves	④	80
1983 Bonnes Mares	⑤	85
1983 Bourgogne Hautes Côtes de Nuits	②	80
1983 Chambertin Clos de Bèze	⑤	87
1983 Clos Vougeot	⑤	83
1983 Corton Clos du Roi	④	83
1983 Corton Clos des Vergennes	④	85
1983 Côte de Nuits-Villages Domaine Chevillon	②	82
1983 Fixin	②	78
1983 Fixin Clos de la Perrière	③	80
1983 Nuits St.-Georges Clos des Thorey	④	86
1983 Nuits St.-Georges Les Richemondes	⑤	86
1983 Romanée St.-Vivant	⑤	86
1983 Volnay Clos des Chênes	④	85
1983 Vosne-Romanée Les Beaux Monts	④	83
1983 Vosne-Romanée Les Malconsorts	④	83

These wines I tasted from Moillard show several things. One, this firm produces consistently above-average wines; there were no bad wines tasted. Second, while the wines are not great, there are some very fine, fleshy, rich, dense, chunky selections that offer plenty of palate pleasure. The two best values are the Côte de Nuits-Villages and Bourgogne Haute Côtes de Nuits. To briefly summarize the highlights here, the Romanée St.-Vivant and Bonnes Mares have the most complexity and reflected their appellation the best. The Chambertin Clos de Bèze was the biggest and most concentrated, with an easy ten year lifespan ahead of it. The two wines from Nuits St.-Georges, Moillard's home base, the Richemondes and Clos des Thorey, are both big, thick, jammy, almost opaque wines. Both were rather atypical Pinot Noirs but offered dense, smoky, very rich fruit, and full body. The Volnay Clos de Chênes has aromas and flavours of black cherries, is alcoholic and rich; the Corton Clos des Vergennes is quite good, spicy, deep, fat, rich, and long. Both wines should be cellared for five years. As for the other wines, it was difficult to tell them apart (except that some were more intense than others).

DOMAINE MOINE-HUDELOT
CHAMBOLLE-MUSIGNY ★ ★ ★ ★

This tiny estate is run by Daniel Moine-Hudelot, the mayor of Chambolle-Musigny. He is a philosophical chap who explains quite succinctly why Burgundy is so expensive and irregular in quality – too much demand, not enough quantity, and too much illegal stretching by means of blending in the wine from weak, overcropped, inferior vineyards with that of better vineyards. Moine-Hudelot is a serious winemaker, but he makes so little wine that only tiny quantities are exported.

1983 Chambolle-Musigny **80**
1983 Chambolle-Musigny Les Amoureuses............. **85**
  Both wines have deep ruby colour and a pronounced raspberry-like bouquet. The Chambolle-Musigny is a little dry and astringent in the finish; the Les Amoureuses ripe, full-bodied, alcoholic, and rich. Give both four to five years.

DOMAINE MONGEARD-MUGNERET
VOSNE-ROMANÉE ★ ★ ★ ★

Jean Mongeard is the master architect behind this estate, which can make truly superb Burgundies. To my taste, they have everything I really want in a wine – the scent of ripe fruit and violets, lush, deep, berry flavours, a touch of oak and a super finish. Mongeard is a believer in very hot vinifications, long ageing in small oak (of which 50% is new), and absolutely no filtration. His 1983s are great successes, as are his 1985s, particularly Richebourg and Grands-Echézeaux. He also made very good 1984s, especially his Grands-Echézeaux. However, his wines are not always the model of consistency. His 1979s were disappointing.

1983 Clos Vougeot .... ⑤ **90**
1983 Echézeaux .... ⑤ **88**
1983 Fixin .... ⑤ **82**
1983 Grands-Echézeaux .... ⑤ **92**
1983 Vosne-Romanée... ④ **85**
  All of Jean Mongeard's wines have great colour and clean, ripe, deeply scented bouquets. His Fixin offers a lighter-weight version of his more serious wines. Broad, ripe, alcoholic flavours are complex and soft in this medium-bodied

wine; it will be mature by 1990. The Vosne-Romanée has excellent colour and depth and the richness of most growers' Premiers Crus. Deeply flavoured, full-bodied, high in alcohol with moderate tannins, this delicious wine will also be ready to drink by 1990. The Echézeaux, Clos Vougeot, and great Grands-Echézeaux are wines to lay away for ten years. The Echézeaux is wonderfully fruity, chewy, fleshy and very concentrated. Its bouquet is one of vanillin, violets, and ripe berry fruit. It is potentially outstanding, but next to the spectacular Clos Vougeot and Grands-Echézeaux, it is overwhelmed. Mongeard's Clos Vougeot has remarkable intensity, great depth of flavour, superb richness, and is altogether a great young wine. Give it eight years. The Grands-Echézeaux is, along with several of the DRC 1983s and Ponsot's Clos de la Roche Vieilles Vignes, among the greatest red Burgundies of the vintage. The bouquet is filled with complex scents of flowers, plums, oak, and exotic spices. Incredibly rich and concentrated with layers of fruit, this is a great wine that should be at its best between 1990 and 2000. Mongeard thinks it is his best wine since the 1949.

DOMAINE ALBERT MOROT *BEAUNE* ★ ★ ★ ★

This old estate is surely going to get a strong following as the quality of its wines becomes better known. Madame Chapin runs the business from the old, rather run-down Château de la Creusotte in Beaune. The wines are all from her own vineyards. Having tasted through the 1964s, 1972s, and 1979s, these are full-throttle, natural Burgundies that age well, have excellent flavours, and are not filtered. The prices are very reasonable.

1983 Beaune Bressandes	③	86
1983 Beaune Cent Vignes	④	87
1983 Beaune Grèves	④	86
1983 Beaune Marconnets	③	86
1983 Beaune Theurons	③	85
1983 Beaune Toussaints	③	84
1983 Savigny-Vergelesses	③	85

This is an impressive array of Beaune wines. For elegance and drinking in four to five years, the Savigny-Vergelesses and Beaune Toussaints would be my choices. The most tannic wine, and most backward at the moment, is the Beaune Theurons, which is dark ruby, medium- to full-bodied, but very tannic. Don't touch it before 1993. The Beaune Marconnets needs five to eight years, but has excellent colour, a big, tarry, berry-scented bouquet, long, ripe flavours, and firm tannins. The Beaune Bressandes is very similar, perhaps slightly more fruity, but deep and broad, particularly for a

Beaune. The Beaune Cent Vignes tastes the richest and most concentrated, with just something extra in the bouquet and flavour. Again, it would be a shame to drink it before 1993. The Beaune Grèves is excellent, has deep colour, no trace of rot or hail damage, firm tannin, and rich, jammy fruit with medium to full body. Looking for some unadulterated Pinot Noir to lay away for ten to fifteen years at a reasonable price? Then consider these very fine offerings from Albert Morot.

DOMAINE GEORGES MUGNERET
VOSNE-ROMANÉE ★ ★ ★ ★

This is a very serious domaine run by Dr. Georges Mugneret, who has retired from the medical profession to make wine. Only new oak barrels are used to age the wine, and this estate refuses to filter its wines. The two best wines are almost always the Ruchottes-Chambertin and Clos Vougeot. Several of the 1982s of Georges Mugneret are excellent and his 1983s very good. Mugneret's wines are beginning to obtain a cult following, so make reservations now for his splendid 1985s, which he feels are the best he has made.

1983 Clos Vougeot	⑤	**90**
1983 Echézeaux	⑤	**86**
1983 Nuits St.-Georges Les Chaignots	④	**85**
1983 Nuits St.-Georges Les Vignes Rondes	④	**80**
1983 Ruchottes-Chambertin	⑤	**86**
1983 Vosne-Romanée	④	*81*

When I visited Mugneret in 1984, I feared that his use of 100% new oak barrels for the 1983s was a mistake. The wines were already very tannic and they hardly needed any additional wood tannins. Well, the wines have turned out to be very good, with the Clos Vougeot potentially outstanding. The Vosne-Romanée has a roasted, ripe, spicy bouquet, very good concentration, a trace of astringence, but should age well for five to eight years. The Nuits St.-Georges Les Vignes Rondes tasted less concentrated, a little too hard and dry. It has good, ripe fruit, but I worry about it drying out before it matures. On the other hand, the Nuits St.-Georges Les Chaignots, despite the presence of very aggressive tannins, has a ripe, roasted character, deep colour, and a long finish. It must have ten years of cellaring. The Echézeaux, another wine that requires a ten-year wait before drinking, is dark ruby, very spicy, quite robust and concentrated, but very, very tannic. The Ruchottes-Chambertin has less charm than the lovely, seductive 1982, but is a very big wine, dark in colour; it is potentially better than scored, but is extremely tannic. The Clos Vougeot gets my nod as Mugneret's best. It is very intense and powerful with mouth-searing tannins, but also oodles of ripe, plummy fruit. It should be sublime between 1995 and 2005.

1982 Echézeaux .... ⑤ **85**
1982 Ruchottes-Chambertin .... ④ **88**
With respect to the best 1982s, one might say they are composed of 'sugar and spice and all things nice'. No doubt that the 1982s have been chaptalized to give them a fat, fruity, alcoholic character, and if a grower was meticulous with his/ her selection process, the diluted, watery lots of wine were discarded. Well, both these 1982s are extremely alluring. Round, sweet, and spicy, with captivating aromas, lush, gentle flavours, and surprising concentration, this is the type of red Burgundy that is easy to drink and easy to understand. The 1982 Ruchottes-Chambertin should drink well for three to four years and then fade quickly. However, it is a top 1982. The Échézeaux is a trifle tannic and may last four to six years, but it should be viewed as a hedonistic red Burgundy for drinking soon.

NAIGEON-CHAUVEAU *GEVREY-CHAMBERTIN* ★★
DOMAINE DES VAROILLES ★★★

The Domaine des Varoilles has a loyal following for its long-lived wines, particularly those from Gevrey-Chambertin. The owners are the Naigeon-Chauveau family, who also sell wines as a *négociant* under their own labels. The 1984s here are not very promising, but the 1983s are quite good, very tannic, deeply coloured, true *vins de garde*. The quality of the wines under the Domaine des Varoilles label is vastly superior to those under the *négociant* label, Naigeon-Chauveau. Burgundy enthusiasts should make a special search for the Clos des Varoilles Cuvée Vieilles Vignes and Clos des Meix Ouches Cuvée Vieilles Vignes.

Naigeon-Chauveau

1983 Chassagne-Montrachet .... ③ **78**
1983 Côte de Beaune-Villages .... ③ **73**
1983 Côte de Nuits-Villages .... ③ **69**
1983 Nuits St.-Georges .... ④ **79**
1983 Nuits St.-Georges Les Damodes .... ④ **80**
1983 Nuits St.-Georges Les Pruliers .... ④ **83**
1983 Santenay Le Passe Temps .... ③ **78**
None of these wines are bad, but none of them are particularly interesting. The Nuits St.-Georges Les Pruliers had the most colour and concentration, but was somewhat dull and overly tannic. The others are quite aggressively tannic, raising serious questions about whether they would dry out before the tannins subside.

Domaine des Varoilles

1983 Bonnes Mares	⑤	**87**
1983 Charmes-Chambertin	⑤	**85**
1983 Clos Vougeot	⑤	**87**
1983 Gevrey-Chambertin	④	**82**
1983 Gevrey-Chambertin Champonets	④	**87**
1983 Gevrey-Chambertin Clos de Couvent	④	**85**
1983 Gevrey-Chambertin Clos de Meix Ouches Vieilles Vignes	④	**88**
1983 Gevrey-Chambertin Clos de Prieur	④	**82**
1983 Gevrey-Chambertin Clos des Varoilles	④	**86**
1983 Gevrey-Chambertin Clos des Varoilles Vieilles Vignes	④	**89**
1983 Vosne-Romanée La Romanée	⑤	**84**

Given the fact that the wines of the Domaine des Varoilles are made in a tight, lean, hard style that takes most of a decade to open and develop, the 1983s provided the precise natural products this estate needed. These are very tannic, backward wines. I would guess that 1995 or beyond will be a good time to take another look at these wines to see if they are mature. Even the lower-level wines, such as the Gevrey-Chambertin are eight to ten years away from maturity. The Gevrey-Chambertin Clos de Prieur seemed to lack richness and colour, and the Vosne-Romanée La Romanée is good, but somewhat light, particularly for a 1983. Otherwise, the Gevrey-Chambertin Clos de Couvent, made from 40-year-old vines, is dark in colour, with good body and rich fruit to balance out its considerable tannic clout. The excellent Gevrey-Chambertin Champonets may need ten years, but it has the requisite concentration to outlast the tannins, and is nearly as good as the Clos des Meix Ouches Vieilles Vignes, which has oodles of ripe, sweet Pinot Noir fruit, a spicy, rich, but restrained bouquet, and tough tannins. The Clos des Varoilles Vieilles Vignes is probably better than the 1978 version of this wine; at least it is more powerful and tannic. It will need ten to fifteen years, but it has excellent concentration and makes a powerful impression on the palate. The regular Cuvée of the Clos des Varoilles is not as rich not as tannic; it may be ready by 1995. As for the Grands Crus, the Charmes-Chambertin is a typical, very good 1983, big and rich, but so tough and tannic. The Bonnes Mares had tons of tannin but deeper fruit and better colour than the Charmes-Chambertin. The Clos Vougeot is the most precocious of this latter trio, has excellent ripeness, full body, and a long finish, provided you are willing to cellar it for ten years.

DOMAINE PERNOT-FOURRIER
GEVREY-CHAMBERTIN ★ ★ ★ ★

Over the years I have tasted some marvellous wines from this estate, particularly the 1964s, 1969s, and 1971s. They have broad, lush Pinot flavours and smoky, quite fragrant bouquets. Normally the wines from Pernot-Fourrier need five to eight years to develop fully, though I suspect the 1983s will need ten to fifteen years. This estate made several good 1982s and their 1984s are certainly successful. The wines of Pernot-Fourrier are filtered prior to bottling, but, interestingly, they are never fined while ageing in the cask. His 1983s are extremely tannic and several of them are problematic.

1983 Gevrey-Chambertin	④	**70**
1983 Gevrey-Chambertin Clos St.-Jacques	⑤	**87**
1983 Gevrey-Chambertin Combe aux Moines	⑤	**86**
1983 Gevrey-Chambertin Premier Cru	④	**72**
1983 Griottes-Chambertin	⑤	**78**
1983 Vougeot Premier Cru	⑤	**85**

These are real macho wines. In fact, several may be far too tannic to ever develop properly. The Gevrey-Chambertin tastes severe and astringent. I will pass on judging it. The Gevrey-Chambertin Premier Cru is even more abrasively tannic and its future is suspect. The Griottes-Chambertin has plenty of ripe, rich, sweet fruit, but the musty taste of rot is present. That is a shame, because the wine has a lot of power and richness. Some growers claim that with extended aeration this smell blows off. Perhaps you are willing to take that chance, I am not. As for the others, the Vougeot is very tannic and full-bodied, but also has a lot of rich, ripe, deep fruit. It should peak in eight to ten years. The Combe aux Moines is another tannic titan, but has very fine concentration, some lush, sweet fruit in the mid-range, and eight to ten years of evolution ahead. The Clos St.-Jacques is the best of these wines, a big, alcoholic, rich, deep, tannic wine that has balance and depth. However, it begs for eight to ten years.

DOMAINE PONSOT *MOREY ST.-DENIS* ★ ★ ★ ★

Jean-Marie Ponsot and his son make some of Burgundy's richest and most concentrated wines. However, the estate is far from consistent; the 1984s are weak and feeble here, the 1985s excellent. They still hold to the opinion that 1983 is 'an extraordinary year' and the best since 1947 and 1949. For several of their wines, they may be right. Some of their 1983s are, quite frankly, unbelievably concentrated and powerful. Consequently, they did not bottle their 1983s until early 1986. Some of the 1982s produced here are good, but by Ponsot's own admission they were not happy with the quality of their 1984s. Ponsot's wines can be truly great – the 1980 Clos de la Roche Vieilles Vignes is one of the greatest young Burgundies I have ever tasted. In addition to their superb Clos de la Roche, the Latricières-Chambertin and Clos St.-Denis are the top wines from this estate. Ponsot never filters its wines.

1983 Chambertin...	⑤	**85**
1983 Clos de la Roche.....................................	⑤	**88**
1983 Clos de la Roche Vieilles Vignes	⑤	**96**
1983 Clos Saint-Denis.....................................	⑤	**91**
1983 Griottes-Chambertin.............................	⑤	**87**
1983 Latricières-Chambertin.......................	⑤	**88**

These wines are all very good, even spectacular, in quality, but they differ considerably in style and will be ready to drink at different times. The Griottes-Chambertin is fairly precocious, with oodles of supple, yet soft, ripe tannins. It is so rich it is almost jammy. Drink it between 1990 and 1995. The Chambertin, a greater name but not greater wine, is rather light in colour, especially for a Ponsot wine, has soft, classy, complex flavours, and is ready to drink. It is extremely long in the mouth but too light for a Chambertin. The regular Clos de la Roche (250 cases produced) is very dark in colour, with a huge aroma of black cherries, apricots, and spicy oak. Quite full-bodied, deep and concentrated, this excellent wine should be at its best between 1990 and 1998. The Latricières-Chambertin is similar: dense, dark, almost jammy, with full body, a long, rich, deep texture, and excellent concentration. It is more exotic and fragrant than the Clos de la Roche and should peak between 1992 and 2000. As for the two sensational wines of Ponsot, the Clos Saint Denis (75 cases produced) combines power with finesse, has a voluptuous, deeply concentrated, long taste, is highly aromatic, and superbly flavoured. It can be drunk now, but promises to be extraordinary in five to seven years. Then we have the monument of the 1983 red Burgundies, the Clos de la Roche Vieilles Vignes (200 cases produced). It is in the same class as the staggering 1980, only the wine is more powerful – the alcohol is 14.5% – and denser. It simply must be tasted to be believed. This is an old heavyweight style of red Burgundy that no one but Ponsot produces any more. It should be mature by 1993 and last at least several decades. The concentration of flavour and length have more in common with a Guigal La Mouline or Pétrus than any red Burgundy I have ever tasted.

DOMAINE POTHIER-RIEUSSET *POMMARD* ★ ★ ★ ★

Virgile Pothier is one of those charming, red-cheeked vignerons who makes a visit to his cellars a memorable stop. Pothier made several great wines in 1983 and appears to have triumphed again in 1985. His 1984s are quite light, but clean and fruity; his 1982s are relatively disappointing given the standards here. Pothier's wines are not filtered.

1983 Beaune Boucherottes	④	**84**
1983 Bourgogne	③	**82**
1983 Bourgogne Grand Ordinaire	②	**78**
1983 Pommard	④	**86**
1983 Pommard Clos des Vergers	④	**89**
1983 Pommard Epenots	④	**88**
1983 Pommard Rugiens	④	**90**

The basic Bourgogne Grand Ordinaire, which is made from Gamay, not Pinot Noir, is a pleasant, rather simple, but fruity wine. The Bourgogne is a step up in quality and interest. Pothier's Bourgognes generally have been excellent values (his 1979 and 1980 are very nice) and the 1983 actually needs two to three years to fully develop. It is spicy and fruity, with good body and length. The Beaune Boucherottes is, of course, a more serious wine. It will be ready to drink soon for a 1983, probably by 1990. It has a lovely Pinot fragrance, good, ripe, round, spicy fruit, medium body, and soft, moderate tannins. The real specialities of this house are the Pommards, and all of them are stunning in 1983. The Pommard has plenty of ripe, sweet fruit, a long, rather unctuous finish, round tannins and very forward, precocious personality. It should be at its best between 1989 and 1996. The Pommard Epenots has a ripe, exotic aroma, deep, rich, long, broad flavours of raspberries tinged with vanillin oakiness, and moderate tannin. It should be delicious by 1989 and hold for a decade. Although the Epenots is good, the two stars are the Pommard Clos des Vergers and Pommard Rugiens. In both 1982 and 1983 these two wines stood out as greats of the vintage. The Clos des Vergers is perhaps the more classically structured. It has 13.5% alcohol without chaptalization, a staggering perfume of cedarwood, truffles, flowers, and ripe berry fruit. Full-bodied, rich and lush with good supporting tannins, the Clos des Vergers can be drunk in five years or cellared for ten to twenty years. The Rugiens is, by comparison, a more extroverted, exotic, fleshy wine. Sweet, oaky aromas intermingled with ripe plums fill the olfactory senses. On the palate, it has stupendous richness and none of the harsh, astringent tannins frequently found elsewhere. Pothier thinks it is the best Rugiens since his 1949 (which is a legendary wine). I am not quite sure when to drink this wine. By 1990 it will be outstanding, but it already has oodles of ripe fruit showing.

1982 Beaune Boucherottes	③	78
1982 Bourgogne	②	77
1982 Pommard	③	80
1982 Pommard Clos des Vergers	④	82
1982 Pommard Rugiens	④	82

These are all rather light, fruity, pleasant wines, but except for a good Clos des Vergers and Rugiens they are simple. Even the latter two are rather shallow and watery for Pothier.

GÉRARD POTEL—DOMAINE DE LA POUSSE D'OR
VOLNAY ★ ★ ★ ★

I have a great deal of admiration for Gérard Potel and his lovely estate perched in Volnay with a full view of the vineyards. His wines have been textbook examples of elegant, refined, complex Burgundies that show very well young but age beautifully. At a vertical tasting at the domaine covering the vintages 1964–1983, I was struck by the splendid velvety richness these wines attain in vintages such as 1980, 1978, 1976, 1971, 1969, 1966, and 1964. The two greatest vintages for this property were 1964 and 1976. As for the 1983s, they are not among my favourites; while certainly good, they are perhaps too dry and tannic. I prefer his 1980s to his 1983s. Potel has begun to filter his wines.

1983 Pommard Les Jarollières	④	??
1983 Santenay Clos d'Audignac	④	77
1983 Santenay Clos Tavannes	④	80
1983 Volnay Bousse d'Or	④	84
1983 Volnay Les Caillerets	④	83
1983 Volnay Les Caillerets 60 Ouvrées	④	85

In general these wines are medium ruby in colour, quite hard and tannic, and several, notably the Pommard Les Jarollières, are just too severe and unpleasant to judge at the moment. Neither Santenay greatly impressed me as they both had a light colour and a dry (*sec*) finish. The Volnay Caillerets has more obvious depth and fruit, but needs eight to ten years of cellaring. Certainly the Volnay Bousse d'Or and Volnay Les Caillerets 60 Ouvrées show richer and greater fruit, more depth and richness, and long finishes. Don't drink either until 1993.

DOMAINE CHARLES QUILLARDET *MARSANNAY* ★ ★

This estate makes wines that I find clumsy, dull, and very Rhône-like. They are dark in colour, chewy, sometimes too barnyard-like in aroma, but rarely do I find accurate Pinot Noir flavours. Nevertheless, the wines have a certain following and are fairly priced, save for the Chambertin, which is always overpriced, regardless of who produces it. The 1983s are pretty mediocre wines. I do have a very good note on the 1982 Chambertin, but the price is too high.

1983 Bourgogne Les Grands Vignes	②	**72**
1983 Bourgogne Montre Cul	②	**60**
1983 Chambertin	⑤	**83**
1983 Fixin	②	**75**
1983 Gevrey-Chambertin	③	**82**
1983 Gevrey-Chambertin Le Bel Air	④	**82**
1983 Gevrey-Chambertin Champeaux	④	**83**

The problem is that all the wines from Gevrey-Chambertin taste alike. The prices are different, but I see little or no difference between the *village* Gevrey-Chambertin and the Chambertin. I would also like to know how Quillardet gets Pinot Noir to produce wines with this colour and such a chunky, dense, heavy character. The Montre Cul is a wine that is truly in poor taste, from its adolescent label (drawn with a woman's derrière in full view) to its heavy, coarse flavours.

1982 Chambertin	⑤	**85**

This is quite a lovely wine. Ready to drink, with rich, spicy, fat, deep flavours, medium to full body, and an earthy, truffle-like aroma, I find this quite an attractive offering from Quillardet.

DOMAINE HENRI REBOURSEAU
GEVREY-CHAMBERTIN ★ ★ ★

This is an historic old property that the now ancient General Rebourseau made famous. The late Frank Schoonmaker claimed the 1929s from Rebourseau to be among the greatest Burgundies he had drunk. Now the younger Rebourseau runs the show, and the wines are certainly less rich and full-bodied than in the past. The 1983s are very difficult wines to judge. They are suspiciously light in colour, but do make a powerful, heady, alcoholic impact on the palate. However, after 20–30 minutes in the glass, mouldy smells of rot emerge, and after an hour these smells have overtaken everything in the glass. I went to the trouble and expense to taste these wines three separate times to be sure I was right. My conclusion is that they are badly affected by rot and are flawed. The 1984s also seem poor, but for different reasons such as dilution and inferior winemaking.

1983 Chambertin	⑤	**60**
1983 Charmes-Chambertin	⑤	**55**
1983 Clos Vougeot	⑤	**65**
1983 Gevrey-Chambertin	③	**70**
1983 Mazis-Chambertin	⑤	**73**

These wines, though quite alcoholic and powerful on the palate, are very light in odour, browning at the edges, and after 20–30 minutes in the glass take on the unmistakable mouldy smell of rot. The Mazis and Clos Vougeot are less afflicted, the Charmes totally flawed. Some tasters may not object to this character – it resembles the smell and taste of a 'corked' bottle.

REMOISSENET *BEAUNE* ★★★

This is unquestionably one of the wealthiest domaines in Burgundy. Roland Remoissenet is the gregarious genius behind this empire. The quality of wines here has always been quite good, perhaps not so exciting as the prices charged for the wines suggest, but nevertheless ripe, round Pinot Noir-flavoured wines. While tasting through the line of Remoissenet wines, I got the impression that Roland Remoissenet thinks 1983 is a good vintage. The quality level in 1983 at Remoissenet is good, but I found no great red Burgundies, adding evidence to my feeling that 1983 is by no means a super vintage. Remoissenet did not bottle his wines until December 1985, in order to soften the tannins as much as possible. His wines are quite expensive.

Côte de Beaune *Remoissenet*

1983 Beaune Grèves	④	**85**
1983 Beaune Marconnets	④	**87**
1983 Beaune Touissants	④	**84**
1983 Bourgogne Passe Tout Grains	②	**74**
1983 Corton Clos du Roi	⑤	**86**
1983 Givry Baron Thénard	④	**83**
1983 Mercurey Clos Fourtoul	④	**75**
1983 Pommard	④	**76**
1983 Le Renommée	②	**72**
1983 Santenay Gravières	④	**75**
1983 Volnay	④	**80**

The range of Remoissenet wines from the Côte de Beaune was surprisingly mediocre. Only five wines stood out. The 1983 Givry from Baron Thénard, always a good value from Remoissenet, is robust, fruity, substantial on the palate and interesting. Look for it to be fully mature between 1988 and 1994. Several of the Beaune wines are quite good. The Beaune Touissants has a lovely black cherry bouquet, spicy, rather hard, tannic flavours, and medium body, and at least five to eight years of positive evolution ahead. The Beaune Marconnets was my favourite Côte de Beaune wine from Remoissenet. Rich, ripe cherry and spicy oak aromas inundate the nose. On the palate, the wine is dense and concentrated, moderately tannic, and simply longer and deeper in flavour than the other wines. Give it six to eight years of cellaring. The Beaune Grèves has broad flavours, but not the length or complexity of the Beaune Marconnets. The Corton Clos de Roi is the biggest and most alcoholic of these wines. Deep, fat, but also hard and tough in the finish, it should make a fine bottle in eight years or so.

Côte de Nuits *Remoissenet*

1983 Charmes-Chambertin	⑤	**78**
1983 Clos Vougeot	⑤	**86**
1983 Gevrey-Chambertin	④	**70**
1983 Gevrey-Chambertin Aux Combottes	⑤	**87**
1983 Gevrey-Chambertin Clos St.-Jacques	⑤	**87**
1983 Grands-Echézeaux	⑤	**84**
1983 Mazis-Chambertin	⑤	**83**
1983 Nuits St.-Georges	④	**84**
1983 Nuits St.-Georges Les Perdrix	④	**86**
1983 Richebourg	⑤	**72**
1983 Vosne-Romanée Les Beaumonts	⑤	**80**

Remoissenet's wines from the Côte de Nuits show somewhat better quality than the wines from the Côte de Beaune. That is not to say there are not any disappointments. The Gevrey-Chambertin is thin and hard; the Charmes-Chambertin totally one-dimensional and musty in flavour. The Vosne-Romanée Les Beaumonts smelled herbaceous and stemmy. Lastly, the Richebourg tasted uncommonly harsh and astringent. As for the good news, the Nuits St.-Georges exhibits a smoky, earthy richness, deep colour, good body and six to eight years of life ahead. The Nuits St.-Georges Les Perdrix is even better, rich, smoky, dark in colour, full-bodied, tannic, and powerful. Give it eight to ten years. The Gevrey-Chambertin Clos St.-Jacques is a definite winner, deep in colour, full-bodied, ripe, intense, rich, and quite loaded with fruit. I like the Gevrey-Chambertin Aux Combottes equally for its spicy, rich, very complex bouquet, ripe, dense, alcoholic, powerful flavours and excellent finish. It is quite a big impact wine that needs seven to ten years of cellaring. The Grands-Echézeaux is delicious, but rather light and not as concentrated as one might expect. The Clos Vougeot, while very tannic and in need of ten years of cellaring, is rich in extract, spicy, full-bodied, with a long, deep finish.

DOMAINE DANIEL RION *NUITS ST.-GEORGES* ★★★

I have tasted most of Rion's wines over the last four vintages; the wines have shown considerable consistency and now avoid the lapses in quality that plagued them in the late seventies. The Rion wines tend to be round, ripe, and fruity, with moderate levels of tannins. For the last several years, the Nuits St.-Georges Les Hauts

Pruliers, Clos Vougeot, and Vosne-Romanée Les Beaumonts have tended to be the best wines from this domaine.

1983 Clos Vougeot	⑤	**87**
1983 Côte de Nuits-Villages	③	**81**
1983 Nuits St.-Georges Les Hauts Pruliers	④	**86**
1983 Vosne-Romanée	④	**84**
1983 Vosne-Romanée Les Beaumonts	④	**84**

These 1983s are more forward and accessible than many wines from this vintage. I would expect them to peak around 1990 and last a half-dozen more years. Rion's wines generally are not very long-lived; a tasting in the summer of 1985 of the 1978s showed them to be drying out. The 1983 Côte de Nuits-Villages is a solid, chunky, straightforward wine with moderate tannins and some elegant Pinot Noir character. It should last for five years. The Vosne-Romanée is a lively, medium-bodied wine with a suppleness and pleasing lushness that give it appeal now. It should be drunk over the next three to four years. Curiously, the Vosne-Romanée Les Beaumonts has a similar character and, while more tannic, seems too close in style and quality to the Vosne-Romanée to merit the additional price. I liked both the Nuits St.-Georges Les Hauts Pruliers and Clos Vougeot considerably more than the other Rion wines. The Nuits St.-Georges Les Hauts Pruliers has a lot of spicy oak in its bouquet as well as some ripe plums. On the palate, it is deep and relatively rich, with very good length and depth. It is quite a deep wine. The Clos Vougeot is even better, with a dense-looking, dark ruby colour, a very fragrant plum and oak bouquet, fat, rich fruit, full body, and moderate rounded tannins. Both the Les Hauts Pruliers and Clos Vougeot should be at their best between 1990 and 1995.

DOMAINE DE LA ROMANÉE-CONTI
VOSNE-ROMANÉE ★ ★ ★ ★ ★

After a number of years of futile efforts, I was finally permitted to visit this domaine in 1985. I can appreciate the domaine's feelings that certain writers have maliciously criticized this estate, which produces Burgundy's most expensive and sometimes its most remarkable wines. However, the domaine should be able to accept constructive criticism. I was the very first writer to praise highly their excellent 1980s, but when I criticized several of the 1981s, I was *persona non grata*. In any event, since 1978 this estate has produced many of the greatest wines in Burgundy; the 1978s are superb, the 1979s excellent, the 1980s exceptional, the 1981s somewhat mixed, and the 1982s very, very good. The 1983s here are outstanding, but begin to save your money for them now since they are extremely expensive.

1983 Echézeaux	⑤	85
1983 Grands-Echézeaux	⑤	90
1983 Richebourg	⑤	90
1983 Romanée-Conti	⑤	92
1983 Romanée-St.-Vivant	⑤	87
1983 La Tâche	⑤	92

The 1983 vintage for this domaine, or the DRC as it is often called, was a very tough year. First there was hail, then the advent of rot in August because of tropical heat and humidity. When the harvest occurred, the DRC instructed its pickers to pick only the grapes, not the whole bunches, by hand and to discard all the rotten grapes. The results are splendidly concentrated and rich wines, but wines that are also extremely expensive. They need at least a decade of cellaring, as they are not showing well at present because they are so tannic. At the summit of quality is the Romanée-Conti and La Tâche, two sensational wines with rich yet youthful fragrances, long, deep flavours, and plenty of body. The Richebourg is closed, the Grands-Echézeaux the most velvety and forward, and, given its quality, also the best value for a DRC wine. The Romanée-St.-Vivant is very spicy, a little rustic, but tannic and big. The Echézeaux is the lightest, and while good, not terribly exciting. Yet despite their obvious success, these wines all need seven to ten years of cellaring, except for the Echézeaux.

1982 Echézeaux	⑤	83
1982 Grands-Echézeaux	⑤	87
1982 Richebourg	⑤	87
1982 Romanée-Conti	⑤	88
1982 Romanée-St.-Vivant	⑤	86
1982 La Tâche	⑤	88

The fact that the DRC is on top in Burgundy is well evidenced by these 1982s. Considering the vintage, they are remarkably rich, deep, broadly flavoured wines. They are expensive, but certainly extremely high in quality. The Echézeaux is rather light and slightly herbaceous, but aromatic, very spicy, and ready to drink. It will keep for five to seven years. The Grands-Echézeaux is normally the 'best buy' (for a DRC wine) and in 1982 it seems to offer the most for your money. It has surprisingly deep colour, a big, rich, open-knit bouquet of exotic spices, plums, and wood. On the palate it is rich, medium-bodied, and fairly heady, with moderate tannins. It should be at its best between 1988 and 1994. The Romanée-St.-Vivant is intensely spicy, round, and fruity, with plenty of complexity, moderate tannins, and five to seven years of evolution. The Richebourg actually needs five years to mature fully. It is deep in colour (in fact one of the darkest 1982s), quite long and rich on the palate, with a lush, rich finish, and some firm tannins clearly noticeable. Give it four to five years. The La Tâche and Romanée-Conti are both very, very fragrant. Exotic spices, new oak, and ripe berry fruit all intermingle to create an orgy of wonderful scents. Both wines need three to five years to lose some of their tannic bite, but they are surprisingly deep, rich, and well-coloured wines for this vintage. The DRC clearly looks to have made some of the finest wines of the 1982 vintage.

DOMAINE ROUMIER *CHAMBOLLE-MUSIGNY* ★★★★

When I first looked at the 1983s at Roumier, I thought they were among the very best of the vintage. There is no reason to change my opinion now, though I wish Roumier had not bowed to pressure from his American importer and filtered his 1983s. Roumier's wines were pre-sold by a number of retailers, so I doubt that his greatest wines are still available, as he did not make much wine in 1983 due to hail and rot. Several of Roumier's 1982s are also attractive for drinking now. His 1985s look very good rather than great.

1983 Bonnes Mares	⑤	**92**
1983 Chambolle-Musigny	④	**84**
1983 Chambolle-Musigny Les Amoureuses	⑤	**88**
1983 Clos Vougeot	⑤	**90**
1983 Morey St.-Denis Clos de la Bussière	④	**87**
1983 Musigny	⑤	**90**
1983 Ruchottes-Chambertin	⑤	**93**

Roumier always makes top-quality Burgundy, but the 1983s are the best I have ever tasted from him, including the sensational wines he produced in 1976 and 1969. His 1983s have an opulence and richness to go with their power and firm tannins. They are not likely to be fully mature until 1992–2000. These are truly great red Burgundies – worth a search of the marketplace to find. The Morey St.-Denis Clos de la Bussière is an excellent red Burgundy by any standard, but when tasting it alongside the other top wines here it gets lost. It has dark ruby colour, an intense, sweet fruitiness, medium to full body, and firm tannins. It should be ready by 1992. The Chambolle-Musigny is a bit more tough and tannic, and while the colour and concentration are excellent, the wine has some dry, astringent tannins in the finish that suggest hail or rot problems; it is the only Roumier wine I noticed this in. The Chambolle-Musigny Les Amoureuses (only 200 cases made) is rather powerful and alcoholic, but extremely deep and concentrated. Give it ten years. The great wines produced by

Roumier include a staggeringly rich Clos Vougeot that is packed with ripe Pinot Noir fruit. This powerful, rather massive red Burgundy is so complex and aromatic that it will not be fully mature for ten years. Roumier's Musigny is also a great wine, more sensual and elegant, but extremely ripe and rich, dark in colour, with an intense, supple lushness to its fruit. It has great balance and should drink beautifully between 1992 and 2000. Two of the very greatest wines are the Bonnes Mares and Ruchottes-Chambertin. I truly don't think one can taste better Burgundy. The Bonnes Mares tastes denser and richer than the Musigny. The Ruchottes-Chambertin is a monument, a prodigious and magnificent wine of incredible power, richness, and depth.

1982 Bonnes Mares	⑤	82
1982 Chambolle-Musigny	④	78
1982 Clos Vougeot	④	82
1982 Musigny	⑤	84

These are good wines, light, fruity, clean, and supple, but the prices for Burgundy are so high that, unless the wine is truly superb, your money is better spent elsewhere. The Musigny is clearly the best; it has a vivid, oaky, and cherry-scented bouquet, but compared to the 1983 is rather light and watery.

DANIEL SENARD *ALOXE-CORTON* ★ ★ ★

In America one hears little about this fine estate in Aloxe-Corton. Senard's speciality is Corton, but for connoisseurs of the unusual, he makes a tiny amount of white wine from the Pinot Gris grape called Corton Blanc. It is an exotic, rich wine. Senard's red 1983s are typical for the vintage, big, backward, dry, tannic, and undeveloped. Hopefully ten to twelve years of cellaring will see the fruit emerge from behind the wall of tannin.

DOMAINE ARMAND ROUSSEAU
GEVREY-CHAMBERTIN ★ ★ ★ ★

This is a very serious domaine, where Charles Rousseau makes altogether classic long-lived wines. They are expensive and hard to find, but very much deserve their acclaim and price. Rousseau compares the 1983 to the 1976, only he admits that the grapes were much more difficult to deal with. Some of the 1983s here are exceptional, but very tannic; some have noticeable rot problems. Rousseau says they need a minimum of fifteen years of cellaring.

1983 Chambertin	⑤	67
1983 Chambertin Clos de Bèze	⑤	90
1983 Charmes-Chambertin	⑤	70
1983 Clos de la Roche	⑤	70

1983 Gevrey-Chambertin.. ④ *82*
1983 Gevrey-Chambertin Clos St.-Jacques .... ⑤ *90*
1983 Gevrey-Chambertin Les Cazetiers................... ⑤ *85*
1983 Mazis-Chambertin.. ⑤ *72*
1983 Ruchottes-Chambertin.. ⑤ *88*

> With the exception of the Gevrey-Chambertin, which may be mature by 1990, all of these wines require a minimum of ten years of cellaring. However, the tannins are ripe and hard, not the dry and astringent tannins caused by rot. All the wines are very deep in colour, especially the Clos de Bèze, Clos St.-Jacques, and Ruchottes. The most forward wine is the Clos de la Roche, but it still needs ten years. The most backward wine is the Chambertin. If I had just one of these wines to buy, it would be the Clos St.-Jacques, which has layers of sweet fruit and is significantly less expensive than the Clos de Bèze or Chambertin. If you have a good cellar and plenty of discretionary income, the Clos de Bèze will be superb in ten to fifteen years. The others may or may not turn out well. Rot definitely appears to be a problem.

1983 Corton... ⑤ *70*
1983 Corton Bressandes.. ④ *86*
1983 Corton Clos du Meix .... ④ *85*
1983 Corton Clos du Roi .... ⑤ *87*

> Patience is required here ... a lot of it. With the exception of the Corton, which I found awkward to judge because of the mouth-searing tannins and apparent absence of ripe fruit, the other three Cortons, though tannic and hard, do seem to have the concentration of fruit for balance. The Corton Clos du Roi is the most impressive since it has the finest deep colour and density of fruit, with a promising bouquet of vanillin oak and ripe cherries. Give it ten years of storage. The Corton Bressandes is a trifle more supple, medium-weight, yet a fragrant, ripe, medium- to full-bodied wine that also needs five to ten years of cellaring. The Corton Clos du Meix is similarly styled, yet very tannic and in need of twelve to fifteen years of ageing. It does have plenty of ripe fruit and a rustic, alcoholic punch.

BERNARD SERVEAU *MOREY ST.-DENIS* ★★★★

I have begun to visit Serveau regularly as I regard his wines as benchmark examples of the elegant, graceful, supple style of Burgundy winemaking. His wines are made to be drunk young, as they are never tannic, alcoholic, or full-bodied enough to age past seven to eight years. The 1985s are excellent, the 1984s also well above average, but the 1983s generally less impressive than his 1985s. However, the 1983 Chambolle-Musigny Les Amoureuses should prove to be a winner.

1983 Chambolle-Musigny Les Amoureuses.............. ⑤ *88*
1983 Chambolle-Musigny Les Sabiots........................ ④ *84*
1983 Morey St.-Denis Les Sorbets .... ④ *83*

The Morey St.-Denis Les Sorbets has lost colour, but still retains a pleasing ripeness and sweetness of Pinot Noir fruit. It is a delicate rather than powerful 1983, and should be drunk over the next four to five years. The Chambolle-Musigny Les Sabiots has a trifle more concentration, surprising suppleness for a 1983, and very good ripeness. It should be ready to drink by 1987. The Chambolle-Musigny Les Amoureuses is quite fine, dark in colour, with an expansive, fragrant, ripe bouquet of flowers and plums. This silky, medium-bodied wine has very good concentration and moderate, rather gentle tannins. It should be at its peak between 1990 and 1995.

ROBERT SIRUGE *VOSNE-ROMANÉE* ★ ★ ★

This small grower in Vosne-Romanée produces elegant, supple wines that generally mature quite quickly. His 1983s are above average to good wines, with the exception of the Grands-Echézeaux, which is outstanding.

1983 Grands-Echézeaux .... ⑤ *90*
1983 Vosne-Romanée .... ④ *80*
1983 Vosne-Romanée Les Petits Monts .... ④ *84*

The *village* Vosne-Romanée is a light to medium ruby in colour, with a pleasing oaky, spicy bouquet, a strong lashing of tannin, and a powerful alcoholic punch to it. It needs five to six years of cellaring. The Vosne-Romanée Les Petits Monts is darker in colour, ripe, and alcoholic, but finishes hard and dry with a touch of the *goût de moisi*, which, in essence, is a taste of mouldy, damp cardboard from rot-damaged grapes. It is certainly a good wine, but its development must be watched. The Grands-Echézeaux is quite outstanding, dark ruby in colour with a really superb, intense bouquet of very ripe fruit and spicy oak. It is quite concentrated, very deep and rich, with good tannins that add firmness rather than astringence. It should be at its best between 1992 and 2000.

DOMAINE GABRIEL TORTOCHOT
GEVREY-CHAMBERTIN ★ ★ ★

Tortochot is a serious winemaker. His wines are not filtered and therefore, if not cared for properly, can become unstable. His 1983s are very big, full-bodied wines with an almost roasted ripeness. Like most of the big 1983s, the wines will require significant cellaring.

1983 Chambertin... ⑤ *89*
1983 Clos Vougeot .... ⑤ *84*

1983 Gevrey-Chambertin Lavaux St.-Jacques .... ⑤ *83*
1983 Mazis-Chambertin .... ⑤ *88*
Both the Gevrey-Chambertin Lavaux St.-Jacques and Clos
Vougeot tasted closed and tough, but had good concentration,
and some underlying suppleness, although a tannic toughness
in the finish. They showed no signs of rot damage. They
definitely need six to eight years of cellaring. The Mazis-
Chambertin and Chambertin are very old-style wines, thick,
rich, full-throttle Burgundies with roasted, spicy, intense
bouquets, rich, sweet, almost creamy flavours, full body, and
ripe, round tannins. They are approachable now, but please
cellar them for six to eight years for their potential to be
realized.

DOMAINE LOUIS TRAPET *GEVREY-CHAMBERTIN* ★★★

I have not always been pleased with the Trapet wines. They certainly
have an excellent reputation, but in some vintages they have turned
out too light and have had a tendency to turn brown in colour at an
early age. They are aged fifteen to eighteen months in oak barrels, of
which one-third are new. Jean Trapet, the current Trapet in charge,
is a short, affable man. His 1983s were bottled in May 1985, after a
slight filtration. Trapet used the new 'Bouteille Bourgogne' for his
1983s, an ugly, cheap-looking bottle that resembles the bottle used
for generic Côtes du Rhône wines, which does no justice to the
product. The style of wine produced here is generally lighter than
that made at such domaines as Leclerc, Rousseau, Clair-Daü, and
Varoilles. The 1983s from Trapet are very, very good, probably the
best wines I have yet tasted from this estate.

1983 Chambertin .... ⑤ *86*
1983 Chambertin Cuvée Vieilles Vignes .... ⑤ *90*
1983 Chapelle-Chambertin .... ④ *86*
1983 Latricières-Chambertin .... ④ *86*
All of these wines have a light to medium ruby colour. They
also exhibit very broad, ripe, smoky, sweet Pinot flavours.
Firm tannins are present, but these wines are much more
accessible and forward than most 1983s. I expect all of them
to be drinking well by 1990 and lasting five to ten years. The
Chapelle-Chambertin is quite rich, round, and fruity, with a
complex, smoky, deep bouquet. The flavours are lush and
intense. It should be ready in three to four years. The
Latricières-Chambertin is less evolved and more obviously
tannic, yet develops beautifully in the glass, revealing scents of
toffee, caramel, and hickory. It has a velvety texture and very
long finish, and should be drunk by 1990; no later than 1996.
The Chambertin is the most closed and tannic of these four

wines. It is spicy and rich, but for the moment does not reveal the same depth and complexity of flavour of the other wines. The Chambertin Cuvée Vieilles Vignes, produced from 80-year-old vines and made on an average of only once every decade (there were 100 cases in 1983) is a decadently rich and opulent Pinot Noir. It has the deepest colour (although it is not very dark) and concentration, with a huge scented bouquet of smoky fruit and crème brûlée. Sweet, ripe, long, and very expansive on the palate, this medium- to full-bodied wine is already tasting exceptionally fine. However, five to six years of bottle age should reveal even more character.

COMTE DE VOGÜÉ *CHAMBOLLE-MUSIGNY* ★ ★

This estate in Chambolle-Musigny is certainly one of the most famous in all of Burgundy. Burgundy collectors continue to rush to buy these wines, even though the quality has slipped considerably. I have not tasted a great Vogüé wine since the 1972s. Yet the price is as high as ever and the wines more often than not extremely light, sometimes insipid, overly filtered and, in truth, a total embarrassment. The 1983s are better than many of the wines made in the dismal 1973–1982 period, but are not anywhere close to being considered among the best in this variable vintage. The 1982s are no better than most white Zinfandels on the market; in fact, they lack the colour of most blush wines.

1983 Bonnes Mares..	⑤	*84*
1983 Chambolle-Musigny	⑤	*75*
1983 Chambolle-Musigny Les Amoureuses..............	⑤	*83*
1983 Musigny..	⑤	*85*

For fear of tainting the macerating grape juice with the *goût de moisi* from rot and hail-scarred grapes, the decision was made to pull the skins off after only a week. Several other producers made similar decisions and the results were rather lightly coloured, elegant, fruity wines that lacked depth and concentration. The *village* Chambolle-Musigny is very light, but clean and pleasant. The Chambolle-Musigny Les Amoureuses has considerably more fruit and flavour, decent body, some attractive vanillin oakiness, and a good, lush finish. It should be at its best by 1990. The Bonnes Mares is very precocious-tasting, has medium body, good concentration, an underlying, pleasing suppleness, and four to six years of evolution ahead of it. The Musigny is darker in colour, with more tannin and slightly more concentration. Its tannins are soft, the bouquet dominated by the smell of new oak and cherries. The Musigny should reach full maturity between 1990 and 1994.

1982 Bonnes Mares.. ⑤ **73**
1982 Chambolle-Musigny Les Amoureuses.............. ⑤ **72**
1982 Musigny... ⑤ **74**
There is not much flavour or colour to these wines, so all I will say is that they look and taste like simple, pleasant rosés with some faint Pinot Noir character in the distant background. How any respectable producer, particularly the Comte de Vogüé, could release such overpriced mediocrities under a famous label is beyond my comprehension. *Caveat emptor!*

BEAUJOLAIS

Beaujolais, produced from the Gamay grape, will never be a great or profound wine, but it has the potential to be one of the most flexible, enjoyable, and seductive wines. At its best, served slightly chilled (50°F is a perfect temperature), it is a heady, perfumed, intensely fruity, soft, lush wine that can be rapaciously gulped down without feeling any guilt for not commenting on its bouquet, complexity, or finesse. Simple, lush and delicious, Beaujolais can be a hedonistic summer pleasure for wine drinkers.

The Beaujolais hierarchy is simple. At the lowest echelon is 'straight' Beaujolais, followed by Beaujolais-Villages, which is usually better. At the top level of quality are the nine Crus, each supposedly offering the inimitable soft, lush fruitiness that has made Beaujolais so popular, but each slightly different in style.

Today the difference between a Moulin-à-Vent, historically the fullest, most ageworthy and richest Beaujolais Cru, and Brouilly, the lightest Cru, is not always so apparent as the textbooks say. However, the other seven Crus are Chiroubles, always one of my favourites for decadently fruity wines; Juliénas, fleshy and rich; St.-Amour, very fruity and supple; Morgon, among the most ageworthy; Fleurie, lush, silky, and fruity; Côtes de Brouilly, light and delicate, and Chénas, full, darkly coloured, and potentially excellent.

Most Beaujolais will be at their best one to three years after the vintage. Some will last longer. Despite this possibility of longevity, the wines do lose fruit and change in character as the freshness and zesty, exuberant fruitiness of the wines dissipates. They may taste good in three years, but clearly their effusively fruity character begs for them to be drunk up over the first few years.

Recent Vintages

As for recent vintages, 1985 is the best bet since the wines are ripe, fragrant, rich, and supple. They should be drunk up by the end of 1987. Avoid the 1984s, which are hollow and lack charm. The rather large-proportioned 1983s were atypical Beaujolais — tannic, full-bodied, rich, but 'too big'. The best Morgons, Fleuries, and Moulin-à-Vents from 1983 can still be drunk with great pleasure. However, given a choice, I would definitely opt for the 1985s. The Beaujolais from 1986 are firmer, more tannic wines than the 1985s, as well as less concentrated. They are certainly good, but they lack the fat and flesh of the remarkable 1985s.

A GUIDE TO BEAUJOLAIS' BEST PRODUCERS

★ ★ ★ ★ ★ Outstanding Producers

J. P. Bloud	Jacky Janodet
Michel Chignard	Petit Perou
B. Diochon	Bernard Sauté
Georges Duboeuf	

★ ★ ★ ★ Excellent Producers

Serge Aujas	Domaine Matray
Jean Bédin	Jean-Paul Ruet
Louis Champagnon	Domaine Savoy
Jacques Depagneux	Thevenet
Pierre Ferraud	Château Thivin
Château des Jacques	Trenel
Mathelin	Georges Trichard

★ ★ ★ Good Producers

Paul Beaudet	Chanut Frères
Georges Boulon	Jaffelin
Domaine Dalicieux	André Large
Joseph Drouhin	Moillard
Henry Fessy	Piat
Sylvain Fessy	Roger Rocassel

★ ★ Average Producers

Loron	Pasquier-Desvignes
Mommessin	Paul Sapin
Robert Pain	Louis Tête

The King of Beaujolais

No other person dominates a wine region of France as Georges Duboeuf, le grand roi de Beaujolais, does there. The reasons for his remarkable success are simple – fair prices, consistently high quality, and a huge production. His famous 'flower-labelled' bottle has inspired a new colourful era of wine labels and his single domaine-designated Beaujolais wines are the best that money can buy. In recent vintages Duboeuf's wines have been priced very reasonably, and his 1985s are the finest he has made to date. Duboeuf's wines are always in demand.

RATING DUBOEUF'S BEST SINGLE-VINEYARD BEAUJOLAIS

Outstanding

Chiroubles Desmeures	Morgon Jean Descombes
Fleurie Les Deduits	Moulin-à-Vent Herrtiers Tagent

Excellent

Beaujolais Regnie (du Potet)	Fleurie (Quatre Vents)
Beaujolais-Villages (Grand Grange)	Juliénas (des Mouilles)
	Juliénas (des Vignes)
Brouilly (de Nervers)	Morgon (Princesse Lieven)
Brouilly (du Prieuré)	Morgon (des Versauds)
Chénas (La Combe Remont)	Moulin-à-Vent (des Caves)
Chénas (Manoir des Journets)	Moulin-à-Vent (La Tour du Brief)
Chiroubles (de Javernand)	
Chiroubles (de Raousset)	St.-Amour (du Paradis)

WHITE BURGUNDY

The Price of Glory

Puligny-Montrachet, Chassagne-Montrachet, Meursault, Corton-Charlemagne

There can be no doubt that the tiny region of southern Burgundy, centred around the small towns of Puligny-Montrachet, Chassagne-Montrachet, and Meursault, produces the world's greatest dry white wine from the Chardonnay grape. However, the production is strictly limited by law, and insatiable worldwide demand has caused prices for white Burgundy in 1987 to reach such absurd levels that one is hard pressed to recommend any of these wines. However, I have provided a rating of the growers for those willing to spend the small fortune necessary for a bottle of white Burgundy.

Chablis

Located at Burgundy's northernmost end, Chablis is not always fully appreciated. Chablis wines, less opulent, fat, buttery and rich than white Burgundy made further south, are crisp, sometimes flinty, often austere and tart, but in great years are classic examples of tightly knit Chardonnay ripeness and crisp acidity. In most years, a huge quantity of wine is made here, all of it white and all of it from Chardonnay vines spread out around the town of Chablis. But this is a risky area since the vineyards lie quite far north and it is cool in Chablis. Consequently, the frequent spring frosts can occur very late, thereby putting a tragic halt to vine growth and significantly curtailing production. Yet, when the climate is hospitable from March through October, Chablis at its best has a remarkable richness of fruit, a firm, fresh acidity that gives it a zesty taste and a penetrating bouquet. The best Chablis comes from several Grand Cru vineyards (which represent less than 5% of the total produced), but some Chablis Premiers Crus from vineyards such as Montée de Tonnerre, Fourchaume, and Vaillons can, in the hands of the best growers, be as good. Chablis, which has had its name bastardized by both the California and Australian wine industry, is not a wine to seek out in cold, rainy years, since the wines then tend to be too acidic, lean, and hard. But in the great vintages, 1985, 1983, 1978, and 1975, Chablis can last and improve in the bottle for five, ten, even fifteen years in some cases. Prices here too have rocketed in the last two years and Chablis at the top levels (Premier or Grand Cru) is now very, very expensive.

When choosing a top Chablis, I recommend staying away from straight Chablis except in the ripe, sunny vintages. It is often a green, very neutral wine with an acid-like character. Decide whether you like a toasty oaky character to your Chablis or want pure, uninfluenced, crisp Chardonnay fruit to taste. If you like the barrel-fermented, aged-in-cask 'traditional', buttery, toasty, ripe style of Chablis, no one does it better than Dauvissat, Raveneau, and Long-Depaquit, but expect to pay upwards of £15 a bottle for Grands Crus from these producers. For pure Chardonnay fruit that never sees a trace of oak ageing, Louis Michel's wines are brilliant expressions.

QUICK VINTAGE GUIDE

1986 An excellent, perhaps outstanding vintage of ripe, well-balanced wines with good acidity was produced. In many cases, the wines are more classic examples of Chablis in the sense that they are austere, flinty, racy wines when compared to the opulent, low acid 1985s. Thankfully, prices are dropping after reaching outrageously high levels for the 1985s.

1985 An outstanding year for Chablis, a very good year for Puligny, Chassagne, and Meursault. Forward, lush, soft wines were made that have good, not excessive alcohol content, relatively low acidity, and no trace of any annoying rot or hail damage. Unfortunately, prices are at absurd levels and show no signs of dropping. The crop size was below average in Chablis due to a severe winter. A vintage to buy if you can afford it.

1984 The tiny crop of wine was maligned for no reason prior to this harvest, but for Chablis and Puligny, Chassagne, and Meursault, medium-bodied, clean, fresh, lively wines were produced that will drink nicely for three to four years. They are not great wines, but neither are they poor. The wines have begun to lose some of their annoyingly high acidity and greenness, but they lack fruit and flesh.

1983 The best year for Chablis since the great vintage of 1978. For Puligny, Chassagne, and Meursault, a very irregular year of rather massive, high-alcohol wines. Where balancing acidity is present, the wines are spectacular. When it is not, they are heavy, clumsy, and grotesque. The top wines from Chablis are explosively rich, powerful, and alcoholic, but they are slightly out of balance and though immensely enjoyable, should be drunk before the end of this decade.

1982 A prolific crop of lush, rich, very fruity, low-acid wines was produced in Chablis and also in Puligny, Chassagne, and Meursault. Some wines, particularly from the growers/producers who over-cropped or made no selections, are watery and light. The best, however, are voluptuous, lush, elegant, and ideal for drinking over the next two to three years. A very good, sometimes outstanding vintage, but it will not keep long.

1981 Initially considered a classic year of slow-to-mature, high-acid, lean, angular wines that just needed time to develop, though some wines lack flesh and charm and will never develop. Those that have the requisite intensity and richness will be long-lived and classic. The wines from Chablis are good, but a trifle austere and in some cases very lean. This is a vintage in which one should pay particular attention to the producer.

1980 A dull summer led to adverse pre-harvest publicity that doomed the reputation of the vintage. The wines are solid, reliable, but rather uninspiring. They should be drunk up.

1979 A huge crop everywhere and the wines show a lack of depth as well as low acidity. They all should be drunk up; only a few of the big wines from the best growers are worth holding on to.

1978 In the last ten years, the only uncontested and consistently great vintage for Chablis and for Puligny, Chassagne, and Meursault. The wines are both powerful and graceful, with splendid balance, rich, ripe flavours, and further evolution ahead of them.

Older Vintages

I suspect few consumers give the best white Burgundies and top Chablis much of a chance to prove their remarkable longevity. Older vintages of the best producers can be eye-opening in their freshness. The best 1978s are presently in full bloom, revealing all of their majestic ripeness and richness, unquestionably a great year. The 1979s should have been consumed by now (examples from cool cellars can be wonderful). The 1976s were ripe, alcoholic, and similar to the 1983s, but all 1976s should be drunk up. The 1975s from Chablis are still classics, and the wines of Chablis were certainly France's best-kept secret in this vintage.

A GUIDE TO THE BEST PRODUCERS OF PULIGNY-MONTRACHET, CHASSAGNE-MONTRACHET, MEURSAULT, AND CORTON-CHARLEMAGNE

★ ★ ★ ★ ★ Outstanding Producers

Coche-Dury	Leroy
Louis Jadot	André Ramonet
Comtes Lafon	Etienne Sauzet
Vincent Leflaive	

★ ★ ★ ★ Excellent Producers

Bitouzet-Prieur	Delagrange-Bachelet
Bonneau de Martray	Joseph Drouhin
Louis Chapuis	Gagnard
Chartron and Trébuchet	Jaffelin

François Jobard
Louis Latour
Lequin-Roussot
Château de Maltroye
Château de Meursault
Michelot-Buisson
Albert Morey

Niellon
Prieur-Brunet
Ramonet-Prudhon
Remoissenet
Ropiteau
Guy Roulot

★ ★ ★ Good Producers

Robert Ampeau
Henri Boillot
Bouchard Père
Bouzereau-Gruère
Caillot
Coche-Debord

Duc de Magenta
Joseph Matrot
Moillard
Charles Moncaut
Jean Monnier

A GUIDE TO CHABLIS' BEST PRODUCERS

★ ★ ★ ★ ★ Outstanding Producers

René Dauvissat
Long-Depaquit

Raveneau

★ ★ ★ ★ Excellent Producers

Paul Droin
William Fèvre
Louis Michel

Louis Pinson
Guy Robin
Robert Voceret

★ ★ ★ Good Producers

La Chablisienne
Jean Colin
Domaine Defaix
Joseph Drouhin
Marcel Duplessis
Domaine de L'Eglantière
Alain Geoffrey

Lamblin
Domaine Laroche
Moillard
J. Moreau
Albert Pic
A. Regnaud

WHERE ARE BURGUNDY'S WHITE WINE VALUES?

If one is willing to be a bit adventurous and avoid the glamorous appellations of white Burgundy, values can be found. The little-known Saint-Romain, Auxey-Duresses, Saint-Aubin, and Santenay provide four appellations where it is still difficult to find a white Burgundy for more than £10 a bottle. Further south in the area called the Chalonnais, the white wines of Rully and Montagny are where the values are produced. Further south of the Chalonnais, just to the north of Lyon, is the Mâconnais, the consumer's best chance for enjoying fruity, crisp Chardonnay wines for £5–£7. The Mâcon-Villages wines and neighbouring wines of St.-Veran are increasingly well made, and represent very fine values. The following is a list of the best producers of these wines. Vintages should be regarded as approximately the same as in Puligny, Chassagne, Meursault, and Corton Charlemagne.

Burgundy's Best White Wine Values

Delorme (Rully)

Domaine de la Folie (Rully)

Duboeuf (Mâcon-Villages)

Duboeuf (St.-Veran)

Guffens-Heynen (Mâcon-
  Pierreclos)

J. Lamy (St.-Aubin)

Lequin-Roussot (Santenay)

Leroy (Auxey-Duresses)

Leroy (St.-Romain)

Prunier (Auxey-Duresses)

Vachet (Montagny)

CHABLIS, PULIGNY-MONTRACHET, CHASSAGNE-MONTRACHET, MEURSAULT, CORTON-CHARLEMAGNE ● A BUYING STRATEGY

Unless you have the riches of a successful movie star, the glories of the outstanding 1985 Chablis will seem, justifiably, too expensive an indulgence. Another small crop has caused prices to rocket. If that is discouraging news, I can hardly recommend the lean, acidic 1984s that are not only rather unattractive wines, but also expensive. The 1983s are drinking beautifully, but I will bet that the top wines have long disappeared from the marketplace. Wine from the bountiful crop of 1982 can still be found, but unless you can find those from the top producers, these wines too are beginning to show a little fatigue. In short, this is not a good time to buy white burgundy unless you want to pay the outrageously high prices asked for the 1985s, and that seems senseless to me, given the numerous high-quality, less expensive alternatives.

CHAMPAGNE

A vast amount of Champagne, the festive wine par excellence, is purchased and drunk by consumers. For the last few years, Champagne buyers have never had it so good. Bumper crops of solid-quality wine in Champagne, and intense price competition by importers, wholesalers and retailers all combined to drive prices down and for a time it was a wonderful buyer's market. However, this has all changed. A small, mediocre crop in 1984, a top-quality but quite small crop in 1985, and a sagging American dollar have caused an upward surge in Champagne prices. The shift was first noticed in 1986, as prices soared higher – a good 20% – 40% in many cases. Price instability appears to be the rule now, but those who stocked up in 1985 can consider themselves fortunate, since prices now are considerably higher.

In luxury Champagne, I recommend paying close attention to the following rules.

1 The luxury or prestige Cuvées of the Champagne houses are almost always over-priced. The pricing plays on the consumer's belief that higher price signifies a higher level of quality. In many cases it does not.

2 Purchase your Champagne from a merchant who has a quick turnover in stock. More than any other wine, Champagne is particularly vulnerable to poor storage and bright shop lighting. Buying bottles that have been languishing on the shelves of retailers for two to three months can be risky business.

3 Don't hesitate to try some of the best non-vintaged Champagnes recommended herein. The best of them are quite comparable to the best luxury Cuvées, but sell for a quarter to a fifth of the price.

4 There has been a tremendous influx of high-quality Champagnes from small firms in Champagne. Although many of these wines may be difficult to find some of these small houses produce splendid wine worthy of a search.

5 The technical terms that appear on the label of a producer's Champagne can tell you several things about the wine. **Brut** Champagnes are dry, but legally can have up to 1.5 grammes per litre sugar (dosage) added. **Extra Dry** Champagnes are those that have between 1.5–3.5 grammes per litre sugar added. Most tasters would call these Champagnes dry, but they tend to be rounder and seemingly fruitier than Brut Champagnes. The terms **Ultra Brut, Brut Absolu or Dosage Zéro** signify that the Champagne has had no sugar added and is bone dry. These Champagnes are rarely seen, but can be quite impressive as well as austere and lean tasting.

AISNE

VESLE

Saint-
Gilles

Ville-en-
Tardenoi

A4

Vincelles   Vandières

Rueil

A4   Château-
Thierry   Dormans

N3   Reuilly-
Savigny

Montreuil-
aux-
Lions

le Breuil

Orbais-l'Abbaye

MARNE

Saacy-
sur-
Marne

D1

Montmirail

Champagne

0   5   MILES

0   5   10   KILOMETERS

Champagne AOc area
Vineyard areas
• Centers of production
— Route de Champagne

Champagne

Recent Vintages

The idea of vintage-dated Champagne representing only the very best years has become somewhat of a farce. It seems as though most Champagne producers now claim that 'every year is a vintage year'. For example, in the fifties there were four vintage years, 1952, 1953, 1955, and 1959; in the sixties five vintage years, 1961, 1962, 1964, 1966, and 1969. In the seventies, every year has been a vintage except 1972 and 1977. In the current decade, 1980, 1981, 1982, 1983 are all vintage years. If you insist on vintage Champagne, 1975, 1976, 1978, 1979, and 1982 are the only recent years that are truly vintage quality. The 1979 may well turn out to be the sleeper vintage of this quintet; not highly regarded at first, many of the 1979s seem to have excellent balance and grace, as well as flavour.

CHAMPAGNE · FINDING THE BEST WINES

Non-vintage Brut

Ayala
Bollinger
Charbaut Blanc de Blancs
Clicquot
Gratien
Legras

Mumm Crémant
Bruno Paillard Crémant
J. Perrier Cuvée Royale
Pol Roger
Rapeneau
Louis Roederer Prémier

Rosé

N.V. Billecart
1979 Clicquot
N.V. Krug
1975 Moët et Chandon
    Dom Pérignon
1979 Perrier-Jouët

N.V. Roederer
1978 Dom Ruinart
1976 Taittinger
    Comtes de Champagne
1979 Taittinger
    Comtes de Champagne

Vintage Brut

1979 and 1982 Billecart
    Blanc de Blancs
1982 Bonnaire Blanc de Blancs
1979 Charbaut Blanc de Blancs
1978 Clicquot
1979 H. Germain
    Blanc de Blancs

1979 Gratien
1976 Bruno Paillard
1979 Pol Roger
1976 Pol Roger

Luxury Cuvées

1979 Billecart Cuvée Billecart
1975 Bollinger R.D.
N.V. Cattier Clos du Moulin
1976 Charbaut Certificate
1979 Clicquot La Grande Dame
1979 Deutz Wm. Deutz

N.V. Gosset Réserve
1979 Heidsieck Monopole
    Diamant Bleu
1979 Henriot Rothschild
1969 Jacquesson
    Late Disgorged

N.V. Krug Grand Cuvée
1978 Laurent-Perrier Grand
  Siècle
N.V. Laurent-Perrier Ultra Brut
N.V. Lechere Blanc de Blancs
N.V. Lechere Orient Express
1978 and 1980 Moët et
  Chandon Dom Pérignon
1975 Pol Roger
  Blanc de Chardonnay

1979 Pol Roger
  Winston Churchill
1979 and 1981 Louis Roederer
  Cristal
1976 Taittinger
  Comtes de Champagnes
1979 Taittinger
  Comtes de Champagnes

A GUIDE TO CHAMPAGNE'S BEST PRODUCERS

★ ★ ★ ★ ★ Outstanding Producers

Bollinger (Full-bodied)
Veuve Clicquot (Full-bodied)
Krug (Full-bodied)

Pol Roger (Medium-bodied)
Louis Roederer (Full-bodied)
Taittinger (Light-bodied)

★ ★ ★ ★ Excellent Producers

·Billecart-Salmon (Light-bodied)
Bonnaire (Light-bodied)
Charbaut (Light-bodied)
Gosset (Full-bodied)
Alfred Gratien (Full-bodied)
Henriot (Full-bodied)
J. Lassalle (Light-bodied)

Laurent-Perrier
  (Medium-bodied)
Lechere (Light-bodied)
Moët et Chandon
  (Medium-bodied)
Dom Ruinart (Light-bodied)

★ ★ ★ Good Producers

Ayala (Medium-bodied)
Paul Bara (Full-bodied)
Barancourt (Full-bodied)
Cattier Brut (Light-bodied)
Deutz (Medium-bodied)
H. Germain (Light-bodied)
Charles Heidsieck
  (Medium-bodied)
Heidsieck Monopole
  (Medium-bodied)
Jacquesson (Light-bodied)

Lanson (Light-bodied)
Launois Père (Light-bodied)
R. & L. Legras (Light-bodied)
Bruno Paillard (Light-bodied)
Joseph Perrier (Medium-bodied)
Perrier-Jouët (Light-bodied)
Philipponnat (Medium-bodied)
Piper Heidsieck (Light-bodied)
Pommery and Greno
  (Light-bodied)

★ ★ Average Producers

Beaumet (Light-bodied)
Besserat de Bellefon
  (Light-bodied)
Boizel (Light-bodied)
Nicholas Feuillatte
  (Light-bodied)
Goldschmidt-Rothschild
  (Light-bodied)
Michel Gonet (Medium-bodied)

Jacquart (Medium-bodied)
Jestin (Light-bodied)
Guy Larmandier
  (Medium-bodied)
Mumm (Medium-bodied)
Oudinot (Medium-bodied)
Rapeneau (Medium-bodied)
Alfred Rothschild (Light-bodied)
Marie Stuart (Light-bodied)

CHAMPAGNE · TODAY'S BUYING STRATEGY

One should have stocked up in 1985 and early 1986, before prices began to climb. However, what do you do now? For vintage Champagnes, unless you are dealing with those producers who make long-lived, full-bodied Champagnes (e.g. Bollinger, Pol Roger, Krug, Veuve Clicquot), you are advised to avoid vintages before 1978. Concentrate on the 1979s, which are very good and the best vintage for drinking until the 1982s appear on the market. Also concentrate on the top non-vintage Champagnes listed. Most experienced tasters cannot begin to tell the difference between a vintage and non-vintage Champagne when tasted blind, yet the price differential is considerable. Lastly, if you think Champagne prices are too high, don't ignore the fine sparkling wines made in Alsace or the Loire Valley. The best of them offer attractive and inexpensive alternatives.

AYALA (Medium-bodied) ★★★
Brut Non-Vintage .... ③ 86

This is a very good Champagne that is quite inexpensive. Quite dry, medium-bodied, and frothy with crisp acidity, this is a fairly aromatic, spicy, toasty Champagne with a dramatic bouquet and well-balanced, dry taste.

PAUL BARA (Full-bodied) ★★★
1979 Brut .... ④ 85

Bara's style makes his among the most forceful, aggressive, and full-bodied Champagnes. His 1979 is relatively rich, toasty, spicy, and full, and for that reason should be served with food rather than as an apéritif.

BARANCOURT (Full-bodied) ★★★
1979 Cuvée des Fondateurs .... ⑤ 84

This is a well-made, rather tightly knit, austere yet large-framed Champagne at a rather ridiculous price. It needs several years of ageing to shed its tartness and austere qualities.

BEAUMET (Light-bodied) ★★
Brut Blanc de Blancs Non-Vintage .... ③ 85
Brut Non-Vintage .... ③ 78
1979 Brut Rosé .... ③ 75

This is a very reasonably priced line of light-bodied, clean, fresh, straightforward Champagnes. The Non-Vintage Brut is acceptable, but rather bland; the 1979 Brut Rosé has little character other than freshness and pretty packaging. The

Non-Vintage Blanc de Blancs is fresh, has a moderately intense, toasty, buttery bouquet, lovely, fresh, light flavours, and a good lingering finish.

BESSERAT DE BELLEFON (Light-bodied) ★★
Brut Non-Vintage .... ③ **78**

Quite light, rather tart and lean with some annoyingly high acidity in the finish, this wine has good freshness, but suffers in comparison with the other non-vintage Champagnes on the market.

BILLECART-SALMON (Light-bodied) ★★★★
1979 Blanc de Blancs .... ⑤ **90**
1982 Blanc de Blancs .... ⑤ **88**
Non-Vintage Brut .... ④ **83**
1979 Cuvée Billecart .... ④ **89**
1982 Cuvée Billecart .... ④ **?**
Rosé Non-Vintage .... ④ **92**

One cannot say too many good things about this small house that produces wonderfully light, elegant, yet flavourful Champagnes. In every one of my Champagne tastings, Billecart has shown exceptionally well. This year the remarkable Rosé edged out the wonderful but superexpensive Taittinger Comtes de Champagne Rosé and Perrier-Jouët Flower Bottle Rosé and Perrier-Jouët Blason Rosé wines. As for the Non-Vintage Rosé, it is a gorgeously balanced, light salmon-coloured wine with pinpoint bubbles, faint yet noticeable aromas of framboises and strawberries, lovely, light yet flavourful and frothy character. The Blanc de Blancs is an equal match for the Rosé in terms of finesse and gracefulness. It is dry and steely, but has very crisp, light flavours, a zesty, refreshing acidity, and dry finish. In contrast, the 1979 Cuvée Billecart is rounder and has a creamy, toasty richness to it that one does not find in the Blanc de Blancs. It is fuller and fruitier than the Blanc de Blancs, but lacks equal finesse. The Non-Vintage Brut is light and serviceable, but less interesting than previous releases. On a negative note, two out of three bottles of 1982 Cuvée Billecart tasted flabby and out of balance.

BOIZEL (Light-bodied) ★★
Brut Réserve Non-Vintage .... ③ **74**
1978 Joyau de France .... ④ **84**

The Non-Vintage is neutral, quite bland, cleanly made, but has no focal point of interest. The 1978 Joyau de France is richer, medium-bodied, with a hint of buttery fruit, fully mature, and rather attractive.

BOLLINGER (Full-bodied) ★ ★ ★ ★ ★

1973 Année Rare	⑤	**85**
1979 Grande Année Brut	⑤	**85**
1979 Grande Année Rosé	⑤	**86**
1975 R.D.	⑤	**92**
Special Cuvée Non-Vintage	④	**87**
1979 Vieilles Vignes Françaises	⑤	**90**

Bollinger is clearly one of Champagne's most respected and celebrated houses. The wines are very high in quality and made in a full bodied, dry style with considerable character. The Non-Vintage is fermented in stainless steel, but the other Champagnes are still fermented in oak. On the negative side, the prices for Bollinger Champagnes are high and the availability tight. As for these new offerings from Bollinger, the 1979 Vieilles Vignes is listed for academic purposes only. Less than 150 cases were produced and a third of these were sent to America. The 1979 is lighter than other vintages I have had the pleasure of tasting, but still rather full, with authoritative flavours and good body for a Champagne. The bubbles are extremely small and well defined, which is always a sign of high quality. However, the price is ludicrous. The 1975 R.D., despite spending nine years on its lees, tastes remarkably young and undeveloped. It is full-bodied for a Champagne, deeper in colour than the other Bollinger Champagnes, quite dry and austere, very complex and outstanding. The 1973 Année Rare spent eleven years on its lees and though refined and obviously well made, it tastes lean, a trifle too tart and acidic. My notes show it has a pH of 2.95, which is extremely low. As for the two Grande Année releases from Bollinger, the 1979 Grande Année Rosé is very dry, quite austere, medium-to full-bodied, with tiny pinpoint bubbles. The 1979 Grande Année Brut is medium-bodied, a trifle tart and reserved, but very stylish. Lastly, the Non-Vintage Bollinger Special Cuvée surprisingly showed more of the famed Bollinger full-bodied, creamy, toasty style than the more expensive bottlings. I found it quite tasty and complex. Overall, Champagnes from Bollinger, always among my favourites, tasted lighter and less extroverted than I expected, and I wonder if the house style is lightening up a bit.

BONNAIRE (Light-bodied) ★ ★ ★ ★

1982 Blanc de Blancs	④	**89**
1981 Blanc de Blancs Cuvée Anniversaire	③	**87**
Cramant Non-Vintage	③	**83**

This is quite a good producer of Champagne from the village of Cramant. The 1982 is toasty, with spicy, yeasty-scented aroma, good, clean, crisp flavour, medium-body, and good, lingering effervescence. The Cuvée Anniversaire is a special bottling to honour the famous New York wine merchant Sam Aaron of Sherry Lehmann. It is identical to the 1981 Bonnaire Blanc de Blancs (which was almost as good as the 1982) only less expensive. The Non-Vintage Cramant is a good, dry, yeasty brut Champagne.

CATTIER BRUT (Light-bodied) ★ ★ ★

1979 Brut .... ④ **80**
Brut Non-Vintage .... ③ **81**
Clos du Moulin Non-Vintage .... ④ **86**

This house produces quite light, rather flowery Champagnes. The Non-Vintage is straightforward, frothy, light, and gentle on the palate. The 1979 Brut is also light, a trifle dull and unexciting, but pleasant. The Non-Vintage Clos du Moulin exhibits considerably more style and interest. Delicate and subtle, with a flowery, clean bouquet, light yet flavourful palate impression, the Clos du Moulin is an ideal Champagne to serve as an apéritif.

CHARBAUT (Light-bodied) ★ ★ ★ ★

1979 Blanc de Blancs Brut .... ④ **87**
Brut Non-Vintage .... ④ **84**
Brut Blanc de Blancs Non-Vintage .... ④ **87**
Brut Rosé Non-Vintage .... ④ **86**
1976 Certificate Blanc de Blancs Tête de Cuvée .... ⑤ **90**

These releases from Charbaut were among the surprises in my series of blind tastings of Champagne. This is a house that I have always regarded as producing reliable, middle-of-the-road, fruity, soft Champagnes that lacked excitement and drama. However, these wines may well suggest a move to a higher plateau of quality; all turned in very good performances. At the top level, the 1976 Certificate, made from 100% Chardonnay, tastes like a buttery, flavourful yet effervescent white Burgundy, spicy with soft, impeccably balanced, rich, delineated flavours. It will not age well, so enjoy it now while it is showing its best. Very similarly styled is the 1979 Blanc de Blancs Brut, which showed much of the same subtle, spicy, buttery character as the 1976 Certificate. However, it is less than half the price. It has a frothy effervescence, a graceful Chardonnay fruitiness, and crisp, clean finish. Remarkably, even the Brut Non-Vintage Blanc de Blancs has plenty of Chardonnay character and a creamy, buttery, medium-bodied feel on the palate. The Brut Non-Vintage does not have the finesse or broad richness of the other wines, but is a good, soft, fruity, non-vintage Champagne that is very cleanly made. The Brut Non-Vintage Rosé is one of the very best rosé Champagnes on the market and undoubtedly one of the better values in the generally exorbitantly priced rosé Champagne marketplace. It has a lovely pink salmon colour, a subtle, complex, berry fruit aroma, and crisp, light- to medium-bodied texture.

VEUVE CLICQUOT (Full-bodied) ★★★★★

1978 Brut	⑤	88
Brut Extra Dry Non-Vintage	④	67
1979 Brut Rosé	⑤	89
1976 La Grande Dame	⑤	70
1979 La Grande Dame	⑤	90
Ponsardin Brut Non-Vintage	④	88
1980 Texas Sesquicentennial Cuvée	⑤	85

This excellent firm is generally regarded as a producer of rather full-bodied, creamy, large-scaled Champagnes that can age well, and recent vintages continue this style. This is a house I like quite a bit, and the recent Champagnes are certainly very well made in a medium- to full-bodied style. The wines are more richly flavoured than most other Champagne houses. As for the two disappointments, the Brut Extra Dry tasted like ginger ale, soft, slightly sweet, and oddly perfumed. The 1976 La Grande Dame is tired and, in this vintage, better named the Senile Dame. Otherwise, the current offerings are delectably full, fruity, yeasty, rich, and interesting. The Ponsardin Brut Non-Vintage is light golden, spicy and full with excellent flavour concentration. Among the bigger, boldly flavoured Champagnes on the market, it is one of the very best. The 1979 Brut Rosé is quite delicious and rather full-bodied and full-flavoured for a rosé. The 1979 La Grande Dame is in top form, rich, round, toasty, and creamy, with fine length and tiny bubbles that linger and linger. The 1978 Brut is the most robust Champagne in this group, with plenty of flavour, a mouthfilling, toasty, spicy richness, and crisp finish. Lastly, the special Cuvée of Champagne to honour the 150th birthday of Texas is good, very attractively packaged, but obviously a marketing gimmick. Because of their fullness, these Champagnes are better drunk with food than as apéritifs.

DEUTZ (Medium-bodied) ★★★

1978 Blanc de Blancs	⑤	82
1976 Brut	④	78
Brut Non-Vintage	④	78

1981 Brut Rosé..	④	*80*
1979 Cuvée G. Mathieu..	⑤	*84*
1979 Cuvée William Deutz..	⑤	*90*

Somewhat to my surprise, the Deutz Champagnes did not fare so well in my tastings as I had expected. While the 1979 Cuvée William Deutz is excellent, frothy, elegant, medium-bodied, and delicious, the others tasted one-dimensional, almost too mild and bland. They are dry, light in body, and, though clean and crisp, seemed to offer little excitement or flavour interest. Oddly enough, the 1981 Brut Rosé had almost no bouquet whatsoever.

NICHOLAS FEUILLATTE (Light-bodied) ★★

Brut Non-Vintage..	③	*75*
Rosé Non-Vintage..	③	*85*

I have had little tasting experience with these Champagnes. The labels are pretty, but with the exception of the very charming and captivating Non-Vintage Rosé, I have been unimpressed by the other Champagnes. The Rosé is light, frothy, and dry, with a bouquet vaguely reminiscent of strawberries.

H. GERMAIN (Light-bodied) ★★★

1979 Blanc de Blancs	④	*87*
Brut Non-Vintage..	③	*85*

This small house is highly reputed in France and it is easy to see why. Both the above Champagnes showed well in my tastings. The Brut Non-Vintage has a rather full-blown, spicy, yeasty, intense bouquet, good, elegant, dry flavours, medium body, and a crisp finish. The 100% Chardonnay 1979 Blanc de Blancs was even more impressive, with a complex, fruity, spicy, moderately intense bouquet, clean, well-defined, crisp flavours, tiny, uniform bubbles, and good effervescence.

MICHEL GONET (Medium-bodied) ★★

1981 Blanc de Blancs Brut	③	*85*

With Champagne prices going up, one suspects that buys like this will not be available much longer. This is a Blanc de Blancs, and a light one at that, but it does have considerable finesse, clean, light intensity, toasty Chardonnay scents, light to medium body, and an overall refreshing character. It is perfect as an apéritif Champagne.

GOSSET (Full-bodied) ★★★★

Réserve Brut Non-Vintage	④	*84*
Special Réserve Brut Non-Vintage.............................	⑤	*89*

The Special Réserve Brut is a classic Champagne, rich, creamy, deep, complex, full-bodied, yet impeccably balanced and graceful. One is hard pressed to find a better non-vintage Champagne. As for the regular Réserve Brut Non-Vintage, it has plenty of flavour, but seems slightly tired and oxidized. Those with an English palate for mellow, well-aged Champagne will like it better than I did.

ALFRED GRATIEN (Full-bodied) ★★★★
1979 Brut .... ④ **88**
Brut Non-Vintage .... ④ **87**
Brut Rosé Non-Vintage .... ④ **85**
One of the few Champagne firms to still ferment their wines in small barrels, the wines of Gratien are rather traditional and full-flavoured. The Brut Non-Vintage Rosé has plenty of depth, well-defined bubbles, a crisp, dry, but not tart or acidic finish. The Brut Non-Vintage has toasty, creamy, yeasty flavours, good body, an assertive personality and real style. The 1979 Brut is richer, perhaps softer on the palate, but complex, flavourful, and quite effervescent.

CHARLES HEIDSIECK (Medium-bodied) ★★★
Brut Non-Vintage .... ④ **85**
1979 Cuvée Charlie .... ⑤ **85**
Here is an example of a luxury Cuvée, Cuvée Charlie, that for three times the price is no better than the good Brut Non-Vintage. Charlie, affectionately named (presumably) after the founder of this firm, Charles-Henri Heidsieck, is a light, delicate, quite restrained, medium-bodied Champagne that is obviously well made, but in quality more like a £10 bottle of Champagne than a £25 bottle. The Brut Non-Vintage is more dramatic, if only because it is more fruity, spicy, and possesses a soft, creamy texture.

HEIDSIECK MONOPOLE (Medium-bodied) ★★★
Brut Non-Vintage .... ④ **84**
1976 Diamant Bleu .... ⑤ **78**
1979 Diamant Bleu .... ⑤ **88**
Extra Dry Non-Vintage .... ④ **75**
The luxury Cuvée from Heidsieck Monopole, the Diamant Bleu, has generally been one of the most fairly priced Tête de Cuvée Champagnes. The 1975 was a long-time favourite of mine, while the 1976 is rather light, dull, and a trifle too tart and acidic. However, the 1979 Diamant Bleu is quite a stylish, delicate wine with tiny bubbles, a creamy, graceful, well-balanced texture, and a good, crisp finish. The Brut Non-

Vintage is fuller-bodied, somewhat toasty and spicy, and a seemingly bigger, more aggressive style of Champagne. The Extra Dry Non-Vintage has a straightforward, fruity bouquet, and somewhat dull flavours.

HENRIOT (Full-bodied) ★★★★

Brut Non-Vintage	④	85
1976 Réserve Baron Philippe de Rothschild	⑤	90
1979 Réserve Baron Philippe de Rothschild	⑤	90

For their price, it is hard to beat the quality of these three Champagnes from Henriot. But be warned, those who prefer light, flowery Champagnes will no doubt find these too rich, dramatic, and creamy for their tastes. The 1976 Réserve Baron Philippe de Rothschild is fully mature but has a full-blown, spicy, toasty bouquet, round, nutty flavours and very fine length. The 1979 is very similar, only slightly lighter and more elegant. The Brut Non-Vintage is very similarly structured and styled – creamy, toasty, ripe, and quite dramatic. It, too, is fully mature, and should be drunk rather than aged.

JACQUART (Medium-bodied) ★★

Brut Non-Vintage	③	82
Extra Dry Non-Vintage	③	75

The Brut Non-Vintage is fruity, soft, cleanly made and very straightforward in style. It lacks personality, but is satisfying. The Extra Dry Non-Vintage is quite soft, slightly sweet, a little tiring to the taste, but serviceable.

JACQUESSON (Light-bodied) ★★★

Blanc de Blancs Brut Non-Vintage	④	84
1979 Brut	④	85
1969 Brut Late Disgorged	⑤	90
Brut Non-Vintage	③	70
Brut Rosé Non-Vintage	④	80
1976 Brut Signature	⑤	86

The Jacquesson Champagnes are very reasonably priced and made in a very light, delicate style not unlike that of Taittinger. The Brut Non-Vintage is musty in the nose, has fairly insipid flavours and no finish. The 1979 Brut is quite light, but also complex and flavourful, with subtle toasty, yeasty aromas, soft, very refined flavours, and a good lingering effervescence. The Blanc de Blancs Brut Non-Vintage is one of the lightest Champagnes I have ever tasted. In fact, its lightness is an attribute and a curse. Delicate, almost ethereal, and unbelievably light, it seems to disappear on the palate once in the mouth. It is probably a controversial Champagne, but very cleanly made and an ideal apéritif. The 1976 Brut Signature is also made in the very light, delicate style but has more flavour, some hint of toasty, aged fruit, and is still very fresh and crisp. It is good value for a luxury Cuvée. The Brut Rosé Non-Vintage is standard quality, but the rare 1969 Brut Late Disgorged is a super, very complex, interesting, provocative Champagne with considerable interest in both flavour and bouquet.

JESTIN (Light-bodied) ★★
Brut Non-Vintage .... ③ 78
Brut Rosé Non-Vintage .... ③ 78

There is little to comment on here. These are dry, cleanly made, crisp, tart straightforward Champagnes at very reasonable prices. In fact, the prices are all that should draw some interest to these Champagnes.

KRUG (Full-bodied) ★★★★★
1976 Brut .... ⑤ 91
1979 Brut .... ⑤ 90
Grand Cuvée Non-Vintage .... ⑤ 88
Rosé Non-Vintage .... ⑤ 88

In the first year (1978) that Krug launched the Grand Cuvée Non-Vintage, the batch released in America was sublime. Since then, this Champagne has vacillated from tart, green, and austere to light, elegant, and graceful. It is impossible to know when a new blend is released, but the Krug Grand Cuvée I purchased in November 1985 from a shop with a huge turnover of stock is back to top form. Lighter and more elegant than one would assume from the reputation Krug's wines have, the new batch of Grand Cuvée is very flavourful, very elegant, with scents of vanillin and toast, medium body, and long, crisp, yet gentle flavours. The new 'Rosé Non-Vintage from Krug sets a new benchmark in price absurdity, but otherwise is rather full-bodied, quite well made, rather deeply flavoured, with crisp acidity and tiny bubbles. Both vintage Champagnes (1976 and 1979) get top marks because they have even more character, exquisite noses of fruit and toast, and loads of refined flavours.

LANSON (Light-bodied) ★★★
Brut Black Label Non-Vintage .... ③ 84
1979 Brut Red Label .... ④ 86

Lanson's Brut Black Label Non-Vintage continues to represent a good value. It is very consistent in style, with a soft, light, lively fruitiness, light to medium body, crisp acidity, and adequate finish. It is a good party Champagne, not too austere, not too flabby and soft. The 1979 Brut Red Label is a classier Champagne. It tastes as if it has plenty of Chardonnay in it, it is delicate yet flavourful, cleanly crisp, medium-bodied, and well made.

GUY LARMANDIER (Medium-bodied) ★★
Blanc de Blancs Non-Vintage..................................... ④ **86**

Not for those who prefer soft, round Champagnes, this austere, 100% Chardonnay-based wine exhibits plenty of character, a chalky, clean, refined bouquet, average effervescence, medium body, a dry, firm, interesting texture, and very crisp finish. It tastes quite dry, like an ultra or zéro brut.

J. LASSALLE (Light-bodied) ★★★★
1979 Blanc de Blancs.. ④ **86**

This small producer produces a lovely, delicate, flavourful, and graceful wine. The 1979 Blanc de Blancs is crisp, aromatic with scents of fresh wheat and dough. On the palate, it is medium-bodied, zesty, and fresh, with well-delineated flavours and a lovely finish.

LAUNOIS PÈRE (Light-bodied) ★★★
1980 Blanc de Blancs.. ④ **71**
Blanc de Blancs Non-Vintage...................................... ③ **65**

Both of these Champagnes showed poorly in my tastings. The 1980 Blanc de Blancs is watery and rather thin. The Blanc de Blancs Non-Vintage has a bizarre, almost artificial perfumed character and little character on the palate.

LAURENT-PERRIER (Medium-bodied) ★★★★
Cuvée Speciale Brut Non-Vintage.............................. ③ **85**
Cuvée Ultra Brut Non-Vintage.................................... ④ **91**
1978 Grand Siècle... ⑤ **88**

For the last few years the Non-Vintage Laurent-Perrier has represented one of the great bargains in high-quality Champagne. The Cuvée Speciale Non-Vintage Brut is less bold and toasty than previous renditions, as well as a little lighter and noticeably more flowery. It is still a very good Champagne. The Cuvée Ultra Brut Non-Vintage is a gloriously refined, flavourful Champagne that is better than the very good Grand Siècle (and at half the price). Light golden with a rich, toasty, fragrant bouquet, it has tiny bubbles, good effervescence, a crisp yet medium- to full-bodied feel on the palate, and a very impressive finish. It is hard to find a better Champagne at any price. The 1978 Grand Siècle is also quite an elegant, graceful, refined Champagne, crisp and fruity, yet so delicate, with aromas of vanillin and bread dough, it lingers on the palate and has a good measure of flavour.

LECHERE (Light-bodied) ★ ★ ★ ★
Blanc de Blancs Non-Vintage...................................... ④ **88**
Orient Express Non-Vintage...................................... ④ **90**
Rosé Brut Non-Vintage.. ④ *84*

The special Cuvée called the Orient Express (because it is served on that famous European train) is an ethereal, sublime Champagne. It is outstanding, light golden with a toasted wheat, spicy, vanillin bouquet, crisp, well-focused flavours, and a lovely, lingering effervescence. For the sheer delicacy of its flavours, it is stunning. The Blanc de Blancs Non-Vintage is very similar, only slightly lighter and perhaps a trifle more tart on the palate. The Rosé Brut is good, dry, crisp, but a trifle too understated; it is not in the same league as the others.

R. & L. LEGRAS (Light-bodied) ★ ★ ★
1979 Blanc de Blancs.. ④ **86**
Blanc de Blancs Non-Vintage.. ④ **86**

These are both very polished, refined, lighter-styled Champagnes that are produced from 100% Chardonnay grapes. Given the choice, why not save money and opt for the Non-Vintage? Both are similar: elegant, flowery, and subtle, but crisp, flavourful, fresh, and light- to medium-bodied. The 1979 has, however, some toasty, spicy notes in its bouquet that I could not find in the Non-Vintage.

MOËT ET CHANDON (Medium-bodied) ★ ★ ★ ★
1980 Brut Imperial.. ⑤ *78*
Brut Imperial Non-Vintage...................................... ④ *82*
1980 Brut Imperial Rosé.. ⑤ *85*
1978 Dom Pérignon .... ⑤ **90**
1980 Dom Pérignon .... ⑤ **88**
1975 Dom Pérignon Rosé .... ⑤ **90**
White Star Extra Dry Non-Vintage.................... ④ *73*

The largest producer of Champagne, Moët et Chandon's products are visible in virtually every hotel, wine shop, and restaurant in the world. Dom Pérignon is, of course, Champagne's most famous wine, and the ultimate for those who collect labels. It can be superb, as it was in 1964 and 1971. The 1978 Dom Pèrignon is back to top-notch form, the 1980 slightly lighter, but elegant and very tasty. The 1978 has authoritative, impeccably balanced flavours, a very classy, refined, yeasty, spicy bouquet, and lovely, moderately rich flavours. The 1975 Dom Pérignon Rosé is quite outstanding as well, but good luck finding a bottle. Only 400-500 cases are produced, and its rich, strawberry fruitiness, captivating colour, and crisp flavours as well as its super-snob appeal make it the hardest Champagne in the world to find. As for the other Champagnes, they offer the prestige of the Moët et Chandon name, but little else. The rather sweet-tasting White Star Extra Dry Non-Vintage is heavy and cloying. I liked the Brut Imperial Non-Vintage, yet it is hardly a classic Champagne in the sense that it relies too much on softness and a puffy, frothy character for its appeal. The 1980 Brut Imperial is hardly the stuff of vintage Champagne – it is lean, light, a little green, and does not have much of a finish. As for the 1980 Brut Imperial Rosé, it has surprisingly deep colour for a rosé, a tomato, herb-scented bouquet, rather fat, round, slightly soft flavours, and some character.

MUMM (Medium-bodied) ★★

1979 Cordon Rouge	⑤	80
Cordon Rouge Brut Non-Vintage	④	83
Crémant de Cramant Blanc de Blancs Non-Vintage	⑤	90
1979 René Lalou	⑤	83

I have never been a great admirer of the Mumm Champagnes, which I find rather average in quality and rarely exciting. The luxury Cuvée René Lalou can often be terribly mediocre; the 1979 René Lalou is above average to good, but given the outrageous price, hardly a bargain. Austere, a trifle tart and too lean, one is hard pressed to find enough to like to merit the price. The 1979 Cordon Rouge is even more bland and simple, with straightforward, fruity flavours. The Cordon Rouge Non-Vintage Brut shows as much character as the luxury Cuvée. It has a more interesting, spicy, vanillin, fruity nose and is less austere. My favourite Mumm Champagne is the gorgeously well-balanced, light, delicate, but rare and expensive, 100% Chardonnay Crémant de Cramant. This is a frothy, very refined wine of considerable finesse. It is a shame the other Mumm wines don't show this style and class.

OUDINOT (Medium-bodied) ★★

Blanc de Blancs Brut Non-Vintage	④	78
1976 Brut	③	75
1976 Gold Label Brut	④	80

The Oudinot Champagnes seem to be quite standard in quality, not objectionable, but simple, straightforward, and light- to medium-bodied. The 1976 Gold Label Brut has some pleasant, spicy, fruity, yeasty scents in its aroma, and clean, decent flavours. These are rather light, innocuous Champagnes.

BRUNO PAILLARD (Light-bodied) ★★★

1976 Brut	④	87
1979 Brut	③	85
1975 Brut Blanc de Blancs	④	79
Brut Non-Vintage	③	83
Brut Rosé Non-Vintage	④	85
Brut Zéro Non-Vintage	③	85
Crémant Blanc de Blancs Non-Vintage	③	87

This is a new house in Champagne that has quickly moved upward in the ranks of Champagne producers because of the reasonable prices charged for its well-made Champagnes. First, the mediocrities. The Non-Vintage Brut Rosé is clean, soft, but lacks style and has absolutely no character. The 1975 Brut Blanc de Blancs is beginning to tire a bit, and has an annoying greenness to it. The Non-Vintage Brut is well above average in quality, sensibly priced, but one can still do better for the money with Lanson or Laurent-Perrier. The stars of Bruno Paillard are the austere, totally dry, classy Non-Vintage Brut Zéro, which (for those who like really dry Champagne) is very nice in an elegant, leaner style. The 1976 Brut should be mandatory drinking for anyone on a high-fibre diet. It smells like toasty bran flakes, has a marvellous, frothy appeal, medium body, and lovely balance. It is a real bargain among the lighter yet flavourful Champagnes on the market. The Non-Vintage Crémant Blanc de Blancs is a real winner. It tastes like a very good Puligny Montrachet with bubbles. Creamy, very obviously Chardonnay in taste, with small pinpoint bubbles, it is a delicious Champagne that, because of its lightness and creamy texture, is just perfect as an apéritif. Lastly, the 1979 Brut is light, frothy, and quite flavourful. It tastes like it has a good measure of Chardonnay in it. Medium-bodied, dry and yeasty, its price should cause considerable interest.

JOSEPH PERRIER (Medium-bodied) ★★★

1979 Brut	④	86
Cuvée Royale Non-Vintage Brut	④	87

The 1979 Brut is well made, straightforward, pleasant, with faint, toasty, vanillin aromas, some good, crisp acidity in the finish, good effervescence, and medium body. As difficult as it is to comprehend, the Cuvée Royale Non-Vintage Brut is richer, more flavourful, and has more to it. Slightly fuller, quite tasty, with subtle, yeasty, buttery, toasty flavours, medium body, and good, well-defined bubbles that last, it is a very fine Non-Vintage Champagne.

PERRIER-JOUËT (Light-bodied) ★★★

Blason de France Rosé Non-Vintage.......................... ⑤ **90**
1979 Flower Bottle Brut .... ⑤ **?**
1979 Flower Bottle Rosé.. ⑤ **90**
Grand Brut Non-Vintage .... ④ **81**

I have enjoyed many a bottle of Perrier-Jouët Champagne. This house is owned by Mumm and controlled by Seagram. The Champagnes are made in a light, rather delicate style. The famous Flower Bottle luxury Cuvée was an ingenious marketing invention to publicize their best Champagnes. Their 1979 Flower Bottle Rosé is outstanding, delicate, very subtle in flavour, with hints of berry fruit, spice and yeast. The 1979 Flower Bottle Brut can merit 87–88 points: delicate, charming, light, frothy Champagne. It can also taste tart, green, and acidic. At its extravagant price, I expect consistency. Apparently, the Blason de France Rosé Non-Vintage suffers from the same malady. It too can be sublime; however, one bottle I tasted was tired and oxidized, while a second was stunningly crisp, flavourful, and quite excellent. Since it can be 90–92-point Champagne, it may be worth the risk. The Grand Brut Non-Vintage is soft, round, quite fruity and obvious in style.

PHILIPPONNAT (Medium-bodied) ★★★

1980 Blanc de Blancs .... ④ **84**
Brut Rosé Non-Vintage.. ④ **78**
1978 Clos de Goisses .... ⑤ **82**

This house has a considerable reputation, but I was left unmoved by how these Champagnes showed. The Brut Rosé Non-Vintage was standard in quality, dry, pleasant, a touch high in acidity. The single vineyard Clos de Goisses tasted very tart, lean, and surprisingly reserved. Perhaps time will see it emerge from its rather dormant, closed personality. The 1980 Blanc de Blancs has more character. Spicy, yeasty, Chardonnay aromas exhibited style and subtlety. It is dry, medium-bodied, and pleasant rather than sublime.

PIPER HEIDSIECK (Light-bodied) ★★★

1976 Année Rare .... ⑤ **83**
1979 Brut Sauvage.. ⑤ **77**
Cuvée des Ambassadeurs Non-Vintage .... ④ **83**
1976 Pink .... ⑤ **74**

This house rarely makes exciting Champagne. There was a tremendous amount of hoopla about the release of the 1976 Année Rare, which is quite light, crisp and tart, but, all things considered, should sell for a much, much lower price. The rosé Champagne called Pink (I appreciate the firm's candour in naming this Champagne) is already tired and taking on the colour of an old Tavel from the Rhône. It still has flavour, but is a little flat and not very interesting. The Cuvée des Ambassadeurs Non-Vintage is pleasant, dry, light- to medium-bodied, with a decent, frothy, yeasty character. It is a better Champagne than the expensive wines for Piper Heidsieck. The ultra-dry Brut Sauvage is steely, very austere, lean, and a trifle green and tart. The Champagnes are hardly inspiring and, for the most part, notably overpriced.

POL ROGER (Medium-bodied) ★ ★ ★ ★ ★

1975 Blanc de Chardonnay	⑤	**90**
1976 Brut	④	**88**
1979 Brut	④	**88**
Brut Non-Vintage	④	**86**
1979 Cuvée Winston Churchill	⑤	**87**

Pol Roger is one of the best producers of classic, rich, flavourful Champagnes, which can also be particularly long-lived. In my tastings there were no disappointments. The Brut Non-Vintage is medium-bodied, creamy, and rich, has plenty of flavour, a lot of bubbles, and considerable style. As for the other Champagnes, both the exquisite 1975 Blanc de Chardonnay and 1979 Cuvée Winston Churchill need two to three years of cellaring. They are impeccably made, dry, toasty, medium-bodied, loaded with fruit and tiny, symmetrical bubbles, but are extremely unevolved and young. If I were Pol Roger, I would have waited and released them in 1989. The 1976 Brut is fully mature, creamy, rich, toasty, and has a wonderfully complex bouquet. The 1979 Brut is more or less a younger version of the 1976. It is rich and creamy, medium-bodied, but could benefit handsomely from several years of cellaring. Pol Roger's Champagnes are among the most consistent in quality on the market.

POMMERY & GRENO (Light-bodied) ★ ★ ★

1981 Brut	④	**77**
Brut Rosé Non-Vintage	④	**80**
Brut Royal Brut Non-Vintage	③	**85**
1979 Cuvée Speciale-Louise Pommery	⑤	**87**

The 1981 Brut is very frothy, very light, and lacks flavour. The Brut Rosé Non-Vintage is straightforward, dry, very light, with a nice pale salmon colour, crisp finish, and lively acidity. The Brut Royal Brut Non-Vintage is usually one of Pommery's best Champagnes and best values. It has medium body, a crisp, refreshing, dry fruitiness, yeasty, clean bouquet, and adequate finish. The newly released luxury Cuvée is toasty, rather unevolved, and backward in taste and aroma, but has quite long, lingering flavours. Give it two to three years of cellaring.

RAPENEAU (Medium-bodied) ★★

1979 Brut	③	86
Brut Blanc de Blancs Non-Vintage	③	85
Brut Cuvée L'Escalape Non-Vintage	④	86

This new entry into the ranks of Champagne producers offers both notable quality and value. Rapeneau's Champagne seems to fall in style between the light-bodied, fluffy Champagne of Taittinger and the fuller-bodied, robustly flavoured Champagne of Veuve Clicquot. The 1979 Brut has a buttery, almond-scented nose, crisp, medium-bodied flavours, and impressively small, symmetrical bubbles. The Brut Blanc de Blancs Non-Vintage is crisp and flavourful, and the Brut Cuvée L'Escalape Non-Vintage is spicy, clean, with good intense flavours in a medium-bodied format.

LOUIS ROEDERER (Full-bodied) ★★★★★

Brut Non-Vintage	④	88
Brut Premier Non-Vintage	④	87
1979 Cristal	⑤	88
1981 Cristal	⑤	90
Extra Dry Non-Vintage	④	75
Rosé Brut Non-Vintage	④	87

Roederer's Champagnes are usually among the best made; they are rather full-flavoured and assertive, with aromas of nuts, toasted wheat and spices. Both the 1979 and 1981 Cristal are obviously overpriced, but aside from that, excellent Champagnes. The 1979 is lighter than previous vintages, but has the telltale personality of Roederer – the toasty, hazelnut-scented aroma, ripe flavours, and great balance and finesse. I was also quite surprised by how good the dry Rosé Brut Non-Vintage is. It is very pale coloured, yet has a lovely, complex, faint berry fruitiness, soft yet lively flavours, and good length. The Brut Non-Vintage is surprisingly soft, with a sweet yeasty nose. I found it rather atypical of Roederer's style. I peferred the new Non-Vintage Brut Premier, which is quite elegant and full-flavoured and one of the best of its type on the market. The Extra Dry Non-Vintage was sweet and rather diffuse in character.

ALFRED ROTHSCHILD (Light-bodied) ★★
1979 Brut .... ④ *72*
Brut Réserve Non-Vintage .... ④ *80*
> The 1979 Brut is acidic and sharp on the palate and, though cleanly made, has little redeeming social value. The Brut Réserve Non-Vintage is soft, round, fruity, quite frothy, and easy to like, albeit very simple.

DOM RUINART (Light-bodied) ★★★★
1976 Blanc de Blancs .... ⑤ *75*
1978 Blanc de Blancs .... ⑤ *87*
1976 Rosé .... ⑤ *90*
1978 Rosé .... ⑤ *90*
> The 1976 Blanc de Blancs is lean, tart, lacking fruit and interest, and quite tired. On the other hand, the 1978 has plenty of elegantly rendered fruit, a crisp, dry, yeasty, toasted wheat scent, and a good dry finish. It is the best Dom Ruinart since the lovely 1971. The 1976 Rosé is a gorgeous Champagne, medium-bodied, quite aromatic with scents of strawberries, and is round, crisp, and quite flavourful, with good, zesty acidity. The 1978 Rosé is just as good, perhaps lighter, but also fresher and still remarkably elegant and flavourful.

TAITTINGER (Light-bodied) ★★★★★
1980 Brut Millésime .... ⑤ *77*
1976 Comtes de Champagne Blanc de Blancs .... ⑤ *90*
1979 Comtes de Champagne Blanc de Blancs .... ⑤ *91*
1976 Comtes de Champagne Rosé .... ⑤ *91*
1979 Comtes de Champagne Rosé .... ⑤ *90*
La Française Brut Non-Vintage .... ④ *80*
1978 Vasarely Collection Series Brut .... ⑤ *88*
> Taittinger's top-of-the-line *tête de Cuvée*, the Comtes de Champagne, is one example of a luxury Champagne that rarely disappoints. In fact, it is consistently ethereal, light, and delicate as well as impeccably made. Both the 1976 and 1979 Comtes de Champagne Blanc de Blancs (made from 100% Chardonnay) are remarkably light, frothy, delicate, and complex Champagnes that exemplify the words breed and finesse. I believe I detect even more character in the 1979. The Comtes de Champagne Rosé is quite rare and of course expensive, but is among the most delicate and delicious of the luxury Cuvée Champagnes on the market. It is rounder in texture than the Blanc de Blancs, but stunningly crisp, subtle, and sublime. The 1979 is slightly lighter than the 1976, but both are truly superb. The 1978 Vasarely Collection Series

Brut is, in essence, the Comtes de Champagne Blanc de Blancs (there was no specific bottling of 1978 Comtes de Champagne). It is quite light, with soft, gorgeous flavours, some complex, toasty wheat notes in its bouquet, and a round finish. As for the other selections from Taittinger, the 1980 Brut Millésime is quite light, rather thin and tart, and, for Taittinger, a disappointment. The Brut Française Non-Vintage is soft, creamy, very light, and rather sweet for a brut Champagne.

LOIRE VALLEY

Most wine drinkers can name more historic Loire Valley châteaux than Loire Valley wines. It's a pity, really, because the Loire Valley regions offer France's most remarkable array of wines. The wine-producing region stretches along one-third of the meandering 600-mile river, and the astonishing diversity of grapes planted in this valley is far greater than that in the better-known wine-growing regions of Burgundy or Bordeaux.

The Sauvignon Blanc grape makes distinctive and delicious wines in the most eastern part of the valley, around the towns of Gien, Briare, Sancerre, and Pouilly-sur-Loire. At the western end, surrounding the city of Nantes, the Muscadet reigns supreme. Midway between these two areas is the historic cathedral city of Tours, where the Chenin Blanc grape is king. Certainly, these three white grape varieties are the most frequently encountered when sampling Loire wines, but there are other varieties that are also widely planted in this vast wine region. The Chardonnay, Pinot Gris, Arbois, and Gros Plant are the other white grape varieties found in abundance. And for red and rosé wines, there are the Gamay, Cabernet Franc, Cabernet Sauvignon, Malbec, Pinot Noir, and Pinot Meunier.

MUSCADET

Muscadet is made from the grape of the same name in an area just southeast of the city of Nantes in the western Loire Valley. The best Muscadet is called Muscadet de Sèvre-et-Maine, after the two local rivers. Muscadet is really the perfect white wine for shellfish, particularly briny clams and oysters. Muscadet must be drunk young, always within two to three years of the vintage, when its best attributes can be fully appreciated. Textbook Muscadet is exuberantly fruity, extremely fresh, totally crisp, dry, and light- to medium-bodied. Consumers in search of top Muscadet should bypass any of the stale 1982s (with the exception of the long-lived Château de Chasseloir) or older vintages that remain on retailers' shelves. Look instead for the highly successful 1985s, because of their excellent freshness and crisp fruitiness – these are rounder and fuller than usual – and for the recently released 1986s, which are more typical of the Muscadets normally turned out in a good vintage. Finally, don't buy more Muscadet than you will drink over the next year; these wines don't improve in the bottle.

QUICK VINTAGE GUIDE

1986 Not as good as 1985, considered by most growers to be above average in quality. The wines are less fruity and fat than the extroverted 1985s.

1985 A very good vintage, very similar in style to the 1982s, but perhaps superior. Soft, fruity, and delicious the wines must be drunk before the end of 1987.

1984 Lean, tart, high-acid wines that will last two to three years, but in general lacking charm and flavour.

1983 Ripe, fruity, soft, very flavourful wines that are now beginning to tire a bit.

A GUIDE TO MUSCADET'S BEST PRODUCERS

★★★★ Excellent Producers

André-Michel Bregeon
Château de Chasseloir
Marquis de Goulaine

Château La Noë
Sauvion Cardinal Richelieu
Sauvion Château du Cléray

★★★ Good Producers

Domaine de la Botinière
Château de la Bretesche
Domaine de la Fevrie
Domaine de la Fruitière
Domaine de la Gautronnière
Domaine de la Grange

Domaine de l'Hyvernière
Château de la Jannière
Louis Metaireau
Château l'Oiselinière
Château de la Ragotière
Sauvion (other cuvées)

ANJOU-SAUMUR

At last count, over eleven million cases of wine were produced annually in the 25 Anjou-Saumur appellations of the Loire Valley. Most of the wines made here are rosés, which can be quite good, but they never quite match the great rosés made in the Tavel in the southern Rhône Valley and in Bandol in Provence. However, there is one Loire rosé that does stand out, and that is the Rosé d'Anjou from Château de Tigné. In any case, this area's reputation is based not so much on its rosés as on its sweet white wines.

Curiously, the dry white wines of the Savennières appellation are hardly known even in France. Just southwest of the intriguing city of Angers, Savennières has a winemaking history that dates back to the twelfth century, when monks planted the first vines in the steep, slate-covered hillsides. The grape variety is Chenin Blanc, which here reaches an aristocratic level of excellence unmatched elsewhere in the world. No one makes Savennières any better than Madame Joly, who produces a rare, extremely dry, powerful and

The Loire Valley
and
Central France

N
W · E
S

SARTHE

LOIRE-
ATLANTIQUE

MAINE-
ET-

LOIR

LOIRE

N171

SARTHE

1
A11

N165

Angers

2

D952

St-Nicolas-
de-Bourgueil

Saint-
Nazaire

LOIRE

Ancenis

Savennières

Bourgueil

N23

Nantes

LOIRE

2

LAYON

2

Saumur

Chinon

3

1

D960

D147

MAINE

VENDÉE

D937

N160

SÈVRE-NANTAISE

Thouars

VIENNE

DEUX-
SÈVRES

Neuville-
du-Poitou

la Roche-
sur-Yon

Fontenay

Poitiers

0   10   20   30 MILES

0   20   40 KILOMETERS

Paris
Orléans
LOIRE

Orléans 4 N60
LOIRE
Vendôme
LOIRET
N10
A10
Gien
Blois
N20
LOIR-ET-
CHER
Mesland
3
LOIRE
D940
N7
Sancerre
Pouilly-
Sur-
Loire
Tours Vouvray
Amboise
N76
Vierzon
Ménetou-
Salon
3
Quincy
Valençay
INDRE-
ET-
LOIRE
5
Reuilly
Bourges
Nevers
INDRE
N20
D976
CHER
INDRE
Châteauroux
CHER
VIENNE
CREUSE
ALLIER

1 Vins du Pays Nantais 3 Vins de Touraine
2 Vins d'Anjou et   4 Vins de l'Orléanais
  Vins de Saumur   5 Vins du Centre

rich, ageworthy wine from seventeen acres that are entitled to their very own appellation. The Joly Savennières-Coulée-de-Serrant, from her estate called Clos de la Coulée de Serrant, is a wine that does not reveal all of its charms until it is at least seven or eight years old. One suspects that the mouth-puckering acidity and steep price will keep many a wine adventurer from ever experiencing what a great treasure this wine can be when it is fully mature.

Less expensive, but still quite interesting, are Savennières from the Château d'Epiré and La Bizolière. Both of these wines are dry, clean, yet remarkably fresh and fruity, with mouth-bracing acidity.

There are three other estates to know of in this region of the Loire Valley, all noteworthy because they produce very high-quality, sweet wines. From the Coteaux du Layon appellation there is the Touchais family, from the Quarts de Chaume appellation the Domaine des Baumard, and from the Bonnezeaux appellation the Château de Fesle. All three estates make surprisingly rich, luscious wines that can often rival the better-known wines from the Sauternes/Barsac region of Bordeaux.

The most remarkable thing about these sweet wines, in addition to their quality, is that few people know they even exist; still fewer realize that they will last for thirty or more years without losing their freshness, delicacy, sweetness and vigour, and hardly anyone realizes that they are made from the Chenin Blanc grape. These wines are splendid with foie gras, poached chicken, mildly sweet desserts, or when served as an apéritif.

Like the famous Sauternes/Barsac of Bordeaux, the sweet wines from these Loire appellations can be produced only in years when the climatic conditions are perfect for the Chenin Blanc grape to be attacked by the famed fungus *Botrytis cinerea*. Consumers can still find older vintages of the Touchais Coteaux du Layon wines back to 1959, which are all in marvellous condition. Other excellent vintages for the Coteaux du Layon, the Quarts de Chaume, and the Bonnezeaux are 1978, 1976, 1971, 1969, and 1964. These limited-production wines are not cheap, but most of the recent vintages sell for £7 and upwards, which is far less than their qualitative equivalent from Bordeaux.

Before leaving the Anjou-Saumur area, it is necessary to mention the booming, sparkling-wine industry of Saumur. A number of firms specialize in producing surprisingly good, low-priced, sparkling wines from the Chenin Blanc grape, but no one does it better than Bouvet-Ladubay in St.-Hilaire-St.-Florent. Their sparkling Saumur, promoted under the name Bouvet Brut is a high-quality alternative to Champagne – dry, lively, medium-bodied, and fruity.

QUICK VINTAGE GUIDE

1986 The rain in the last two weeks of October ruined the chance for a top quality crop of sweet wine, but the dry and sparkling wines should be good as their grapes were picked under good conditions before the rains came.

1985 The best vintage since 1978 – rich, long-lived, sweet wines from the Coteaux du Layon, Quarts de Chaume, and Bonnezeaux, and remarkably long-lived dry white wine from Savennières.

1984 The balance between fruit and acidity is missing in 1984; the wines lack fruit and are too high in acidity.

1983 Wonderfully mature, ripe grapes produced fat, rich, big wines that lack a little finesse, but have plenty of flavour and intensity. For the sweet wines, this could turn out to be a great vintage.

A GUIDE TO ANJOU-SAUMUR'S BEST PRODUCERS

★ ★ ★ ★ ★ Outstanding Producers
Coulée de Serrant (Savennières) ★

★ ★ ★ ★ Excellent Producers
Domaine des Baumard
  (Quarts de Chaume)
Château de Chamboureau
  (Savennières) ★
Philippe Delesvau
  (Coteaux du Layon)

Château de Fesles (Bonnezeaux)
Château de Plaisance
  (Coteaux du Layon)
Touchais (Anjou)

★ ★ ★ Good Producers
Jacques Beaujeau
  (Coteaux du Layon)
Château de Bellerive
  (Quarts de Chaume)
Château de la Bizolière
  (Savennières) ★
Château Bonin
  (Coteaux du Layon)
Domaine du Closel
  (Savennières)
Domaine de la Croix
  de Mission (Bonnezeaux)

Diot-Autier (Coteaux du Layon)
Château d'Epiré (Savennières) ★
Vincent Goizel
  (Coteaux du Layon)
Château de la Guimonière
  (Coteaux du Layon)
Logis du Prieuré
  (Coteaux du Layon)
Château des Rochettes
  (Coteaux du Layon)
Château de Tigné (Anjou)

★ Denotes dry wines with little or no amounts of residual sugar.

TOURAINE

Chinon is the first appellation that one encounters in this part of the Loire Valley after leaving Anjou-Saumur to head up-river. Chinon's historic château is reason enough to visit this beautiful area, but Chinon makes the Loire Valley's best red wine, as well as some distinctly fresh, fruity rosés. The region also makes white wines, but they do not compare favourably with the white wines from other parts of the Loire.

The best-known producer of Chinon is the firm Couly-Dutheil. Although I have found some of Jacques and Pierre Couly's white wines not impressive enough to warrant their high reputation, their red wines from Chinon and Bourgueil, produced from the Cabernet Franc grape, can be surprisingly complex and interesting. Look for the following trio of fruity, spicy, slightly herbaceous, complex wines, with scents of wild strawberries and vanillin oak: the Chinon Domaine de Versailles, the Clos de l'Echo and the Bourgueil Réserve des Closiers are all quite well-made wines and represent excellent value.

My favourite Chinon producer is Charles Joguet. He makes a marvellous rosé; try his stunningly refreshing, lively, fruity Chinon Rosé and you will see what I mean. His loyal following, however, is based on his inexpensive red wines – all rich, full, complex and savoury – that require five to six years of ageing to show their real character. This is especially true of his best wine, the Chinon Cuvée Clos de la Dioterie Vieilles Vignes. The 1978 version of this wine could have been confused with an excellent St.-Emilion. Other selections from Joguet to look for are his Chinon Cuvée Clos du Chêne Vert, Chinon Cuvée des Varennes du Grand Clos, and Chinon Cuvée du Clos du Curé.

The other major Loire Valley appellation in Touraine is Vouvray, which is famous for its white wines. They are produced from the Chenin Blanc grape, and range in style from dry to sweet, as well as bubbly. I have enjoyed immensely the Vouvrays from the largest producer of this appellation, Château Moncontour; the Vouvray Sec is a brilliantly made wine, with its vivid, ripe fruitiness counterbalanced against crisp, taut acidity. The small growers of Vouvray, such as Gaston Huet at the Domaine de Haut-Lieu, produce excellent Vouvrays, as does A. Foreau at his property called Clos Naudin. Interestingly, Foreau's Brut Réserve is one of the best sparkling Vouvrays I have tasted, resembling, believe it or not, rich, old vintages of Champagne. Foreau also does a nice job with his dry (or *sec*) style of wine. The regular Vouvray is clean, stylish, fruity, with good acidity and at least five to six years of positive evolution.

QUICK VINTAGE GUIDE

1986 Again, the rains which came in the last weeks of October ruined the chances for a top crop of sweet wine, but the red wines should be adequate, although less intense and flashy than their 1985 counterparts. They will all be more tannic and austere.

1985 A potentially great year for the sweet wines of Vouvray, and certainly at the very least a very good year for the dry white wines and an excellent year for the red wines.

1984 A poor vintage, with the wines lean, acidic, and thin.

1983 An excellent vintage for Vouvray, both dry and sweet wines, and a very good vintage for the red-wine producers since everything ripened well.

1982 The dry white wines are fading quickly. The red wines are perfect for drinking now, the sweet whites are above average but overshadowed by the recent vintages of 1983 and 1985.

Older vintages

Gaston Huet's sweet Vouvrays from 1959 and 1962 were tasted last year and are in suberb condition. Why don't more people realize just how fine these wines are? Charles Joguet's best Cuvées of red wine from his Chinon vineyards, unfiltered and rich, can easily last ten years. His 1978s are excellent now. The same can be said for Olga Raffault's Chinons. Otherwise, the wines from other producers in Touraine should be drunk within their first five to six years of life for their freshness.

A GUIDE TO TOURAINE'S BEST PRODUCERS

★ ★ ★ ★ ★ Outstanding Producers
Gaston Huet (Vouvray)
Charles Joguet (Chinon)

★ ★ ★ ★ Excellent Producers
Couly-Dutheil (Chinon)
A. Foreau (Vouvray)
Château Moncontour (Vouvray)

★ ★ ★ Good Producers
Audebert (Bourgueil)
Marc Brédif (Vouvray)
Caves Coopèratives de Haut Poitou (Touraine)
Domaine de la Charmoise (Touraine)
Le Clos Neuf des Archambaults (Cobeaux)
La Croix de Mosny (Touraine)
Jean-Pierre Freslier (Vouvray)
Sylvain Gaudron (Vouvray)
Lamé-Delille-Boucard (Bourgueil)
Jean Louet (Touraine)
J. M. Monmousseau (Vouvray)
D. Moyer (Vouvray)
Prince Poniatowski (Vouvray)
Olga Raffault (Chinon)

UPPER LOIRE

The upper Loire Valley is synonymous with Sauvignon Blanc. There are other grape varieties planted here, the bland Chasselas and some Pinot Noir, but the real glories are the Sauvignon Blanc-based wines from such appellations as Sancerre and Pouilly-Fumé and from the two little-known appellations of Quincy and Ménétou-Salon. Sauvignon Blanc, when grown in these appellations, produces dry white wines that are very aromatic, sometimes too aggressively pungent for some tastes, but always smoky, herbal, earthy and distinctive. They are usually medium- to full-bodied wines, with crisp, high acidity, plenty of fruit, and a dry finish. They are marvellous with fish, poultry and, not surprisingly, the freshly made goat cheeses of the area.

Happily, 1985 was an especially kind vintage to these appellations, which often produce wines too high in acidity and too abrasively sharp and angular in texture. The hot summer and autumn rendered wines slightly lower in acidity than normal, yet rich and lush with Sauvignon Blanc fruit. From Sancerre and Pouilly-Fumé, the following producers' 1985s are excellent choices. First, J. C. Chatelain's Pouilly-Fumé Cuvée Prestige is loaded with intense, ripe Sauvignon fruit, very aromatic, and quite long in the finish. Another excellent Pouilly-Fumé is Ladoucette from Château du Nozet, but this wine tends to be more expensive than other Pouilly-Fumés.

From Sancerre, the pickings are even better. Five producers have consistently made excellent, estate-bottled Sancerres that stand far above their peers. All were extremely successful in both 1984 and 1985. Jean Reverdy's Domaine de Villots, Vincent Delaporte's Sancerre from Chavignol, Lucien Crochet's two Sancerres Clos du Chêne Marchand and Clos du Roy Blanc, Jean-Max Roger's Clos Derveau, and Lucien Thomas's Clos de la Crele all have the pungent, herbaceous bouquet and dry, lively, fruity flavours that one expects from a fine Sancerre. They usually sell for between £6 and £9 a bottle, making them attractive wines for the price. All of these 1985s will keep and drink well through the end of 1988. Keep in mind, however, that the 1985s, being lower in acidity, are full, fleshier wines than the 1984s, which are more typical, but more austere, leaner wines.

Last, the two tiny wine hamlets of Quincy and Ménétou-Salon also make Sauvignon Blanc-based wines, which can be almost impossible to distinguish from a fine Sancerre. (They also have the advantage of probably being unknown to your wine-smart guests.) From Quincy look for the wines of the highly acclaimed producer Raymond Pipet. In Ménétou-Salon, Henri Pellé makes excellent wines. His 1985 and 1984 Ménétou-Salons are quite spicy, pungently herbaceous, dry, medium-bodied, fruity wines, with crisp acidity. They would do justice to any fish or fowl dish. One thing is certain in this area – the overall quality of winemaking is by far the best of any in the Loire Valley area.

QUICK VINTAGE GUIDE

1986 The Upper Loire had a successful vintage in 1986. The Sauvignon grape matured well and was harvested long before the damaging rains of October. In quality, the wines will be just behind the excellent vintage in 1985.

1985 This is a very fine vintage in the same style as the 1982s – fat, ripe, juicy wines that are a little low in acidity. They have more finesse and freshness than the heavy-handed 1983s, and more charm and fruit than the 1984s. Drink them over the next one to three years.

1984 High-acid wines were made that will keep several years in the bottle, but may lack fruit. However, the best wines of this vintage will turn out to be surprisingly good, but they need time to drop some of their sharp acidity.

1983 Ripe, alcoholic, rather ponderous wines were produced in 1983. When first released, they tasted quite good, if more powerful than normal. However, they are now just beginning to turn the corner and should be consumed soon.

1982 Somewhat similar to the 1985s in style, these wines should be drunk up.

Older Vintages

The 1976 and 1978 were excellent vintages, but the wines of Sancerre, Pouilly-Fumé, Ménétou-Salon, and Quincy are made intentionally to be drunk within the first three to four years and are appreciated for their zesty, tart, lively fruitiness. They will keep longer, but they won't get any better.

THE LOIRE VALLEY · TODAY'S BUYING STRATEGY

The wines of the Loire Valley, as popular as they are in France, particularly Paris, have never been considered exceptional glamour wines elsewhere in the world. Consequently, their prices have remained stable, and there are numerous fine values, particularly among the sweet wines of Coteaux du Layon, Bonnezeaux, Quarts de Chaume, and Vouvray. Wines here that are five, ten, even fifteen years old (and in impeccable condition) can be purchased for under £12, the starting price for a Barsac or Sauternes of similar quality. Among the dry white wines, the exuberant, fresh Muscadets from the 1985 vintage should never cost over £5; the top Sauvignon Blancs from Sancerre, Pouilly-Fumé, and Ménétou-Salon in 1985 should cost under £9. The red wines, except for those of Charles Joguet and Olga Raffault, have never struck me as terribly interesting, but if you can find the Chinons from these two producers, they are worth trying. For vintages, if you are indulging your palate with a nectar-like sweet wine, you can go back to 1959 with no problem, but for the dry white wines make it 1985 or nothing at all; for the red wines you can consider 1983, but avoid 1984.

A GUIDE TO THE UPPER LOIRE'S BEST PRODUCERS

★ ★ ★ ★ ★ Outstanding Producers
J. C. Chatelain (Pouilly-Fumé)
Paul Cotat (Sancerre)

Château du Nozet
   (Pouilly-Fumé)

★ ★ ★ ★ Excellent Producers
Lucien Crochet (Sancerre)
Vincent Delaporte (Sancerre)
Gitton (Sancerre)
Jean Reverdy (Sancerre)

H. Reverdy (Sancerre)
Jean-Max Roger (Sancerre)
Lucien Thomas (Sancerre)

★ ★ ★ Good Producers
Roger Neveu (Sancerre)
Henri Pellé (Ménétou)
Raymond Pipet (Quincy)

Château de Tracy (Sancerre)
Clos de la Poussie (Sancerre)

PROVENCE

For many, Provence is known as France's vacation land and not as a source of high-quality wine. Such a statement may have had a great degree of truth a decade ago, but of all the viticultural areas of France, none has made greater progress than Provence. Long regarded for its excellent, crisp, fresh, dry rosé wines, Provence is beginning to win many converts for its up-and-coming red and white wines. Many producers in this region produce three wines – rosé, white, and red. For the most part, the high quality of the best estates of Provence has yet to be appreciated outside the region; consequently this is a splendid area for bargain hunters.

QUICK VINTAGE GUIDE

Given the area's constant sunshine and heat, one can expect every year to be at least good. Although this is generally true, certain years can be too hot and dry, which in Provence creates more of a problem than cooler, wetter years. For the white and rosé wines, I know of none that should not be consumed within two to three years of the vintage. They are best when fresh, lively, and vibrant. In short, don't drink anything before 1984, and concentrate on 1985s and 1986s. As for the red wines, those from the top estates itemized here can last in the top vintages for ten or more years, but most are in their full prime by the time they are five to six years old. Of recent vintages, 1985 and 1982 are superb, 1983 very good, and 1984 mediocre. For the white and rosé wines, 1985 gets first place, followed by 1986 and 1984.

A GUIDE TO PROVENCE'S BEST PRODUCERS

★ ★ ★ ★ ★ Outstanding Producers

Domaine Richeaume
(Coteaux d'Aix)
Domaine Tempier
(Bandol)

Domaine de Trevallon
(Coteaux de Baux)
Château Vignelaure
(Coteaux d'Aix)

★ ★ ★ ★ Excellent Producers

Château de Crémat (Bellet)
Château de Fonscolombe
(Aix-en-Provence)
Mas de la Rouvière (Bandol)
Domaines Ott (Côtes de
Provence)
Commanderie de Peyrassol
(Côtes de Provence)
Château Pradeaux (Bandol)

St.-André de Figuière
(Côtes de Provence)
Domaine de St.-Jean
de Villecroze (Coteaux Varois)
Château Simone (Palette)
Château Val-Joanis
(Côtes du Luberon)
La Vieille Ferme
(Côtes du Luberon)

Provence

KILOMETERS

MILES

A 7

St-Rémy-
de-Provence

Plan d'Orgon

les Baux

Eygalières

1

2

DURANCE

Arles

N 7

Salon-de-
Provence

Lambesc

N 113

Meyrargues

Eguilles

2

Rians

RHÔNE

N.568

Istres

2

La Fare-les-Oliviers

Vauvenargu

Aix-
en-Provence

N 7

4

3

Palette

A 8

BOUCHES-
DU-RHÔNE

ÉTANG DE BERRE

Rognac

Vitrolles

Trets

Martigues

A 55

A 57

4

A 52

St-
Zachari

Allauch

A 50

Marseille

7

4

A 50

M E D I T E R R A N E A N

Cassis

La
Ciotat

Bandol

Paris

Provence
Marseille

1 Coteaux des Baux   5 Coteaux Varois
2 Coteaux d'Aix   6 Bandol
3 Palette   7 Cassis
4 Côtes de Provence   8 Bellet

Villars-sur-Var

D 202

St·Roman-
de·Bellet

VAR

8

A 8

Nice

Seillans

Tavernes   Salernes
             5

S 60

Draguignan   4

A 8

5   VAR   N 555

4   Lorgues   Le Muy

St·Maximin-
la·Ste·Baume   St·Raphaël

N 98

N 560   Brignoles   N 7   A 8

La   Le Luc   N 98

Roquebrussanne Besse·sur·Issole

La Garde-Freinet

5   D 5

4   St·Tropez

Collobrières   La
                  Foux
Cuers

Le Beausset

6   Solliès·
Pont   La Verrerie   D 559

Toulon

N 98   Hyères   Le Lavandou

4   N

S E A   W   E

S

PROVENCE · *TODAY'S BUYING STRATEGY*

For the white and rosé wines, 1985 is the year. For the red wines, 1982, 1983, and 1985 are all first-rate. Prices are extremely reasonable for the wines of Provence. Domaine Tempier's splendid long-lived reds go for £6–£8, as do Domaine de Trevallon's voluptuous red wines. Most Provençal wines retail for £4–£7.

CHÂTEAU DE CRÉMAT *BELLET* ★ ★ ★ ★

1985 Blanc	③	*84*
1985 Rosé	②	*84*
1982 Rouge	③	*84*
1983 Rouge	③	*82*

Anyone who has enjoyed a bottle of wine in a good restaurant in Nice has probably noticed the wines of Château de Crémat on the wine list. This property sits in the hills above Nice and has been run by the Bagnis family since 1957. They produce the best wines of Bellet. The red wine tends to be a little high in alcohol, jammy and heavy, but the white wine is fresh, with scents of nuts, apple blossoms, and fresh fruit. The rosé is a rather full-bodied wine, but fresh, deliciously fruity, and long on the palate.

CHÂTEAU DE FONSCOLOMBE
COTEAUX D'AIX-EN-PROVENCE ★ ★ ★ ★

1985 Blanc	①	*83*
1985 Red	①	*84*
1985 Rosé	①	*84*

This estate, situated north of Aix-en-Provence, seems to be increasingly garnering more respect for its fine, fresh, lively, modern-style wine. The 1985s are much better than the 1984s. The white is fresh and exuberant, medium-bodied, rather neutral on the nose, but good. The 1985 rosé is downright delicious, very fresh and vivacious, dry, perfumed, and has a lovely balance and length. The red wine is plummy and ripe, with aromas and flavours of blackberry fruit. It is meant to be drunk now.

MAS DE LA ROUVIÈRE *BANDOL* ★ ★ ★ ★

1985 Bandol Rosé	②	*85*
1981 Bandol Rouge	②	*84*
1982 Bandol Rouge	②	*86*

This up-and-coming estate in Bandol excels with its supple, spicy, rich, full-bodied red wine. The 1981 is fully mature with a raspberry-scented bouquet; the 1982 is even better as it is a richer, deeper, more fragrant wine. It should keep well for five to ten years. The 1985 rosé is fresh, crisp and flavourful.

Their white wine is reputedly one of the best of Bandol, but I have not had it.

DOMAINES OTT *CÔTES DE PROVENCE* ★★★★

1983 Bandol Rosé	②	83
1984 Bandol Rosé	②	85
1983 Bandol Rouge	②	85
1984 Côtes de Provence Rosé	②	83
1985 Côtes de Provence Rosé	①	84
1985 Cuvée Comtes de Provence Blanc de Blancs	①	85
1983 Cuvée Comtes de Provence Rouge	②	85
1984 Château de Selle Blanc	①	84

Provence's most famous and successful winery, Domaines Ott's wines are on virtually every important wine list in France. Their success is well earned. The rosé wines are crisp, fragrant, fresh and lively; the white wines rich, full-bodied and made to stand up to a big, spicy, garlic-scented soupe de poissons or bouillabaisse. In the last five years, Ott's red wines have improved dramatically in quality and have intense aromas of Provençal herbs, black cherries and cassis. Ott's white and rosé wines should be drunk up before they are four years old. The reds will keep well for five to seven years.

CHÂTEAU PRADEAUX *BANDOL* ★★★★

1978 Bandol Rouge	②	84
1981 Bandol Rouge	②	81

This particular Bandol usually is aged three to four years in oak casks prior to bottling and represents a rather big, rustic style of wine. The 1981 is a trifle coarse, but a big, fleshy mouthful. The 1978 has a cedary, rich, intense personality, full body, and long, alcoholic finish.

DOMAINE DE RIMAURESQ *CÔTES DE PROVENCE* ★★★★

1982 Rouge	①	84
1983 Rouge	①	84

This estate makes round, generously flavoured, very fruity, supple wines that should be drunk within their first five to six years of life. They are notable values and resemble in style a very good Côtes du Rhône. The estate began producing wine in 1981.

ST.-ANDRÉ DE FIGUIÈRE *CÔTES DE PROVENCE* ★★★★

1983 Blanc de Blancs	①	83
1984 Blanc de Blancs	①	83
1982 Cuvée du Marquis Rouge	①	86
1982 Cuvée Speciale Rouge	①	84

One of France's few wineries dedicated totally to organically produced wine, St.-André uses no insecticides or chemical fertilizers in the vineyards. The wines, particularly the reds, tend to be rich and robust with powerful, exotic aromas and fleshy flavours. The vintages I have tasted were at their best after three to four years. Certainly, both the 1982s are fully mature but will last for four to five more years. The white wines have flowery, peach-scented aromas, soft, voluptuous flavours, and a lush finish; they should be drunk up as they will not get any better.

DOMAINE DE ST.-JEAN DE VILLECROZE *COTEAUX VAROIS* ★★★★

1982 Cabernet Sauvignon	①	85
1982 Cuvée de l'Heritier	①	78
1984 Rosé	①	84
1983 Syrah	①	86

This is a serious estate that was established in the early 1970s by an American and his French wife. The wines are organically made; no insecticides or chemical fertilizers are used. Like many Provence rosés, this wine is fresh, lively, and loaded with fruit, as well as dry. The Syrah, aged in oak barrels, is quite impressive, rich, deep, and full-bodied, with four to six years' ageing potential. The Cabernet is round, generously flavoured, and shows the potential for this grape in the south of France. The Cuvée de l'Heritier is straightforward, fruity, soft, and pleasant, but lacks complexity.

CHÂTEAU SIMONE *PALETTE* ★★★★

1981 Blanc	③	81
1982 Blanc	③	83
1982 Rosé	②	78
1981 Rouge	③	83
1982 Rouge	③	85

Palette, located just south of Aix-en-Provence, is one of France's smallest appellations. The Rougier family runs Simone with great care and makes three very distinctive wines. The rosé is, to my taste, a trifle oaky and heavy. The Blanc is spicy, rich in fruit and body, with a long, fleshy finish. Much of Simone's fame is based on its Rouge, a herb-scented, spicy, red wine that has medium to full body, and is generally quite tannic and long-lived. For both the white and red, 1982 and 1985 are the two best recent vintages.

DOMAINE TEMPIER *BANDOL* ★★★★★

1982 Bandol La Migoua	④	90

1982 Bandol La Tourtine	④	**90**
1984 Bandol Rosé	②	**85**
1985 Bandol Rosé	③	**86**
1982 Bandol Rouge	③	**86**
1983 Bandol Rouge	③	**85**

Domaine Tempier is considered by many knowledgeable authorities to be the finest estate not only in Bandol but in all of Provence. Certainly their splendidly complex, refreshing rosé is the best of its type I have ever tasted. Tempier makes no white wine, but their red Bandol is a very complex, long-lived wine that in vintages such as 1961, 1970, 1975, and 1982 can last fifteen to twenty years. Their regular Bandol is a ripe, rich, powerful wine with excellent concentration. The two single-vineyard wines, La Migoua and La Tourtine, are wonderfully complex, rich wines that are fragrant, deep, and velvety on the palate. The 1982s will be particularly long-lived.

DOMAINE DE TREVALLON *COTEAUX DE BAUX* ★★★★★

1981 Rouge	②	**85**
1982 Rouge	②	**90**
1983 Rouge	②	**91**
1984 Rouge	②	**86**

These marvellous wines, made from a blend of 60% Cabernet Sauvignon and 40% Syrah, are among the shining new stars of Provence. The wines, dense in colour, are very richly perfumed with fascinating aromas of cassis, apricots, and thyme. They are full-bodied, rich, very concentrated wines that exhibit great complexity and potential. The proprietor, Eloi Durrbach, planted the vineyards fifteen years ago and is now realizing the full fruits of his labour, for this winery is surely an up-and-coming superstar of France.

CHÂTEAU VAL-JOANIS *CÔTES DU LUBERON* ★★★★

1985 Blanc	①	**82**
1985 Rosé	①	**82**
1985 Rouge	①	**84**

This estate has received a remarkable amount of favourable publicity in recent years. The vineyards, planted only in 1978, are still very young, but the ambitious efforts and fresh, lively wines made here are sure to please. The 1985s are better than the 1984s. The Rouge is light, fruity, with a vibrant raspberry-scented bouquet, and soft, round flavours. The Rosé is clean, fresh and best drunk within its first one to two years of life, and the Blanc is round, crisp, and quite fruity. This is a property to keep an eye on.

CHÂTEAUX VIGNELAURE
COTEAUX D'AIX-EN-PROVENCE ★ ★ ★ ★ ★

1979 Rouge	③	**85**
1981 Rouge	③	**84**
1982 Rouge	③	**85**
1983 Rouge	③	**88**

This Provençal estate is one of the most famous properties in Provence. The proprietor, Georges Brunier, gained fame by resurrecting a renowned Bordeaux château, La Lagune, to prominence. He now runs this property with equal care and, not surprisingly, his wines have an affinity with those of Bordeaux. The 1979 is velvety and fully mature; the 1981 is round, generous, and elegant with five more years of evolution ahead of it; the 1982 is a more muscular, richer, fuller-bodied effort. Brunier thinks the 1983 is the finest wine yet made at Vignelaure. Vignelaure is usually at its best within six to nine years of the vintage.

LANGUEDOC

For years, this vast, sun-drenched area running parallel to the Mediterranean between Perpignan near the Spanish border and Arles in Provence was considered the major supplier of inexpensive, high-alcohol, red wines for the French supermarket trade. Much of the wine from this area still finds its way into these grapy, thick blends, but a few producers are trying to rise above the tide of mediocrity and produce something with more class and distinction. There are many viticultural regions and appellations in this enormous area, but five seem to have the most potential – Costières du Gard, Faugères, Minervois, Corbières, and Fitou. None produce particularly refined, graceful, long-lived wines, but the best producers make immensely satisfying, round, generous, fruity wines that are very inexpensive and meant to be drunk within their first four to five years of life. Don't hesitate to slightly chill any of these red wines, as many seem to taste better when served at a cool temperature. Lastly, there is one red wine producer that is not in an approved French appellation but is widely recognized for making the greatest wine of the Languedoc region, and one of the greatest of all France. The red wine of Mas de Daumas Gassac in L'Herault (which is legally only a *vins de pays*) is an extraordinary wine with great potential for longevity of fifteen to twenty years. It is primarily a Cabernet Sauvignon-based wine made in a distinctly Bordeaux style. The first vintage was 1978, the most recent 1985, and all have been stunningly rich, powerful, potentially very long-lived wines. To date they have sold at low prices, but given both the quality and demand, one wonders how much longer this price can hold.

RECENT VINTAGES

Heat and sun are constants in this region. Vintages are incredibly consistent and the quality of most wines has more to do with the availability of modern technology to keep the grapes and grape juice from overheating in the intensely hot temperature. Nevertheless, recent vintages that stand out are 1985, 1983, and 1982, with 1984 the closest thing this area has had to a mediocre year.

A GUIDE TO LANGUEDOC'S BEST PRODUCERS

★ ★ ★ ★ ★ **Outstanding Producers**
Mas de Daumas Gassac (L'Hérault)

★ ★ ★ ★ **Excellent Producers**
St.-Jean de Bebian (L'Hérault)

★ ★ ★ **Good Producers**
Gilbert Alquier (Faugères) Domaine du Bosccaute (L'Hérault)

Domaine de Fontsainte
(Corbières)
Château de Gourgazaud
(Minervois)
Château de Grezan (Faugères)
Haut Fabrèges (Faugères)
Domaine de la Lecugne
(Minervois)
Domaine de Mayranne
(Minervois)

Caves de Mont Tauch (Fitou)
Château de Nouvelle (Fitou)
Château de Paraza (Minervois)
Cuvée Claude Parmentier
(Fitou)
Château de Queribus
(Corbières)
St.-André (L'Hérault)
Château de Villerambert-Julien
(Minervois)

LANGUEDOC · *TODAY'S BUYING STRATEGY*

For serious collectors, the Mas de Daumas Gassac is a revelation and
a highly desirable addition to any wine cellar. For the other wines,
stick to younger vintages, avoiding anything older than 1982. Expect
to pay under £5 a bottle for a wine from any of the recommended
producers.

THE RHÔNE VALLEY

France's Least-Known Great Wines

The Rhône's top wines continue to represent France's least-known and most undervalued great wines.

The Rhône Valley offers something vinous for everyone from soft, round, plump, fruity generic Côtes du Rhône selling for under £3, which provide the wine consumer with immediate thirst gratification and value, to the stunning and profound hand-crafted estate-bottled wines that collectors must cellar for eight to ten years before seeing their full majestic richness.

QUICK VINTAGE GUIDE

1986 About 20% of the grapes in the Rhône Valley had not been harvested when the area was inundated with heavy rains on October 12 and the weather that followed over the next two weeks was equally miserable. However, the early pickers should have done quite well and in both the northern and southern Rhône, quality should at least be good. Production was less than in the bountiful year of 1985, but because of the late-harvest deluge selection will be critical and one can expect a great deal of irregularity in the range of quality.

1985 My initial tastings indicate that this vintage has produced excellent wines in the northern Rhône, and very good wines in the south. For Côte Rôtie, it is a great vintage. The wines are very deep in colour, quite rich, but not particularly tannic. The overall impression is one of wines fully ripe, rich in fruit, very opulent in style, and quite forward. Overall the vintage is very close in quality to 1978. In Côte Rôtie and Châteauneuf-du-Pape it is better than 1983. Everywhere it is certainly better than 1982, 1981, and 1980. The white wines are very powerful and rich.

1984 A rather mediocre vintage of light-to medium-bodied wines that will offer straightforward, one-dimensional drinking for the near future. There are many surprisingly good wines from Châteauneuf-du-Pape and Gigondas, and the white wines of the entire region are quite good.

1983 An outstanding vintage in the north, a very good yet irregular vintage in the south. A hot, dry summer resulted in fully mature grapes loaded with sugar, flavour extract, and hard tannins. For Hermitage, Crozes-Hermitage, and St.-Joseph, the wines are clearly the best since 1978 and 1961, neither so

269

massive and rich as the 1978s nor as opulent as the 1985s, but more elegant and potentially very long-lived. The southern Rhônes should be moderately long-lived as they are ripe, yet full of tannin. In Châteauneuf and Gigondas, 1983 is just behind 1978, 1981, and 1985 in quality.

1982 Initially believed to be outstanding in the north but mediocre in the south, only the latter half of the early prognosis has held true. The great heat during the harvest created significant problems and those growers not equipped to keep the fermenting grapes cool had problems with volatile acidity. The northern Rhônes are very flavourful but quite forward and will mature quickly. Most will keep until the early nineties, but not much longer. At present, they are 'showing' better than the more tannic, more sought-after 1983s. The southern Rhône had many more problems with both the heat and the huge crop. The wines are rather frail and somewhat unstable. However, there are some pleasant surprises, yet one must tread carefully here.

1981 A much better vintage in the southern than northern Rhône, where many vineyards lacked fully mature grapes. Most of the big red wines from Hermitage, Côtes Rôtie, and Cornas are lean and lack charm; however, exceptions do exist. In the south it is a very good, even excellent vintage for both Gigondas and Châteauneuf-du-Pape, the best between 1978 and 1985. The wines here are quite powerful, deep in colour, and offer excellent value.

1980 A large crop of easy-to-drink, medium-weight wines was produced in 1980. They are all relatively mature today and if stored well will continue to provide delicious drinking for the rest of this decade. Both the north and south were equally successful in this attractive, commercial vintage of fruity, soft, medium-bodied wines. Clearly, in 1980, the Rhône was France's most successful viticultural district.

1979 A very underrated, yet consistently excellent year in both the northern and southern Rhône. The 1979 had the misfortune to follow 1978, the Rhône's greatest vintage since 1961. The wines are just now entering their mature period (where the best of them should remain for another seven to ten years). They are rich, full-bodied, deep in colour, and quite flavourful and scented. The 1979s can still be found at very low prices.

1978 An undeniably great vintage in both sectors of the Rhône Valley. Most of the top wines, even though they are just short of their tenth birthday, are still not mature, yet can be drunk with pleasure because of their explosive fruit and remarkable depth. The 1978s are collectors' items and the well-cellared examples of Côte Rôtie, Hermitage, Cornas, and Châteauneuf-du-Pape will easily make it into the next century.

1977 Between 1976 and 1986, this is the Rhône's worst vintage. The wines are light, a little green, and lack character and charm. Some of the white wines from the northern Rhône, particularly those of Hermitage, which were very acidic when young, have opened up, but this is by and large a vintage to ignore.

1976 Some reports called this a great vintage, but time has taken its toll on these wines that in reality lacked depth from the beginning. Côte Rôtie was by far the most successful appellation, but many other northern Rhônes were problematic and the southern Rhônes in most cases lacked balance and were excessively tannic. Whereas 1979 is the Rhône's most recent underrated vintage, 1976 is its most overrated.

A GUIDE TO NORTHERN RHÔNE'S BEST PRODUCERS

★ ★ ★ ★ ★ Outstanding Producers

J. L. Chave (Hermitage)
A. Clape (Cornas)
A. Dervieux Thaize (Côte Rôtie)
Gentaz-Dervieux (Côte Rôtie)
E. Guigal (Côte Rôtie)

Paul Jaboulet Aîné (Hermitage)
R. Jasmin (Côte Rôtie)
R. Rostaing (Côte Rôtie)
N. Verset (Cornas)

★ ★ ★ ★ Excellent Producers

G. Barge (Côte Rôtie)
R. Burgaud (Côte Rôtie)
Delas (Hermitage)
P. Dumazet (Condrieu)

P. Multier (Condrieu)
J. Pinchon (Condrieu)
H. Sorrel (Hermitage)
Vidal-Fleury (Côte Rôtie)

★ ★ ★ Good Producers

G. de Barjac (Cornas)
Caves des Clairmonts
  (Crozes-Hermitage)
E. Champet (Côte Rôtie)
M. Chapoutier (Hermitage)
R. Clusel (Côte Rôtie)
Courbis (St.-Joseph)
Coursodon (St.-Joseph)
Desmeures (Hermitage)
A. Drevon (Côte Rôtie)
E. Duclaux (Côte Rôtie)
B. Faurie (Hermitage)

Fayolle (Hermitage)
Ferraton (Hermitage)
E. Florentin (Crozes-Hermitage)
A. Gerin (Côte Rôtie)
Gray (Hermitage)
Château Grillet (Condrieu)
J. L. Grippat (Hermitage)
J. Jamet (Côte Rôtie)
M. Juge (Cornas)
B. Levet (Côte Rôtie)
J. Marsanne (St.-Joseph)
R. Michel (Cornas)

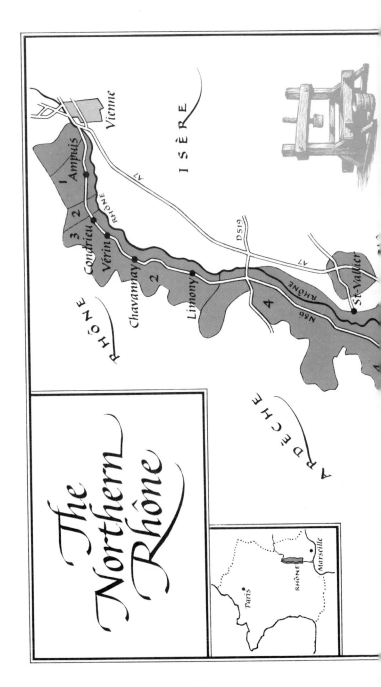

The Northern Rhône

Vienne

ISÈRE

Ampuis

Condrieu

Vérin

Chavannay

Limony

St-Vallier

RHÔNE

RHÔNE

ARDÈCHE

Paris

Marseille

RHÔNE

Côtes-du-Rhône

1 Côte Rôtie
2 Condrieu
3 Château-Grillet
4 St-Joseph
5 Crozes-Hermitage
6 Hermitage
7 Cornas
8 St-Péray

MILES

KILOMETERS

Domaine Pradelle
  (Crozes-Hermitage)
C. Tardy (Crozes-Hermitage)
R. Trollat (St.-Joseph)

Vallouit (Côte Rôtie)
Georges Vernay (Condrieu)
A. Voge (Cornas)

★★ **Average Producers**

A. Fumat (Cornas)
J. Lionnet (Cornas)
R. Roure (Crozes-Hermitage)

J. Teysseire (Cornas)
Union des Propriétaires
  (Hermitage)

NORTHERN RHÔNE

The northern Rhône viticultural district begins just south of the historic city of Vienne and winds south along both sides of the Rhône, running through Côte Rôtie, Condrieu, Château Grillet, St.-Joseph, Crozes-Hermitage, Cornas, and St.-Peray, concluding at the large commercial city of Valence. The total distance is only 42 miles.

CÔTE RÔTIE

Côte Rôtie can be France's most magnificent wine. Produced from the Syrah grape, Côte Rôtie can by law also have up to 20% of the highly perfumed white Viognier grape blended in. Producers use considerably less than the maximum Viognier permitted, but do use some for its aromatic personality.

The top Côte Rôties will handsomely repay eight to ten years of cellaring, yet for most consumers, the greatest difficulty is finding the top wines from the small, excellent producers such as Jasmin, Gentaz-Dervieux, Rostaing, and Jamet. Fortunately, the wines from the four major *négociants*, E. Guigal, P. Jaboulet, M. Chapoutier, and Vidal-Fleury, can be found in most major metropolitan markets.

What does a mature Côte Rôtie taste like? Imagine the scent of rich, ripe raspberry fruit, combined with exotic spices, floral aromas, the scent of vanillin from oak wood, and smoky hickory wood. In texture and palate impression, imagine rich, opulent, silky fruit that coats the mouth and just lingers and lingers.

GILLES and PIERRE BARGE ★★★★

1981 Côte Rôtie	③	**78**
1982 Côte Rôtie	③	**84**
1983 Côte Rôtie	④	**88**
1984 Côte Rôtie	④	**82**

Little of Barge's rustic, deeply coloured Côte Rôtie makes it to Britain, but this traditional winemaker, who works his craft off a back street of Ampuis, consistently makes fine, tannic, robust Côte Rôtie. His wines lack the finesse and grace of a Jasmin, Rostaing, or Guigal, but they do offer chunky, spicy fruit, full body, and a tough, tannic overlay. I was somewhat surprised that the 1982 did not show more concentration. The 1981 needs one to two years to reach full maturity, but for now, its attractive and spicy nose is more interesting than the overly tannic, compact palate impression. The 1982 needs four to six years. The star, however, is the 1983, a powerful, rich, dark ruby wine with a scent of bacon fat, full body and five to ten years of further ageing potential. The 1984 has a complex bouquet, but is high in acidity and lean. The 1985 will be a sensation when released in late 1987.

ROGER BURGAUD ★★★★
1983 Côte Rôtie.. ④ **88**
1984 Côte Rôtie.. ④ **88**
One of the youngest growers in Côte Rôtie, Burgaud is making people take notice of his talents. The 1983 is very tannic and rich; the 1984 one of the top successes of the vintage in Côte Rôtie. Both wines could use three to four more years, particularly the 1983.

E. CHAMPET ★★★
1982 Côte Rôtie.. ④ **86**
1983 Côte Rôtie.. ④ **87**
1984 Côte Rôtie.. ④ **85**
I have had experience with only a few vintages of Champet's wines; they are very good, rustic, rich, earthy examples of Côte Rôtie. The wines have a dark ruby colour with pleasant, berryish, leathery, fruity bouquets, moderately tannic, straightforward, medium- to full-bodied flavours, and tannic finishes. The 1983 is very ripe, tannic, a little low in acidity, but clearly a Côte Rôtie to drink after at least five to six years of bottle age. The unreleased 1985 is a little more concentrated and tannic; it will need five to six years. Champet's 1984 is quite good for the vintage.

CHAPOUTIER ★★★
1981 Côte Rôtie.. ③ **82**
1982 Côte Rôtie.. ③ **84**
1983 Côte Rôtie.. ③ **84**
The ebullient Max Chapoutier seems to have succeeded in the last couple of years in upgrading the quality of this family's wines, which have slipped noticeably. Nevertheless, the best Cuvées of Châteauneuf-du-Pape, Côte Rôtie, and Hermitage are still blended together and sold under the firm's top-of-the-line label, the non-vintage Gran Cuvée. The vintage offerings from Chapoutier show good fruit, an attractive,

woodsy, raspberry-scented bouquet, medium- to full-body, and soft, easy-going textures. Both the 1983 and 1982 are rounder, riper, richer, and overall just have more to them. They should drink well for five to six years.

R. CLUSEL ★★★
1983 Côte Rôtie.. ④ 86
1984 Côte Rôtie.. ④ 78

The 1983 is ripe, rich in fruit, and powerfully scented with the smell of raspberries. This seductive wine can be drunk now or held for five to six years. The 1984 is light yet pleasant.

ALBERT DERVIEUX-THAIZE ★★★★★
1983 Côte Rôtie Fongent .... ④ 87
1984 Côte Rôtie La Garde... ④ 84
1983 Côte Rôtie La Viaillère .... ④ 92
1984 Côte Rôtie La Viaillère .... ④ 84

The affable Albert Dervieux has been president of the Côte Rôtie growers and for years his well-placed vineyards have made a very traditional, rich, deep, tannic wine. His 1983s are top successes, but his 1985s look to be even greater. His 1984s are good, a trifle lean, but interesting, complex wines. His best wine is his La Viaillère, a tiny vineyard on the Côte Brune with vines that average 55 years old. Dervieux's wines are best drunk between six to fifteen years after the vintage.

GENTAZ-DERVIEUX ★★★★★
1982 Côte Rôtie Côte Brune .... ③ 90
1983 Côte Rôtie Côte Brune .... ④ 91
1984 Côte Rôtie Côte Brune .... ④ 87

Here are spectacular 1982 and 1983 Côte Rôties, and a great success in 1984 as well. In 1982, Gentaz-Dervieux harvested his tiny vineyard (1.25 hectares on Côte Rôtie's precipitous Côte Brune) in the morning to avoid the intense heat and probability of overheated grapes, which could cause vinification problems. His 1982 is extremely dark in colour, has a powerful, jammy, framboise-scented aroma, with exotic aromas of smoky hickory wood and black pepper. Quite rich and full-bodied, with firm, plentiful tannins, this wine will need seven to ten years of cellaring. Don't despair if you miss the wonderful 1982, because the 1983 is even better. It is even more concentrated, dense, very aromatic, but again in need of five to seven years of cellaring. Even the 1984, with its profound aromas of raspberries and dense fruit, is excellent. This is another grower who made a truly great 1985.

GERIN ★ ★ ★

1978 Côte Rôtie	③	72
1980 Côte Rôtie	③	75
1982 Côte Rôtie	③	84

The Domaine Gerin has a badly situated vineyard, on the level ground above the Côte Rôtie hill, and the vines are still young, particularly by the standards of most ancient Côte Rôtie vineyards. Perhaps these are the reasons for the quality and style of these wines, which, except for the 1982, are lacking in richness and character. Both the 1978 and 1980 exhibit annoyingly high acid levels and sinewy, compact personalities. The 1978 is especially distressing in view of the greatness of the vintage. As the vines get older, the wine here may get better.

GUIGAL ★ ★ ★ ★ ★

1979 Côte Rôtie	③	85
1980 Côte Rôtie	③	85
1981 Côte Rôtie	④	83
1982 Côte Rôtie	④	89
1983 Côte Rôtie	④	90
1980 Côte Rôtie La Landonne Côte Brune	⑤	95
1981 Côte Rôtie La Landonne Côte Brune	⑤	90
1982 Côte Rôtie La Landonne Côte Brune	⑤	95
1983 Côte Rôtie La Landonne Côte Brune	⑤	100
1980 Côte Rôtie La Mouline Côte Blonde	⑤	96
1981 Côte Rôtie La Mouline Côte Blonde	⑤	90
1982 Côte Rôtie La Mouline Côte Blonde	⑤	98
1983 Côte Rôtie La Mouline Côte Blonde	⑤	100

It is obvious that I admire Guigal's wines, but I admire even more his philosophy of making wine naturally and not over-manipulating it. My only fear is that his recently found superstar status will, as with so many who have become stars before him, cause him to forget the reasons for his success. Guigal owns vineyards only in Côte Rôtie. He purchases wine from growers for his other products and does a superb job of blending. His Côte Rôties are his best – his 1982s were the most successful northern Rhônes I tasted. The two rare, single vineyard wines, La Mouline and La Landonne, are among the world's greatest half-dozen wines. La Mouline is more volup-tuous and lush, La Landonne more brawny and tannic. Both should benefit nicely from three to six years of cellaring, but both have otherworldly concentration and aroma. The regular 1982 Côte Rôtie is spicy, quite aromatic, richly fruity, very concentrated and opulent in texture, soft, and long. It can be drunk now or aged for four to eight years. The 1981s, though not the greatest La Mouline and La Landonne ever made, are excellent wines, particularly in view of the difficult vintage conditions. The 1981 La Mouline is more precocious in style than the 1980, 1979, and 1978. The fragrant, open-knit, gorgeous bouquet of ripe blackberry fruit, oak, and violets lingers and lingers. It is firm on the palate, with very good fruit and a hint of the great lush, silky quality this wine is famous for; expect it to mature in seven to eight years. In contrast, the 1981 La Landonne is closed in, tannic, dark in colour, with a tarry, blackberry fruitiness, and impressive weight, but it is currently austere. It will need a full decade to show its best. The 1980 regular Côte Rôtie is quite successful, more supple and accessible than the tannic 1979, and of course not so profound and tannic as the 1978. Quite spicy, richly fruity, lush, the 1980 Côte Rôtie is quite concentrated, smooth and round, and can be drunk now or cellared for six to seven years. The 1981 regular Côte Rôtie does not quite have the concentration and lush, rich fruitiness of the 1980 or the structure, body, and potential of either the great 1978 or very fine 1979 Côte Rôties. However, it is round, very attractive, with soft, ripe fruit, light tannins, and immediate appeal. The 1983s are monumental wines here and the 1983 La Mouline and 1983 La Landonne, two of the greatest wines one could ever hope to encounter, should both last and evolve for 20–30 years.

PAUL JABOULET AINÉ ★ ★ ★ ★ ★

1981 Côte Rôtie Les Jumelles... ③ **74**
1982 Côte Rôtie Les Jumelles... ③ **85**
1983 Côte Rôtie Les Jumelles... ③ **86**
1984 Côte Rôtie Les Jumelles... ③ **78**

Louis and Gérard Jaboulet do a lovely job with Côte Rôtie, and while it rarely matches the sheer majesty of their famed Hermitage La Chapelle, it can be quite good. Vintages such as 1970, 1976, and 1978 were quite successful for the Jaboulet Côte Rôtie Les Jumelles, as anyone who has cellared these gorgeously succulent wines knows. The 1981 is a satisfying bottle of wine, but it lacks the richness and breadth that one normally expects. It is now ready to drink. The 1982 is my sensual favourite. It bursts forth from the glass, revealing scents of raspberry fruit, flowers, and spices. Supple, round, medium-bodied, quite elegant and seductive, this precociously styled wine should be drunk over the next five years. Not so the 1983, which has a big, tannic clout, full body, surprising strength and power, and good length. It is the best Côte Rôtie Les Jumelles since the wonderful 1976. It will need five to six years before it can be drunk. The 1984 is light, ready to drink, but simple.

R. JASMIN ★★★★★

1981 Côte Rôtie	③	*81*
1982 Côte Rôtie	③	*87*
1983 Côte Rôtie	④	*90*
1984 Côte Rôtie	④	*83*

The affable Robert Jasmin makes Côte Rôtie's most elegant and fruity wine. It is delicious from the barrel or the bottle, but is best drunk up within six to eight years of the vintage, since it rarely has the stamina to last much beyond a decade. Jasmin has the habit of keeping a barrel or two of his best Côte Rôtie from his oldest vines for his personal consumption, and those who have had the pleasure of visiting his private wine cellar under the kitchen floor will be amazed how concentrated and rich this wine can be, and lament that it is not blended into his Côte Rôtie for 'l'exportation'. The 1981 Jasmin Côte Rôtie is pleasant, too straightforward and light to merit high marks, but certainly a charming, fully mature wine. His 1982 is from a much better vintage but again lacks a bit of grip, richness and depth, however, it is quite fruity, spicy, generous, warm and round, and apt to please virtually any taster. It should be drunk over the next five years. The 1983, which Jasmin said was the 'best in quality and quantity since 1947', was clearly his finest wine since 1978 and until the 1985. Dark ruby with an expansive bouquet of ripe, rich fruit, and vanillin oak, the 1983 is quite perfumed, fat, and concentrated, and long and silky in the finish. Moderate tannins are present, but they are simply overwhelmed by the fruit. It should be drunk over the next ten years. The 1984 is ready to drink, quite charming, and light. His 1985, to be released in the autumn of 1987, is exceptional.

B. LEVET ★★★

1983 Côte Rôtie	④	*88*

This is an extremely impressive wine in need of five to six years of cellaring. Rich, dense in colour, it has aromas and flavours of ripe raspberries, pepper, and chocolate.

R. OGIER ★

1980 Côte Rôtie	②	*60*

Côte Rôtie? This large *négociant* has made an unsavoury wine with hot, southern Rhône flavours, plenty of alcohol, and not one trace of the character of Côte Rôtie. Need I say more?

R. ROSTAING ★ ★ ★ ★ ★
1981 Côte Rôtie Côte Blonde .... ③ 87
1983 Côte Rôtie Côte Blonde .... ④ 87
1984 Côte Rôtie Côte Blonde .... ④ 90
1981 Côte Rôtie Côte Brune et Blonde.................... ③ 83
1983 Côte Rôtie La Landonne Côte Brune.............. ④ 87
1984 Côte Rôtie La Landonne Côte Brune.............. ④ 86

One of the new up-and-coming producers in Côte Rôtie, Rostaing's first releases have been quite impressive. They have their own unique style, and are not copycat versions of Guigal or Jasmin, but something quite individual. They seem exotic and especially spicy for Côte Rôtie, with full-blown, peppery, raspberry aromas. Both 1983s need five to seven years of bottle age, but both are impressive wines of grace, richness, and excellent flavour. The 1983 Côte Blonde is more open and more obvious at this time; the 1983 La Landonne deeper, more tannic, and more peppery and spicy. The 1981 Côte Blonde is really quite excellent – velvety, long, rich, and ideal for drinking over the next five years. The other 1981 is tight, austere yet promising, but not possessed of the fruit of the 1981 Côte Blonde. His 1984 Côte Blonde is the top Côte Rôtie of the vintage, a decadently rich, gorgeously scented, wine. The 1984 La Landonne is more tannic and hard. His 1985s are simply incredible – make your reservations now.

VIDAL-FLEURY ★ ★ ★ ★
1983 Côte Rôtie... ③ 84
1979 Côte Rôtie La Chatillonne .... ③ 83
1980 Côte Rôtie La Chatillonne .... ③ 81

In the late seventies and early eighties, the venerable firm of Vidal-Fleury was in one of those awkward periods where effective leadership and management were missing, and the lack of direction was reflected in the wines, which were still solid and reliable but lacked the majesty of previous efforts. Côte Rôtie enthusiasts who have cellared Vidal-Fleury's Côte Rôties of 1966, 1969, 1971, and 1978, realize how stunning these wines can be. Certainly the 1978, which, for the lucky few who have some, still needs a good six to eight years of cellaring, was the last great Côte Rôtie from Vidal-Fleury. Change is certain, since the firm of Guigal purchased Vidal-Fleury and is now making great efforts to rebuild its reputation. The 1985s made here confirm this. Both of the above wines are from Vidal-Fleury's best vineyard on the Côte Blonde sector of the famous terraced hillside of Côte Rôtie. The 1979 La Chatillonne is medium ruby with a spicy, woody, ripe berryish bouquet, medium to full body, and good concentration. It should be fully mature in two to three years. The 1980 La Chatillonne is straightforward, plummy, enjoyable, but lacking character and complexity, as is the 1983. One will have to wait for the release of this firm's 1985s to see the obvious potential this old house has.

CHÂTEAU GRILLET AND CONDRIEU

Just several minutes drive south from Ampuis is the sleepy hamlet of Condrieu; several miles further still is the famed Château Grillet. The wines produced in both appellations are intensely perfumed, viscous, individualistic wines made from one of the rarest white wine grapes in the world, the Viognier. Condrieu is an opulent wine, intense, rich, and full-bodied, with a viscous texture, astonishing density of fruit, and a bouquet that suggests pears, peaches, tropical fruit, roses, and lychees. With such a glowing and enticing description of the wine, why isn't Condrieu better known? Scarcity and price are two reasons. There are only 35 acres to the Condrieu appellation, and a scant 7.5 acres to the Château Grillet appellation. The result is very tiny quantities of Condrieu available for worldwide distribution, which has kept the price for Condrieu in the high priced to luxury class, and for Château Grillet, the price is always in the luxury bracket. The difficulty with Condrieu is that it can overwhelm most foods. In Condrieu, the preferred dish is quenelles of river fish with a Nantua sauce. Condrieu also goes well with foods grilled over mesquite, particularly salmon and bass.

P. DUMAZET ★ ★ ★ ★
1984 Condrieu .... ④ 82
1985 Condrieu .... ⑤ 89

The 1984 here is light and a little short, but the 1985 is explosively rich, lush, with a deep, ripe, intense fragrance of spring flowers and lychees.

CHÂTEAU GRILLET ★ ★ ★
1982 .... ⑤ 86
1983 .... ⑤ 82
1984 .... ⑤ 80

For the last few years, the wines of the fabled Grillet vineyard have not been all that their precious reputation would seem to suggest. The wine is obviously overpriced, simply because the property makes so little wine. The 1982 is the best wine since 1978. Full-bodied, rich, honeyed, viscous, ripe, and fruity, it is very similar to a fine Condrieu (made just a few kilometres away). Drink over the next four to five years. The 1983 is more austere and lacks the richness of the 1982. The 1984 is lean and a bit acidic.

E. GUIGAL ★ ★ ★ ★ ★

1983 Condrieu .... ④ 89
1984 Condrieu .... ④ *84*
1985 Condrieu .... ④ **90**

The progress Guigal has made with white wines is amazing. His Condrieu is now one of the best of this appellation. Guigal toned down the oaky character of the 1983 (his 1982 was delicious, but too oaky) and to my palate, the results are excellent. All of these wines, particularly the 1985 and 1983, are highly perfumed with aromas suggesting honey, flowers, and apricots. Silky, loaded with fruit, opulent and exciting, these luscious wines will make excellent drinking over the next two years. The 1984 is pleasant, but lacks the richness of the 1983 and 1985.

PAUL MULTIER ★ ★ ★ ★

1982 Condrieu Château du Rozay .... ④ **90**
1983 Condrieu Château du Rozay .... ④ 88
1984 Condrieu Château du Rozay .... ④ 82
1985 Condrieu Château du Rozay .... ⑤ 87

The late Paul Multier was one of Condrieu's finest wine-makers, and if there is just one Condrieu to purchase, it is Château du Rozay. The 1982 and 1983 are absolutely superb with bouquets suggesting lychees, apricots, and lilacs; the wines have great density, richness, viscosity, and lushness on the palate. Both are best drunk now for their glorious, exuberant characters. The 1984 is reticent and shy in comparison, with a slight amount of *petillance*. It has plenty of punch and the heady, perfumed quality that makes Condrieu wonderful, as well as the lush, rich texture on the palate, and it is much thinner than the 1982. The newest vintage, 1985, is very rich, and opulent, with decadent flavours and a tremendous depth of fruit.

J. PINCHON ★ ★ ★ ★

1982 Condrieu .... ④ **90**
1983 Condrieu .... ④ 86
1984 Condrieu .... ④ 85
1985 Condrieu .... ④ **90**

Pinchon's Condrieu can rival Multier's Château du Rozay, but unfortunately Pinchon makes such a tiny quantity that little escapes France. The 1982 is one of the best-knit Condrieu wines, and if I were going to cellar one of these wines for four or five years, it would be the Pinchon. A bouquet of ripe pears and tropical fruits is enticing enough. On the palate, the wine has surprisingly good acidity, a very rich, intense, honeyed texture, and a long, long finish. The 1985 is very similar in style. The 1983 is a smaller-scale model of the 1982 and 1985, yet still wonderfully fruity and exotic. Pinchon's 1984 was the best Condrieu that I tasted from that difficult vintage.

G. VERNAY ★★★

1982 Condrieu	④	85
1983 Condrieu	④	87
1983 Condrieu Coteau de Vernon	④	88
1984 Condrieu Coteau de Vernon	④	83
1985 Condrieu Coteau de Vernon	⑤	92

Condrieu's best-known name, as well as its largest producer, Vernay is quite good, but in most vintages not quite at the same level of brilliance as Pinchon or Multier. However, if you can latch on to his top Cuvée of Condrieu (Coteaux de Vernon) from old hillside vines, it is extremely unctuous, rich, lush, and opulently fruity. However, the 1984 lacked length and tasted a trifle too acidic. The 1983 Vernay is very fresh, with a wonderful perfume of roses and spices. Fresh, intensely fruity, medium- to full-bodied, with layers of fruit, it is a round, sumptuous wine for drinking over the next one to three years. The 1982 is at its peak, lush and fruity, full-bodied, and a trifle alcoholic, but the heady perfumed bouquet of peaches, pears, and flowers is extremely seductive.

HERMITAGE (RED)

The most panoramic view a wine enthusiast gets of the famed Hermitage 'hill' is from across the bridge over the Rhône on the Tournon side, and it is simply spectacular. Steep, huge and jutting up from the ground behind the small, commercial town of Tain L'Hermitage is a massive outcropping of granite covered with vines and the huge painted white walls advertising the names of two of Hermitage's great producers, Paul Jaboulet Aîné and M. Chapoutier.

The wine of Hermitage used to be, in great years, closest in texture and richness to a vintage port. Despite the fact that many growers have lightened up in style and routinely filtered their wines, Hermitage is still a very big, rich, full-bodied, full-tilt, winter-weight wine. Even the minuscule quantities of white wine produced here are expansive, big, ripe, and viscous. Red Hermitage mandates game or beef on the table, but it can go splendidly well with strong cheese as well and it is big and distinctive enough to stand up to the pungent aromas of grilled foods.

M. CHAPOUTIER ★★★

Hermitage Le Pavillon Non-Vintage	⑤	88

1981 Hermitage La Sizeranne... ③ **82**
1982 Hermitage La Sizeranne... ③ **84**
1983 Hermitage La Sizeranne... ④ **84**
 The 1981 Chapoutier Hermitage is quite fat, supple, with good colour and fruit, a chunky, ripe cherry aroma, and a full-bodied, solid finish. It lacks complexity and style, but is quite satisfying. The 1982 is fuller, deeper, and more concentrated, richly fruity, with a blackberry taste and soft tannins. It should mature rapidly. The 1983 is very similarly styled, perhaps slightly firmer; it may be Chapoutier's best vintage of Hermitage since the early 1960s. The non-vintage luxury Cuvée, Le Pavillon, is very rich, long, deep and has an aged complexity to its flavour.

J. L. CHAVE ★★★★★
1981 Hermitage.. ③ **84**
1982 Hermitage.. ③ **90**
1983 Hermitage.. ④ **93**
1984 Hermitage.. ④ **87**
 Unquestionably one of the most respected growers in the Rhône, Chave is also one of the great wine drinkers and gourmets of the entire region. His propensity to talk enthusiastically about his most recent culinary innovation often leaves questions concerning the latest vintage or Rhône Valley gossip unanswered. Despite his remarkable reputation, his wines are not quite the model of consistent excellence that might be suggested. His 1976 and 1969 are two vintages that I find to be lacking in fruit and entirely too austere. However, his 1978 is a monumental wine, and his 1982 and 1983 wines are top flight. The 1981 Chave is certainly good for the vintage, rather precocious, medium-weight, charming, and fruity, with a pleasant spicy character. It needs two to three years to be fully mature. The 1982 has altogether more to it. It is quite dark ruby, rich and full-bodied, with a powerful, ripe berry, blackcurrant aroma, deep, viscous, fat, fruity flavours and firm tannins. Acidity is average; the wine should mature fully in ten years. Consumers should make a note to look for the 1983, Chave's best Hermitage since 1978. The 1984 is a top success for the vintage and very similar to Chave's excellent 1979.

DELAS ★★★★
1979 Hermitage Cuvée de la Tourette...................... ④ **87**
1983 Hermitage Cuvée de la Tourette...................... ④ **91**
 This firm tends to assume a very low profile and consequently its wines are not nearly as well known as they should be. Their

Hermitage is top-drawer in quality. The 1979 is just beginning to open, displaying rich aromas of cassis and smoky, tarry fruit. It has excellent concentration. The 1983 is sweet, smoky, with gobs of fruit, a cedary, ripe, rich, very complex bouquet, and five to ten years of further evolution ahead.

B. FAURIE ★★★

1982 Hermitage .... ③ **85**
1983 Hermitage .... ④ **87**

I have found Faurie's wines to be good. Both the 1982 and 1983 are quite full-bodied, supple, spicy, with a rich black cherry fruitiness, full body, plenty of power and alcohol, and excellent colour. They should be mature by 1990.

J. FAYOLLE ★★★

1982 Hermitage Les Dionnières .... ③ **89**
1983 Hermitage Les Dionnières .... ④ **87**

Except for 1983, 1982 is considered the best vintage for Hermitage after 1978, provided the grower could properly handle the vinification, which took place in torrid heat. Fayolle, a tiny grower, has produced a blockbuster wine, inky ruby/purple with huge, chewy, viscous fruit, a very intense blackberry bouquet, moderate tannins, and an amazing finish. A winter wine for serving with game, stews, and ripe cheeses, this excellent Hermitage, produced by the only winemaking twins I know of in the Rhône Valley, will be mature by 1987-1990. The 1983 has shown considerable bottle variation, so judgement is somewhat reserved; the good bottles have been rich and port-like, but the bad suffer from off aromas.

FERRATON ★★★

1981 Hermitage La Cuvée des Miaux .... ③ **86**
1982 Hermitage La Cuvée des Miaux .... ③ **?**
1983 Hermitage La Cuvée des Miaux .... ④ **89**

A small grower, Ferraton produces tiny amounts of Hermitage and Crozes-Hermitage. His 1981 is an excellent wine in a vintage that was mediocre for the area. Still very young, this deep ruby/purple wine has an intense, spicy, oaky, plummy aroma with the gamy scent of Syrah very evident. Rich, full-bodied, and quite tannic, this big, rich, complex wine will handsomely repay those who have the foresight to buy it and the patience to cellar it for five to eight years. The 1982, which should easily surpass the 1981, was quite poor on the two occasions I tasted it. Intolerable levels of volatile acidity make me wonder if all of Ferraton's 1982 Hermitage is flawed. The

1983, however, is smoky, rich, very concentrated, full-bodied, with great depth. Ferraton's 1985 looks to be even better.

E. GUIGAL ★ ★ ★ ★ ★

1979 Hermitage	③	87
1980 Hermitage	③	82–86
1981 Hermitage	③	86
1982 Hermitage	④	87
1983 Hermitage	④	90

I am impressed with the consistency in style and quality of Guigal's wines of Hermitage. He purchases the grape juice for these wines and then 'brings it up (*élévage*) in his wine cellars in Ampuis. The 1982 is rich and supple, with a big blackberry, licorice-scented bouquet, and long, lush flavours. It should drink nicely for five to eight years. The 1983 is Guigal's finest red Hermitage to date—a profound wine of great depth and stature. The 1979 is still on the market, and is the best of these three wines. Richer, fuller-bodied, and more concentrated than either the 1980 or 1981, it still has plenty of tannin to shed, but is loaded with ripe cassis fruit and lingers on the palate. The 1980 is actually two different wines because there are two separate lots. Unfortunately, there is no way to tell which lot you may be getting. One lot of 1980 is good but harshly tannic and austere, with a short, compact finish; the other lot has a much greater concentration of fruit, is still very tannic, but is rich and well balanced. Guigal's 1981 is a great success in this mixed vintage. A wonderful cassis aroma is followed by a big, deep, rich, full-bodied wine that has more in common with the 1979 than one would expect for the vintage.

PAUL JABOULET AINÉ ★ ★ ★ ★ ★

1981 Hermitage La Chapelle	③	80
1982 Hermitage La Chapelle	③	90
1983 Hermitage La Chapelle	⑤	96
1984 Hermitage La Chapelle	④	85
1985 Hermitage La Chapelle	④	89

I was surprised that Gérard Jaboulet decided to declare a La Chapelle in 1981, because the first time I tasted his 1981 Hermitage he said the quality wasn't high enough to be called La Chapelle. However, his initial reaction to the wine has obviously changed, because it does indeed exist. It is a light, charming wine with soft, blackcurrant fruit and light tannins. It should be drunk over the next two to four years. The 1984 is similarly styled, but noticeably richer and deeper in colour. As for the 1983, Gérard Jaboulet thinks this wine is one of the very best he has ever made. I doubt whether it is better than the extraordinary 1978 or 1961 La Chapelles, but it looks to be a real winner. Opaque and ruby/purple in colour, this full-bodied wine has an intense aroma of black cherry fruit, hickory wood, freshly ground black pepper and cassis. Voluptuous and full-bodied on the palate, with layers of silky, lush, viscous, chewy fruit, moderate tannin, and average acidity, this big, potentially great wine will mature in five to eight years, well before Jaboulet's stunning 1978. Both the 1982 and 1985 are similarly styled—quite deep, rich, full-bodied, but very precocious, fruity, and lush. Both should drink well young, and last eight to twelve years. People who buy and cellar great Hermitage will be shocked at how sensational they will be at maturity. It can be a great value.

H. SORREL ★★★★

1982 Hermitage Le Greal	④	**60**
1983 Hermitage Le Greal	④	**90**
1984 Hermitage Le Greal	④	**85**

The ancient Monsieur Sorrel has passed away, and with him the talent to produce great Hermitage from his splendid parcel of vines on the Le Méal sector of the Hermitage hill. His son at first let things get out of hand, but one suspects that he found the right winemaker to assist him in 1983 and quality has returned. His 1983 is vastly superior in quality, exhibiting rich, deep fruit, and a long, tannic finish. It needs five to six years. The 1982 is spoiled by excessive volatile acidity, not to mention faulty winemaking.

UNION DES PROPRIÉTAIRES ★★

1982 Hermitage	②	**75**
1983 Hermitage	③	**72**

The 1982 bottling from this cooperative is soft, gamy, grapy, and simple, but fruity and pleasant. Drink up. The 1983 is very tannic and hard.

VIDAL-FLEURY ★★★★

1979 Hermitage	③	**83**

This offering from Vidal-Fleury is a robust, spicy, chunky wine, with good colour, a ripe, black cherry bouquet, full body, and a brawny, hefty texture. The tannins are beginning to mellow, so this plump wine should be ready to drink in two to three years.

HERMITAGE (WHITE)

White Hermitage can be remarkable, long-lived, rich, intense wine.

Last year I drank the 1955 and 1929 white Hermitage from the firm of Chapoutier, which Max Chapoutier poured in a tasting of his old vintages. I was also lucky enough to drink the 1929, 1952, and 1969 of Gérard Chave. These wines smell of grilled almonds; their intense, lively fruit, incredible length and richness reinforce the fact that they are almost always drunk too young. I use these examples not to suggest that you cellar white Hermitage for twenty or more years before consuming it, but to consider latching on to a few older bottles, because they can be truly great wines.

White Hermitage is produced from two grapes, the Marsanne and Roussanne. Most growers primarily use the Marsanne, since it is easier to cultivate and more prolific. Traditionally, the top producers of white Hermitage have been Chave, Chapoutier, and Grippat. Paul Jaboulet Aîné, for all the splendid success with reds, has lagged behind in quality with the firm's white wines, although the white 1983s and 1985s of Jaboulet are very good. Guigal also makes white Hermitage, and it can be quite good.

M. CHAPOUTIER ★★★
1982 Hermitage Chante Alouette	③	84
1983 Hermitage Chante Alouette	③	87
1984 Hermitage Chante Alouette	③	87
Hermitage Cuvée l'Orvée Non-Vintage	⑤	92

Chapoutier's vintage white Hermitage, called Chante Alouette, is one of this firm's very best wines. The 1982 is soft, flavourful, ripe, and generous. It should be drunk now and over the next five years for its full-bodied, fleshy texture. Both the 1983 and 1984 are very powerful wines, very deep, very full, and Max Chapoutier thinks they are among his finest in the last two decades. They linger and linger on the palate, and seem to have the potential to last for at least ten years. His luxury blend of white Hermitage, the Cuvée l'Orvée, is an extraordinary wine of great depth and dimension, and must be tasted to be believed.

J. L. CHAVE ★★★★★
1981 Hermitage	③	86
1982 Hermitage	③	87
1983 Hermitage	③	90
1984 Hermitage	④	87
1985 Hermitage	④	92

Chave's white Hermitage is made to last and last, and with few exceptions will keep and improve for fifteen or more years. The 1981 is the lightest of this trio, and lacks the power and richness of the subsequent two years. It shows charming mineral-scented fruit, a medium-weight texture, and crisp acidity; it is rather light for Chave, but stylish and flavourful. The 1982 is very accessible, unusually opulent for a young wine from Chave, with ripe, intense, soft, fat flavours. It is a trifle deficient in acidity, so consumers should drink it up over the next seven to ten years. It is extremely flavourful, full, and rich. The 1983 is even bigger than the large-scaled 1982, but has better acidity and superb balance. It is very concentrated, quite full-bodied, very firm, and is a stunning example of white Hermitage. The 1984 is stylistically similar to the 1981; the unreleased 1985 is absolutely stunning in its power and graceful harmony.

B. FAURIE ★★★

1982 Hermitage .... ③ **83**

This 1982, like many of the white Hermitage wines of this vintage, is a trifle low in acidity, but has a full-intensity aroma of hazelnuts and ripe fruit. On the palate, the wine is full-bodied, ripe, viscous, a bit heavy, and has a long finish. Drink over the next two to four years.

FERRATON ★★★

1982 Hermitage La Reverdy .... ③ **50**
1983 Hermitage La Reverdy .... ③ **70**
1985 Hermitage La Reverdy .... ④ **85**

Two bottles of the 1982 revealed the same inexcusable problem – excessive volatile acidity. Dark golden and quite flawed, this wine should never have been released by Ferraton. The 1983 is also a trifle odd and bizarre, but clearly more palatable. However, the 1985 is crisp, well balanced, and has no technical problems.

GRAY ★★★

1978 Domaine de l'Hermite .... ③ **88**
1980 Domaine de l'Hermite .... ③ **75**

The elderly Gray made a great, viscous, ripe, heavyweight old style Hermitage in 1978 that may still be available from some wine merchants. It's a marvellous example of a big, rich, decadently powerful and full Hermitage. The 1980 suffers not only by comparison, but tastes flat and too low in acidity, although it has solid, fruity flavours and full body.

GRIPPAT ★★★

1982 Hermitage .... ③ **87**
1983 Hermitage .... ③ **90**
1984 Hermitage .... ③ **85**
1985 Hermitage .... ④ **90**

Grippat makes excellent white Hermitage and the 1982, 1983, and 1985 are among his best. Quite full-bodied with a big, luscious, ripe pear- and almond-scented aroma, deep, fat, alcoholic, rich flavours that coat the palate with oodles of fruit, Grippat's white Hermitage usually needs five years to show its best. However, there is no reason not to enjoy this big, rich wine now.

E. GUIGAL ★ ★ ★ ★

1981 Hermitage	③	79
1982 Hermitage	③	84
1983 Hermitage	④	87
1984 Hermitage	④	83

Guigal's style of Hermitage leans towards an austere, tightly knit, well-structured wine that should improve with age. Unfortunately, the oldest white Hermitage of his that I have tasted is the 1978, which is just now beginning to unfold. The 1981 and 1984 are lean, closed, medium-bodied and tight. Two to three years of cellaring should prove beneficial, but they are not big, highly concentrated Hermitages. The 1982 is also tightly knit and closed up, but has more weight, length, and concentration. The 1983 looks to be the best of the four.

PAUL JABOULET AINÉ ★ ★ ★ ★ ★

1982 Hermitage le Chevalier de Sterimbourg	③	82
1983 Hermitage le Chevalier de Sterimbourg	③	85
1984 Hermitage le Chevalier de Sterimbourg	③	78
1985 Hermitage le Chevalier de Sterimbourg	④	86

For over a decade and a half, the weakest link in the Jaboulet family's strong Rhône wine line-up has been the white wines. However, over the last five years there has been a strengthening in character and richness in these wines, and the 1983 and 1985 white wines are Jaboulet's best in memory. The 1982 is a good white Hermitage, but makes no pretensions of challenging the quality of a Chave, Chapoutier, or Grippat. It is a clean, fresh, fruity, straightforward wine that should be drunk over the next five years. The 1983 is much more concentrated, powerful, very deep and fruity, with a nose suggesting straw, almonds, and mineral scents. Quite full-bodied, it should last at least a decade. The 1984 is tart, rather light, but fragrant and fruity.

CROZES-HERMITAGE AND ST.-JOSEPH

Both Crozes-Hermitage and St.-Joseph are the stepchildren of the northern Rhône. If the wines of Hermitage and Côte Rôtie are notoriously underrated and under-valued, then you can imagine how little credibility the wines from these two appellations receive. However, they are the great values of the northern Rhône, since they rarely will cost the consumer more than £4 a bottle. Consequently, the top red wines from these communes are almost always drunk too young by consumers who think that £4 wine will not keep. In fact, good Crozes-Hermitage and St.-Joseph is usually best at four to six years after the vintage, and in great vintages like 1978 and 1983 can last ten or more years. As for white wines, they too are little known except by real Rhône wine enthusiasts, who know what great, under-valued finds they can be.

CROZES-HERMITAGE AND ST.-JOSEPH (RED)

CAVES DES CLAIRMONTS ★★★
1983 Crozes-Hermitage... ② **84**
> A ripe, round, supple, very lovely wine with very good richness for drinking over the next four to five years.

COURBIS ★★★
1981 St.-Joseph.. ② **82**
1983 St.-Joseph.. ② **84**
> Both the 1981 and 1983 are chunky, big, spicy, fruity wines with plenty of cherryish fruit, full bodies and long finishes. They are not complex, but substantial and satisfyingly full. Drink them over the next two years.

DESMEURES ★★★
1983 Crozes-Hermitage.. ① **81**
> Dark in colour, rich, rather deep, but still savage and raw, this is a very traditional backward wine for drinking in two to three years.

FAYOLLE ★★★
1982 Crozes-Hermitage Pontaix.................................... ① **84**
1983 Crozes-Hermitage Pontaix.................................... ② **?**
> The 1982 wine could easily be mistaken for most producers' Hermitage. The ripe, tarry, game-like aroma is full and interesting. On the palate, the wine has excellent concentration, big, thick flavours, and a soft, long finish. Drink over the next three to four years. The 1983 has proved itself to be both very good and very bad.

E. FLORENTIN ★★★
1981 St.-Joseph Clos de l'Arbalestrier...................... ② **78**
1982 St.-Joseph Clos de l'Arbalestrier...................... ② **82**
1983 St.-Joseph Clos de l'Arbalestrier...................... ② **84**

The 1981 is a trifle tight, hard and lean, but seems to have the depth of fruit to outlast its tannins. Hold for two to three years before drinking. It is above average in quality, but too angular. The 1982 has more to it, greater ripeness and length, but top among this trio is the 1983, a rustic, rich, authoritative wine with plenty of body and length.

J. L. GRIPPAT ★★★

1982 St.-Joseph	②	84

A velvety wine with rich cherry and strawberry fruit flavours, medium to full body, this soft, round, plump wine has a lush texture, lingering finish, and is ideal for drinking over the next four years.

PAUL JABOULET AINÉ ★★★★★

1982 Crozes-Hermitage Thalabert	②	83
1983 Crozes-Hermitage Thalabert	②	86
1984 Crozes-Hermitage Thalabert	②	83
1985 Crozes-Hermitage Thalabert	②	86
1982 St.-Joseph Le Grand Pompée	①	83
1983 St.-Joseph Le Grand Pompée	②	83
1984 St.-Joseph Le Grand Pompée	②	72
1985 St.-Joseph Le Grand Pompée	②	84

The 1982, 1983, and 1985 vintages were extremely successful for the firm of Paul Jaboulet. The 1982s are lower in acidity and much more forward, the 1983s are dark, broodingly tannic, and loaded with potential. As for the Grand Pompée, the 1982 is a perfect wine for casual drinking. Decadently fruity and lush, with lots of round, silky raspberry fruit and an intensely perfumed bouquet, it is a real crowd-pleaser. The 1983 is atypically big, dense, full, and rich. It will need two to four years of cellaring. The 1982 Crozes-Hermitage Thalabert, usually the best wine of this appellation, was the best wine from the Thalabert vineyard since 1978. Dark ruby, with a wild, spicy, plummy, game-like aroma, soft, richly fruity flavours and medium body, it should be drunk over the next three to four years. However, the 1983 and 1985 Thalaberts are the best Thalaberts I have ever tasted, including the much heralded 1978. Tasting like a really big Hermitage, it is quite black/ruby in colour, very ripe, rich, full-bodied and tannic, and has everything going for it. It should last ten to twelve years. The 1984s are light and ready to drink now. The 1985s are much more opulent and loaded with ripe fruit.

R. ROSTAING ★★★★★

1982 St.-Joseph	①	75

I am fond of Rostaing's Côte Rôtie, but his St.-Joseph is only average in quality, with a straightforward, simple, fruity bouquet and average-intensity flavours. Drink over the next one to two years.

C. TARDY ★ ★ ★
1981 Crozes-Hermitage Domaine des Pierrelles .... ① **82**
1983 Crozes-Hermitage Domaine des Pierrelles .... ① **82**
Both the 1981 and 1983 are very solid and substantial wines with good body and concentration, plenty of spicy Syrah fruit, and excellent colour. They lack a little complexity, but offer gutsy, mouth-filling flavours.

R. TROLLAT ★ ★ ★
1982 St.-Joseph .... ② **84**
1983 St.-Joseph .... ② **85**
These offerings from the very fine 1982 and 1983 vintages in the northern Rhône, from the highly respected grower Trollat, have more in common with a good Burgundy than with a wine made from the Syrah grape. Medium to dark ruby in colour, with lovely, moderately intense bouquets of crushed raspberries and strawberries, on the palate the wines are lush, very concentrated, medium- to full-bodied, clean, dry, with lingering finishes, and that ability to make one come back time and time again for another glass ...isn't that what is called complexity?

CROZES-HERMITAGE AND ST.-JOSEPH (WHITE)

COURBIS ★ ★ ★
1982 St.-Joseph .... ② **84**
This fine offering exhibits big, robust, deep flavours of buttered nuts, ripe, spicy fruit, and a powerful finish. A chunky, fat wine with a lush, weighty feel on the palate, this is an excellent, robust wine for drinking with full-flavoured dishes.

FAYOLLE ★ ★ ★
1982 Crozes-Hermitage Pontaix .... ② **83**
1983 Crozes-Hermitage Pontaix .... ② **82**
Full-bodied, quite aromatic, very fruity, dry and surprisingly powerful (14% alcohol), the 1982 Fayolle white Crozes-Hermitage is a big, juicy, well-balanced white wine for having with grilled fish or poultry. The 1983 is almost as good, but a little more angular. Drink over the next one to two years.

GRIPPAT ★ ★ ★
1982 St.-Joseph .... ② **85**

1983 St.-Joseph..	②	**86**
1984 St.-Joseph..	②	**84**
1985 St.-Joseph..	②	**86**

These wines are beautiful white St.-Josephs with more of a resemblance to fine, expensive Condrieus than to lesser-known white Rhônes. In particular, the 1985, 1983, and 1982 have perfumed bouquets of ripe apricots, pears, and floral scents. On the palate, these wines are round and very lush, with a heady, high-alcohol content, long finish, and layers of fruit. The 1984 is the lightest and is slightly less concentrated. Drink over the next two years.

PAUL JABOULET AINÉ ★★★★★

1982 Crozes-Hermitage La Mule Blanche................	②	**83**
1983 Crozes-Hermitage La Mule Blanche................	②	**84**
1984 Crozes-Hermitage La Mule Blanche................	②	**78**
1985 Crozes-Hermitage La Mule Blanche................	②	**86**

These are the best examples of white Crozes-Hermitage that Jaboulet has made in recent memory. The 1982 and 1983 are similar in style, with rich, aromatic, spicy bouquets, luxurious, fruity flavours, and lovely balance. The 1982 is a trifle softer. The 1983 is fuller, bigger in size, and more concentrated; the 1985 even richer and more powerful than the 1983. The 1984 is tart, pleasant, but austere. I yearn for a grilled salmon or bass when I taste them.

RAYMOND TROLLAT ★★★

1981 St.-Joseph..	②	**83**
1982 St.-Joseph..	②	**84**

Always reliable and fairly priced, Trollat's wines tend to be elegant for the northern Rhône, with lovely peach-like bouquets. A moderately intense, fruity, slightly spicy, perfumed aroma is followed by a wine that has good acidity, a fleshy, interesting texture, and supple, generous flavours. Both are fine choices for fowl or fish. The 1982 is a trifle longer on the palate.

CORNAS

I doubt there is any writer alive today who has argued the case for Cornas as fervently as I have. Of course, I have no interest other than gustatory pleasure in seeing that the savage and wild wines of Cornas find a place in your cellar. I believe passionately in these wines, because they are anachronisms in the new world of wine – Cornas producers have yet to realize the technology of the twentieth century. A visit to the caves of Cornas growers such as Clape, Michel, Juge, Barjac and Voge is like stepping into a time machine and getting off a century or so earlier. The wines produced make no compromises to consumers who want supple, forward, easy-to-drink wine. Cornas is broodingly dark, rustic, sometimes coarse, massively proportioned in great vintages such as 1978 and 1983, brutally tannic and nasty to taste, but after eight to twelve years, the wine has a majestic perfumed nose, rich, long, savoury flavours, and just enough tannic kick to remind you of its origins. Properly mature Cornas is one of the great gustatory treasures. John Livingstone Learmonth, in his excellent book *The Wines of the Rhône* (Faber and Faber, 1983), comments, 'the sight of a mature Cornas tumbling into a broad-based wine glass is unforgettable. What richness, vigour and virility are portrayed in that startling dash of colour – and the heady scent of blackcurrant and raspberry that accompanies it is sufficient to surprise the most cosmopolitan of wine tasters'. Indeed it is!

With respect to vintages, 1981 was not an especially good vintage for Cornas, although Juge, Clape, and Barjac did well. The 1982 had the potential to be good, but the tremendous heat during the harvest and vinification caused problems. Verset's 1982 Cornas looks to be the one outstanding success of this vintage. In 1983 the conditions were perfect, and virtually everyone made a wine that they claimed to be the best since 1978, perhaps better. The 1984 was a more sobering type of vintage, but 1985 is again excellent. This recent vintage provides an excellent opportunity to become acquainted with the wines of Cornas.

G. DE BARJAC ★★★

1981 Cornas	②	86
1982 Cornas	②	83
1983 Cornas	②	87
1984 Cornas	②	82

Barjac makes one of the most robust and coarse wines of Cornas. There is neither fining nor filtration here, and consequently he gets wines that are opaque in colour, throw a heavy sediment, and age endlessly. The 1981 is a fiercely tannic, full-bodied, savage wine loaded with Syrah fruit, peppery, blackcurrant flavours, and abrasive tannins. Give it six to ten years. The 1982 is much softer, will mature much earlier, and does not have the depth of the 1981. The 1983 is black in colour, thick, deeply concentrated, and brutally tannic. It will live for decades. The 1984 is good, given the vintage, and can last three to four years.

A. CLAPE ★★★★★

1981 Cornas	③	84
1982 Cornas	③	83
1983 Cornas	③	90

1984 Cornas.. ③ **87**
1985 Cornas.. ③ **90**

Unquestionably the finest producer of Cornas, Clape's wines tend to have the best balance and lack the ferocious tannins found in the wines from his peers. His 1981 is a good wine for the vintage, dark ruby, with a spicy, peppery bouquet and good, solid, deep flavours as well as full body. The 1984 is similar but lighter. Neither is as good as the 1978, 1979, and 1980, but both should be very attractive by 1990. The 1982 is a little light in colour, of medium weight, surprisingly soft, and a trifle diffuse. Surprisingly, it is not as good as the 1981. On the other hand, the 1983 is a blockbuster of a wine, with a gorgeous perfumed aroma of peppery, blackberry fruit and spicy oak. Massive in size with tremendous power and extract, and a tannic, long, rich finish, it is a Rhône wine collector's item. It will need six to ten years of cellaring. The 1985 is just as concentrated and deep, but not nearly so tannic as the 1983.

A. FUMAT ★★

1981 Cornas.. ② **75**

Peppery, slightly herbaceous, and medium ruby in colour, this is a satisfactory wine, but it lacks interest and character. Surprisingly, for a Cornas, it is ready to drink.

PAUL JABOULET AINÉ ★★★★★

1981 Cornas.. ② **80**
1982 Cornas.. ② **84**
1983 Cornas.. ③ **88**
1984 Cornas.. ② **78**
1985 Cornas.. ③ **86**

Jaboulet's Cornas tends to get overlooked in his fine line-up of Rhône Valley wines, but it can be fabulous. The 1962, 1972, and 1978 are vivid examples of Cornas at its best. The 1983 is one of the greatest Cornas wines from Jaboulet that I have ever tasted. Impenetrably black, with a colossal aroma of cassis, truffles and pepper, it is both voluptuous and firm on the palate, and in weight and richness resembles some of the 1982 Pomerols. It is worth waiting in line for. The 1982 is a very good, typical Cornas, virile, tough, brawny, a trifle coarse, but rich, very full-bodied, and has the standard mouth-shattering tannin. It needs ten years of cellaring. The 1981 is lighter, pleasant, and in need of three to four years of cellaring, but is not nearly on the level of quality of the 1982s and 1983s. The 1984 is light, simple, and ready to drink; the 1985 is fat, ripe, loaded with fruit, and much more accessible than normal.

MARCEL JUGE ★★★

1981 Cornas	②	**86**
1982 Cornas	②	*84*
1983 Cornas	③	*88*
1984 Cornas	③	**86**

Juge's cellar is well worth a visit, not only because of the good wine he makes, but also because he has the only alcoholic dog I have ever seen. This dog has a voracious appetite for young Cornas wine, and actually drinks from Juge's pipette or 'wine thief'. As he is another who believes neither in fining nor filtration, Juge's Cornas has more finesse than the wines of other producers. The 1981 won't be mature until 1988 or later, but it is a very flavourful, stylish wine with excellent texture and fruit. The 1982 is more successful than others, but the 1983 is absolutely superb and its huge structure and density of both fruit and tannin will require quite a wait. The 1984 is lighter, but an unqualified success. Juge made a special hillside Cuvée in 1985 that looks to be one of the greatest wines of Cornas I have tasted – keep an eye out for it.

N. VERSET ★★★★★

1982 Cornas	②	**86**
1983 Cornas	②	**90**
1984 Cornas	②	**86**

The 1983 Verset Cornas is the best wine I have tasted from this small grower. The 1983 is a beauty, and appears to be among the best wines made in Cornas in 1983. The wine has a dark black/ruby colour, a ripe, gamy aroma intermingled with ripe cassis flavours, moderate tannins, and a clean, long, savoury finish. It should be fully mature by 1990. The 1982 is similarly styled, rich, lush, long, and very seductive. The 1984 is somewhat of a sleeper, a broadly flavoured, rich, supple, deeply fruity wine. Verset's 1985 is stupendous—buy it.

A. VOGE ★★★

1982 Cornas	②	*84*
1983 Cornas	②	*87*

I have very fond memories of the splendid 1978 Voge Cornas, and the excellent 1979, but since then the wines have lost some concentration as the winemaking style seems to have changed. However, the 1982 is quite drinkable now. Very attractive, the bouquet suggests hickory wood and frying bacon; the flavours are not very tannic, but open-knit, spicy, fruity, and quite round and generous. The 1983 is a blockbuster of a wine, very tannic, very backward, and in need of seven to eight years of cellaring.

A GUIDE TO SOUTHERN RHÔNE'S BEST PRODUCERS

★ ★ ★ ★ ★ Outstanding Producers

Beaucastel (Châteauneuf)

Le Bosquet des Papes
  (Châteauneuf)

Clos des Papes (Châteauneuf)

Fortia (Châteauneuf)

Les Gouberts (Gigondas)

Rayas (Châteauneuf)

Vieux Télégraphe (Châteauneuf)

★ ★ ★ ★ Excellent Producers

Barrot (Châteauneuf)

Beaumet Bonfils (Gigondas)

Beaurenard (Châteauneuf)

Brunel (Châteauneuf)

Les Cailloux (Châteauneuf)

Chante Perdrix
  (Châteauneuf)

Les Clefs d'Or (Châteauneuf)

Clos du Mont-Olivet
  (Châteauneuf)

Georges Faraud (Gigondas)

Fonsalette (Côtes du Rhône)

Font de Michelle (Châteauneuf)

Grand Tinel (Châteauneuf)

Longue Toque (Gigondas)

Mont-Redon (Châteauneuf)

La Nerthe (Châteauneuf)

Les Pallières (Gigondas)

Raspail (Gigondas)

St.-Gayan (Gigondas)

Roger Sabon (Châteauneuf)

Senechaux (Châteauneuf)

Cuvée du Tastevin
  (Châteauneuf)

Cuvée du Vatican (Châteauneuf)

Vieux Donjon (Châteauneuf)

★ ★ ★ Good Producers

Aqueria (Tavel)

P. Archimbaud (Gigondas)

P. Berard (Châteauneuf)

Busset (Côtes du Rhône)

Cabasse (Côtes du Rhône)

Cabrières (Châteauneuf)

Chante Cigale (Châteauneuf)

Chapoutier (Châteauneuf)

Clos de l'Oratoire (Châteauneuf)

Clos St.-Jean (Châteauneuf)

Combe (Gigondas)

Coudelet (Côtes du Rhône)

Devoy (Lirac)

Durieu (Châteauneuf)

Fines Roches (Châteauneuf)

Font du Loup (Châteauneuf)

Forcadière (Tavel)

La Fourmone (Côtes du Rhône)

La Gardine (Châteauneuf)

Genestière (Tavel)

Guigal (Châteauneuf)

Haut des Terres Blanches
  (Châteauneuf)

Paul Jaboulet Ainé (Châteauneuf)

Marcoux (Châteauneuf)

Montmirail (Gigondas)

Nalys (Châteauneuf)

Père Caboche (Châteauneuf)

J. Quiot (Châteauneuf)

Relagnes (Châteauneuf)

St.-Anne (Côtes du Rhône)

St. Roch (Lirac)

Ségriès (Lirac)

La Solitude (Châteauneuf)

Trignon (Côtes du Rhône)

Trinquevedel (Tavel)

Trintignant (Châteauneuf)

Vaudieu (Châteauneuf)

La Vieille Ferme (Côtes du Rhône)

Vieux Chêne (Côtes du Rhône)

Vieux Lazaret (Châteauneuf)

★ ★ Average Producers)

Anselme (Châteauneuf)

RHÔNE · TODAY'S BUYING STRATEGY

For the wines of the northern Rhône, those who have the patience to cellar them should be looking for the remaining yet very tannic 1983s and newly arriving 1985s. For the Côte Rôties in 1985, a special effort is needed to secure some of these exceptional wines. Avoid 1984 as a general rule. For drinking now, the 1982s, powerful, rich 1981s, 1980s, and 1979s are the vintages in which to concentrate your efforts. The 1978s, should you be lucky enough to find any, are rare and extraordinary.

For the southern Rhône, all the Côtes du Rhônes are made to be drunk within four to five year of the vintage. So look for the 1982s, 1983s, and delicious 1985s. Anything older is definitely a risk unless it is a great Côtes du Rhône such as Fonsalette or Coudelet. For Gigondas and Châteauneuf-du-Pape, the vintages to buy are 1981, 1983, and 1985. Some 1982s can offer charming drinking, but the best two vintages for mature drinking over the next few years are 1979 and 1980. If you are lucky enough to see any 1978s or 1981s languishing on retailers' shelves, you may want to acquire them, for they can represent the pinnacle of winemaking in Châteauneuf. Some 1985s will have the potential to be as good as the greatest 1978s, 1979s, 1981s, or 1983s. The 1985 white wines from Châteauneuf are excellent, but should be drunk up over the next year.

SOUTHERN RHÔNE

CHÂTEAUNEUF-DU-PAPE

With an average production of a million cases, Châteauneuf-du-Pape easily has the largest production of the serious wines of the Rhône Valley. It is also the unofficial capital of this vast wine region. The wonderful city of Avignon, a major tourist attraction, is only fourteen kilometres to the south, so many a traveller has tasted the roundness and heady power of a Châteauneuf-du-Pape.

Up until four or five years ago, the highest-quality Châteauneuf-du-Pape wines, produced from single vineyards and estate-bottled, were difficult to find. What were usually encountered on the retailers' shelves were *négociant* wines, many of which were simple, grapy trash, hideously thick and heavy, and excessively high in alcohol. Many of these wines still remain, but the new wave of quality-conscious importers and growing numbers of smarter wine consumers have resulted in easier access to a plethora of top-

The Southern Rhône

quality Châteauneuf-du-Papes that offer outstanding value and quality. The truth is that there are at least three dozen estates here making serious, delicious, excellent wine.

The wine consumer, in order to understand the wines of Châteauneuf-du-Pape, must first realize that, like all wine-producing regions, the range in quality is vast, but just as important, the styles of wines in Châteauneuf-du-Pape can be dramatically different. If you seek a round, generous, soft wine that is ready to drink when released, there are numerous estates – Clos de l'Oratoire des Papes, Maucoil, Vieux Lazaret, Domaine de Nalys, Marcoux, Domaine de Beaurenard, Domaine du Père Caboche, and Vieux Télégraphe (since 1980) among them – producing wines that are ideal for immediate gratification. If you prefer a rich, full-bodied, complex, intense wine that must be cellared for five to ten years after the vintage in order to develop fully, look to Beaucastel, Les Cailloux, Clefs d'Or, Bosquet des Papes, Clos des Papes, Fortia, La Nerte, Rayas, Chante Cigale, and Chante Perdrix, a few of the properties that produce very full, tannic, deep wines that require ageing.

Châteauneuf-du-Pape's appellation laws permit thirteen different grape varieties to be grown, but in practical terms, most estates use no more than three or four major grapes for their red wines. Topping the list in grape popularity is the ubiquitous Grenache, followed by Mourvèdre, Syrah, and Cinsault. The red grape varieties that some growers proclaim will be planted in more abundance in the future are Vaccarèse and Counoise. The Grenache grape provides alcohol and fleshiness, yet its shortcoming is its vulnerability to oxidation. Mourvèdre provides great colour, great firmness, tannic richness, and the ability to age, but in its youth it is nasty to taste and often eccentric to smell. The Syrah provides rich fruit, firmness, and complexity, and Cinsault gives a certain dimension to a wine's bouquet but lacks colour and richness. A small amount of white wine is made in Châteauneuf-du-Pape, and where the vinification is done properly, the wine can be extremely full, flavourful, and quite interesting. Vieux Télégraphe, Nalys, Père Caboche, Mont Redon, and Font de Michelle make some of the best modern-style white Châteauneuf-du-Pape available. However, white Châteauneufs rarely age past four to five years, and the general rule of thumb, unless you are drinking a Beaucastel or Clefs d'Or, is to drink them within three to four years of the vintage.

Red Châteauneuf is an autumn and winter wine; its full-bodied strength (13.5% alcohol and up is normal) makes it a perfect match for game, beef, lamb, stews, and grilled meats. White Châteauneuf would overpower a delicate fish course, and it is too full for using as an apéritif, but when matched with fowl or with grilled foods, particularly charcoal-grilled fish and chicken, it is a marriage that is likely to provide a lasting memory.

CHÂTEAUNEUF-DU-PAPE (RED)

L. BARROT ★★★★

1979 Cuvée du Tastevin	②	88
1980 Cuvée du Tastevin	②	84
1981 Cuvée du Tastevin	②	87
1983 Cuvée du Tastevin	②	88

There are two growers'associations in Châteauneuf-du-Pape in which the producers share bottling and storage premises. One is Les Reflets and the other is Prestige et Tradition. Barrot belongs to the latter and is one of the top growers of this group. His wines have good ageing potential as well as the typical Châteauneuf-du-Pape fullness and peppery, spicy bouquet. The 1979, 1981, and 1983 are all quite full-bodied, with big, peppery, blackberry bouquets, ripe yet tannic flavours, a large frame, and ageing potential of five to seven years. The 1980 is even more tannic, and is quite full-bodied; it is surprisingly backward for a 1980, yet has potential. The 1981 is the best of this trio, black/ruby, rich, full-bodied, deep, with ten to twelve years' further ageing potential.

BEAUCASTEL *PERRIN* ★★★★★

1981	②	93
1982	②	84
1983	③	92
1984	③	87

Beaucastel makes Châteauneuf-du-Pape's longest-lived and most profound and complex wine. It is also one of the greatest of France. Perhaps the most memorable tasting I have ever attended was a vertical tasting of Beaucastel from 1942 to 1978, which for those in attendance proved beyond a reasonable doubt that at around age eight or nine a red Beaucastel begins to unfold its richness and complexity, at age twelve to fifteen is simply magnificent, and at 20–25 years is one of the truly great gustatory pleasures. It is, however, a wine for collectors since it needs considerable time, unless of course, the vintage produced light-bodied, soft wines. That's just the case in 1982 and 1984. I had expected Beaucastel to declassify its entire crop in 1982, but after an extremely strict selection (50% was sold to *négociants*) a small amount of 1982 was produced; it has turned out much better than I anticipated. Resembling the 1973, only lighter, the 1982 is fruity, soft, charming and, unlike most Beaucastels, can be drunk immediately. It is an ideal wine for restaurants. The 1984 is similarly styled, only a trifle deeper. The 1981 is the best Châteauneuf-du-Pape of the vintage and has enormous potential. Dark ruby/purple with a bouquet of blackberries, pepper, flowers, and tarry scents, this full-bodied, deeply concentrated wine should be at its best in 1991 and last for another fifteen to twenty years. The 1983 is superb, rich, intense, full-bodied, and will be quite long-lived. The 1984 is slightly higher in acidity than normal, but rich and complex, with five to ten years' ageing potential.

BEAURENARD *COULON* ★ ★ ★ ★

1981	③	**84**
1982	②	**78**
1983	③	**85**

I would like to score Beaurenard higher, because I sincerely enjoy the wine for its charm, soft, exuberant fruitiness and round, warm, generous flavours. However, it is a strightforward wine with little complexity. Made in a style that is clearly aimed for early consumption, Beaurenard is supple, fruity, with plenty of silky, lush flavours suggesting ripe black cherries. The 1982 is too much like a simple grapy Beaujolais, but has charm. It should be drunk over the next two years. The 1981 and 1983 are virtually identical in style, full-bodied, gushing with soft, round fruit, a savoury, long finish, and very few tannins. However, the 1983 is a trifle more rich.

BOSQUET DES PAPES ★ ★ ★ ★ ★

1983 Bosquet des Papes	③	**90**
1984 Bosquet des Papes	③	**86**
1985 Bosquet des Papes	③	**91**

The 1985 white wine is cleanly made, simple but lacking in character. The 1985 Châteauneuf-du-Pape is explosively rich, deeply coloured, has oodles of blackberry fruit, a powerful presence on the palate, long, deep and quite impressive. The balance, depth and complexity are there; it will need five to six years. The 1984 is, along with Vieux Télégraphe and Beaucastel, one of the best I tasted, gloriously lush and fruity and hardly the type of wine one suspects was produced from an 'off year'. It has excellent colour, a fragrant perfume of rich, chocolaty, plummy fruit, a forward personality and soft, lush finish. Drink it over the next five to six years while you await the considerable pleasures of the 1983. A year and a half ago, the 1983 stood out in a big tasting of Châteauneuf-du-Papes put on for me by the growers. It continues to impress me greatly. Dark ruby in colour with a gorgeous fragrance of blackcurrants, fruit, tobacco and exotic spices, it is quite rich on the palate, moderately tannic and impeccably balanced. I would defer gratification to 1987 and beyond.

BRUNEL ★★★★

1980 Les Cailloux	②	**80**
1981 Les Cailloux	②	**84**
1983 Les Cailloux	③	**87**
1984 Les Cailloux	③	**84**

The 1980 has average colour, and a herbaceous, spicy, peppery, faintly fruity bouquet. On the palate it is well structured but a trifle austere and lean. It is ready to drink now. The 1981 has more richness and concentration, a moderately intense, peppery, spicy bouquet, medium to full body, and a good finish. It can easily be drunk now, but will get better over the next one to two years. The 1983 is the best of this trio, full-bodied, rich, with a spice-box aroma. The 1984 is a success for the vintage.

CHANTE CIGALE ★★★

1978	④	**88**
1979	②	**82**
1981	③	**86**
1983	③	**78**

I always find an intensely herbal, olive-scented aroma intermingled with blackberry fruit, spices, and earthy scents in the wines of Chante Cigale. The 1978 is top-class, still big, broodingly opaque, chocolaty, herbal, peppery, and very full-bodied and rich on the palate. The wine can be drunk now, but try to keep your hands off it until 1988–1989. The 1979, which the proprietor, Favier, thinks is better, is overtly herbaceous, minty, and very, very peppery. It is good, but lacks the dimension of the 1978. The 1981 is closer in style to the 1978 and the 1979, rich, supple, with plenty of fruit and length on the palate. The 1983 is not a success here as it lacks some colour and is rather weak on the palate.

CHANTE PERDRIX ★★★★

1979	③	**86**
1981	③	**86**
1982	③	**80**
1983	③	**90**
1984	③	**88**

Chante Perdrix produces Châteauneuf-du-Pape wines that by any standards of this appellation are huge, chewy, and deep ruby-coloured, loaded with viscous, blackberry, occasionally herbal-scented and flavoured fruit, as well as a hefty dose of alcohol. Sometimes the wines can be overpowering, and even when well balanced Chante Perdrix is a wine to reserve for cheese. The 1982 showed very poorly at a big tasting put on for me in Châteauneuf-du-Pape in 1984, but in recent tastings it has fared much better. However, the 1984, 1983, 1981, and 1979 are authentic examples of Chante Perdrix's powerful style of Châteauneuf-du-Pape. Very deeply coloured, with thick, chocolaty, herbaceous flavours, quite full-bodied and spicy, peppery, and chocolaty to smell, these big, aggressive wines are unique, yet may be too much for some people. I thought the 1981 and 1983 had an edge in complexity and balance over the 1979, but these wines are big and chewy and will last for five to nine years. Look out for the 1984, a great success for the vintage.

CHAPOUTIER ★★★

La Barbe-Rac Non-Vintage .... ⑤ **89**
1978 La Bernardine .... ③ **70**
1982 La Bernardine .... ② **76**
1983 La Bernardine .... ② **83**

Two of these Châteauneuf-du-Papes are quite mediocre. The 1982, from a mediocre to poor vintage, is shockingly better than the 1978, which is from a great vintage. The 1978 is tired, flat, and lacking interest. The 1982 is soft, straightforward, fruity, and charming in an innocuous way. The 1983, however, offers more flesh and muscle with much better depth of fruit. Chapoutier's limited edition, luxury Cuvée, the Barbe-Rac, is quite rich and intense, with great length.

LES CLEFS D'OR *DEYDIER* ★★★★

1979 .... ③ **85**
1980 .... ③ **83**
1981 .... ③ **86**
1982 .... ② **83**
1983 .... ③ **87**

One of my favourite producers of Châteauneuf-du-Pape, the reclusive Deydier produces an old-style, ripe, rich, full-bodied wine with a lot of extract, power, and ageing potential. Even in a light year such as 1982, Deydier obtained a measure of concentration, a ripe berry, tarry fruitiness, and enough tannin to warrant two to three years of cellaring. The 1981 is much richer, with a deep-scented, spicy aroma, full-bodied, black cherry flavours, and firm tannins. It needs five more years to be at its best. The 1980 is a marriage of styles between the lighter 1982 and fuller, bigger 1981. It should be aged for four years. The 1979 is similar to the 1981, only a trifle less rich and more austere, but very well made and interesting. The 1983 is Deydier's best wine since his great 1978. It is a rich, concentrated wine with at least a decade of ageing potential.

CLOS DU MONT-OLIVET *SABON* ★ ★ ★ ★

1981	② 85
1983	③ 87
1984	③ 85

Clos du Mont Olivet is normally an excellent Châteauneuf-du-Pape, but it rarely comes my way. The 1978 and 1976 were especially notable, particularly the latter, in a year when the wines of the southern Rhône were notoriously irregular. Both the 1981 and 1983 are quite backward, tannic, and will probably merit a higher score in five to six years when they are mature. The bouquet of oak and ripe cherries is first-class; full-bodied, tannic, and needing time, these are wines for the patient. Keep an eye out for this domaine's 1985, an astonishingly great wine that most observers feel is the best of the vintage.

CLOS DE l'ORATOIRE *AMOUROUX* ★ ★ ★

1978	② 83
1979	② 82
1983	③ 82

One of the great names of Châteauneuf-du-Pape, the wine of Clos de l'Oratoire has changed considerably in style over recent years, moving further and further away from a big, rich, dense, traditional style to a Beaujolais-like, soft, very fruity and charming wine that is best drunk within five to six years of the vintage. The 1978 is such a wine, effusively fruity, with a bouquet and flavour of jammy cherry fruit. It is fully mature. The 1979 and 1983 are quite similar, only lighter, but very fruity, quite attractive, and best consumed over the next year.

CLOS DES PAPES *AVRIL* ★ ★ ★ ★ ★

1980	③ 84
1981	③ 88
1982	② 82
1983	③ 87

A highly respected estate, Paul Avril's Clos des Papes produces tannic, ageworthy wines in a very traditional manner. The 1982 is light yet very fruity and charming. The 1981, however, is a big, ripe, dense wine with excellent colour, a seductive bouquet of ripe black cherries and wood, firm, full-bodied flavours, and a healthy dosage of tannin. It should be given three to four years of cellaring. The 1980 is also a success, with a ripe, spicy, cherry-scented bouquet, and richly fruity, full-bodied flavours admirably backed by tannin. The 1983 is also very promising, with a rich black cherry, peppery bouquet and full-bodied flavours.

FONT DU LOUP *MELIA* ★ ★ ★

1981	③	**89**
1982	③	**80**

Two very attractive wines for drinking over the next one to two years. The 1982 is medium ruby, with an intense aroma of strawberries. On the palate, it is easy-going, charming and soft. The 1981 has much deeper colour, a ripe aroma of peaches and oranges, a ripe Grenache smell, and is quite full-bodied, with an alcoholic kick and soft, lush finish: it is splendidly concentrated.

FONT DE MICHELLE *GONNET* ★ ★ ★ ★

1981	②	**86**
1982	②	**83**
1983	②	**87**
1984	②	**85**

An up-and-coming estate that first began to estate-bottle its wines in 1974, Font de Michelle has consistently impressed me in tastings. The 1982, one of the top wines of this difficult vintage, is loaded with attractively ripe, plummy fruit, has surprisingly good colour for the vintage, and a round, richly fruity texture. Drink it over the next two years. The 1981 and 1983 continue their impressive tradition with rich, full-intensity bouquets of ripe fruit, black pepper, and spices. Full-bodied, generously flavoured and heady, these big wines will keep for five to eight years. The 1984 is also above average, a peppery, spicy, fruity, straightforward sort of wine.

FORTIA ★ ★ ★ ★ ★

1980	③	**85**
1981	③	**88**
1983	③	**87**

Historically the most significant Châteauneuf-du-Pape estate, Fortia is the property of Baron LeRoy de Boiseaumarié, whose father founded the *appellation contrôlée* system in France. The wine is generally one of the best in Châteauneuf-du-Pape, almost on the level of Beaucastel or Rayas. The 1978 is a marvellous wine; 1983 rivals it. The 1981 is one of the top 1981s, rich with a ripe bouquet of raspberries and violets; this wine is big, tannic, full-bodied, and in need of three to four years of cellaring. The 1980 Fortia has a tell-tale, intense raspberry, peppery bouquet, lush, ripe flavours, and a good, deep, dark colour. The 1983 is even deeper and more age-worthy, very perfumed and rich, a top success for the vintage.

LA GARDINE ★★★

1978	②	**80**
1981	②	**85**
1983	②	**84**

La Gardine produces a chunky, smoky, heavy style of wine that is impressively coloured, very weighty and alcoholic, with chewy, viscous flavours. The 1978 is thick, ripe, almost port-like, and interesting, although it is hard to imagine drinking this wine with food. The 1981 is this estate's strongest effort in five or six years – a rich, chewy, leather-scented wine with a lot of muscle. The 1983 is much in the same style, though not so concentrated.

GRAND TINEL *JEUNE* ★★★★

1979	②	**85**
1980	②	**82**
1981	③	**90**
1982	③	**78**
1983	③	**87**

Grand Tinel makes consistently fine Châteauneuf-du-Papes that are usually characterized by a very dark colour, a ripe peach and raspberry-scented bouquet, and full-bodied, relatively rich, concentrated flavours. Most Grand Tinels need a least five to six years of cellaring, and are best drunk before they reach age twelve. The 1979 is very full, with a complex bouquet of smoky raspberry fruit, and rich, full-bodied flavours. It will improve for three to five more years. The 1980 is good, but straightforward and rather one-dimensional. The 1981 has excellent depth, and is a savoury, full, and very attractive, big-styled wine for drinking over the next three to five years. The 1983, rich and full-bodied, is potentially the best of this group, a very powerful, long, deep wine made in a very traditional style.

GUIGAL ★★★

1979	③	**84**
1981	③	**86**
1982	③	**87**

Guigal's Châteauneuf-du-Papes have the house style imprinted on them. The wines are very dark in colour, with ripe, rich berry aromas, solid tannic, full-bodied flavours, and good finishes. They are lush, deep, opulent wines yet are clearly capable of ageing seven to ten years in the bottle. The 1982 has the most concentration of the above trio and looks to be the best wine from this appellation, an irony given the fact that most people tend to think that the growers can do a better job in off years than a *négociant*.

HAUT DES TERRES BLANCHES *DIFFONTY* ★ ★ ★

1979	②	**86**
1981	②	*84*

Rémy Diffonty produces very stylish, complex wines with plenty of flavour, tarry, earthy, almost truffle-scented bouquets and round, soft, lush textures. The 1979 is top-notch, but has quickly disappeared from the marketplace; it is better than Diffonty's 1978. The 1981 is lighter in colour, less rich and fruity, but still very attractive, with plenty of peppery, berry fruit, a bouquet suggestive of caramel and spices, and soft, lush, nicely concentrated flavours. Drink the 1981 over the next three years, the 1979 over the next six.

PAUL JABOULET AINÉ ★ ★ ★

1980 Les Cèdres..	③	*84*
1982 Les Cèdres..	③	*83*
1983 Les Cèdres..	③	*82*
1985 Les Cèdres..	③	*84*

Jaboulet's Châteauneuf-du-Pape seems to get overlooked when the firm's wines are discussed. However, his Les Cèdres can be magnificent. The 1961 is still stunning, as is the 1967. The 1982 Les Cèdres will certainly be considered a success for the vintage. Fresh, fruity, with oodles of fat, supple flavours, and light tannins, this wine is destined to be drunk young, preferably within three years. The 1980 is slightly richer, with a big, ripe raspberry-dominated bouquet, a peppery, spicy quality, and solid, rich, ripe fruit. The 1983 and 1985 have good black cherry fruit, full body, and a long finish, though the 1985 is slightly more concentrated.

MONT-REDON ★ ★ ★ ★

1978	③	*84*
1980	③	*75*
1981	③	*86*
1982	③	*80*
1983	③	*86*

For those who remember the old-style Mont Redon wines from such vintages as 1949, 1955, and 1961, all of which remain quite lively and brilliant examples of Châteauneuf-du-Pape, the new, lighter style this estate adopted in the seventies will prove a disappointment, for it has robbed Mont Redon of much of its character. At times the wine has resembled a sound, run-of-the-mill Côtes du Rhône, which is a tragedy to say the least. The 1978, 1980, and 1981 taste mature, fruity, soft, and very pleasant. The 1978 and 1981 should continue to drink well for two years; the 1980's future is now – they are clean, technically correct, but less intense than in the past. However, all this may be changing, since the excellent 1981, 1983, and 1985 are clearly the finest wines this estate has made in over a decade; all have a rich, smoky, raspberry-scented nose, and long, lush flavours. An estate on the rebound.

LA NERTHE ★ ★ ★ ★

1980	③ 84
1981	③ 87
1983	③ 86

La Nerthe is one of the very best estates of Châteauneuf-du-Pape, with wine that is quite full-bodied, unusually high in alcohol, with a first-class aroma of floral and ripe raspberry/blackberry scents. They tend to be powerful wines that are clearly very traditionally made and normally require five to seven years to be at their best. Neither the 1980 nor the excellent 1981 are up to the superb 1978 or 1979 La Nerthes. However, both are serious wines that clearly merit the interest of Rhône wine enthusiasts. The 1983 is full and rich in the nose. Rich, extroverted, powerful, and voluptuous, it is the best La Nerthe since 1978 and 1981.

PÈRE CABOCHE ★ ★ ★

1981	② 83
1983	② 84
1981 Elisabeth Chambellan	③ 85

The enthusiastic Jean-Pierre Boisson runs the Domaine Père Caboche, which makes Châteauneuf-du-Pape in a forward, rich, ripe, fruity style. Given this style, the wines are best drunk within five to six years of the vintage. The 1981 and 1983 wines of Père Caboche are soft, direct, quite enjoyable, fruity, medium- to full-bodied, with hardly any tannins. The best wine of the trio is the 1981 Elisabeth Chambellan, which is filled with concentrated, round, spicy, peppery, black cherry fruit. It is full-bodied, has a long, rich, lush finish, and should be drunk over the next two years.

JÉRÔME QUIOT ★ ★ ★

| 1981 | ② 82 |

1982 .... ② **80**
1983 .... ② **78**

The 1981 and 1983 are extremely pleasing styles of Châteauneuf-du-Pape. Quiot has produced a fragrant, ripe, almost sweet wine, with round, generous, voluptuous, fruity flavours that show little tannin, but with a very pleasing, soft texture, and long finish. Both wines are delicious now and should be drunk over the next two years. The 1982 is soft, fruity, very pleasant and charming, but simple and a trifle one-dimensional.

RAYAS ★ ★ ★ ★ ★
1978 .... ④ **93**
1979 .... ③ **91**
1981 .... ④ **90**
1983 .... ④ **91**

The reclusive and eccentric Jacques Reynaud oversees what some observers feel is the best wine of Châteauneuf-du-Pape. These four wines do justice to the fame Rayas has among Châteauneuf-du-Pape fanciers. The 1978 has been available for some time, but the high price has kept it from jumping off merchants' shelves, because it is certainly not lacking in quality. Still very young, very deep ruby in colour, with a very concentrated, powerful, weighty feel on the palate, this big wine is simply loaded with potential. Lay it away for at least five to six more years. In comparison, the 1979 is actually more attractive now; while being every bit as rich, full-bodied, and complex as the 1978, the tannin is less intrusive. The 1979 should drink beautifully and improve for at least seven to ten years. The 1981 is gorgeously aromatic now, with layers of ripe, decadently rich fruit. It should drink well for ten years. The 1983 is very forward, yet still packed with fruit and flavour, and while quite outstanding, will not have the ageing potential of the other three vintages. Consumers should look for the seond label of Rayas which is Pignan. In vintages such as 1981 and 1983 Pignan is difficult to distinguish from Rayas.

RELAGNES ★ ★ ★
1982 .... ③ **83**
1983 .... ③ **85**

In 1982 the Domaine des Relagnes produced a very attractive wine in a vintage that was generally unkind to the *vignerons* of Châteauneuf-du-Pape. It has a bouquet of ripe cherries and peppery spice that is quite seductive and intense. On the palate, the wine is ready to drink with clean, soft, very fruity flavours, and a surprisingly good, lengthy finish. The 1983, a knockout from the cask, rich, dense, spicy, and very complex, is closed in and less impressive from the bottle. This little-known estate merits much more attention.

ROGER SABON ★ ★ ★ ★

1981 .... ② **86**
1983 .... ② **86**

The 1981 from Sabon is a classic Châteauneuf-du-Pape. This big, tightly knit wine has a firm but promising bouquet of berry fruit, black pepper, and tarry scents. On the palate, the wine is deep, rich, yet tannic and still quite youthful. The 1983 is very Burgundy-like, with an expansive bouquet of cherry fruit and spices – it is very seductive.

VIEUX LAZARET ★ ★ ★

1981 .... ② **83**
1983 .... ② **84**

Vieux Lazaret produces very fruity, round, supple wines that are meant for immediate consumption. Both the 1981 and 1983 are quite fruity, medium- to full-bodied, with plenty of ripe berry fruit in the bouquet and flavour, a certain sweetness, and a generous, soft finish. A good, charming, rather uncomplicated style of Châteauneuf-du-Pape, both should be drunk over the next three years.

VIEUX TÉLÉGRAPHE ★ ★ ★ ★ ★

1981 .... ② **85**
1982 .... ② **84**
1983 .... ② **90**
1984 .... ② **86**

Although Brunier has significantly lightened his style of Châteauneuf-du-Pape (the magnificent 1978 was the best of the old style), his wines remain among the most consistently well-made and delicious Châteauneuf-du-Papes produced. The 1981 is a lush, full-bodied, deeply fruity wine with enough stuffing and tannin to provide enjoyable drinking over the next five to six years. The 1982 vies for the top wine of the appellation in that vintage. It has very good colour, a big, plummy, spicy, leafy-scented aroma, fat, round, generous, sweet flavours, and little tannins in evidence. It is undoubtedly a top success in this difficult vintage and should be drunk now. The 1983 is Brunier's best wine since the 1978; it is a big, fragrant, supple, and rich wine. The 1984 is well balanced, fruity, elegant, and should drink well for four to five years.

CHÂTEAUNEUF-DU-PAPE (WHITE)

Only a tiny amount of white Châteauneuf-du-Pape is made, but when it is vinified at cool temperatures and quickly bottled and quickly drunk, it can be quite delicious. Not surprisingly, Beaucastel, which makes the wine that lasts the longest, Vieux Télégraphe, Clefs d'Or, Nalys, Quiot, Font de Michelle, and sometimes Père Caboche and La Nerthe, are the top producers of white Châteauneuf-du-Pape. Generally, the 1985s and 1983s are superior to the 1984s.

BEAUCASTEL *PERRIN* ★ ★ ★ ★ ★
1983	③	86
1984	③	83
1985	③	90

Beaucastel's white wine, which is 80% Roussanne, is the longest-lived dry white wine of the southern Rhône. I recently tasted the 1954, 1962, and 1971, which were all in stunning condition. The 1983, while not so opulent and rich as the 1982, has an intriguing bouquet of straw, mineral scents, and pears. On the palate, it is full-bodied, admirably concentrated, and quite well balanced. It needs two to three years to really open up. The 1984 is light, pleasant, and crisp, but, due to the vintage, lacks some concentration. The 1985 is powerful, rich, and truly outstanding.

LES CAILLOUX *BRUNEL* ★ ★ ★ ★
1985	③	86

Deep, intensely fruity, ripe, long, and alcoholic, this is the best white wine yet from Les Cailloux. A solid, powerful wine that has no flaws, but little to distinguish it.

LES CLEFS D'OR *DEYDIER* ★ ★ ★ ★
1985	③	85

A highly aromatic wine with a full-blown bouquet suggesting tropical fruit, the 1985 Clefs d'Or is an exotic wine with a bit too much alcohol in the finish, but is ripe, full, and distinctive. Drink over the next two years.

NALYS ★ ★ ★
1985	③	85

This is a delicious wine with clean, fresh, fruity aromas of light intensity, crisp acidity, and good depth. It is solid, crisp, and direct. Drink over the next one to two years.

LA NERTHE ★ ★ ★ ★
1983	③	82
1985	③	85

La Nerthe's popularity for big, rich, full-tilt red wines seems to have carried over to the 1985 white wine, which has interesting pear and pineapple flavours, plenty of body, and a hefty dose of alcohol. In contrast, the 1983 has a sweet cotton candy-like bouquet, good acidity, and despite some heady alcohol in the finish, it seems a much better wine.

R. OGIER ★
1984 .... ② **55**

This white Châteauneuf-du-Pape could be a wine from anywhere in the world. It is simple, lacking in flavour, high in alcohol, and just downright poor.

PÈRE CABOCHE *BOISSON* ★★★
1983 .... ② **75**
1985 .... ③ **84**

One of the better producers of white Châteauneuf-du-Pape, Père Caboche usually makes aromatic, fresh, lively, rich wines. The 1983 showed quite an unexpected degree of mediocrity, with high acidity and average-intensity, non-descript flavours. On the other hand, the 1985 is fragrant, full-bodied with nicely concentrated fresh fruit and floral scents and flavours. It should be drunk over the next two years.

JÉRÔME QUIOT ★★★
1985 .... ② **82**

A fresh, very correct wine, with a plump, fat, alcoholic feel on the palate, a slightly perfumed bouquet, and good, crisp acidity and balance; the 1985 Quiot should be drunk over the next two years.

VIEUX TÉLÉGRAPHE *BRUNIER* ★★★★★
1985 .... ③ **90**

Brunier produced only 300 cases of this white Châteauneuf-du-Pape. Made entirely from the Grenache Blanc grape, it tastes as if it came from the Viognier grape. Full-bodied (13.5% alcohol) luxuriously opulent, decadently fruity, this round, silky wine has layers of fruit. Like most good white Châteaunef-du-Papes, this wine is a perfect choice for dishes cooked over a charcoal grill.

GIGONDAS

The name Gigondas has such a nice, easy ring to it that I am surprised the wines of this region – adjacent to and just slightly to the northeast of Châteauneuf-du-Pape – have not attained more success. Like the wines of Châteauneuf-du-Pape, they are excellent value, and contrary to what most people think, can live and improve for a decade or more when vinified traditionally. Gigondas is almost always a big, full-bodied, alcoholic wine, so it is best treated as a robust and generously flavoured Châteauneuf-du-Pape.

GOUR DE CHAULE *BEAUMET-BONFILS* ★ ★ ★ ★

1979	②	**87**
1981	②	**86**
1982	②	**84**

A sensational producer of Gigondas, these wines have bouquets of cedary, ripe fruit, and are lively, robust wines filled with aromas and flavours of black cherry and pepper. Luscious and fat on the palate, with a wonderfully rich, full, well-balanced feel, these big, complex Gigondas are as good as they come. The 1981 and 1979 are better than the 1982.

R. COMBE ★ ★ ★

1982 L'Oustaou Fauquet	①	**80**

Attractive berry fruit and spicy, herbal, fennel aromas intermingle to provide a nice backdrop. On the palate, the wine is solid, medium- to full-bodied, and cleanly made. The short finish detracts from an otherwise decent effort.

GEORGES FARAUD ★ ★ ★ ★

1981	②	**85**
1982	②	**87**
1983	②	**86**

This ancient winemaker produces inky-coloured, very peppery, very concentrated wines that can age and improve for ten or more years. Both his 1983 and 1982 are extremely powerful wines, cedary, peppery, with interest and personalities, layers of flavour, and quite full-bodied. The 1982 is the richest of the wines. The 1981 is a little vegetal in aroma, but ripe and backward.

LES GOUBERTS ★ ★ ★ ★ ★

1979	②	**90**
1980	②	**86**
1981	②	**90**
1983	②	**83**
1984	②	**87**

Virtually every Rhône wine observer agrees that this is an up-and-coming estate, meticulously run by Jean-Pierre Cartier, and fully capable of making exquisite Gigondas. His wines are nearly black in colour, with a full-blown, peppery, intense blackcurrant bouquet, a dense, deep, very concentrated, chocolaty fruitiness. His 1979 and 1981 Gigondas are monumental wines, his 1983 somewhat dilute by his high standards. His 1984 is a notable success and his 1985 a smashing success which will not be released until 1988.

GUIGAL ★★★

1981	②	**86**
1982	②	**87**
1983	②	**89**

Marcel Guigal's Gigondas seem to get better with each vintage. The 1981 is loaded with peppery, rich fruit, is full-bodied, quite complex and very long on the palate. Drinkable now, but destined to live four to seven more years. The 1982 is loaded with peppery scents and raspberry fruit, is opulent and luscious on the palate. The 1983 is truly outstanding, long, rich, dense, with great extract and character.

PAUL JABOULET AINÉ ★★★

1978	③	**83**
1979	②	**86**
1983	②	**84**
1985	②	**84**

The wine to get is the 1979, which is still very young, robust, rich, and full. The 1978 is more evolved with an attractive, gamy, raspberry fruitiness, and full body. The 1983 and 1985 are straightforward in style, peppery, spicy, and not yet as complex as either the 1979 or 1978.

LONGUE-TOQUE ★★★★

1981	②	**76**
1982	②	**84**

Longue-Toque is a very highly regarded estate, particularly by John Livingstone Learmonth in his book *The Wines of the Rhône* (Faber & Faber, 1983). The 1981 Longue-Toque is an above-average wine, but is hardly inspirational. A leafy, stalky aroma and high-acid flavours are surprisingly austere. Certainly an interesting wine, but nothing special in 1981. The 1982 is much fruitier, long, ripe, and supple. The unreleased 1985 looks to be spectacular in quality.

MONTMIRAIL ★★★

1978	②	**83**
1979	②	**80**
1981	②	**84**

Montmirail produces big, chunky, densely coloured wines that seem to lack complexity and for some reason are overpriced compared with Gigondas wines. The 1978 is a huge, heavy wine that has plenty of power and character, but becomes a little overbearing in the glass. The 1979 is quite big, but does not have the depth of the 1978. The 1981 is big, tough, and rich. These are solid, sturdy wines that are certainly good, but overpriced.

R. OGIER ★
1981 Luc de Mayreuil .... ① **52**

Hot, very alcoholic, and oxidized aromas are hardly the stuff that dreams or even good wines are made of. A poor wine with no resemblance to Gigondas. Avoid.

LES PALLIÈRES ★★★★
1979 .... ② **85**
1981 .... ② **88**
1982 .... ② **85**
1983 .... ② **91**

Difficult to find, Les Pallières is a genuine old-style Gigondas, rustic, full-flavoured, big, and spicy, with lots of cedary, earthy, ripe fruity flavours, full body, a hefty dosage of alcohol, and a long finish. Les Pallières is usually held two and a half to three years in cask before being released, and can easily age for five to eight years. The 1981, 1983, and the unreleased 1985 are all excellent, but also quite special for their intensity and distinctive style.

RASPAIL *AY* ★★★★
1981 .... ② **86**
1982 .... ② **86**
1983 .... ② **87**
1984 .... ② **78**

An outstanding producer of long-lived Gigondas, Raspail's 1964, 1966, and 1971 are wines that are still in excellent condition today. The 1981 and 1983 are the best vintages for Raspail since the excellent 1978, although the 1985 is potentially the finest Raspail in two decades. Black/purple, peppery, intensely concentrated, and full bodied, these generous, plummy, deep wines can be drunk now, but five years of cellaring will add extra joy.

ST.-GAYAN *MEFFRE* ★★★★
1980 .... ② **86**
1981 .... ② **86**
1982 .... ② **82**
1983 .... ② **85**

One of the best producers of Gigondas, St.-Gayan has a sumptuous style of winemaking that produces black/purple wines with explosive bouquets of blackberry fruit, truffles, and smoky, hickory scents. Both the 1980 and 1981 are enormously rich, full-bodied wines with layers and layers of rich, ripe fruit, long, rich finishes and, I suspect, head-dizzying alcohol contents. Big, lusty, and intensely aromatic, both these wines will live for five to eight more years. The 1982 is ready to drink, a little unstructured by this producer's standards, but fruity and soft. The 1983 is fat, plummy, and ripe, and the unreleased 1985 this property's best wine since 1978.

TRIGNON ★ ★ ★
1981 .... ① **84**

André Roux makes an assortment of southern Rhône wines. His Gigondas is a robust yet finely balanced wine with good colour, a spicy, robust fruitiness, and full body. Drink over the next two to three years.

LIRAC AND CÔTES DU RHÔNE-VILLAGES, RASTEAU, CAIRANNE, ETC.

This vast wine-producing area in the southern Rhône can offer the shrewd wine consumer the finest red wine values that exist in the world. The range of quality is enormous in the Côtes du Rhône-Villages appellations and its most noted wine-producing towns, Séguret, Vacqueyras, Sablet, Cairanne, Rasteau, Visan, and Chusclan. The high-quality Côtes du Rhônes from the area's best producers are almost always priced less than £6 a bottle and, when well chosen, offer sumptuous, rich, full-blown flavours and, far more important, immediate gustatory pleasure. The 1985 is the best recent vintage for both red and white Côtes du Rhônes since 1978. The following red Côtes du Rhônes are listed alphabetically by the name of the estate or wine.

D'Aigueville
1985 Côtes du Rhône .... ① **78**

Normally a reliable producer of chunky, rustic-styled Côtes du Rhône, the 1983 is surprisingly light for d'Aigueville, but has straightforward, pleasant fruitiness and soft, easy-going texture. Drink over the next year.

Berthete
1983 Côtes du Rhône .... ① **82**

Another producer of high-quality Côtes du Rhône to keep an eye out for, Berthete's 1982 is moderately rich, full-bodied, fruity, and deep. It can be drunk now or aged for two years.

Brusset 1982 Cairanne Côtes du Rhône-Villages.... ① **83**
Brusset 1983 Cairanne Côtes du Rhône-Villages.... ① **83**

One of the best Côtes du Rhône domaines, Brusset produces full-flavoured and full-bodied, deeply coloured wine with a smoky, hickory-scented bouquet, rich, plummy fruit, a velvety texture, and spicy, rich finish. The 1982 is a trifle more fruity than the 1983, which has a little more ageing potential. They should be consumed over the next two to three years.

Cabasse Réserve 1983 Séguret Côtes du Rhône-Villages .... ① **85**
Cabasse Réserve 1985 Séguret Côtes du Rhône-Villages .... ① **85**

Two really outstanding wines for Nadine Latour's Domaine de Cabasse, these wines have the strength, richness, and vigour of a Gigondas or Châteauneuf-du-Pape. Deep ruby/purple, with a first-class bouquet of ripe black cherry and peppery fruit, these powerful, full-bodied wines have the depth and tannin to age for at least five or more years. Quite impressive.

Caves des Vignerons du Rasteau 1983 Côtes du Rhône.. ① **82**
Caves des Vignerons du Rasteau 1985 Côtes du Rhône.. ① **83**

Produced from one of the best co-operatives in France, these lovely, soft, very generously flavoured, spicy wines have robust, peppery, herbaceous bouquets, attractive fruit flavours, and soft, delicious, surprisingly long finishes. Drink over the next few years.

Chantegril 1982 Côtes du Rhône.............................. ① **76**
Chantegril 1983 Côtes du Rhône.............................. ① **78**

A ripe Grenache bouquet of peaches and apricots is immediately noticeable in both of these wines. On the palate, the wines are quite soft, round, and simple, but offer warm, easy-to-swallow flavours. Produced by the excellent Lirac estate of Saint-Roch.

Cru de Coudelet 1982 Côtes du Rhône...................... ① **81**
Cru de Coudelet 1983 Côtes du Rhône...................... ① **85**
Cru de Coudelet 1984 Côtes du Rhône...................... ① **85**

Coudelet is produced by the famous Beaucastel estate in Châteauneuf-du-Pape, and its vineyard is separated from the Châteauneuf-du-Pape appellation by only a two-lane road. The Coudelet wines are big, smoky, robust, intense wines. The 1978 still needs two to three more years of cellaring. Both the 1983 and the surprisingly good 1984 are top-flight Côtes du Rhônes for drinking over the next three to four years. The 1982, from a very difficult vintage, is quite charming. But the 1983 and 1984 are loaded with easy-to-drink, strawberry and raspberry fruit; they are medium-bodied wines that should be drunk over the next five to seven years.

Devoy 1980 Lirac... ① **80**
The wines of Lirac are consistently good, usually better than most Côtes du Rhônes, yet very cheap. This 1980 is quite peppery and spicy, but has oodles of blackberry fruit, some subtle herbal components, and a robust, gutsy texture. Drink over the next year.

Fonsalette 1978 Côtes du Rhône................................. ② **85**
Fonsalette 1979 Côtes du Rhône................................. ② **87**
Fonsalette 1981 Côtes du Rhône................................. ② **86**
Fonsalette 1982 Côtes du Rhône................................. ② **87**
Fonsalette 1983 Côtes du Rhône................................. ② **87**
Fonsalette 1978 Côtes du Rhône Syrah.................... ③ **90**
Fonsalette 1983 Côtes du Rhône Syrah.................... ③ **90**
Château Fonsalette is a likely candidate for criticism because of the unusually high prices fetched for its wines, as well as the bizarre behaviour exhibited by its owner, Jacques Reynaud. However, one taste of these Côtes du Rhônes leaves no doubt that they are equal to, if not better than, 80% or more of the wines from Châteauneuf-du-Pape and Gigondas. The 1978 Côtes du Rhône is drinking beautifully now, showing a complex, cedary, plummy, savoury bouquet, big, velvety, complex flavours and a top-notch finish. As good as they are, the 1979, 1982, and 1983 Côtes du Rhônes are better – very fragrant with scents of cedar, violets, blackcurrants and oak, they are opulent on the palate with a wonderful texture and gorgeous peppery bouquets. They would have been the greatest Côtes du Rhônes I have tasted except for the 1978 and 1983 Côtes du Rhône Syrahs, special Cuvées of 100% Syrah from old vines. Both are blockbuster wines with incredible depth and richness, and black/purple colour; they promise to be magnificent in ten to fifteen years.

**La Fourmone 1981 Vacqueyras Réserve du
Paradis**... ① **83**
**La Fourmone 1982 Vacqueyras Réserve du
Paradis**... ① **82**
Roger Combe, the proprietor of La Fourmone, is both a winemaker and poet. His wines from Vacqueyras (he also

makes Gigondas) are always black/purple in colour and have a
deep bouquet of blackberry fruit and spicy oak. They would
appear to be heavy and viscous from their impenetrable
colour, yet are not. Quite manageable on the palate with
lively, plummy, ripe fruit flavours, they are usually at their
best three to four years after the vintage. The 1982 is already
quite attractive, soft, fruity, and very flavourful. The 1981 is
bigger, more robust, but seems to harmoniously combine
strength with elegance and ripe, rich fruit.

Goubert 1983 Côtes du Rhône	①	**85**
Goubert 1981 Côtes du Rhône Beaumes des Venise	②	**90**
Goubert 1983 Côtes du Rhône Beaumes des Venise	②	**86**
Goubert 1984 Côtes du Rhône Beaumes des Venise	①	**85**
Goubert 1981 Côtes du Rhône Sablet	①	**84**
Goubert 1984 Côtes du Rhône Sablet	①	**84**

The Domaine Goubert has quickly emerged as one of the
shining superstars in the southern Rhône. The proprietor,
Jean-Pierre Cartier, makes a Gigondas under the Côtes du
Rhône appellation of Beaumes de Venise as well as the finest
Gigondas of the appellation. His wines are broodingly deep in
colour with a big, spicy, hickory, earthy, smoky bouquet.
These full-bodied, robust wines have impressive concentration, a long finish, and can easily handle three to four years of
cellaring for the Côtes du Rhônes and ten or more years for
the Gigondas.

Guigal 1980 Côtes du Rhône	①	**83**
Guigal 1981 Côtes du Rhône	①	**85**
Guigal 1982 Côtes du Rhône	①	**85**
Guigal 1983 Côtes du Rhône	①	**86**

Guigal makes lovely Côtes du Rhônes. All three have lovely,
seductive, clean and pure bouquets of ripe berry fruit and
peppery spices. On the palate, the wines exhibit savoury,
multidimensional, fruity flavours, shocking length, and good
balance. The 1981 and 1982 have a little more length to them;
the 1983 is excellent, opulent and rich, his best wine yet from
this appellation.

Paul Jaboulet Aîné 1983 Parallèle 45 Côtes du Rhône	①	**83**
Paul Jaboulet Aîné 1985 Parallèle 45 Côtes du Rhône	①	**83**

Paul Jaboulet Aîné 1982 Vacqueyras Côtes du Rhône... ① *80*

The 1982 Parallèle 45 is quite plummy and fruity, with a substantial, full-bodied attack on the palate. Though it is one of the best Parallèle 45s in years, the 1983 is even better. The Vacqueyras has an intensely peppery, spicy aroma, full body, and a straightforward, plummy, briary fruitiness.

Ogier 1979 Calandry Côtes du Rhône .... ① *60*
Ogier 1982 Vacqueyras Côtes du Rhône.................. ① *56*

Ogier's wines are consistent – consistently inferior. Rarely do I find a wine nasty and unpleasant, but these two wines are abrasive on the palate and seem to have just one outstanding component in them: hot, high alcohol. Stay away.

Rabasse-Charavin 1982 Cairanne Côtes du Rhône.. ① *82*
Rabasse-Charavin 1983 Cairanne Côtes du Rhône.. ① *84*
Rabasse-Charavin 1984 Côtes du Rhône .... ① *84*

This producer made a superb 1983 Côtes du Rhône with oodles of rich, deep, soft, lush fruit, a complex, cedary, ripe black cherry-scented bouquet, and wonderful finish. It should be drunk over the next year. The 1982 is lighter, with an intense, charming fruitiness, medium body; it has some hot alcohol in the finish, but is very agreeable and fruity. The generic 1984 Côtes du Rhône is peppery, with plenty of raspberry fruit and a soft texture. This is a domaine to search out.

St.-Anne 1983 Cuvée Notre Dame des Cellettes Côtes du Rhône... ① *82*
St.-Anne 1984 Cuvée Notre Dame des Cellettes Côtes du Rhône... ① *85*

One of the top domaines in the Côtes du Rhône, St.-Anne has in 1983 produced a firm, medium-bodied wine with good colour, concentration, and firm tannins. Well structured, this stylish well-balanced wine will be better in six months, although it is quite attractive now for its berry fruitiness and lengthy finish. Curiously, the 1984 is even better: rich, spicy, deeply fruity, with surprising length.

St.-Maurice L'Ardoise 1978 Côtes du Rhône .... ① *76*

Very peppery, somewhat herbaceous, this medium-bodied Côtes du Rhône has a robust, chunky fruitiness and average length.

St.-Paul 1982 Côtes du Rhône..................................... ① **75**

The 1981 Caves St.-Paul Côtes du Rhône was one of the finest Côtes du Rhônes I have ever tasted. However, the 1982 is somewhat diffuse and light, but still attractively fruity, soft, supple, and ready to drink.

St.-Roch 1980 Lirac... ① **80**
St.-Roch 1981 Lirac... ① **82**
St.-Roch 1982 Lirac... ① **84**
St.-Roch 1982 Lirac Cuvée Ancienne Viguerie....... ② **84**

Along with Château Ségriès in Lirac, Antoine Verda's beloved domaine called St.-Roch produces the finest wines of this appellation. His Liracs tend to have in common a big, intense perfume of apricots, peaches, and berry fruit, soft voluptuous flavours, and a lush, almost sweet texture on the palate. The 1980 is a good wine, direct, fruity, ripe, and round, but the 1981 and 1982 are better. They are round and generous wines, with oodles of sweet berry fruit. Both, like the 1980, should be drunk over the next one to two years. The 1982, a special Cuvée of the estate's best lots, is more concentrated and more interesting.

Treilles 1982 Côtes du Rhône..................................... ① **81**

Quite delicious, this medium ruby-coloured wine has a silky, luxurious texture, a lovely ripe berry quality to its bouquet, and good concentration. It is perfect for drinking now and over the next twelve months.

Trignon 1982 Côtes du Rhône..................................... ① **78**
Trignon 1983 Rasteau Côtes du Rhône-Villages..... ① **83**
Trignon 1982 Sablet Côtes du Rhône-Villages........ ① **83**

André Roux is one of the most innovative producers of fine Côtes du Rhône wines. Using a modified carbonic maceration method that employs much higher temperatures for extraction of colour and fruit, and eschewing the use of wood barrels for ageing, Roux obtains wines that are remarkably fruity and supple, ready to drink young, yet with an uncanny ability to age well. The 1982 Côtes du Rhône is a good, straightforward wine with attractive berry fruit and good spice. However, for a few pennies more, you should move up to the 1983 Rasteau and 1982 Sablet. Both have a lot of ripe, tasty, peppery, blackcurrant fruit, supple, easily appreciated flavours, and enough tannins to warrant cellaring for three to five years.

Vidal-Fleury 1982 Cairanne Côtes du Rhône .... ① **84**
Vidal-Fleury 1983 Les Ronvières Côtes du Rhône . ① **83**

Always well made, Vidal-Fleury's Côtes du Rhône 1983 is nowhere near a match for the wonderful 1978, but it does offer charming, soft, berry fruit and adequate length. The 1982 Côtes du Rhône from the village of Cairanne is wonderfully plump, rich, ripe, long, and loaded with fruit.

La Vieille Ferme 1983 Côtes du Ventoux.................. ① **82**
La Vieille Ferme 1982 Gold Capsule Côtes du Rhône.. ① **83**
La Vieille Ferme 1983 Réserve Côtes du Rhône...... ① **83**
La Vieille Ferme 1984 Réserve Côtes du Rhône...... ① **83**

The best red wines from La Vieille Ferme in quite a few years. Jean-Pierre Perrin has apparently gone back to a bigger, richer style with more body and stuffing. The result is obviously a success. Rich, peppery fruit jumps from the glass. On the palate, the wines are full, lush, interesting, and very delicious to drink. The Côtes du Ventoux is a little lighter. Drink over the next three to four years.

Vieux Chêne 1985 Côtes du Rhône........................... ① **82**
Vieux Chêne 1985 Cuvée Haie aux Grives Côtes du Rhône.. ① **84**

This domaine has consistently provided me with some deliciously fruity, plump bottles of Côtes du Rhône. My favourite Cuvée from Vieux Chêne has been the Haie aux Grives. The 1985 has a ripe, peach-scented bouquet, juicy, ripe fruity flavours, medium body, and a good, silky finish. It should be drunk over the next three years. The straight Côtes du Rhône lacks the richness and extra ripeness of the aforementioned special Cuvée, but is soft, fruity, easy to drink, and very pleasant.

MUSCAT DE BEAUMES DE VENISE

These largely unknown, marvellous Rhône wines are intensely perfumed, sweet dessert wines produced from the Muscat grape. They are rich and lively wines, and despite their alcohol content – upwards of 20–21% – I find them much easier to drink and fresher than the Sauternes and Barsacs. The wines are perfect for after-dinner sipping or, better yet, served with an open fruit tart. They are wines that are best drunk within three to four years of the vintage, when they retain their remarkable freshness, intense, exuberant fruitiness, and incredible perfume of ripe pears and peaches.

Domaine de Coyeaux 1985... ② **85**

Light golden orange, with a moderate aroma of almonds, apricots, and lychees, this sweet, rich, viscous wine is not heavy at all but vibrant, alive, and zesty. It is, however, heady, with a dizzying alcohol content of 16%. Drink over the next year, and serve it with fresh fruit or fruit desserts.

Domaine Durban Non-Vintage .... ② **87**
Domaine Durban 1985 .... ② **90**
The Domaine Durban has perhaps the highest reputation for Muscat de Beaumes de Venise, with ripe orange, apricot, and nut scents, and flavours of almond. The Non-Vintage wine is rich and concentrated on the palate, intense and decadent. The 1985 has all of these qualities but more acidity and a more complex bouquet.

Paul Jaboulet Aîné 1985 .... ③ **90**
A sensational bouquet of ripe tropical fruit, as well as scents of peaches, almonds, and apricots fill the nose. On the palate, this light orange-coloured wine is sweet but extremely well balanced, with really crisp acidity, and a lovely, lush, concentrated feel on the palate. Despite its richness and sweetness, the wine is quite easy and refreshing and never becomes cloying, heavy, or tiring to drink. A total success.

Domaine St.-Sauveur 1985 .... ② **85**
Medium orange gold in colour with a big, ripe, intense aroma of ripe tropical fruit and floral scents; on the palate, the wine is a trifle heavy, but loaded with rich, ripe fruit.

THE WINES OF FRANCE'S SOUTHWEST

There is little known about this remote area of vineyards spread out between the Spanish border, the Correre to the north, and the Lot Valley to the south. Even for frequent tourists to France, this area is largely uncharted territory. Yet there are some very serious, very good wines produced here. For red wine enthusiasts there are plenty of wines to choose from—the fruity, light, casual wines of Bergerac, the stern, tannic, dark, remarkably cheap, long-lived red wines of Madiran, and the progressive, modern-style, supple, fruity Bordeaux-like wines of Cahors. While there is less to choose from among the white wines, crisp, dry, fruity whites are available from Bergerac, and France's most curiously named white wine, the Pacherenc du Vic Bihl, is also delicious, crisp and lively.

RECENT VINTAGES

Vintages in this vast area are hardly ever discussed or rated but since the weather closely resembles that of Bordeaux, the years tend to be similar in style. Consequently, 1982 and 1985 stand out, closely followed by 1983, 1981, 1978, and 1979.

A GUIDE TO SOUTHWEST FRANCE'S BEST PRODUCERS

★ ★ ★ ★ Excellent Producers

Château d'Aydie-Laplace
   (Madiran)
Clos de Gamot (Cahors)
Clos de Triguedina Prince
   Phobus (Cahors)

Château la Jaubertie (Bergerac)
Château Montus (Madiran)

★ ★ ★ Good Producers

Château Bellevue (Bergun)
Château de Cayrou
   (Cahors)
Chambert (Cahors)
Château Court-Les-Mûts
   (Bergerac)
Haute Serre (Cahors)

Château Michel de
   Montague (Bergerac)
Château du Perron
   (Madiran)
Château de Peyros (Cahors)
Château St.-Didier
   Parnoux (Cahors)

SOUTHWEST FRANCE · TODAY'S BUYING STRATEGY

For the light white and red wines of Bergerac, don't risk drinking anything older than 1983. The 1984s are disappointing for this area,

327

but 1985 is very good and is the year to search out now. Madiran is a fertile hunting ground for shrewd, bargain-conscious consumers; try a red Madiran or white Pacherenc du Vic Bihl. The 1982s from Madiran are very good, as are the 1983s and 1985s. The top Madirans from these vintages will last seven to ten years without any difficulty. For the rare white wine, Pacherenc du Vic Bihl, stick to the most recent vintage.

CHAPTER TWO

ITALY

The wines of Italy may be at once the most bewildering, frustrating, and sometimes fascinating group of wines to taste and evaluate. Italy produces more wine than any country in the world, and the Italians still drink more wine than anyone else, a hefty average 92 litres of wine per man, woman, and child. Compare that figure with the average British consumption of 10+ litres per person.

The range of wines produced in Italy is staggering. There are many wines still made with nineteenth-century techniques and that are, unfortunately, still exported. These wines are often oxidized, have excessive amounts of volatile acidity, and taste dirty, coarse, and sharp. On the other hand, there are also increasing amounts of wines produced in shiny, sparkling clean, stainless steel tanks, their vinification temperature regulated by computers. From the sun-drenched and baked wine regions of Sicily, Campania, Basilicata, and Calabria to the cool Alpine climates of Trentino, northern Lombardy, and Piedmont, there is a remarkable diversity of wines, winemaking styles, grape varieties, and flavours. More so than elsewhere, there is a dichotomy to Italian wines. Italy's greatest wines compete with the finest produced anywhere in the world, yet the bad wines of Italy are among the world's worst.

Following are my observations about the current state of affairs of Italian wines.

1 Italy's greatest red wines are either the product of the Nebbiolo or Sangiovese grape. There are a handful of exceptions. Nebbiolo finds its greatest heights in the wines of Piedmont, the pastoral, hilly section of northern Italy. It is here that Italy's two greatest wines are produced, the stern, tannic, rich, full-bodied Barolo and the more elegant Barbaresco. Although the Sangiovese grape is equally reputed and can reach supreme heights in the hands of careful, skilled winemakers, it most frequently yields good but rarely great Chiantis and Brunello di Montalcinos.

2 Italy's new breed of crisp, light, dry, fruity white wines made with modern technology, particularly Chardonnay, Pinot Grigio, Bianco di Custoza, Pinot Bianco, Vernaccia di San Gimignano, Orvieto, and Trebbiano represent outstanding values and have no peers for lightness, freshness, and immediate charm in drinking, provided of course that they are vinified at cool temperatures, made in stainless steel, and bottled very early to capture their fruitiness and vivacity.

3 Italian experimentation with new styles of red wine, often aged in small oak casks as in Bordeaux and produced from various blends of Cabernet Sauvignon, Cabernet Franc, Merlot, and Sangiovese, has resulted in a number of stunning new wines that have the potential to be considered world-class red wines.

4 Italian winemakers are getting very serious about making complex, sparkling wines that can rival top French Champagnes. Virtually all of the serious efforts in this area are taking place in Lombardy, where producers such as Ca Del Bosco, Bellavista, and Berlucchi are making very good, very interesting, dry sparkling wines in the *méthode champenoise* manner.

5 For the most part, Italy's serious red wines spend too much time ageing in wood containers. From the smell of some of them, I'd guess the wood is also not terribly clean. The result is far too many oxidized, dried-out wines deficient in the ripe fruit that they once had. Gradually, some of the winemakers are seeing the folly of their ways, but shorter ageing periods – one to three years rather than the three to ten years in some instances – would render wines richer in fruit and less prone to oxidation. Bottling the entire crop at the same time, à la Bordeaux, would also be a welcome change and would eliminate the extreme bottle variation that now exists between a producer's Chianti bottled after three years of ageing in wood vats and the same wine bottled after six or seven years of wood vats. This results in totally different wines and is confusing to the wine consumer.

6 Italy's red wines, at least the big, serious wines of Piedmont, Tuscany, and a handful of others from Umbria, Abruzzi, and Campania, require, as a general rule, one to two hours of aeration after decanting into a clean container. I am generally opposed to extended breathing of wines, but my tastings time and time again confirmed that the big reds of Italy improve significantly with some airing.

7 Italy's wine scandal of 1986, involving the criminal adulteration of wine by the addition of potentially harmful, even deadly, chemicals such as methanol and diethylene glycol, significantly tarnished many great winemakers in Italy. Only a tiny percentage of Italy's winemakers were involved in this criminal activity and none of their wines are reviewed herein.

Northern
Italy

KILOMETERS
MILES

WINE
REGIONS
1 Valle d'Aosta
2 Piedmont
3 Liguria
4 Lombardy
5 Veneto
6 Trentino-
  Alto Adige
7 Friuli-
  Venezia Giulia
8 Emilia-
  Romagna

Southern
Italy

WINE
REGIONS
1 Campania
2 Puglia
3 Basilicata
4 Calabria
5 Sicily

TYRRHENIAN SEA

Central Italy

0 ____ 60
MILES
0 ____ 50 ____ 100
KILOMETERS

ADRIATIC
SEA

LIGURIAN
SEA

CORSICA

TYRRHENIAN SEA

•Lucca
•Pisa   •Firenze
•Livorno Arrezo•
  Siena•
      1
•Grosseto

8
•Pesaro
    •Ancona
3   2   •Macerata
Perugia•
   •Spoleto Ascoli Piceno•
  Terni•
Viterbo•   L'Aquila• •Pescara
      5   4   •Chieti
   •Roma   Isernia•
      •Latina   •6

Olbia•
•Sassari
•Alghero
    Nuoro•
•Bosa 7
   Tortoli•
•Oristano

•Cagliari

N
W—E
S

WINE REGIONS
1 Tuscany   5 Lazio
2 Marche   6 Molise
3 Umbria   7 Sardinia
4 Abruzzo   8 San Marino

PIEDMONT

Italy's Finest Wine Region

One will get no disagreement from this writer that Piedmont is Italy's greatest wine region and that Barolo and Barbaresco are frequently Italy's two best red wines. The great intellectual and rich, powerful, sensory pleasures that a great Barolo or Barbaresco can provide have been well established in wine literature.

Both Barolo and Barbaresco are produced in a bucolic, hilly terrain that serves double duty as the white truffle kingdom of Italy. The drab town of Alba is the closest thing to a commercial city centre for this viticultural region that has the sharp hills of Barolo to its south and the more gently rolling slopes of Barbaresco to its northeast.

Part of the reluctance on the part of many wine enthusiasts to jump at the opportunity to purchase many of the exquisite Barolos and Barbarescos on the market is that these big, brawny wines are often forbidding and savage in their youthful rawness. Certainly Barbaresco is the more tame, but the grape they are made from, the aforementioned Nebbiolo, is quite capable of rendering furiously tannic, unyielding wines that beg for ten years' ageing to reveal their complex aromas of peppery spices, rich truffle-scented fruit, leather, tar, and tobacco. Barbaresco has the reputation of being the most approachable in its youth and is less robust and tannic, but such generalizations fall short of doing justice to the divergent styles of wine found in these two regions, as well as the different soils and micro-climates that will affect the style, texture, taste, and personality of the wines.

With respect to Barolo, it is Italy's most robust, powerful, full-bodied, tannic, and, by most accounts, memorable wine. However, there are different schools of winemaking in Barolo that result in quite differently styled wines. Barolo enthusiasts will add that the style of many Barolos can also be predicted from the vineyard in which the grapes are grown. Certainly, one of the most obvious trends over the recent decade has been the emergence of single-vineyard-designated Barolos. This trend is also very obvious in Barbaresco. However, in Barolo and Barbaresco, like Burgundy in France, different growers often use grapes from the exact same vineyard, yet vinify and handle the wines in different manners. Consequently, the consumer is often confronted with wines from the same vineyard and vintage that taste totally different. At present, virtually everyone agrees that the top Barolo vineyards are Marcenasco, Monprivato, Villero, Bussia Soprana, Cannubi, Brunate, Rocche, Monfortino, Monfalletto, Lazzarito, and Rionda. However, just knowing the vineyards is not enough. One must also know the winemaking styles of the top Barolo and Barbaresco producers.

If Barolo and Barbaresco are two of Italy's greatest wines, then the smooth, fruity Dolcetto is one of that country's most delicious but misunderstood wines. It is not sweet, as many wine enthusiasts think, but quite dry, though in top vintages like 1983 it is intensely fruity, lush and oozing with plummy fruit.

Wines called Nebbiolo d'Alba are sometimes a producer's declassified Barolo or Barbaresco, but are almost always good value. Barbera d'Alba, Grignolino and Freisa are Piedmont's weakest wines. The first is often abhorrently sharp and acidic except in the hands of a producer such as Vietti, Giacosa, or Pio Cesare; the second is innocuously light and bland; the third is a totally repugnant wine, frothy, sweet, and acidic.

North of Alba and the famous Barolo/Barbaresco zone, in full view of the Alps, are several other red wine regions of Piedmont. Carema, Gattinara, Spanna, Ghemme, and Donnaz are the best of these wines, all bred from the Nebbiolo and all capable of producing very good wines in the hands of the best producers.

QUICK VINTAGE GUIDE

1986 A good to very good vintage, the 1986s are not nearly as concentrated or as full-bodied as the 1985s, but should prove superior to the irregular but sometimes good 1983s. The top wines have elegance and attractive levels of good, ripe fruit. This year may turn out to resemble the elegant, stylish 1979s.

1985 Gaja, Ceretto and their peers are already calling it one of the greatest vintages this century. I believe they said the same thing about 1982, 1978, and 1971. Nevertheless, broker Neil Empson claims it is better than either 1982 or 1978, which is difficult for me to imagine, given the superlative quality of the latter two years. Unfortunately, no one will see a bottle of the best red wines until 1988, with most *riservas* not reaching the market until 1990–1992. Since top Barolos and Barbarescos need twelve to fifteen years of cellaring the best wines of 1985 won't be ready until 2000–2010. Will you have the discipline to wait?

1984 Maligned by the press corps (as was the case everywhere in Europe) this vintage in Piedmont is claimed to be average in quality, with the wines light yet forward and flavourful.

1983 A good vintage of rather tannic, stern wines, the 1983s may turn out to be similar to the unyielding but overall potentially good 1974s.

1982 A very great vintage. The wines are loaded with ripe, rich fruit, have plenty of tannins, full body, and real alcoholic punch to them. They are tasting surprisingly forward, and since most great vintages of Barolo and Barbaresco need ten to fifteen years of bottle age to mature, this might be the opportunity to enjoy a rich, dense, ripe fruity Barolo or Barbaresco before the age of ten. Despite the accessible nature of this vintage, the top wines should keep 25 or more years. A year to buy.

1981 Rain during September ruined what could have been a very good year. Many of the best growers declassified their entire crops. My initial tastings have turned up fruity, compact, short wines that are rather plain.

1980 Somewhat of a sleeper vintage, the 1980s are medium-bodied, rather light wines, but the good growers have produced wines with plenty of fruit, soft tannins, and charm. It is a vintage to drink over the next four to five years. If priced right, 1980 is worth considering.

1979 One of the best vintages for current drinking. Elegant, ripe, fruity wines were produced. They may lack the muscle, power, and great concentration of a vintage such as 1978 or 1982, but they offer plenty of finesse and complexity. Not to be overlooked.

1978 This is a great vintage of very long-lived wines, huge in structure, very tannic, very concentrated, and the best of them are still a good ten years away from maturity. The crop size was small, the style of the wines aggressive, rich, and tough. They have developed very slowly, causing impatient critics to down-grade them. The 1982s show more ripe, intense fruit than the 1978s did at a similar stage, but this is a great vintage that just needs plenty of time.

1977 A horrendous year of rain and cold weather. Most good growers declassified their entire crops.

1976 Another bad year; the wines lacked ripeness, had excessive tannins, and are now drying out.

1975 The first of a trio of consecutive poor vintages, the 1975s I have tasted have had aromas of tea, light intensity flavours and shallow personalities.

1974 This is a highly rated vintage, but one I find overrated; the wines are too hard and tannic, and lacking in ripeness and richness. Perhaps time will prove me wrong, but most of the Piedmont wines from 1974 lack length, grace, and charm.

1973 Relatively easy to drink, soft, pleasant, light wines were produced in 1973. All should have been drunk by now.

1972 As in most of Europe's viticultural regions, rain was the ruination of this vintage.

1971 Until the advent of the remarkably promising 1982s, the 1971s had been what I consider a classic Piedmont vintage. Rich, perfumed, and deeply concentrated, these wines are now entering their plateau of maturity, which should easily last for another ten to fifteen years. A great vintage.

Older Vintages

The 1970s are very good eclipsed in stature by the admittedly greater 1971s; the 1969s are average in quality and best drunk up. The 1968s are disastrous; the 1967s very good, but now beginning to slip; the 1966s and 1965s below average to poor; the 1964 another great vintage. Well-stored bottles of 1964 Piedmontese wines are gloriously rich and scented.

A GUIDE TO PIEDMONT'S BEST PRODUCERS

★ ★ ★ ★ ★ Outstanding Producers

Angelo Gaja (Barbaresco)

Bruno Ceretto
   (Barolo/Barbaresco)

Clerico (Barolo)

Bruno Giacosa
   (Barolo/Barbaresco/Arneis)

Renato Ratti (Barolo/Dolcetto)

★ ★ ★ ★ Excellent Producers

Castello di Neive (Barbaresco)

Pio Cesare (Barolo/Barbaresco)

Cogno-Marcarini (Barolo)

Aldo Conterno
   (Barolo/Dolcetto)

Giacomo Conterno (Barolo)

Fontanafredda (Barolo)

Marchesi di Gresy (Barbaresco)

G. Mascarello (Barolo)

Produttori di Barbaresco
   (Barbaresco)

Francesco Rinaldi (Barolo)

L. Sandrone (Barolo)

Valentino (Barolo/Dolcetto)

Vietti (Barolo/Dolcetto)

★ ★ ★ Good Producers

Mario Antoniolo (Gattinara)

Brovia (Barolo)

Carretta (Barolo)

Deassilani (Gattinara, Spanna,
   Ghemme)

Dosio (Barolo)

Luigi Einaudi (Barolo)

Giovannini Moresco
   (Barbaresco)

Pasquero-Secondo (Barbaresco)

Pelissero (Barbaresco)

Prunotto (Barolo)

Ravizza (Gattinara)

Giuseppi Rinaldi (Barolo)

Roagna (Barbaresco)

Scarpa (Barolo)

Vallana (Spanna/Gattinara)

★★ Average Producers

Borgogno (Barolo)
Agostino Brugo (Gattinara)
Damilano (Barolo)
Deforville (Barbaresco)

Franco-Fiorina (Barolo)
Elli Giacosa (Barolo)
Spinona (Barbaresco)
Travaglini (Gattinara)

★ Other Producers

Guido Bara (Gattinara)
Bersano (Barolo)
Bil Colle (Barbaresco)
L. Caldi (Barolo)

Kiola (Barolo)
Marchesi di Barolo (Barolo)
Oddero (Barolo)
A. Scavino (Barolo)

PIEDMONT · A BUYING STRATEGY

If you can find some of the outstanding 1978s on the shelves of retailers, they should be gobbled up – not for drinking now, but for cellaring until 1990. This is particularly true for the best Barolos and Barbarescos from top producers. The 1979 is the best vintage for current consumption, and the 1982s, destined to be great classics, will be arriving over the next several years and, of course, merit significant interest. As for the white wines of Piedmont, look for the excellent 1985s and avoid older vintages which are now showing signs of losing their fruit.

MARIO ANTONIOLO *GATTINARA* ★★★

1974 Gattinara	③	83
1975 Gattinara	③	60
1978 Gattinara Osso San Grato	③	86
1979 Gattinara Osso San Grato	③	84
1974 Gattinara San Francesco	③	83
1976 Gattinara San Francesco	③	75
1978 Gattinara San Francesco	③	85
1979 Gattinara San Francesco	③	85

One of the best producers of Gattinara. Antoniolo's best wines come from two specific vineyards, Osso San Grato and San Francesco, and are so-called on the label. I was disappointed in the 1974s from Antoniolo, but his 1978s and 1979s are good.

Both 1974s display complex, leathery, earthy aroma and decent fruit, but finish short and have excessive tannin levels making further ageing a gamble. The 1976 is austere and severe and going nowhere. The 1975 has some spicy, leathery, earthy fruit in the nose, but tastes bitter and clumsy on the palate. The 1978s are rich and fruity, show a sweet ripeness and good tannic backbone. They can be drunk now or cellared for another two to three years. The 1979s are less powerful than the 1978s, but are medium-bodied, elegant, spicy, attractive wines for drinking over the next one to two years.

GUIDO BARRA *GATTINARA* ★

1974 Gattinara .... ② **82**
1979 Gattinara .... ② **74**
1978 Spanna... ② **72**
1981 Spanna... ② **78**

I have not had a great deal of tasting experience of Barra's wines. Those I have tasted have been rather old-style, coarse, somewhat oxidized wines that lacked fruit and complexity. The best Barra wine I have tasted is the 1974 Gattinara, which is fully mature, spicy, and aromatic.

AGOSTINO BRUGO *GATTINARA* ★ ★

1975 Gattinara .... ② **76**
1976 Gattinara .... ② **82**
1979 Gattinara .... ② **85**
1975 Spanna... ① **83**
1976 Spanna... ① **78**

Brugo's wines are generally robust, soundly made, and flavourful. They are usually rustic in style and, though lacking in finesse and elegance, are nevertheless good, rich, savoury wines. Brugo produces wine under the Gattinara, Ghemme, and Spanna labels. Among the Spannas, the 1976 is ready to drink, spicy, tarry, medium-bodied, and robust. The 1975 has more richness and fruit, and a pungent, earthy, tarry bouquet. It can age for one to three more years. Of the Gattinaras, the best is the 1979, which has a medium ruby colour, a richly scented bouquet of cherry fruit and fresh leather, a medium body, and good length. It should keep well for two to three years. The 1975 is lean and somewhat dry and tannic, whereas the 1976 is plump, simple, but satisfying in a robust, way.

CARRETTA *BAROLO* ★ ★ ★

1978 Barolo Cannubi .... ③ **87**
1979 Barolo Cannubi .... ③ **85**
1983 Bianco del Roero .... ① **82**
1985 Bianco del Roero .... ① **84**
1978 Nebbiolo d'Alba...................................... ① **83**
1980 Nebbiolo d'Alba...................................... ① **75**

Carretta is a fine producer who seems to get overlooked when discussing top Barolo producers. Perhaps it is because his wines tend to be savagely tannic and backward when young, and it is nearly impossible to judge if they have sufficient fruit to outlast the huge, raw tannins. Certainly his 1970 and 1971 were brilliant examples of Barolo when tasted in 1985 in a comparative tasting of these two vintages. I regard his 1970 as the best Barolo produced in that vintage.

True to form, Carretta's new releases, 1978 and 1979, are both eight to ten years away from maturity. That alone will, I suspect, be enough to deter most interested parties. Carretta also produces a small amount of good, crisp white wine called Bianco del Roero. Both the 1982 and 1985 are quite lively, fresh, stylish, dry wines that ideally complement fish and chicken. Carretta's Nebbiolo d'Alba is also considered to be among the best; it, too, takes at least seven to eight years of cellaring to reach drinkability. The 1978 Barolo will last 25-40 years. I cannot see it reaching its peak before 2000. It is loaded with fruit but brutally tannic and really unpleasant on the palate, although those accustomed to judging young wine will see its immense potential. The 1979 is similar, but not as concentrated. It needs until 1992–1995 to reach its peak. Both the white wines are for consumption now.

CASTELLO DI NEIVE *BARBARESCO* ★ ★ ★ ★

1978 Barbaresco Santo Stefano	③	**87**
1979 Barbaresco Santo Stefano	③	**85**
1981 Barbaresco Santo Stefano	②	**75**
1983 Dolcetto Basarin	②	**85**
1982 Dolcetto Messoirano	②	**82**
1983 Dolcetto Messoirano	②	**78**

This is an excellent producer of Piedmontese wine that rarely seems to get the publicity it deserves. The wines are rich, fragrant, deep, and concentrated, without the excess of tannin so commonly found in many wines of this region. The Barbaresco Santo Stefano is usually the top wine here. Santo Stefano is one of the great vineyards of Piedmont. The 1978 Santo Stefano is drinkable now but ideally should receive another four to five years of cellaring. It has a rich, full-intensity bouquet of cedar, ripe cherries, spices and leather. Ripe and full-bodied, still quite tannic and youthful, it is an excellent wine that may with time become outstanding. The 1979 Santo Stefano is a less tannic, slightly less full-bodied version of the 1978. It has a full-blown bouquet of spicy, leathery, tarry fruit and deep flavour. Among the Dolcettos, the 1983 Basarin is a textbook wine, rich, plummy, fleshy, and very fruity. It is delicious for drinking now. The 1982 Messoirano is more tannic and robust, but has less lushness. The 1983 Messoirano is herbaceous with the scent of ripe tomatoes and plenty of tannin and acidity. It lacks the charm of the other two Dolcettos.

BRUNO CERETTO *BAROLO/BARBARESCO* ★ ★ ★ ★ ★

1982 Barbaresco Asij	④	**88**

1979 Barbaresco Bricco Asili	⑤	**90**
1980 Barbaresco Bricco Asili	⑤	**86**
1982 Barbaresco Bricco Asili	⑤	**92**
1983 Barbaresco Bricco Asili	⑤	**88**
1982 Barolo Bricco Rocche, Bricco Roche	⑤	**91**
1980 Barolo Brunate	④	**78**
1982 Barolo Brunate	④	**89**
1979 Barolo Prapo	④	**89**
1980 Barolo Prapo	⑤	**89**
1982 Barolo Prapo	⑤	**89**
1980 Barolo Rocche	④	**81**
1979 Barolo Zonchetta	④	**88**
1982 Barolo Zonchetta	⑤	**87**
1985 Dolcetto d'Alba	②	**86**
1982 Nebbiolo d'Alva	②	**84**

The Cerettos are justifiably proud of their wines, particularly their. Barolo, which comes from specific vineyards called Prapo, Brunate, Rocche and Zonchetta, and their Barbaresco, from a highly regarded vineyard called Bricco Asili. The style of wines is classic, relying on modern equipment and facilities to produce wine full of fruit yet with no excess of tannin nor suggestion of oxidation. I find the wines among the most accessible and easy to drink when young, since they possess a core of very good fruit that, along with their very aromatic character, is one of their personality traits. I cannot assess how they age because I have not tasted anything older than 1978, but they have good balance and sufficient fruit. Interestingly, Ceretto's 1979s seem more successful than his 1978s.

All of the 1982s are very, very successful, led by the sublime, gorgeously scented, rich, supple 1982 Barbaresco Bricco Asili and absurdly priced yet rare 1982 Barolo Bricco Rocche, Bricco Roche. Both will improve for another five to ten years. The 1982 Barbaresco Asij and Barolo Brunate offer contrasting styles, the Barbaresco rich, velvety, and deep, yet very accessible, the Barolo backward, very rich, and full, but in need of seven to eight years of cellaring. Both the excellent 1982 Barolo Zonchetta and Prapo need seven to ten more years. The 1979 Barbaresco Asili, the 1979 Barolo Prapo, and 1979 Barolo Zonchetta are delicious to drink now, ripe, very fragrant, rich, and quite well balanced. The aromas of ripe cherries and leather and the seductively lush, almost sweet, ripe fruit palate sensations are top-notch. Less profound but very good is the 1980 Barbaresco Bricco Asili. The 1980 Barolo Prapo is a trifle too hard, tannic, amd slightly vegetal. The 1982 Nebbiolo d'Alba is easy to drink, fruity, direct, rather soft, and quite pleasant. Of recent releases, the 1985

Dolcetto d'Alba is gloriously fruity, fat, soft, and loaded with character. The famed 1983 Barbaresco Bricco Asili continues the tradition of excellent wines from this vineyard.

PIO CESARE *BAROLO/BARBARESCO* ★★★★

1974 Barbaresco Riserva	③	75
1978 Barbaresco Riserva	④	88
1979 Barbaresco Riserva	④	84
1980 Barbaresco Riserva	④	70
1978 Barolo Riserva	④	86
1979 Barolo Riserva	④	87

For years this firm in Alba produced very traditional, old- style wines fermented at hot temperatures for very long periods in old wooden vats. Now stainless steel has replaced the wood and temperature control is observed. If anything, these changes have been for the better. The wines are still big, well proportioned, potentially long-lived examples of their type. I find the weakness of this firm lies in off vintages where the wines sometimes do not turn out as well as might be expected. Certainly in top vintages such as a 1978, Pio Cesare does not miss the mark. Unlike many other producers in Piedmont, Pio Boffa, the administrator of the firm, does not believe in single vineyard wines, preferring to blend wines from different vineyards, claiming that this is what gives a wine balance. The top-rated wines, the 1978 Barbaresco Riserva and 1979 Barolo Riserva, have classic Nebbiolo scents of tar, leather, earth, and ripe big cherries. Both show surprisingly rich, supple fruit, good length, and further ageing potential of six to eight years. The 1978 Barolo Riserva exhibits good richness and, though it won't be fully mature before 1990, already tastes well, with plenty of ripe fruit, spice, leather, and tobacco. The 1979 Barbaresco Riserva is light but tasty and ready; the 1974 Barbaresco is quite harsh and severe and just seems to lack fruit. The 1980 Riserva may be in a dumb stage, but it too tastes short and deficient in fruit and is entirely too tannic.

CLERICO *BAROLO* ★★★★★

1980 Barolo Bussia	③	87
1982 Barolo Bussia	③	90
1982 Barolo Ginestra	③	90

This small producer makes outstanding Barolo from the Ginestra and Bussia vineyards. The 1980 Barolo Bussia is a very good wine from this rather mediocre vintage. The 1982s need ten to fifteen years of cellaring, but they are explosively rich, intense wines with exceptional concentration, length, and balance. The Ginestra is a touch more supple than the Bussia, but both should prove to be fabulous wines with a decade or more of cellaring potential.

COGNO-MARCARINI *BAROLO* ★★★★

1980 Barolo Brunate .... ③ *83*
1980 Barolo La Serra .... ③ *81*

This producer is quite highly regarded, but I have always found the wines somewhat light and a trifle diluted rather than delicate, elegant, and suave. His 1971 is over the hill, and his 1978s were a disappointment, particularly in view of the excellence of the vintage; so one wonders why all the acclaim? These two 1980s are decently made, fruity, soft, with pleasant cherry fruit flavours and some spice. They are supple and ready to drink. The Brunate has more fruit, depth, and length.

ALDO CONTERNO *BAROLO/DOLCETTO* ★★★★

1980 Barolo Colonnello .... ④ *86*
1982 Dolcetto d'Alba .... ① *85*

Only Ratti produces a better Dolcetto than Aldo Conterno. However, it is Conterno's Barolos for which he is most famous. I recall vividly his 1971 Barolo Bussia Colonnello, tasted only once, but what a gorgeously proportioned wine, and how it oozed with fruit! For some reason, his wines are hard to find. I felt when I last visited Conterno that his obsession with the modern style of winemaking had gone a little far, since the 1978s tasted surprisingly fruity and did not seem to have sufficient tannin for eight to ten years of cellaring. However, more recently tasted wines have all shown well. The 1980 Barolo Colonnello is a top success for this rather maligned vintage. It is quite rich with a tarry, plummy, supple fruitiness. It should be drunk over the next two to three years. His 1982 Dolcetto d'Alba is a stunningly lush, richly fruity wine that is about as good a Dolcetto as one can find.

GIACOMO CONTERNO *BAROLO* ★★★★

1979 Barbera d'Alba .... ② *79*
1971 Barolo Monfortino .... ⑤ *92*
1974 Barolo Monfortino .... ⑤ *78*
1978 Barolo Monfortino .... ⑤ *92*
1971 Barolo Riserva .... ⑤ *90*
1973 Barolo Riserva .... ④ *75*
1979 Barolo Riserva .... ④ *82*

Giovanni Conterno, who runs this firm, is probably Piedmont's most traditional and stubborn winemaker. His nineteenth-century winemaking philosophy produces some of this region's most dramatic wines, but his inflexibility and blind commitment to tradition can also result in some oxidized, overly tannic wines with little charm and fruit. Unlike his brother Aldo, who bottles his Barolo after two years of ageing, Giovanni rarely bottles before ten years of cask ageing. He is a perfectionist when it comes to quality, never hesitating to produce no wine in years when the grapes don't measure up. However, his predilection for keeping some of his lots of wine a decade or more in wood has caused some wines to taste dry, volatile, or oxidized. Conterno's best wine may be the special Barolo called Monfortino, unquestionably Barolo's single greatest and most dramatic wine. The classic vintages for Monfortino are 1964, 1967, 1971, and 1978, the last and best of which has not yet been released. I have not been impressed with the 1974 Monfortino; its mouth-searing tannins seem entirely too excessive for its fruit. His Barolo Riservas, aged only a mere four to six years in wood, can also be excellent. The 1971 is superb, chewy, intense, and extremely full-bodied. In Conterno's Barolos one finds the essence of Barolo: scents of tar, leather, tobacco, ripe fruit, a massive, chewy texture, and gobs of tannins. The 1971 Riserva needs five to eight more years of cellaring; the 1971 Monfortino and the 1978 Monfortino need a decade.

DEFORVILLE *BARBARESCO* ★ ★

1980 Barbaresco	③	**87**
1983 Dolcetto d'Alba	②	**83**
1983 Grignolino d'Asti	①	**60**

This producer's best wines are his fleshy, deeply coloured 1983 Dolcetto and stylish Barbarescos. The 1980 Barbaresco is a real sleeper, rich, supple, fully mature, with an expansive, tarry, smoky, ripe fruity bouquet, and lush flavours.

DESSILANI *GATTINARA/SPANNA/GHEMME* ★ ★ ★

1978 Caramino Riserva	②	**84**
1974 Gattinara Riserva	②	**85**
1979 Gattinara Riserva	②	**83**
1978 Ghemme Riserva	②	**84**
1982 Spanna	①	**80**

Dessilani's wines offer good value. They are generally direct, robust, deeply fruity wines that lack finesse but more than make up for that deficiency with richness and unabashed fruitiness. On occasion, one seems to find a dirty, flawed wine. These are not cerebral wines, but drinking wines. The 1982 Spanna is robust, full-bodied with mushroom scents and flavours of black cherries. The 1978 Caramino has rich, chocolaty fruit, smoky flavours and an intense concentration of fruit. Let it breathe for one to two hours to allow some barnyard aromas that appear initially to blow off. The 1978 Ghemme is another rustic, large-scaled wine oozing with tarry, plummy, rich aromas and full-bodied flavours. The 1974 Gattinara is a more elegant, complex wine. It has rich, tarry, ripe, fruity flavours complemented nicely by the smell of damp earth and flowers. The 1979 Gattinara is similar, a touch lighter, but well made.

DOSIO *BAROLO* ★★★

1971 **Barolo Riserva**	④	**82**
1974 **Barolo Riserva**	④	**77**
1978 **Barolo Riserva**	④	**87**
1979 **Barolo Riserva**	③	**79**
1981 **Dolcetto d'Alba**	①	**80**
1983 **Dolcetto d'Alba**	①	**82**

I have had plenty of experience of tasting Dosio's wines. I find them good, sometimes irregular, but generally fairly priced. The best Dosio wine I have tasted is the 1978 Barolo, a rich, deep but forward wine that can be drunk now or cellared for another three to seven years. Dosio's Dolcetto d'Alba is usually a soundly made wine. Both the 1981 and 1983 have the requisite lush, plummy fruit that makes this wine easy to drink.

LUIGI EINAUDI *BAROLO* ★★★

1980 **Barolo**	④	**85**
1981 **Barolo**	③	**80**
1983 **Dolcetto**	②	**82**

Einaudi's style of Barolo is one that provides plenty of body, very good colour, and rich, ripe, rather soft, fruity flavours. The 1980 Barolo is delicious now, and shows good depth for this vintage. The 1981 is fruity but lighter. His Dolcetto is always made in a big, ripe, soft style. The 1983 merits interest.

FONTANAFREDDA *BAROLO* ★★★★

1978 **Barolo Bianca**	③	**85**
1978 **Barolo Delizia**	③	**88**
1978 **Barolo Gattinera**	③	**86**
1978 **Barolo Lazzarito**	③	**88**
1978 **Barolo La Rosa**	③	**87**

This modern winery perched in the hills of Barolo makes very good Barolo that can be applauded for its reasonable prices as well as high quality. The style of Fontanafredda's Barolos is classic – the wines take a good eight to ten years of cellaring *after* release to shed sufficient tannins. Somewhat confusing for the consumer is that Fontanafredda produces at least six different single-vineyard Barolos in top years such as 1978. The differences in taste are marginal, at least at this early stage of their lives. All the 1978s of Fontanafredda are dark in colour, with full body, gobs of hard tannins, excellent concentration, and tarry, rich, spicy bouquets. The difference in scores is negligible and largely attributable to the higher-ranked wines having more complex aromas. I would suggest cellaring them until at least 1992–1995. They will last for twenty years.

ANGELO GAJA *BARBARESCO* ★ ★ ★ ★ ★

1979 Barbaresco	④	85
1982 Barbaresco	⑤	87
1979 Barbaresco Costa Russi	⑤	85
1982 Barbaresco Costa Russi	⑤	93
1979 Barbaresco San Lorenzo	⑤	86
1982 Barbaresco San Lorenzo	⑤	90
1979 Barbaresco Sori Tilden	⑤	90
1982 Barbaresco Sori Tilden	⑤	95
1982 Cabernet Sauvignon Darmagi	⑤	84

I have on occasion been critical of Gaja's pricing policy, but I am a great admirer of this man, who has done so much to bring attention to the top Italian wines. His wines remain expensive; one must remember that they are rare items and it only takes one visit to his modern winery in Barbaresco to see that Gaja spares no expense in making wine. He is a pioneer in small cask ageing (as practised in Bordeaux) of his best wine, a practice that has been criticized by some but in general has had a major impact on some of Italy's best winemakers. He is at the forefront of his profession, and while it may take a decade to see if his small barrel ageing methods are best for Italy's top red wines, Gaja's results to date speak for themselves. His wines are grandiose examples of winemaking at its best and most adventurous. Gaja's 1982 Barbarescos are to me his greatest wines to date; his new experiments with Chardonnay and Cabernet Sauvignon in the foothills of Piedmont look promising – as well as disconcerting – to his neighbours. His 1979 ordinary Barbaresco can still be found quite inexpensively, compared with the 1982; it is drinking well now and is a good introduction to the Gaja winemaking style. As for the 1982s, the Barbaresco is quite impressive with a rich, ruby colour, a toasty vanillin, oaky scent to the bouquet, some of the tell-tale tarry character of Nebbiolo, and excellent length. There is plenty of tannin to this full-bodied wine, so give it eight to ten years of cellaring. The San Lorenzo is a denser wine than the regular Barbaresco, has even more depth and tannin, an outstanding aroma of ripe fruit and new oak, and ten to twenty years of evolution ahead of it. The most forward wine is the Costa Russi, a rich, very concentrated wine with an intense perfume of plummy, ripe fruit and oak. It has a good lashing of tannin but a more velvety, unctuous texture. It is a great Barbaresco that can use six to eight years of cellaring. Lastly, the Sori Tilden has awesome potential, provided one can wait a minimum of ten or more years. Very dark, very backward, but oh, so promising, this spectacular wine has layers of concentrated fruit, ripe tannins, a powerful, long finish, and a dramatic personality. The single-vineyard Barbarescos are rare (approximately 1,000 cases of each were produced) but the ordinary Barbaresco is more readily available. Gaja also produces a Cabernet Sauvignon that is quite overpriced, but well made, fruity, too obviously oaky, but encouraging.

BRUNO GIACOSA *BARBARESCO/BAROLO/ARNEIS* ★ ★ ★ ★

1980 Barbaresco Gallina	③	89
1982 Barbaresco Gallina	⑤	88
1978 Barbaresco Santo Stefano	⑤	95
1979 Barbaresco Santo Stefano	④	90
1980 Barbaresco Santo Stefano	④	89
1978 Barolo Bussia	⑤	88
1979 Barolo Bussia	⑤	90
1980 Barolo Rionda	⑤	84
1978 Barolo Rionda-Serralunga	⑤	94
1978 Barolo Rocche	⑤	90
1980 Barolo Rocche	③	89
1978 Barolo Villero	④	88
1979 Barolo Villero	④	90
1980 Barolo Villero	④	87

When I first wrote about Bruno Giacosa I called him Piedmont's best-kept secret. I have continued to follow his wines with an obsession befitting a man with the touch of genius he has. He owns no vineyards, preferring to purchase his grapes from Piedmont's best vineyards in the top vintage years; in lesser years he simply makes no wine. The quality of the wines is extraordinary; I have never tasted anything less than great wine from Giacosa. They are wonderfully opulent, highly aromatic, complex wines with layers and layers of ripe fruit and good, but not excessive, tannic backbones. If I said his top Barbarescos and Barolos can rival a great vintage of Pétrus for richness and complexity, few, I suspect, would believe it. However, Giacosa's wines are on that level; though hard to find and expensive. Giacosa's best wines are undoubtedly his Barbarescos from the Santo Stefano, Montefico, and Gallina vineyards, but I know of no Barolo producer who is able to get such a voluptuous richness and tannic clout to his wines as he somehow does. His Barolos from such single vineyards as Bussia, La Rocche, and Villero are sensational wines. His 1978 Barolo Serralunga from the Rionda vineyard is one of the greatest Barolos ever produced and is destined to live and improve for 15–25 years. Italy's greatest winemaker? For me, yes. His 1971 and 1978 Barbaresco Santo Stefanos are still the greatest Italian wines I have ever tasted.

All the above wines are available in small quantities. Because of his winemaking style, his wines can be drunk young but improve for ten to fifteen years after their release.

MARCHESI DI GRESY *BARBARESCO* ★★★★

1979 Barbaresco Martinenga...	③	**84**
1980 Barbaresco Martinenga...	③	**84**
1982 Barbaresco Martinenga...	④	**85**
1979 Barbaresco Martinenga Camp Gros..................	④	**89**
1982 Barbaresco Martinenga Camp Gros..................	⑤	**88**
1982 Barbaresco Martinenga Gaiun	⑤	**90**
1984 Martinenga...	③	**82**

I have only tasted three vintages of the di Gresy wines, but have been impressed by their harmony and elegance. They are not as rich and powerful as those of Bruno Giacosa, Gaja, or Castello di Neive, but lean stylistically towards the Barbarescos produced by Ceretto from his Bricco Asili vineyard. Gresy produces his Barbarescos from a vineyard called Martinenga. Within that vineyard he separately vinifies two choice lots called Camp Gros and Gaiun. All the wines offer high quality and surprising complexity and finesse. Curiously, I thought the 1979 Martinenga Camp Gros, with its rich cherry fruit, spicy, leather-scented bouquet, and ripe flavours, a worthy rival of the 1982s, the latter of which are from a much more highly touted vintage. Top marks did, however, go to the 1982 Marinenga Gaiun, a beautifully made wine that needs five to six years to soften and shed its tannins, but has a super bouquet of ripe cherry fruit, spicy oak, and tobacco. The 1982 Martinenga Camp Gros is similarly styled, only more backward and closed, but rich and elegant. I liked the 1982 Martinenga quite a bit, but it does not have the concentration of the aforementioned wines; it should be ready by 1990–1992. For current drinking, in addition to the 1979 Martinenga Camp Gros, the regular 1979 Martinenga Barbaresco is supple, fragrant, and tasting quite good. The 1980 Martinenga is equally good, a trifle firmer and more compact, but very well made. Lastly, the intensely fruity and elegant 1984 Martinenga is light but smells of cherry jam and is delicious on the palate. These are impressive Barbarescos.

G. MASCARELLO *BAROLO* ★★★★

1978 Barbaresco Bernadotti	③	85
1979 Barbaresco Chirella	③	83
1979 Barbera Ginestra	②	84
1978 Barolo Monprivato	③	90
1979 Barolo Monprivato	③	87
1978 Barolo Villero	③	87
1979 Barolo Villero	③	84
1982 Dolcetto Boscarello	②	78

Mascarello's wines are among the deepest-coloured, richest, and most tannic produced in Barolo. One suspects that if Giacomo Conterno bottled his Barolo after four or five years rather than ten, it would look as ruby/purple and be as dense and backward as those of G. Mascarello. His best wine is the Barolo from the Monprivato vineyard, which in vintages such as 1978 will last 30–40 years and not be drinkable until 1995 or later. It is a monumental wine. The 1979 Monprivato is only a shade lighter and should be mature by 1990. The other Mascarello wines are cut from the same cloth, dark, rich, rather boldly styled, and very tannic. Mascarello's 1979 Barbera from the Ginestra vineyard, normally a variety I find too acidic and austere, is quite good in this instance. Before you rush out to buy a Mascarello wine, be sure you have the requisite patience to wait for it to mature, especially the Barolos and Barbarescos.

GIOVANNINI MORESCO *BARBARESCO* ★★★

1978 Barbaresco Pajore	④	85
1979 Barbaresco Pajore	④	86

To my knowledge, Moresco produces only Barbaresco. The three vintages I have tasted have been good – elegant, spicy, clean wines that in style resemble those of di Gresy and Ceretto. Moresco's Barbaresco comes from a single vineyard, Podere de Pajore. The 1967, tasted in 1985, seemed more like a great Burgundy than a Barbaresco. His 1978, acclaimed in his native Piedmont, is good, and certainly flavourful, with ripe cherry fruit in evidence. The 1979 shows more concentration and perfume than the 1978, and the promise of complexity and a velvety richness if cellared to 1987-88.

Given the three wines of Moresco that I have tasted, I would question his exalted status among Barbaresco's élite winemakers.

PASQUERO-SECONDO *BARBARESCO* ★★★

1979 Barbaresco d'Paytin	③	76
1980 Barbaresco d'Paytin	③	75
1982 Barbaresco d'Paytin	③	86

This tiny producer produces gentle, supple, medium-weight Barbarescos of which the best come from the Sori d'Paytin vineyard. His 1978 is excellent, a benchmark standard for the more elegant, less robust and muscular style of Barbaresco that is most consistently practised by di Gresy and Ceretto. Since 1978, his wines have been good but hardly inspiring. The 1982 Sori d'Paytin is very promising. It is supple, deeply fruity, with ripe, very fleshy, forward flavours of ripe black cherries, medium to full body, and a good, long finish. It should be ready by 1989–1990. Neither the 1980 nor the 1979 exhibit sufficient fruit to warrant interest. Both are dry, rather lean, austere wines.

PELISSERO *BARBARESCO* ★★★

1978 Barbaresco	③	84

The only vintage I have tasted is 1978: a powerful, very full-bodied, broodingly backward, dark and tannic wine. Its cherry, ripe, sweet fruit more than balances out the huge tannic clout; however, I wouldn't dare drink it before 1990–1992.

PRODUTTORI DI BARBARESCO *BARBARESCO* ★★★★

1979 Barbaresco Asili	③	89
1979 Barbaresco Moccagatta	③	87
1979 Barbaresco Ovello	③	85
1979 Barbaresco Pora	③	85
1979 Barbaresco Rabaja	③	87
1979 Barbaresco Rio Sordo	③	85

Many wine enthusiasts take a dim view of co-operative-produced wines. There are indeed growers' co-operatives that are poorly run, but this co-operative of upwards of 50 Barbaresco growers is considered by many to be one of the finest in the world. Should you find any of Produttori's 1978 Barbarescos still languishing on the shelves, don't hesitate to grab the Moccagatta, Pora, Montefico, and Rabaja vineyard-designated Barbarescos. All could use cellaring until 1990–1995. As for the 1979s, they are an impressive group as well, though marginally less concentrated and tannic than the 1978s. While none is fully mature, they all have such ripeness of fruit that they are accessible. The Asili has a striking bouquet of rich cherry fruit, saddle leather, and flowers. Rich and supple with layers of fruit, it is the standard bearer for the class of 1979 Produttori wines. The Rabaja is dark and rich, more muscular and closed; it needs until 1990 to reach its peak. The Ovello, Pora, Rio Sordo, and Moccagatta are still quite youthful, closed, and young. Of these four wines the Moccagatta looks to be the most impressive. I would keep an eye out for the 1982s when they are released as these wines represent outstanding values.

PRUNOTTO *BAROLO* ★★★

1978 Barolo	③	78
1979 Barolo	②	82
1978 Barolo Bussia	③	84
1979 Barolo Bussia	③	85
1978 Barolo Cannubi	③	80
1979 Barolo Cannubi	③	83
1978 Barolo Ginestra	③	86
1979 Barolo Ginestra	③	86

A very traditional producer of Piedmontese wines, Prunotto's wines tend to be hard, very dry and tannic, and sometimes coarse. I was not fond of the firm's 1974s and even the 1971s were less successful than other producers. All the grapes for Prunotto wines are purchased, and the wine is aged for a long time in large oak casks. The wines are dense and chewy, and those who like this rough-and-tumble, macho style of Barolo may score them higher than I do. Curiously, I thought Prunotto's 1979s more fruity and successful than his 1978s, an overall better vintage. In both vintages, I preferred the Ginestra because it has an extroverted, rich, chewy, fruity character, and has plenty of tannin. The 1978s should peak between 1990 and 2005; the 1979s between 1987 and 1995.

RENATO RATTI *BAROLO/DOLCETTO* ★★★★★

1979 Barolo	②	78
1978 Barolo Marcenasco	④	90
1979 Barolo Marcenasco	④	85
1980 Barolo Marcenasco	④	84
1981 Barolo Marcenasco Conca	④	84
1979 Barolo Marcenasco Rocche	④	87
1980 Barolo Marcenasco Rocche	④	85
1981 Barolo Marcenasco Rocche	④	86

Ratti's sensibly made wines combine richness with lushness, power with finesse at a consistently high level of quality, even in difficult vintages such as 1980 and 1981. There is almost a sweetness to his wines as a result of picking his grapes at a very high level of maturity. His wines are produced in temperature-controlled stainless steel vats and aged in casks only for the minimum time mandated by Italian law. Unlike some of his peers, who appear to have gone too far with their compromises to the modern taste for soft, ready-to-drink wines, Ratti's wines are not wimpish but rich, full-bodied, intense wines with ten to fifteen years ageing potential in the top vintages. However, since he retains such a marvellous balance and depth of fruit to the wines, they are approachable when young. His Barolos are wines to search out, particularly the special Marcenasco Vineyard wines that occasionally list the subsections of that vineyard, Conca and Rocche, as well. His 1978s can be drunk now, but need another four to five years of cellaring. His 1979s are fully mature, his 1980s almost mature, and his 1981s great successes for the vintage. His Dolcetto from the Colombe vineyard is the benchmark standard for all other Dolcettos in Piedmont. Unfortunately, too little of it is available – it is a captivating, lush, fruity wine that is a joy to drink.

GIUSEPPI RINALDI *BAROLO* ★ ★ ★

1982 Barbera d'Alba	①	65
1970 Barolo Brunate	⑤	72
1971 Barolo Brunate	⑤	88
1974 Barolo Brunate	⑤	86
1978 Barolo Brunate	④	87
1979 Barolo Brunate	④	78
1980 Barolo Brunate	③	75
1982 Barolo Brunate	⑤	88

One taste of this man's wine reveals a very traditional approach to Barolo winemaking. These are rather huge, intense, very aromatic, very chewy, very tannic, and very large-scaled wines that may well intimidate neophyte tasters. The three stars are the 1978, 1974, and 1971. The surprise is the 1974, a vintage that the Piedmontese congnoscenti hold in high regard, but in which the reality is often far less encouraging. Rinaldi's 1974 is almost mature; rich, chocolaty, smoky, tarry notes are pervasive in its bouquet. Rich, deep, and full-bodied, it should age well for another four to five years. The 1971 is at its peak; rich, chewy, lush flavours, an altogether overwhelming array of aromas ranging from mushrooms to road tar to spring flowers. Massive on the palate, with some volatile acidity present, it is a textbook, big, old-style Barolo. Both the 1978 and 1982 may turn out, circa 1995–2000, to be the best wines. Both have layers of ripe, dense fruit, huge body, and mouth-searing tannins. The 1970 was totally oxidized and could not be judged, the 1979 was bitterly tannic, and the 1980 was excessively volatile. G. Rinaldi looks to be a hit-or-miss producer, but in the top vintages he seems right on target.

ROAGNA *BARBARESCO* ★ ★ ★

1982 Barbaresco	③	**78**
1979 Crichet Pajè	③	**86**
1982 Crichet Pajè	③	**80**
Opera Prima Non-Vintage	③	**60**

I have enjoyed Roagna's wine, so I was surprised to see the new releases do so poorly. The 1979 Crichet Pajè is an extremely elegant Barbaresco for dinking now. Loaded with spicy vanillin oak and ripe cherry fruit, this wine has excellent balance and a surprising measure of finesse. However, the 1982 Barbaresco is lean, quite short and insubstantial on the palate, and really atypical for the vintage. The 1982 Crichet Pajè should, given the vintage, be a bigger, richer, better wine than the 1979. It is not. It tastes lean, and, while it has a nice, attractive bouquet, seems disappointing for Roagna and the vintage. The new non-vintage Opera Prima, vinified and aged in small oak casks, tastes sour, with the new oak totally obliterating any trace of Nebbiolo fruit. It is an experiment that seems to have missed its mark by quite a lot.

L. SANDRONE *BAROLO* ★ ★ ★ ★

1980 Barolo	③	**84**
1981 Barolo	③	**82**
1982 Barolo	③	**90**
1984 Dolcetto d'Alba	②	**80**
1985 Dolcetto d'Alba	②	**85**

Sandrone is a very small producer of both Barolo and Dolcetto. His wines are very dark in colour, quite rich, robust, and, in the case of his Barolo, very tannic and potentially very long-lived wine. The superstar is the 1982 Barolo, a chewy, very concentrated, full-bodied wine exuding scents of chocolate, leather, and road tar. It is explosively rich and deep, lingers and lingers, and should be quite a stunning Barolo circa 1995–2000. Don't miss the 1985 Dolcetto either.

VALENTINO *BAROLO/DOLCETTO* ★ ★ ★ ★

1978 Barolo	③	**89**
1979 Barolo	③	**87**
1980 Bricco Manzoni	②	**85**

1985 Dolcetto d'Alba .... ② **84**

An excellent producer whom I have only followed since 1978, but whose wines show top-flight winemaking skills. Furthermore, the prices are extremely reasonable. His blended wine, Bricco Manzoni, is ripe, earthy, quite delicious, and full-bodied. It is meant to be drunk over the next three to four years. The 1978 and 1979 Barolos are rich, smoky, tarry-scented wines, quite full-bodied, very cleanly made, with broad, ripe flavours. The 1979 is for drinking now and over the next five to six years; the 1978 is for cellaring until 1990 and then enjoying for the next decade. Don't overlook the exuberant, intense, very fruity, rich, blackberry-scented and flavoured Dolcetto. It is ideal for drinking over the next few years.

VALLANA *SPANNA/GATTINARA* ★ ★ ★

1978 Barbera	①	**83**
1978 Boca	②	**74**
1980 Bonarda	①	**73**
Bucciarossa Non-Vintage	①	*81*
1979 Gattinara	⑤	**85**
1966 Spanna Montalbano	③	**89**
1967 Spanna Montalbano	③	**85**
1969 Spanna Montalbano	③	**86**
1974 Spanna Montalbano	②	**85**
1977 Spanna Montalbano	②	**84**
1966 Spanna Piemonte	④	**87**
1968 Spanna Piemonte	③	**85**
1974 Spanna Piemonte	②	**86**
1976 Spanna Piemonte	②	**85**
1978 Spanna Piemonte	②	**87**
1967 Spanna Traversagna	③	**86**
1977 Spanna Traversagna	②	**82**

One of the most extraordinary individuals I have ever met was Vallana. I can vividly remember him telling me that if he could hold a glass of wine parallel with his abdomen and smell its bouquet, the vintage was great. Some of his wines have been among the finest Italian red wines I have ever drunk. His 1958, 1961, and 1964 Spannas Campa Raudii were superb wines that are still evolving and continue to be outstanding today. Vallana's peers in Piedmont always accused Vallana of illegally blending in juice from southern Italy; an allegation that was never proven, and whether it is true or not, the bottom line was that no one in Gattinara or Spanna (and few in Barolo or Barbaresco) have produced such majestic wines. Reports are that Vallana and his wines have slipped, but as the scores above attest, his 1978 Spanna is excellent and 1979 Gattinara better than any his winemaking rivals in Gattinara have produced. His wines are not very elegant, but rather very rich, dense, powerful, deeply coloured, somewhat rustic wines, that age beautifully for 15–25 years.

Of the above wines, all are quite ready to drink except for the 1979 Gattinara, which is quite dark in colour, rich, chewy, robust, and quite tannic. It should hit its peak between 1990 and 2000. The 1978 Spanna is excellent, with a rich, intense bouquet of cedar, tobacco, chocolate, and smoky, tarry fruit. It has layers of fruit and will improve for at least another four to five years. Both 1977 Spannas are good, particularly in view of the horrible vintage conditions. Among the older wines, the 1974, 1969, 1967, and 1966 Spanna Montalbanos are lush, rich, very aromatic wines with bouquets of sweet cedar, smoke, coffee, and ripe, tarry fruit. Only the 1966 Spanna Piemonte smells a little odd at first, but with two to three hours of breathing, cleans up, and becomes intensely perfumed with scents of tar, hickory, fennel, and ripe, plummy fruit. It is very rich and concentrated on the palate. Vallana's wines are among the most individualistic produced. They are very old-style, rich, chewy, unfiltered wines that must be rested and decanted one to two hours before serving.

VIETTI *BAROLO/DOLCETTO* ★ ★ ★ ★

1982 Barbaresco	③	82
1981 Barbaresco Masseria	③	80
1982 Barbaresco Masseria	③	86
1980 Barbera Rocche	①	78
1978 Barolo Briacca	③	87
1980 Barolo Briacca	②	81
1978 Barolo Rocche	③	88
1980 Barolo Rocche	②	80
1982 Barolo Rocche	④	90
1985 Dolcettto	②	85
1985 Dolcetto Disa	②	85
1982 Dolcetto San Giorgio	①	86
1982 Fioretto	②	78
1982 Nebbiolo d'Alba	①	84

Alfredo Currado is the proprietor and winemaker of the Vietti winery and in addition to being one of the most respected talents of the region is a remarkably gentle and gracious man. He continues to increase the number of different bottlings of wine, preferring to vineyard designate everything on his distinctive artistic labels. His best wines are his Barolos, which usually need ten to fiteen years of cellaring. In all of Vietti's wines, he achieves a dense, rich colour and avoids excessive cask ageing that can lead to oxidation and volatile acidity problems. His 1971 Briacca was still not fully mature when tasted in October 1985. His 1971 Rocche is just now entering its plateau of maturity. His 1978 Barolos are outstanding successes and his 1982s perhaps his finest wines to date, particularly the fabulously rich, full-bodied, dense Rocche. His Dolcettos are usually quite deeply coloured and fruity. The 1982 Dolcetto San Giorgio is as good as Dolcetto can get: plummy, soft, decadently fruity and opulent. The 1985s are also gorgeously fruity and supple, and significantly better than his disappointing 1984 Dolcetto. The Fioretto, a blended wine that Vietti has introduced, is impressively dark in colour, but rather dull and flat on the palate and clearly in need of some acidity. His 1982 Barbaresco is forward but supple, very fruity and deep with at least a decade of cellaring potential. His 1982 Barolo Rocche is the best Barolo I have yet tasted from Vietti – a profound wine.

PIEDMONT'S WHITE WINES

Piedmont does produce a handful of interesting white wines. Of course, the region also makes an ocean of Asti Spumante, the ever-popular, sweet, sparkling wine that can be good but has lost favour among serious wine enthusiasts because so much of it is cloyingly sweet, dull, and heavy. The serious dry white wines of Piedmont are the Gavi white wines made from the Cortese grape and the Arneis white wines produced from the grape of the same name. There are also experimental plantings of Chardonnay, with Angelo Gaja's being the most promising, and a very low-alcohol, delicious, fresh, very fragrant, slightly sparkling Muscat-based wine called Moscato d'Asti, which in the hands of producers such as Vietti, Giacosa, and Vignaioli Santo Stefano of Ceretto puts any Asti Spumante to shame.

ARNEIS DEI ROERI

1985 Castello di Neive .... ③ **87**
1985 Ceretto .... ③ **86**
1985 Giacosa .... ③ **88**
1985 Rabino S. Vittoria .... ① **82**
1984 Vietti .... ② **75**

Arneis is a wine with a historical reputation and with perhaps as much potential as any white grape yet planted in Piedmont. The quantities produced to date have been very small. Both Castello di Neive and Giacosa produced very fine 1983, 1984, and 1985 Arneis wines. Giacosa's is lighter and more elegant; Castello di Neive's richer, fatter and a more powerful wine.

Vietti also produces Arneis, which is quite dry with a taste and scent of almonds, good body, and loads of fresh fruit – however, I have been unimpressed with it. The famous red wine producer Ceretto made an Arneis in 1985, and it is excellent, fresh, loaded with fruit, but requires drinking over the next one to two years.

GAVI AND CORTESE DI GAVI

1983 Broglia Fasciola	③	85
1983 Pio Cesare	②	85
1984 Pio Cesare	②	82
1985 Pio Cesare	③	85
1984 Contratto	②	84
1984 Gallo d'Oro	②	84
1983 La Scolca	④	84
1984 Villa Sparina	③	84

Gavi white wines have had considerable acclaim but, while generally pleasant, dry, austere wines, they are considerably overpriced when looked at with respect to what is available elsewhere from Italy. In style, they have an austerity and a bone-dry, almost severe character that is vaguely reminiscent of a French Chablis that has been tank-fermented and not exposed to any ageing in wood casks. The 1983s are still on the shelves and are better wines from a fruitier, riper, richer vintage than the new releases. The 1984s are by and large ungenerous and too severe. The 1985s are excellent but are just now coming on the market. Certainly, Pio Cesare's Cortese di Gavi confirmed the vintage's fine reputation. Should you still be interested, I recommend the above wines, keeping in mind that the 1983 is better as a general rule than the 1984, and 1985 potentially the best yet.

MOSCATO D'ASTI

1985 Ceretto Santo Stefano	②	87
1985 Dogliotti Caudrine	①	84
1985 B. Giacosa	②	85
1985 Rivetti	②	87
1985 Vietti	②	85

These exquisitely scented, moderately sweet Muscats are very low in alcohol (5%–7% is normal,) have intense bouquets of apricot, peaches, and other summer fruit, are light in body, and slightly sparkling. They are so fresh and youthful that they are a joy to drink either as an apéritif or with a fruit dessert. Fresh, vivacious, and lively, I recommend the above producers highly. These wines must be drunk within two years of their vintage; they will not keep.

TUSCANY

Tuscany's Reds • Brunello Di Montalcino, Chianti, etc.

The red wines of Tuscany are even more famous than the red wines of Piedmont. The diversity in winemaking styles, not to mention the range of quality, is enormous. This popular tourist region is of course most famous for its Chianti, the light to medium ruby-coloured wine of which I find the great majority frail, pale, and quite insipid. However, top-quality Chianti wine is made. Monsanto, Capannelle, Monte Vertine, Badia a Coltibuono, Ruffino, Castello di Rampolla, and Isole e Olena are a handful of producers who make world-class, serious wine of flavour and character.

Tuscany is also the home base for Italy's most expensive red wine, Brunello di Montalcino. This is an interesting wine, and usually over-oaked because of the ridiculous law that requires a minimum of three and a half years in wood. There are a lot of under-achievers in Brunello with famous names and expensive wines. Ironically, some of the best producers of Brunello di Montalcino are some of the least known and least publicized.

Other Tuscan red wines to take note of include a wine called Carmignano, in taste not distinguishable from a Chianti, and Vino Nobile di Montepulciano, another legendary Tuscan wine that only rarely lives up to its historical reputation of quality.

Yet the most interesting wines being produced in Tuscany may well turn out to be wines made outside the Italian wine laws and not entitled to appellation status. Over the last decade, many top producers inspired by oenological practices in Bordeaux, and also by Piero Antinori of Tuscany and Angelo Gaja in Piedmont, have been making more and more wines that are either 100% Sangiovese (the basic red grape of Chianti and Brunello) or Sangiovese/Cabernet blends. These wines, often aged à la Bordeaux in small new oak casks, have proved to be exceptionally good, ageworthy and, despite high price tags, very popular with wine enthusiasts. Most of them are infinitely better, richer wines than the great majority of Chiantis. At present, I am most impressed by such wines as Monte Vertine's Le Pergole Torte, Il Palazzino's Grosso Senese, Castello di Volpaia's Coltassaia, Antinori's Tignanello, Villa Cafaggio's Solatio Basilica, Avignonesi's Grifi, San Guido's Sassicaia, Castello di Rampolla's Samarco, and the Monte Antico. Given the high quality of many of these wines and the enthusiastic reaction they have received from consumers, one can expect many more like them to appear on the market even though they can legally only be called Vino da Tavola. These revolutionary new wines are, however, not cheap – expect to pay £7-£15 a bottle for them.

QUICK VINTAGE GUIDE

1986 Not nearly up to the quality of the exceptional 1985s, the 1986s from Tuscany are lighter yet fruity, medium-bodied wines that will provide good drinking early on.

1985 As in Piedmont, there is great enthusiasm for this vintage. No one yet has said it is the vintage of the century, but it is expected to be one of the very best vintages in the last 20–25 years. It was a hot, drought year.

1984 A dreadful year, much worse in Tuscany than in Piedmont to the north. Rain and a paucity of sunshine were the culprits. No doubt the trade will say the wines are light and commercial, but at this point this looks to be a vintage to pass up.

1983 Quite highly regarded, Tuscany had weather conditions similar to those experienced in Bordeaux hundreds of miles to the west. A drought year of intense heat caused sugars and the consequent alcohol level to skyrocket in the grapes. The reports are that the wines are ripe, alcoholic, fat, low in acidity, and jammy, with deep layers of fruit.

1982 Considered more classic than 1983, which I suppose means less powerful and less opulently fruity and rich wines. Certainly a very good vintage with firm tannins, good depth, and ripeness. My tasting notes indicate that the vintage is the best since 1975, maybe 1971. A year to be taken seriously. For Brunello di Montalcino, it is the best vintage since 1970.

1981 An average vintage of light, pleasant, rather frail wines. Most are fully mature. Only a handful will get better.

1980 An average vintage of light, soft, easy-to-drink wines. They require drinking up.

1979 A good vintage of wine with more flesh and stuffing than either 1980 or 1981. As in most of Europe, a gigantic crop was harvested.

1978 Rather highly regarded, but I have never found the wines to be terribly exciting, either in Brunello or Chianti.

1977 Rather successful, particularly in view of the negative publicity surrounding this vintage in Europe. Most Brunellos and Chiantis have more fruit and character than the more highly rated wines of 1978.

1976 For Tuscany a disastrous vintage because of heavy rains that diluted the grapes.

1975 A very good vintage, 1975 was initially claimed by the producers of Chianti and Brunello to be a great vintage, but it is not. All of the wines are fully mature and should be drunk up over the next few years.

1974 An average year of pleasant but rather charmless wines that have lacked flesh and fruit. Most are now too old to drink.

1973 It has been a good five years since I last tasted a 1973 Chianti or Brunello. The wines were never very attractive, were excessively light and feeble, and I would suspect are now totally decrepit.

1972 Like most of Europe, a wet, cold summer precluded the grapes from reaching maturity. Most of the better producers did not declare a vintage, preferring to declassify their entire crop. A disaster.

1971 Arguments among Chianti-lovers have long raged as to which was the greater vintage, 1971 or 1970. The 1971s, rich, alcoholic, sumptuous wines, drank well young but are now tiring. They can when well stored, be delicious, voluptuous, rich wines that are full of fruit, but even the best-preserved examples of this vintage should be drunk immediately.

1970 Unquestionably a greater vintage for Brunello di Montalcino than 1971, but in Chianti most observers have given 1971 the edge. However, the 1970 Chiantis, less flashy and flamboyant in their youth, have opened and blossomed in ageing. The Chiantis from this vintage, overshadowed by the 1971s, can offer many surprises. The best Brunellos are sensational and will last at least another decade.

A GUIDE TO TUSCANY'S BEST PRODUCERS OF CHIANTI, BRUNELLO, AND VINO NOBILE DI MONTEPULCIANO

★★★★★ Outstanding Producers

Altesino (Brunello)
Campogiovanni (Brunello)
Constanti (Brunello)
Monsanto (Chianti)
Pertimali (Brunello)
Il Poggione (Brunello)
Castello di Rampolla (Chianti)

★★★★ Excellent Producers

Antinori (Chianti)
Avignonesi (Vino Nobile)
Badia a Coltibuono (Chianti)
Berardenga (Chianti)
Boscarelli (Vino Nobile)
Capannelle (Chianti)
Carparzo (Brunello)
Castello de Castellina (Chianti)
Fontodi (Chianti)
Isole e Olena (Chianti)
Lisini (Brunello)
Monte Antico (Tuscany)

Monte Vertine (Chianti)
Il Palazzino (Chianti)
Ruffino (Chianti)

San Guido (Tuscany)
Castello di Volpaia (Chianti)

★ ★ ★ Good Producers

Barbi (Brunello)
Biondi Santi (Brunello)
Casale del Bosco (Brunello)
Camigliano (Brunello)
Capezzana (Vino Nobile)
Caprili (Brunello)
Fanetti (Vino Nobile)
Fassati (Vino Nobile)
La Fortuna (Brunello)

Montesodi (Chianti)
Castello di Nipozzano (Chianti)
Nozzole (Chianti)
Riecine (Chianti)
San Filippo (Brunello)
Savignola Paolina (Chianti)
Villa Cafaggio (Chianti)
Villa Selvapiana (Chianti)

NEW BREED REDS · A QUICK REFERENCE GUIDE TO THE BEST SANGIOVESE- OR CABERNET-BASED WINES

Borro Cepparello
  Isole e Olena (Chianti)
Brusco di Barbi
  Barbi (Brunello)
Ca del Pazzo
  Carpazo (Brunello)
Capannelle Rosso
  Capannelle (Chianti)
Coltassala
  Castello di Volpaia (Chianti)
Flaccianello della Pieve
  Fontodi (Chianti)
Grifi *Avignonesi* (Vino Nobile)
Grosso Senese
  Il Palazzino (Chianti)
Le Pergole Torte
  Monte Vertine (Chianti)

Sangioveto Grosso
  Monsanto (Chianti)
Il Sodaccio
  Monte Vertine (Chianti)
Monte Antico
  Monte Antico (Tuscany)
Palazzo Altesi
  Altesino (Brunello)
Sammarco
  Castello dei Rampolla (Chianti)
San Giorgio *Lungarotti* (Umbria)
Sassicaia *Antinori* (Tuscany)
Solaia *Antinori* (Tuscany)
Solatia Basilica
  Villa Cafaggio (Chianti)
Tignanello
  Antinori (Chianti)

TUSCANY · A BUYING STRATEGY

The buying strategy for Tuscany is simple – buy without hesitation the 1982s and 1983s, this area's best overall vintages since 1970 and 1971. These fruity, ripe, rich wines will give great pleasure for most of the next five years. The top Brunellos and new-breed Sangiovese- or Cabernet-based wines will provide fascinating drinking for at least the next decade. As for Chianti, unless you are buying wine from a great producer like Monsanto in a great vintage, you are best advised to steer clear of anything older than four to five years for the simple reason that Chianti is a notoriously short-lived wine. In short, your first choice should be the 1982s from Tuscany and second choice the 1983s. For Tuscany's white wines, the 1985s are vastly superior to the 1984s.

ANTINORI ★★★★

1980 Tignanello	③	83
1981 Tignanello	③	88
1982 Tignanello	③	90

Tignanello, a blend of roughly 80%–85% Sangiovese and 15%–20% Cabernet, is one of the most successful new breeds of Italian wines. Unfortunately, its price continues to escalate. The 1982 and 1981 are the best Tignanellos released yet. Both have sweet, oaky, ripe, fruity, complex bouquets, supple but firm, deep flavours, and medium to full body. The 1981 can be drunk now but will likely improve for four to five years. The 1982, a richer, more tannic wine, ideally needs three to four years. The 1980 is less opulent and charming with a more compact feel on the palate, but still flavourful and attractive. I would drink the 1980 over the next two to three years.

AVIGNONESI ★★★★

1981 Grifi	③	87
1982 Grifi	③	86
1983 Grifi	③	88

This wine is the product of the fine Avignonesi winery. It is also a blend of Sangiovese and Cabernet with the Sangiovese representing 70%–75% of the total. The three vintages released to date have all been very impressive yet differently styled. The 1981 is rich but very elegant. It exhibits cherry fruit, oak, flowers, and vanillin in its bouquet. Lush and rich on the palate, it should continue to drink well for four to five years. The 1982 is reputedly better, but in two separate tastings it had plenty of potential, a deeper, richer-looking colour, more tannin and oak, but just does not 'sing' as my English counterparts would say. It definitely needs two to three years more of bottle age. At present, the most impressive wine of this trio is the 1983. It has a very complex bouquet of cigar box spices, ripe, rich cherry fruit, and noticeable oak; this is a full-bodied, tannic wine with plenty of rich, supple fruit and an alcoholic clout to its finish. It should age well for upwards of a decade.

CAPEZZANA ★★★

1980 Ghiaie Della Furba	③	86

From the best producer of Carmignano in Tuscany, Capezzana also produces a tiny amount of this wine, a 70%

Cabernet Sauvignon, 30% Merlot blend. The 1980 has a textbook blackcurrant, cedary, olive-scented bouquet, good firm tannins, and a medium body.

CARPARZO ★★★★

1982 Ca del Pazzo... ④ **82**
1983 Ca del Pazzo... ④ **86**

Produced by the excellent Brunello producer Carparzo, from a 50-50 blend of Cabernet Sauvignon and Sangiovese, the 1982 has dark ruby colour, good depth and ripeness of fruit, but lacks complexity and tastes a bit dull and one-dimensional. The 1983 seems to show greater depth, richness, and more complexity in its bouquet. Both should age for five to seven years.

CASTELLARE DI CASTELLINA ★★★★

1982 I Sodi di S. Niccolo... ④ **87**

A 100% Sangiovese wine, the 1982, the only vintage I have tasted, was quite impressive. The bouquet suggests very ripe black cherries and chestnuts. Medium- to full-bodied, long, with good richness and length, this wine should continue to improve for at least four to six more years.

ISOLE E OLENA ★★★★

1982 Cepparello.. ③ **85**

A 100% Sangiovese wine with a very Bordeaux-like personality, the 1982 Cepparello has a dark ruby, deep colour, spice-box, rich, fruity bouquet, moderate levels of tannin, excellent ageing potential of five more years, and a clean, well-balanced feel. A young, promising wine.

MONSANTO ★★★★★

1974 Sangioveto Grosso... ④ **75–85**

Tasted twice, this 100% Sangiovese from Chianti's finest producer proved disappointing first but very good a second time. From the good bottle, the wine smelled like a textbook Graves, with a tobacco-scented, smoky, earthy bouquet. On the palate, the wine was rich, alcoholic, and quite big and aggressive. Will the real Sangioveto Grosso please come forth?

MONTE ANTICO ★★★★

1981 .... ① **86**
1983 .... ② **86**
1978 Riserva.. ② **86**
1979 Riserva.. ② **84**
1980 Riserva.. ② **87**

1981 Riserva .... ② **87**

This Tuscan wine is one of today's great values in complex, rich, savoury wines. It is made from 100% Sangiovese grapes grown on a vineyard adjacent to Brunello di Montalcino. In quality it challenges and even surpasses many Brunellos and virtually all of the medium-priced Chianti Classicos. Both the 1978 and 1979 Riservas are quite mature with rich, sweet, broad flavours, full-intensity bouquets of oriental spices, rich, berry fruit, smoked meats, and cinnamon. Both have a good deal of sediment and are obviously unfiltered wines, so care must be taken to decant them. The 1980 Riserva is similar, only darker in colour, a little firmer on the palate, but complex and aromatic, with sweet, ripe fruit displayed in abundance. The 1981 and 1983 are, given their complexity and quality, among the greatest Italian red wine values on the market. Both have a complex, cedary, roasted chestnut, spicy bouquet, long, deep, soft, lush flavours, and one to two more years of evolution ahead. The 1981 Riserva is styled similarly to the 1981 ordinary wine, perhaps a trifle less expansive on the palate, and capable of evolving four to five years.

MONTE VERTINE ★★★★

1982 Il Sodaccio .... ④ **83**
1979 Le Pergole Torte .... ④ **87**
1980 Le Pergole Torte .... ④ **84**
1982 Le Pergole Torte .... ③ **87**

Virtually anything produced by this grower in Tuscany is of high quality, from his Chianti Classicos to the limited bottlings of 100% Sangiovese Le Pergole Torte and Il Sodaccio. The best two vintages of Le Pergole Torte to date have been the 1979 and 1982. The 1979 is a delicious wine with an uncanny resemblance to an intensely fruity, spicy Zinfandel. It is richly scented and just now reaching its plateau of maturity. The 1980 is good, but has less length and dimension than the other vintages. The 1982, the new release, is quite exciting, with a toasty new oak bouquet filled with the scents of ripe cherry fruit. The impression on the palate is one of balanced richness, moderate tannins, and four to five years of further evolution. The 1982 Il Sodaccio is good but rather light and lacks the richness and dimension of the 1982 Le Pergole Torte.

IL PALAZZINO ★★★★

1982 Grosso Senese .... ③ **88**

A 100% Sangiovese wine from the excellent Chianti producer Il Palazzino, this wine is aged in small oak casks. Explosively rich on the palate with big, rich, fat, cherry and strawberry

flavours wrapped in spicy, toasty oak, this is a rather voluptuous wine, full-bodied, rather heady and high in alcohol, but
loaded with flavour and character. Drink over the next three
to four years.

CASTELLO DI RAMPOLLA ★ ★ ★ ★

1980 Sammarco..	④	**86**
1981 Sammarco..	④	**88**
1982 Sammarco..	④	**90**

A blend of 75% Cabernet Sauvignon and 25% Sangiovese, the
1980 is a rather forceful, rich, aggressive wine that exhibits a
lot of character and richness, has medium to full body, and a
tannic finish. It needs two to four more years to develop. The
1981 is richer, with a rounder, lusher texture. It has immense
appeal and should develop well for at least four to seven years.
The 1982 is a profound wine, rich, intense, with great length,
depth, and ten to fifteen years of ageing potential.

SAN GUIDO ★ ★ ★ ★

1980 Sassicaia..	④	**86**
1981 Sassicaia..	④	**91**
1982 Sassicaia..	⑤	**91**

This wine, which has gained something of a cult following, is a
blend of 95% Cabernet Sauvignon and 5% Cabernet Franc. It
is an excellent wine, to date the finest Cabernet wine made in
Italy. It is also very long-lived. A vertical tasting of the 1982,
1981, 1980, 1979, 1978, 1976, 1975, and 1971 I attended in
January 1986 proved quite conclusively that the 1981 and
1982 are the finest Sassicaias to date. Both are stunningly rich
wines not unlike great Médocs and both need ten to twelve
years of cellaring to peak. Following the 1981 and 1982, the
1978 and 1975 stand out. The 1980, which is widely available,
can be held five to six years, is dark ruby, elegant, and
showing well already. It does not have the concentration and
depth of the 1981, 1978, or 1975. Sassicaia remains hard to
find.

VINATTIERI ROSSO

1982	③	**83**

This wine was acquired in Italy, so I am not sure if it is
exported. The bouquet is richly fruity, oaky, and interesting.
On the palate, the wine is medium-bodied but rather short in
the finish and somewhat lacking in the mid-range. A blend of
Sangiovese and Cabernet that just misses the mark (perhaps
made from young vines).

CASTELLO DI VOLPAIA ★★★★

1981 Coltassala .... ③ *84*
1982 Coltassala .... ③ *87*

The Volpaia estate makes good Chianti and the Coltassala is the name of their 100% Sangiovese, small cask-aged Tuscan wine. The 1981 is a very good wine, oaky with plenty of black cherry fruit present, medium-bodied, rather graceful, and with a supple, lush finish; it can be drunk now or aged two to four more years. The 1982 is altogether a bigger, denser, deeper wine, medium to dark ruby with a ripe cherry, spicy, oaky bouquet, tannin, and medium- to full-bodied flavours. The 1982 needs three to five more years to reach its zenith.

BRUNELLO DI MONTALCINO AND ROSSO DI MONTALCINO

Tuscany's and Italy's most expensive red wine is, in reality, rarely worth its stiff price. That is not to suggest that good Brunello cannot be found, but the romantic and historical accounts of this wine seem to have more to do with its legendary status than the reality of its flavour depth, dimension, and complexity. I have tasted a lot of Brunello di Montalcino and can remember only four great bottles ever tasted: the 1970 Constanti, 1970 Il Poggione, 1970 Barbi, and 1975 Altesino. That is a rather pitiful percentage for a great wine, yet it confirms the fact that Brunello di Montalcino is the Chambertin of Italy – always outrageously priced and overrated, but rarely great. The most famous producer, Biondi Santi, gets outrageously high prices for recent vintages of his wines and they are among the most disappointing wines of this region. From a consumer's perspective, I would advise strongly to boycott these wines unless you can find the top wines of Brunello, which unfortunately are among the hardest to find since three of the top five producers, Altesino, Pertimali, and Constanti, have very limited quantities to sell.

ALTESINO ★★★★★

1979 .... ④ *89*
1980 .... ④ *85*

The only difference in these two wines is that the 1979 tastes richer, more intense, and has a more complex bouquet. The 1980 is rather light for Altesino, but quite supple, very fruity, with smoky, ripe, plummy fruit, medium body and a good finish. The 1979 is quite rich and full-bodied, deep with layers of tarry, smoky fruit, and five to eight more years of improvement ahead of it. Altesino also produces an excellent single-vine-yard-designated Brunello that I have not tasted since 1975.

BARBI ★★★

1977	⑤	85
1978	④	78
1979	④	80
1978 Riserva	⑤	83

This producer was my benchmark Brunello producer before I discovered the likes of Il Poggione, Altesino, and Carparzo. Some of the older vintages are excellent. The 1964, 1971, and fabulous 1970 are memorably good Brunellos. Since the mid-seventies, the style of wine here has been lightened up and, while Barbi used to be one of the best, they are now in the second tier of Brunello producers. Perhaps this is only a temporary thing. Of the above wines, the 1979 and 1978 regular bottlings are pleasant, light, rather straightforward wines. They lack richness and depth. The 1978 Riserva shows some potential, but again does not have much of a finish or depth. The best current vintage is the regular 1977, which has an expansive, Burgundian, earthy, richly fruity bouquet, medium body, and lush fruit.

BIONDI SANTI ★★★

1977	⑤	82
1978	⑤	77
1979	⑤	70
1970 Riserva	⑤	86
1971 Riserva	⑤	85
1975 Riserva	⑤	87
1977 Riserva	⑤	80

This estate is an easy target for criticism. Prices for their wines are quite absurd, and while the wines are not bad (in fact the 1975 Riserva is very good) there are far too many mediocre wines. Not once have I tasted a great wine from Biondi Santi, although cask samples of the 1982 and 1985 looked superb. At a blind tasting several years ago, Biondi Santi vintages in the sixties and early seventies did not fare well against the competition. Of course, much is made of the fact that these wines need 2–24 hours of aeration, but I have done that only to find that they get more astringent and bitter in the glass, not better. For me the problem with these wines (forgetting the high prices) is that they are far too tannic and the tannins too often are dry and bitter. In short, the wines are unpleasant to drink, and one wonders how the wine can command the price it does. Of the above vintages opened and examined over a 48-hour period, only one wine improved in the glass – the 1975 Riserva – and it was very good when it was first poured. The 1979 and 1978 are deficient in fruit. The 1977 is spicy with scents of minerals and leather and decent fruit, although not very deep or concentrated. The 1975 Riserva needs six to ten years, but shows good colour and sufficient fruit to balance out the tannin. The 1971 Riserva is quite good, the 1970 Riserva richer and more powerful. It is dark in colour, and seems to have reached full maturity. Only about 1,200 cases of Riserva are made and 3,200 cases of standard Brunello, so the limited availability no doubt keeps the prices for these wines extremely high.

CASALE DEL BOSCO ★★★

1979 .... ④ *84*

This looks to be a well-made Brunello, quite backward, dark in colour, very spicy with the tell-tale aroma of saddle leather. The 1979 del Bosco needs six to ten years of cellaring as the tannins are immense at the moment. Hard, tough, and inaccessible, it may ultimately merit a higher score.

CAMIGLIANO ★★★

1974 Riserva	③	**65**
1978 Riserva	③	**85**
1980 Riserva	③	**82**
1983 Rosso	②	**82**
1984 Rosso	②	**55**

This producer can be a good choice for inexpensive Brunello; however, as the scores demonstrate, consistency is often a problem. The 1975 is the best Camigliano Brunello I have tasted and still needs another three to four years of cellaring. The 1980 and 1978 have good, smoky, ripe, pleasant fruit and are ready for drinking. The 1983 Rosso is a good value: smoky, ripe supple wine with plenty of cherry fruit. Otherwise, the 1984 Rosso is thin, acidic, and bitter. The 1974 has a flawed, musty, cheesy aroma that does not blow off.

CAPRILI ★★★

1979	④	**86**
1981	④	**86**

Both wines are similar and very tannic yet quite impressive Brunellos that seem to have all the depth and ripe fruit to carry the tough tannins that are present. The bouquets are quite intense with chocolaty, smoky, earthy scents; the wines are quite full-bodied and rich, but six to ten years away from maturity.

CARPARZO ★★★★

1978 .... ④ **85**

1980	④	**82**
1981	④	**86**
1979 La Casa..	⑤	**90**
1980 La Casa..	⑤	**89**
1979 Riserva..	⑤	**86**
1981 Rosso...	①	**76**
1982 Rosso...	①	**80**

This is a very reliable producer of very good, and if the 1979 and 1980 La Casas are any indication, potentially great, Brunello di Montalcino. The 1979 La Casa has a stunning bouquet of rich, tarry fruit and fresh saddle leather, with some oriental spices intermingled. On the palate it explodes with a deep, rich fruitiness. Quite full-bodied and long, it was the number one Brunello in all my tastings. It can be drunk now but promises to be better in four to six years. The 1980 La Casa is a shade less concentrated but has the same rich, smoky, complex, broadly flavoured character. The 1979 Riserva is also impressive, but the tannins are quite pronounced; yet the rich, dense fruit and concentration of this wine suggest a higher-rated wine than I have scored it, provided one can wait five to eight more years. The 1978 regular bottling is quite tarry, stemmy, and ready to drink. The 1981 shows considerably more depth and length. The two Rossos are supple, easy to drink, and very pleasant.

CONSTANTI ★ ★ ★ ★ ★

1979	⑤	**89**
1980 Riserva..	⑤	**88**

In 1985 I tasted this producer's 1970, a superb Brunello that did justice to the historical reputation this region's wines have. The two current releases both have considerable merit. Both of these vintages are less tannic and backward than normal. The 1980, along with the Pertimali, is one of the leading Brunellos of that vintage. Sweet, ripe, intense aromas of leather, tar, and tobacco gush from the glass. On the palate the wine is fat, quite round and supple. It should drink well for five to six years. The 1979 is similarly styled, more obviously fruity and perhaps less smoky-scented in its bouquet, but still very attractive for drinking over the next four to six years.

LA FORTUNA ★ ★ ★

1979	④	**85**

This is a very good Brunello. It has characteristic harshness and aggressive tannins are present, but the bouquet exhibits some tarry, ripe, earthy scents and the palate impression is one

of richness, heavy tannins, and clean winemaking. Cellar until
1990–1992.

LISINI ★ ★ ★ ★
1977 .... ⑤ **84**
1978 .... ⑤ **82**

This estate was one of my favourite producers, having made
excellent Brunellos in 1975, 1971, 1970, and even in 1973, a
difficult vintage. The 1977 is a good Brunello, but not a great
wine. It is full-bodied, ripe, and impressively coloured, but
hard and bitter in the finish. I find it awkward and lacking
grace and finesse. Perhaps five to six years of cellaring will be
beneficial. The 1978 is plump, rather forward, with a
moderately intense bouquet of tobacco and earthy fruit. It is
an above-average wine, but not special.

PERTIMALI ★ ★ ★ ★ ★
1979 .... ④ **88**
1980 .... ④ **86**

This small, excellent producer's wines are well worth seeking
out. They seem to be made in a more sensible modern style
without excessive oak ageing and consequently retain much
more fruit and richness than other Brunellos. Both vintages of
Pertimali offer a deep, dark colour (among the darkest in
colour of any Brunello), rich, hickory, smoky-scented bouquets, full body, deep, concentrated flavours and plenty of
tannin. The wines are very cleanly made and need five to seven
years of cellaring. The 1979 tastes a trifle more concentrated.

IL POGGIONE ★ ★ ★ ★ ★
1979 .... ④ **88**
1977 Riserva .... ④ **89**
1978 Riserva .... ⑤ **89**
1982 Rosso .... ② **85**

One wishes there were more Brunellos like those of Il Poggione. Rich, intense, broadly flavoured wines with balance,
complexity, and character, this producer seems to extract
flavour and interest out of his grapes even in the most difficult
vintages. The 1982 Rosso is a forward, relatively rich, spicy,
robust wine for dinking over the next three to four years. It is
one of the best Rossos I have drunk. The 1979 Brunello
exhibits exotic, ripe, rich, lush fruit, medium to full body and
a well-developed, complex bouquet of tar, smoked nuts, and
ripe fruit. The 1978 and 1977 Riservas are two of the finest
Brunellos of their respective vintages. Both have full-intensity,

ripe, smoky, tarry, deep bouquets, full body and surprisingly rich, lush, fruity flavours, and excellent length. The 1978 is deceptively easy to drink and seems close to maturity, although there are good, ripe tannins in the finish. Il Poggione is one of the best of the Brunello producers.

SAN FILIPPO ★★★

1980 .... ④ **85**

Dark ruby with a ripe, tarry fruit, leather-scented, spicy bouquet, this wine has a supple, accessible richness, good length, and complexity. Not a great Brunello, but certainly a very good wine that can be drunk now and over the next four to five years.

VILLA BANFI

1979 .... ④ **74**
1980 .... ④ **75**

There are great hopes for the huge fortunes invested in this estate, but at present the vineyard is very young and the wines no doubt show the effect. The 1980 is very dry and lacks mid-range and length. It is a compact, rather simple wine. The 1979 is similarly styled, pleasant and innocuous with less tannin than the 1980.

CHIANTI

There are hundreds of producers of Chianti. It is Italy's best-known wine (along with the ubiquitous Lambrusco and Asti Spumante) though sadly only on occasion is it delicious and sublime. More often than not, it is pale in colour, diluted in flavour, and possessed of not more than two to three years of bottle life. While not expensive at £2 to £3 a bottle, neither is it good value. However, from a handful of producers, Chianti can be an excellent wine – but producers who make fine Chianti charge a lot for it, so top-quality Chianti is not the value it is perceived to be.

I have tasted well over 100 Chiantis and have found the quality to be generally average to below average. In fact, I have tasted only three Chiantis in my life that I would call great: the 1970 and 1971 Monsanto Il Poggio Chianti and the Berardenga 1970. Out of several hundred producers, that is a very poor record of quality. Who are the best Chianti producers? In order of my findings, Monsanto stands in a class by itself, followed by Ruffino's Gold Label Riserva Ducale, Capannelle, Il Palazzino, Berardenga, Monte Vertine, Badia a Coltibuono, and Castello di Rampolla.

Here are my notes on the current releases from the top eight estates.

BADIA A COLTIBUONO ★★★★

1974 Riserva	③	**75**
1978 Riserva	③	**85**
1979 Riserva	③	**82**

Coltibuono produces rather rustic Chiantis, lacking a touch in finesse, sometimes a little inconsistent, but usually intense and rather dramatic. The 1974 is tired and has an annoying bitterness and musty character that is off-putting. The 1979 is above average, a trifle too tannic and surprisingly orange at the rim. The winner is the 1978. A robust, rustic, slightly earthy herbaceous bouquet is followed by a wine that is rich, rather alcoholic, and powerful for a Chianti. It finishes long in the mouth.

BERARDENGA FATTORIA DI FELSINA ★★★★

1977	②	**80**
1981	①	**84**
1970 Riserva	④	**90**
1974 Riserva	③	**84**
1975 Riserva	③	**85**
1979 Riserva	②	**75**

With the exception of the 1979 Riserva, which has an attractive bouquet but tasted a little tart on the palate, these were all elegant, ripe, round Chiantis with a prominent raspberry-scented fruitiness and medium body. The 1970 is a stunning, great wine and, given its great concentration and depth, one cannot help but wonder if Berardenga has lightened the style in recent vintages. The 1970 is available and will last at least another four to five years. Both the 1974 Riserva and 1975 Riserva are fully mature, nicely scented, cleanly made wines with good fruit, medium body, and elegance. The 1977 is supple, but short on the palate. No doubt because of the raspberry fruitiness of these wines, I find a vague resemblance to Burgundy.

CAPANNELLE ★★★★

1975 Riserva	④	**85**
1977 Riserva	④	**86**
1980 Riserva	④	**85**
1982 Riserva	④	**84**

The Capannelle Chiantis are among the best wines produced, and perhaps the most expensively packaged too in heavy glass bottles with very stylish labels. I have even seen a limited-edition bottle with a solid silver label. The wines, while expensive, do indeed deliver clean, rich, cherry and strawberry fruit, rich, toasty, spicy, oaky aromas, and good length.

The 1975 Riserva is still a lovely mouthful of Chianti. The 1977 is even better: sweet, savoury, lush, and quite seductive. The 1980 is not as expansive or as deeply fruity as the 1977, but offers a very good introduction to the top class of Chianti. The 1982 is good, but given the vintage less impressive than one might have expected.

MONSANTO ★★★★★

1975 Il Poggio	④	86
1977 Il Poggio	④	87
1978 Il Poggio	④	80
1979 Il Poggio	③	85
1981	③	85

At present, the Monsanto estate is at the head of the pack in Chianti. The 1970 and 1971 Monsanto Chiantis from the Il Poggio vineyard continue to represent truly great wine, but I have seen nothing from Monsanto since then that appears capable of equalling them. The 1973 and 1974 Il Poggios were certainly uninspiring. More recently, the 1975 is quite good, still young but with a rich, smoky, mineral-scented bouquet, a lovely sweetness of fruit and firm tannins backing up a medium- to full-bodied texture. The 1977 is also quite young, but has impressive credentials, though I would be surprised if it equals the 1970 or 1971. Dark ruby with a big, smoky, tobacco-scented bouquet, tannic, full-bodied flavours and very good length, it needs one to three years of cellaring. The 1978 is dark in colour, but dull and slightly bitter and astringent. If it is going to get better, it needs another three to four years of cellaring. The 1979 is neither as hard and astringent as the 1978 nor as promising as the 1977. Nevertheless, it is forward, with Monsanto's tell-tale, smoky, earthy, ripe bouquet, medium body, and soft finish. It should be drunk over the next three to four years. The 1981, not from the Il Poggio vineyard, is a deeply coloured and broadly flavoured wine with character.

MONTE VERTINE ★★★★

1982	③	83
1981 Riserva	③	85

Monte Vertine is a very reputable producer of Chianti as well as of two single-vineyard wines called Le Pergole Torte and Il Sodaccio. The 1981 Riserva Chianti is drinking well today and should continue to hold well for several years. It has spicy vanillin oak and ripe berry fruit abundantly displayed in a medium-bodied, softly textured format. The 1982 regular bottling is fruity, soft, easy to drink, but lighter and less deep than the 1981 Riserva.

IL PALAZZINO ★ ★ ★ ★

1981	②	**84**
1982	②	**85**
1982 Riserva	②	**86**

The only three Chiantis I have tasted from this estate have been very good. It is a relatively new estate that also makes the 100% Sangiovese wine, Grosso Senese. The style of Chianti produced is marked by the smell of new oak barrels, a ripe, rich, cherry fruitiness, good firm tannins, and very clean, well-delineated flavours. They are impressive Chiantis with colour and flavour, to be drunk between age four and eight.

CASTELLO DI RAMPOLLA ★ ★ ★ ★

1979 Riserva	②	**85**
1980 Riserva	②	**85**
1981 Riserva	②	**86**
1982 Riserva	②	**86**
1983 Riserva	②	**85**

One of my favourite Chianti producers, whose wines represent the new school of winemaking in Chianti. The wine is partially aged in small barrels and small percentages of Cabernet Sauvignon are blended in. All three vintages above are strong efforts with plenty of flavour interest, body, and character. Unlike most pale-coloured Chiantis, the Rampolla wines have good colour. The 1981 and 1982 are the most ageworthy of the above wines. Both can use two to four years of cellaring, but have a rich, cedary, spicy, fruity nose, good colour, medium body and firm tannins. The 1980 and 1983 are more open and aromatic with good, ripe fruit, some spicy oak in evidence, and good length. The 1979 is slightly herbaceous, but ripe and cedary, medium-bodied, and is now mature.

RUFFINO ★ ★ ★ ★

1978 Gold Label	③	**86**
1979 Gold Label	③	**83**

One of the most famous producers, Ruffino's Gold Label (their best wine) can be found easily and older vintages frequently show up. The 1979 is fat and supple, with easy-to-drink flavours and some high alcohol showing through in the finish. The 1978 tastes like many a Brunello. It has a big, ripe, rich, leather-scented bouquet. Full-bodied, heady and rich it is a rather big-proportioned Chianti for drinking over the next five to six years.

THE SIX BEST VALUES IN CHIANTI

While these six firms do not produce Chianti on as sublime a level of quality as that of the aforementioned eight growers, their wines have consistently demonstrated a very high rapport in quality/price. They are the best values for Chianti and the wines generally sell for £4-£6 a bottle. Look for the 1982s and 1983s from these producers.

Castello di Volpaia   Dr. Gracciano
Fontodi   Di Pancole
Fossi   Villa Cafaggio

OTHER TUSCAN RED WINES · VINO NOBILE DI MONTEPULCIANO, CARMIGNANO

Brunello di Montalcino may be Tuscany and Italy's most expensive and overrated wine, and Chianti may be Tuscany and Italy's best-known red wine, but there are several other red wines of merit produced there. Carmignano is not terribly well known but can be a good wine. It is made, as are most Chiantis, from a blend of red wine grapes (Sangiovese, Canaiolo Nero, and Cabernet Sauvignon) as well as white grapes. The top producer is Capezzana. The other red wine of importance is Tuscany's Vino Nobile di Montepulciano. There are four good producers of this Chianti-like, tasty wine – Avignonesi, Boscarelli, Fanetti, and Fassati. I have read excellent things about Buonsignori, but I have never seen a bottle of his wine.

Both Carmignano and Vino Nobile, when well made, taste like very good Chiantis. Neither wine is particularly good value. In my tastings, three wines stood above the rest – the 1983 and 1982 Avignonesi Vino Nobile di Montepulciano and the 1981 Carmignano Riserva from Capezzana.

AVIGNONESI ★★★★
1982 Vino Nobile di Montepulciano............................ ④ **87**
1983 Vino Nobile di Montepulciano............................ ③ **86**
I find this producer's wines consistently very good, and both of these wines are well made. The 1982 is more powerful, with very good colour, enough stuffing and tannin to age seven to eight years, and plenty of ripe black cherry fruit. It is one of the best Vino Nobiles I have ever tasted. The 1983 is a less powerful version of the 1982, stylish, graceful, ripe, and medium- to full-bodied. Both are serious wines that should improve for seven to eight years.

CAPEZZANA ★★★
1981 Carmignano Riserva.. ③ **85**
Approachable now, this wine has a complex, sweet, cedary, ripe, fruity bouquet. Quite cleanly made, fruity, and medium-

bodied, this is a very attractive wine for drinking over the next three to four years.

FASSATI ★★★

1979 Vino Nobile di Montepulciano............................ ② **84**
1980 Vino Nobile di Montepulciano............................ ② **83**

These are two good wines, although not quite on the level of those of Avignonesi. The 1980 has chocolaty, ripe, spicy nose, good colour, some attractive, sweet fruit in the flavour, and a soft, medium-bodied texture. It should be drunk over the next two to three years. The 1979 is slightly more concentrated, with an aroma of ripe cherries, spicy oak, and firmer, more aggressive tannins noticeable on the palate. It needs two to three years before consumption as it is relatively unevolved.

THE WHITE WINES OF TUSCANY

Over recent years much has been made of the new Tuscan white wines. There is the Pomino from Frescobaldi, the Galestro of Antinori, the inexpensive Bianco di Pitigliano, and, of course, numerous white wines usually made from Trebbiano by the Chianti producers. Italy does indeed make lovely white wines today, but the only Tuscan white I can stand behind and recommend enthusiastically is the Vernaccia di San Gimignano. Thankfully, it is not made from the bland, tart Trebbiano grape, but rather from the Vernaccia grape, and it comes from the remarkable medieval fortified hill town of San Gimignano. All the Vernaccias today are made in stainless steel, temperature-controlled tanks and the results are refreshingly crisp, light yet flavourful dry wines that seem to perfectly match, and are easy to drink with fish and chicken. The 1983 was an excellent vintage for Vernaccia, but most 1983s should be drunk up. The vintage in 1984 was not so good, but the 1984 Vernaccias, if not as fruity and solid as the 1983s, are still extremely enjoyable wines. The 1985s are better than the 1983s. The best Vernaccias year in and year out, are the wines from Falchini, Ponte a Rondolino, Strozzi, di Pancole, and Pietraserena. Of these five excellent producers, I find Strozzi's the fruitiest, Falchini's and di Pancole's the lightest, and Ponte a Rondolino and Pietraserena the fullest. A double pleasure about Vernaccia di San Gimignano is the price – it costs no more than £5 a bottle.

1985 Falchini Vernaccia di San Gimignano .... ① **85**
1985 di Pancole Vernaccia di San Gimignano .... ① **84**
1985 Pietraserena Vernaccia di San Gimignano ..... ① **84**
1985 Ponte a Rondolino Vernaccia di San
   Gimignano .... ① **85**
1985 Strozzi Vernaccia di San Gimignano .... ① **86**

OTHER SIGNIFICANT RED WINES OF ITALY

Italy's Least-known Great Red Wines

Piedmont and Tuscany are not the only serious red wine regions of Italy. Following are reviews of the best red wines from several other regions of Italy. But first, some observations. The red wine of Campania called Taurasi from Mastroberardino is probably's Italy's most famous and renowned wine produced outside of Tuscany and Piedmont, but it is not, in my opinion, the best. In the hilly, pastoral province of Umbria, Giorgio Lungarotti produces three red wines that rival the greatest reds made in Italy. The Rubesco, the Rubesco Riserva from the vineyard Monticchio, and the San Giorgio Cabernet Sauvignon are not only better than the highly publicized Taurasi, but are truly world-class wines. In the wild and primitive province of Abruzzi, just to the south of Umbria, two men, Edoardo Valentini and Emilio Pepe, produce uncommonly rich and powerful red wines called Montepulciano d'Abruzzo. In the southern provinces of Italy there are a number of great wines. In Apulia, the Salice Salentino of Dr. Cosimo Taurino is first-rate. In Basilicata on the slopes of Mount Vulture, the robust, fleshy, Aglianco del Vulture is made. Even in the wilderness of Sicily, a red wine called Regaleali from Giuseppe Tasca d'Almerita, a rich, classy, powerful wine is made. Also, the much-maligned Valpolicella, in the hands of a grower such as Quintarelli, can become an expansive, rich, flavourful wine. There are others, but these grand reds compete with and in many cases surpass the best wines that Italy can produce in the famous regions of Piedmont and Tuscany.

GIUSEPPE TASCA D'ALMERITA *SICILY* ★★★
1981 Regaleali.. ③ **85**

What this wine lacks in finesse, it compensates for in richness, power and full body. Dark ruby and very fleshy, on the palate the wine is fat, rich, alcohlic, and loaded with clean, plump, black cherry fruit flavours. Although not complex, it is rather substantial. It is quite drinkable now, but given its hefty constitution, will last at least another four to six years.

LUNGAROTTI *UMBRIA* ★★★★
1978 Rubesco... ② **85**

1979 Rubesco	② **83**
1975 Rubesco Riserva Monticchio	④ **90**
1978 San Giorgio	④ **86**
1979 San Giorgio	④ **89**

The San Giorgio Cabernet, produced from a vineyard planted in 1971, seems to get better with each passing vintage. The 1978 is not yet mature, but impressively dark ruby in colour, with a moderately intense, blackcurrant, subtle, herbaceous bouquet, medium to full body, and firm tannins. It should peak between 1988 and 1992. The 1979 is better and much more forward. It is every bit as concentrated as the 1978, but more accessible with blackcurrant fruit, rich tobacco and smoky scents, intertwined in a complex, fragrant bouquet. Full-bodied, rich and moderately tannic, the 1979 San Giorgio is the best Cabernet produced yet from Lungarotti, and rivals the legendary Sassicaia. As for the Rubescos, the 1978 is mature, has ripe, rich, supple, spicy, earthy fruit, medium to full body, good length and a Bordeaux-like bouquet. The 1979 is similarly proportioned but is less evolved and not yet ready to drink. The superstar here is the single-vineyard 1975 Monticchio vineyard Rubesco; few wine enthusiasts seem to realize how fine this wine is. Already eleven years old, it needs another five to be fully mature and will last another ten to twenty years. Intense black cherry scents, this intense, opulent, full-bodied wine is extremely impressive and potentially a great wine.

MASTROBERARDINO *CAMPANIA* ★ ★ ★ ★

1981 Taurasi	② **84**
1982 Taurasi	③ **82**
1968 Taurasi Riserva	⑤ **90**
1971 Taurasi Riserva	⑤ **82**
1973 Taurasi Riserva	⑤ **84**
1977 Taurasi Riserva	⑤ **80**
1978 Taurasi Riserva	⑤ **78**
1979 Taurasi Riserva	④ **84**
1980 Taurasi Riserva	③ **86**

This wine is generally considered one of Italy's half-dozen best red wines. I wonder if the greatness of the 1968 Taurasi has caused some to have an over-inflated view of this wine, or whether recent vintages have not been as successful. Or has the style of vinification lightened up? Whatever the reason, in tasting through these wines the common element was an earthy, cheesy nose that I suspect most tasters would find a little unusual. Curiously, it was missing in the superb 1968. The 1968 remains relatively young, but splendidly rich with a deep, ripe, earthy bouquet, long, dense flavours and fine balance. The 1980 and 1979 Riservas show promise for good (not great) drinkability in seven to eight years as their tannin level is quite aggressive at the moment. The 1977 is reputedly excellent, but the wine had a rather stewed, baked nose, very high acidity and a hard, lean texture with little charm. The 1978 tasted one-dimensional except for a cheesy, Burgundy nose. The 1973 showed a lovely, moderately intense cherry fruit, medium body, and some hard tannins in the finish. It should be drunk over the next five to six years. The 1971 had an interesting earthy nose, rather light to medium colour, but tasted off in the mouth with plenty of tannin left. The 1981, not a *riserva*, was youthful, clean, with plenty of ripe cherry fruit in a medium-bodied format. The same thing could be said for the rather compact, straightforward 1982.

EMILIO PEPE ★ ★ ★ ★

1974 Montepulciano d'Abruzzo	④	86
1978 Montepulciano d'Abruzzo	④	72

Pepe produces a deep, aromatic, ripe, full-bodied Montepulciano d'Abruzzo. The 1974 has a spicy, cigar-box bouquet, a deep, full-bodied, rustic feel on the palate, and has exceptional richness. It is ready to drink now but will hold. The 1978 is impressively dark, but flawed from excessive volatile acidity.

QUINTARELLI ★ ★ ★ ★

1979 Rosso Ca' Del Merlot	②	85
1980 Valpolicella	②	86

One has never tasted Valpolicella until one has tried one produced by Quintarelli. His Valpolicella is loaded with velvety, ripe cherry flavours, has good length and depth, and a spicy, berry-scented bouquet. It is ideal for drinking now and over the next one to three years. The 1979 Rosso Ca' Del Merlot is also ripe, fat, supple, and deliciously fruity. Both wines are very cleanly made, stylish, and very good values.

DR. COSIMO TAURINO ★ ★ ★ ★

1975 Patriglione Rossol	②	?
1979 Salice Salentino Riserva	①	84

This man produces the best Salice Salentino and it is great value. The 1979 Riserva is a straightforward, robust, ripe cherry-scented wine with good fruit, a medium- to full-bodied texture, and decent finish. On the other hand, the 1975 Patriglione is extremely high in alcohol, tastes like an overblown, heavy-handed Amarone, and is so viscous that it is almost sickening to drink.

EDOARDO VALENTINI ★ ★ ★ ★

1974 Montepulciano d'Abruzzo.................................... ④ **86**
1975 Montepulciano d'Abruzzo.................................... ③ **88**

A young man who left the practice of law to pursue wine-making, Valentini is considered the finest producer of Montepulciano d'Abruzzo. He obviously believes in rich, unfiltered, intense wines that need a decade of ageing to reveal their multidimensional personalities. Both these wines remain relatively young, especially in view of their age. They are rich, alcoholic, viscous wines that, despite their size, have very good balance and complex bouquets of wood and cherries. Both still have a good measure of tannin, but because of low acidity are very enjoyable now. Valentini's wines are very rare but worth a search to find.

OTHER
SIGNIFICANT
WHITE WINES OF
ITALY

Friuli-Venezia Giulia: Italy's Best-Made and Most Delicious
Inexpensive White Wines

White wines are made everywhere in Italy, but for today's modern taste, the crisp, light, fruity, fresh whites of Friuli-Venezia Giulia are, in my opinion, Italy's most enjoyable white wine resource. Modern technology is abundant here and what one usually gets for less than £5 a bottle is a deliciously vibrant wine, dry yet lively, fruity and often with just a trace of effervescence from some carbon-dioxide intentionally left in. Pinot Grigio, Tocai, Pinot Bianco, Malvasia, Chardonnay, Müller-Thurgau, Sauvignon, Ribolla and Riesling Renano are never great, profound, complex white wines, but in the hands of the best producers are among the most easy to drink and refreshingly light white wines produced on the face of the earth. Picilet, the ultra-rich, sweet dessert wine, is supposedly this area's challenge to the Barsacs and Sauternes of France. In fact, it is an outrageously over-priced mediocrity that I urge you to bypass without hesitation. Friuli-Venezia Giulia also produces light, fresh red wines. The Cabernet is always fruity but also invariably herbaceous and vegetal. Better bets are the soft, light, fruity Merlot made here and the native Refosco.

THE BEST PRODUCERS IN FRIULI-VENEZIA GIULIA

Abbazia di Rosazzo
An outstanding producer of crisp, fresh, technically flawless white wines. The 1983s and 1985s are excellent across the board. The 1984s, like most producers' wines, are more lean, acidic and tart, but good. The Ridge-like label is controversial. Best wines: Pinot Bianco, Tocai, Ronco Acacie, Sauvignon.

Borgo Conventi
Vibrant, fresh, delicious wines that are light, very cleanly made, and still flavourful are commonly found with this producer. The 1983s are richer, fuller than the lean 1984s. Best wines: Pinot Grigio, Tocai, Pinot Bianco.

Bortoluzzi

Of all the 1984 Friuli wines, Bortoluzzi's were clearly the best. I never tasted his 1983s, but can enthusiastically recommend the fresh, surprisingly rich, crisp 1984s and his multi-flavoured 1985s. Best wines: Pinot Grigio, Foian Blanc, Chardonnay, Riesling Renano.

Enofriulia

I did not see the 1984s, but both the 1983s and 1982s were excellent. Light, deliciously fruity, crisp, vibrant wines with style and character. Best wines: Müller-Thurgau, Pinot Bianco, Pinot Grigio.

Livio Felluga

Felluga is a very well-known producer who makes good but generally expensive wine from Friuli. Best wines: Pinot Grigio, Tocai, and perhaps the only Picolit to merit some acclaim.

F. Furlan

Among the richest wines, the wines of Furlan are intense, sometimes a trifle low in acidity, but always among the most distinctive of this region. Best wines: Ribolla Gialla, Pinot Grigio, Tocai and Malvasi. The 1985s and 1983s are superior to the 1982s.

Ronchi di Fornaz

The Tocai and Pinot Bianco are delicious here, particularly the 1985s.

Ronco del Gnemiz

A tiny producer with an impeccable reputation. The 1983s from Gnemiz were stunningly fresh, fruity and stylish. The 1984s were the best tasted after those of Bortoluzzi, and his newly released 1985s exceptionally good. Best wines: Pinot Grigio, Müller-Thurgau, Tocai Friulano, Chardonnay.

THE WHITES OF LOMBARDY AND TRENTINO

Italy's Most Serious Sparkling Wines and Santa Margherita

Lombardy and Trentino both produce good red wines. In fact, some are excellent. The Teroldego Rotaliano of the Baron de Cles and the new Cabernet-based wines of Bellavista come to mind immediately. And, of course, there is the famous Giorgio Gray, a mystical, reclusive oenologist from Bolzano who is reputed to have produced a superlative array of wines, but I have never seen a bottle of his wine. However, it is the white wines that merit most attention from this area, particularly the sparkling wines from Ca' del Bosco and Bellavista and the exceptional white wines of Santa Margherita. The following are my notes on their wines.

BELLAVISTA ★★★

1982 Cabernet Sauvignon Solestine (RED)	③	84
1984 Chardonnay Uccellanda	③	84
Cuvée Brut Non-Vintage	②	86
1982 Franciacorta Cuvée Brut.................................	③	85
1981 Gran Cuvée Pas Opere....................................	④	86

This luxurious estate in Lombardy specializes in sparkling wine, Cabernet Sauvignon aged in small casks, and oak-aged Chardonnay. The results are impressive. The sparkling wines are a match for the Ca' del Bosco wines that have long set the benchmark for high-quality Italian sparklers. The Non-Vintage Cuvée Brut is very French-like, with a crisp, clean, yeasty aroma, elegant flavours and good finish. I liked it at least as much as the vintage-dated, more expensive bottlings. The 1982 Franciacorta Cuvée Brut is fuller, more austere, quite dry, medium-bodied, and very well made. The 1981 Gran Cuvée is a very yeasty, austere, sparkling wine with considerable finesse. It comes in a bottle very reminiscent of the Krug Champagnes of France. The single vineyard Chardonnay Uccellanda is a good beginning. It is quite oaky, but shows good apple-like fruit with a suggestion of butter.

BERLUCCHI ★★★

Brut Cuvée Imperiale Non-Vintage	③	80
1981 Brut Cuvée Imperiale	④	86
Pas Dose Cuvée Imperiale Non-Vintage	③	78
Rose Cuvée Imperiale Non-Vintage...........................	③	80

Berlucchi is a very highly respected producer of sparkling wines. The star here is the 1981 Vintage Brut, which surpasses in complexity, finesse, and quality many a French Champagne. It has a yeasty bread-dough scented bouquet, very good effervescence, tiny bubbles and a crisp, fresh, lively finish. How good it is to see Italian sparkling wine of this quality.

CA' DEL BOSCO ★★★

Brut Spumante Non-Vintage	④	84

This producer can make excellent sparkling wine on a par with very good French Champagne. It used to have no competition, but the Bellavista winery is now also doing special things. The above Non-Vintage Brut is yeasty and toasty, with clean, fresh, medium-bodied flavours, good effervescence, and small, lingering bubbles. The wine is dry and very cleanly made.

SANTA MARGHERITA ★★★

1984 Chardonnay	②	85

1985 **Chardonnay** .... ② 86
1985 **Luna dei Feldi** .... ③ 86
1984 **Pinot Grigio** .... ② 84
1985 **Pinot Grigio** .... ② 85
This estate in Trentino produces a considerable amount of wine. The importer markets it aggressively, as a look at most Italian restaurant wine lists attests. However, the white wines of Santa Margherita are the most striking examples I have tasted of the new breed of Italian whites, richly fruity, very crisp, impeccably clean, stylish wines that have just enough varietal character. Perhaps their greatest attribute is the one that is impossible to articulate properly – you just want to keep drinking them. The 1984s are among the most successful white wines I tasted in this difficult vintage. The Luna dei Feldi is excellent, dry, so fresh and vibrant, yet so fruity and tasty. The 1985s are richer, fuller wines that continue to drink beautifully today. If you want a quality benchmark for Italian white wines, these are your reference point.

OTHER RECOMMENDED ITALIAN WHITE WINES (THE BEST OF THE REST)

ANSELMI ★ ★ ★ ★
1985 **Soave Anselmi** .... ② 85
1985 **Soave Capital Foscarino** .... ② 85
If you are like me, you probably think of Soave as a watery, thin, inoffensive wine. Well, these two Soaves are the finest two I have ever drunk. Both are dry but have plenty of fresh fruit, a lot of flavour, medium body, crisp acidity, surprising ripeness and length, and outstanding balance. For Soave, these are wines as perfect as one can get. They are vibrant, refreshing, and a treat to drink.

BIGI ★ ★ ★
1985 **Orvieto Classico** .... ① 84
I had always preferred to remember this beautiful town for its lovely cathedral and breathtaking situation atop an outcropping of rocks rather than as a place for interesting white wine. The 1984 Bigi Orvieto may cause me to take the wines seriously. It is a crisp, quite dry and fruity, vibrant wine that should be drunk over the next year.

MASO POLI ★ ★ ★
1985 **Chardonnay** .... ② 84
1985 **Pinot Grigio** .... ① 85
The 1985 Pinot Grigio has surprising richness, ripeness, and character, and is an excellent bargain as well. Spicy, richly

fruity and medium-bodied, this wine will drink very well for at least another twelve months. The Chardonnay is lighter, more delicate and very pleasant in an understated way.

MIRAFIORE ★★★
1985 Soave .... ① **83**

Until I tasted the Anselmi Soaves reviewed above, I thought this was the best Soave on the market. It remains a deliciously alive, tasty wine with surprising character.

GUERRIERI RIZZARDI ★★★★
1985 Dogoli .... ② **85**

The Dogoli is an elegantly wrought wine that may not represent the value that some of the others in this section do, but it is a delicious, very aromatic, flowery scented, vivacious, fruity wine that begs attention because of its charm and freshness. Medium-bodied, exuberant, and just plain delicious to sip, this wine should go handsomely with grilled or steamed fish.

CASTEL SCHWANBURG ★★★★
1985 Chardonnay .... ② **86**
1985 Pinot Bianco .... ② **85**

This estate draws its grapes from the Alto Adige and the 1985s are delicious – rich and fruity, impeccably clean and crisp, with good varietal character and plenty of pure ripe fruit. They should be drunk over the next two to three years.

J. TIEFENBRUNNER ★★★★
1985 Chardonnay .... ① **86**
1985 Gewürztraminer .... ① **86**
1984 Pinot Grigio .... ① **74**
1985 Pinot Grigio .... ② **86**
1985 Rhine Riesling .... ① **76**

Forget the lean, citric, deficient 1985 Riesling, and the flabby, loosely knit, oxidized 1984 Pinot Grigio. However, the other three Tiefenbrunner wines represent excellent values and are extremely attractive wines. The 1985 Pinot Grigio is a serious wine with broad, lush fruit, a fresh, lively feel and good finish. The 1985 Chardonnay is intensely fruity, long and ripe in the mouth with good acidity. The 1985 Gerwürztraminer is lovely, delicate, quite flavourful and really impressive.

VALENTINI ★★★★
1982 Trebbiano d'Abruzzo .... ③ **88**

The finest dry Italian white wine I have ever tasted, this rich Burgundian imitation is produced from a grape I usually despise – the ubiquitous Trebbiano. However, in the hands of Signori Valentini the wine has an uncommon power, richness and depth of character that I had heretofore believed was reserved for only the best French white Burgundies. This is a fascinating wine that is still quite young and potentially will get even better. Very rare – unfortunately.

VILLA BANFI ★★

1985 Pinot Grigio San Angelo .... ② *82*
1984 Chardonnay Fontanelle .... ② *82*
1985 Gavi Principessa .... ③ *70*

The Gavi is virtually tasteless except for a pronounced citrusy character. The other two offerings show some style and flavour interest. The Pinot Grigio is also a touch citrusy, but has good fruit present, is very fresh and quite charming in a simple way. The Chardonnay is lemony, light- to medium-bodied, fresh, cleanly made and the perfect 'food' wine.

CHAPTER THREE

GERMANY

It is rather sad that Germany's finest wine producers are rarely accorded the recognition and respect that their peers in Bordeaux or Napa Valley receive. There appear to be a multitude of reasons why this is the case. First, German wine laws and the hierarchy of quality are extremely difficult to understand. Second, the German language itself is more troublesome to comprehend and read than French or Italian. Third, German wine labels are overzealous – there is simply too much information on them, which only complicates matters for the consumer. Finally, there is the prevailing image – or should I say myth that German wines are cloyingly sweet and therefore fattening and simply not serious enough to merit attention.

Unfortunately, none of these preconceptions about German wines are likely to change. Despite the tremendous publicity for Germany's outstanding 1983 vintage, few wine drinkers other than the hard-core German wine enthusiasts jumped at the opportunity to purchase what are excellent wines at amazingly reasonable prices. Nevertheless, consider the following points and comments and try to taste at least a half-dozen of the 1983 or excellent 1985 Rieslings from the best producers. Perhaps then you will learn why German Rieslings, with their fresh acidity, low alcohol, crisp fruitiness, and lightness, are such wonderful wines.

WHAT YOU NEED TO KNOW

1. The Germans grade their wines based on the ripeness of the grape. There are seven levels of ripeness, and therefore sweetness. In ascending order of ripeness and sweetness, as well as price, these seven levels in the German wine hierarchy are:

    i)   Tafelwein
    ii) Qualitätswein
    iii) Kabinett
    iv) Spätlese
    v)   Auslese
    vi) Beerenauslese
    vii) Trockenbeerenauslese

2. There are three other generic categories of German wine. The Trocken and Halbtrocken wines are the two generic types of dry German wine. The Trockens tend to be dryer, but also boring, thin wines with little body or flavour. Halbtrockens also taste dry but are permitted to have slightly more residual sugar and are also slightly more interesting. I rarely recommend either because they are not very good and they are commercial creations made to take advantage of the public's demand for 'dry' wine. The third type of wine is called Eiswein, Germany's rarest and most expensive wine. It is made from frozen grapes, generally picked in December or January, or even February. It is quite rare, and a very, very sweet wine, but has remarkably high acidity and can last and improve in the bottle

for decades. It does have great character, but one must usually pay an unbelievably steep price to experience it.

3. There are at least two dozen grape varieties legally permitted in Germany. However, with all due respect and acknowledging that certain varieties such as Müller-Thurgau, Silvaner, Scheurebe, and Rulander can, in some cases, produce something special, most interested consumers can concentrate on only one variety – the Riesling. In Germany, it reaches heights of complexity that are unparalleled anywhere else in the world.

4. There are eleven major wine-producing zones in Germany. Within these zones there are three sub-districts, the most general of which is called a Bereich. This is used to describe a wine from anywhere within the boundaries of that particular Bereich. An analogy that may help facilitate this distinction would be the closest French equivalent, a wine entitled to Appellation Bordeaux Contrôlée or Appellation Bourgogne Contrôlée. Within the Bereich there are more specific boundaries called Grosslagen, whereas the closest French equivalent would be the generic appellation St.-Julien Contrôlée or Appellation Morey St.-Denis Contrôlée. These would be wines that are not from a specific château or specific vineyard but from a specific region or collection of sites for vineyards. There are 152 different Grosslagen in Germany. The most specific zone in Germany is called an Einzellage, which is a specific site or vineyard. There are 2,600 of them and again, by analogy, the closest French equivalent would be a specific St.-Julien château such as Ducru-Beaucaillou, or a specific Premiér Cru or Grand Cru vineyard in Morey St.-Denis such as Clos des Lambrays. Perhaps this will help one to understand the breakdown of the German wine zones. However, few people have the patience to memorize the best Einzellagens or Grosslagens, so it is much more important to try to remember the names of some of the best producers.

5. The majority of the best producers in Germany are located in four of the eleven German wine zones. They are the Mosel-Saar-Ruwer, the Rheingau, the Rheinhessen, and the Rheinpfalz. While there are certainly good wines, even some outstanding wines, made in the other seven wine zones, by far and away the great majority of the finest German wines are produced in these four regions, with the Mosel-Saar-Ruwer being the very best region of all.

6. The best German wines are those produced at the Kabinett, Spätlese, Auslese, Beerenauslese, and Trockenbeerenauslese levels of ripeness and sweetness. Most consumers tasting a Kabinett wine would not find it particularly sweet, although there is residual sugar in the wine. Because of the high natural acidity found in German wines, a Kabinett generally tastes fresh, fruity, but not sweet to most palates. However, most tasters will detect a small amount of sweetness in a Spätlese, and even more with an Auslese. All three types are

West Germany

WINE REGIONS
1 Mittelrhein
2 Ahr
3 Mosel-Saar-Ruwer
4 Rheingau
5 Nahe
6 Rheinhessen
7 Franken
8 Rheinpfalz
9 Hessische-Bergstrasse
10 Württemberg
11 Baden

Rheingau

ideal wines to have as an apéritif or with food, whereas the wines entitled Beerenauslese and Trockenbeerenauslese designations are clearly dessert wines, very rich and quite sweet. One should keep in mind that the alcohol level in most German wines averages between 7%–9%, so one can drink much more of this wine without feeling its effects. One of the naïve criticisms of German wines is that they do not go well with food. However, anyone who has tried a fine Kabinett, Spätlese, or Auslese with oriental cuisine, with roast pork, or even with certain types of fowl such as pheasant or turkey can tell you that these wines work particularly well, especially Spätlese and Auslese.

7. The best German wines age like fine Bordeaux. In great vintages, such as 1983, one can expect a Kabinett, Spätlese, or Auslese from a top producer to evolve and improve in the bottle for five to ten years. A Beerenauslese or a Trockenbeerenauslese has the ability in a great vintage to improve for two or three decades. This is a fact, not a myth, to which those who have recently tasted some of the great Ausleses from 1959 can easily attest. German wines at the top levels, from the top producers, do indeed improve remarkably in the bottle, though the trend among consumers is to drink them when they are young, fresh, and crisp.

RECENT VINTAGES

1985 The German wine trade has touted this year rather highly, but except for a handful of wines it in no way compares to the outstanding 1983 vintage. Nevertheless, it is a good to very good year with a rather smallish production of wines with good acidity and more typical textures and characteristics than the opulent, rather richly fruity yet sometimes overblown 1983s. Like 1983, the dryness during the summer and autumn prevented the formation of botrytis cinerea. The Rieslings in many cases can be very good, but will be firmer and slower to evolve and less open than the more precocious, overt, fruity 1983s. Overall, the 1985s should be at their best between 1988 and 1995. Reports indicate that the top successes were in the middle Moselle with potentially great wines from villages such as Urzig and Erden.

1984 Fresh, light, very pleasant, straightforward wines that are neither green nor too acidic were produced in this vintage of average quality, and below-average quantity. They will not keep, so drink the 1984s over the next three to four years. The Mosel estate of Dr. F. Weins-Prüm Erben made excellent wines in 1984, as did Monchof.

1983 This vintage has received the most publicity since the 1976 vintage. Most growers seem to feel that it is certainly the best since the 1976. It was a very large crop throughout all viticultural areas of Germany, but it was especially large and exceptional in quality in the Mosel-Saar-Ruwer region. The wines have excellent concentration, very fine levels of tartaric rather than green malic acidity, and a degree of precocious ripeness and harmonious roundness that gives the wines wonderful appeal now. However, because of their depth and overall balance, they should age well for at least ten or more years. The vintage seemed strongest at the Spätlese level, since there were very little Auslese, Beerenauslese, and Trockenbeerenauslese wines produced. The 1983 was also a great year for Eiswein, where, as a result of an early freeze, above normal quantities of this nectar-like, opulent wine were produced. However, despite larger quantities than normal, the prices are outrageously high for the Eisweins, although very realistic and reasonable for the rest of the wines.

1982 In the 1982 the Germans harvested a record crop of wine. The wines are ready to drink, fruity, somewhat soft, and, on occasion, somewhat diluted because of the huge crop, but are very cleanly made and fresh. Very few wines at the Auslese level and above were produced. Overall, 1982 is a big, commercial vintage with plenty of appeal, and is priced quite reasonably.

1981 The Mosel was particularly blessed in 1981 with a number of excellent Kabinett and Spätlese wines. There was a little bit of Eiswein produced in the Rheingau of outstanding quality.

1980 A somewhat maligned vintage but, as in the rest of Europe, there are many successful wines, though few great ones. Certainly the Mosel and Rheingau seem to have produced better wines than elsewhere in Germany. These wines are now fully mature and should be drunk before the end of the decade.

1979 Between 1976 and 1983, this is certainly the most successful overall vintage for all of Germany. The quality in the Mosel was very good, even excellent, and the wines extremely well balanced with very good acidity, and wonderfully fresh, nicely concentrated fruit flavours that are rounding into the full bloom of maturity at the moment. The top Rieslings are fully mature and should be drunk before the end of this decade.

Older Vintages

The great vintage that can still be found in the marketplace is 1976, a vintage that by German standards produced incredibly ripe, intense, opulent wines, with a significant amount of wine produced at the Auslese and Beerenauslese levels. These tend to be very sweet and are drinking sensationally well at the moment. The top wines should continue to last for another five to eight years. Some critics have disputed the greatness of this vintage, saying that the 1976s are low in acidity, but that seems to be a minority point of view. The wines remain reasonably priced at the Auslese level, but the Beerenausleses and Trockenbeerenausleses from this vintage are soaring into the stratosphere in price. The 1977 vintage should be avoided, and 1978, unlike in France, was not a particularly successful year in Germany. Well-kept 1975s can provide great enjoyment, as can the wines from another great vintage, 1971. I would avoid the wines from 1972, and, of course, the 1973s, which were good in the mid-seventies but are now tiring quite a bit.

A GUIDE TO GERMANY'S BEST PRODUCERS

★ ★ ★ ★ ★ Outstanding Producers

Geltz-Zilliken
  (Mosel-Saar-Ruwer)
F. W. Gymnasium
  (Mosel-Saar-Ruwer)
Monchof
  (Mosel-Saar-Ruwer)

Egon Müller
  (Mosel-Saar-Ruwer)
Müller-Catoir (Rheinpfalz)
J. J. Prüm (Mosel-Saar-Ruwer)
Von Schubert
  (Mosel-Saar-Ruwer)

★ ★ ★ ★ Excellent Producers

Adelmann (Württemberg)
Aschrottsche Erben (Rheingau)
A. Babach Erben (Rheinhessen)
Bassermann-Jordan
(Rheinpfalz)
Bischofliches Konvikt
  (Mosel-Saar-Ruwer)
Bischofliche Priesterseminar
  (Mosel-Saar-Ruwer)
H. Braun (Rheinhessen)
Brentano (Rheingau)
Dr. Burklin-Wolf (Rheinpfalz)
Christoffel-Berres
  (Mosel-Saar-Ruwer)
Hans Crusius (Nahe)
Deinhard (Mosel-Saar-Ruwer
  and Rheinpfalz)
O. Dunweg
  (Mosel-Saar-Ruwer)
Eser (Rheingau)
Dr. Fischer (Mosel-Saar-Ruwer)
Forstmeister-Geltz-Erben
  (Mosel-Saar-Ruwer)

Freiherr von Heddesdorff
  (Mosel-Saar-Ruwer)
Graf zu Hoensbroech
  (Baden)
F. Haag (Mosel-Saar-Ruwer)
F. Heyl (Rheinhessen)
Hohe Domkirche
  (Mosel-Saar-Ruwer)
Koehler-Ruprecht (Rheinpfalz)
Landgraf von Hessen (Rheingau)
Lauerburg (Mosel-Saar-Ruwer)
Licht-Bergweiler
  (Mosel-Saar-Ruwer)
Licht-Kilburg (Rheingau)
Dr. Loosen
  (Mosel-Saar-Ruwer)
Milz-Laurentiushof
  (Mosel-Saar-Ruwer)
Dr. R. Muth (Rheinhessen)
Dr. Nagler (Rheingau)
Pleffingen (Rheinpfalz)
A. S. Prüm-Erben
  (Mosel-Saar-Ruwer)

E. Reverchon
(Mosel-Saar-Ruwer)
Ruetter Kunz
(Mosel-Saar-Ruwer)
St. Johannishof (Rheingau)
Schloss Johannisberg (Rheingau)
Schloss Plettenberg (Nahe)
Dr. A. Senfter (Rheinhessen)
G. Siben Erben (Rheinpfalz)
Staatlichen Weinbaudomanen
(Mosel-Saar-Ruwer)
Staatsweinguter Eltville
(Rheingau)
J. H. Strub (Rheinhessen)

Vereinigte Hospitien
(Mosel-Saar-Ruwer)
von Hoevel (Mosel-Saar-Ruwer)
von Kanitz (Rheingau)
von Kesselstatt
(Mosel-Saar-Ruwer)
von Mummisches (Rheingau)
von Simmern (Rheingau)
Dr. Heinz Wagner
(Mosel-Saar-Ruwer)
Weins-Prüm Erben
(Mosel-Saar-Ruwer)
H. Wirsching (Franken)
Dr. Zenzen (Mosel-Saar-Ruwer)

★ ★ ★ Good Producers

S. Adler (Baden)
F. Altenkirch (Rheingau)
P. Anheuser (Nahe)
Bergweiler-Prüm
(Mosel-Saar-Ruwer)
F. Baumann (Rheinhessen)
Graf von Neippergsches
(Württemberg)
L. Guntrum (Rheinhessen)
Johann Hart
(Mosel-Saar-Ruwer)
D. Hermann
(Mosel-Saar-Ruwer)
Irsch-Ockfen
(Mosel-Saar-Ruwer)
Josefinegrund
(Mosel-Saar-Ruwer)
Josephshof
(Mosel-Saar-Ruwer)
Jostock-Thul
(Mosel-Saar-Ruwer)
J. Koch (Mosel-Saar-Ruwer)
Kurfurstenhof (Rheinhessen)
Lehneit-Veit-Erben
(Mosel-Saar-Ruwer)
Max Markgraf (Baden)
Oekonomierat Piedmont
(Mosel-Saar-Ruwer)
Oekonomierat Rebholz
(Rheinpfalz)

F. Reh (Mosel-Saar-Ruwer)
P. Scherf (Mosel-Saar-Ruwer)
Schloss Groenesteyn (Rheingau)
Schloss Reinhartshausen
(Rheingau)
Schloss Vollrads (Rheingau)
F. Schmitt (Rheinhessen)
R. Schmitt (Franken)
Schumann-Nagler (Rheingau)
B. Simon (Mosel-Saar-Ruwer)
Studert-Prüm
(Mosel-Saar-Ruwer)
H. Taprich (Mosel-Saar-Ruwer)
Erbhof Tesch (Nahr)
Dr. Thanisch
(Mosel-Saar-Ruwer)
Usinger-Gunderlach
(Rheinhessen)
Van Volxem
(Mosel-Saar-Ruwer)
von Buhl (Rheinpfalz)
von Hessisches (Rheingau)
von Prittwitz
(Mosel-Saar-Ruwer)
R. Weil (Rheingau)
S. Weiland (Mosel-Saar-Ruwer)
Würzburg Staalichen Hofkeller
(Franken)
W. Zahn (Mosel-Saar-Ruwer)

GERMANY · TODAY'S BUYING STRATEGY

There are plenty of bargains at the Kabinett and Spätlese levels from the good producers for both the two most recent exciting vintages, 1983 and 1985, starting in price from £4 per bottle for Kabinett and from £6 per bottle for Spätlese. At the level of Auslese, the prices start at around £7.50 and can go as high as £12-£15 for some wines. Therefore, the best Spätleses and Kabinetts from 1983 and 1985 represent the best values. The 1984s are not bad wines, but are simply overshadowed by the two surrounding vintages. The 1982s can be good if well stored, but again, the best of them are not as good as the 1983s and 1985s. Should you want to indulge in a great, nectar-like Beerenauslese, Trockenbeerenauslese, or Eiswein from recent vintages such as 1971, 1981, 1983 or 1985, expect to pay upwards of £40 for one bottle.

CHAPTER FOUR

PORTUGAL

DRY RED TABLE WINES

Except for the unctuous, rich, almost decadent joys of vintage port, Madeira, and one of the greatest nectars of all, Muscatel de Setubal, the potential for fine wine from Portugal has yet to be discovered by most wine enthusiasts. Of course, the ubiquitous, spritzy, rather sweet Portuguese rosés are known the world over and are what many consumers first drink when they deem themselves too old or too sophisticated for soda pop. But Portugal produces some good red wines that could even be superb if winemaking was not still adhering to nineteenth century practices, as well as a few lively, crisp, tart white wines, the best of which are the *vinho verdes*. For dry red wine, the best are from Dão, Bairrada, and the Douro.

QUICK VINTAGE GUIDE

Vintages in Portugal seem to have relevance only to the port trade. For the dry red table wines, none of the wineries seem to think vintages matter a lot, but certainly 1977, 1980, 1982, and 1983 would be recent years in which grapes were reputed to ripen evenly and reach perfect maturity.

A GUIDE TO PORTUGAL'S BEST PRODUCERS OF DRY RED TABLE WINE

★★★★ Excellent Producers

Carvalho, Ribeiro, Ferreira (Dão, Serradayres, Garrafeira)
Ferreira (Barca Velha)

J. M. da Fonseca (Periquita)
João Pires (Cabernet and Muscat)

★★★ Good Producers

Caves Alianca (Vinho Verde)
Caves St. Jão (Garrafeira)
Caves Velhas (Dão, Romeira)

Grao Vasco (Dão)
Quinta da Aveleda (Vinho Verde)

A BUYING STRATEGY

First, the intense, rich, full-bodied Barca Velhas from Ferreira are expensive at about £8 a bottle, but they compete with the elegant, seductive, voluptuous Periquitas of Fonseca for honours as Portugal's top dry red table wine. The Periquitas cost about £3.50 a bottle. The excellent firm of Carvalho, Ribeiro, and Ferreira produces three fine reds, all selling for around £3 a bottle. Their supple, generously flavoured Dão from Conte de Santar, their claret-like, stylish Serradayres, and old, robust, yet sometimes coarse Garrafeira are all worth a try. Lastly, the Quinta de Bacalhoa near the famous Sintra castle makes modern-style, Bordeaux-inspired Cabernet Sauvignon for about £3.50.

For white wines, the tart, light, exuberant Vinho Verde – if drunk within two years of the vintage from producers such as

Quinta da Aveleda and Carvalho, Ribeiro, Ferreira – is a refreshingly crisp, lively wine for around £2.50-£3.50 a bottle. Lastly, if you are able to find any, the Muscat from João Pires is a lovely wine: dry, flowery and deliciously fruity.

PORT

The pleasures of port are justifiably legendary. Good vintages are said to need ten even fifteen years of cellaring before they can be drunk. However, the truth is that vintage port is terribly appealing even when consumed in its youth, though port fanatics would consider that infanticide. The major port houses all have their specific styles yet the level of quality of these houses is remarkably high. In addition to vintage port, which seems to be declared in only three to four vintages a decade, there are other types of port, the best of which is old tawny port. I find ruby port rather one-dimensional, late-bottled port lacking in character, and white port a rather grotesque aberration. For me, it is vintage port and tawny port or nothing, and consequently that is what I shall write about.

QUICK VINTAGE GUIDE

The great recent vintages for port are 1963, 1970, 1977, and 1983. Other years have been declared and are quite good, such as 1966, 1975, 1980, and 1982, but they do not have the level of sheer intensity and richness of the first four referenced vintages, nor do they have the ageing potential.

A GUIDE TO PORTUGAL'S BEST PRODUCERS OF PORT

★ ★ ★ ★ ★ Outstanding Producers

Dow	Graham
Fonseca	Taylor Fladgate & Yeatman

★ ★ ★ ★ Excellent Producers

Cockburn	Quinta do Noval
Croft	Sandeman
Ferreira	Warre

★ ★ ★ Good Producers

Calem	Offley Forrester
Delaforce	Poças Junior
Gould Campbell	Ramos-Pinto
Martinez	Smith-Woodhouse

A BUYING STRATEGY

Since the port producers do not release their production figures, and since most of them rarely declare a vintage more than four times a decade, quantities of vintage port are believed to be rather small. Prices for port usually do not begin to become expensive until the

Spain and Portugal

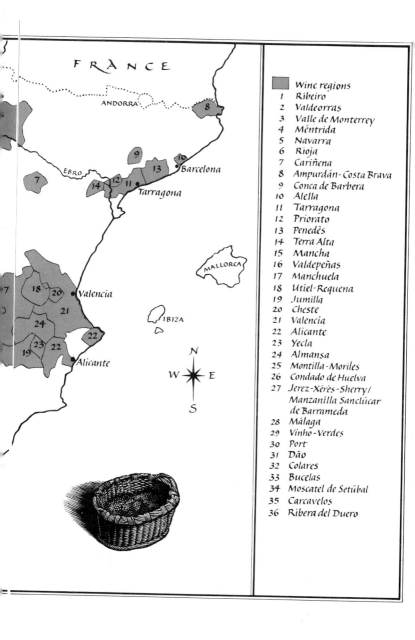

Wine regions
1 Ribeiro
2 Valdeorras
3 Valle de Monterrey
4 Méntrida
5 Navarra
6 Rioja
7 Cariñena
8 Ampurdán-Costa Brava
9 Conca de Barbera
10 Alella
11 Tarragona
12 Priorato
13 Penedès
14 Terra Alta
15 Mancha
16 Valdepeñas
17 Manchuela
18 Utiel-Requena
19 Jumilla
20 Cheste
21 Valencia
22 Alicante
23 Yecla
24 Almansa
25 Montilla-Moriles
26 Condado de Huelva
27 Jerez-Xérès-Sherry/
    Manzanilla Sanclúcar
    de Barrameda
28 Málaga
29 Vinho-Verdes
30 Port
31 Dão
32 Colares
33 Bucelas
34 Moscatel de Setúbal
35 Carcavelos
36 Ribera del Duero

wine reaches its tenth birthday, the time when port fanciers begin to seriously imbibe a given vintage. Demand for vintage port continues to grow at a rapid pace and my advice is to stock up on the remaining 1977s that exist because this is the greatest vintage since 1963, though the 1983s are not far behind in quality. As for the 1983s, I would take a serious look at them. At the moment they are priced very reasonably, but their prices can only go up once the quality of the vintage is more widely known. The 1963s and 1970s are very expensive, but the 1975s, forward, lighter-weight wines that are delicious now are somewhat undervalued in the scheme of things.

The other type of port I would not hesitate to try would be the mellow, fully mature, old tawny ports offered by the better houses. Tawny ports are aged ten, twenty, sometimes thirty or forty years in cask and have a very complex, mellow, savoury, nutty, berry fruit character. Many cheaply made, blended tawny ports have given this type of port a bad name, but the old authentic tawny ports from firms such as Taylor Fladgate and Yeatman, Dow, Graham, and Ferreira are truly superb.

COCKBURN ★ ★ ★ ★

1963	⑤	**86**
1970	⑤	**87**
1975	④	**82**
1983	④	**88**

This house tends to produce quite full-bodied, rich, alcoholic, spirity vintage ports that never have a great deal of complexity or finesse but offer meaty, chocolaty, spicy, full-bodied, alcoholic flavours at the expense of elegance. The 1977 has always tasted a bit awkward but shows enormous depth, power, and richness. One should wait until the end of this century before drinking it. The 1975 is light, a little alcoholic, and not terribly distinguished. The 1970 is big and powerful and just now reaching maturity. The 1963 is fully mature, spicy, with a chocolaty, meaty texture and a somewhat hot, short finish.

CROFT ★ ★ ★ ★

1963	⑤	**86**
1966	⑤	**87**
1970	⑤	**85**
1975	④	**87**
1977	④	**88**
1982	④	**90**

Croft never seems to get much publicity as the wines, while always very good, sometimes even excellent, never quite reach the superb level of the top houses in Oporto. However, Croft seems to do surprisingly well, often rivalling the top ports in the less glamorous vintages such as 1975 and 1966. The 1975 is almost as good as Croft's 1977. Both are rich, creamy, intense ports that should be fully mature within ten to twelve years, relatively soon for a vintage port. The 1970 is quite good, but in the context of the vintage, marginally disappointing. The 1966 is a sleeper: complex, rich, very aromatic, with long, deep flavours. The 1963, one of the great vintages for port, is good, but unexciting. However, the 1982 is superb, a powerful broadly flavoured wine with exhilarating depth and richness on the palate, and at least 25 years of life ahead of it.

DELAFORCE ★ ★ ★

Emminence's Choice 16-year-old Tawny Port	③	85
1966	⑤	86
1970	⑤	84
1975	④	82
1978 Quinta da Corte	⑤	85
1982	④	85

This house tends to make good port and sell it at rather reasonable prices. The 16-year-old Tawny is soft and pleasant but lacks a bit of character. The 1978 single-vineyard port, Quinta da Corte, is straightforward and chunky, with good length but not much complexity; the same can be said for the 1975 and 1970, both of which are fully mature. It has been several years since I have tasted a 1966, but my recollection is that it is the best Delaforce port I have had.

DOW ★ ★ ★ ★ ★

Boardroom 15-year-old Tawny	③	87
Gold Label 30-year-old Tawny	⑤	90
1963	⑤	92
1966	⑤	88
1970	⑤	86
1975	④	85
1977	⑤	93
1980	④	88
1983	⑤	90

This is an extraordinary house that seems to have been particularly successful with its vintage ports since 1977. Of course, the 1963 is a classic, a monumental, rich, still tannic wine that will last at least another 30 years. The 1966 is also a top success for that vintage; in fact, it would be hard to find a better port that year. The 1970 is good, but for some reason has never blossomed and developed any complexity, and the same can be said for the fully mature, fruity, soft 1975.

However, starting with the 1977 Dow has hit its stride. The 1977, still a baby, is fabulously scented, very rich and concentrated, and has a potential longevity of at least another 30–50 years. The 1980 is very, very good and certainly better than what this house produced in 1975 and 1970. It should mature relatively fast and be ready to drink by 1992. The newest vintage port, the 1983, is rich, concentrated, very fruity, and magnificently perfumed, suggesting that it is going to mature early, long before the 1977. As for the tawny ports from Dow, they can also be superb. The 30-year-old Tawny has a scent of sweet saddle leather, hazelnuts, and rich fruit. The 15-year-old Tawny, for a third of the price, is a somewhat lighter but no less interesting version.

FERREIRA ★ ★ ★ ★

Duque de Bragança 20-year-old Tawny	④	88
1970	⑤	85
1975	④	86
1977	⑤	87
1980	④	85
1983	④	88

This house is terribly underrated when top ports are mentioned. Their vintage ports tend to lack a bit in complexity and majesty of aromas, but do offer rich, robust, concentrated flavours of chocolate, spices, and deep, plummy fruit. However, their 20-year-old Tawny, Duque de Bragança, must certainly be one of the top tawny ports made in Portugal and is well worth seeking out by those who want something to drink immediately.

FONSECA ★ ★ ★ ★ ★

Bin '27	③	84
Fonseca 10-year-old Tawny	③	86
1963	⑤	96
1966	⑤	88
1970	⑤	93
1975	④	89
1977	⑤	93
1980	⑤	87
1983	⑤	92

Fonseca is clearly one of the great port lodges making, to my palate's taste, the most exotic and most complex port of them all. If Fonseca lacks the sheer weight and power of a Taylor, Dow, or Warre, or the opulent sweetness and intensity of a Graham, it excels in its magnificently complex, intense bouquet of plummy, cedary, spicy fruit and long, broad, expansive flavours. One might call it the Pomerol of vintage ports, with its lush, seductive character. When it is young, it often loses out in blind tastings to the heavier, weightier, more tannic wines, but I always find myself up-grading my opinion of Fonseca after it has had seven to ten years to age. If there is a disappointment for me, it is their tawny ports. However, for vintage ports, the newly released 1983 is magnificently scented, full-bodied, creamy, rather forward, but showing great length and character. The 1980 is very good, possibly excellent, but tasted lighter than some of the best ports from that vintage. The 1977 has developed magnificently in the bottle, and while it clearly needs another decade to reach its summit, it is the best Fonseca since the 1970 and 1963. Fonseca's 1975, which is fully mature, shows just how good this house can be; it is a port to seek out since the vintage does not have the reputation or the price tag that 1977 and 1970 do. It should drink magnificently for another decade or more. The 1970, of course, is a powerful Fonseca, with an exotic bouquet and lush, creamy, multidimensional flavours. The 1966, a top success as well, is fully mature, but will hold for fifteen or more years; the 1963, one of the great modern-day classics of vintage port, is an incredibly aromatic, sublime, majestic port that simply defines Fonseca's style perfectly.

GOULD CAMPBELL ★★★

1977	④	84
1980	③	85
1983	④	82

My experience with this house is limited to one vintage port, which I found rich, full-bodied, well-coloured, but not complex or terribly distinctive.

GRAHAM ★★★★★

Emperor Tawny 20-year-old	③	85
Prince Regent's 10-year-old Tawny	⑤	88
1963	⑤	92
1966	⑤	88
1970	⑤	93
1975	④	82
1977	⑤	96
1980	⑤	88
1983	⑤	95

Graham is another one of the great port houses, producing one of the deepest-coloured and sweetest styles in vintage port. Along with Taylor and Fonseca, Graham has probably been the most consistent producer of great port in the post-

World War II era. Their tawnys are quite good rather than exceptional, but their vintage ports are truly sublime and sumptuous. The 1983, like most vintage ports, seems more forward than normal, but has a great depth of very ripe, viscous, unctuous, plummy, tarry fruit and significant tannin in its very long finish. It is black/purple in colour. I doubt that it will be as profound or as long-lived as the great 1977, but it is certainly one of the top two or three ports of this vintage, and better than the excellent 1980 that Graham produced. The 1970 is a monumental vintage port and one of the greats of that vintage. It begs to be drunk now, although it will last for at least another two decades. The 1966, which I initially thought rather mediocre, has developed beautifully in the bottle and is a much finer vintage port than I originally suspected. It should be drunk now since it is not likely to get any better. The 1975 is the only recent vintage of Graham that I find disappointing. It is rather light in colour, finishes very short on the palate, and obviously lacks depth and ripeness.

MARTINEZ ★★★

1963	⑤	78
1967	④	85
1975	⑤	86
1982	④	84

This house is little known and I was unimpressed with the example of the 1963 that I once had in a comparative tasting. However, the two most recent notes I have are for the 1967 and 1975; both were good, medium-weight, tarry, plummy ports without a lot of character, but with good ripeness and clean winemaking.

OFFLEY FORRESTER ★★★

1970	⑤	86
1972	④	83
1977	④	86
1980	④	83
1983	④	85

Offley Forrester produces medium-weight ports that, given their reasonable price, offer value rather than great complexity and richness. Curiously, the 1972, a vintage not declared by most port shippers, produced a very good wine and I have good notes on the 1970. I have not tasted either of the two most recent top vintages, 1977 and 1983.

QUINTA DO NOVAL ★★★★

1963	⑤	82

1970	⑤ *84*
1975	④ *85*
1978	⑤ *84*
1982	⑤ *87*

The beautiful Quinta do Noval is undoubtedly the most famous port producer, largely because their 1931 and 1927 were to vintage port what the 1947 Cheval Blanc and 1945 Mouton Rothschild were to the Bordeaux trade—divine, monumental wines of extraordinary depth of flavour. Also, the Quinta do Noval produces a rare vintage port from a small vineyard of ungrafted, prephylloxera vines called Nacional. It is so rare that I have never seen, much less tasted, a bottle of what is supposedly a great port. However, the truth of the matter is that recent vintages of Quinta do Noval have not been nearly as impressive as they should be. Commentators have described the wines as light, elegant, and charming when in fact they lack richness and depth of flavour. The 1963 and 1970, two great vintages for port, are disappointing. The 1975 has turned out charming, fruity, and actually better than the 1970 or 1963, which is inexplicable. The two most recent vintages, 1978 and 1982, two vintages not declared by most port houses, have shown more richness of flavour and character in bouquet and aroma. Perhaps this estate is taking its winemaking a bit more seriously now, but it remains one of Oporto's most conspicuous under-achievers.

RAMOS-PINTO ★★★

Quinta da Bom Retiro Tawny 20-year-old	④ *86*
Quinta da Ervamoira Tawny 10-year-old	③ *85*
1970	④ *86*
1980	③ *84*
1983	③ *85*

I know little about this firm other than that both their tawnys are excellent and offer considerable value, and that the two vintage ports currently on the market show a style not unlike that of Fonseca, a lush mellowness and complex, plummy, chocolaty bouquet. Their 20-year-old Tawny, the Quinta da Bom Retiro, is really quite sumptuous.

SANDEMAN ★★★★

Founder's Reserve	③ *80*
Royal Tawny Non-Vintage	③ *83*
1970	⑤ *84*
1975	⑤ *84*
1977	⑤ *87*
1980	④ *82*

1982 .... ④ **87**

Sandeman is one of the biggest and most conspicuous of the port houses, with extensive interests in the sherry business as well. They advertize significantly and their products are well-represented in virtually every marketplace. The quality is quite good given the quantity of wine produced, but rarely does a Sandeman tawny or vintage port hit the true heights that a Dow, Fonseca, Taylor, or Graham will. Their Royal Tawny has an attractive, nutty, ripe black cherry character. Their Founder's Reserve, which is highly publicized, is good, inexpensive, straightforward port of little complexity but with plenty of mellow, savoury, sweet flavours. Their vintage ports have been a bit light, but the 1977 and 1982 show considerable strength and richness. However, the 1980, 1975, and 1970 are good rather than exciting in quality.

SMITH-WOODHOUSE ★ ★ ★

1980 .... ④ **85**

My experience with Smith-Woodhouse is limited, but I was impressed with a 1980 vintage port that showed a lovely, supple, ripe, rich, fruity character in an early-maturing style. I continue to hear good things about their tawnys, but have not had the opportunity to taste them.

TAYLOR FLADGATE & YEATMAN ★ ★ ★ ★ ★

Tawny Non-Vintage	③	**85**
10-year-old Tawny	④	**87**
20-year-old Tawny	⑤	**90**
30-year-old Tawny	⑤	**87**
1963	⑤	**95**
1966	⑤	**88**
1970	⑤	**96**
1975	④	**87**
1977	⑤	**96**
1980	④	**89**
1983	④	**94**

This house must certainly be the Latour of Portugal. Their ports are remarkably backward yet still impressive when young. Of all the vintage ports, those of Taylor need the longest time to mature and even when fully mature seem to have an inner strength and firmness that keep them going for decades. Their tawnys are also among the very best, though somewhat expensive. For current drinking, the 10-year-old Tawny is a wonderfully fragrant, nutty-scented wine of great character and complexity. Among their vintage ports there has not been an unsuccessful year since 1963. The 1963 is quite fabulous yet still seemingly capable of developing for another decade or more. The 1966 is drinking well now and is a very good rather than exceptional Taylor. The 1970 is fabulous, a broodingly dense-coloured and backward port, yet it has all the signs of future greatness, provided one is willing to cellar it until the early 1990s. The 1975 has turned out richly fruity, supple, and offers delicious drinking for the near future. The 1977 has consistently been at the top of my list of vintage ports in this great vintage, although the Dow, Graham, and Fonseca are equally splendid. It is a mammoth, opaque, statuesque vintage port of remarkable depth and power, but it should not be touched before 2000. The 1980 is probably the best port of the vintage, and the 1983 is wonderfully aromatic and perfumed (a characteristic of this charming vintage) yet powerful, long, and deep on the palate. It gives every indication of being an early-maturing Taylor, but I wouldn't want to drink it before 1995.

WARRE ★★★★

Nimrod Tawny	④	85
1963	⑤	87
1966	⑤	86
1970	⑤	87
1975	④	86
1977	⑤	92
1980	④	88
1983	④	90

This house makes rather restrained, yet rich, flavourful vintage port and a very good tawny called Nimrod. Their vintage ports seem slow to develop, and while they never have quite the voluptuous richness of a Dow, Graham, or Fonseca, they have their own unique mineral-scented character that gives them their own complexity and style. The 1983 is richly perfumed and fragrant, which is so typical of the ports from this vintage, and is seemingly more forward than normal. The 1980 is backward, firm, and has yet to reveal its true personality; the 1977 is quite powerful, very deep and intense, particularly for Warre; and the 1975 is soft, supple, and clearly mature. Of the older vintages, the 1970 remains rather unyielding but still impressive, the 1966 fully mature and good but not exciting, and the 1963 very, very good and now fully mature.

CHAPTER FIVE

SPAIN

SPAIN'S WINES

An Awakening Giant

RED WINES

Ask a French wine producer in Bordeaux what wine region in the world has the best chance of competing qualitatively with his, and the answer will be Spain.

The potential for great red wine in Spain's top three viticultural regions, the Rioja, Penedès, and Ribera del Duero, all in northern Spain, is considerable. Yet most wine enthusiasts probably think of inexpensive sparkling wines and sherry rather than fine red table wines when the topic of Spanish wine production comes up.

Admittedly, the high-quality sherries made in the hot, arid southern region of Jerez de la Frontera offer considerable diversity in style and appeal, but for centuries little has changed in the making of sherry. In the red wine regions, however, there is considerable revolution in winemaking and growers and producers are committed to making fine wine; I predict that they will have a significant positive impact on the future and image of Spain's red wine.

The consumer should remember that there are three constant conditions that exist for Spanish red wines. First, an obviously sweet, oaky taste, which the Spanish palate adores; second, except for a handful of super-expensive wines, Spain offers the very finest rapport in quality/price of any red wine produced today; third, traditional practice dictates that the wineries release their wines when they are ready to drink. All of Spain's wines are relatively mature when released but the best of them keep well in the bottle.

QUICK VINTAGE GUIDE

1985 Virtually every wine-producing region of Spain reported 1985 to be a very successful, high-quality vintage.

1984 This vintage has a terrible reputation because of a poor, cool European summer, but the wines of Spain may turn out to be the best made in Europe.

1983 A hot, dry year caused some problems, but early reports indicate a very good year.

1982 For Rioja and Ribera del Duero, the finest vintage since 1970, and largely regarded as a great year.

1981 A very good vintage.

1980 An average-quality year.

1979 A good year in the Penedès area, but only average in Rioja.

1978 For Rioja, Penedès, and the Ribera del Duero, the best overall vintage between 1970 and 1982.

Older Vintages

The 1977 vintage was a great one for most of northern Spain. Prior to that, 1964 was another superb vintage. Well-kept bottles of 1970 and 1964 red wines from Rioja and the Ribera del Duero can be excellent examples of Spanish red wines.

A GUIDE TO SPAIN'S BEST PRODUCERS

★ ★ ★ ★ ★ Outstanding Producers

Pasquera (Ribera del Duero)
La Rioja Alta (Rioja)
Torres Black Label Coronas
   (Penedès)

Vega Sicilia (Ribera del Duero)

★ ★ ★ ★ Excellent Producers

CVNE (Rioja)
Laserna (Rioja)
Jean León (Penedès)
Marqués de Griñon (Rueda)

Muga (Rioja)
Remelluri (Rioja)
Torres Gran Coronas (Penedès)

★ ★ ★ Good Producers

Bilbainas (Rioja)
Campo Viejo (Rioja)
Castillo de Tiebas (Navarra)
Faustino Martinez (Rioja)
Lar de Barros (Tierra de Barros)
Lopez de Heredia Viña
   Tondonia (Rioja)
Marqués de Cáceres (Rioja)

Marqués de Murrieta (Rioja)
Marqués de Riscal (Rioja)
Mont Marcal (Penedès)
Olarra (Rioja)
Rioja Vega-Muerza (Rioja)
Señoria de Sarria (Navarra)
Torres Gran Sangre de Toro
   (Penedès)

★ ★ Average Producers

Age-Unidas (Rioja)
Masia Bach (Penedès)
R. Barbier (Penedès)
Berberana (Rioja)
Beronia (Rioja)
Domaine Domecq (Rioja)
Franco Españolas (Rioja)

Gran Condal-Bodegas Santiago
   (Rioja)
Lan (Rioja)
Montecillo (Rioja)
Federico Paternina (Rioja)
Viño Pedrosa
   (Ribera del Duero)

SPAIN • TODAY'S BUYING STRATEGY

For the most part, Spanish wines are aged, mostly in oak vats, but also in bottle a long time before release. The Spaniards like to buy and drink their wine when it has mellowed and is close to maturity. Consequently, most Spanish wines are ready to drink when released, although they may not yet be fully mature. Prices over recent years have been remarkably stable, and the best of these wines continue to represent great bargains in mature red wines. Except for a handful of the rarer, more sought-after Spanish red wines, the Vega Sicilia, Pesquera, and Torres Black Label Gran Coronas, I buy Spanish wines not to cellar but to drink immediately. Keep in mind that 1978, 1981, and the great 1982 are the three best recent vintages. Most of the top 1982s are just now coming on the market and these three vintages are those on which to concentrate.

A COMMENT ON SPANISH SPARKLING WINES

The Spanish sparkling wine business is large and best at producing solid, reliable, unexciting, sparkling wines at remarkably low prices. If they do not provide inspiring drinking, they are certainly adequate and, most important, cheap. The best producer of sparkling wine is Juve and Champs, followed by Codorníu, Freixenet, Penelada, and Segura Viudas. Over 90% of the Spanish sparkling wine is produced in Penedès and the two largest firms, Codorníu and Freixenet, account for the great majority of the sparkling wine produced in Spain.

Following are my notes for all the top producers of Spain's red wine-producing regions.

AGE-UNIDAS *RIOJA* ★★

1981 Siglo.. ① **65**

This winery can produce good wine, but most comsumers will probably remember the wines more for the burlap bag in which the wine bottle is encased. The best vintage I ever tasted was the 1961, which was soft and fruity and held for a number of years. The 1981 is quite light and a little stale-tasting.

RENÉ BARBIER *PENEDÈS* ★★

1978 Cabernet Sauvignon... ① **78**
1983 Red Wine.. ① **80**
1983 Reserva... ① **75**

René Barbier produces rather straightforward, fruity, medium-bodied wines that are meant to be drunk young. The prices are reasonable but the wines often lack a focal point of interest as is the case for the three selections above.

BERBERANA *RIOJA* ★★

1981 Carta de Oro... ① **82**
1975 Gran Reserva... ② **80**
1978 Gran Reserva... ② **83**
1980 Reserva... ① **78**

These Riojas are all average to slightly above average quality wines and are fully mature. The 1981 Carta de Oro is light ruby with a moderately intense, oaky, strawberry and cherry-scented bouquet and light flavours. The 1980 Reserva is light, with a cardboard-type aroma and decent flavours. Between the other two Reservas, the 1978 is spicy with nice cherry fruit, medium body and decent length. The 1975 is just beginning to dry out in fruit and should be drunk up. These are decent, rather lightweight Riojas.

CAMPO VIEJO *RIOJA* ★★★

1975 Gran Reserva... ② **85**
1970 Gran Reserva Villamagna............................ ③ **86**
1973 Gran Reserva Villamagna............................ ③ **85**
All three of these Riojas showed quite well in my tastings. They have good colour, plenty of richness and length, mature, well-developed bouquets, and good character. The 1975 has a rich, intense bouquet of coffee, spices and leather, medium body, soft, generous flavours, and a good finish. The 1973 has an aged Rioja smell of sweet, oaky aromas, and soft, cherryish fruit. It is a medium-bodied, mellow, rather good Rioja. The 1970, from a great vintage for the area, has a deep colour, a spice-box, cedary, sweet, oaky bouquet, rich, fleshy flavours that have a round, plump texture, and good finish. These are attractive, well-made, interesting Riojas.

CVNE *RIOJA* ★★★★

1982 Clarete .... ① **84**
1978 CVNE.. ① **80**
1975 Reserva Imperial .... ② **84**
1976 Reserva Imperial .... ② **83**
1980 Viña Real.. ① **82**
1975 Viña Real Gran Reserva............................ ② **84**
This producer is still among the top Rioja houses. The 1982 Clarete is supple and loaded with fruit. One can only anticipate with great desire just how good the 1982 Reserva Rioja will be, given the success of this lighter-styled Clarete. The 1980 Viña Real has good colour, a spicy, plum fruitiness, bigger body but not the charm of the 1982. The 1978 CVNE has a spicy, fruity, complex bouquet, medium body, but finishes short. The 1975 Viña Real (in the Burgundy-shaped bottle) is a rich, medium, to full-bodied wine with good concentration, a round texture, and good length. The 1976 Reserva Imperial (in the Bordeaux-shaped bottle) is more angular, lean, and lacks the richness of the 1975 Viña Real. The 1975 Reserva Imperial is better than the 1976, with more body, depth, and richness of fruit. It is fully mature and should keep well for two to five years.

DOMAINE DOMECQ *RIOJA* ★★

1976 .... ② **70**
1980 .... ① **70**
This winery makes inexpensive but soft, fruity, light-bodied wines for drinking upon release. They show no evidence of any ability to improve within the bottle.

FAUSTINO-BODEGA MARTINEZ *RIOJA* ★★★

1970 Faustino .... ③ **85**
1976 Faustino .... ② **84**
I have tasted a range of older Rioja Reservas from this firm that were well made, not terribly complex or profound, but spicy, fruity, soft, velvety wines that exhibited quality winemaking. The 1976 Faustino, the vintage currently available, is quite an alluring wine. A moderately intense bouquet of sweet oak and ripe cherry fruit is pleasant. On the palate, the wine is supple, lush, and fully mature. The 1970, which is still commercially available, is slightly richer, with a deep, more complex bouquet.

GRAN CONDAL-BODEGAS SANTIAGO *RIOJA* ★★

1976 Reserva Rioja .... ② **76**
1978 Reserva Rioja .... ② **72**
1983 Rioja .... ① **75**
1984 Rioja .... ① **78**
All four of these wines are light, insubstantial, and fairly bland. The 1984 is the most appealing, with a charming, light-intensity strawberry fruitiness. The 1978 Reserva has an aged maturity but short, thin finish. The 1976 Reserva has a decaying, leafy, vegetal smell and short, light flavours.

LAR DE BARROS *TIERRA DE BARROS* ★★★

1982 Tinto Reserva .... ② **85**
To date, this is the best red Spanish wine I have tasted outside of the famous viticultural areas of Rioja, Penedès, Navarra, Ribera del Duero, and Rueda. It is a very good wine with an exotic bouquet suggesting chocolate cherry candy, it has the texture of a lush Pomerol and a smooth, velvety finish.

VINÍCOLA LASERNA *RIOJA* ★★★★

1975 Contino .... ② **87**
1978 Contino .... ② **88**
1980 Contino .... ② **86**
This is one of the few estates to use a specific vineyard for its wine. The winery is largely unknown, but the quality of the wines is among the best in Spain and the potential enormous.

All of these wines have very good colour, very fragrant, oaky, voluptuous, deep, intense bouquets, loads of fruit and concentration, and long finishes. The wines have the sweet oakiness so common in Spanish red wines as well as a lush Pomerol fruitiness. An estate to watch carefully.

JEAN LEÓN *PENEDÈS* ★ ★ ★ ★

1978 Cabernet Sauvignon .... ② **86**
1979 Cabernet Sauvignon .... ② **86**

This winery continues to turn out very fine Cabernets at very modest prices. However, despite their prices, these wines need cellaring as they are made in a very rich, deep, tannic, full-bodied style. For example, older vintages such as the 1974 and 1975 are still not fully mature. The 1978 and 1979 are deeply coloured, medium- to full-bodied wines loaded with aromas and flavours of toasty new oak, blackcurrants, and exotic spices. Both can be drunk now, but given their structure and depth, I would imagine five to six years of cellaring might just yield some shockingly complex, rich wines.

LOPEZ DE HEREDIA VIÑA TONDONIA *RIOJA* ★ ★ ★

1978 Viña Tondonia .... ② *80*
1979 Viña Tondonia .... ① *75*

This winery makes two styles of wine, a Viña Tondonia in a Bordeaux-shaped bottle and a more robust, richer Viña Bosconia in a Burgundy-shaped bottle. Older vintages from the fifties and sixties were beautiful examples of Rioja at its best; however, recent vintages have a tendency to be fruity, soft, light and rather straightforward in style, as typified by the above examples.

MARQUÉS DE CÁCERES *RIOJA* ★ ★ ★

1975 Reserva .... ② *84*
1981 Tinto .... ① *82*

The Cáceres style of Rioja represents the very modern style that draws its inspiration from Bordeaux. The wines are fruity, supple, straightforward and not oaky. Both of these wines, while lacking a little depth and character, are still good wines with clean, soft, generous, ripe cherry flavours, medium body, and pleasant finishes. Both should be drunk over the next several years.

MARQUÉS DE GRIÑON *RUEDA* ★ ★ ★ ★

1982 Tinto de Crianza .... ② *87*
1983 Tinto de Crianza .... ② *85*

The inspiration for this wine from Rueda is Carlos Falco, an agricultural engineer and graduate of the University of California at Davis. His 1982 is 90% Cabernet Sauvignon and 10% Merlot, aged two years in American oak. (The famous Professor Peynaud and Alexis Lichine are consultants here.) The 1982 is a rich, deeply flavoured wine with a complex bouquet of cedarwood and ripe plums. On the palate, the wine is rich, supple, quite drinkable now, but shows every indication of being able to live for five to ten years. It is extremely impressive. The 1983 is very similar in style but slightly less fat and deep. Both are excellent examples of the newer styles of Spanish red wines.

MARQUÉS DE MURRIETTA *RIOJA* ★★★

1978	②	**82**
1978 Castillo de Ygay....................................	②	**85**

The Marqués de Murrietta is one of the oldest Bodegas in Spain. The winery has an excellent reputation, although I have found the quality of the wines to be rather spotty and inconsistent. The above two wines are both fully mature, show a great deal of oak ageing, and have round, soft, supple flavours. Neither is likely to improve any further and should be drunk up.

MARQUÉS DE RISCAL *RIOJA* ★★★

1978	②	**82**
1980	②	**74**
1981	②	**78**

The Marqués de Riscal is one of Rioja's most famous wineries from which I have had some wonderfully rich, complex, old vintages. Recent wines have not shown nearly as well and have tasted significantly lighter than some of the older vintages; however, should you come across any of their Gran Reservas, which usually have a hefty portion of Cabernet Sauvignon added in, they are worth a try.

MONT MARCAL *PENEDÈS* ★★★

1982 Cabernet Sauvignon	②	**?**
1981 Tinto Reserva..	②	**?**

There are some attractive components to these wines, but also some disturbing flawed qualities. The 1982 Cabernet has a slight barnyard aroma that spoils a wine that otherwise has a lovely, lush, rich texture and deep fruit. The 1981 Tinto Reserva has an aroma of overripe black cherries and sweaty leather and seems rather unstable in the bottle. Neither is worth a gamble.

MONTECILLO *RIOJA* ★★
1981 Lumbrero .... ① *80*
1978 Monty .... ② *82*
This winery produces Rioja in the very modern, fruity, soft style that eschews excessive amounts of wood ageing. The wines are straightforward, fruity, soft and cleanly made.

MUGA *RIOJA* ★★★★
1978 Muga .... ① *84*
1976 Prado Enea .... ② *86*
This is one of my favourite Bodegas in Rioja. Their wines are very traditionally made, tend to be quite oaky and light in colour, but are very aromatic, with sweet, long, ripe flavours. The 1978 Muga has ripe, plummy fruit and a generous bouquet of expansive, spicy oak and rich cherry fruit. The 1976 Prado Enea is deeper, more complex, and certainly one of the finest Riojas on the market. Both are ready to drink now.

OLARRA *RIOJA* ★★★
1980 Cerro Añon .... ① *82*
1982 Cerro Añon .... ① *75*
1978 Cerro Añon Reserva .... ② *78*
1981 Tinto .... ① *80*
1975 Tinto Gran Reserva .... ② *82*
1978 Tinto Reserva .... ② *83*
Several years ago, in tasting through the Olarra wines, I was very impressed with their quality and reasonable prices, and certainly these wines have enjoyed and deserved a great deal of success. But more recent offerings have been only average in quality, and seem less impressive than those first tasted four or five years ago. All of the above wines are soundly made but rather dull.

FEDERICO PATERNINA *RIOJA* ★★
1964 Gran Reserva .... ④ *65*
1966 Gran Reserva .... ④ *67*
1968 Gran Reserva .... ④ *62*
1970 Gran Reserva .... ③ *75*
The Paternina Bodega is certainly one of the Rioja's most famous names. In fact, I can remember some grand old wines from vintages in the fifties and early sixties. However, the 1964, 1966 and 1968 Gran Reservas all suffered from the same problem: an objectionable cardboard smell I associate with filter pads. However, I would think that given the eight to ten years these wines spent in oak, they hardly needed to be

filtered for clarity. Whatever the reason, the wines tasted short, were terribly deficient in fruit on the palate, and were rather dried out. The 1970 had some fruit left to it. What a shame for this fine old Bodega to release such inferior wines.

PESQUERA *RIBERA DEL DUERO* ★★★★★

1982 Pesquera	③	92
1983 Pesquera	③	90
1984 Pesquera	③	85
1975 Pesquera Reserva	⑤	92
1982 Pesquera Reserva	⑤	95

The new star in Ribera del Duero is the Pesquera of Alejandro Fernandes. With vineyards next to Vega Sicilia, this wine is aged only two to two and a half years in cask (à la Bordeaux) and then bottled. The results are stunning. Both the 1982s are staggeringly immense wines, rich, unctuous, with the depth and texture of a great Pomerol such as Pétrus or L'Evangile, plenty of ripe, round tannins, the sweet oaky smells that typify Spanish reds, and unbelievable length. The 1983 is identical, but slightly less open and opulent; the 1984 is just a shade lighter and less concentrated. The 1975, just released, is another fine effort, very rich and, despite its luxurious texture, it has the depth and harmony to improve for another two decades. A 1972 Pesquera tasted recently was sublime. Pesquera's wines must be tasted to be believed. They should last five to fifteen years, but because of their massive fruit can be drunk young. The Pétrus of Spain?

REMELLURI *RIOJA* ★★★★

1979 La Bastida de Alava	②	86
1980 La Bastida de Alava	②	85
1982 La Bastida de Alava	②	87

Remelluri is one of only a handful of Rioja estates to produce and estate-bottle their wines from their own vineyards. The proprietor, Don Jaime Rodriquez Salis, believes in elegant, complex wines, and that is what one finds – wines with a refined fragrance and gentle suppleness and lushness that are more akin to Burgundies than Bordeaux. His wines are aged three to four years in oak casks and then bottled. This is a very serious estate and, after the Bodegas La Rioja Alta in Haro, perhaps the region's second-best producer. All three of these wines are similarly styled – medium-bodied, graceful, stylish wines with smooth, harmonious, generous flavours. The 1982, Rioja's first great vintage since 1970, is more concentrated, but ready to drink. The 1980 is slightly lighter but has a lovely bouquet of ripe berry fruit and sweet oak. The 1979 is virtually identical in style, but I thought it just a bit longer on the palate. I am not sure whether these wines will improve in the bottle, but they will keep easily for three to five years.

LA RIOJA ALTA *RIOJA* ★★★★★

1970 Reserva 890...	④	**90**
1973 Reserva 904...	②	**89**
1983 Viña Alberdi..	①	**75**
1976 Viña Ardanza..	②	**86**
1978 Viña Ardanza..	②	*84*

This is the top Rioja winery, and the demand for its products, and consequently the prices, reflect it. However, I know of no one who has ever tasted these wines to complain about the price – they are that good. La Rioja Alta is a practitioner of the old school of Rioja winemaking. The wines are kept six, eight, even ten years in cask and only released when the winery deems them 'ready'. The 1983 Viña Alberdi is quite undistinguished, but the other wines certainly have plenty to offer. I marginally prefer the 1976 to the 1978 Viña Ardanza only because the 1978 is still a little tannic. Both are spicy, rich in fruit, medium-bodied, with cedary aromas and excellent balance. The top-of-the-line Cuvées, the 1973 Reserva 904 and the 1970 Reserva 890, are both quite exceptional. The Reserva 904 is fully mature, light in colour and with a gorgeous fragrance of ripe, rich fruit and smooth, complex, almost Volnay-like flavours. It will keep for four to five years, but I know of nowhere in the world where you can find this level of mature, sublime complexity for such a reasonable price. The 1970 Reserva 890 is altogether outstanding – from its full-intensity bouquet that suggests roasted chestnuts, tobacco, and a fine Graves, to its long, rich, smooth, medium- to full-bodied flavours that linger and linger on the palate.

RIOJA VEGA-MUERZA *RIOJA* ★★★

1975 Reserva	②	*84*
1978 Reserva	①	*84*
1981 Tinto..	①	*80*

This winery has in recent years consistently provided good wine at rather low prices. Of the three current releases, the 1981 is a little dull and one-dimensional, but for the price no one will complain about the quality. Both the 1978 and 1975 are a big step upward. The 1978 is light ruby in colour, has a moderately intense, rather seductive raspberry-scented bouquet, soft, supple flavours, and nice balance. It is ready to drink. The 1975 is a more serious wine, but more tannic with a sterner, rougher framework, and slightly less charming. If you prefer charm, try the 1978; if you like power, the 1975.

SEÑORIA DE SARRIA *NAVARRA* ★★★

1982	①	**80**
1973 Reserva	②	**85**
1978 Tinto	①	**84**
1978 Viña del Lerdon	②	**85**

This well-run Navarra winery produces rather light-coloured wines, but don't let that mislead you. They are spicy, fragrant, and redolent with scents of sweet oak, cherries and flowers. The 1982 is light, fruity, supple and a very attractive value. Both 1978s have more richness, medium body, supple, elegant textures. The Viña del Lerdon tasted longer on the palate. The 1973 Reserva is beginning to tire a bit (at least the bottle I tried was fatigued) but is still a delicious mouthful of savoury, oaky, fruity, easy-to-drink yet complex and elegant Spanish wine.

TORRES *PENEDÈS* ★★★★

1982 Coronas	①	**83**
1979 Gran Coronas Reserva	②	**87**
1981 Gran Coronas Reserva	②	**88**
1982 Gran Coronas Reserva	②	**89**

The 1982 Coronas is one of the great red wine values in today's market. It is remarkably consistent from bottle to bottle. A moderately intense, black cherry bouquet intermingled with scents of spice is very appealing. Round and generously flavoured, this medium-bodied, dry wine has soft tannins, good concentration and character. Serve it blind and most tasters will think it is a much more expensive bottle of wine. The 1979, 1981, and 1982 Gran Coronas Reservas are astonishing bargains. Their rich, complex bouquets of ripe plums, spicy oak, and vanillin are top-flight. On the palate, they are full-bodied, deep, savoury and quite long, with layers of fruit. A Spanish Lynch-Bages? Perhaps. Both should drink and improve for at least five to six more years. They are blends of 60% Cabernet Sauvignon and 40% Tempranillo, the dominant red wine grape of Penedès and Rioja.

1981 Sangre de Toro	①	**79**
1982 Sangre de Toro	①	**83**
1978 Sangre de Toro Reserva	①	**85**

I suspect more Spanish restaurants use the Sangre de Toro in their Sangria than any other wine. In a way it does a disservice to the wine. For its low price, it offers plenty of rich, chunky, supple fruit and is similar to a good generic Côte du Rhône. The 1981 is chunky, deep in colour, but one-dimensional. I would go for the 1978 Reserva, which has a fragrant, ripe, spicy bouquet, big, rich flavours and a long, supple finish. It's a fleshy, rich wine made from 65% Grenache and 35% Carignane. It is Spain's answer to a good Châteauneuf-du-Pape.

1977 Gran Coronas Black Label.................................. ③ **90**
1978 Gran Coronas Black Label.................................. ③ **92**
1981 Cran Coronas Black Label.................................. ④ **90**
The 1978 is the first Black Label to be 100% Cabernet Sauvignon. These are truly extraordinary wines and among the world's greatest. Their prices are, quite frankly, unbelievable and not likely to remain low once the wine-consuming public realizes how great these wines can be. The 1977 has a wonderful bouquet of toasty vanillin oak, ripe blackcurrants, and leather. On the palate, it is velvety, supple, deeply flavoured, and oh, so long. It should be drunk over the next five to six years. The 1978 is, I think, the greatest Black Label yet produced. It is 100% Cabernet Sauvignon, and the bouquet explodes from the glass with complex aromas of oak, cassis, coconuts, violets, truffles and leather. Very concentrated, moderately tannic, fleshy and deep, it has the concentration and texture of a great vintage of Pétrus. Yes, the score is correct; I feel there are few red wines in the world from the 1978 vintage that can top this marvellously balanced, impeccably vinified wine. It should develop and last for at least eight to ten years. The newly released 1981 continues the splendid line of successes from Torres. It is reminiscent in style of the 1977, but has slightly more richness and fragrance.

1975 Gran Coronas Reserva .... ② **83**
This new release, a commemorative bottling, is showing a spicy, tobacco and earthy bouquet, rather tannic, hard flavours, and an angular personality. I prefer the recent Gran Coronas Reservas to this older vintage.

VEGA SICILIA *RIBERA DEL DUERO* ★★★★★
1960 Unico Reserva.. ⑤ **87**
1965 Unico Reserva.. ⑤ **80**
1966 Unico Reserva.. ⑤ **92**
1972 Unico Reserva.. ⑤ **90**
1976 Valbuena.. ④ **85**
1978 Valbuena.. ④ **88**
1979 Valbuena.. ④ **89**
1980 Valbuena.. ④ **87**

1982 Valbuena... ⑤ **87**

Vega Sicilia is reputed to produce Spain's greatest red wines. Because of the high prices charged, the estate has been a target for criticism. However, the wines I tasted, except for the 1965 Vega Sicilia, ranged from excellent to superb. The top wine is the Vega Sicilia Unico Reserva; it is expensive and produced in very limited quantities. Given their quality, age, and rarity, the price is not unfair. The 1960 has a full-intensity, sweet, oaky bouquet dominated by the smell of rich, plummy fruit on the palate. The wine is expansive, lush and flowing, like a great old Pomerol. It is very concentrated and so well-balanced. Since the Vega Sicilias are kept at least ten years in cask prior to release, I doubt much ageing takes place in the bottle. The 1965 is awkward, rather compact, and lacking in personality. I tasted it twice and was left surprised by its rather mediocre character. The 1966 is fabulous: a rich, spicy, sweet, oaky bouquet with rich, opulent, voluptuous flavours, an incredible finish, and remarkable complexity. It can hardly get any better. The newest Unico Reserva is the 1972, another rather profound wine with the tell-tale sweet, oaky, richly fruity, full-blown bouquet and ripe, voluptuous, opulent flavours and length. The wine is all the more remarkable given the fact that 1972 was a terrible vintage in Europe.

Before you invest in a Vega Sicilia Reserva, an excellent introduction to the style of this winery is its Valbuena, which spends only five, rather than ten, years in oak. It is very similarly styled with the same lush, intense opulence of fruit, the fragrant, sweet, oaky smells, and the easy-to-drink yet very complex style. The 1978, 1979, and 1980 are all excellent; the 1976 less concentrated, a trifle too oaky. The wines of Vega Sicilia are exotic, dramatic, and intensely rich.

VIÑA PEDROSA *RIBERA DEL DUERO* ★★

1983 Tinto Pedrosa... ② **78**
1982 Tinto Reserva Pedrosa... ③ **84**
1985 Viña Pedrosa .... ② **83**

The best wine I tasted from Pedrosa was the 1985 Viña Pedrosa, a rich, supple, explosively fruity wine that must be Spain's answer to Italy's Dolcetto or France's Beaujolais. It is meant to be drunk young and it is quite delicious. The 1983 Tinto had a fine dark color but a rustic, coarse texture. The 1982 Tinto exhibited more charm and character.

CHAPTER SIX

NORTH AMERICA

CALIFORNIA

While California does indeed produce some world-class wines, particularly Cabernet Sauvignon, Chardonnay, and the nectar-like, decadently sweet, late harvest Riesling, much of the self-serving, overly exaggerated publicity about the greatness of California wines (both from the trade and chauvinistic West Coast wine press) is quite excessive and easily refutable.

For decades the prevailing philosophy, spawned by so-called wine wizards at the University of California at Davis (the California equivalent of the University of Bordeaux), was that grapes could grow virtually anywhere in California with great success because of the exceptional climate that the state enjoys. Soil and the density of vines per acre, two extremely critical considerations for most of Europe's winemakers, were thought to be of secondary significance. Fortunately, these ill-founded beliefs are now under intense scrutiny by more serious segments of the wine industry concerned with the quality of California wines and their ageing potential. Yet there is no doubt that many vineyards of Riesling, Gewürztraminer, Pinot Noir, and Chenin Blanc were planted in areas too hot for producing premium wines of finesse and good flavour. In addition, the obsession of many California winemakers with state-of-the-art technology to sculpture and produce extremely clean, often very innocuous examples of wine, has resulted in many of these same wines lacking personality, as well as charm and a focal point of flavour. For every bold, dramatic, interesting, world-class California Chardonnay and Cabernet Sauvignon produced, there are at least five or six times that number of wines produced that are sterile, one-dimensional and bland, which taste as if they have been made by winemakers according to a formula where the only goal was that of perfect acidity and a perfect pH. Perhaps the wild swings in winemaking style that have characterized California from the early 1970s through the early 1980s are symptomatic of an industry that for a large majority of its members is still not even a decade old. But, the basic fact remains that California has much to learn, and even more to prove before it can, as a region, be considered a top-rank producer of consistently great wines.

Nevertheless, the top producers in California do indeed make majestically flavoured wines, although given the cost of shipping to the United Kingdom as well as the current exchange rates between the dollar and the pound, they will never represent the value that the better European imports do.

AN OVERVIEW OF THE MAJOR CALIFORNIA VARIETALS

White Wine Varietals

Chardonnay

The great superstar of the white wines, Chardonnay at its best can produce majestically rich, buttery wines with layers of flavours suggesting tropical fruits, apples, and peaches. It flourishes in all of California's viticultural districts. The trend in California has been to pick the grapes earlier to achieve higher natural acidities. Even though Chardonnay definitely produces California's finest white wines, far too many, though technically flawless, tend to lack character and taste like imitations of each other. This will hopefully change as winemakers and owners become more confident. Chardonnay is generally aged in oak barrels for several months to a year. They can be long-lived wines in the hands of producers such as Trefethen, Sonoma-Cutrer, Stony Hill, Mayacamas, or Kalin, but the great majority of these wines require drinking up before they turn five years old. Anyone who tells you anything different clearly does not have your best interests in mind. One trend to pay particular attention to is the bevy of top-quality, low-priced Chardonnays that have appeared on the market. Labels to look for are Glen Ellen, Stratford, and Liberty School.

Chenin Blanc

This maligned, generally misunderstood grape can produce lovely apéritif wines both dry and slightly sweet, but in either style, fruity, delicate, perfumed, and light-bodied. However, sagging sales have caused many premium wineries to abandon it. Dry Creek, Chappellet, Preston, Alexander Valley, and Hacienda make some of the best.

French Colombard

Like the Chenin Blanc, another varietal that is rarely accorded respect by consumers. Its charm is its aromatic character and crisp, light-bodied style. Parducci and Chalone consistently prove its credentials.

Gewürztraminer

Highly promoted and encouraged by the California wine press, this varietal, made in the dry, slightly sweet, and late-harvest (very sweet) style, is to my palate a watery, vague resemblance to the spicy, exotic, flamboyant Gewürztraminers made in Alsace, France. Wineries that have captured some authentic Gewürztraminer character in their wines are Evensen Napa, Joseph Phelps Napa, and Château St.-Jean Sonoma.

Muscat

This is a terribly underrated and under-appreciated varietal that produces at the top levels slightly sweet, remarkably fragrant,

California

Wine regions

1 Napa Valley
2 Sonoma
3 Mendocino
4 Solano
5 Sierra Foothills
6 El Dorado
7 Amador
8 Alameda
9 Santa Clara
10 Santa Cruz
11 Monterey
12 San Benito
13 San Luis Obispo
14 Santa Barbara
15 Los Angeles
16 Riverside
17 San Diego
18 Imperial Valley

NEVADA

MOJAVE
DESERT

San
● Bernardino

COLORADO

16

SALTON
SEA

San
Diego

17   18

MEXICO

| 0 | 50 | 100 | 150 |
KILOMETERS

| 0 | 50 | 100 |
MILES

perfumed wines that are usually loaded with tropical fruit aromas and flavours. Robert Pecota, Louis Martini, and Bonny Doon all achieve special results with this grape.

Pinot Blanc
Often indistinguishable from Chardonnay in a blind tasting, Pinot Blanc is usually a more steely, crisper, firmer wine than Chardonnay. Chalone makes the best Pinot Blanc in California, followed by Congress Springs, Mirassou, and Bonny Doon.

Sauvignon Blanc
In the last several years, the trendy California wine scene made this grape the 'great white hope', and now that wineries have taken up its cause, it seems to be falling out of fashion. It is often called Fumé Blanc. It is a crisp wine with a subtle earthy, herbaceous quality that in many examples becomes grotesquely vegetal, although examples of blatantly vegetal wines are much less extensive today than several years ago. It is a remarkably flexible wine with an assortment of foods and the level of quality across the board is quite high. Yet, rather unfortunately, far too many wineries aim for the middle-of-the-road, safe style of wine and, as with Chardonnay, one finds an excessive number of fairly neutral, bland, innocuous examples of this wine. Sauvignon is often blended with Semillon to give it more body and a creamy character. Some of California's best Sauvignons or Fumé Blancs are produced by Robert Mondavi, Dry Creek, Kalin, Matanzas Creek, Château St.-Jean, Spottswoode, and Glen Ellen.

Semillon
This is clearly one of the up-and-coming white varietals of Califor-nia. It is the perfect partner when added to the crisp, lean, acidic, Sauvignon because it seems to always have plenty of body and a creamy richness. It is difficult to handle entirely by itself, but Kalin Cellars of Marin County has produced a ravishing string of Semillons from old vines planted in Livermore, and Beringer has produced a decadently sweet dessert wine from this varietal.

White Riesling or Johannisberg Riesling
With over 8,000 acres of this varietal planted in California, the wine industry is not likely to tear out the vines; nevertheless, except for the world-class, late-harvest sweet Rieslings made by Joseph Phelps, Château St.-Jean, Raymond and a handful of other wineries, the attempts at making dry Kabinett or Spätlese-styled Rieslings have generally produced dull, heavy wines with little character. The simple truth of the matter is that most of the Riesling is planted in areas where the soil is too rich or the climate too hot. With only a handful of exceptions, Jekel, Kendall Jackson, Château St.-Jean are three that come to mind – the conditions are only suitable for great,

sweet, dessert-style Rieslings. No one wants to hear it, but its drier versions have largely been failures.

Red Wine Varietals

Cabernet Franc

Now being used by more and more wineries to give complexity to their wines' bouquet, Cabernet Franc is a cedary, herbaceous-scented wine that is much lighter in colour and body than either Cabernet Sauvignon or Merlot. It rarely can stand by itself, but used judiciously in a blend, it can provide an extra dimension. Two great California wines with significant proportions of Cabernet Franc that have stood the test of time are the 1971 Robert Mondavi Reserve Cabernet and the 1977 Joseph Phelps Insignia red wine. The Santa Cruz winery of Congress Springs has recently demonstrated success with this varietal.

Cabernet Sauvignon

This great red wine grape has found a hospitable home in many areas of California. It reaches its heights in Napa, the Santa Cruz Mountains, and Sonoma. It renders wines dense in colour, with high tannins, and a rich blackcurrant-flavoured fruitiness often inter-twined with subtle, spicy, herbaceous scents. While wines made from Cabernet Sauvignon can be remarkably long-lived – fifteen to twenty years in a few instances – most California Cabernets should be drunk before they attain the age of eight. However wines, from the top wineries can certainly last twelve to fifteen years before fading. But beware: many California Cabernets, primarily those made from grapes in Santa Barbara, San Luis Obispo, Monterey, and Lake counties, have extremely vegetal aromas and flavours. This defect even afflicts certain Sonoma and Napa Cabernets. Don't let anyone tell you this is a peculiar personality trait of California Cabernet. It is a major defect, and many wineries have to face the fact that their vineyards are planted in improper soils and regions – a hard fact to accept when it costs upwards of $20,000 an acre to purchase, clear, and plant a vineyard.

Merlot

The higher-alcohol, fleshier, more supple stablemate of Cabernet Sauvignon, Merlot can stand by itself and be enjoyed for its opulence, or blended with Cabernet Sauvignon to provide a softer, lusher texture. Some wineries are now offering Merlot on its own, and the results have generally been quite good.

Petite Sirah

Unfortunately, this varietal has fallen from grace. Though not the true Syrah, it can produce richly coloured, very tannic, intense wines with peppery, cassis-scented bouquets. The Ridge and Freemark Abbey Petite Sirahs from Napa's York Creek Vineyard prove the outstanding potential of this grape when planted in the proper soils and grown and vinified with care.

Pinot Noir

Largely a failure in California's North Coast regions, the Pinot Noir has probably broken more winemakers' hearts than anybody or anything else. Grapes grown in the cool Carneros region have consistently shown promise, as have grapes grown in Monterey and other areas of the Central Coast. One must always approach California Pinot Noir with the greatest degree of caution, for the bad, or should I say bad and bizarre, examples of this wine are repugnant. Yet progress continues to be made. In the north, Robert Mondavi, Acacia, Hanzell, and the two emerging superstars, Saintsbury and Kalin, have somehow found the secret. South of San Francisco, Chalone, Calera, Thomas Fogarty, Edna Valley and a handful of other wineries have also found the elusive formula for Pinot Noir.

Syrah

The great red grape of the Rhône Valley. Few California wineries have toyed with this varietal, which may be more suitable for the climate and soils of most California viticultural districts than any other varietal. Joseph Phelps produces a Syrah in a light, fruity, Beaujolais style, but Bonny Doon in the Santa Cruz Mountains has made exquisite wines from Syrah in 1983, 1984, and 1985, and Qupé is another pioneer with this varietal. Perhaps these wineries will finally prove that outstanding wines from this varietal can be made in California.

Zinfandel

The perennial whipping boy of the wine press, Zinfandel all but disappeared from the popularity charts in the late seventies and early eighties. It can be a remarkably satisfying wine, rich, bold and dramatic. It can also cause rampant confusion because it appears in so many different styles – from light, zesty Beaujolais-inspired wines to heavy, port-like, late-harvest monsters. The best Zinfandels have properly balanced richness and harmony. The two best practitioners, Ridge and Ravenswood, continue to be in a class by themselves.

QUICK VINTAGE GUIDE

1986 All of the reports indicate a good quality crop for Chardonnay and Cabernet Sauvignon, although only a handful of producers seem to think the quality will be up to the exceptional level reached in 1985 and the very good level obtained in 1984. Rain complicated matters prior to the harvest. Barrel samples of the red wines tasted have shown wines that are tannic, a trifle austere, but well coloured and balanced. The Chardonnays look to be very good rather than exceptional.

1985 The finest vintage for California Cabernet Sauvignon, Chardonnay, and Sauvignon Blanc since 1974. A perfect growing season preceded near-perfect conditions for harvesting. Napa and Sonoma look to be the best, Santa Cruz and Mendocino just behind in quality. The Cabernets should be both rich and long-lived, less extroverted and opulent in their youth than the 1984s, but certainly longer-lived. This could prove to be the best overall vintage since 1970.

1984 An excellent year, somewhat overshadowed by 1985, 1984 was one of the hottest years on record, with temperatures frequently soaring over 100°F during the summer. An early flowering and early harvest created problems, since many grape varietals ripened at the same time. The style of the Chardonnays and Cabernets is one of very good to excellent concentration, with engaging, opulent, forward fruitiness that gives the wines appeal in their infancy, and good overall balance. Mendocino is less successful than elsewhere, but the ripe, rich, forward character of the wines of this vintage gives them undeniable charm and character. The majority of winemakers call 1985 a more classic year, 1984 a more hedonistic year. Certainly 1984 and 1985 are California's best two back-to-back vintages since 1973 and 1974.

1983 An average year for most of California's viticultural regions, though the Chardonnays from Napa are very good, even excellent. The Cabernets are medium-bodied, rather austere, and lack the flesh and richness found in top years. Nevertheless, some stars are to be found, but overall the quality of Napa and Sonoma Cabernets is disappointing. The white wines should be drunk before the end of 1987; the red wines will keep for at least another four to six years.

1982 The growing season was plagued by heavy rains, then high temperatures. The press seemed to take a cautionary approach to the vintage, and as it turns out, justifiably so. Sonoma is more consistent than Napa, and Santa Cruz is surprisingly weak in 1982. The Sonoma red wines are ripe, rich, very forward, and much more interesting than those of Napa, which range in quality from outstanding to out of balance. Chardonnays are mediocre, diluted, and lacking depth and acidity. They should have been drunk up by now.

1981 Like 1984, a torridly hot growing season that had all varietals ripening at once and the harvest commencing very early.

Many fine, ripe, rich, dramatic Chardonnays were produced but they should have been drunk by now. The Cabernets are good rather than exciting, with the best of them having a decade of life. Most 1981 Cabernets, because of their forward character, should be drunk before 1991–1992.

1980 A relatively long, cool growing season had wineries predicting a classic, great vintage for both Chardonnay and Cabernet. As the wines have matured, the Chardonnays are indeed excellent, but not as good as in 1984 and 1985. The Cabernets are very good, but hardly great. The Cabernets do however, have good acidity levels and seem by California standards to be evolving rather slowly. A vintage that has a top-notch reputation but which in reality appears to be a very fine rather than monumental year.

Older Vintages
Since I fervently believe that California's Chardonnays and Sauvignon Blancs rarely hold their fruit or improve after four to six years, older vintages are of interest only with respect to California red wines, principally Cabernet Sauvignon.

1979 This year produced a good vintage of tannic, well-endowed wines that are now fully mature.

1978 An excellent vintage from a hot year that produced very concentrated, rich, plummy, dense wines that have aged quite quickly. In all but a few cases, they should be drunk up before the end of this decade.

1977 An above-average vintage that rendered elegant, fruity, supple wines that are now just beginning to tire a bit.

1976 A hot, drought year in which production yields per acre were very small. The wines are very concentrated and tannic, sometimes out of balance. Nevertheless, the great examples from this vintage (where the level of fruit extract matches the ferocity of the tannins) should prove to be among the longest-lived Cabernets of this generation. Despite irregularity here, there are some truly splendid Cabernets.

1975 After the great vintage of 1974, few people wanted to believe California could have another good vintage. The wines, noticeably lighter and less alcoholic and opulent than the 1974s, are all fully mature now. They are refined, fruity, very well-balanced Cabernets, but they should be drunk up.

1974 A great vintage of very rich, very big, deep, dramatic, intense wines that have shown well from their first release. Some of the lesser stars have started to fade, and even the greatest wines from this vintage are not likely to get much better. However, 1974 offers wine enthusiasts flamboyant, rich, intense wines that should continue to drink seductively and well for at least another five to six years.

1973 A very fine vintage of classically structured Cabernet with plenty of fruit, some finesse, and ten to twelve year life-lines. These wines should be drunk up.

1972 A rain-plagued, terrible year except in the Santa Cruz area, which produced a bevy of fine wines.

1971 A mediocre year, although Mondavi's Reserve and the Ridge Montebello are two of the greatest Cabernets I have ever tasted.

1970 Along with 1968, 1974, 1984, and 1985, this is one of California's most successful vintages. The top 1970s are still in great form, with a decade of life left in them at the top levels.

1969 A good vintage, but the wines did not have the stamina or extract to last more than ten years. I know of nothing from this vintage that should not have been drunk up by now.

1968 A great vintage: powerful, rich, deep, dense wines that when stored well are close to perfection today.

A GUIDE TO CALIFORNIA'S BEST PRODUCERS OF CABERNET SAUVIGNON, MERLOT, OR BLENDS THEREOF

★ ★ ★ ★ ★ Outstanding Producers

Beaulieu Private Reserve
  Georges Latour (Napa)
Carmenet (Sonoma)
Caymus Special Selection (Napa)
Château Montelena (Napa)
Diamond Creek (Napa)
Dominus (Napa)
Duckhorn Three Palms
  Vineyard Merlot (Napa)
Dunn Howell Mountain (Napa)
Forman (Napa)

Groth (Napa)
Heitz Martha's Vineyard (Napa)
William Hill Reserve (Napa)
Lyeth (Sonoma)
Mayacamas (Napa)
Robert Mondavi Reserve (Napa)
Opus One (Napa)
Joseph Phelps Eisele (Napa)
Ridge Monte Bello (Santa Cruz)
Spottswoode (Napa)
Stag's Leap Cask 23 (Napa)

★ ★ ★ ★ Excellent Producers

Beringer Private Reserve (Napa)
Burgess (Napa)
Chappellet (Napa)
Conn Creek (Napa)
Girard (Napa)

Inglenook Reserve (Napa)
Laurel Glen (Sonoma)
Matanzas Creek Merlot (Sonoma)
Mount Eden (Santa Cruz)
Joseph Phelps (Napa)

| Ravenswood (Sonoma) | Rubicon (Napa) |

★ ★ ★ Good Producers

Alexander Valley (Sonoma)	Gundlach Bundschu (Sonoma)
David Bruce (Santa Cruz)	Jordan (Sonoma)
Carneros Creek (Napa)	Charles Krug (Napa)
Clos du Bois (Sonoma)	Charles Lefranc (San Benito)
Clos du Val (Napa)	Louis Martini (Napa)
Congress Springs (Santa Clara)	Newton (Napa)
Dehlinger (Sonoma)	Raymond (Napa)
Dry Creek (Sonoma)	Sebastiani (Sonoma)
Eberle (Paso Robles)	Shafer (Napa)
Fetzer (Mendocino)	Silverado (Napa)
Flora Springs (Napa)	Simi (Sonoma)
Glen Ellen (Sonoma)	Sterling (Napa)
Grgich Hills (Napa)	Trefethen (Napa)

★ ★ Average Producers

Christian Brothers (Napa)	Gallo (Stanislaus)
Clos du Val (Napa) (since 1979)	Paul Masson (Monterey)
Far Niente (Napa)	Parducci (Mendocino)
Freemark Abbey (Napa) (since 1974)	Spring Mountain (Napa)

A GUIDE TO CALIFORNIA'S BEST PRODUCERS OF CHARDONNAY

★ ★ ★ ★ ★ Outstanding Producers

Chalone (Monterey)	Robert Mondavi Reserve (Napa)
Château Montelena (Napa)	Mount Eden (Santa Clara)
Château St.-Jean (Sonoma)	Sonoma Cutrer (Sonoma)
Forman (Napa)	Stony Hill (Napa)
Kalin (Marin)	Trefethen (Napa)
Matanzas Creek (Sonoma)	

★ ★ ★ ★ Excellent Producers

Acacia (Napa)	Groth (Napa)
Clos du Bois (Sonoma)	Monticello (Napa)
Congress Springs (Santa Clara)	Newton (Napa)
De Loach (Sonoma)	Raymond (Napa)
Edna Valley (San Luis Obispo)	Saintsbury (Napa)
Flora Springs (Napa)	Simi (Sonoma)
Girard (Napa)	ZD (Napa)
Grgich (Napa)	

★ ★ ★ Good Producers

William Baccala (Mendocino)	Buena Vista (Sonoma)
Beringer (Napa)	Burgess (Napa)
David Bruce (Santa Cruz)	Chappellet (Napa)

Château Bouchaine (Napa)
Dry Creek (Sonoma)
Eberle (Paso Robles)
Far Niente (Napa)
Fetzer (Mendocino)
Glen Ellen (Sonoma)
William Hill (Napa)
Inglenook (Napa)
Jekel (Monterey)

Leeward (Central Coast)
Charles Lefranc (San Benito)
Mayacamas (Napa)
Joseph Phelps (Napa)
Shafer (Napa)
Smith-Madrone (Sonoma)
Sterling (Napa)
Stratford (Napa)

★★ Other Producers

Clos du Val (Napa)
Conn Creek (Napa)
Firestone (Santa Barbara)
Freemark Abbey (Napa)
  (since 1978)
Gallo (Central Coast)

Jordan (Sonoma)
Lords and Elwood (Napa)
Michton (Sonoma)
Pellegrini (Sonoma)
Sebastiani (Sonoma)
Rodney Strong (Sonoma)

A GUIDE TO CALIFORNIA'S BEST PRODUCERS OF SAUVIGNON BLANC AND SEMILLON

★★★★★ Outstanding Producers

Kalin (Marin)
Lyeth (Sonoma)

Matanzas Creek (Sonoma)
Robert Mondavi Reserve (Napa)

★★★★ Excellent Producers

Acacia (Napa)
Beaulieu (Napa)
Château St.-Jean (Sonoma)
Dry Creek (Sonoma)
Duckhorn (Napa)

Glen Ellen (Sonoma)
Karly (Amador)
Simi (Sonoma)
Spottswoode (Napa)
Sterling (Napa)

★★★ Good Producers

Beringer (Napa)
Carmenet (Sonoma)
Château Bouchaine (Napa)
Congress Springs (Santa Cruz)
Fetzer (Mendocino)

Flora Springs (Napa)
Gallo (California)
Parducci (Mendocino)
Joseph Phelps (Napa)
Stratford (Napa)

A GUIDE TO CALIFORNIA'S BEST PRODUCERS OF PINOT NOIR

★★★★ Excellent Producers

Bonny Doon (Santa Cruz)
Calera (San Benito)
Chalone (Monterey)

Edna Valley (San Luis Obispo)
Kalin (Marin)
Saintsbury (Napa)

★★★ Good Producers

Acacia (Napa)
Beaulieu (Napa)

Robert Mondavi (Napa)
Monticello (Napa)

Mount Eden (Santa Cruz) Joseph Swan (Sonoma)
Robert Stemmler (Sonoma) Trefethen (Napa)

A GUIDE TO CALIFORNIA'S BEST PRODUCERS OF ZINFANDEL

★ ★ ★ ★ ★ Outstanding Producers
Ravenswood (Sonoma) Ridge (Santa Cruz)

★ ★ ★ ★ Excellent Producers
Calera (San Benito) Rafanelli (Sonoma)
Château Montelena (Napa) Shenandoah (Amador)
Grgich (Napa) Joseph Swan (Sonoma)
Joseph Phelps Alexander
  Valley (Sonoma)

★ ★ ★ Good Producers
Burgess (Napa) Fetzer (Mendocino)
Caymus (Napa) Story (Amador)
De Moor (Napa) Sutter Home (Amador)
Dry Creek (Sonoma)

CALIFORNIA · TODAY'S BUYING STRATEGY

In devising an intelligent buying strategy for California wine, it is obviously to your advantage to know the finest producers of each major varietal. However, there are several other factors that are also important. California excels in making lusciously fruity, crisp, lively white wines from Chardonnay and Sauvignon Blanc. Vintages do differ in quality, but rarely is there a complete disaster. With few exceptions, all of California's white wines are best drunk within three to four years of the vintage. Their winemakers don't like to admit such things, but who really cares? The quality level of Chardonnay and Sauvignon Blanc is very high and they drink so well young, why should anyone worry if they are not long-lived? The cardinal rule then is to concentrate on buying white wines from the best two recent vintages, 1985 and 1984, and generally avoid anything older.

For California's rosé or blush wines, Chenin Blancs, and dull, poor Rieslings, the rule is even more strict – buy and drink the 1986s and 1985s immediately and avoid anything older. The only exception would be the sweet, nectar-like, late-harvest Rieslings from top producers such as Château St.-Jean, Joseph Phelps, Austin Cellars, Raymond, and Milano, which exhibit the potential to last and improve in the bottle for five to eight years, perhaps longer.

As for the red wines produced in California, one generally has a great deal more flexibility. The attraction of many California red wines is their grapy, exuberant, fleshy, forward character. Even though they may not be fully mature or have developed secondary bouquets, most California red wines are undeniably attractive to drink young. For California Pinot Noir, the good ones should be drunk within five to six years of the vintage. Concentrate on the 1984s and 1985s, which are splendidly ripe and opulent, and the 1983s of Chalone and Calera.

For Zinfandels, these again are wines to drink within five to seven years of the vintage. The principal exceptions are the wines produced by Ridge, which can last in the bottle for eight to ten years with no difficulty. The two vintages to get excited about for Zinfandel are 1984 and 1985.

For the Cabernet Sauvignon, Merlot, and proprietary blends thereof, the two best vintages are 1984 and 1985. The 1984s are more forward, supple, richly fruity, velvety wines that have enough backbone to ensure their longevity for eight to twelve or more years, but they are also wines that have great appeal in their youth. The 1985s best Cabernets are not likely to appear on the market until 1988–1989, but this is unquestionably the year with the greatest potential for California Cabernet since the outstanding 1970s and 1974s. The 1985s will be less accessible and opulent in their youth than the 1984s, but they should prove to be relatively long-lived by California standards. As for 1982 and 1983, both vintages produced many fine wines, but they are very irregular in quality (especially 1983), and neither year can pretend to have either the peaks or the consistency of 1984 or 1985.

ACACIA *NAPA*

1985 Chardonnay *Napa*	③	*83*
1985 Chardonnay Carneros *Napa*	④	*86*
1985 Chardonnay Marina Vineyard *Napa*	④	*87*
1985 Chardonnay Winery Lake Vineyard *Napa*	④	*87*
1983 Pinot Noir Iund *Napa*	④	*83*
1983 Pinot Noir Lee Vineyard *Napa*	④	*80*
1983 Pinot Noir Madonna *Napa*	④	*85*
1983 Pinot Noir St.-Clair *Napa*	④	*84*
1983 Pinot Noir Winery Lake *Napa*	④	*84*
1985 Sauvignon Blanc *Napa*	③	*86*

Acacia was sold in 1986 to Chalone, so the level of quality should remain quite high. This winery, which made its first wine in 1979, quickly gained a strong following for its vineyard-designated, stylish yet flavourful Chardonnays and interesting, sometimes very good Pinot Noirs. In 1984, Sauvignon Blanc and tiny quantities of Merlot were added to its stable, and have also proved to be among the best made in California. As for the Chardonnays, the 1985s show the very forward, lush ripeness of the vintage, with the Winery Lake and Marina showing deeper, richer fruit than the other offerings. As for the Pinot Noirs, the 1984s promise to be better than the 1983s, but of the 1983s the Madonna and St.-Clair are certainly the best of the pick at this moment. In tracking this winery's performance in Pinot Noir over the last few years, the Winery Lake tends to be the most French in style and the Madonna and St.-Clair the two densest and richest in extract. As for the Sauvignon Blanc, it is wonderfully filled with ripe, fresh, subtly herbaceous fruit, a touch of oak, and a lot of depth and character. Acacia, in its short history, has a proven track record of fine winemaking.

ALEXANDER VALLEY VINEYARD *SONOMA*

1982 Cabernet Sauvignon *Alexander Valley*	③	86
1984 Cabernet Sauvignon *Alexander Valley*	③	88
1984 Chardonnay *Alexander Valley*	③	83
1985 Chardonnay *Alexander Valley*	③	86
1985 Chenin Blanc *Alexander Valley*	②	84
1984 Merlot *Alexander Valley*	③	87

The Alexander Valley Winery in Sonoma County rarely seems to get the publicity it clearly merits for its very reasonably priced, well-made wines. Its Chenin Blanc is always made with a lot of appeal – a fruity, soft wine with good acidity. Its Chardonnays can range from some of the best to merely good wines. The 1985 looks to be excellent, with the right amount of oak in its character. The 1984, for whatever reason, has always tasted rather lean and delicate when in fact this winery is known for rather bold, toasty, buttery Chardonnays. Of the recent Cabernets, the 1982 clearly stands out with plenty of ripe berry fruit, full body, and a lush texture. The 1983 is similarly styled but lacks the depth and richness of the 1982. However, both the 1984 Cabernet and 1984 Merlot, both with fabulous richness, appear to be the best red wines yet made here.

WILLIAM BACCALA *MENDOCINO*

1983 Chardonnay *Mendocino*	③	85
1984 Chardonnay *Mendocino*	③	85

This winery has obtained a quick reputation for its style of lush, reasonably priced Chardonnays. Both the 1983 and 1984 Chardonnays showed liveliness, fragrance, and crisp acidity with moderately intense, well-focused, varietal fruit. Both are the type of Chardonnays that beg to be drunk within the first three years of their lives. Production has averaged 15,000 cases.

BEAULIEU *NAPA*

1982 Cabernet Sauvignon Beau Tour *Napa* .... ② **82**
1980 Cabernet Sauvignon Private Reserve *Napa*..... ④ **90**
1981 Cabernet Sauvignon Private Reserve *Napa*..... ④ **85**
1982 Cabernet Sauvignon Rutherford *Napa*............ ③ **83**
1984 Chardonnay Beaufort *Napa*................................ ③ **84**
1984 Chardonnay Los Carneros *Napa* .... ④ **85**
1984 Sauvignon Blanc *Napa*... ② **86**

Beaulieu has a deserved reputation for being one of California's greatest wineries. Its fame is largely based on its remarkable Private Reserve Cabernet Sauvignon, which has never strayed from its style of great ripeness and opulence, marked by the significant amount of time it spends ageing in new American oak barrels. Certain vintages have been monumental wines – 1968, 1970, 1976, and more recently 1980, as well as the unreleased 1984. Other vintages have sometimes been curiously light and underwhelming – 1977 and 1978 for example. The lighter Cabernet Sauvignon is represented by the Beau Tour, made to be drunk young, and the Rutherford, which tends to be a bit richer than Beau Tour but, to my taste, no more interesting. Both of the lower-level Cabernets are distinctly different from the Private Reserves. The 1980 Private Reserve will easily last ten to fifteen years, but the 1981 seems tannic and closed, and somewhat disappointing given the great reputation this wine has. As for the Chardonnays, the winery seems to be making increased quality efforts as the 1984 Los Carneros as well as the 1983 Los Carneros are two of the best Chardonnays that the winery has released in almost a decade. Beaulieu's Sauvignon Blanc is always excellent: fruity, crisp, with a subtle herbaceousness in the background. Another wine to look for, which is made in very limited quantities, is the Special Pinot Noir from Los Carneros, which never reminds me particularly of Pinot Noir, but which I nevertheless enjoy immensely.

BERINGER *NAPA*

1982 Cabernet Sauvignon Knight's Valley................ ② **82**
1981 Cabernet Sauvignon Private Reserve.............. ④ **86**
1980 Cabernet Sauvignon Private Reserve
    Lemmon-Chabot .... ④ **90**
1984 Chardonnay *Napa* .... ② **80**
1984 Chardonnay Gamble Ranch *Napa*..................... ③ **85**
1983 Chardonnay Private Reserve *Napa*................... ④ **86**
1984 Fumé Blanc *Napa*....................................... ③ **83**

This famous old winery, located in the heart of Napa Valley, tends to produce a consistently good range of wines; its two best wines, the Private Reserve Cabernet and Chardonnay are particularly intense and marked by long ageing in oak barrels. The Fumé Blanc is herbaceous, fruity, and an above-average rather than an exciting example of its type. The 1980 Private Reserve Cabernet Sauvignon from the Lemmon-Chabot branch is outstanding: a rich, dense, ripe wine that should mature early because of low acidity. The 1981 Private Reserve does not have quite the richness of the 1980, but has the typically rich, chocolaty, spicy flavours that one finds in many of the Beringer Private Reserve Cabernets. The 1982 Knight's Valley Cabernet tends to be much softer and much lighter in style, but is straightforward and well made. Of the Chardonnays, the barrel-fermented Gamble Ranch Napa can often resemble an oaky, buttery, French Meursault. The Private Reserve always seems to have the better balance, is well marked by oak, made in a big, rich style, and is typically Californian in its proportions. Visitors to the winery should also ask if any of the limited production, splendidly sweet, Semillon-based wine made by retired yet still active winemaker Myron Nightingale is available. The 1980 and most recent vintage, 1983, are wonderfully rich wines not unlike an excellent sweet wine from the Sauternes region of France.

BONNY DOON VINEYARD *SANTA CRUZ*

1983 Cabernet Sauvignon *Anderson Valley*	③	85
1984 Le Cigare Volant	③	87
1985 Pinot Blanc Monterey	②	85
1983 Pinot Noir *Bethel Heights, Oregon*	④	87
1985 Pinot Noir *Bethel Heights, Oregon*	④	88
1983 Syrah	③	86
1984 Syrah	③	88
1985 Vin Gris de Grenache	②	85

This is one of the most distinctive and unique winery operations in all of California. Winemaker Randall Graham clearly marches to the beat of a totally different drummer. In search of the secret for making wines modelled after the great Rhône classics of France (Châteauneuf-du-Pape, Hermitage, and Côte Rôtie), Graham is producing California's finest Syrah-based wine and his interpretation of Châteauneuf-du-Pape, the historic 1984 Le Cigare Volant, shows wonderfully rich, raspberry, peppery fruit and remarkable character. Virtually everything from this winery is of great interest, including the late-harvest, rich Muscat dessert wine that resembles a Beaumes de Venise from the Rhône, and the remarkable rosé produced here called Vin Gris of Grenache that is remarkably similar to a Tavel. Graham's talents are obvious, yet he rarely seems to get the publicity and accolades his considerable winemaking skills deserve. Even his Pinot Noir, which he buys from the excellent Bethel Heights Vineyard in Willamette Valley, Oregon, is among the finest made in California, though not in truth a California wine. Bonny Doon's wines should be sought after by any wine enthusiast for their distinctive, unique qualities.

DAVID BRUCE WINERY *SANTA CRUZ*

1982 Cabernet Sauvignon *California*	③	**82**
1983 Chardonnay *California*	③	**72**
1984 Chardonnay *California*	③	**78**

Older vintages from David Bruce seemed to be hit-or-miss propositions, often fabulously rich, intense, full-bodied wines that, while never lacking character, had as many virtues as flaws. Recent vintages have gone completely in the other direction; they have shown remarkable restraint, to the point that they lack interest. The 1982 Cabernet seems remarkably tannic and lean on the palate. The 1983 and 1984 Chardonnays also seem to be rather thin – the 1983 in fact is rather flat and out of balance, whereas the 1984 has a toasty, pineapple-scented, tropical fruit bouquet but seems to fade in the glass with a rather watery, tart, high-acid finish. One wishes for a return to the old style practised here.

BUENA VISTA *SONOMA*

1981 Cabernet Sauvignon Special Selection		
Sonoma	④	**85**
1983 Chardonnay *Sonoma*	②	**75**
1984 Chardonnay *Sonoma*	③	**80**
1985 Fumé Blanc *Lake*	②	**84**

This winery, with a significant production in excess of 100,000 cases, has been German-owned since 1979. Its colourful history goes back to the middle of the nineteenth century (it is California's oldest winery). The wines tend to be straightforward, commercial examples of their type, which rarely disappoint but are not exciting either. The Chardonnays tend to be lean, compact, slightly varietal examples without much depth of character. The Cabernets tend to be rather tannic and dark and show little charm, although the 1981 Special Selection has the best depth and complexity I have experienced from Buena Vista Cabernet. The winery made a delicious, soft, intensely fruity Fumé Blanc in 1985. My gut feeling is that this winery should be doing better.

BURGESS CELLARS *NAPA*

1981 Cabernet Sauvignon Vintage Selection *Napa* . ④ 84
1982 Cabernet Sauvignon Vintage Selection *Napa* . ④ 88
1983 Chardonnay Vintage Reserve *Napa* .... ③ 72
1984 Chardonnay Vintage Reserve *Napa* .... ③ 86

Tom Burgess, the owner of this medium-sized winery that produces 30,000 cases of wine per year, seems to be content to do his job quietly but steadily. His Cabernets have ranged from among the best in California to merely good. His 1974, 1976, 1978, and more recently the 1982, have certainly been among the top several dozen Cabernets made in those vintages. His Cabernets tend to be tannic and backward, but the 1982 shows a very accessible, charming, lush quality though it has a decade of life ahead of it. The Chardonnays at Burgess started off in the mid-seventies as huge, oaky, alcoholic wines that seemed to fall apart after a couple of years. The more recent examples have shown remarkable restraint, crisp acidity, and a much lighter touch with the oak, with the 1984 the best of the current offerings. Perhaps they lack the drama and flamboyance of the earlier Chardonnays, but they are better balanced and better examples of this type of wine. Burgess wines may not be expensive, but they are generally quite well made. The winery also makes a good, rather tannic, deeply coloured Zinfandel.

CALERA WINE CO. *SAN BENITO*

1984 Chardonnay Santa Barbara................................. ③ 82
1982 Pinot Noir Jensen.. ⑤ 86
1983 Pinot Noir Jensen.. ④ 87
1982 Pinot Noir Reed .... ⑤ 87
1983 Pinot Noir Reed .... ④ 84
1982 Pinot Noir Santa Barbara .... ③ 74
1983 Pinot Noir Santa Barbara .... ③ 72
1982 Pinot Noir Selleck .... ⑤ 88
1983 Pinot Noir Selleck .... ④ 86
1984 Pinot Noir Selleck .... ④ 87

At present, the tiny Calera Winery is making some of California's best and most intriguing Pinot Noirs. They are rich, aromatic, rather intense, unique wines. The production is tiny, the costs of production high, so the prices for the final product look expensive. However, you are not likely to be disappointed, particularly if you are in search of flamboyant and intense, exotic Pinot Noirs. The 1982s are intensely smoky, spicy, fragrant, rich wines that some might call the Chambertins of California. They are unfiltered and, whether for that reason or not, seem to swell and develop in the glass as they sit. Usually the Selleck is the most evolved and the Reed and Jensen the most tannic and presumably ageworthy. All three of the 1982 wines can be drunk now for their extroverted, full-intensity, complex bouquets, although they show the potential to improve for several more years. The 1982 Santa Barbara, made from purchased grapes, is very weedy and vegetal, and not to my liking. The 1983s continue the success this winery has had with this fickle varietal. They are similar to the 1982s, perhaps slightly less exuberant and intense, and are immensely interesting wines. The Selleck again is the most advanced and the Reed and Jensen more backward, with spicy, leathery, exotic bouquets. Of the three, the Jensen looks to be the star. Again, the Santa Barbara, made from purchased grapes, is excessively vegetal and of little interest. The 1984 Selleck showed more restraint but still plenty of flamboyant, spicy, fragrant Pinot Noir character. Calera also makes an inexpensive Zinfandel that can be very good – although my experience is that it is inconsistent from vintage to vintage – and a sound, fruity, straightforward Chardonnay.

CARMENET VINEYARD *SONOMA*

1983 Sauvignon Blanc *Edna Valley*	②	86
1984 Sauvignon Blanc *Edna Valley*	②	82
1982 Sonoma Red Table Wine	④	87
1983 Sonoma Red Table Wine	④	84
1984 Sonoma Red Table Wine	④	90

Carmenet is the new winery constructed by the famous Chalone corporation; its first several wines, a Sauvignon Blanc and a proprietary blend of Cabernet Sauvignon, Cabernet Franc, and Merlot, have been instant successes. The Sauvignon in 1983 showed intense, exotic, herbaceous-scented fruit and loads of flavour. The 1984 seemed to border on being excessively vegetal, but nevertheless interesting. Among the great successes would appear to be their red wines. The 1982, the first vintage, has developed a rich, fragrant, ripe plummy bouquet, deftly married with spicy oak. It still shows a great deal of tannin but has an excellent concentration and length and should be a good candidate for at least seven to ten more years of ageing. The 1983 is equally dense, but quite closed and tannic and at the present is showing less of its potential. The 1984 looks to be the best wine yet from Carmenet, a rich, opulent, intense wine with loads of fruit, plenty of body, and at least a decade of life ahead of it. Prices are moderately high here but quality is clearly present.

CARNEROS CREEK WINERY *NAPA*

1981 Cabernet Sauvignon *Napa* .... ③ **84**
1982 Cabernet Sauvignon *Napa* .... ③ **83**
1983 Cabernet Sauvignon *Napa* .... ③ **78**
1983 Chardonnay *Napa* .... ③ **79**
1984 Chardonnay *Napa* .... ③ **83**
1982 Merlot *Napa* .... ③ **72**
1983 Pinot Noir *Napa* .... ④ **84**

The smallish winery of Carneros Creek began production in 1971 and left many critics immensely pleased with the excellent Cabernet Sauvignons, Zinfandels, and occasionally delicious Chardonnays. In 1977, Carneros Creek made a truly outstanding Pinot Noir that had heads buzzing. Nevertheless, the great hope that this winery promised in the early seventies has not carried into the eighties for reasons that are yet to be identified. Certainly the quality remains average to above average, but in recent vintages the wines have shown much less intensity and character and seem to be made in a very commercial style aimed at offending the least number of people. The rich, intense, dramatic Cabernets have given way to a lighter, rather innocuous style, as have the Chardonnays. The great success of the 1977 Pinot Noir has been followed by rather mediocre wines with little interest, with the possible exception of the 1983. This is all rather unfortunate.

CAYMUS VINEYARD *NAPA*

1981 Cabernet Sauvignon *Napa* .... ④ **87**
1982 Cabernet Sauvignon *Napa* .... ④ **87**
1983 Cabernet Sauvignon *Napa* .... ④ **85**
1981 Cabernet Sauvignon Grace Family
    Vineyards *Napa* .... ⑤ **91**
1982 Cabernet Sauvignon Grace Family
    Vineyards *Napa* .... ⑤ **90**
1980 Cabernet Sauvignon Special Selection *Napa* .. ⑤ **90**
1981 Cabernet Sauvignon Special Selection *Napa* .. ⑤ **88**
1984 Chardonnay *Napa* .... ③ **84**
1984 Sauvignon Blanc *Napa* .... ② **84**

The Caymus Winery, owned and run by Charles Wagner and his son, has been one of the great success stories of California. The production remains under 40,000 cases and the quality of their wines across the board ranges from at least good to extraordinary in the case of their Cabernet Sauvignons. Their secondary label, the Liberty School, is one to seek out for good values, particularly in Cabernet Sauvignon and Chardonnay. Caymus also produces some Pinot Noir that I do not find up to the level of quality of their other wines, and Zinfandel that tends to be rich, spicy, and loaded with berry fruit. If the winery has room for improvement, it is probably with their Chardonnay and Sauvignon Blanc, which are good examples of their types, but rarely have the character, sheer intensity, and flavours of their red wines. The 1984 Chardonnay and Sauvignon Blanc are attractive examples, easy to drink, easy to like, and satisfying. Their regular Cabernets tend to be rich, supple, loaded with blackcurrant fruit, quite concentrated, and always made with enough backbone to age for seven to ten years. They are consistently among the best Cabernets produced in California. At the top echelon of quality are the two luxury Cabernets produced by Caymus – the Special Selection, a monumental Cabernet aged three and a half years in small oak barrels, and the Grace Family Vineyard Cabernet, made in exactly the same manner by Caymus in very limited quantities. Both of these wines show remarkable concentration and surprisingly are not as oaky as one would suspect from their long sojourn in barrels. They represent the pinnacle of quality of what one can find from California; certainly the 1982 and 1981 Grace Family Vineyard and 1980 and 1981 Special Selection Cabernets are worthy additions to anyone's cellar. Older great vintages of the Caymus Special Selection Cabernet are the 1979, 1978, 1976, and 1975.

CHALONE VINEYARDS *MONTEREY*

1983 Chardonnay *California*	④	*84*
1984 Chardonnay *California*	④	*90*
1985 Chardonnay *California*	④	*91*
1983 Chardonnay Reserve *California*	⑤	*90*
1984 Chardonnay Reserve *California*	⑤	*92*
1983 Pinot Blanc *California*	③	*83*
1984 Pinot Blanc *California*	③	*87*
1985 Pinot Blanc *California*	④	*88*
1981 Pinot Noir *California*	④	*87*
1982 Pinot Noir *California*	④	*85*
1983 Pinot Noir *California*	④	*86*
1981 Pinot Noir Reserve *California*	⑤	*88*

The tiny Chalone Vineyard, which produces less than 15,000 cases of wine, is located in the remote Gavilan Mountains about a 40-minute drive from Soledad, California. The wines here have been distinctive, rich, original expressions of the winemaking art at its best. The Chardonnays have, in certain vintages, been perhaps the single best white wines produced in California. The Pinot Noirs are smoky, rich, intense and always interesting, and the Pinot Blancs pacesetters as well. As production increased, the Chardonnays and Pinot Blancs at first seemed to have taken on a slightly lighter style, with the reserve bottlings seeming to get the best juice from the oldest vines. Both the 1983 Chardonnay and Pinot Blanc were good wines, but disappointing by the high standards of Chalone. Certainly, the 1984s and 1985s were a return to the style one expects from Chalone, which is barrel-fermented, oaky, buttery, intense, complex wines with great depth of flavour. The Reserve wines are among the finest in California, but one must get on Chalone's private mailing list to be able to reserve a few bottles of them. The Pinot Noirs have been brilliant, with a fabulous 1978 that is still drinking well, and a 1980 that is still not mature; both are among a handful of great Pinot Noirs made in the last decade in California. Of recent vintages that are still available commercially, the 1981, 1982, and 1983 are very, very good, and the unreleased 1984 a superstar Pinot Noir. The Pinot Noir Reserves are simply richer and more ageworthy. This is a great winery that has had remarkable success throughout the country for its unwavering commitment to quality wines. One would like to see more California wineries emulating the style of Chalone Vineyards. The prices are high, but you won't be disappointed.

CHAPPELLET VINEYARD *NAPA*

1980 Cabernet Sauvignon *Napa*	④	**88**
1982 Cabernet Sauvignon *Napa*	④	**87**
1983 Chardonnay *Napa*	③	**85**
1984 Chenin Blanc *Napa*	②	**84**

This lovely winery, tucked away in the hills east of Rutherford, produces on average just under 30,000 cases of wine, all of which can be recommended with enthusiasm. The Chenin Blanc is among the best made in California, as well as among the most expensive. Most consumers turn their noses up at Chenin Blanc, but one taste of Chappellet's reveals just how fresh, exuberant, and satisfying this wine can be as an apéritif. The Chardonnay is always a graceful, stylish, elegant wine that has good, crisp acidity and an understated character, but always enough flavour interest to keep one going back for another glass. The 1983 looks to be one of the better Chardonnays that Chappellet has made in the last several years. The pride of this house, and rightfully so, are the ageworthy Cabernets, which are deep in colour, somewhat austere in the beginning of their lives, but attractive, well-made, elegant wines with plenty of flavour. The 1980, a long-time favourite, is still not fully mature; the 1982 is a lusher, more forward, accessible version of the 1980. Prices for Chappellet's wines are on the high side, but then so is the quality.

CHÂTEAU BOUCHAINE *NAPA*

1983 Chardonnay *Carneros*	④	**86**
1984 Chardonnay *Carneros*	④	**85**
1983 Chardonnay *Napa*	③	**78**
1984 Chardonnay *Napa*	③	**75**
1983 Pinot Noir *Carneros*	③	**72**
1983 Pinot Noir *Winery Lake*	④	**80**
1984 Sauvignon Blanc *Napa*	②	**84**

The Château Bouchaine Winery always seems to play it safe, preferring middle-of-the-road, good wines to dramatic artistic expressions of Napa viticulture. Their Chardonnays tend to be their best wines, no doubt because if you get good grapes there is little harm (given competent winemaking, of course) that you can do to them. Both the 1983 and 1984 Chardonnay Carneros merit interest for their satisfying, straightforward varietal character, good length, and likeable format. The Sauvignon Blanc tends to be a bit grassy to my taste and I would like to see that aspect toned down, but it is a decently made, interesting wine. The Pinot Noirs, which this winery has touted from the beginning, seem to be made with the restaurant trade in mind – squeaky clean, overly filtered wines that are totally predictable; nevertheless, they are clean, with a little bit of cherry fruitiness, a little bit of oak, and a pleasant finish. One wishes they would take a little bit more risk here rather than settling for something that is good but hardly exciting.

CHÂTEAU MONTELENA *NAPA*

1980 Cabernet Sauvignon *Napa*	④	**87**
1982 Cabernet Sauvignon *Napa*	④	**92**
1982 Cabernet Sauvignon Silverado *Napa*	③	**84**
1983 Chardonnay *Alexander Valley*	④	**87**
1984 Chardonnay *Alexander Valley*	④	**87**
1983 Chardonnay *Napa*	④	**88**
1984 Chardonnay *Napa*	④	**89**
1982 Zinfandel *Napa*	③	**86**

This Calistoga-based firm, with its fortress-like winery, is one of California's most consistent producers of top-quality wines across the board. Their Chardonnays, always exuberantly rich and oaky, are brilliant expressions of California winemaking. Their Zinfandel remains one of the best of its type: a rich, intense, briary, full-bodied wine with plenty of extract and flavour. And their Cabernet Sauvignons have emerged since the late seventies as among the very best in all of California. One wishes that there were more than 25,000 cases produced here as the wines are hard to find. Of the recent Chardonnays, both the 1984s and 1983s are excellent, the Alexander Valley having a slightly lusher, more accessible, buttery style than the more firmly structured Napa. The 1982 Zinfandel is a powerful, rich, lush, intense wine with great flavour. Their second label, Silverado Cellars, produced a wonderfully rich, supple, fat Cabernet in 1982 for early drinking. And of course, both the 1982 and 1980 Montelena Cabernets show plenty of tannin, great concentration, and at least eight to ten years of ageing potential. Prices are on the high side, but the quality here seems to get better with each passing vintage.

CHÂTEAU ST.-JEAN *SONOMA*

1983 Chardonnay *Sonoma*	③	78
1984 Chardonnay *Sonoma*	③	*81*
1983 Chardonnay Belle Terre Vineyards *Alexander Valley*	④	*82*
1984 Chardonnay Belle Terre Vineyards *Alexander Valley*	④	*84*
1983 Chardonnay Frank Johnson Vineyards *Alexander Valley*	④	*84*
1984 Chardonnay Frank Johnson Vineyards *Alexander Valley*	④	*84*
1983 Chardonnay Robert Young Vineyards *Alexander Valley*	④	*83*
1984 Chardonnay Robert Young Vineyards *Alexander Valley*	④	*87*
1985 Fumé Blanc *Sonoma*	②	*82*
1984 Fumé Blanc La Petite Etoile *Sonoma*	③	*82*
1985 Gewürztraminer *Sonoma*	②	*82*
1984 Selected Late-Harvest Semillon-Sauvignon St.-Jean Vineyards	④	*90*

From the very beginning Château St.-Jean has produced a bevy of high-quality white wines ranging from intensely herbaceous, grassy Fumé Blancs that have become more subtle as their winemaking evolved, to rich, intense, vineyard-designated Chardonnays, of which the best consistently have been the Robert Young, Belle Terre, and Frank Johnson. The winery also makes a fairly bland Gewürztraminer, a good value in its 'Vin Blanc' generic wine, and every once in a while a bit of Cabernet that tends to be rather rich but heavy-handed and excruciatingly tannic. Perhaps the best wine made by St.-Jean is its late-harvest, decadently rich Riesling from both the Belle Terre and Robert Young vineyards. The 1978 was a remarkably rich Trockenbeerenauslese-styled wine. The 1982s were also remarkably hedonistic in their nectar-like richness and sweetness. In 1984, an impressive Sauternes-like, sweet, late-harvest Semillon/Sauvignon Blanc was added to the line-up. Château St.-Jean has also got involved in the production of sparkling wines, which have been incredibly overpriced; they are rather bland, tart, neutral-tasting wines that I cannot recommend. Fortunately, the lofty debut price has dropped. In 1984 the winery was sold to the Japanese group Suntory and reports are that the quality will continue at the present level. Of the current releases, the 1984 vintage was a much greater success than the 1983. The 1983 wines here, particularly the Chardonnays, lacked richness and length, but the 1984s are filled with ripe aromas and flavours of tropical fruits with a touch of spicy oak, and are very flavourful. The Fumé Blancs have taken on a less grassy character and now are better made than ever. For all the success Château St.-Jean has had with its white wines, with the exception of the late-harvest Rieslings that seem to have a ten-year life potential, the Chardonnays and Fumé Blancs are best drunk within the first three to four years of their lives since they have rarely shown the ability to age and retain their fruit beyond that period. (The 1980 and 1982 Robert Young Chardonnays, for example, both intense and delicious when released, are now drying out, with the alcohol becoming more and more noticeable.) Prices are on the high side.

CHRISTIAN BROTHERS WINERY *NAPA*

1980 Cabernet Sauvignon *Napa* .... ② **76**
1982 Chardonnay .... ② **75**
1980 Zinfandel .... ② **70**

The huge Christian Brothers Winery, which produces in excess of one million cases a year, has a wonderful location in Napa Valley, but the quality of the wines is hardly inspiring. In a positive sense, one can say that they are inexpensive, modestly priced, and never bad examples of their types. But they rarely have much varietal character and sometimes seem remarkably watery in taste. Despite their modest prices, there are no values to be found here.

CLOS DU BOIS WINERY *SONOMA*

1981 Cabernet Sauvignon *Alexander Valley* .... ③ **84**
1980 Cabernet Sauvignon Briarcrest *Alexander Valley* .... ③ **77**
1981 Cabernet Sauvignon/Merlot Marlstone *Alexander Valley* .... ④ **86**
1984 Chardonnay Barrel-Fermented *Alexander Valley* .... ③ **80**

1983 Chardonnay Calcaire Vineyard *Alexander Valley* .... ④ 85

1984 Chardonnay Calcaire Vineyard *Alexander Valley* .... ④ 87

1983 Chardonnay Flintwood Vineyard *Dry Creek* ... ③ 90

1984 Chardonnay Flintwood Vineyard *Dry Creek* ... ④ 90

1984 Chardonnay Proprietor's Reserve *Alexander Valley* .... ④ 88

1983 Merlot *Sonoma* .... ③ 82

1980 Pinot Noir Proprietor's Reserve *Sonoma* .... ② 75

1982 Pinot Noir *Sonoma* .... ② 70

1985 Sauvignon Blanc Barrel-Fermented *Alexander Valley* .... ② 85

Clos du Bois prides itself on having won more medals than any other California winery. With a production in excess of 100,000 cases, this winery has achieved a high degree of success due to both the quality of its wines and its remarkable owner, Frank Woods. The wines, which have been produced here since 1974, have a good reputation, though my tasting notes always show the Chardonnays to be the best wines of the Clos du Bois stable, particularly the Flintwood, Calcaire Vineyards, and Proprietor's Reserve. The Flintwood is always more austere, but oozing with character, and the Calcaire is a very California-style Chardonnay, with plenty of tropical fruit and toasty oak. As for the Cabernets, they tend to be good rather than exciting, although the luxury proprietary blend of Cabernet Sauvignon, Merlot, and some Cabernet Franc, Marlstone, in 1981 was the best I have tasted yet from Clos du Bois. The other Cabernets come under such vineyard names as Woodleaf and Briarcrest, and they tend to be very forward, soft, rather ripe wines that are surprisingly herbaceous but always fruity and supple. The Pinot Noirs have, to my mind, been disappointing and typical of many California Pinot Noirs in that they are overly vegetal, sometimes minty, but hard and lacking charm. The winery also produces a relatively sweet, decent Gewürztraminer, and a dull Johannisberg Riesling, and with each vintage has shown more and more progress with its barrel-fermented Sauvignon Blanc, which was excellent in 1985.

CLOS DU VAL WINE CO. *NAPA*

1982 Cabernet Sauvignon *Napa* .... ③ 67

1981 Cabernet Sauvignon *Napa* .... ③ 76

1982 Chardonnay *Napa* .... ③ 74

1983 Chardonnay *Napa* .... ③ 82

1984 Chardonnay *Napa* .... ③ 80

1983 Merlot *Napa* .... ③ **75**
1984 Semillon *California* .... ② **84**
Clos du Val has been another California success story since its first vintage. Its Bordeaux-trained winemaker, Bernard Portet, has captured the hearts of many California wine enthusiasts and comes from a Bordeaux family famous for their expert winemaking. The wines of Clos du Val seem to get much greater reviews on the West Coast than I have been able to give them. Why the difference? For one, this winery seems, in my opinion, to excel in producing basically bland, straightforward, undramatic wines that seem overly filtered and lacking character. This was not always the case for the Cabernets in the period 1972–1978 had both flavour and character. More recently, the only exceptions to blandness have been the 1983 Chardonnay, the best Chardonnay this winery has produced in almost a decade, and the very good Semillon, which Clos du Val seems to routinely produce. The Cabernets since 1978 have been clean, technically correct, but largely devoid of character and personality. Perhaps the 1984s and 1985s will see a return to the style of Cabernets made in 1974 and 1975, which are still in good condition today. Sometimes I even pick up the smell of cardboard, which suggests an overzealous use of filter pads. I am at a loss to understand why I seem to be in a minority, but having had these wines many times, I will stand by my opinion that while this is one of California's most successful wineries, it remains a very overrated producer of fine wines.

CONGRESS SPRINGS VINEYARD *SANTA CLARA*
1984 Cabernet Franc *Santa Cruz* .... ③ **86**
1982 Cabernet Sauvignon *Santa Cruz* .... ③ **78**
1984 Cabernet Sauvignon *Santa Cruz* .... ③ **85**
1984 Chardonnay *Santa Clara* .... ③ **86**
1985 Chardonnay *Santa Clara* .... ③ **88**
1984 Chardonnay Private Reserve *Santa Cruz* .... ④ **91**
1985 Chardonnay Private Reserve *Santa Cruz* .... ④ **90**
1985 Pinot Blanc *Santa Clara* .... ② **84**
1982 Pinot Noir Private Reserve *Santa Cruz* .... ④ **84**
Located in the mountains near Saratoga, this winery, with a relatively tiny production of 6,500 cases, seems to produce very interesting, distinctive wines whether they be Cabernet, Chardonnay, or Pinot Noir. The Chardonnays are marked by plenty of time spent in oak, but they are also loaded with wonderful aromas of tropical fruit and have a creamy, rich, luxurious palate impression. They are not timid wines by any means. The Private Reserve bottlings from Santa Cruz seem to

have more of the buttery, butterscotch flavours than the straight Santa Clara bottlings. The 1984 and 1985 Reserves are fabulous, two of the great Chardonnays made in California. The winery's Cabernets tend to show a great deal of oak with rather uncomplicated fruit flavours, but demonstrate good winemaking and lush, ripe fruit. They are clearly wines to be drunk within their first six to seven years of life. The 1984 is particularly good. The 1982 Pinot Noir had plenty of smoky, ripe Pinot fruit, but it just missed the mark because of too long a sojourn in oak barrels, which gave it an overly woody character. Nevertheless, this winery, which also makes a fine Semillon, Pinot Blanc, and one of the best Cabernet Franc-based wines in California (try the 1984), is worth searching out for the quality of all its wines – particularly its Chardonnays, which are among the very finest in California.

CONN CREEK WINERY *NAPA*

1980 Cabernet Sauvignon *Napa*	④	87
1981 Cabernet Sauvignon *Napa*	④	85
1982 Cabernet Sauvignon *Napa*	③	75
1982 Chardonnay Château Maja *Napa*	②	72
1983 Chardonnay Château Maja *Napa*	②	82
1984 Chardonnay Château Maja *Napa*	③	75

Conn Creek first burst on the scene with a fabulous 1974 Cabernet Sauvignon made from grapes that were grown in the famous Milton Eisele Vineyard near Calistoga. Since that time the winery quickly developed an excellent reputation for its rich yet oaky, intense, tannic, long-lived Cabernet Sauvignons. The 1974 was followed by top-notch successes in 1976, 1978, and 1980. The Chardonnays have been a different animal altogether, always rather flabby, unstructured, and lacking character. The winery has also produced from time to time a very alcoholic, big, rich, husky, alcoholic Zinfandel that seems appropriate for drinking with cheese at the end of a meal. The winery was sold in 1985 and hopefully the fine Cabernets that have been a permanent asset of this winery will continue uninterrupted.

DE LOACH VINEYARDS *SONOMA*

1984 Chardonnay Reserve (O.F.S.) *Sonoma*	④	89
1985 Chardonnay Reserve (O.F.S.) *Sonoma*	④	90
1984 Chardonnay Russian River *Sonoma*	③	85
1985 Chardonnay Russian River *Sonoma*	③	87
1982 Pinot Noir *Sonoma*	③	82
1983 Pinot Noir *Sonoma*	③	78
1983 Zinfandel Russian River *Sonoma*	②	80

De Loach Vineyards is making excellent white wines and adequate red wines. The Chardonnays tend to be the best product from this moderately sized winery in Santa Rosa, California. They have such wonderful opulence and ripeness that some have accused them of being slightly sweet. They are very seductive, lush wines and both the 1984s and the 1985 are deliciously succulent, lush, buttery, appley, rich, ripe Chardonnays that have immense crowd appeal. These wines are meant to be drunk within two to three years of the vintage. The Pinot Noirs are adequate, with little varietal character, but as red wines are pleasant and drinkable. The Zinfandels here tend to be high in alcohol with plenty of briary, berryish fruit, but again lack complexity and seem overly one-dimensional. The winery also makes one of California's best blush wines, a white Zinfandel of which the 1985 is a classic – richly fruity, fresh, lively, and altogether quite good. My advice is to stick to the Chardonnays and blush wines and wait for the reds to improve in quality.

THE JOHN DANIEL SOCIETY *NAPA*

1983 Dominus .... ⑤ **93**
1984 Dominus .... ⑤ **91**

One of the hottest new winemaking ventures in all of California is this partnership between Christian Moueix, the co-proprietor of a bevy of Bordeaux châteaux, the most famous of which is Pétrus, and the two daughters of the late, legendary John Daniel, Marcia Smith and Robin Lail. Making a proprietary luxury blend of Cabernet Sauvignon, Cabernet Franc, and Merlot from old, established vineyards in the valley, the first release was the 1983 Dominus, a monumental wine that is rich yet firmly structured and remarkably complex. The 1984 is a more opulent, lusher example of the 1983 and should mature sooner. Dominus is a great wine, made by one of the most talented winemakers of our day; moreover, Dominus is a brilliant example of using California's superb raw materials and applying the traditional winemaking philosophy of Bordeaux to them. Production is expected to grow to an excess of 5,000 cases, but no matter what and despite their high prices, these wines will be eagerly snapped up by anyone who calls himself a connoisseur of wine.

DEHLINGER WINERY *SONOMA*

1982 Cabernet Sauvignon *Sonoma* .... ③ **85**
1983 Cabernet Sauvignon *Sonoma* .... ③ **80**
1984 Chardonnay Russian River *Sonoma* .... ③ **82**
1985 Chardonnay Russian River *Sonoma* .... ③ **86**

1982 Pinot Noir Russian River *Sonoma* .... ③ **70**
1985 Pinot Noir Russian River *Sonoma* .... ③ **86**

This small winery in Sonoma seems to do a very fine job with Cabernet Sauvignon but is less successful with other varietals. The Chardonnays tend to be refined and polite, but one wishes there was more intensity of flavour and character. I must admit to being impressed with the 1985. While the 1982 Pinot Noir had more in common with a rich yet clumsy Zinfandel, the 1985 Pinot Noir had remarkable character, finesse and charm, and is a clear success. The winery can make good Zinfandel that is often blended with a percentage of Petite Sirah. It tends to be peppery, tannic, ripe, and intense. The winery's best recent efforts, in addition to the 1985 Pinot Noir, have been the 1985 Chardonnay and the 1982 Cabernet Sauvignon, which has a slightly herbaceous, oaky aroma but is a deeply fruity wine with plenty of richness, length and depth.

DIAMOND CREEK VINEYARDS *NAPA*

1982 Cabernet Sauvignon Gravelly Meadow *Napa*. ④ **87**
1983 Cabernet Sauvignon Gravelly Meadow *Napa*. ④ **86**
1984 Cabernet Sauvignon Gravelly Meadow *Napa*. ⑤ **90**
1982 Cabernet Sauvignon Red Rock Terrace *Napa*
.... ④ **88**
1983 Cabernet Sauvignon Red Rock Terrace *Napa*
.... ④ **85**
1984 Cabernet Sauvignon Red Rock Terrace *Napa*
.... ⑤ **90**
1982 Cabernet Sauvignon Volcanic Hill *Napa* .... ④ **88**
1983 Cabernet Sauvignon Volcanic Hill *Napa* .... ④ **85**
1984 Cabernet Sauvignon Volcanic Hill *Napa* .... ⑤ **92**

This small winery in the hills south of Calistoga produces some of California's greatest Cabernet Sauvignons from three separate vineyard locations. The production runs between 1,800–2,500 cases for each vintage, so there is not much to go around and knowledgeable connoisseurs for years have been snapping up these very rich, unfiltered, intense wines that seem to have no trouble ageing and improving for ten to twelve years. The 1982s are very forward by Diamond Creek standards but wonderfully lush, rich, and loaded with blackcurrant fruit and spicy oak. The Red Rock Terrace and Volcanic Hill are the two best in 1982, as the Gravelly Meadow seems slightly less concentrated. The 1983 was not one of this winery's top vintages, but the wines are certainly well made, just overshadowed by the excellent 1982s and superb 1984s. Of the 1983s, the Gravelly Meadow seems to have more depth than the other two wines. In 1984 all three wines were superb and the owner/winemaker Al Brounstein thinks they are the finest wines he has ever made. They are all wonderfully opulent, rich, intense, majestic wines with explosive bouquets and plenty of tannic backbone and spine for at least eight to ten years' ageing potential. Despite what looks to be high prices, these are the kind of Cabernets that make California's reputation for producing world-class wine well justified.

DOMAINE CHANDON *NAPA*

10th Anniversary Reserve Non-Vintage.....................	④	85
Blanc de Noirs Non-Vintage...	③	84
Brut Napa Non-Vintage	③	84

With a production close to 400,000 cases, this operation, which was founded in 1973 by the French company Moët-Hennessy, has inspired a plethora of other sparkling wine operations in California. Yet, to date, Domaine Chandon sparkling wines still remain the best though they hardly compete with the top level of French Champagne. So far the wines have been light in body, easy to drink, crisp, but somewhat austere and acidic, as are many of their California competitors. The Blanc de Noirs is generally my favourite of their less expensive wines, with a light salmon colour and yeasty bouquet. Their special Anniversary Reserve has a bit more complexity and roundness since it was aged longer on its lees. These are good sparkling wines, but they have yet to reach the class of the top echelon of non-vintage or vintage Champagnes from France. Domaine Chandon also makes a tiny quantity of an apéritif liqueur called Panache, which is pleasant and enjoyable before a meal.

DRY CREEK VINEYARD *SONOMA*

1982 Cabernet Sauvignon *Sonoma*................................	②	84
1983 Cabernet Sauvignon *Sonoma*................................	②	83
1984 Chardonnay *Dry Creek*......................................	②	84
1985 Chenin Blanc *Dry Creek*....................................	②	83
1982 David Stare Reserve *Dry Creek*	④	87
1983 David Stare Reserve *Dry Creek*	④	80
1984 Fumé Blanc *Dry Creek*.......................................	②	85
1985 Fumé Blanc *Dry Creek*.......................................	②	86

The jovial David Stare has been making wine at Dry Creek since 1972 and was one of the first, along with Robert Mondavi, to promote and believe in the quality of the Sauvignon Blanc grape. It is called Fumé Blanc here and it is one of the best made in California, always crisp, subtly herbaceous, medium-bodied, and one of the few that seems capable of ageing beyond three to four years, although I still prefer to drink it young. Stare often produces 30,000+ cases of this wine and that in itself is a remarkable achievement, particularly in view of the fact that he sells it all. His 1984 and 1985 are two of the best vintages yet. He also makes a dry, fruity, soft Chenin Blanc that is one of the better examples of its type. His Chardonnay tends to be straightforward in style but attractive and easy to drink. If this house has a weakness, it is their Cabernet Sauvignons, which tend to be a bit mixed and lacking in real complexity and character. Though the 1982 David Stare Reserve (which was primarily a Merlot wine) had incredible flavour extract and a wonderfully lush, opulent texture reminiscent of a fine Pomerol, the 1983 tasted gawky and excessively alcoholic. Stare's wines have always been modestly priced and his white wines are worth trying.

DUCKHORN VINEYARDS *NAPA*

1982 Cabernet Sauvignon *Napa*	③	**83**
1983 Cabernet Sauvignon *Napa*	④	**88**
1984 Cabernet Sauvignon *Napa*	④	**86**
1982 Merlot *Napa*	③	**85**
1983 Merlot *Napa*	④	**80**
1984 Merlot *Napa*	④	**84**
1983 Merlot Three Palms Vineyard *Napa*	④	**86**
1984 Merlot Three Palms Vineyard *Napa*	④	**88**

It is hard to believe that this winery was founded in 1976 and produced its first wines in 1978. The quality of their wines from the beginning has been very good to exceptional. The 1978 Cabernets and Merlots were outstanding, followed by equal successes in 1979 and 1980. Of the recent releases, the 1982s are good but exceptionally tannic and hard and not quite as successful as other vintages for Duckhorn. However, 1983, generally a less successful vintage in Napa than 1982, is a clear-cut success for two of the three red wines made by Duckhorn. The tiny production of Merlot from the Three Palms Vineyard is a broad and rich but still tannic, young wine, and the 1983 Cabernet is one of the top Cabernets from Napa in this vintage. Both wines need an additional two to four years of ageing to round out, as do most of the Duckhorn wines, which seem to have the potential to last ten or more years in the bottle. The 1984s all show considerable amounts of tannin, including the Merlot and Cabernet Sauvignon. The wine to get in line for should be the Merlot from the Three Palms Vineyard, which has exceptionally broad, deep flavours and also plenty of tannin. The 1984s can use three to five years of ageing. The production at Duckhorn Winery is around

10,000 cases and the wines are sold out on allocation each vintage. Since they are dealing with mostly purchased grapes, one wonders if they can continue their great success by simply buying the top grapes each year. The winery introduced a Sauvignon Blanc in 1982 and the recent vintages, 1984 and 1985, have shown that their magical touch with red wine can be transferred to making a white wine.

DUNN HOWELL MOUNTAIN *NAPA*

1982 Cabernet Sauvignon *Napa* .... ③ **85**
1981 Cabernet Sauvignon *Napa Howell Mountain*..... ④ **90**
1982 Cabernet Sauvignon *Napa Howell Mountain*..... ④ **92**
1983 Cabernet Sauvignon *Napa Howell Mountain*..... ④ **87**
After learning his trade as the full-time winemaker at Caymus, Randy Dunn left there in 1984 to concentrate his efforts on his own tiny vineyard on Howell Mountain. He produces only a dense, incredibly concentrated, broodingly dark, potentially superb Cabernet. His first vintages were sold out to connoisseurs yearning for the old-style Cabernet – unfiltered, dramatically rich, and flamboyant. The early vintages, 1980 and 1981, were both superb, the 1982 Howell Mountain another fabulous wine that is arguably the best Cabernet made in California in that vintage. Upcoming vintages, including the excellent 1983 and 1984, look equally successful. The production has averaged around 1,000 cases so there is little to go around. However, there is no doubt that this is one of the great Cabernets made in California. Most vintages to date seem to suggest that ten years of cellaring is required.

EDNA VALLEY VINEYARDS *SAN LUIS OBISPO*

1984 Chardonnay *Edna Valley* .... ③ **87**
1985 Chardonnay *Edna Valley* .... ③ **89**
1982 Pinot Noir *Edna Valley* .... ③ **86**
1983 Pinot Noir *Edna Valley* .... ④ **86**
1981 Pinot Noir Reserve *Edna Valley* .... ④ **87**
The Edna Valley Vineyard is part of the Chalone Vineyard's empire and produces wines similar in style to those of Chalone – intense, full-bodied, highly extracted wines with great character and flamboyance. The Chardonnays have been the stars to date, and are made in a big, rich, toasty, buttery, broadly flavoured style that makes splendid drinking in the first two to three years of their lives. The Pinot Noirs have not yet competed with those from Chalone, but are well-made, rich, intense wines with explosive bouquets of smoky, earthy, ripe, Pinot Noir fruit. The winery also produces small amounts of Reserve Pinot Noir.

FAR NIENTE *NAPA*

1982 Cabernet Sauvignon *Napa*	⑤	82
1983 Cabernet Sauvignon *Napa*	⑤	82
1982 Chardonnay *Napa*	④	85
1983 Chardonnay *Napa*	④	87
1984 Chardonnay *Napa*	④	82
1985 Chardonnay *Napa*	④	86

There is no question that the Far Niente Winery has high aspirations. The prices asked for the wines, given the up-and-down performance record, are somewhat ridiculous, but one look at the packaging and you will see that much of the promotion here is on the surface. The Chardonnays have ranged from excellent to mediocre, with the 1983 and 1985 being the best Chardonnays yet from this winery, which was founded in 1979. Recently, Far Niente has added Cabernet Sauvignon to its stable of wines and has priced it about three times its real value given the average to above average quality level. Both the 1982 and 1983 show a dense colour but have very weedy, blackcurrant fruit and a very high, tart acidity. They do not seem capable of improving and are not particularly attractive at the moment. This is an estate that apparently lives by the motto 'Why pay less?' Their Chardonnay is worth a try in certain vintages, if you don't mind spending a lot of money.

FETZER VINEYARD *MENDOCINO*

1983 Cabernet Sauvignon *Lake*	②	67
1983 Cabernet Sauvignon *Mendocino*	②	83
1982 Cabernet Sauvignon Home Vineyard *Mendocino*	③	84
1984 Chardonnay Barrel Select *Mendocino*	②	85
1985 Chardonnay Barrel Select *Mendocino*	②	85
1984 Chardonnay Selected Reserve *California*	②	84
1985 Chardonnay Sundial *Mendocino*	②	85
1985 Chenin Blanc *Mendocino*	②	80
1985 Fumé Blanc *Valley Oaks*	②	85
1985 Gewürztraminer *Mendocino*	②	84
1985 Sauvignon Blanc *Mendocino*	②	84
1983 Zinfandel Ricetti Vineyard *Mendocino*	③	82

The Fetzer Vineyard, with a production now in excess of 600,000 cases, has retained a strong following for the quality/price rapport that its wines have always represented. The philosophy here has been to bottle the white wines as quickly as possible and get them on the market. It has emphasized the fresh, fruity character of each varietal. One can hardly fault that strategy since all the Chardonnays, from the crisp, non-

oak-aged, wonderfully fresh, lemony, citrusy Sundial Chardonnay to the barrel-fermented, rich, oaky toasty, buttery
Barrel Select Chardonnay, are fairly priced and consistently
successful regardless of vintage. The Sauvignon Blanc is herbaceous but fresh and fruity, the Gewürztraminer, Chenin
Blanc, and Riesling rather simple, fruity, and pleasant. Among
the reds, the Lake County Zinfandels and Cabernets can often
represent good values, though the 1983s seemed rather disappointing for this quality-conscious winery. The Cabernet from
Fetzer, both 1982 and the 1983 Mendocino, has always
represented very good value, with supple, easy-to-drink and
easy-to-understand blackcurrant fruit well displayed. The
Zinfandels have ranged from the lighter style in Lake County
to the intense, rich, tannic monsters and vineyard-designated
Zinfandels of Ricetti and, in years past, Scharffenberger,
Lolonis, and, more recently, the Home Vineyard Zinfandel.
Fetzer is still one of the better Zinfandel producers in California, though the quality level of their Zinfandels does not
match what it was in the late seventies. The winery also
produces a rather vegetal Pinot Noir that they like much more
than I do, and one of California's better Petite Sirahs, a
peppery, rich, ripe, interesting wine that is always worth
considering. The wines under their secondary label, Bel
Arbres, are good value, particularly the blush wines.

FIRESTONE VINEYARDS *SANTA BARBARA*

1977 Cabernet Sauvignon *Santa Ynez*	③	**55**
1982 Cabernet Sauvignon *Santa Ynez*	②	**70**
1978 Cabernet Sauvignon Reserve *Santa Ynez*	③	**59**
1979 Cabernet Sauvignon Reserve *Santa Ynez*	③	**69**
1984 Chardonnay *Santa Ynez*	③	**50**
1981 Merlot *Santa Ynez*	②	**70**
1979 Pinot Noir *Santa Ynez*	②	**55**
1980 Pinot Noir *Santa Ynez*	②	**65**
1983 Sauvignon Blanc *Santa Ynez*	②	**62**
1984 Sauvignon Blanc *Santa Ynez*	②	**80**

This large winery, with a production in excess of 75,000 cases,
is jointly owned by the Japanese Suntory Group and the
Firestone family of tyre fame and fortune. The quality record
here borders on dismal and unfortunately things seem to be in
need of a major overhaul if this winery is to compete in an
ever-increasing competitive and quality-conscious wine
business. The white wines have lacked varietal character, fruit
and concentration. The red wines are even worse, with many
of them showing both excessive vegetal characteristics and
jammy, thick, over-ripe fruity characters. It is a shame,

because the prices seem fair and the owners certainly pleasant, but the quality is just not in the bottle.

FLORA SPRINGS WINE CO. *NAPA*

1982 Cabernet Sauvignon *Napa*	③	*81*
1983 Cabernet Sauvignon *Napa*	③	*78*
1984 Chardonnay *Napa*	③	*86*
1983 Chardonnay Barrel-Fermented *Napa*	④	*90*
1984 Chardonnay Barrel-Fermented *Napa*	④	*90*
1985 Sauvignon Blanc *Napa*	②	*85*
1984 Triology *Napa*	⑤	*89*

This small winery with a 15,000-case production has, since its opening in 1978, excelled with its two white wine varietals, Chardonnay and Sauvignon Blanc. The regular Chardonnay is very fruity and well structured, but the barrel-fermented takes on the character of a fine Puligny-Montrachet, with wonderful structure and toasty oak integrated into gobs of Chardonnay fruit. The 1985 Sauvignon Blanc continues the success that Flora Springs has enjoyed with this varietal, having a crisp austerity but plenty of character and freshness. Both the 1982 and 1983 Cabernet Sauvignons are rather lean and unyielding with rather tough, tannic, austere flavours. However, the launching in 1984 of the new proprietary wine, Triology, a Cabernet Sauvignon, Merlot, Cabernet Franc blend (33% of each), will propel this winery into the élite of red wine producers in California. There is a real quality effort being made here and this is undoubtedly a winery to keep an eye on.

LOUIS FOPPIANO WINE CO. *SONOMA*

1981 Cabernet Sauvignon *Sonoma*	②	83
1982 Cabernet Sauvignon *Sonoma*	②	85
1981 Cabernet Sauvignon Fox Vineyard *Sonoma*	③	85
1983 Chardonnay *Sonoma*	②	83
1984 Chardonnay *Sonoma*	②	84
1984 Sauvignon Blanc *Sonoma*	②	84

For whatever reason, the Foppiano Winery never seems to get the accolades it deserves for offering the wine consumer well-made, fresh, fairly interesting wines that are easy to drink young and have both character and quality. The prices remain among the most reasonable for California and with a production in excess of 150,000 cases, the wine is widely available. Virtually everything I have tasted from Foppiano has seemed well made and good value, from the crisp, fruity, lemony, citrusy Chardonnays to the tart, slightly herbaceous, fruity, medium-bodied Sauvignon Blancs. Even the reds are well made, with lush, medium-bodied, supple flavours, particularly the 1982 Cabernet Sauvignon. The 1981 Cabernet from the Fox Vineyard is more ageworthy and can be drunk or held for another five to six years. The secondary label of Foppiano, Riverside Farm, produces wines that also offer good value, although they are very straightforward in style.

FORMAN WINERY *NAPA*

1983 Cabernet Sauvignon *Napa*	④	**90**
1984 Cabernet Sauvignon *Napa*	④	**90**
1984 Chardonnay *Napa*	④	**90**
1985 Chardonnay *Napa*	④	**88**

Ric Forman has had numerous winemaking jobs over the last decade; he was the winemaker behind the fabulous string of Sterling Cabernets and Merlots between 1973 and 1976, wines that are still drinking beautifully today as well as great expressions of California winemaking art. He has now settled into his own winery and the debut releases, a barrel-fermented, rich, toasty, buttery 1984 Chardonnay and classically structured, rich, tannic, beautifully made 1983 Cabernet Sauvignon, show just how much talent Mr. Forman continues to have. His second releases, the 1985 Chardonnay and 1984 Cabernet Sauvignon, are no less impressive. His Chardonnays are oak-influenced but show wonderful buttery, pineapple fruit, a medium- to full-bodied format, and impeccable balance. His Cabernets are much like the ones he made at Sterling in the mid-seventies – rich, tannic, very ageworthy wines with impeccable balance and plenty of character. This is an up-and-coming star in the California wine world.

FREEMARK ABBEY *NAPA*

1981 Cabernet Sauvignon Bosché *Napa*	④	**82**
1982 Cabernet Sauvignon Bosché *Napa*	④	**78**
1983 Chardonnay *Napa*	③	**78**
1984 Chardonnay *Napa*	③	**82**
1982 Edelwein Gold *Napa*	⑤	**88**

Freemark Abbey is one of the older California wineries, having been founded in 1967. Production has been maintained at a modest 30,000 cases a year and the winery specializes in four wines – an oaky, rich Chardonnay, a late-harvest, decadently sweet Johannisberg Riesling called Edelwein Gold, a regular Cabernet Sauvignon, and a single-vineyard Cabernet Sauvignon from the famous highly respected Bosché Vineyard near Rutherford. (They also make a Petite Sirah from the York Creek Vineyards in Napa Valley that is generally peppery, rich, and one of the better of its type.) The older vintages of

Freemark Abbey, the 1960s and early 1970s have been wonderful wines, but I have found recent vintages rather dull and
more disappointing than pleasing. The 1983 Chardonnay is a
bit flat and overly oaky. The 1982 Cabernet Sauvignon Bosché
is straightforward and medium-bodied, with a slightly vegetal
bouquet, and seems to lack richness and depth, relying more
on its one-dimensional fruit than any kind of complexity that
the price suggests it should have. The 1981 Bosché is a bit
better, with more fruit and a bit more complexity. Given the
wonderful wines this vineyard produced for Freemark Abbey
in the late sixties and early seventies, it appears to be only a
shadow of its former self today.

E. & J. GALLO WINERY *MODESTO*

1978 Cabernet Sauvignon	②	78
Chablis Blanc Non-Vintage	①	79
Chardonnay Non-Vintage	①	76
Chenin Blanc Non-Vintage	①	72
Hearty Burgundy Non-Vintage	①	77
Sauvignon Blanc Non-Vintage	①	75
1984 Sauvignon Blanc Special Release	①	*84*

Gallo, with a production of 60,000,000+ cases a year, or as
they advertise, 250,000 cases a day, is a remarkable success
story. Wine enthusiasts tend to turn up their noses when
Gallo wines are mentioned, but quite honestly, no winery,
given this kind of production, is more consistent in quality
than Gallo. No, the wines are not the complex or sublime
renditions that some of the smaller wineries can turn out but,
for the value, the Hearty Burgundy and the Chablis Blanc are
really quite remarkable wines when one considers their prices.
The varietal wines range from a fairly dull, flat Chenin Blanc to
a decent yet uninspired non-vintage Sauvignon Blanc and
Chardonnay, a supple, fruity 1978 Cabernet Sauvignon, and a
very good Loire Valley-inspired 1984 Sauvignon. If you
haven't tried Gallo's inexpensive Hearty Burgundy or Chablis
Blanc, you might be surprised. Of course, the winery does
much more than this, producing a line of wines called Polo
Brindisi, a number of sparkling wines under the André label
that are cloyingly sweet, fat, and to my taste rather unpleasant, and the very soundly made Carlo Rossi wines. Gallo also
produces sherries and ports that are heavy but adequate.

GIRARD WINERY *NAPA*

1982 Cabernet Sauvignon *Napa*	③	86
1983 Cabernet Sauvignon *Napa*	③	*84*
1984 Cabernet Sauvignon *Napa*	③	86

1984 Cabernet Sauvignon Reserve *Napa* .... ④ **90**
1982 Chardonnay *Napa* .... ③ **80**
1983 Chardonnay *Napa* .... ③ **87**
1984 Chardonnay *Napa* .... ③ **87**
1984 Sauvignon Blanc *North Coast* .... ② **84**

The Girard Winery started off strongly this decade with several outstanding releases, particularly the 1981 Chardonnay. That has been followed up by an increase in quality of Cabernet Sauvignon with each vintage. At present, the three major wines in the Girard line-up are all at least very good and in certain cases outstanding. The 1983 Chardonnay, while not quite up to the great 1981, is still a wonderfully intense Chardonnay with a fragrant bouquet of toasty oak, butter, apples, and lemons. The 1984 is similarly styled. The Sauvignon Blancs tend to be rather opulent and aggressively herbaceous, but are loaded with fruit. Of the Cabernet Sauvignons, the 1982 was a wonderful start for Girard followed by a very good, interesting 1983, and two excellent wines in 1984, particularly the Reserve, which is Girard's finest Cabernet to date – a backstrapping, rich, intense, tannic, yet beautifully structured wine for ageing ten or more years. Prices are moderately high, but the quality here has been consistently excellent since the beginning. The production has inched up towards 15,000 cases. (The winery also makes a little bit of Chenin Blanc, which I have never tasted.) Its secondary label is called Stephens.

GLEN ELLEN *SONOMA*
1983 Cabernet Sauvignon Proprietor's Reserve
  Sonoma... ② **80**
1984 Cabernet Sauvignon Proprietor's Reserve
  Sonoma... ② **82**
1984 Chardonnay Estate *Sonoma* .... ② **85**
1984 Chardonnay Proprietor's Reserve *Sonoma* ...... ② **78**
1985 Fumé Blanc Estate *Sonoma* .... ② **86**

It's hard to believe that the Glen Ellen Winery was founded only in 1981. The owners, the Benziger family, took a bold stand with their Proprietor's Reserve Chardonnay and Cabernet Sauvignon by producing wines easy to drink and easy to understand at a remarkably high level of quality. They have had astounding success with these two wines, which has forced as well as inspired other wineries to lower their prices as well. Today the Glen Ellen Proprietor's Reserve Cabernet Sauvignon is still one of the best buys on the market, and the Chardonnay Proprietor's Reserve, while not quite as interesting as the Cabernet, is nevertheless a fruity, lighter-styled, lean, compact wine that is easy to drink. The 1984 and 1985 estate bottlings of Sauvignon Blanc and Chardonnay are both extremely well made and reasonably priced. This winery rarely makes a mistake and their wines always represent good values. Production is now in excess of 45,000 cases.

GRGICH HILLS CELLARS *NAPA*

1981 Cabernet Sauvignon *Napa*	④	85
1982 Cabernet Sauvignon *Napa*	④	87
1983 Chardonnay *Napa*	④	88
1984 Chardonnay *Napa*	④	88
1984 Fumé Blanc *Napa*	③	78
1982 Zinfandel *Alexander Valley*	③	85
1983 Zinfandel *Alexander Valley*	③	84

This winery is run with great enthusiasm by one of California's most respected winemakers, Miljenko Grgich, who built his reputation during the mid-seventies by making splendid wines at the Château Montelena. His Napa winery produces just over 20,000 cases of wine and has done extremely well with a big, rich, oaky, intense, lush, very concentrated Chardonnay that has been superb in vintages such as 1983 and 1984. The Zinfandel, made from grapes purchased in Alexander Valley, is another winner here – intense, spicy, loaded with berry flavours, and deftly touched by a sojourn in oak barrels. The Cabernet Sauvignons from Grgich, both the 1981 and 1982, have been tannic, fairly intense wines with a heavy overlay of tannin and spicy oak. The 1981 is perhaps the firmer, more structured wine, capable of seven to eight years of ageing; the 1982 is lusher, richer, and more supple. Grgich wines are hardly values at their high prices, but they are expressive examples of high-quality winemaking that rarely disappoint.

GROTH VINEYARDS AND WINERY *NAPA*

1982 Cabernet Sauvignon *Napa*	③	87
1983 Cabernet Sauvignon *Napa*	③	85
1984 Cabernet Sauvignon *Napa*	④	90
1982 Chardonnay *Napa*	③	84
1983 Chardonnay *Napa*	③	87
1984 Chardonnay *Napa*	③	87
1984 Sauvignon Blanc *Napa*	②	84

The Groth Winery, founded in 1982, has already raised its production to 30,000 cases, but the smartest decision it has made to date was to hire the brilliant winemaker Nils Venge away from Villa Mount Eden Vineyard. Venge has an impeccable track record for producing some of California's best

Cabernets and Chardonnays, and the genius he demonstrated at Villa Mount Eden has hardly stopped now that he is working for Dennis Groth. The first releases have been remarkably impressive and, for their quality, very reasonably priced. Venge is a big believer in dramatic wines made from fully ripe grapes. His Cabernets have gone from one strength to another, starting with an excellent 1982 Cabernet Sauvignon loaded with blackcurrant fruit and married beautifully with oak. The 1983, while less concentrated and a trifle more herbaceous, is still rich and very fruity, with quite a long finish. His 1984 looks to be his best yet for the Groth Winery. It is an opulent, very rich, intense wine with layers of fruit. Nils Venge thinks his 1985 is even better; so it appears we have plenty to look forward to from this young but emerging star in Napa Valley.

HEITZ CELLARS *NAPA*

1980 Cabernet Sauvignon *Napa*	③	79
1981 Cabernet Sauvignon *Napa*	③	75
1980 Cabernet Sauvignon Bella Oaks *Napa*	⑤	87
1981 Cabernet Sauvignon Bella Oaks *Napa*	④	84
1980 Cabernet Sauvignon Martha's Vineyard *Napa*	⑤	87
1981 Cabernet Sauvignon Martha's Vineyard *Napa*	⑤	86
1980 Chardonnay *Napa*	③	65
1981 Chardonnay *Napa*	③	55
1982 Chardonnay *Napa*	③	60

Heitz Wine Cellars is one of the magical names of Napa Valley and, in fact, their Cabernets can be among the best wines of Napa. However, that hardly excuses the rest of the stable here, which includes some very poorly made Chardonnays and some inexpensive wines like its Grignolino, a terribly disappointing wine, as well as their Chablis, which lacks character. Undoubtedly, the fame of this winery is the Cabernet Sauvignon from Martha's Vineyard. For whatever reason, the wines have a unique character that can be recognized by smell alone because of their intense minty, chocolaty, eucalyptus-styled aroma. The great vintages of this wine have been the 1968 and 1970, which continue to age magnificently while losing none of their minty character. The 1974 is also a candidate for excellence. Recent vintages have not lived up to the above-mentioned ones. The 1978 was disappointing, the 1979 somewhat better, and the 1980 and 1981 good wines but hardly the type of quality to justify the price asked. Heitz also has begun to purchase grapes from another excellent vineyard, the Bella

Oaks Vineyard in Napa Valley, and this wine can also be excellent, as it was in 1977, 1979, and 1980. The 1981, however, is a disappointment. The regular Cabernets have taken on a very commercial, straightforward style and while not extravagantly priced are hardly good values. As for the Chardonnays, they are consistently thin, acidic, and lacking in varietal character. One wonders how such a great red wine-maker can show so little ability with a white varietal that seems to be easy to make elsewhere. The Grignolino is a poor effort for a cash flow wine and is best served chilled, but its high-acid character makes it very unattractive. Heitz, of course, remains an institution in Napa Valley, but proceed with caution since the great reputation here is not always justified by the quality or the price of the wine in the bottle.

THE WILLIAM HILL WINERY *NAPA*

1980 Cabernet Sauvignon Gold Label *Napa*.............. ④ **90**
1981 Cabernet Sauvignon Gold Label *Napa*.............. ④ **87**
1982 Cabernet Sauvignon Gold Label *Napa*.............. ④ **87**
1983 Cabernet Sauvignon Gold Label *Napa*.............. ④ **86**
1981 Chardonnay Gold Label *Napa*............................ ④ **87**
1982 Chardonnay Gold Label *Napa*............................ ④ **82**
1983 Chardonnay Gold Label *Napa*............................ ④ **86**

Bill Hill is a fervent believer in mountain vineyards, with their cooler temperatures and higher natural acidity in the grapes. His winery, which started with an excellent 1978 Cabernet and huge, oaky style of Chardonnay, has continued to evolve in style. In the short ten years that the winery has been in existence, it has built an impeccable reputation with Cabernet Sauvignon and good Chardonnay. The production is inching its way up towards 40,000 cases. The winery also makes a less expensive, ready-to-drink Chardonnay and Cabernet under what they call a Silver Label, versus the Reserve Gold Labels that are now on the market. The Chardonnays, after being too oaky and heavy (as in 1980), have moved towards a crisper, more restrained style, but as Bill Hill promised, they have aged well in contrast to most California Chardonnays. The 1981 Reserve has developed a Meursault-like, buttery, subtle oak character and is drinking beautifully at the moment. The 1982 Reserve is a good bit less impressive, but the 1983 looks to be another Chardonnay that can live five to six years in the bottle, a long time by California standards. However, the glories of this house are the beautifully made Cabernet Sauvig-nons that start off life rather lean and austere but seem to develop richness and character as they age. After the very successful 1978 and more supple, fruity, open style of 1979,

468

the 1980, which seemed tight and hard when first released, has developed magnificently into a truly great California Cabernet that may have at least another ten years of life ahead of it. It can still be found on the market, so run, don't walk, to get a few bottles for your cellar. The 1981 is a more supple, fruity style of Cabernet and the 1982 again lusher but showing good structure and a very seductive texture, with at least five to ten years' future. Hill's Cabernets are well worth seeking out by those who have the patience to wait for them to develop, as they exhibit wonderful blackcurrant fruity flavours, an intelligent dosage of oak, and plenty of concentration and tannin. This is definitely one of the premier producers of Cabernet in California.

INGLENOOK VINEYARDS *NAPA*

1980 Cabernet Sauvignon *Napa* .... ② **84**
1981 Cabernet Sauvignon *Napa* .... ② **78**
1982 Cabernet Sauvignon *Napa* .... ② **72**
1983 Cabernet Sauvignon Kabinett Selection
Napa .... ② **73**
1980 Cabernet Sauvignon Reserve Cask *Napa* .... ④ **88**
1981 Cabernet Sauvignon Reserve Cask *Napa* .... ④ **88**
1982 Cabernet Sauvignon Reserve Cask *Napa* .... ④ **87**
1983 Cabernet Sauvignon Reserve Cask *Napa* .... ④ **86**
1982 Charbono *Napa* .... ② **85**
1983 Chardonnay Reserve *Napa* .... ④ **?**
1984 Chardonnay Reserve *Napa* .... ④ **85**
1982 Merlot *Napa* .... ② **78**
1981 Merlot Limited Cask Reserve *Napa* .... ③ **75**
1983 Merlot Reserve Cask *Napa* .... ④ **?**
1984 Sauvignon Blanc Reserve *Napa* .... ② **78**

Inglenook is one of the great old names in California and was one of the pioneers in producing world-class, outstanding Cabernet Sauvignons under the legendary John Daniel. Much has been made of the fact that when the winery was sold to Heublein in the mid-sixties production was expanded significantly and the quality suffered immensely. Certainly, anyone who had tasted the old Inglenook Cabernets from the fifties and early sixties realized how great California Cabernets could be. However, since 1980 the winery has been putting its best foot forward in trying to regain some of its lost prestige and stature. The wines have a new label (which actually resembles the old label used back in the fifties) and the quality seems to be on the rise again. Certainly, 1980 was a very successful vintage for the winery's Cabernets, and the Reserve Casks from 1981, 1982, and 1983 all look very good, particularly the flamboyant blackcurrant, cedary-scented, supple 1981 and the exotic, multi-dimensional 1982. The new Kabinett selections from Inglenook are inexpensive, lighter-styled wines that are simple and straightforward, and of course the winery produces a significant amount of jug wine under the Navalle label. The Chardonnays continue to be a little disappointing in the scheme of things, rather light, citrusy and lemony with just a touch of oak, but one would like to see more intensity. The Sauvignon Blanc Reserve has looked quite good, has a lot of fruit, depth, and character, but the 1984 was surprisingly devoid of flavour intensity. The winery also continues to make a bit of Chenin Blanc, Gewürztraminer, Riesling, Pinot Noir, Petite Sirah and Charbono. One of the most interesting wines in the Inglenook line-up that rarely gets the credit it should is Charbono, of which the 1982 is one of the better examples since the mid-seventies. It is a beefy, rich, spicy, peppery wine with a considerable amount of character. Inglenook's production of 150,000 cases of varietals and another 100,000+ cases of generics puts it among the leaders in terms of total production of wine in California. This winery clearly looks to be on the rebound and merits following to see what new vintages offer.

IRON HORSE RANCH AND VINEYARDS *SONOMA*

1983 Blanc de Noirs *Sonoma*	④	84
1983 Blanc de Noirs Wedding Cuvée *Sonoma*	④	84
1982 Brut *Sonoma*	④	83
1983 Brut *Sonoma*	④	83
1981 Brut Late Disgorged *Sonoma*	④	85
1981 Cabernet Sauvignon *Sonoma*	④	72
1982 Cabernet Sauvignon *Sonoma*	④	65
1984 Chardonnay *Sonoma*	③	78
1985 Fumé Blanc *Sonoma*	③	85

Iron Horse is doing one of the best jobs in California with its sparkling wines, though the prices remain a bit stiff. One can find French non-vintage Champagne that is superior for less money. Nevertheless, these beautifully labelled wines are certainly worth a try and I applaud the idea of a late-disgorged wine, which adds character and body to the product. With regard to the other wines, the Fumé Blanc tends to be very lean, tart, austere, yet interesting. The 1985 seems less successful than the 1984. The Chardonnay is in the same style, rather herbaceous for a Chardonnay, with lean, tart, citrusy flavours. It is not a style I personally prefer, but it is cleanly made and pleasant. The Cabernet Sauvignon tends to be lean, austere, and rather thin. The 1981 was acceptable, but the

1982 tasted more like a Beaujolais and was also spoiled by cardboard aromas in its bouquet.

JEKEL VINEYARD *MONTEREY*
1982 Cabernet Sauvignon *Monterey*............................. ③ ?
1981 Cabernet Sauvignon Private Reserve
Monterey.. ④ ?
1982 Chardonnay Reserve *Monterey*........................... ③ 84
1983 Chardonnay Reserve *Monterey*........................... ③ 86
1984 Johannisberg Riesling *Monterey* .... ② 85
1985 Johannisberg Riesling *Monterey* .... ② 87

This winery, which has a fairly large production of 50,000 cases, started in 1978 and quickly built a reputation for its Riesling. Since then they have added a very powerful, oaky, richly buttery Chardonnay and an intense, very rich, but, to my taste, excessively vegetal Cabernet Sauvignon. I like and applaud the individualistic style that owner Bill Jekel is aiming for with his rich, dramatic, flamboyant wines, but the Cabernet, as much as I adore its texture, power, and balance on the palate, is difficult to give high marks to because of its pungent vegetal aromas. Both the 1981 Reserve and 1982 are impressive on the palate but bizarre to the smell. One wine that Jekel seems to consistently do an excellent job with is the Johannisberg Riesling. It was this wine that in 1978 won such plaudits from critics that the name Jekel began to be bantered about in wine circles. I am not a great admirer of California Riesling, which tends to lack acidity and to be heavy and dull, but this Riesling has a wonderfully fragrant bouquet, and soft, delicious, fruity flavours balanced by nice acidity in the background. The newly released 1985, made in a true Kabinett style, is as good a dry Riesling as you are likely to find from California.

JORDAN VINEYARD AND WINERY *SONOMA*
1980 Cabernet Sauvignon *Alexander Valley* .... ④ 85
1981 Cabernet Sauvignon *Alexander Valley* .... ④ 86
1982 Cabernet Sauvignon *Alexander Valley* .... ④ 79
1982 Chardonnay *Alexander Valley* .... ④ 75
1983 Chardonnay *Alexander Valley* .... ④ 59

The Jordan Winery, which was built to resemble a Bordeaux château, is one of the top tourist sites in Sonoma County. The first vintage of Cabernet Sauvignon was the 1976, which pleased people when it was released because of its supple, very lush, forward charms. The subsequent vintages of Jordan have continued in the same very supple, plummy, easy-to-drink style, with a noticeable herbaceous note to the wines. The prices are high for what one actually gets, but the wines have been quite well promoted. They are appealing young, but be forewarned, five to six years seems to be the best one can hope for in longevity for these wines, although the 1980 may last until 1990. Longevity has been compromised for the sake of immediate drinkability; I certainly won't complain, but you should be aware of that before you stock up on cases of Jordan Cabernet expecting it to mature like a fine Bordeaux. As for the Chardonnay, it is straightforward, dull, and quite overpriced for what one receives.

KALIN CELLARS *MARIN*

1980 Cabernet Sauvignon *Santa Barbara*	③	67
1982 Cabernet Sauvignon Reserve *Santa Barbara*	④	86
1984 Chardonnay *Potter Valley*	③	87
1983 Chardonnay Cuvée D *Sonoma*	④	90
1983 Chardonnay Cuvée L *Sonoma*	③	87
1984 Chardonnay Cuvée L *Sonoma*	③	91
1982 Pinot Noir Cuvée DD *Sonoma*	③	87
1984 Sauvignon Blanc *Potter Valley*	②	87
1984 Sauvignon Blanc Reserve *Potter Valley*	③	90
1984 Semillon *Potter Valley*	③	90

Kalin consistently turns out some of the most interesting and well-made complex wines in all of California. Perhaps this is due to the fact that owner and microbiologist Terry Leighton is one of the world's great specialists in yeast and believes in making wines very naturally, not centrifuging or filtering them, resulting in highly intense, original, complex wines with great style. If there is a disappointment, it tends to be occasional vintages of Cabernet Sauvignon that are made from grapes purchased in Santa Barbara. The 1980 was extremely vegetal, spicy, and unattractive. However, the 1982 showed great depth and intensity, with the vegetal component tamed down considerably. This winery makes California's best Semillon wine, with an incredible waxy, lush richness that stands out in vintages such as 1985 and 1984. One can't recommend this dry, Graves-like wine enough. The Sauvignon Blanc Potter Valley is another knockout and potentially one of the great Sauvignons made in California, with some toasty oak in the background and rich, deep flavours that are reminiscent of the great white Graves château Laville-Haut-Brion. The Chardonnays have ranged from a very good Potter Valley Chardonnay in 1984 to absolutely superb Chardonnays from Sonoma, the Cuvée L and Cuvée D. These are unfiltered Chardonnays that actually throw some sediment after several years in the bottle, but they have remarkably intense, rich, buttery, appley, lemony fruit married brilliantly with toasty oak and are as close to the style of a great French Chassagne-Montrachet as one is likely to find from California. The Pinot Noir is tannic but shows every bit of the potential expected of an earthy, smoky, Chambertin-styled wine that can age from five to ten years. A tiny amount of decadently rich sweet wine called Cuvée d'Or is made, but your best chance of finding a bottle of this is to buy it directly from the winery or one of its outlets in California. The production of Kalin is now up to 5,000 cases, hardly enough to go around once the splendid quality of the wines being made here is known. This to me is one of the great underpublicized wineries in California, and Terry Leighton, one of California's most adventurous and successful winemakers, is willing to take a risk to make something special. One wishes more California wineries would follow in his footsteps.

CHARLES KRUG *NAPA*

1981 Cabernet Sauvignon	②	82
1974 Cabernet Sauvignon Lot F1	⑤	87
1978 Cabernet Sauvignon Vintage Selection		
Napa	③	84
1983 Chardonnay *Napa*	②	78
1983 Johannisberg Riesling *Napa*	②	68

Charles Krug's wines, which are made by one segment of the omnipresent Mondavi family in California, get very little publicity and could use a good PR expert to give them a bit more status in the wine world today. The reds tend to be the best wines here; I find the Riesling rather dull and too acidic, and the Chardonnay bland and lacking varietal character. However, the Cabernet can be quite good. The 1978 Vintage Selection Cabernet Sauvignon has a rich black cherry nose dominated somewhat excessively by oak, but it has good flavours and should be drunk now since it appears to have reached full maturity. The 1974 Cabernet Sauvignon Lot F1, which has been reintroduced into the market, is a very good, even excellent example of a wine from a great vintage for California Cabernet. It has a wonderfully rich, expressive bouquet, dramatically deep, intense flavours, and seems to be at its plateau of maturity now. One suspects that the Krug Cabernets can hold their own against some of the best from California, but it's a shame they don't get more attention from retailers and the press. The production of this winery has topped one million cases, of which a large part is in their jug wine production under the label C. K. Mondavi.

LAUREL GLEN *SONOMA*

1981 Cabernet Sauvignon *Sonoma Mountain* .... ③ **87**
1983 Cabernet Sauvignon *Sonoma Mountain* .... ③ **81**
1984 Cabernet Sauvignon *Sonoma Mountain* .... ④ **90**
1982 Merlot *Sonoma* .... ② **75**

Winemaker/owner Patrick Campbell is producing close to 5,000 cases of wine which were the first to have the appellation 'Sonoma Mountain' on them. Before he opened his winery, he sold his grapes to several Sonoma wineries. His debut wine, the 1981 Cabernet Sauvignon, was a rich, beautifully made, well-structured wine with intense fruit, full body, and deep layers of flavour, and with five to seven more years of ageing potential. This was followed by the 1982 Merlot, which was rather feeble in colour, light in body, and rather herbaceous, with somewhat diluted flavours. However, the 1983 Sonoma Mountain Cabernet Sauvignon was a return to the more impressive style of the 1981. Campbell's 1984 Cabernet Sauvignon, his best produced yet, is a rich, opulent, intense wine with great flavour concentration and plenty of backbone for ageing five to ten years. So far this winery has been content to produce only Merlot and Cabernet Sauvignon, and aside from the off year of 1982, three of the four first vintages have been considerable successes and merit serious attention from wine enthusiasts.

CHARLES LEFRANC — ALMADEN *SAN JOSE*

1981 Cabernet Sauvignon *San Jose* .... ② **84**
1982 Cabernet Sauvignon *San Benito* .... ② **83**
1983 Cabernet Sauvignon *San Benito* .... ② **85**
1984 Chardonnay *Napa* .... ④ **85**
1984 Chardonnay *Tepusquet* .... ② **78**
1984 Pinot Noir *Cienga Valley* .... ③ **85**
1984 Premium Red *California* .... ② **83**
1985 Premium White *California* .... ② **82**
1982 Sauvignon Blanc Late-Harvest *San Benito* .... ③ **84**

The huge Almaden Winery in San Jose with a production in excess of eight million cases a year, is separating more and more its premium line of wines called Charles Lefranc away from the bulk wine production of Almaden. Winemaker Klaus Mathes has been given greater independence and flexibility to produce wines of high quality for Charles Lefranc. The first evidence of this was the 1981 Cabernet Sauvignon, the best Cabernet produced yet by Almaden under their premium Charles Lefranc label. A rich, densely coloured wine, it should drink and evolve well for another five or more years. The 1982 is somewhat less impressive, but still a good wine; the 1983 is the best yet from this winery, deserving prestige and respect. The Chardonnays that have been released include an impressive, expensive Napa Chardonnay in 1984 that had a complex bouquet of hazelnuts and toasty, buttery fruit. The palate impression was one of balance and restrained elegance. The other 1984 Chardonnay from grapes grown in the Santa Barbara area from the Tepusquet Vineyard was a more tart wine with scents of tropical fruit, particularly pineapples. The Late-Harvest Sauvignon Blanc that Charles Lefranc is producing also looks to be a winner, as does their 1984 Pinot Noir. Most serious wine consumers turn their heads the other way when looking at some of the huge wineries that are primarily involved in jug wine production; Almaden, however, is clearly setting new standards with their Charles Lefranc label and they bear watching as the wines are released. The new Premium generic red and white table wines are delicious: the white is supple, lush, very fruity; the red is cherry-scented and obviously Cabernet-dominated. Both offer quality and value.

LYETH VINEYARD AND WINERY *SONOMA*

1981 Red Table Wine *Alexander Valley*	④	86
1982 Red Table Wine *Alexander Valley*	④	87
1983 Red Table Wine *Alexander Valley*	④	85
1984 Red Table Wine *Alexander Valley*	④	90
1982 White Table Wine *Alexander Valley*	②	87
1983 White Table Wine *Alexander Valley*	②	86
1984 White Table Wine *Alexander Valley*	②	86

The Lyeth Winery, which was founded only in 1981, is one of the new breed of California wineries that has taken the varietal name off the label and featured a proprietary blend for both its red table wine (composed of Cabernet Sauvignon, Merlot, and Cabernet Franc) and its white wine (Sauvignon Blanc and Semillon). The quality clearly matches the price for the red; and the white wine represents a good value. The style aimed at here is very Bordeaux in orientation, the white wine resembling a very fine Graves, with a percentage of Semillon blended in for its creamy, soft qualities. The red table wines have a good deal of Cabernet Franc and Merlot blended in and have shown remarkable elegance in 1981, more power and tannin in 1982, a more austere quality in 1983, and the wonderful, opulent, rich, layered quality of a fine Pomerol in 1984. Their label is one of the more interesting in California, with engraved gold etching on the face of the bottle. This winery plans to get their production up in the region of

30,000 cases and if the quality continues at the current level they should have no problem selling them. I'm impressed.

LOUIS M. MARTINI *NAPA*

1980 Barbera *California*	②	72
1982 Burgundy *California*	①	70
1982 Cabernet Sauvignon *North Coast*	②	74
1981 Cabernet Sauvignon La Loma *Napa*	④	84
1980 Cabernet Sauvignon Monte Rosso *Sonoma*	④	86
1978 Cabernet Sauvignon Special Selection *Napa*	②	86
1984 Chardonnay *North Coast*	②	84
1983 Chardonnay Los Vinedos Russian River *Sonoma*	③	84
1983 Chardonnay Vineyard Selection *Napa*	③	82
1983 Merlot *North Coast*	②	72
1980 Merlot Private Reserve *Napa*	②	84
Non-Vintage Moscato Sparkling Wine *California*	②	87
1983 Pinot Noir *Napa*	②	65
1980 Pinot Noir Las Amigas *Napa*	①	73
1983 Zinfandel *North Coast*	②	72

The strength of Martini has always been its red wines – some old vintages of Cabernet Sauvignon and Barbera from the fifties and sixties can still be marvellous today. The style produced here is very light by northern California standards, and since the mid-seventies my notes also show a surprising inconsistency. Yet in certain vintages Martini's Barbera can still be one of California's best wine buys. (For example, the 1979 is very, very good, the 1980 quite mediocre.) The other two great bargains here include the Special Selection Cabernet Sauvignon – the 1978 is fully mature, rich, cedary, and supple – and the Chardonnay from the Los Vinedos Vineyard – the current release, the 1983, is fresh, lively, and filled with fruit. Martini has two single-vineyard Cabernet Sauvignons that also merit attention, although they are not bargains. The La Loma from Napa Valley and the Monte Rosso from Sonoma are Martini's two richest, densest-coloured wines, meant to take at least ten years of ageing. My notes have consistently shown a preference for the richer, more complex Monte Rosso over the La Loma. If you visit the winery, be sure to ask for Martini's remarkably vibrant, fruity, flowery, absolutely delicious sparkling Moscato, which can only be purchased there. One wishes he would make much more of this wonderful wine. Over recent vintages, the other wines here (particularly the feeble Pinot Noirs) have been consistently dull, very light, somewhat oxidized, and often too dominated by the smell of redwood. However, chosen carefully, Martini's wines, particularly the Special Selections, can offer considerable quality/price rapport.

PAUL MASSON VINEYARDS *SANTA CLARA*

1981 Cabernet Sauvignon *California*	②	**69**
1982 Cabernet Sauvignon *Sonoma*	②	**73**
1984 Chardonnay *Monterey*	③	**77**
1984 Emerald Dry	①	**74**
1984 Sauvignon Blanc Pinnacles Selection *Monterey*	②	**80**

Paul Masson Winery, located in Monterey, produces a staggering 8,000,000 cases of wine. Owned by the Seagrams Wine Co., the prices range from inexpensive to moderately expensive for their top-of-the-line Chardonnays and sparkling wines. The quality has improved somewhat with the inauguration of their best lots of wine, which appear under the Pinnacles Estate Selections. In addition, in 1983 they began to buy their Cabernet Sauvignon from growers in Sonoma County. The wines tend to have very light-intensity flavours, unfocused varietal characters, and often rather soft, slightly sweet flavours. The proprietary wine, Emerald Dry, is a slightly sweet but fresh, very light, casual wine. The Chardonnays have tasted like some sort of generic white table wine, totally lacking varietal character, which is somewhat amazing given the fact that they come from Monterey, where splendid Chardonnay grapes can be produced. The Sauvignon Blancs have been up and down in quality, and are often very herbaceous and green. The Cabernet Sauvignons, under the California appellation, tend to be rather cooked and pruny, not bad, but not good either. The 1982 Cabernet Sauvignon shows an increase in quality; although it is very light and watery, it does have simple, fruity flavours. The sparkling wines are generally sweet, flabby, and terribly uninteresting. One can't question the commercial success of operations like this, but the quality level of the wines is hardly inspirational.

MATANZAS CREEK WINERY *SONOMA*

1983 Chardonnay *Sonoma*	③	**88**
1984 Chardonnay *Sonoma*	④	**86**
1983 Chardonnay Estate *Sonoma*	③	**90**
1984 Chardonnay Estate *Sonoma*	④	**87**
1983 Merlot *Sonoma*	③	*81*
1984 Merlot *Sonoma*	③	**89**
1984 Sauvignon Blanc *Sonoma*	③	**87**

This winery, with a tiny production of only 6,000 cases, has a well-deserved reputation for producing some of California's greatest Chardonnays and certainly one of its very finest Sauvignon Blancs. The Chardonnays come in two types, one made from purchased grapes in Sonoma, the other an estate-bottled Chardonnay. They are brilliant examples of marrying the wonderful, opulent, ripe Chardonnay fruit obtained in California's best vineyards with toasty oak, balanced beautifully by crisp acidity. The Estate always seems to be a little richer and longer. The 1983s are superb; the 1984s are slightly less so, but still excellent and well worth a special trip to find. The 1984 Sauvignon Blanc is loaded with wonderful fruit, good acidity, and a lushness that one rarely finds in this wine. The 1983 Sauvignon Blanc, which should now be drunk up, was one of the greatest Sauvignon Blancs I have ever tasted from California. The red wines here have always lagged behind the quality of the whites. Interestingly, the Cabernet Sauvignon has now been dropped from the winery's offerings. The Merlots have shown steady improvement, the 1983 being angular but with moderately intense, supple fruit. The 1984 looks to be a real winner, since winemaker David Ramey seems to have learned his lessons well by working in Pomerol with Christian Moueix. The 1984 Merlot is a wonderfully opulent, ripe, fleshy-textured wine with super depth and remarkable appeal. Now that some of California's finest white wines are produced here, it looks as if their Merlot will enter the top league and put Matanzas Creek on the map for top-quality red wine as well.

MAYACAMAS VINEYARDS *NAPA*

1978 Cabernet Sauvignon *California*	④	87
1980 Cabernet Sauvignon *California*	④	85
1981 Cabernet Sauvignon *California*	④	83
1982 Cabernet Sauvignon *California*	④	88
1983 Chardonnay *California*	④	85
1984 Sauvignon Blanc *California*	③	85

Mayacamas is one of Napa's oldest wineries, having been originally founded in 1889 and resurrected by the Travers family in 1941. The reputation of this house has been built on California's longest-lived Cabernet Sauvignon, a wine that ages as slowly as the great Latour in Pauillac. A vertical tasting attended recently showed such wines as 1968, 1970, and 1974 still evolving, and the last vintage not yet close to being ready to drink. Recent vintages have performed less spectacularly than such greats as the 1974, 1973, and 1968, but one always wonders (when tasting this wine) if its true personality and flavour intensity are really showing through since it is such a notoriously slow starter. Of the recent vintages, certainly the

1982 looks like a big winner, but it should not be drunk until the mid-1990s. It has more accessibility than most Mayacamas Cabernets, while the 1981 seems particularly hard, backward, and without the inner core of strength and muscle this wine normally exhibits. The unreleased 1984, tasted from cask, looks to be a pretty stunning wine with all the muscle and tannin as well as the opulence that a great Napa Cabernet should have. The Chardonnays are also remarkably slow developers. The 1975 remains in healthy condition, proof that not every California Chardonnay begins to fall apart after three or four years. It remains one of the great Chardonnays I have ever tasted. Recent vintages have not shown the same character, but then, I always ask myself, am I drinking them too soon? The Sauvignon Blanc is married nicely with toasty, spicy oak, shows good fruit, and seems to be the only Mayacamas wine that one must drink in its first four or five years. One should also keep an eye out for the late-harvest Zinfandel that this winery occasionally makes. It can be the best example of late-harvest Zinfandel produced in California.

MIRASSOU VINEYARD *SANTA CLARA*

1980 **Blanc de Blancs** *Monterey*	③	**78**
1981 **Blanc de Noir** *Monterey*	③	**82**
1981 **Brut Champagne** *Monterey*	③	**58**
1982 **Brut Champagne** *Monterey*	③	**82**
1982 **Cabernet Sauvignon Harvest Reserve** *Napa*	③	**85**
1984 **Chardonnay Harvest Reserve** *Monterey*	③	**80**
1984 **Fumé Blanc Harvest Reserve** *Monterey*	②	**72**
1984 **White Burgundy** *Monterey*	①	**84**
1985 **White Burgundy** *Monterey*	①	**84**
1981 **Zinfandel Harvest Reserve** *Monterey*	②	**80**

The Mirassou Winery is one of the great old historic wineries in California, having been founded in 1854. It remains family-owned in a time when wineries this size (300,000+ cases) are being gobbled up by large corporations. The quality of the wines here ranges from good to occasionally below average. One of the great buys offered by Mirassou has consistently been their white Burgundy, a wine made from Pinot Blanc grown in Monterey County. It has been a consistent success in every vintage I have tried, with the 1984 and 1985 fresh, loaded with fruit and broad flavours, and, unquestionably a 'best buy'. The top wines are called Harvest Reserve and the Chardonnays have tended to be rather oaky and buttery, with a certain earthy character. In certain vintages they have turned out slightly thin and vegetal. The Fumé Blanc tends to be very vegetal and smoky, but is certainly interesting. Among the red wines, the Cabernets have been consistent disappointments, extremely herbaceous and green and rather unpleasant to drink. After decades of drawing their grapes from Monterey for Cabernet, the Mirassous in 1982 began to put their Harvest Reserves under a Napa appellation and the 1982 Cabernet Sauvignon is their best Cabernet in memory. The winery also dabbles a bit with Zinfandel, which tends to be very high in alcohol, rich, lush, and intense (as is the 1981). The winery has also made some Pinot Noir, a rather big wine but again painfully green and herbaceous. Sparkling wines are also part of the huge stable of offerings at Mirassou—I have had remarkably thin and again vegetal-tasting wines as well as rather odd, unidentifiable-smelling, sparkling wines. However, the 1982 Brut Champagne and 1981 Blanc de Noir seem to be harbingers of better and more interesting sparkling wines. We shall see with the release of their 1983s. Many wine consumers tend to dismiss this winery as not making serious wine, but they can do very well with certain varietals; their decision to go to Napa for their Cabernet Sauvignon can only be looked upon as a positive step in the right direction.

ROBERT MONDAVI WINERY *NAPA*

1982 Cabernet Sauvignon *Napa*	③	**82**
1978 Cabernet Sauvignon Reserve *Napa*	⑤	**91**
1979 Cabernet Sauvignon Reserve *Napa*	⑤	**86**
1980 Cabernet Sauvignon Reserve *Napa*	⑤	**87**
1981 Cabernet Sauvignon Reserve *Napa*	⑤	**87**
1982 Cabernet Sauvignon Reserve *Napa*	⑤	**90**
1984 Chardonnay *Napa*	③	**82**
1984 Chardonnay Reserve *Napa*	④	**91**
1984 Fumé Blanc *Napa*	③	**83**
1983 Fumé Blanc Reserve *Napa*	④	**86**
1984 Moscato d'Oro *Napa*	②	**84**
1980 Pinot Noir Reserve *Napa*	④	**84**
1981 Pinot Noir Reserve *Napa*	④	**86**
1982 Pinot Noir Reserve *Napa*	④	**86**

It's hard to believe that Robert Mondavi only started his winery in 1966. It seems as if he has been around forever – he has become an American institution and certainly one of the greatest influences on the California wine scene. There are those who often find some trivial matter to criticize him for, but looking at what he has accomplished, it is hard to find fault with anything he has done, with the possible exception of the bold pricing policy established here. The quality of his wines at the reserve level is outstanding, and many of the regular bottlings, while more commercial in orientation, are still very drinkable, well-made wines with which one is rarely disappointed. The production at his Oakville winery, pictured on the label, is up to 300,000 cases, with over one million cases produced at his plant in Woodbridge. Yet most people tend to think that the Robert Mondavi Winery is one of those small, quality-conscious, boutique Napa Valley wineries. Needless to say, his marketing staff has promoted the right image. Certainly his Fumé Blanc Reserve, made in a rich, opulent, oaky, intensely concentrated style, is one of the most unique and greatest wines of its type in California, and with it he has led the way with regard to the potential of the Sauvignon Blanc grape. The Chardonnays – from the regular, rather pleasant but straightforward bottling to the luxuriously rich, buttery, oaky, exotic, reserve bottlings – have been superb in vintages such as 1981, 1983, and 1984 where they are truly world-class Chardonnays. They have even tended to last five to six years in the bottle, a lot longer than many California Chardonnays. His regular Cabernets have been increasingly dull after a splendid Regular Cabernet in 1974, which today is still drinking beautifully; perhaps one will have to wait for the wonderful regular bottling of 1984, which has not yet been released, to again experience such quality. However, at the reserve level Mondavi does not miss a step. Great vintages for his reserve Cabernets have been 1971 (still an astonishing wine in its full bloom of maturity); 1974, a rather controversial, minty, chocolaty wine that may not prove to be as great as he predicted; the 1975, an elegant Bordeaux-style wine that is ready to drink; the 1978, a wine that continues to get richer and more complex as it ages and may prove to be one of his greatest successes; the 1981, rich, velvety and complicated; and the 1982, another very opulent, ripe, rich wine that shows exceptionally well now and should last for seven to eight years. Mondavi can also turn a trick or two with his Pinot Noirs, with which he is constantly experimenting. He seems to be moving closer and closer to an elegant, ripe cherry fruitiness married with new, toasty, vanillin oak in such vintages as the 1981 Reserve, a wine remarkably similar to a fine Volnay. Zinfandel was unfortunately dropped by the winery, although they never seemed to give it the attention it deserved. The other wines to look for from Mondavi include a flowery, fruity, seductive Chenin Blanc that is slightly sweet but one of the very best on the market, and his wonderfully fragrant, slightly sweet Moscato d'Oro. Of course, there are many other Mondavi wines, including the generic wines of white and red which are simple and straightforward, but Mondavi has in twenty years established remarkably high quality standards and all the success he has attained seems, in my opinion, well deserved.

MONTICELLO CELLARS *NAPA*

1982 Cabernet Sauvignon Corley Reserve *Napa*......	④ **80**
1982 Cabernet Sauvignon Jefferson Cuvée *Napa*.....	③ **76**
1983 Cabernet Sauvignon Jefferson Cuvée *Napa*.....	③ **90**
1984 Chardonnay Estate *Napa*..	③ **85**
1984 Chardonnay Jefferson Reserve *Napa*.................	④ **88**
1985 Chevrier Blanc *Napa*...	② **86**
1984 Pinot Noir *Napa*...	② **87**
1985 Sauvignon Blanc *Napa*..	② **84**

This winery, which has been built to look like the famous Virginia home of Thomas Jefferson, was founded in 1980 and seems to be showing dramatic improvement in the quality of its wines with each passing vintage. The unreleased 1984 Reserve Cabernet Sauvignon looks to be the best wine yet from Monticello Cellars, and the 1984 Pinot Noir from Napa, of which only 175 cases were made, is a wonderfully complex, rich, berry-fruited wine with a remarkable similarity to a top Volnay with its sweet, broad, round flavours. The 1982 Cabernets, both the Corley Reserve and the Jefferson Cuvée, hardly do justice to the memory of Thomas Jefferson. They are tart, lean, angular wines with good colour, rather hard tannins, but little personality charm. While the same can be said for the 1984 Sauvignon Blanc, the 1984 Chardonnays are both very good, with a toasty, buttery richness, good balance, and lively fruit. The 1985 Sauvignon Blanc is much better than the 1984, and the 1985 Chevrier, with its 80% Semillon, a very interesting wine of character and elegance. The newly released 1983 Cabernet Sauvignon is superb with at least a decade of life ahead of it, and a barrel sample of the 1984 Cabernet Sauvignon Reserve looks even better. This is surely a winery to watch.

MOUNT EDEN VINEYARDS *SANTA CLARA*

1982 Cabernet Sauvignon *Santa Cruz Mountains*......	④ **78**
1983 Chardonnay *Santa Cruz Mountains*.....................	④ **90**
1984 Chardonnay *Santa Cruz Mountains*.....................	④ **90**
1982 Pinot Noir *Santa Cruz Mountains*........................	④ **81**
1983 Pinot Noir *Santa Cruz Mountains*........................	④ **84**

Mount Eden Winery has always had a cult following for some of California's most spectacular Chardonnays, which are ripe, buttery, toasty, and very much in the full-bodied, barrel-fermented style of winemaking. The Pinot Noir has, in my opinion, been somewhat overrated, but some of the vintages can be particularly aromatic, spicy, smoky, at least interesting if not always in total harmony. I have had less experience with the Cabernet Sauvignons, but the 1982 (not a good vintage in this area) is quite herbaceous, soft, and obviously over-priced. This is a winery that has gone through tremendous change of winemakers and managers since it was founded in 1961. The production of 3,500 cases does not go far, but I would seek out with great enthusiasm any of the Chardonnays produced here, even the secondary Chardonnay that is sold under the MEV label from purchased grapes from the Ventana Vineyard in Monterey County.

NEWTON VINEYARDS *NAPA*

1981 Cabernet Sauvignon *Napa*	③	**84**
1982 Cabernet Sauvignon *Napa*	③	**87**
1983 Chardonnay *Napa*	④	**87**
1984 Chardonnay *Napa*	④	**87**
1982 Merlot *Napa*	③	**87**
1984 Sauvignon Blanc *Napa*	③	**82**

The Newton Vineyard, founded in 1978 by one of the former partners of Sterling Vineyards, is clearly trying to stylize its wines in a French fashion with barrel-fermented, rich Chardonnays, oaky Sauvignons, and tightly knit, well-made, potentially very promising Cabernet Sauvignons and Merlots. The Chardonnays have been very good for those who prefer the toasty, oaky style of wine since the wines have plenty of vanillin toasty oak but also plenty of flavour, depth, and concentration. The 1984 is a bit more restrained than the 1983. The Sauvignon Blancs have been similarly styled and are among the more unique Sauvignons produced in California, with an oaky character and a similarity to the richer, oaky style of white Graves wines. The Cabernets have tended to be very closed and tight, so their ratings may sometimes be a bit ungenerous given their obvious potential for seven to ten years of further evolution and improvement in the bottle. Both the 1981 and 1982 show good acidity, plenty of spicy oak, and rich, berry-like flavours tightly integrated with plenty of tannin and acidity. The 1982 is lusher and riper, but both wines need until the end of this decade to reach maturity. The 1982 Merlot is one of the best I have tasted from Napa, yet needs until 1988-1990 to reach full maturity.

NIEBAUM-COPPOLA ESTATES *NAPA*

1978 Rubicon *Napa*	⑤	**88**
1979 Rubicon *Napa*	⑤	**90**

1980 Rubicon *Napa* .... ⑤ **90**

This winery, founded in 1978, is dedicated to producing luxury-priced, proprietary wines from blends of Cabernet Sauvignon, Cabernet Franc, and Merlot from an old-established vineyard in Napa Valley. It is owned by the famous movie producer/director Francis Ford Coppola, who has said that he wants his wines to last 100 years. They are certainly impressive wines, rich, full-bodied, intense, with power and character. The 1979 was released first and has a rich bouquet with a tarry, black cherry fruit note. It is very concentrated, full-bodied, and while drinkable now will keep for at least eight to ten more years. The unreleased 1978 is an even bigger wine, still a little rough around the edges, but loaded with black cherry fruit, cedar and tar scents. There is enough tannin and acidity to easily last another decade. The 1980 looks to be the best of the first three vintages of Rubicon; rich yet graceful, powerful, but with finesse, it should be quite long-lived. Prices have been high, but with a production of 3,500 cases and winemaking that seems to spare no expense and make no compromises, these dramatic, unique, distinctive wines will attain quite a following among wine enthusiasts.

OPUS ONE *NAPA*

1979 Opus One *Napa* .... ⑤ **87**
1980 Opus One *Napa* .... ⑤ **89**
1981 Opus One *Napa* .... ⑤ **87**
1982 Opus One *Napa* .... ⑤ **90**

No wine has received more publicity in the last ten years in California than the Opus One, a joint venture between Napa's famous Robert Mondavi and Bordeaux's equally famous and flamboyant Baron Philippe de Rothschild. The first vintages have been made at Robert Mondavi's winery in Napa, although plans have been proposed for construction of a separate facility to house Opus One. The price of the wine has been criticized throughout the country, but the quality of the wine has ranged from excellent to outstanding. The best vintage to exemplify the combination of the rich Napa Valley grapes and the broad winemaking experience of the French has been the 1982, an elegant yet still powerful, rich wine that shows impeccable winemaking and looks to be the best Opus One to date. The 1980 is very Californian in style, having plenty of power and richness but also plenty of depth. The 1979 and 1981 are lighter-styled wines with a little bit less concentration, but still very good (and very pricy as well). In spite of the prices asked for the wines and the hoopla surrounding them, it remains to be seen if these wines can fully live up to all of their advance publicity. However, the quality has been very good to excellent, and reports are that both the 1983 and 1984 are even better than the outstanding 1982. Whatever people may think, this operation has generated a tremendous amount of attention for the California wine business.

PARDUCCI WINE CELLARS *MENDOCINO*

1982 Cabernet Sauvignon *Mendocino*	②	84
1980 Cabernet Sauvignon 50th Anniversary *Mendocino*	②	84
1984 Chardonnay *Mendocino*	②	84
1983 Chardonnay Cellarmaster *Mendocino*	③	84
1985 French Colombard *Mendocino*	①	83
1985 Gewürztraminer *Mendocino*	②	78
1978 Petite Sirah Cellarmaster *Mendocino*	②	84
1985 Sauvignon Blanc *Mendocino*	②	85

The Parducci clan have long fought for recognition of Mendocino as one of the better viticultural areas of California. The winery, founded in 1932, has grown by leaps and bounds to produce over 300,000 cases of wine. The style of the wine here rarely disappoints the taster – they are fruity, with their varietal character well displayed, they are cleanly made, and always enjoyable. Their Sauvignon Blanc, which often suggests that a slight amount of residual sugar is still left, is wonderfully fruity, round, lush, and altogether captivating. The same can be said for their very aromatic, off-dry French Colombard, one of the best of its type made in California for this grape varietal and a lot more appealing than most consumers have realized. The Chardonnays tend to be mostly fruit, are straightforward in style, always well made, clean, with no oxidation and no overly oaky character. The Gewürztraminer has always been rather lean and insufficient to my taste, but the Cabernet Sauvignons are fat, grapy, immensely fruity, delicious wines that all seem to be drunk while young, though a 1970 drunk last year showed that they can age surprisingly well. Cellarmaster selections are meant to be the pick of the bunch from this winery. By no means ignore the often criticized Petite Sirah from Parducci, a peppery, densely coloured wine in which Parducci seems to extract more fruit than tannin, making it wonderfully appealing but also capable of ageing for seven to eight years. I find little to criticize from this winery, which makes remarkably sound yet interesting, fruity wines that have immense crowd appeal and are sold at realistic prices.

JOSEPH PHELPS VINEYARDS *NAPA*

1981 Cabernet Sauvignon *Napa*	③	80
1982 Cabernet Sauvignon *Napa*	③	80
1981 Cabernet Sauvignon Bacchus *Napa*	⑤	84
1983 Cabernet Sauvignon Bacchus *Napa*	⑤	87
1981 Cabernet Sauvignon Eisele *Napa*	⑤	87
1982 Cabernet Sauvignon Eisele *Napa*	⑤	85
1983 Cabernet Sauvignon Eisele *Napa*	⑤	88
1981 Cabernet Sauvignon Insignia *Napa*	⑤	87
1982 Cabernet Sauvignon Insignia *Napa*	⑤	86
1982 Chardonnay *Napa*	③	78
1983 Chardonnay *Napa*	③	75
1983 Chardonnay Sangiacomo *Sonoma*	③	85
1983 Delice du Semillon *Napa*	④	90
1985 Gewürztraminer *Napa*	②	84
1985 Johannisberg Riesling Late-Harvest *Napa*	⑤	88
1985 Sauvignon Blanc *Napa*	②	83
1985 Scheurebe Late-Harvest *Napa*	④	87
1979 Syrah *Napa*	③	84
1982 Syrah *Napa*	②	75
1980 Zinfandel *Alexander Valley*	②	87
1982 Zinfandel *Napa*	②	70
1985 Zinfandel *Napa*	②	82

The Joseph Phelps Winery is unquestionably one of the great California wine producers. Since their inception, when much of the wine world praised the winery for its great late-harvest white wines, there has been a remarkable succession of both great late-harvest Rieslings and, starting in 1974, fabulous Cabernets and, every once in a while, a sensational Zinfandel. The record in the seventies was one of unparalleled brilliance and consistency. The top-of-the-line Cabernets are all vineyard-designated, including one of the first luxury proprietary red wines launched in California, the Insignia. The other top Cabernets include the fabulously rich, tannic, monumental wine from the Calistoga vineyard of Milton Eisele and, since 1977, the Bacchus Vineyard designated Cabernet from Napa. So in essence there are four Cabernets offered – the regular, the Eisele Vineyard, the Bacchus Vineyard, and the proprietary luxury blend, Insignia. In addition, there are two Zinfandels, the Napa Valley Zinfandel and the Alexander Valley Zinfandel, of which the last has been the most interesting and even fabulous in years like 1975, 1976, and 1980.

The Phelps Winery in the seventies produced a bevy of great Cabernet Sauvignons that stand out in the history of California winemaking. The 1974 Insignia, the 1975 Eisele, the 1976 Insignia, the 1977 Insignia and Eisele, the 1978

Eisele, and the 1979 Eisele are all very special wines. Regular Cabernets that were sensational included the 1975 vintage. Despite this fabulous record of success, recent vintages, especially the 1982, have shown a slight drop in quality. However, the 1983s and 1984s from Phelps look to be a return to the top rank, particularly the 1984 red wines. The 1980s were good, the 1981s also good, but the 1982 vintage for this winery was somewhat plagued by problems. The Bacchus Vineyard Cabernet Sauvignon was never released because of a technical problem with the wine; the Eisele was somewhat of a disappointment for that particular wine, and the regular Cabernet was fruity and soft but lacking complexity. Even the Insignia is not up to its normal quality.

As for the Chardonnays here, this has never been a winery that has greatly impressed me with its ability to make top-notch Chardonnays. The best has generally been the barrel-fermented Chardonnay from San Giacomo Vineyard in Sonoma, whereas the non-barrel-fermented Shellville tends to be rather straightforward and fruity but lacking in complexity. However, if there was a little slump in the early eighties, the Late-Harvest Rieslings and Scheurebes made by this winery have been consistently superb, particularly the Late-Harvest or Select Late-Harvest wines which resemble respectively Beerenauslese and Trockenbeerenauslese wines. They are decadently rich, intense and fragrant, and can challenge the greatest of the German late-harvest sweet wines. In 1983, Phelps added a sweet 1983 Delice, produced from 75% Semillon and 25% Sauvignon Blanc. It is a brilliant achievement and has a frightening resemblance to a great Sauternes.

The Sauvignon Blanc here has taken on more complexity and richness with the addition of Semillon, and the Gewürztraminer, a varietal that I find does not do very well in California, can be one of the best made in California. Phelps also has experimented with the true Syrah grape, with mixed results. The 1979 showed some of the peppery, Rhône-like character one would expect, but the 1982 tastes like a dilute Beaujolais with little character and a somewhat stinky nose. All in all, this remains a great winery despite an off year in 1982. The 1984 Cabernets across the board are the best overall vintage for Joseph Phelps since 1978, and this winery, where production has remained around the 60,000-case level, is certainly one to always take note of.

RAVENSWOOD WINERY *SONOMA*
1983 Cabernet Sauvignon *Sonoma*............................... ③ **83**
1984 Cabernet Sauvignon *Sonoma*............................... ③ **83**

1983 Merlot *Sonoma*	③	87
1984 Merlot *Sonoma*	③	90
1982 Zinfandel *Napa*...	②	84
1982 Zinfandel Dickerson Vineyard *Napa*	②	84
1984 Zinfandel Dickerson Vineyard *Napa*	②	89
1981 Zinfandel Dry Creek Benchland *Sonoma*	②	86
1984 Zinfandel Old Hill Vineyard *Sonoma*...............	③	90
1984 Zinfandel Vintner's Blend *Sonoma*....................	②	87
1981 Zinfandel Vogelsen Vineyard *Sonoma*	②	86
1984 Zinfandel 60% Sonoma, 40% Mendocino.......	②	86

Ravenswood, with a production of only 5,000 cases, has been causing quite a bit of talk in wine circles. Winemaker Joel Peterson seems to have the magical touch with both Zinfandel and Merlot. His Cabernet Sauvignon can be good but it never seems to be a match for his handcrafted, intense, wonderfully ripe and opulent Zinfandels and his Merlots, which seem to get more spectacular with each vintage. Perhaps the best wine made yet by Ravenswood is the 1984 Merlot, a wine of unbelievable richness and stunning opulence that should drink beautifully for its first seven to eight years of life. The 1983 Merlot is also an excellent wine, with an almost gamy, exotic, Rhône-like nose, and loaded with luscious berry fruit and a soft, unctuous texture. Of the Zinfandels, it is almost impossible to make a mistake with any from this winery. They are all densely coloured, high in extract, with rich, berry-like flavours of raspberries and cassis, and lush, long textures. They come from different vineyards but always keep an eye out for the Ravenswood Vintner's Blend, an inexpensive Zinfandel made from purchased grapes. The 1984 might be one of the great wine buys from California. It is one of four super Zinfandels Ravenswood produced in 1984. All in all, it seems as if one can hardly make a mistake with a Ravenswood wine – they represent the best of what California should be doing more frequently – producing individualistic, dramatic wines with plenty of personality. Prices can only go up since the demand already exceeds the supply, so move quickly to try the very special wines of Ravenswood, and make a mental note to jump on the 1984s as they appear.

RAYMOND VINEYARD AND CELLAR *NAPA*

1981 Cabernet Sauvignon Reserve *Napa*	④	87
1983 Chardonnay *Napa*	③	85
1984 Chardonnay *Napa*	③	82
1984 Chardonnay California Selection *Napa*............	③	83
1984 Chardonnay Reserve *Napa*	④	85
1982 Johannisberg Riesling Late-Harvest *Napa*.......	③	86

The family-owned Raymond Winery has been a success from its founding in 1970. Production has climbed towards 60,000 cases and the hallmark of this house has always been the oaky, buttery, opulently styled Chardonnay that is never shy but always loaded with fruit as well as plenty of vanillin, spicy, toasty oak. All the recent vintages have generally been solid, including the 1983 and 1984 Reserve, although the 1984 California selection seemed a bit dull. Raymond can also do interesting things with Cabernet Sauvignon, but most of the time the wine tends to be fairly straightforward, ripe, and intense, without a lot of complexity. However, the 1981 Cabernet Sauvignon Reserve is one of Raymond's best Cabernets to date and shows that when he puts his mind to it he can make top-notch Cabernet. Its lushness and richness dictate drinking over the next three to four years. The winery also makes a little Zinfandel that I find average in quality, but every once in a while a splendid Late-Harvest Johannisberg Riesling is made. The current version (1982) has a wonderful bouquet of caramel and pineapples and is rich and sweet on the palate. It is a perfect dessert wine. Raymond made a great classic in 1978 when he produced a Trockenbeerenauslese-styled wine of great intensity and depth that is still drinking well today.

RIDGE VINEYARDS *SANTA CLARA*

1981 Cabernet Sauvignon *Napa*	③	**78**
1982 Cabernet Sauvignon Howell Mountain *Napa*	④	**85**
1983 Cabernet Sauvignon Howell Mountain *Napa*	④	**82**
1980 Cabernet Sauvignon Monte Bello *Santa Cruz*	⑤	**86**
1981 Cabernet Sauvignon Monte Bello *Santa Cruz*	⑤	**90**
1982 Cabernet Sauvignon Monte Bello *Santa Cruz*	⑤	**84**
1983 Cabernet Sauvignon Monte Bello *Santa Cruz*	⑤	**88**
1981 Cabernet Sauvignon York Creek *Napa*	③	**85**
1982 Cabernet Sauvignon York Creek *Napa*	③	**75**
1984 Chardonnay *Santa Cruz*	④	**84**
1981 Petite Sirah York Creek *Napa*	②	**85**
1983 Petite Sirah York Creek *Napa*	③	**86**
1982 Zinfandel Geyserville *Sonoma*	②	**86**
1983 Zinfandel Geyserville *Sonoma*	③	**87**
1984 Zinfandel Geyserville *Sonoma*	③	**90**
1984 Zinfandel Lytton Springs *Sonoma*	③	**90**
1982 Zinfandel York Creek *Napa*	③	**86**
1984 Zinfandel York Creek *Napa*	③	**84**

Ridge Vineyards and its winemaker, Paul Draper, are justifiably very highly respected, not only in the United States but in the world. Paul Draper has consistently produced spectacular, long-lived Cabernet Sauvignons that have fifteen to twenty years ageing potential, and usually California's finest Zinfandels from a half-dozen or so vineyard locations. A little Chardonnay is also made here that tends to be oaky and often not terribly interesting, but the 1984 showed very well. The reasons for Ridge's success are numerous, but they believe in no (or minimum) handling of the wine once it has been made, resulting in wines that are generally made with wild yeasts from the vineyards; their wines receive the minimum of fining, and no filtration whatsoever. Consequently, they all have character and plenty of flavour-intensity. The jewel of this house is its Cabernet Sauvignon from the Monte Bello Vineyard next to the winery, which sits strategically and beautifully overlooking Silicone Valley and San Jose. The drive up to Ridge is both beautiful and steep. The Ridge Monte Bello Cabernets start off life almost like Château Latour Cabernets do in Bordeaux. Many writers dismiss them as being too tannic and too lean when in truth there are layers and layers of flavour underneath. The great Monte Bellos have been the 1964 (still in spectacular condition when I last tasted it in 1985), the 1968, the 1970, an incredibly great 1971, the 1974, and a monumental 1977 that needs another ten years to reach its peak. In the 1980s, the vintages have been slightly less successful, although the 1984 tasted from the cask looked to be outstanding and both the 1981 and 1983 are very strong. The Ridge Monte Bello Cabernet is a wine that has rich fruit, an almost gravelly, mineral extract, and it develops like no other Cabernet I have experienced in California. I have consistently mistaken a ten- or twelve-year-old Ridge Monte Bello for a first-growth Bordeaux. The other Cabernets made here range from the fairly chunky, medium- to full-bodied York Creek made from grapes purchased in Napa to a fairly tannic, closed, rather reserved yet very ageworthy Howell Mountain Cabernet also made from purchased grapes in Napa.

The winery has always done a great job with Zinfandels, and until the Ravenswood Winery in Sonoma got started, Ridge rarely had any competition for producing the best Zinfandels in California. Their Zinfandels come from a horde of different locations, but the best ones have consistently been the Zinfandels produced in Sonoma called Geyserville and Lytton Springs. The 1984s are the best in recent memory. These wonderfully rich Zinfandels are loaded with berry fruit and age beautifully. Perhaps the next best Zinfandel is that from the York Creek Vineyard in Napa, which often contains a little bit of Petite Sirah. This again is a rich, intense, long-lived Zinfandel that can seemingly last for eight to ten years with no difficulty. Other Zinfandels are from Fiddletown

Vineyard in Amador, which tends to be a robust, rich wine, the Dusi Ranch in Paso Robles, and, every once in a while, the Jimsonmare Ranch, which is located lower down the mountain from Ridge. The 1970 Jimsonmare Zinfandel remains for me the single greatest bottle of Zinfandel I have ever tasted. Having had it several years ago, I can report with great astonishment that it is still not fully mature. The winery also makes a splendid Petite Sirah that is deep, dark, rich, and loaded with peppery extract and blackcurrant, cassis flavours. The best Petite Sirah always comes from the York Creek Vineyard in Napa Valley. Sometimes Paul Draper adds a dollop of Zinfandel to give it some additional character. In fact, a 1974 Petite Sirah York Creek drunk in 1984 had an astonishing resemblance to a great Côte Rôtie from Guigal. So perhaps this wine has even more potential for ageing than any of us have ever given it credit for.

SAINTSBURY WINERY *NAPA*

1984 Chardonnay *Carneros*	③	**87**
1985 Chardonnay *Carneros*	③	**87**
1984 Pinot Noir Carneros *Carneros*	②	**87**
1984 Pinot Noir Garnet *Carneros*	②	**84**
1985 Pinot Noir Garnet *Carneros*	②	**84**

The Saintsbury Winery is proving that very good, even stunning Pinot Noir can be made from grapes grown in the cool region of Carneros. The two young owners, David Graves and Richard Ward, seem to have learned their lessons well and with each vintage the quality improves. The 1984 and 1985 Chardonnays are their best Chardonnays to date, with wonderful complex, toasty, buttery, moderately intense bouquets of spices and ripe apple fruit. Both wines show remarkable balance, medium body, long flavours, and seem very French in their orientation. The winery produces two Pinot Noirs. The lighter-styled Garnet Pinot Noir in 1984 and 1985 seems richer and a trifle firmer than the previous editions, with lush raspberry fruitiness and true Pinot Noir personality. The one to get really excited about however is their 1984 Carneros Pinot Noir, one of the most impressive Pinot Noirs to come out of the Carneros region in the last ten years. It seems to have an ageing potential of five to seven years but can be drunk now for its intense raspberry fruitiness and smoky, rich Pinot Noir character. This winery has sensible prices, and its wines improve in quality with each vintage. I recommend paying more and more attention to it. Production has inched up to 15,000 cases.

SCHRAMSBERG WINERY *NAPA*

1982 Blanc de Blancs	④	**70**
1982 Cuvée de Pinot	④	**71**
1979 Reserve Sparkling Wine	⑤	**75**

Schramsberg of course has a great reputation, but I have never been overwhelmed by the quality of their sparkling wines. Despite all the hype, the reality is that recent releases have been less interesting than many of the releases that pre-date the mid-seventies. This is unfortunate because this historic winery has led the California sparkling wine industry from its founding in 1965, and obviously inspired many a vintner to try his or her hand at making sparkling wine. The 1982 Blanc de Blancs tastes like a green Muscadet that has been carbonated. The nose is odd, there is no middle range of flavour, and it has a sharp finish. The 1982 rosé, the Cuvée de Pinot, has a charming colour but little else. There is no flavour; what is present is clean and crisp, but with absolutely no follow-through. The 1979 Reserve, priced 'modestly', has some body and flavour but no real focal point of interest. Occasionally, Schramsberg can make better sparkling wines than this, but though one gets a famous name here, a higher level of quality can be found in most Vins Mousseux from France as well as the numerous inexpensive Italian and Spanish sparkling wines. This remarkably overrated winery produces approximately 50,000 cases of sparkling wine.

SEBASTIANI WINERY *SONOMA*

1981 Cabernet Sauvignon Eagle Label *Sonoma*	⑤	**84**
1982 Cabernet Sauvignon Eagle Label *Sonoma*	⑤	**84**
1983 Cabernet Sauvignon Eagle Label *Sonoma*	⑤	**85**
1980 Cabernet Sauvignon Proprietor's Reserve *Sonoma*	③	**85**
1984 Chardonnay Proprietor's Reserve *Sonoma*	③	**78**
1984 Sauvignon Blanc Proprietor's Reserve *Sonoma*	③	**81**
1980 Zinfandel Proprietor's Reserve *Sonoma*	③	**84**

One of Sonoma's most famous wineries, with a production in excess of two million cases, the Sebastiani Vineyards (founded in 1904) has gone through a tumultuous period from 1980, when the patriarch of the firm, August Sebastiani died, until 1985, when his son, Sam Sebastiani, was dismissed from the company by his mother. Sam had attempted to give Sebastiani a brand new look, improving the quality and dropping some of the wines that made up the bulk wine production of this winery. At this time, it is too early to know what direction this winery will go, but there are a number of good-quality wines under the Sebastiani label in existence. The strength of the house has always been their red wines, with the Zinfandel especially good, as well as a generally sound Cabernet Sauvignon. The introduction of the super-expensive Eagle Label was met with praise from the critics but had a price too steep for most consumers. It has tended to be an inky, rich, very tannic, intense wine that requires ageing. The winery also produces a range of white wines, with the best being a somewhat underrated Muscat with a slight sweetness but wonderfully perfumed aroma, and a blush wine called Eye of the Swan. The Rosa Gewürztraminer, which has a rosé-type colour, is another wine that has tended to be consistently good. The Pinot Noirs have erred on the light side, the Gamay is dull and uninteresting, and the Chardonnays and Sauvignon Blancs are well behind the quality one expects from this winery. Sebastiani is going through a period of major changes, and it will be interesting to see if the style of the wines produced here changes as well.

SHAFER VINEYARDS *NAPA*

1982 Cabernet Sauvignon *Napa* .... ③ **84**
1983 Cabernet Sauvignon *Napa* .... ③ **65**
1982 Cabernet Sauvignon Reserve *Napa* .... ④ **86**
1982 Chardonnay *Napa* .... ③ **87**
1983 Chardonnay *Napa* .... ③ **84**
1984 Chardonnay *Napa* .... ③ **86**
1983 Merlot *Napa* .... ③ **72**

The Shafer Winery quickly established its reputation for a rich, full-bodied Cabernet Sauvignon and Zinfandel in 1978, the debut vintage. Production has grown to 12,000 cases and the winery continues to specialize in just Cabernet Sauvignon, Chardonnay, and a little Merlot. Unfortunately, the big, rich Zinfandels were dropped from the roster. The 1982 Cabernets were remarkably variable from bottle to bottle, although the best bottles showed wonderful richness and intensity, particularly the Reserve bottling. The 1983 Merlot has never impressed me as it suffers from an intense vegetal aroma and hard, harsh tannins that render it charmless, nor has the vegetal and petrol-scented bizarre 1983 Cabernet. Shafer Vineyards produced one of Napa Valley's very finest Chardonnays in 1982 and followed it with good rather than great efforts in 1983 and 1984. Prices remain moderate for wines that are generally quite soundly made, although I wonder about the variation in quality of the 1982 red wines.

SILVERADO VINEYARDS *NAPA*

1982 Cabernet Sauvignon *Napa*	③	**82**
1983 Cabernet Sauvignon *Napa*	③	**69**
1982 Chardonnay *Napa*	③	**85**
1983 Chardonnay *Napa*	③	**85**
1984 Chardonnay *Napa*	③	**78**
1985 Sauvignon Blanc *Napa*	②	**85**

This winery was started in 1981 by the famous Walt Disney family. Production has peaked at 50,000 cases and the wines are consistently good and fairly priced. The top two wines have been the Chardonnays (although the 1984 was thin and citric) and Sauvignon Blancs, followed by a less impressive but still pleasant (except for the lean, angular 1983) Cabernet Sauvignon. The winery is one of the most beautifully situated in the Napa Valley, overlooking the southern part of the valley on a small ridge next to the Silverado Trail. The Chardonnays tend to be made in the very balanced, correct style, with just enough toasty oak, and the emphasis clearly on the lemony, ripe appley, fruity scents of Chardonnay rather than the big, butterscotchy, barrel-fermented style. The Sauvignon Blanc tends to be fresh and lively, with the aggressive herbaceous character of this varietal well controlled.

SIMI WINERY *SONOMA*

1981 Cabernet Sauvignon *Sonoma*	③	**78**
1982 Cabernet Sauvignon *Sonoma*	③	**85**
1978 Cabernet Sauvignon Reserve *Sonoma*	④	**76**
1980 Cabernet Sauvignon Reserve *Sonoma*	④	**85**
1983 Chardonnay *Mendocino/Sonoma*	③	**85**
1984 Chardonnay *Sonoma*	③	**86**
1981 Chardonnay Reserve *Sonoma*	④	**84**
1982 Chardonnay Reserve *Sonoma*	④	**90**
1985 Rosé of Cabernet *Sonoma*	②	**85**
1984 Sauvignon Blanc *Sonoma*	②	**86**

The historic Simi Winery, founded in 1876, has always made good wine, but the decision to bring on board the outstanding winemaker Zelma Long in 1979 has meant a succession of better wines than ever before from this winery. Zelma Long's speciality is Chardonnay, and one can hardly go wrong with a Chardonnay produced here. The regular Chardonnay, often a blend of both Sonoma and Mendocino grapes, is wonderfully fruity, gently touched by ageing in oak barrels, and consistently successful in every vintage since 1980. The Reserve Chardonnay, released much later, is barrel-fermented and made in the very opulent, rich, full-bodied, oaky style; in vintages like 1982 the balance between fruit and oak is struck;

however in 1981 the oak seemed to play the dominant role. The Cabernet Sauvignon has not matched the quality of the Chardonnays here, but the 1982 regular bottling and the 1980 Reserve, while more tannic and tough, show very good depth and character. The regular bottlings of 1981 and 1982 Cabernet Sauvignon are rather straightforward, simple wines. The Sauvignon Blanc has increased in quality, and the 1984 is certainly the best example yet from this winery. The Rosé of Cabernet is arguably one of the finest rosé wines made in California, remarkably fresh, lively, and with plenty of flavour and character, particularly for a rosé. Prices for the Simi regular bottlings remain fair, although Reserve prices are expensive but in the case of the Chardonnay, they are well worth it.

SONOMA VINEYARDS *SONOMA*

1980 Cabernet Sauvignon Rodney Strong Alexander's Crown	③	**84**
1982 Chardonnay Rodney Strong Chalk Hill	③	**55**
1982 Chardonnay Rodney Strong River West	③	**68**
1983 Sauvignon Blanc Rodney Strong *Alexander Valley*	②	**60**

Sonoma Vineyards produces in excess of 500,000 cases of wine from extensive vineyard holdings in Sonoma. The wines have appeared under a number of different labels, including the Sonoma Vineyards, Windsor Vineyards, and more recently the Rodney Strong labels, alluding rather strongly to winemaker Rodney Strong. The Chardonnays, for whatever reason, seem to be released late on to the market when they are already starting to lose their fruit and have become oxidized. This is precisely the problem with the 1982s. The best wines have been the Cabernet Sauvignon from the excellent Alexander's Crown Vineyard in Sonoma. The 1980 is successful, though not nearly as rich and intense as the great wines made at this vineyard in 1974 and 1976. Another wine to keep a lookout for is the rich, intense, almost late-harvest-style Zinfandel made from old vines of the River West Vineyard in Sonoma. I have not seen a vintage of this since 1978.

SONOMA-CUTRER VINEYARDS *SONOMA*

1983 Chardonnay Cutrer Vineyard *Sonoma*	③	**89**
1984 Chardonnay Cutrer Vineyard *Sonoma*	④	**89**
1983 Chardonnay Les Pierres *Sonoma*	④	**90**
1984 Chardonnay Les Pierres *Sonoma*	④	**90**
1983 Chardonnay Russian River Ranches *Sonoma*	③	**84**

1984 Chardonnay Russian River Ranches *Sonoma*.. ③ 87

The youthful Sonoma-Cutrer Winery has a glittering display of high technology used to make wine in a very traditional way. I have never seen grapes and wines so carefully handled, nor have I seen a winery with any more technology than this showpiece winery in Windsor, California. The results have been brilliant, with the 1983 and 1984 Chardonnays both sensational vintages for this winery. Bill Bonetti, the winemaker here, has a remarkable track record when it comes to Chardonnay, and he has had full control over things at Sonoma-Cutrer. The three Chardonnays that are offered include a fruity, forward, very delicious Russian River Ranches, a rather opulent, tropical fruit-scented, subtly oaky Cutrer Vineyard, and a classic, austere, mineral-scented but long, rich, intense, ageworthy Les Pierres Vineyard Chardonnay. Prices continue to inch up for the 25,000 cases of Chardonnay that are produced, but the wines also continue to be on allocation as demand has simply outstripped supply. These Chardonnays are among the best of their kind in California, three distinctively different wines, of which the Les Pierres and Cutrer are among the handful of California Chardonnays that have the potential and the structure to last and improve in the bottle for more than four or five years. The 1984s tend to be a bit more opulently forward and fruity than the classic 1983s. The winery also plans to produce a sparkling wine after it has spent five to seven years ageing on its lees. This is a Chardonnay producer of the highest quality, and worth every effort to search out and follow.

SOUVERAIN CELLARS *SONOMA*

1982 Cabernet Sauvignon *Sonoma*	②	78
1980 Cabernet Sauvignon Vintage Selection *Sonoma*	③	72
1982 Chardonnay Vintage Selection *Sonoma*	③	70
1982 Zinfandel *Sonoma*	①	70

How things change might be an appropriate comment for this historic winery that was founded by the famous J. Leeland Stewart. Stewart gave the country many excellent Cabernet Sauvignons in the late sixties and early seventies. The last great wine made at Souverain was the 1974 Vintage Selection Cabernet Sauvignon, a wine that today is still remarkably rich and alive. The current crop of offerings is dull, simple, and generally devoid of varietal character. The exceptions tend to be the Cabernet Sauvignons, which have adequate blackcurrant fruit but little else. The Chardonnays are dull and simple, and the same can be said for the Pinot Noirs, Zinfandels, Fumé

Blancs, and Gray Rieslings. The Petite Sirah can provide surprisingly good character, although I have not seen a vintage of it since 1978. The wines are not inexpensive for their mediocre to below-average quality level.

SPOTTSWOODE VINEYARD AND WINERY *NAPA*

1982 Cabernet Sauvignon *Napa* .... ④ **90**
1983 Cabernet Sauvignon *Napa* .... ④ **85**
1985 Sauvignon Blanc *Napa* .... ③ **86**

This winery, which was only opened in 1982, stunned both consumers and critics alike with a great Cabernet from that same vintage. It is a type of Cabernet that one rarely sees from California, rich, tannic with gorgeous balance and enough extract and balance to age gracefully for over a decade. The 1983, while slightly less impressive, was still a good wine and barrel samples of the 1984 and 1985 seem to verify that this winery will make another great wine in 1985 and certainly a very good one in 1984. The winery is also producing small quantities of Sauvignon Blanc, of which the 1985 is very, very good. Production is only 1,500 cases, but the quality level is impeccably high with prices to match.

SPRING MOUNTAIN VINEYARDS *NAPA*

1979 Cabernet Sauvignon *Napa* .... ③ **77**
1980 Cabernet Sauvignon *Napa* .... ④ **72**

This winery, known by television viewers as Falcon Crest, started off in 1968 producing very interesting wines, particularly Cabernet Sauvignon and occasionally Chardonnay. For whatever reason, the wines have become increasingly commercial and dull in style, and recent vintages, though expensive, rarely deliver the complexity and flavour-intensity one would hope for.

STAG'S LEAP WINE CELLARS *NAPA*

1983 Cabernet Sauvignon *Napa* .... ④ **84**
1978 Cabernet Sauvignon Cask 23 *Napa* .... ⑤ **92**
1979 Cabernet Sauvignon Cask 23 *Napa* .... ⑤ **82**
1983 Cabernet Sauvignon Cask 23 *Napa* .... ⑤ **87**
1981 Cabernet Sauvignon Stag's Leap Vineyard
    Napa .... ③ **82**
1982 Cabernet Sauvignon Stag's Leap Vineyard
    Napa .... ③ **78**
1983 Cabernet Sauvignon Stag's Leap Vineyard
    Napa .... ③ **85**
1984 Chardonnay *Napa* .... ③ **85**
1983 Merlot *Napa* .... ③ **85**

1984 Sauvignon Blanc *Napa*.. ② *84*

Stag's Leap Wine Cellars, although only founded in 1972, has a worldwide reputation for making some of California's finest wines, particularly Cabernet Sauvignon. The wine that owner Warren Winiarski built his reputation on is his sumptuous and luscious Cask 23 Cabernet Sauvignon. It is not a wine that I have found to be long-lived, but, given its sheer intensity of flavours and wonderful fleshy suppleness and great rich bouquet, it can be a knockout in vintages such as 1974, 1978, and 1984. It can completely dominate other wines in tastings, not because of its power, but because of its sheer succulence and complexity. The regular Cabernets here have been somewhat light in style and a bit disappointing given the reputation of this winery. The 1981 is beginning to fall apart, the 1982 is rather watery and loosely knit, and the 1983 is somewhat better but very soft, forward, and not terribly complex. However, the 1983 Stag's Leap Vineyard shows fine depth, and the excellent Cask 23, while more austere and tannic than usual, is nevertheless a rich, deep, broadly flavoured wine that will age well for five to eight years. The winery does a nice job with Sauvignon Blanc which often has a little bit of Semillon blended in, and the Chardonnay tends to be slightly toasty, with good lemony, appley, buttery fruit. The secondary label is Hawk Crest, which can often represent good value, particularly in the Cabernet Sauvignon. The performance record over the last decade is surprisingly inconsistent, but for the Cask 23 and for some of the special lots of Cabernet called Lot 1 or Lot 2, this is a winery that can produce world-class, fabulously rich, seductive wines. For the future, the 1984 vintage here looked awfully good and the most consistently successful vintage for this winery's Cabernets since 1978.

STERLING VINEYARDS *NAPA*

1985 Cabernet Blanc *Napa* .... ② *84*

1982 Cabernet Sauvignon *Napa* .... ③ *55*

1982 Cabernet Sauvignon Diamond Mountain *Napa* .... ③ *86*

1983 Cabernet Sauvignon Diamond Mountain *Napa* .... ④ *72*

1984 Chardonnay *Napa* .... ④ *75*

1983 Chardonnay Diamond Mountain *Napa* .... ④ *72*

1984 Chardonnay Diamond Mountain *Napa* .... ④ *85*

1983 Merlot *Napa* .... ③ *80*

1984 Sauvignon Blanc *Napa* .... ③ *85*

1985 Sauvignon Blanc *Napa* .... ③ *85*

Sterling Vineyards, with a production of 75,000 cases, is

unfortunately just a shadow of what it was in the early and mid-seventies when winemaker Ric Forman made an absolutely remarkable string of Cabernets, Merlots, and Chardonnays. When the winery was sold to Coca-Cola in 1978, quality began to slip immediately. In 1983 the winery was again sold, this time to Seagrams, and there seems to be a renewed effort to try to get things back on track, although no red wines made under the new management have yet been released. In any event, one could almost cry when looking at the fabulous Reserve Cabernet Sauvignons of 1973, 1974, 1975, and 1976 and then comparing them to the Cabernets that were made in the late seventies and early eighties. The 1974 Reserve Cabernet remains one of the single greatest California Cabernets I have tasted, and at thirteen years of age it is just now coming into its plateau of maturity. Even the Chardonnays that Ric Forman produced were immensely rich and long-lived by California standards. Today the most consistent wine has been the blush wine called Cabernet Blanc, one of the better of its type made in California. The 1984 and 1985 Sauvignon Blancs also showed quite well in my tastings of this varietal, and their lean yet firm, subtle complexity holds plenty of attraction for Sauvignon Blanc drinkers. The recent Merlots have been rather straightforward, fruity, a little tart, and not ageworthy at all. What a shame when one looks back at the 1974 and 1975 Merlots, which remain in great shape today. The 1982 Cabernet Sauvignon Diamond Ranch shows proof positive that this winery can still turn out top-notch wine. It is rich, ripe, medium- to full-bodied, deep, and long, and should hold well for at least another five to six years. However, the 1983 Diamond Ranch Cabernet is austere and painfully tannic, and the regular 1982 Cabernet Sauvignon was unusually thin and intensely vegetal. Hopefully, Sterling will rebound strongly under its new ownership for it owns a significant amount of acreage and can easily draw from its own well-situated vineyard sources, something that many California wineries do not have the ability to do.

STONY HILL VINEYARDS *NAPA*

1981 Chardonnay *Napa*	④	90
1982 Chardonnay *Napa*	③	80
1983 Chardonnay *Napa*	③	88
1984 Chardonnay *Napa*	④	92

Stony Hill is one of the great old wineries of California, having been founded in 1952 and now run with great enthusiasm by Eleanor McCrea. The Chardonnays are certainly among the handful of exceptions from California in that they actually improve in the bottle for four to five years, longer in some vintages. The 1981 is now fully open and shows the splendid richness and balance that this wine has when mature. The 1982 is a bit of a disappointment, but the 1983, though tightly knit, shows very good underlying richness and ripeness and should be another candidate for extended ageing, as will the 1984, a rich, opulent, yet tightly structured Chardonnay.

SUTTER HOME WINERY *NAPA*
1982 Zinfandel *Amador* .... ② **80**
1985 Zinfandel White *California* .... ② **84**

Sutter Home makes an enormous amount of wine (600,000 cases) and has achieved a great deal of commercial success with its white Zinfandel. It is pale salmon in colour, wonderfully refreshing, fruity, soft, and quite aromatic. In 1985 a sparkling white Zinfandel was added that is slightly sweet but has more character than many of the super-expensive California sparkling wines that are bland and neutral. The Zinfandels here have a good reputation, but I have always been left asking myself why I find them rather straightforward and unimpressive.

JOSEPH SWANN VINEYARDS *SONOMA*
I have not tasted a Joseph Swann wine since some of their Pinot Noirs in the mid-seventies, but the legendary Zinfandels and Pinot Noirs made here continue to elicit rave responses from the few who are lucky enough to try them. The tiny production of 1,200 cases is sold to a mailing list of loyal customers. Prices tend to be very reasonable. The winery also produces Pinot Noir and Chardonnay. Based on the older vintages I have tried, the Pinot Noir is certainly good, though perhaps overrated because of its rarity.

TREFETHEN VINEYARDS WINERY *NAPA*
1982 Cabernet Sauvignon *Napa* .... ③ **82**
1984 Chardonnay *Napa* .... ③ **88**
1983 Chardonnay *Napa* .... ③ **86**
1981 Pinot Noir *Napa* .... ② **80**

With little fanfare the Trefethen Winery has built up to a production of 60,000 cases and specializes in a wonderfully rich yet elegant, understated Chardonnay, one of the handful of wines made from this varietal in California that can age seven to eight years. The 1984, 1983, 1981, 1980, and 1978 are all wonderfully successful. The 1982 proved to be somewhat of a disappointment, given the high level of quality usually obtained here. The winery also produces a Cabernet Sauvignon that I find a bit oaky and a trifle too vegetal to receive high marks, but it is generally richly fruity and supple. A small amount of Pinot Noir is also made that, while not resembling a French Burgundy, does have ripe, plummy fruit and plenty of character. Two of the most successful wines produced by Trefethen are their excellent non-vintage Eschol white and red wines, blends that are expertly put together and offer immediate gratification for a low price.

WENTE BROTHERS WINERY *ALAMEDA*
1984 Chardonnay *California* .... ② **80**
1984 Sauvignon Blanc Estate .... ① **82**

Wente Brothers specializes in inexpensive wines of which the best tend to be their whites, particularly the Sauvignon Blanc and occasionally the Semillon from fairly old vineyards planted in the Livermore Valley. Every once in a while the Chardonnay can also be good. The other wines tend to be dull with little varietal character present.

ZD WINERY *NAPA*
1981 Cabernet Sauvignon *Santa Maria*........................ ③ **68**
1982 Cabernet Sauvignon *California*............................ ③ **84**
1984 Chardonnay *California*.. ④ **91**
1985 Chardonnay *California*.. ④ **90**
1982 Pinot Noir *Napa*... ③ **83**

The ZD Winery has, since 1969, made some of the richest, lushest wines across the entire spectrum of its offerings. Its Chardonnays are excellent and tend to be fat and buttery, with tropical fruit scents and layers of lush, almost decadent fruit. The 1984 continues the line of outstanding Chardonnays produced by this small winery with a production of 10,000 cases. Like all the Chardonnays produced by ZD, it should be drunk within one to two years of its release date, since the wines tend to be a little low in acidity. The Pinot Noirs are rather robust, richly fruity with great density, they are not terribly elegant, but are always deep, fat, bordering on being heavy but nevertheless, unique and distinctive. The Cabernets tend to range widely in quality since the winery buys grapes from all over California, from Santa Maria in the south to Napa in the north. The 1981 Santa Maria is incredibly vegetal and unattractive, but the 1982 has plenty of sweet oak, nice ripeness and richness, and a fat, low-acid style that has plenty of appeal for drinking over the next three to four years. When I think of ZD, I think of good-quality wines, with the Chardonnays usually stunning, the Cabernets somewhat variable, and the Pinot Noirs always interesting, although I don't expect them to taste anything like a good red Burgundy.

OREGON

A New Star?

The good news is that western Oregon may well have the finest potential of any viticultural region in the world outside Burgundy to produce great wines from the fickle and temperamental Pinot Noir grape. Despite the fact that internationally recognized wine authorities such as Hugh Johnson and André Tchelistcheff have written glowing accounts about the wines made by this fledgling industry, the Oregon wine growers have struggled to get the attention of both the media and the wine consumer.

For example, in the late seventies an Eyrie Vineyard 1975 Pinot Noir placed in a blind tasting against Premier and Grand Cru red Burgundies from top producers, and tasted by a French panel, came in second place. It was thought to be a French wine and the results were considered a shock. This tasting made the headlines but, curiously, it did not have the same positive effect on the prestige of Oregon wines that the famed Steven Spurrier Paris tasting of the mid-seventies, pitting California Cabernets and Chardonnays against Bordeaux and Burgundy, had for the reputation and respect of California wines.

Oregon is about to catapult into stardom not just for its startling Pinot Noirs but also for its Chardonnays. The focal point should be the 1983 and 1985 vintages, both perfect growing years for the Pinot Noir and Chardonnay grapes.

For the proud and fiercely independent winemakers of Oregon, the wait for respect and recognition has taken too long. As of 1985, there were 46 bonded wineries and 2,000 acres of vineyards. Most of the wineries are quite small. Even the three largest wineries, Tualatin (83 acres and 18,000-case production), Knudsen Erath (93 acres and 24,000-case production), and Sokol Blosser (45 acres and 23,000-case production), are by California standards rather small. Virtually all of the top wines specializing in Pinot Noir and Chardonnay are located in the Tualatin Valley and Yamhill County just west of Portland. A few wineries are also located to the south of Portland in the Salem and Eugene areas.

The climate in this area is significantly different from that of Mendocino, Napa, Sonoma, and other viticultural regions to the south in California. Cooler weather with more daylight hours (on average, two more than California's north coast per day, as in Burgundy) allows the grapes to mature at a slower pace and thus retain their natural acidity. Unlike California, where the addition of acidity to the finished wine is routinely employed to give the wines balance, in Oregon acidification rarely takes place. In California, only a few Chardonnays are put through a malolactic fermentation to lower acidity, because their acidity levels are already low. In Oregon, all of the Chardonnays go through malolactic and as a general rule are barrel-fermented rather than tank-fermented.

In short, the general style of the wines of Oregon is one with an undeniable European character. The wines develop and improve not only after being poured in the glass, but develop and improve in the bottle. Both the Pinot Noirs and Chardonnays are remarkably similar to their French counterparts, and as my blind tastings proved, often impossible to pick out as being 'made in the U.S.A.'

The best Pinot Noir producers in Oregon look to be Eyrie, Amity, Peter Adams, Adelsheim, Oak Knoll, Ponzi, and Bethel Heights, followed by Rex Hill, Sokol Blosser, and Elk Cove. For Chardonnay producers, Tualatin, Shaker, and Eyrie made stunning wines in both 1982 and 1983, and Peter Adams, Adelsheim, Ponzi, Knudsen Erath, Sokol Blosser, and Alpine have all proved they can do something special with Chardonnay given a good vintage.

Chardonnay and Pinot Noir are not the only top-quality wines made in Oregon. The Riesling one finds in Oregon is light, flowery, crisp, and aromatic. Eyrie Vineyards produces exceptionally good, dry Pinot Gris and Muscat that remind one of these same wines from Alsace. Shafer produces one of this country's best 'blush' wines, a dry, vibrant Pinot Noir blanc, and Oak Knoll produces a sweet raspberry wine that is the Yquem of American fruit wines.

The latest 1986 vintage created numerous problems for the growers in Oregon because of heavy rains before and during the harvest. However, some wines turned out very well depending on the picking date, while others are light and diluted. Although 1986 should certainly prove a better overall vintage than 1984, selection will be critical, and even the top wines will not equal the great success reached by Oregon growers in 1985.

The bad news, however, is that the availability of Oregon wines in the United Kingdom is for the most part non-existent. A few wines have made it to the shops of some of the more innovative retailers, but by and large very little is available from Oregon, and given the tiny production there, it is unlikely that any significant quantity of the outstanding Pinot Noirs from vintages such as 1983 and 1985 will ever get to Britain. However, make a mental note that should you ever see a bottle from one of Oregon's better producers, such as Eyrie, Amity, Peter Adams, Adelsheim, Oak Knoll, Ponzi, Bethel Heights, Rex Hill, Sokol Blosser, or Elk Cove, try it because in all likelihood you will be amazed by its quality and similarity to French wines. Hopefully, with greater interest and investment in western Oregon, there will be increased production and vineyard expansion, and more of the world will be able to taste the potential of Pinot Noir from Oregon.

OTHER PARTS OF THE WORLD

SOUTH

AUSTRALIA

NEW

• Lilydale

Clare
• Watervale
Auburn •
• Waikerie   • Renmark   Buronga •
BAROSSA VALLEY   • Nuriootpa   • Mildura
• Angaston   • Berri
Tanunda •

Adelaide •
SOUTHERN
McLaren • VALES
Vale
• Langhorne
Creek

DARLING

MURRAY

V
I
C   Echuca •
T

Bendigo •

GOULBURN
VALLEY

• Coonawarra   • Great Western

HOPKINS

Melbourne •

Geelong •

Australia

AUSTRALIA

Another Emerging Star

For the next decade, I see three wine-producing countries emerging into stardom and popularity. Spain, Chile, and Australia have all had enormous potential, but the introduction of more modern technology, the explosion of interest in fine wine and fine wine values, and the increasingly expensive top wines of France have all combined to focus more and more attention on these three countries. However, Spain and Chile's strong points are their red wines; in Australia, they can do everything well and they are.

Traditionally, Australia has been red wine country but the new wave of Chardonnays from the Aussies have left me remarkably impressed. In addition, some of the late-harvest, decadently sweet dessert wines and tawny and vintage port look-alikes from here are strikingly beautiful wines. High quality, increasingly good availability, and modest prices should propel Australia's wines into international prominence over the next several years.

RECENT VINTAGES

Vintages are especially hard to appraise because in this vast country there are major differences in climatic conditions in Victoria and New South Wales, the two best-known wine regions, and Queensland, Northern Territory, South Australia, and Western Australia. Most Australian authorities claim that 1982, 1985, and 1986 were the best recent vintages, 1983 the worst. Nevertheless, most of Australia's viticultural regions enjoy a hot, sunny, Mediterranean-type climate.

WHAT YOU NEED TO KNOW

Like any wine-producing region, knowing the finest growers/producers here will give you the maximum benefit. The labels of Australian wines are as confusing as those of Germany. Special 'bin' selections, wines called Riesling that have Chardonnay or Semillon in them, Cabernets blended with Sirah (called Shiraz), and other anomalies are normal here as virtually anything goes. Knowing the finest producers will narrow the risk and ease the pain of making a terrible choice. Therefore, I have concentrated on the producers of the Cabernet and Shiraz as well as the Chardonnay. But there is so much more here. For example, the sparkling wines made by Yellowglen (priced at under £8) put to shame anything coming out of California. The remarkable old fortified Muscats and Tokays of William Chambers and Brown Bros. (£10 upwards a bottle) are among the most sublime after-dinner drinks I have ever tasted. The

Rieslings will not strike any fear in the hearts of German wine-makers, but they are superior to anything produced in North America. However, some of the late-harvest Rieslings, Semillons, and Sauvignon Blancs from producers such as Petaluma, Rosemount, and Peter Lehmann are phenomenal and can successfully rival, sometimes surpass, their German and French counterparts, at one-third of the price.

Yet, it is the Chardonnays and red wines, particularly the Cabernets and Shiraz-based wines, that can compete with the best in the world. When one tastes the likes of a Penfolds Bin 95 Grange Hermitage or a Rosemount Chardonnay, there is no doubt that these two wines are among the world's élite. And there are other firms making wines almost as spectacular as these. For Chardonnay, in addition to Rosemount, look for Leeuwin, Montrose, Tyrrell, Petaluma, and Lindeman. For Cabernet and Shiraz, see the ratings of the producers and growers; there are simply too many fine producers to mention.

A GUIDE TO AUSTRALIA'S BEST PRODUCERS OF CABERNET SAUVIGNON AND SHIRAZ

★ ★ ★ ★ ★ Outstanding Producers

Penfolds (South Australia) | Petaluma (South Australia)

★ ★ ★ ★ Excellent Producers

Alkoomie (Western Australia)	Lake's Folly (New South Wales)
Baileys (Victoria)	St.-Huberts (Victoria)
Balgownie (Victoria)	Seville Estate (Victoria)
Brand's Laira (Coonawarra)	Taltarni (Victoria)
Château Tahbilk (Victoria)	Virgin Hills (Victoria)
Huntington Estate (New South Wales)	Wolf Blass (Victoria)

★ ★ ★ Good Producers

Bowen Estate (South Australia)	Moss Wood (Western Australia)
Brokenwood (New South Wales)	Mount Avoca (Victoria)
Brown Bros. (Victoria)	Redman (Coonawarra)
Fern Hill (McLaren)	Saxondale (New South Wales)
Lindeman (New South Wales)	Vasse Felix (Western Australia)
Mildara (Victoria)	Wrights (Western Australia)
Montrose (Mudgee)	Wyndham Estate (South Australia)

A GUIDE TO AUSTRALIA'S BEST PRODUCERS OF CHARDONNAY

★ ★ ★ ★ ★ Outstanding Producers

Rosemount Estate (New South Wales)

★ ★ ★ ★ Excellent Producers

Arrowfield (New South Wales) Montrose (Mudgee)
Huntington Estate (Mudgee) Moss Wood (Western Australia)
Lake's Folly (New South Wales) Petaluma (South Australia)
Leeuwin (Western Australia) Mark Swann (South Australia)
Lindeman's (New South Wales) Tyrrell (New South Wales)
Miramar (Mudgee)

★ ★ ★ Good Producers

Balgownie (Victoria) Rothbury Estate
Brown Bros. (Victoria) (New South Wales)
Hungerford Hill
(New South Wales)

SOUTH AMERICA

Argentina and Chile dominate winemaking in South America. Argentina seems to have an endless array of incredibly cheap, solid, pleasant wines that, if rarely exciting, are hard to ignore at their ridiculously low prices. On the other hand, Chile has enormous potential but also chronic political instability and nineteenth-century winemaking techniques that have kept them from reaching their full capabilities. Yet Chile is the only major viticultural area in the world that never suffered from the phylloxera plague of the last century, and many of the older vineyards here consist of ungrafted European root stocks that history says produces the greatest wines. Certainly the Cabernet Sauvignons from Cousino Macul and Sauvignon Blancs from Canepa can stand head to head in the best of company.

I have been quite pleased with red wines from Argentina, especially Cabernet Sauvignon and Sirah from Aberdeen Angus, and Cabernet called Cafayate from Etchart. For white wines, things are more tricky, but if you stick to Etchart's Torrontes in only the most recent vintage and the Resero Blanc, from the winery of the same name, you are unlikely to be disappointed.

There are a bevy of wineries that are modernizing and taking their winemaking more seriously than ever, but two merit serious consideration. Chile's and South America's finest wine is the world-class Cabernet Sauvignon Antiguas Reserva from Cousino Macul. The 1978, 1979, and 1980 (about £4.50) all show layers of classic blackcurrant fruit, medium to full body, intense, complex, smoky, cedary bouquets, and enough tannin to continue to evolve gracefully for five to ten years. A 1947 Antiguas Reserva drunk in 1986 showed that in certain vintages this wine can live as long as a top Bordeaux.

Cousino Macul produces two other wines of special significance. Their regular bottling of Cabernet (£3.50) is meant to be drunk upon release. Both the 1981 and 1982 are particularly attractive and supple. The Chardonnay produced here never sees a wood barrel and is bottled quickly to preserve its freshness. It is a soft, creamy, very fruity wine. The 1985s and 1986s must be consumed within two years of the vintage.

Another top grower is José Canepa, a very modern winery that produces an excellent Sauvignon Blanc that I would put up against my favourite California Sauvignons any day. Both the 1986 and 1985 are delicious, full of freshness and character. This fine winery also makes a Gran Brandis Cabernet Sauvignon that is not up to Cousino Macul's standards, but is certainly above average.

Other Chilean wineries to look for are that of Spain's Miguel Torres, Tarapaca, Concha y Toro, and Château Andrew. None of their wines should cost more than £5–£6 a bottle. Wineries that have left me unimpressed are Santa Carolina and Undurraga.

Consider buying Chilean wines very seriously – you are likely to be very favourably impressed.

THE LEBANON

The top wine of the Middle East is a story in itself. Just 30 kilometres (18 miles) from the savage and senseless civil war that has torn apart Beirut is Château Musar, a winemaking estate founded in the thirties, which makes superlative wines from a blend of Cabernet Sauvignon, Syrah, and Cinsault. Owner/winemaker Serge Hochar has had vintages wiped out because no harvesters would risk their lives to pick the grapes, but still he continues. His wine training came from his father and a stint in Bordeaux, but the wines made here remind me of the best and most complex Châteauneuf-du-Papes. They are quite full-bodied, very fragrant, rich and supple enough to drink young, but if the very good 1966 and exquisite 1970 tasted last year are any indication, they will last ten, even twenty years. The vintages now on the market are the 1975, 1977, 1978, and 1979, retailing for less than £7 a bottle, undeniable bargains given the quality here. Between the two, the 1977 is deeper and has more potential, but the 1979 is gorgeously fragrant and velvety. Musar is still relatively unknown; as long as the disastrous civil war continues to rage, one will fear for the future here, but this estate does indeed produce outstanding wine.

HOW TO BUY, STORE, SERVE, AND DRINK WINE

HOW TO BUY WINE

On the surface, having made your choices in advance, buying wine seems simple enough – you go to your favourite wine merchant and purchase a few bottles. However, there are some subtleties in buying wine that must be appreciated in order to ensure that the wine is in healthy condition and unspoiled.

To begin with, take a look at the bottle of wine you are about to buy. Poor storage generally is revealed by the condition of the bottle in your hand. First of all, if the cork has popped above the rim of the bottle and is pushed out on the lead or plastic capsule that covers the top of the bottle, then look for another bottle. Wines that have been exposed to very high temperatures expand in the bottle, thereby putting pressure on the cork and pushing it upward against the capsule. And it is the highest-quality wines, those that have not been overly filtered or pasteurized, that are the most subject to abusive transportation or storage, and they will show the effects in this manner. A wine that has been frozen in transit or storage will likewise push the cork out, and while the freezing of a wine is less damaging than the boiling of it, both are hazardous to its health. Remember: any cork that is protruding above the rim of the bottle is a bad sign and the bottle should be returned to the shelf and never, ever purchased.

Another sign that a wine has been poorly stored is the presence of seepage ('legs') around the rim of the bottle. This is the sometimes sticky, dried residue of wine that has expanded and seeped around the cork and dripped onto the rim. This condition is almost always due to excessively high temperatures in transit or storage. Few merchants take the trouble to wipe this evidence off, and it can often be spotted, particularly in wines that are shipped during the heat of summer. In any case, avoid buying any wine that shows dried seepage legs originating under the capsule and trickling down the side of the bottle.

Also be on the alert if a young wine (less than four years old) has more than half an inch of air space between the cork and the liquid level in the bottle; it may still be a very sound wine, but given modern bottling operations that generally fill the bottle to within a quarter to an eighth of an inch of the cork, more than half an inch of air space, or ullage, is a suspicious sign – why take the risk if there are other bottles with better fills?

Finally, another sign of a badly treated and abused bottle of wine can generally only be determined after the wine has been

512

decanted, though sometimes this culprit can be spotted in the neck of the bottle. Wines that have been exposed to very high temperatures, particularly deep, rich, intense red wines, will often form a heavy coat or film of colouring material on the inside of the glass. One must be careful here because this is the same type of sediment that vintage port regularly throws, and often the huge, rich Rhône wines and Piedmontese wines will do the same thing. But in Bordeaux a coating such as this generally indicates that the wine has been subjected to very high temperatures and has undoubtedly been damaged.

On the other hand, there are two conditions consumers frequently think are signs of a flawed wine, when nothing could be further from the truth. Many consumers return bottles of wine for the very worst reason – because of a small deposit or sediment in the bottom of the bottle. Ironically, this is actually the healthiest sign one could find in most bottles of red wine. However, keep in mind that white wines rarely throw a deposit, and it is rare to see a deposit in wines under two to three years of age. The tiny particles of sand-like sediment that precipitate to the bottom of a bottle simply indicate that the wine has been naturally made and has *not* been subjected to a flavour- and character-eviscerating traumatic filtration. Such wine is truly alive.

Another erroneous reason wine consumers return bottles to retailers is the presence of small crystals called tartrate precipitates. These crystals are found in all types of wines, but appear most commonly in white wines from Germany and Alsace. They often shine and resemble little slivers of cut glass, but in fact they are simply indicative of a wine that somewhere along its journey was exposed to temperatures below 40°F in shipment, and the cold has caused some tartaric crystals to precipitate. These are harmless, tasteless, and a totally natural occurrence in many bottles of wine. They have no effect on the quality and they normally signify that the wine has *not* been subjected to an abusive, sometimes cold stabilization treatment by the winery.

Fortunately, most of the better wine merchants, wholesalers, and importers are more cognizant today of the damage that can be done by shipping wine in unrefrigerated containers, especially in the middle of summer. A general rule is that heat is much more damaging to fine wines than cold. Unfortunately, there are still plenty of wine merchants, wholesalers, and importers who treat wine no differently than they treat beer or liquor, and the wine buyer must therefore be armed with a bit of knowledge before he or she buys a bottle of wine.

HOW TO STORE WINE

Wine has to be stored properly if it is to be served in a healthy condition. All wine enthusiasts know that subterranean wine cellars that are vibration-free, dark, damp, and kept at a constant 55°F are considered perfect for wine. However, few of us have our own castles and such perfect accommodations for our beloved wines. While such conditions are ideal, most wines will thrive and develop well under other circumstances. I have tasted many old Bordeaux wines from cupboards and basements that have reached 65–70°F in summer and the wines have been perfect. In cellaring wine keep the following rules in mind and you will not be disappointed by a wine that has gone over the hill prematurely.

First of all, in order to safely cellar wines for ten years or more keep them at 65°F, and *no* higher. If the temperature gets up to 70°F or higher, then be prepared to drink your red wines within ten years. Under no circumstances should you store and cellar white wines more than one to two years at temperatures above 70°F. Wines kept at temperatures above 65°F will age faster, but unless the temperature exceeds 70°F, will not age badly. If you can somehow get the temperature down to 65°F or below, you will never have to worry about the condition of your wines. At 55°F, the ideal temperature according to the textbooks, long-lived wines actually will evolve so slowly that your grandchildren are more likely to enjoy the wines than you. Constancy in temperature is most essential, and changes, if any, should occur slowly. White wines are far more fragile and sensitive to temperature changes and higher temperatures than red wines. Therefore, if you do not have ideal storage conditions, buy only enough white wine to drink over a one- to two-year period.

Second, be sure that your storage area is odour-free, vibration-free, and dark. A humidity level above 50% is essential; 80%–90% is ideal. The problem with humidity over 80% is that the labels become mouldy and deteriorate. A humidity level below 50% will keep the labels in great shape but will cause the corks to become very dry and the potential lifeline of your wines will be threatened.

Third, always bear in mind that wines from vintages that have produced powerful, rich, concentrated, full-bodied wines travel and age significantly better than wines from vintages that produced lighter-weight wines. It is often traumatic for a fragile, lighter-styled wine from either Europe or California to be transported transatlantic or cross-country, whereas the richer, more intense, bigger wines from the better vintages seem much less travel-worn after their journey.

Fourth, in buying and storing wine I always recommend buying a wine as soon as it appears on the market, assuming of course that you have tasted the wine and like it. The reason for this is that there are still too many wine merchants, importers, wholesalers, and distributors who are indifferent to the way wine is stored. This attitude still persists, though things have improved dramatically over the last decade. The important thing for you as a consumer to remember, after inspecting the bottle to make sure it appears to be healthy, is to stock up on wines as quickly as they come on the market and to approach older vintages with a great deal of caution and hesitation unless you have absolute faith in the merchant from whom you bought the wine. You should be confident that your merchant will stand behind the wine.

HOW TO SERVE WINE

There are really no secrets for proper wine service – all one needs is a good corkscrew, clean, odour-free glasses, a sense of order as to how wines should be served, and a knowledge of whether a wine needs to be aired or allowed to breathe. The major mistakes that most people, as well as most restaurants, make are 1) fine white wines are served entirely too cold, 2) fine red wines are served entirely too warm, and 3) too little attention is given to the glass into which the wine is poured. It might contain a soapy residue or have picked up stale aromas in a closed china closet. All of these things can do much more to damage the impact of a fine wine and its subtle aromas than you might imagine.

Most people tend to think that red wines must be opened and allowed to 'breathe' well in advance of serving. Some even think a wine must be decanted, a rather elaborate procedure but only essential if sediment is present in the bottle and the wine needs to be poured carefully off. With respect to breathing or airing wine, I am not sure anyone has all the answers. Certainly, no white wine requires any advance opening and pouring. With red wines, 15–30 minutes of being opened and poured into a clean, odour- and soap-free wine decanter is really all that is necessary. There are of course examples that can always be cited of wines that improve for seven to eight hours, but these are quite rare and unusual.

While breathing seems to dominate all the discussion in wine circles, to me a much more critical aspect is the temperature of the wine and the glass in which it is to be served. The temperature of red wines is very important, and in generously heated dining room temperatures are often 75°–80°F, more than is good for fine red wine. A red wine served at such a temperature will taste flat and flabby, with its bouquet diffuse and unfocused. The alcohol content will also seem higher than it should be. The ideal temperature for most red wines is from 62°–67°F, light red wines such as Beaujolais should be chilled to 55°F. For white wines, 55°–60°F is perfect; most will show all their complexity and intensity at this temperature, whereas if chilled to below 45°F no one will know if they are drinking a Riesling or a Chardonnay.

In addition, there is the all-important issue of the glasses the wine is served in. An all-purpose, tulip-shaped glass of eight to twelve ounces is ideal for just about any type of wine. But the important thing is that no matter how clean you think the glass might look, be sure to rinse the glass or decanter with unchlorinated well or mineral water just before it is used. A decanter or wine glass left sitting for any time is a wonderful trap for room and kitchen odours that are undetectable until the wine is poured and they yield their off-putting smells. That, and soapy residues left in glasses, has ruined more wines than any defective cork or, I suspect, poor storage from an importer, wholesaler, or retailer. I myself put considerable stress on one friendship simply because I continued to complain at every dinner party about the soapy glasses that interfered with the enjoyment of the wonderful Bordeaux wines being served.

The other critical element in serving wine is to have a sense of the flavour-intensity levels of the different dishes one is serving and to match them with similarly intense wines. The general rule is that delicate courses go best with delicate wines and richer, more exotic, intensely flavoured foods with more intense and dramatic wines. Food and wine combinations are not nearly as important to this writer as to many others; this field has been overly legislated, to the detriment of the enjoyment of wine. Many of the greatest wine connoisseurs I know will serve a great red wine with a seemingly conflicting fish course, the explanation being that they happen to love red wine and they happen to love fish, so they have them together regardless of what everyone says. The point is, red wine often doesn't work so well with fish but there are many more possible combinations than most writers have led people to believe. For me, the rule is simple: if you match the intensity of the dish with the intensity level of flavour in the wine, whether the wine be white or red, you will generally have a successful presentation.

As far as the actual order of wines, I always recommend that one proceed from the lighter, more delicate wines to the richer, more intense wines. If such an order is not followed, a delicate wine will often taste pale and watery having followed a fuller-bodied, richer wine. In addition, I always recommend serving wines from youngest to oldest. This tends to be the traditional manner and I think it makes sense; the grapier, younger, astringent wines show better when followed by mellow, complex, more mature wines.

Much of the material in this book is based upon tastings and research done by Robert Parker in conjunction with the publishing of THE WINE ADVOCATE, an independent consumer's guide to fine wine which is issued six times a year. A one-year subscription to The Wine Advocate costs $28 for delivery in the continental United States, $35 for Canada, and $50 for air mail delivery anywhere in the world. Subscriptions or a sample copy may be obtained by writing to *The Wine Advocate, P.O. Box 311, Monkton, M.D. 21111, U.S.A.*

INDEX